RAMPAGE

ALSO BY JAMES M. SCOTT

Target Tokyo (2015)

The War Below (2013)

The Attack on the Liberty (2009)

RAMPAGE

MacArthur, Yamashita,
and the Battle of Manila

JAMES M. SCOTT

W. W. Norton & Company
Independent Publishers Since 1923
New York London

For information about permission to reproduce selections from
this book, write to Permissions, W. W. Norton & Company, Inc.,
500 Fifth Avenue, New York, NY 10110

For information about special discounts for bulk purchases, please contact
W. W. Norton Special Sales at specialsales@wwnorton.com or 800-233-4830

Manufacturing by Quad Graphics Fairfield
Book design by Lovedog Studio
Production manager: Julia Druskin

ISBN 978-0-393-24694-0

W. W. Norton & Company, Inc., 500 Fifth Avenue, New York, N.Y. 10110
www.wwnorton.com

W. W. Norton & Company Ltd., 15 Carlisle Street, London W1D 3BS

1 2 3 4 5 6 7 8 9 0

For Carmen Scott,
who makes everything possible.

"These children of this Rising Sun:
Look down, dear God, on all they've done."

—CHARLES BROWN, PRISONER OF WAR

CONTENTS

Prologue   1

Part I   7
Part II   125
Part III   253
Part IV   439

Epilogue   507

Acknowledgments   515

Note on Sources   518

Archives and Libraries   522

Notes   525

Select Bibliography   599

Index   609

RAMPAGE

PROLOGUE

"I consider him an officer of most brilliant attainments."

—Maj. Gen. Charles T. Menoher,
Efficiency Report on Douglas MacArthur,
August 28, 1919

Gen. Douglas MacArthur walked out onto the porch of his cottage on the battered Philippine island of Corregidor in the early evening of March 11, 1942, joining his wife Jean and the couple's four-year-old son, Arthur—all packed for that night's perilous escape. The sun had just slipped below the western horizon, silhouetting the nearby Bataan Peninsula where the dormant volcano Mount Mariveles towered majestically almost five thousand feet over the South China Sea. A tropical breeze whipped across Corregidor, one typically filled with the acrid smell of cordite from Japanese bombings and artillery, which had finally let up after a long day of attacks along the waterfront. This tadpole-shaped island that guarded the entrance to Manila Bay had served as MacArthur's last refuge, under siege now for ninety-three days by advancing enemy forces.

The toll of the war showed on the sixty-two-year-old general. The five-foot-ten MacArthur had shed nearly twenty-five pounds on a diet of half rations. His normally close-cropped and thinning hair, which he often hid under his officer's hat, had grown long, and his face was coarse from weeks of shaving with saltwater. Despite that, MacArthur had still insisted each day on dressing in a pressed uniform and shined shoes, a small gesture of normalcy in an environment that deteriorated by the hour. But none of it mattered now as a lone truck grumbled up the bomb-cratered road to retrieve the general and his family for the trip down to the dock. MacArthur's besieged garrison would soon fall. The promised reinforcements had never arrived, and each day the Japanese noose tightened. If he did not leave tonight, MacArthur might never escape.

A patrol-torpedo boat was moored alongside Corregidor's north dock barely a half mile away, ready come nightfall to take the general, his family, and a few senior staffers on a high-speed run south to break the Japanese blockade of the island. Three other navy patrol boats would simultaneously depart Corregidor and Bataan, carrying additional officers on MacArthur's staff for a total party of twenty-one. If successful, this small flotilla would carry the general and his entourage some five hundred miles south over two days to the lush island of Mindanao, where B-17 bombers dispatched from Australia would pick them up at a Del Monte pineapple plantation and fly them to the port city of Darwin. Just as he had told those who had escaped before him, MacArthur knew that the next time he saw the sun, he would be in a whole new world.

The half-ton truck rolled to a halt in front of the gray cottage, where blankets tacked up inside the windows had served as primitive blackout curtains. Only two days earlier MacArthur had sat in the wicker chairs on this same porch with Maj. Gen. Jonathan Wainwright, his wiry second-in-command who answered to the nickname Skinny. That afternoon MacArthur had leveled with Wainwright, informing him that President Franklin Roosevelt had ordered him to evacuate to Australia, a move designed to rob the enemy of the propaganda victory of capturing one of America's most famous generals. Wainwright would remain behind in charge and fight to the end. "I want you to make it known throughout all elements of your command that I'm leaving over my repeated protests," MacArthur had instructed his subordinate.

"Of course I will, Douglas," Wainwright had promised.

"We're alone, Jonathan; you know that as well as I," he said. "If I get through to Australia, you know I'll come back as soon as I can with as much as I can."

"You'll get through," Wainwright assured him.

"And back," MacArthur had insisted.

The general shot a glance at his watch this muggy Wednesday evening, which read seven-fifteen p.m. The patrol boat would depart in just fifteen minutes.

MacArthur could delay no longer.

"Jean," he finally announced. "It's time to mount up."

The general's escape capped a brutal and frantic three months. In December 1941, after the Japanese wiped out America's air and sea power, MacArthur had ordered the evacuation of Manila, hoping to spare the Pearl of the Orient from destruction. Workers had emptied the capital's bank vaults of cash, gold, and securities, while the American high commissioner had pulled down the flag, broken the official seal, and ordered his new air-conditioned car pushed into the bay. The general had no choice but to abandon his own luxurious home in the penthouse atop the Manila Hotel, leaving behind his prized library of some ten thousand volumes, his family silver valued at more than $30,000, and even young Arthur's baby book and birth certificate. MacArthur's forces had fallen back to the Bataan Peninsula and the fortified island of Corregidor, where the general had set up his headquarters in the network of underground tunnels carved deep into the rock. Japanese bombs and artillery had since reduced the lush 1,735-acre island to a barren wasteland, where all that survived of most of the aboveground barracks, offices, and even the hospital were skeletal concrete remains held together by rebar.

Conditions proved far worse for the majority of MacArthur's troops fighting out in the open across the dark waters on Bataan with little more than shallow foxholes for cover. Hunger had forced soldiers there to slaughter and choke down the cavalry's mules and horses, while swarms of mosquitos and flies had spread everything from dengue fever to dysentery. Exhaustion had felled those lucky enough to dodge disease. "Malaria and malnutrition," observed Associated Press reporter Frank Hewlett, "put more soldiers out of service than Jap bullets." Other times Japanese soldiers crept behind Allied lines at night to kill American and Filipino forces, often disemboweling them. "More frequently, the men's genitals were stuffed in their mouths," wrote Steve Mellnik, a captain and artilleryman on MacArthur's headquarters staff. "In one case a victim regained consciousness and begged for a bullet to end his agony!"

The general's starved and battle-weary soldiers on the peninsula quipped that the V chalked on their helmets stood not for "Victory" but for "Victims."

For months, the enemy had humiliated the impotent MacArthur, dumping thousands of leaflets on his forces. "Sir, you are well aware that you are doomed. The end is near," Japanese Gen. Masaharu Homma wrote in one missive addressed directly to MacArthur. "The question is how long you will be able to resist."

Tokyo Rose likewise had aimed her demoralizing broadcasts at the general's troops. "You're out on the end of a 6,000-mile limb. The Japanese Imperial Forces are sawing that limb in two," she warned. "Get smart and give up."

The Japanese and the Germans had mocked MacArthur in other shortwave broadcasts, paying tribute to his struggle as a way to embarrass the United States. "In the name of fair play and chivalry," one broadcast trumpeted, "the Japanese nation demands that the United States give General MacArthur the reinforcements he needs, so he will be able to wage a war that would be to his satisfaction, win or lose."

MacArthur's once-heralded courage that had made him the most decorated American soldier of World War I was now aped by his own men, who called him "Dugout Doug," a ditty sung to the tune of "The Battle Hymn of the Republic."

Dugout Doug MacArthur lies a shaking on the Rock,
Safe from all the bombers and from any sudden shock.
Dugout Doug is eating of the best food on Bataan
And his troops go starving on.

But tonight it would all end.

MacArthur rode in silence from his cottage down to the dock, leaving a trail of dust like the tail of a comet. Mellnik watched as the general climbed down out of the cab. "He removed his droopy garrison cap and turned to peer into the darkness. Involuntarily, we peered with him. But there was nothing to see," Mellnik wrote. "The grim battlefield of Bataan was only a dark blur against the sky to the north. Far-off Manila made a dull glow on the horizon in the east. Across ten miles of mined waters to the south lay Cavite Province. And to the west lay the China Sea."

The general made his way through the rubble toward the pier, where a few men formed a line to see him off. "Good-bye and God bless you," some murmured.

MacArthur paused to shake each man's hand; a few sobbed, no doubt realizing that his departure symbolized what many had come to fear, that this was the end.

Several senior officers had come down to bid him farewell, including Maj. Gen. George Moore, who was in charge of harbor defenses.

"George," MacArthur told him, "keep the flag flying."

MacArthur helped his family into the boat, where Arthur clutched his white stuffed rabbit, nicknamed Old Friend. The general then turned for a final look up at the scorched rock fortress. "Gone was the vivid green foliage, with its trees, shrubs, and flowers," he noted. "Gone were the buildings, the sheds, every growing thing."

The general's eyes fell upon his troops, who stared at him in silence. In addition to his suitcase, musette bag, and walnut cane, MacArthur would take his wife Jean and son Arthur, the two most precious people in his life. He would leave behind thousands of husbands, sons, and brothers of families back home in America.

Families that had trusted him.

Those men would soon face the horrible Death March, followed by years of torture and beatings at the hands of the Japanese. Others would die of starvation, malaria, and dysentery or be crammed inside the bowels of Japan's notorious hellships. Beyond his troops, MacArthur's precious city of Manila was doomed to a brutal three-year occupation that would lead to mass starvation and even the plundering of cemeteries as desperate residents robbed the dead of jewelry, clothes, eyeglasses, and dentures—anything that could be bartered or sold for a few pesos to buy a fistful of rice.

This was defeat.

The general raised his cap in a farewell salute. "The smell of filth thickened the night air," he wrote. "I could feel my face go white, feel a sudden convulsive twitch in the muscles of my face." On the boat, Jean watched her husband, noting his pained expression. "He was just heart broken," she recalled, "just heart broken."

"What's his chance, Sarge?" MacArthur heard a soldier ask.

"Dunno," came the answer. "Maybe one in five."

MacArthur grabbed a piling and climbed down into the boat. "You may cast off, Buck, when you are ready," he told the skipper, Lt. John Bulkeley.

"Aye, sir."

Bulkeley fired up the boat's three 1,500-horsepower engines. Corregidor's searchlights had gone dark, and diversionary fire from the island's guns would soon draw the enemy's attention, allowing MacArthur to escape. Bulkeley guided the seventy-seven-foot boat away from the concrete pier and aimed out to sea to rendezvous with the others. As Corregidor receded in the boat's frothy wake, MacArthur made a solemn promise, one he would announce to reporters upon his safe arrival days later in Australia, a vow that would drive him as the weeks turned to months and then years.

"I shall return."

PART I

"America's army of liberation in the Pacific is here at last."

—Marcial Lichauco,
diary entry, January 9, 1945

The USS *Pennsylvania* leads battleships and cruisers into Lingayen Gulf in advance of America's invasion of Luzon on January 9, 1945.

CHAPTER 1

"In conducting war all of the ferocity of humanity is brought to the surface."

—ARTHUR MACARTHUR,
CONGRESSIONAL TESTIMONY, APRIL 8, 1902

GENERAL MACARTHUR PACED THE DECK OF THE LIGHT cruiser *Boise* as it steamed north along the west coast of the Philippines at ten knots on the afternoon of January 8, 1945. The pulse of the 9,700-ton warship's engines reminded the sixty-four-year-old general of the last time he had plowed through these blue waters, obsessed only with a desire to return. Two years, nine months, and twenty-nine days had passed since MacArthur had climbed aboard the motor patrol boat and slipped away under the cover of darkness, forced to watch in despair as the silhouette of Corregidor vanished on the horizon. His fortunes had since changed dramatically. He had traded the four worn-out patrol boats that had spirited him, his family, and aides to safety for an armada of more than eight hundred aircraft carriers, battleships, cruisers, and transports, the largest invasion force America had ever put to sea in the Pacific.

Despite that power, the same tension that had marked MacArthur's escape years earlier now clouded his return. American forces only weeks earlier had seized the Philippine island of Leyte, followed by Mindoro, but the ultimate prize still eluded MacArthur—the main island of Luzon, home to his beloved Manila. In less than twenty-four hours, the first of more than two hundred thousand soldiers would slog ashore on the beaches of Lingayen Gulf and begin the 110-mile race south to liberate the capital. In advance of the landings, navy carrier pilots had blasted Japanese airfields on Okinawa and Formosa to block any reinforcement of the Philippines before pounding the enemy's airbases scattered across Luzon. Poor weather, however, had limited the success of America's early raids, triggering Japan to unleash its infernal new weapon, kamikazes—a monsoon of metal and flesh that rained down daily on MacArthur's forces.

The threat from suicide planes had crystallized four days earlier when at 5:12 p.m.—just as sailors prepared to sit down to supper— a twin-engine bomber armed with two five-hundred-pound weapons crashed through the wooden flight deck of the escort carrier *Ommaney Bay*. "A tremendous explosion shook the ship so violently it seemed as if a gigantic pile driver had hit us," recalled Chaplain Robert Anderson. The carrier's hangar deck, filled with racks of torpedoes and armed planes fueled to capacity, erupted in an inferno. Fifty-caliber machine-gun rounds exploded, ricocheting off bulkheads. The skipper had no choice but to order his ship abandoned just thirty-eight minutes after the attack. Survivors watched from the water as exploding torpedoes caused part of the flight deck to collapse, a horror captured in the ship's war damage report: "Intensity of fire remained such as to insure that the ship was practically gutted in the next hour."

The destruction of the *Ommaney Bay* foreshadowed MacArthur's troubles. Two days later pilots tore into fifteen ships, including the bridge of the 32,000-ton battlewagon *New Mexico*. The fiery crash killed the skipper along with British Lt. Gen. Herbert Lumsden— Prime Minister Winston Churchill's liaison—and *Time* magazine's Bill Chickering, all of whom were later wrapped in canvas, weighted down with five-inch projectiles, and buried at sea after sunset. "The action was so fast and so continuous that it is hard to sort out the images of what happened," Chickering wrote to his wife only hours before his death. "They came in from all sides." The ferocious kamikazes that would ultimately sink two dozen ships and damage another sixty-seven signaled the strategic and symbolic importance of the coming invasion. This was far more than just the capture of another island in America's push across the Pacific.

MacArthur was coming home.

"If the Lord will let me land this one," the general had announced to his aides that morning over breakfast, "I'll never ask so much of him again."

In the years since he slipped through the Japanese blockade, MacArthur had never let go of the pain of his defeat. Barely one month after his escape, on April 9, Bataan fell, followed by the surrender of Corregidor a little more than three weeks later, cementing his fate. The rugged Philippine peninsula where thousands of MacArthur's men had fought and died had since become an emotional brand burned deep into the general's conscience. "Always Bataan," headquarters clerk Paul Rogers recalled, "never to be forgotten." MacArthur made sure. At his new headquarters in Australia, he had demanded his staff answer the phone with the single word "Bataan," the same name he gave his personal B-17 bomber. But he refused to speak publicly about his loss, except once each year to mark the anniversary of the surrender. "Bataan is like a child in a family who dies," he confided in his aides. "It lives in our hearts."

The Axis powers had ridiculed MacArthur for his escape. Germany's propaganda minister Joseph Goebbels called him the "fleeing general," while the Italian dictator Benito Mussolini labeled him a "coward." The *Japan Times and Advertiser* dubbed him a "deserter" who had "fled his post." MacArthur's secret departure had shocked many of the officers and troops he left behind, most of whom learned of his evacuation only after he was gone. "A foul trick of deception has been played on a large group of Americans by a Commander in Chief and small staff who are now eating steak and eggs in Australia," wrote Brig. Gen. William Brougher, a divisional commander who along with thousands of other Americans ended up as a Japanese prisoner of war. "God damn them!" Troops turned MacArthur's famous vow to return to the Philippines into a joke. "I am going to the latrine," soldiers quipped, "but I shall return."

Army Chief of Staff Gen. George Marshall had countered the negative hype by recommending MacArthur for the Medal of Honor, the prize he had long coveted in his quest to equal his father, a hero of the Civil War. The differences between the father's and son's actions could not have been more stark. The elder MacArthur had led his men to victory in battle; the younger had left his behind. Marshall, who drafted the citation, was blunt with Roosevelt about his motivation in recommending MacArthur for the medal. "This action was taken," he told the president, "among other things, to offset any propaganda by the enemy directed against his leaving command and proceeding to Australia in compliance with your orders." Others saw through the politics, including Gen. Dwight Eisenhower, who later declined his own medal for his role in the North Africa invasion, "because he knew of a man who had received one for sitting in a hole in the ground."

America had rebounded since those dark early days of the war, when MacArthur had begged for bombers, carriers, and destroyers. A nation that had enlisted housewives and even grandmothers in the industrial fight now hammered out as many as eight flattops a month and a plane every five minutes. The navy and the marines meanwhile had battled the Japanese back across the central Pacific, while MacArthur's reconstituted forces had clawed north through the sweltering jungles of New Guinea. But the path to this pivotal moment in the Philippines had required MacArthur to combat more than just the enemy—he had brawled with his own commander in chief.

America's success in the Pacific had led some senior naval leaders to advocate bypassing the Philippines entirely and instead seize the island of Formosa to the north, a move that would have landed U.S. forces even closer to Japan. American B-29 bombers, based on the recently captured islands of Guam, Saipan, and Tinian, had already begun to target Japan's key industrial cities in a campaign that would ultimately incinerate more than fifty square miles of Tokyo. There was no need to risk American lives on a costly invasion of the Philippines when the imminent fall of Japan would end the occupation. The proposal had outraged MacArthur, who viewed the enemy's forces as too perilous to sidestep. More important, failure to liberate the islands would abrogate MacArthur's promise to return. "We must be careful," Marshall had cautioned him, "not to allow our personal feeling and Philippine political considerations to override our great objective, which is the early conclusion of the war with Japan."

But MacArthur had refused to back down.

In a showdown in a beachfront mansion in Hawaii in late July 1944, MacArthur fought to bend American strategy in his favor, going so far as to threaten Roosevelt. "Mr. President," the general warned during a private moment, "if your decision be to bypass the Philippines and leave its millions of wards of the United States and thousands of American internees and prisoners of war to continue to languish in their agony and despair—I dare to say that the American people would be so aroused that they would register most complete resentment against you at the polls this fall." The shocked Roosevelt retreated to bed that night, summoning his physician and demanding an aspirin. "In fact," he said, "give me another aspirin to take in the morning."

For MacArthur, returning to the Philippines—and fulfilling his promise—had become an obsession, as the white whale was to Ahab in Melville's *Moby-Dick*. Brig. Gen. Charles Willoughby, MacArthur's intelligence chief, summed it up best: "Every battle action in New Guinea, every air raid on Rabual or PT boat attack on Japanese barges was a mere preliminary for the reconquest of the Philippines."

The Philippines, for MacArthur, meant one thing: Manila.

And each day—each hour now—he closed in on that goal.

MacArthur needed only to look east to confirm that his story was on the verge of coming full circle. Some sixty miles beyond the *Boise*'s rail, he could make out faint yet familiar landmarks, including Mount Mariveles perched on Bataan. Across from it was the rugged island fortress of Corregidor, whose tunnels had been, in the words of one of the general's aides, "both a refuge and a prison." Beyond them both rose the elegant high-rises of Manila, the city where MacArthur had abandoned his prized family possessions and that still held his remembrances of falling in love with his wife and the birth of his son. MacArthur stood there on the cruiser's deck, transfixed by the view. "One by one, the staff drifted away, and I was alone with my memories," the general recalled of that day. "At the sight of those never-to-be-forgotten scenes of my family's past, I felt an indescribable sense of loss, of sorrow, of loneliness, and of solemn consecration."

MacArthur drew confidence from the powerful warships that punched through the waves, a product of America's industrial might where ninety-six cents of every federal dollar spent went to the war. A convoy of transports stretched over forty miles—a virtual sea of steel—filled with soldiers assembled from sixteen bases across the Pacific. Other ships carried tanks, amphibious tractors, ambulances, and drums of gasoline, everything needed when troops hit the sand in the morning. This was the force MacArthur had dreamed of when Japanese bombs shook the tunnels, filling the humid air with dust. He could not escape noticing the fact that he had been offered a rare second chance, an opportunity to turn defeat into victory. He remembered an old gambling adage: "They never come back." The five-star general filled his corncob pipe. "I had a warm feeling in my heart," he wrote, "that sometimes the betting boys might be wrong."

○　○　○　○

MORE THAN JUST THE BURN of defeat drove Douglas MacArthur. Since his birth on an army base in Little Rock more than six decades earlier, his entire life had been shaped by the powerful influences of his mother and father. He had long held his father up as an icon of the American soldier. The son of a Wisconsin judge, Arthur MacArthur had enlisted in the Union Army in August 1862 at the age of just seventeen. Barely fifteen months later, the teenager seized his regiment's fallen flag—after previous color-bearers were bayoneted, shot, and even decapitated by cannon fire—and led his troops on a victorious charge up Missionary Ridge in Tennessee, earning the Medal of Honor, the nation's highest award for heroism. He went on to fight in thirteen battles and was wounded four times during Gen. William Sherman's march across Georgia. The senior MacArthur was promoted to full colonel at nineteen—the youngest in the Union Army— where his heroics coupled with his youth earned him the nickname the "Boy Colonel."

After the war, Arthur MacArthur decided to practice law but

found the experience anticlimactic, so he climbed back into uniform, albeit with a reduction of his wartime rank. Like that of other professional soldiers, his career languished in the years after the Civil War. He spent twenty-three years as a captain, ricocheting throughout the Southwest and the Dakotas with his young family in tow, fighting during the Indian Wars as American settlers pushed the nation's boundaries west. For the young Douglas MacArthur, the experience was paradise. "It was here I learned to ride and shoot even before I could read or write," he wrote, "indeed, almost before I could walk and talk."

Arthur MacArthur's career prospects improved as America closed in on the twentieth century. He was ordered to Washington in 1889 with the Adjutant General's Department, a move that exposed his son to the political world that would prove vital later in his career. "Washington was different from anything I had ever known," Douglas MacArthur later wrote. "It was my first glimpse at the whirlpool of glitter and pomp, of politics and diplomacy, of statesmanship and intrigue." The senior MacArthur's career reached its climax a decade later, when he helped end more than three centuries of Spanish rule in the Philippines. His success, however, proved short-lived. The voracious reader with a sterling intellect was ultimately felled by his own runaway hubris, a trait that would reverberate through his son's life. He repeatedly clashed in Manila with his civilian counterpart and future president William Taft, resulting in his recall in 1901. The ouster effectively ended his military career, a fate confirmed when he was passed over for chief of staff. "Arthur MacArthur was the most flamboyantly egotistical man I had ever seen," his aide Col. Enoch H. Crowder once remarked, "until I met his son."

Arthur MacArthur's life would come to an end in the same dramatic fashion he had lived it. The sixty-seven-year-old attended the fiftieth reunion of his Civil War regiment in Milwaukee on September 5, 1912, where he regaled about one hundred of his former troops with stories of the Atlanta campaign a half-century earlier, a time when he had led men to victory and himself into history. "Your indomitable courage—"

MacArthur suddenly faltered, raising his hand to his heart.

"Comrades," he finally said. "I am too weak to go on."

The general collapsed into his chair, his eyes closed. "Already his face assumed the pallor of death and he lay back in his chair breathing easily," one witness told the *Milwaukee Sentinel*. "Tenderly we moved him to a couch and everyone stood at a respectful distance while the doctors worked busily."

The regimental surgeon, who had his ear to MacArthur's chest, finally straightened up. "Our commander," he declared, "has gone to his last rest."

A single sob punctured the silence.

The Reverend Paul B. Jenkins, in a voice broken by emotion, began to recite the Lord's Prayer: "Our father, who art in heaven, hallowed be thy name."

The men who had been with Arthur MacArthur that long-ago day on Missionary Ridge encircled their fallen leader and joined in the prayer. When it ended, the adjutant took down from the wall a battle-scarred American flag and draped the Stars and Stripes over MacArthur's fallen body. Overcome by the moment, the adjutant then collapsed, though he later recovered. "He died the death of a soldier," Gen. Charles King told MacArthur's widow that night, "in the midst of his comrades."

For thirty-two-year-old Douglas MacArthur, who would receive word of his father's death by telegraph, life would never be the same. "My whole world changed that night," he recalled. "Never have I been able to heal the wound in my heart."

The job of molding the future of Douglas MacArthur fell that night to the general's mother, the other dominant pillar in his life. Mary Pinkney Hardy, known to most simply as Pinky, had grown up the daughter of a wealthy cotton merchant on the banks of the Elizabeth River outside Norfolk, Virginia. Her family could trace its roots back to Jamestown, the first permanent English settlement in America. She boasted relatives who had served under George Washington in the Revolutionary War and Andrew Jackson in the War of 1812. Her own brothers had fought as Confederate soldiers in the Civil War, two of whom refused to attend her wedding a decade later to a veteran officer of the Union Army.

Life on the dusty plains as the wife of an American soldier proved far different from Pinky's comfortable childhood at her family's Riveredge Plantation. She busied herself educating the couple's three sons, the youngest being Douglas. "Our teaching included not only the simple rudiments, but above all else, a sense of obligation," he recalled. "We were to do what was right no matter what the personal sacrifice might be." The couple's middle son, Malcolm, died at age five of measles, while appendicitis later claimed the life of the oldest, Arthur. With the death of each son, Pinky's focus zeroed in more on Douglas, upon whose shoulders the weight of the family's future legacy rested. She reaffirmed his importance each night when she tucked him in bed. "You must grow up to be a great man," she told him, "like your father."

Pinky did everything in her power to advance her son's studies and later his career. To help secure an appointment to West Point, she hired a local high school principal to tutor him and even relocated the family to a district represented by a congressman who had been a friend of MacArthur's grandfather. When her son's curved spine forced him to fail the physical, she again sprang into action, hiring a Milwaukee specialist who worked with him for a year to correct it. The night before the admissions exam, the anxious MacArthur could not sleep. The next morning he felt nauseous when he arrived at City Hall for the test.

His mother pulled him aside. "Doug, you'll win if you don't lose your nerve," she assured him. "You must believe in yourself, my son, or no one else will believe in you."

MacArthur scored 93.3, besting the next applicant by sixteen points. But his mother's efforts did not stop with his admittance. Rather, she moved to West Point, renting a room for four years at Craney's Hotel, where from her window she could make sure his study lamp burned late into the night. Each day he reported to her for a half hour before supper, allowing the two enough time for an afternoon stroll so she could quiz him on his studies. Pinky's tireless efforts paid off when MacArthur graduated first in the class of 1903 with one of the finest records in West Point's history.

Pinky played an increasingly active role after her son proved his courage in combat and began his climb up the army's ranks. During a standoff between the United States and Mexico in 1914, MacArthur killed seven bandits near Veracruz, a feat that led to his nomination for the Medal of Honor. Three years later he demonstrated his bravery again, this time on the muddy battlefields of France. "The dead were so thick in spots we tumbled over them," he recalled. "The stench was carnal to the point of suffocation." Gassed twice, MacArthur refused to quit, one time climbing out of bed while still vomiting to resume command. For his heroism during World War I, he was again nominated for the Medal of Honor and ultimately earned two Distinguished Service Crosses, a Distinguished Service Medal, and seven Silver Stars. "On a field where courage was the rule," one citation read, "his courage was the dominant feature." One of his soldiers was far more laudatory: "He alone made victory possible."

Once he was home from the war, Pinky assumed the role of host for social events for her unmarried son. She even went so far as to lobby senior officers for promotions, writing to Gen. John Pershing, then America's top soldier, "Won't you be real good and sweet—The 'Dear Old Jack' of long ago—and give me some assurance that you will give my Boy his well earned promotion before you leave the Army?"

Pinky's involvement strayed far beyond her son's professional life. Much to her horror, he fell in love with Louise Cromwell Brooks, a divorced socialite with two children. When MacArthur married her on Valentine's Day 1922, Pinky refused to attend, foreshadowing the marriage's doom seven years later. In his memoir, MacArthur addressed it with a single sentence, failing to even mention his first wife's name: "I entered into matrimony, but it was not successful, and ended in divorce years later for mutual incompatibility." Brooks was far less polite, blaming the couple's split not only on his lack of bedroom skills but more so on his meddling mother. "It was an interfering mother-in-law who eventually succeeded in disrupting our married life."

Douglas MacArthur was not blind to the strong influence his parents exerted on him, though as a dutiful son, he abided. Later in life, however, he admitted it was hard. "My mother put too much pressure on me," he confessed. "Being number one is the loneliest job in the world, and I wouldn't wish it on any son of mine."

MacArthur advanced in part because of his family's connections but also because of his own formidable abilities, demonstrable courage, and hard work. The efficiency reports that filled his personnel file fawned over his many talents.

"A brilliant, young officer of great promise for the future," one report said.

"One of the most efficient, energetic and talented officers I have ever known," stated another.

"Well fitted for positions requiring diplomacy and high-grade intelligence."

At thirty-eight, while fighting in France, MacArthur was promoted to brigadier general, the youngest in the army, a feat he followed up seven years later when he claimed the mantle of America's youngest major general. Along with his advancement in rank came increasingly prestigious assignments. He was appointed superintendent of West Point—again, the youngest—commanded the Manila District, and even served as director of the 1928 Olympic Committee for the games in Amsterdam, where the United States won twenty-four gold medals. In August 1930, while in Manila, MacArthur received a radiogram that the president planned to name him the next army chief of staff, a move that would give him the coveted fourth star on his shoulder and make him the nation's most powerful soldier, not to mention the youngest officer to ever hold that post. It was the job his father had always sought but, because of his own personal failings, had slipped away. "My first inclination was to try to beg off," MacArthur said. "I knew the dreadful ordeal that faced the new Chief of Staff, and shrank from it." Pinky sensed his reluctance and cabled him, demanding he accept. "She said my father would be ashamed if I showed timidity," MacArthur later wrote. "That settled it."

Pinky, of course, was thrilled; her life's work was accomplished.

"If only your father could see you now!" she said. "Douglas, you're everything he wanted to be."

Like his father, MacArthur possessed an impressive intellect. He prided himself on never forgetting a name, while his aides often lauded his uncanny skill to peruse a draft of a speech and recall whole portions of it verbatim. He likewise had a unique ability to boil complex issues down into simple concepts.

"His mind was a beautiful piece of almost perfect machinery," recalled Philip La Follette, who served as a public affairs officer on MacArthur's staff.

"He was a brilliant man," added Maj. Gen. Richard Marshall.

"He was a genius—just a genius," gushed Brig. Gen. Bonner Fellers.

In addition to having a sharp mind, MacArthur was a gifted speaker and storyteller, skills that allowed him to enrapture dinner parties for hours and even helped him charm his second wife, Jean Faircloth. "I never in all my life met a more interesting talker," she wrote in a letter to a friend after meeting him. "I sit there really spellbound."

A couple of quirks marred his rhetorical savvy, including his peculiar habit of speaking about himself in the third person. "The sensation was unusual," recalled Dwight Eisenhower, who served for several years as MacArthur's chief of staff. "In time, I got used to it and saw it not as objectionable, just odd." MacArthur likewise suffered from a tendency to monopolize a conversation. " 'Discuss' is hardly the correct word," Eisenhower added. "Discussion suggests dialogue and the General's conversations were usually monologues." Still, many others, like *Life* magazine photographer Carl Mydans, who often traveled with the general, marveled at his oratorical skills. "Always it was an experience to hear MacArthur talk," the journalist recalled. "He often used archaic words and terms as one might a rare spice for extraordinary flavor."

For all the attributes his parents had given him, the duo had likewise contributed to his greatest flaw, the same one that had toppled his father and that General Pershing singled out in a 1922 efficiency report: "Has an exalted opinion of himself." Pershing wasn't the only one who noticed. Secretary of the Interior Harold Ickes, in a vicious diary entry, captured the feelings of the general's many opponents: "MacArthur is the type of man who thinks that when he gets to heaven God will step down from the great white throne and bow him into his vacated seat." Even those who worked closest with the general, like Eisenhower, suffered under his ego: "MacArthur could never see another sun, or even a moon, for that matter, in the heavens so long as *he* was the sun."

MacArthur's sense of superiority—even destiny—led him to clash with civilian leaders, including his commander in chief. "He talks in a voice that might come from an oracle's cave," President Roosevelt once said of him. "He never doubts and never argues or suggests; he makes pronouncements. What he thinks is final."

On the deck of the *Boise*, one thought indeed consumed MacArthur. His return to Manila.

○ ○ ○ ○

THE SIGNIFICANCE OF MACARTHUR'S return was far greater than just his desire to avenge his personal defeat. The Philippines was like a sun around which MacArthur and his family had revolved for nearly a half-century. His father had been the first one drawn into the volcanic archipelago's orbit, ordered to help drive out the Spanish at the turn of the twentieth century. But even then the seventeen-year-old Douglas had felt the tug of the islands, the promise of adventure, begging his father to allow him to skip his studies at West Point to accompany him. "My son," he said, "there will be plenty of fighting in the coming years, and of a magnitude far beyond this. Prepare yourself."

As much as Douglas MacArthur romanticized his father's legacy in the Philippines, America's early involvement there proved naïve, rudderless, and violent. U.S. troops had landed in the Philippines in 1898 as part of the Spanish-American War, a four-month fight that had begun as a way for the United States to help liberate Cuba, which was then part of the Spanish Empire. The war soon engulfed the Philippines, another colonial Spanish possession whose population likewise hungered for independence. In a sign of how insular America was, President William McKinley confided in a friend that when he received the cable from Rear Adm. George Dewey that the Philippines had fallen, he had to look up the nation's location on a globe: "I could not have told where those darned islands were within two thousand miles." At the war's end, Spain ceded the Philippines, along with Puerto Rico and Guam, to the United States for the sum of $20 million. The acquisition sparked a heated debate over whether America, which had fought a war to cast off its own imperial chains, wanted to become a colonial power. "We have about ten million Malays at two dollars a head unpicked," House Speaker Thomas Reed famously quipped. "Nobody knows what it will cost to pick them."

As history shows, it cost a lot.

McKinley assured the American public, in a speech delivered in Boston on February 16, 1899—one Douglas MacArthur later credited with guiding him during America's postwar occupation of Japan— that control over the Philippines would be short-lived. "No imperial designs lurk in the American mind," he promised. "They are alien to American sentiment, thought and purpose. Our priceless principles undergo no change under a tropical sun." The president later backtracked on that sentiment, deciding that unlike Cuba, which had gained its independence at the war's end, the Philippines were not prepared for self-government, a conviction no doubt colored by the commercial value of America's new Asian acquisition. "There was nothing left for us to do," McKinley said, "but to take them all, and to educate the Filipinos, and uplift and civilize and Christianize them, and by God's grace do the very best we could by them."

Relations between the United States and its new colony deteriorated. Filipino fighters who had teamed up with America to defeat the Spanish turned on it in a conventional conflict that soon devolved into a guerrilla war. Many of the American troops had fought in the Indian Wars, a conflict marked by a deep racial undercurrent and punctuated by massacres and atrocities on both sides, including mutilation, torture, and the burning of villages. The Philippines proved no different. Soldiers derogatorily looked down on Filipinos as racially inferior—no different from Apache, Comanche, and Navajo—often calling them by the same slurs, like "niggers," "injuns," and "savages."

"The country won't be pacified until the niggers are killed off like the Indians," one Kansas soldier told a journalist.

"The only good Filipino is a dead one," explained another.

"No cruelty is too severe for these brainless monkeys, who can appreciate no sense of honor, kindness or justice," a Utah private wrote in a letter.

Many senior officers were similarly racist. Brig. Gen. Robert Hughes, who had served as the provost-marshal-general of Manila and later head of the military department in Visayas, expressed such views openly during testimony before Congress: "These people are not civilized." Brutalities soon escalated, particularly in the wake of various atrocities. One time a captured American soldier was buried alive up to his neck. Guerrillas had propped open the soldier's mouth with a stick and sprinkled a trail of sugar into the woods. "Millions of ants," one report noted, "had done the rest." American troops retaliated, unleashing a reign of terror upon Filipinos that would mirror the horrors executed by the Japanese a half-century later. Soldiers waterboarded suspected guerrillas, herded them by the thousands into concentration camps, destroyed food supplies, and torched villages and towns, the latter referred to by Hughes as "black paint."

"You know what 'black paint' is?" the brigadier general queried gunboat commander Yates Stirling. "I hope you use plenty of it."

Stirling did as ordered. So did many others.

"After we finished up, there was little left to speak of," Stirling recalled. "We burned the villages; in fact, every house for two miles from either bank was destroyed by us. We killed their livestock; cattle, pigs, chickens, and their valuable work animals, the carabaos. It seemed ruthless; yet it was after all war, and war is brutal."

One of the more infamous cases surrounded Brig. Gen. Jacob Smith, known as "Hell-Roaring Jake." After Filipino insurgents overran an American outpost in Balangiga on September 28, 1901, killing forty-eight Americans, Smith ordered Marine Maj. Littleton Waller to turn the island of Samar into a "howling wilderness."

"I want no prisoners. I wish you to kill and burn, the more you kill and burn the better you will please me," Smith instructed Waller. "I want all persons killed who are capable of bearing arms in actual hostilities against the United States."

Waller asked how young.

"Ten years," Smith replied.

"Persons of ten years and older are those designated as being capable of bearing arms?" the surprised officer replied.

"Yes," Smith concluded.

The fight dragged on for three and a half years, sparking a fierce debate in Washington after reports of American atrocities erupted in the press, including a drawing of troops waterboarding a Filipino that ran on the cover of *Life* magazine. The conflict ultimately cost taxpayers $600 million and resulted in more than seven thousand American casualties, including 4,234 killed. The Filipinos paid a much higher price with an estimated 20,000 fighters killed and another 200,000 civilians dead from starvation and disease, the by-product of America's scorched-earth tactics. When asked before a congressional hearing about the lopsided casualties, Arthur MacArthur appeared aloof when he blamed the losses on bad marksmanship. "The Filipino soldier," he testified, "does not know how to shoot." The high price paid by both American troops and Filipinos—in blood, treasure, and, in the case of the United States, principles—seemed to echo the words President McKinley muttered to a friend: "If old Dewey had just sailed away after he smashed that Spanish fleet, what a lot of trouble he would have saved us."

As the fight wore down, Arthur MacArthur, as American military governor, faced the daunting task of stitching the nation back together again. "The U.S. conquest of the Philippines had been as cruel as any conflict in the annals of imperialism," historian Stanley Karnow observed, "but hardly had it ended before Americans began to atone for its brutality." Under the leadership of MacArthur and his successors, the United States began building railways and roads, overhauling the court system, and improving public health, from digging sewers to vaccinating villagers. In addition, more than a thousand teachers arrived from the United States, fanning out across the archipelago. "The educational work under the American military occupation of the Philippines is one of the most romantic chapters in Philippine history," the younger MacArthur later said. "While some countries conquered by means of the Cross, or subjugated by means of the sword, it remained for the United States to colonize through the agency of education."

The senior MacArthur's bullheaded personality, however, sabotaged his tenure after he repeatedly clashed with William Taft, a former federal judge and solicitor general appointed by McKinley to head the Philippine Commission. MacArthur resented the civilian intrusion and bucked protocol, refusing to greet Taft at the port when his steamer arrived, instead sending a colonel. When the two met in the general's office, Taft described his reception as so cold that he "almost stopped perspiring," no easy feat for the more-than-three-hundred-pound commissioner in Manila's sweltering climate. Though initially forgiving, Taft soon soured on MacArthur's acerbity; he derided him in letters to his family and to War Secretary Elihu Root as a "small man" and a "military martinet." His complaints worked. Thirteen months later MacArthur, relieved of his command, boarded a steamer home. In the end, the Philippines had proven both the pinnacle of MacArthur's career and his downfall. "When he died," wrote historian Carol Petillo, "the measure of his bitterness about the situation could be gauged by the fact that he left instructions forbidding a military funeral or burial in the National Cemetery at Arlington, Virginia."

The Philippines likewise had proved a revolving door in the life of Douglas MacArthur, who served four times in the islands, including his first assignment after graduation from West Point. When he first disembarked in Manila from the transport *Sherman*—barely two years after his father departed—the younger MacArthur was amazed at the mix of Asian, Spanish, and American cultures. "The Philippines charmed me," he remembered, "fastened me with a grip that has never relaxed." He hiked the jungles of Bataan, worked on the fortifications at Corregidor, and befriended Manuel Quezon and Sergio Osmeña, two young University of Santo Tomas law graduates who would later lead the Philippines. MacArthur likewise tasted his first adventure when he was jumped on a jungle path by two desperados. "Like all frontiersmen, I was expert with a pistol," MacArthur later said. "I dropped them both dead in their tracks, but not before one had blazed away at me with his antiquated rifle. The slug tore through the top of my campaign hat and almost cut the sapling tree immediately behind me."

Douglas MacArthur returned on future assignments of increasing importance, serving as the commander of the Military District of Manila and later as head of the army's Philippine Department, where he commanded all troops in the islands. He saw in the Philippines the same potential as his father, one the senior MacArthur had articulated best during his 1902 testimony before Congress. "The archipelago," he told lawmakers, "is the finest group of islands in the world. Its strategic position is unexcelled by that of any other position on the globe." Douglas MacArthur shared not only his father's bullishness on the Philippines' future but also his progressive racial views. During his years in the islands, the senior MacArthur had invited Filipinos into his home and admonished officers and spouses who drew the "color line." He appeared insulted during a Senate hearing when a Texas lawmaker asked him to compare Filipinos to African Americans. "I have never made that comparison," Arthur MacArthur chafed. "I have never had any occasion to consider that. I should not want to compare Filipinos with any other people. I might reach conclusions unjust to both."

Douglas MacArthur proved no different, developing deep relationships with Filipino leaders, a fact that triggered resentment and even antagonism from some of his fellow American businessmen and officers who still clung to the idea of white superiority in the islands. The confident MacArthur shrugged it off. "Attitudes die hard," he said, "and the old idea of colonial exploitation still had its vigorous supporters." The general's relations went beyond just friendship. In the wake of his failed first marriage, he found solace with a Filipina mistress, sixteen-year-old Isabel Rosario Cooper, a half-Scottish, half-Filipino vaudeville star known by her stage name Dimples. In his private letters to her, MacArthur often signed them "Daddy," a reference to the three-decade age difference. When he returned to Washington as chief of staff, MacArthur put her up in an apartment in Georgetown. The relationship ultimately was doomed, but as Petillo observed, MacArthur seemed to find both in his romance with Cooper and in his life in Manila an escape from the rigid pressures of Washington officialdom. "For Douglas MacArthur," she wrote, "the Philippines were home."

With MacArthur's tenure as chief of staff about to end in 1935, Philippine president-elect Manuel Quezon visited him in Washington. The United States had agreed to grant the Philippines independence in 1946, and Quezon had questions for MacArthur.

"Do you think that the Philippines can be defended?" he asked.

"I don't think so," MacArthur replied. "I know that the Islands can be protected, provided, of course, that you have the money which will be required."

Quezon then offered MacArthur a job. Would the general return to the Philippines and help build the fledgling nation's new military?

Neither MacArthur nor Quezon could escape the symbolism that hung over the offer. Barely four decades earlier MacArthur's father had fought to pacify the islands; now his son had been invited to return to build it a modern army.

MacArthur accepted.

The opportunity came with the generous salary of $18,000 a year, plus another $15,000 in expenses and a rent-free home in a new air-conditioned penthouse suite to be built atop the luxurious Manila Hotel. MacArthur departed for the Philippines for the fourth time in October 1935 aboard the steamer *President Hoover*, joined by his eighty-three-year-old mother, Pinky, who became ill and spent most of the voyage in her stateroom. Onboard the ship, MacArthur met Jean Faircloth, a beautiful thirty-five-year-old brunette from the small town of Murfreesboro, Tennessee. He sent her a basket of flowers and invited her one morning to coffee. The duo hit it off amid the shipboard festivities, which included evening cocktail parties on deck featuring bowls of ice with caviar in the middle followed by formal dinners and dancing. From an old southern family, Jean was every-thing MacArthur's flapper first wife and his Filipina mistress were not, down to her grandfather's Bible, which she carried in her luggage.

Pinky's health continued to deteriorate after the *Hoover* docked in the Philippines. She died of cerebral thrombosis on December 3, 1935, just five weeks after arriving. Her final breath, as she lay in bed at the Manila Hotel, was of the humid sea air of the Philippines that had come to define the lives of both her husband and her son. MacArthur was crushed, ordering her room to remain empty for a year, the doors locked. Gone was his closest companion, friend, and cheerleader of more than half a century. Dwight Eisenhower, who served as MacArthur's chief of staff, recalled that the general was sullen for months, a grief he expressed in letters to his friend Cal O'Laughlin: "Mother's death has been a tremendous blow to me and I am finding the greatest difficulty in recoordinating myself to the changed conditions." MacArthur followed up a week later. "My loss has partially stunned me and I find myself groping desperately but futilely," he wrote. "For the first time in my life, I need all the help I can get."

MacArthur found that help in Jean, courting her nightly with trips to the movies, often to the Ideal Theater, where the couple sat on the upholstered seats of the center loge. The couple married in a small ceremony at the Municipal Building in New York while on a return trip to the United States on April 30, 1937. The normally loquacious leader was brief in his public comments after the ceremony. "This," he simply declared, "is going to last a long time." Ten months later, at Sternberg Hospital in Manila, the couple welcomed Arthur into the world. MacArthur asked President Quezon, who as a guerrilla had once fought against his father, to be his son's godfather. The christening took place in the family's home atop the Manila Hotel on what would have been Arthur MacArthur's ninety-third birthday. In Manila, freed from the yoke of his parents and with a successful career behind him, Douglas MacArthur found what had evaded him for much of his life—happiness. "With my little family," he wrote, "I would be lonely no more."

But Japan's near simultaneous attacks on Hawaii and the Philippines in December 1941 had in hours destroyed MacArthur's idyllic world. Unlike his War Department counterparts back in Washington, far removed from the capsized battleships at Pearl Harbor and the smoldering airfields around Manila, MacArthur and his family lived on the front lines of America's fight against Japan. From the veranda of his home, MacArthur could see black smoke hovering over the blasted American naval base at Cavite, across the bay and the walled city of Intramuros just blocks away. Japanese fighters and bombers buzzed over the parks he strolled with Jean and the sidewalks where young Arthur rode his new tricycle, an early Christmas gift. On December 22, 1941, the main Japanese invasion force of 43,000 troops sloshed ashore at Lingayen Gulf and began the drive toward the capital. MacArthur felt he had no choice but fall back to Corregidor, declaring the capital an open city. The general wasn't just moving his post.

He was abandoning his home.

On the afternoon of Christmas Eve 1941, Jean rushed to reduce the family's life into a couple of suitcases. Along with food and clothes for Arthur—not to mention his beloved stuffed rabbit—she grabbed a few photos of the general's parents, her grandfather's Bible, and the brown coat with a fur-lined collar she had worn at her wedding. As she prepared to depart, Jean spotted the glass case that held some of her husband's medals and the gold baton President Quezon had presented him when he became field marshal of the Philippine government. She bundled them up in a hotel towel and stashed them inside another suitcase, snapping it closed. Atop the grand piano, Jean eyed two vases given by Emperor Hirohito's grandfather to Gen. Arthur MacArthur during the Russo-Japanese War in 1905, the history of the gifts engraved on their bases. Jean snatched the pair and placed them on a table in the reception hall. "Maybe when the Japanese see it," she said with a half smile, "they will respect our home."

The family boarded the steamer *Don Esteban* for the twenty-seven-mile trip to Corregidor, joined by President Quezon and his wife and children, who traveled aboard the Mayon. Up on deck, members of MacArthur's staff watched the receding lights of the Manila Hotel and the Army and Navy Club, two institutions that had long served as the epicenter of American life in the Philippine capital; an era that was coming to a dramatic end. A bright moon shone down from above as several officers began to sing Christmas carols, including "Silent Night." Capt. William Morse shot a glance at MacArthur, who sat with his head slumped in his hands, the gravity of the situation hanging over him. The city his father had fought to capture, he now fled under the cover of darkness. "Behind us Manila was burning, a spectacular display of sound and light," recalled Paul Rogers, headquarters chief clerk and stenographer. "Fire and smoke illuminated our departure, and exploding munitions dumps added to the sound. Ahead the sky was filled with stars."

MacArthur and his family endured seventy-seven days in the tunnels on Corregidor before evacuating that doomed fortress for Australia. His defeat in the Philippines had shaped MacArthur's entire wartime strategy: every subsequent action was driven solely by his desire to return to Manila. He clawed his way back across the jungles of New Guinea on limited resources that led his staff to describe the fight as the "poor man's war," "Operation Shoe String," and "the Cinderella war." But MacArthur had realized that New Guinea was any commander's nightmare, a tropical island filled with impassable jungles, towering mountains, and disease. Rather than battle the Japanese directly, he turned the island against them, leapfrogging over strongpoints and cutting the enemy off from reinforcements, allowing them to "die on the vine."

"The jungle! Starvation," he told one of his generals. "They're my allies!"

Each successful landing in MacArthur's march north up the coast of New Guinea, his intelligence chief noted, was another milestone on the "road to Manila," where the general had left behind thousands of his troops and his home.

But Japan, for the pending fight for the Philippines, had put a new commander in place. Gen. Tomoyuki Yamashita had defeated the British in Malaya and Singapore in the opening months of the war. Yamashita had then vanished off the battlefield like a ghost; officers in his own army even speculated that he had died. But the Japanese had now resurrected the famous general and sent him to the Philippines to stop MacArthur. As he closed in on his goal, MacArthur likewise changed his strategy. No longer would he bypass the Japanese. The time for battle had arrived. "I'm going to meet the enemy head on," he told one of his generals, "and destroy him."

CHAPTER 2

"There is no weapon against cruelty, against warped minds and warped souls."

—Pacita Pestaño-Jacinto,
diary entry, January 6, 1945

G ENERAL YAMASHITA STEWED IN HIS NEW HEADQUARTERS
in the mountain town of Baguio. The fifty-nine-year-old commander of Japanese forces in the Philippines had relocated his headquarters from Manila to the summer capital some 125 miles north to make his final stand against MacArthur. Built like a bear, Yamashita stood five feet nine inches tall and weighed 220 pounds, his girth often pressing against his green army uniform. He was homely, with a bald, egg-shaped head, wide-spaced eyes, and a flat nose. For years he had worn a short moustache, reminiscent of Adolf Hitler, but as it grayed, he finally opted to shave it. His unattractive looks led the Filipinos to nickname him "Old Potato Face," while an American intelligence report derogatorily described him as "a florid, pig-faced man." Yamashita's banal appearance camouflaged the fact that he was one of Japan's greatest generals. Only three years earlier he had stunned the world by conquering Singapore, earning the nickname the "Tiger of Malaya."

Yamashita understood better than anyone that the war was nearing its climax—and Japan its defeat. The general could only brood over how his nation's fortunes had changed so dramatically since those heady early days of victory when pilots had destroyed much of America's powerful Pacific Fleet anchored in the cool waters of Pearl Harbor. Japanese forces had gone on to capture Guam, Wake, and the

Philippines from the United States, Hong Kong and Singapore from the British, and the oil-rich Dutch East Indies from the Netherlands. In a few short months, Japan had built an empire that stretched across twenty million square miles and seven time zones, putting one-tenth of the world under the control of the bespectacled Emperor Hirohito. But Japan's dream of a Pacific empire had proven an elusive mirage, vanishing with a string of defeats from Midway and Guadalcanal to New Guinea and the Marianas.

With those losses, so, too, went Japan's vital imports. The lack of oil had crippled the nation's war machine, forcing the navy to relegate its once-powerful battleships to antiaircraft duty and leading to the creation of the kamikazes that now crashed down on MacArthur's forces. Japanese civilians likewise suffered. Hungry residents devoured acorns and even sawdust, while new mothers proved too malnourished to nurse. This was the backdrop of Yamashita's pending clash with MacArthur, a battle over the last major geographic roadblock that stood between American forces and the Japanese homeland. Yamashita's job was to turn the Philippines into a tar pit, to bog MacArthur down and give Japan time to dig shelters and prepare. The importance of his mission reflected in the final words Hirohito told him: "The fate of the Empire rests upon your shoulders." Yamashita understood, and just as MacArthur had come to the Philippines to avenge his defeat, so, too, was Yamashita certain of his own destiny.

He had come to die.

Yamashita had traveled a long road to this moment. The son of a rural doctor, he was born on Shikoku—the smallest of Japan's four main islands—in the remote village of Osugi Mura or "Great Cedar." As a child, he thrived in the rugged and isolated environment, where for generations families had worn kimonos and wooden sandals and survived by farming rice and fishing. Yamashita loved hiking, exploring the forests, and writing poetry, adopting the pen name Daisan or "Giant Cedar" after a tree in the family's front yard. "This was a guiding motto for his life," one Japanese historian later wrote. "He wanted henceforth to be a man of upright character and bearing, looking up skyward like the giant cedar." The lull of the wilderness eclipsed his interest in academics, leaving his older brother Tomoyoshi to follow his father into medicine, albeit abandoning a rural practice for a move to Tokyo. "If I had only been cleverer or had worked harder," Yamashita once said, "I would have been a doctor like my brother."

Yamashita's parents instead saw a future for him in soldiering, one he later noted was perhaps his fate. He attended the Cadet Academy in Hiroshima, where his earlier dislike of school vanished. Yamashita's strong performance landed him a spot at the Imperial Japanese Army Academy in Tokyo—Japan's equivalent to West Point—where he graduated fifth in his class of 1908. He applied that same tenacity a decade later at the war college, finishing sixth out of fifty-six officers and earning a sword from the emperor for his achievements. An important lesson for the young officer—one that no doubt hung over him on the eve of his fight against MacArthur—came in 1919, when Yamashita landed as assistant military attaché in Bern, Switzerland. Along with Capt. Hideki Tojo, who would later serve as Japan's war minister and prime minister, Yamashita toured battlefields on the western front and visited Hamburg, witnessing first hand the crippling inflation and food prices that resulted from Germany's defeat.

"If Japan ever has to fight any nation," Yamashita confided in Tojo, "she must never surrender and get herself in a state like this."

Yamashita returned to Europe again several years later as the military attaché in Vienna, an experience that provided a much-needed reprieve after his home life soured. He had invested in a business selling thermometers started by one of his wife's relatives, going so far as to guarantee the loans. The business failed, and bailiffs showed up to seize his home. "For a regular officer to have contracted such a debt, however innocently, was a disgrace," wrote one biographer. "He felt he should resign his commission." Yamashita's brother refused to allow him to quit, instructing him to leave for Vienna, while he resolved his debts. The three years in Europe, Yamashita professed, were the best in life. He studied economics at Vienna University and befriended a Japanese widow, who introduced him to a German woman named

Kitty, with whom he had an affair. "Before Vienna, I knew little of the world outside military life," he later said. "There I read many books and made many good and interesting friends."

Yamashita's reputation as an eccentric officer grew after he returned to Tokyo. He obsessed over hygiene, refusing to eat fruit unless it was thoroughly washed. He likewise avoided ice water, disliked dancing, and never learned to drive a car. His greatest quirk centered on his habit of falling asleep—often in the middle of meetings—with a guttural snore that became legendary throughout the army. But his rising stature faltered when two captains he had mentored helped lead a failed coup of young officers on February 26, 1936, resulting in the deaths of several senior government officials. Yamashita helped mediate a peaceful end to the standoff, but the damage was done. Not only did he fall out of favor with the emperor, but the young captains whom he loved like sons committed suicide. "When I was posted to Korea, I felt I had been given a tactful promotion but that in fact my career was over," he later said. "Even when I was given my first fighting company in North China, I still felt I had no future in the Army, so I was always on the front line, where the bullets flew the thickest. I sought only a place to die."

Yamashita returned to Tokyo in July 1940, where following his success as a frontline divisional commander in the war against China, his fellow officers lauded him as Japan's finest general. Tojo had since ascended to the role of the nation's war minister. One of his first moves was to send a delegation to Germany. Born within three weeks of one another, Tojo and Yamashita shared a long history, stretching back to their days at the Imperial Japanese Army Academy. Unlike Tojo, who was a political animal, Yamashita had little interest outside the army. "My life," he once said, "is that of a soldier; I do not seek any other life unless our Emperor calls me." Despite that, Tojo, who considered Yamashita a "ruthless and forceful commander," saw a potential rival in his former travel partner, and their relationship soured. "I have nothing against Tojo," Yamashita said, "but he apparently has something against me." Near the end of 1940, Tojo tasked Yamashita to lead a team of forty experts on a six-month train tour of Germany and Italy, a move that kept the general out of Tokyo as Tojo solidified his power.

"If you say anything out of place to the newspapers," a fellow officer warned Yamashita, "Tojo will make trouble."

In January 1941, Yamashita met with Adolf Hitler in Germany, passing along messages from Tojo and a silver model of a flying crane. Though he publicly praised Hitler, privately he was unimpressed by the German leader, whom he viewed as a little man. "He may be a great orator on a platform, with his gestures and flamboyant way of speaking," Yamashita said, "but standing behind his desk listening he seems much more like a clerk."

"All our secrets are open to you," Hitler assured him.

Despite that promise, Hitler failed to deliver. "There were several pieces of equipment the Germans did not want us to see," Yamashita said. "Whenever I tried to persuade the German General Staff to show us things like radar—about which we had a rudimentary knowledge—the conversation always turned to something else."

The two clashed on other points, including Hitler's desire for Japan to declare war on America. "My country is still fighting in China, and we must finish that war as soon as possible," Yamashita countered. "We are also afraid that Russia may attack us in Manchuria. This is no time for us to declare war on other countries."

Yamashita met with Field Marshal Hermann Göring, who gave him an overview of the war in Europe. Yamashita fell asleep—as he so often did—and began to snore. Unaware of Yamashita's quirk, Göring cut short his lecture, complaining later that the Japanese general must have been drunk. Yamashita took time off to visit Kitty in Vienna, though the reunion warranted only two sentences in his diary. "I visited my friend the widow and in the afternoon Kitty came to see me," he wrote. "It was memorable."

The trip convinced Yamashita that Japan should stay out of the war, believing that Germany made a grievous error when it invaded Russia in June 1941. The general called the members of his commission together. "You know the results of our inspection as well as I do," he told them. "I must ask you not to express opinion in favor of expanding the alliance between Japan, Germany and Italy. Never suggest in your report that Japan should declare war on Great Britain and the United States. We must not and cannot rely upon the power of other nations. Japan needs more time, particularly as there may be aggression against us from Russia. We must have time to rebuild our defense system and adjust the whole Japanese war machine. I cannot repeat this to you often enough."

Yamashita said much the same in the report he filed upon his return, which infuriated Tojo, who at the time was busy developing plans for war against the United States. Yamashita again landed in exile, this time in Manchuria in July 1941, but his stay in China proved short-lived. In November of that year, Yamashita received orders to report to Tokyo. Despite Tojo's resentment of his former friend, he could not deny that Yamashita was one of the nation's great generals. In the coming war against the United States and Great Britain, Yamashita's services would be vital. He was named commander of the 25th Japanese Army. His orders: seize the Malay Peninsula and the British naval base at Singapore. This was the army general's dream assignment.

The Malay Peninsula snakes seven hundred miles south of Thailand, a rugged sliver of land that constricts at its narrowest point to just sixty miles wide. Mountains split the peninsula in half, climbing as high as seven thousand feet. Malaya produced nearly 40 percent of the world's rubber and almost 60 percent of its tin, both vital resources in war. Just off the peninsula's southern tip sat Singapore, a diamond-shaped island connected to the mainland by a 1,115-yard-long stone causeway. Twenty-six miles long and fourteen wide—or about ten times the size of Manhattan—the island was home to a few villages, rubber plantations, and the city of Singapore, located on the southern coast.

Singapore's biggest asset was the sprawling naval base that guarded passage from the Pacific to the Indian oceans and served, in the words of one reporter, as "the bolt that fastens the back door of the British Empire." Construction of the base atop a mangrove swamp had proved nothing less than an engineering marvel, spanning twenty years and costing a staggering $400 million. Workers diverted a major river, leveled hills to fill in swamps, and drove thirty-four miles of concrete and iron pilings, some as many as one hundred feet deep. The base's towering walls enclosed what amounted to a four-square-mile town complete with churches, cinemas, and recreation facilities, including a swimming pool, seven football fields, and eighteen tennis courts. "The naval base," proclaimed *Life* magazine, "is a bedazzling phenomenon."

Like a jewel thief, Yamashita's job was to snatch this diamond from the British Crown. The general said farewell to his wife at the Japanese Officers Club behind the Imperial Palace. "I pray for your future in battle," she told him and bowed.

Yamashita simply nodded.

The amateur poet Giant Cedar instead captured his thoughts over the pending fight in verse on December 4, 1941, the day he departed for the mission:

> On the day the sun shines with the moon
> Our arrow leaves the bow.
> It carries my spirit toward the enemy.
> With me are a hundred million souls—
> My people from the East—
> On this day when the moon
> And the sun both shine.

The Japanese had long studied Singapore and understood that the so-called "Gibraltar of the Orient" was, as one American reporter noted in 1940, little more than an "empty shell." The cash-strapped British, busy battling Germany in Europe, had no permanent fleet to moor in Singapore, despite offering more than twenty square miles of deep-sea anchorage. "Your American fleet," a British vice admiral quipped to a reporter, "would fit nicely into Singapore." Air support on the peninsula was likewise weak, consisting of outdated planes that were no match for the Japanese. Many of the troops were poorly trained; barely half were English, the rest Indian, Malayan, and Australian. Beyond those deficiencies, Singapore had what Japanese war planners recognized as a fatal blind spot—the base was designed to repel an attack from the sea. Yamashita instead planned to assault the island from the jungle. To make his attack a success, he needed to move fast, opting for a small force of just thirty-six thousand troops. In a war defined by technology and power, Yamashita resorted to an antiquated weapon.

Bicycles.

Japanese forces sloshed ashore on the Malay Peninsula just north of the Thai border, in an invasion timed to coincide with the attack on Pearl Harbor. Yamashita's troops set off south, half in motor vehicles and the rest pedaling eighteen thousand bicycles down paved asphalt highways. Navigation consisted of simple school atlases. "With the infantry on bicycles," wrote chief planner Col. Masanobu Tsuji, "there was no traffic congestion or delay. Wherever bridges were destroyed the infantry continued their advance, wading across the rivers carrying their bicycles on their shoulders, or crossing on log bridges held up on the shoulders of engineers standing in the stream."

The Japanese overwhelmed the poorly trained defenders, some of whom fought back while many others fled, leaving behind stores of food and abandoned trucks, which Yamashita's forces dubbed "Churchill's Allowance." British Lt. Col. Spencer Chapman, hidden along the side of the road, watched hundreds of Japanese troops pedal past. "The majority were on bicycles in parties of forty or fifty, riding three or four abreast and talking and laughing just as if they were going to a football match." Excessive heat, coupled with the eighty pounds of gear each soldier carried, at times popped their bicycle tires. Repair squads mended damaged bikes, though some soldiers simply rode on the rims, which made a metallic rattle that terrified retreating forces.

"Here come the tanks!" troops cried.

The British proved slow to grasp the threat from the Japanese, a sentiment best captured by Singapore governor Sir Shenton Thomas after he learned Yamashita's forces had landed. "Well," he said, "I suppose you'll shove the little men off."

Cities and towns fell one after the other. Japanese forces reached Kuala Lumpur, only to find the British had escaped the night before, which infuriated Yamashita. "I don't want them pushed back," he wrote in his diary. "I want them destroyed."

Prime Minister Winston Churchill fumed over the failure of his forces. Not only had Japanese planes destroyed the battleship *Prince of Wales* and the battle cruiser *Repulse*—the backbone of British naval power in Asia—but now Yamashita's so-called "bicycle blitzkrieg" closed in on the island's rear flank. "Singapore's back door," a United Press reporter wrote, "became its front door." Though many of the island's guns could swivel to face the peninsula, troops realized that the armor-piercing shells designed to punch through ship hulls were worthless in a fight against ground troops. "The possibility," Churchill wrote, "of Singapore having no landward defense no more entered into my mind than that of a battleship being launched without a bottom." The prime minister fired off orders on January 19. "The entire male population should be employed upon constructing defense works," he wrote. "The most rigorous compulsion is to be used, up to the limit where picks and shovels are available."

But it was too late.

Yamashita's forces reached the southern tip of the peninsula by the end of January 1942. In barely eight weeks, his troops had covered some seven hundred miles—an average of more than twelve a day—and fought ninety-five large and small battles. The narrow Johore Strait—barely four feet deep at low tide—was all that stood between Japanese forces and the island. "The Singapore we had once seen in a dream," Tsuji wrote, "we now saw under our eyes." The general gathered about forty of his divisional commanders and senior officers at a rubber plantation to give them orders. The officers then raised canteen caps of Kikumasamune, a ceremonial wine. "It is a good place to die," Yamashita toasted. "Surely we shall conquer."

Conditions inside the city of Singapore deteriorated. Refugees had swollen the population of 550,000 to nearly a million with as many as thirty people packed per room. Japanese artillery rained down, destroying sewers and reducing the flow of freshwater to a trickle as five out of six gallons bubbled out of broken lines. "The whole island seemed afire," wrote one reporter. "It was a pyrotechnical display of unbelievable grandeur and terror." Casualties mounted at a rate of two thousand civilians a day, overwhelming hospitals that stank of blood and entrails and whose lawns were now covered in graves. Between air raids, workers loaded the dead onto trucks for mass burials, while starving dogs feasted on the ones left behind. Troops set fire to oil stores, darkening the skies with a heavy smoke that burned nostrils, teared eyes, and mixed with rain to stain uniforms. "I am sure there is a bright tropic sun shining somewhere overhead," wrote one reporter, "but in my many-windowed room it is too dark to work without electric lights."

British forces destroyed the causeway, but Yamashita's troops had little trouble crossing in collapsible motorboats. Churchill grew desperate, recognizing the stakes were far greater than one island. "There must at this stage be no thought of saving the troops or sparing the population. The battle must be fought to the bitter end at all costs," the prime minister cabled. "Commanders and senior officers should die with their troops. The honour of the British Empire and of the British Army is at stake."

Lt. Gen. Arthur Percival, the bucktoothed commander of British forces, saw the end fast approaching. "It is unlikely that resistance can last more than a day or two," he cabled. "There must come a stage when in the interests of the troops and civil population further bloodshed will serve no useful purpose."

Percival's superiors disagreed, demanding the general fight house to house if necessary. "So long as you are in position to inflict losses and damage to enemy and your troops are physically capable of doing so you must fight on."

But Percival could not.

On February 15, 1942, he sent what would prove to be his final telegram. "Owing to losses from enemy action, water, petrol, food, and ammunition practically finished," he cabled. "Unable therefore to continue the fight any longer."

Shortly before six p.m. that same day—as news cameras rolled— Percival arrived unarmed at the Ford Motor Company factory at Bukit Timah to surrender to Yamashita. The fifty-four-year-old British commander was dressed, this Sunday evening of his daughter Margery's twelfth birthday, in khaki shorts and a shirt and wore a steel helmet. An interpreter and two staff officers accompanied him, one clutching the Union Jack, the other a white flag of surrender, which partially dragged on the ground behind. The men marched through the main entrance of the factory, where the roof had collapsed and explosions had blown out many of the windows. Japanese troops inside had chalked out spots on the concrete floor for the senior officers, cameramen, and reporters.

"Exhausted by the strenuous campaign," one Japanese correspondent observed, "the six-foot Britishers wore haggard expressions." Tsuji noted the same. "The faces of the four English officers," he wrote, "were pale and their eyes bloodshot." Even Yamashita, who arrived a half hour later with his sword in his left hand, was moved by the agony of his vanquished rival, who sat at the table, arms folded in front of him. "Yamashita wanted to say a few kind words to Percival while he was shaking hands with him, as he looked so pale and thin and ill," the general's adjutant wrote that day in his diary. "But he could not say anything because he does not speak English, and he realized how difficult it is to convey heartfelt sympathy when the words are being interpreted by a third person."

The rivals sat down across from each other at a long teak table. The Japanese general kicked off his leather boots, a seemingly arrogant move that masked his fear that the British would discover how small his force really was and that his troops were almost out of ammunition. Shortly before the conference, Yamashita had gambled and ordered his forces to fire a massive barrage at the city, hoping to have a psychological effect on the British. "My attack on Singapore was a bluff—a bluff that worked," Yamashita wrote in his diary. "I had 30,000 men and was outnumbered more than three to one. I knew that if I had to fight long for Singapore, I would be beaten. That is why the surrender had to be at once. I was very frightened all the time that the British would discover our numerical weakness and lack of supplies and force me into disastrous street fighting."

"I want your replies to be brief and to the point," Yamashita began, an interpreter translating his demands. "I will accept only unconditional surrender."

"Will you give me until tomorrow morning?" Percival asked.

Yamashita refused, telling him he would resume the assault that evening. The Japanese general leaned forward, his left hand resting on the hilt of his sword while he brought his open right hand down on the table like a saber chop. Percival asked for just a few more hours, but Yamashita again balked, his patience waning.

"Yes or no," Yamashita finally barked.

Percival sat in silence.

"I want to hear a decisive answer," Yamashita pressed, "and I insist on unconditional surrender."

The gravity of the situation hung over Percival. Not since Gen. Charles Cornwallis surrendered at Yorktown in 1781 during the American Revolution had the British suffered such a significant defeat. "We were," as Gen. Sir Henry Pownall noted in his diary, "frankly outgeneralled, outwitted and outfought."

"Yes," Percival finally muttered.

With that one word, Yamashita had won.

In just seventy-three days, the son of a rural Shikoku doctor had crushed the British, a feat he accomplished with a force a fraction of the size of his adversary, though with the benefit of air and naval dominance. "With the fall of Singapore," lamented *Life* magazine, "an era of empire ended."

Yamashita's stunning battlefield victory, however, was marred by a series of atrocities his forces committed, a barbarism that would echo three years later during the general's desperate fight to hold the Philippines. Near the town of Parit Sulong, Japanese forces killed about 150 wounded Australian and Indian troops, beheading some and shooting others before dousing them in fuel and setting them ablaze. In another case, troops shot and bayoneted more than three hundred doctors, nurses, and even bedridden patients at the Alexandra Hospital, including one on the operating table.

But the worst would come in the weeks after the battle, when Yamashita ordered the "severe disposal" of thousands of Chinese, who were believed hostile to his forces. Over several weeks, troops rounded up and transported Chinese residents—mostly military-aged men—outside the city and slaughtered them in what became known as the Sook Ching Massacre. Japan would later admit to killing five thousand, though leaders of Singapore's Chinese community would place the number closer to fifty thousand.

Back in Japan, euphoria over the capture of Singapore seized the public. Members of the House of Representatives erupted in shouts of "Banzai," schools suspended classes, and newspapers published special "Victory Supplements." Despite rationing, the government announced each family would be given two bottles of beer, rubber goods, and red beans; children under thirteen would receive caramel drops.

"Singapore has fallen!" trumpeted the *Japan Times and Advertiser.* "Let joy be unrestrained."

"The ruin of the British Empire is at hand," announced the *Chugai.*

"The downfall of Singapore," declared *Osaka Mainichi*, "has definitely decided the history of the world."

Yamashita's victory earned him the nickname the Tiger of Malaya, which he personally despised. "I am not a Tiger," he once barked at a German attaché. "The tiger attacks its prey in stealth but I attack the enemy in a fair play."

Japan's capture of the British citadel reverberated around the world. Winston Churchill called it "the worst disaster and largest capitulation in British history" while Australian prime minister John Curtin warned the defeat jeopardized the "fate of the English-speaking world." For the first time, the American press speculated that the Allies might lose the war. "There can now be no doubt," observed a *New York Times* reporter, "that we are facing perhaps the blackest period in our history."

Yamashita had little time to celebrate.

Many of Japan's generals wanted Yamashita appointed war minister, a move that threatened Prime Minister Hideki Tojo, who feared any potential rival. Tojo retaliated, ordering Japan's feted war hero back to Manchuria. On the surface, the assignment appeared worthy as Yamashita would serve as the first line of defense against a possible

Russian invasion. But since the two nations had signed a neutrality pact in April 1941, and Russia was bogged down fighting the Germans, immediate war appeared unlikely. In reality, Tojo had parked Yamashita on the war's sidelines.

Yamashita's fate, in many ways, mirrored MacArthur's, who despite his own fame was destined to fight only in the war's Pacific backwater while his former subordinates achieved glory in Europe. Tojo's humiliation of Yamashita went further. The prime minister barred him any leave in Tokyo, preventing him from visiting his wife as well as from delivering a speech he had written for the emperor. Yamashita instead stopped off in Formosa en route to his new post, where an aide sent him three geishas.

"I know they want to please me with these girls," the dispirited general said, "but send them back—and don't forget to tip them."

The Tiger of Malaya maintained a low profile in Manchuria, positioning his desk, as always, to face the Emperor's Palace back in Tokyo. He ordered that his dining room be enlarged, and he avoided restaurants. When he was promoted to full general, he celebrated with sweet bean cakes and sake.

As the months turned to years—and Japan's fortunes fell—Yamashita was powerless to intervene from his perch in the war's hinterlands.

"I suspect things are not going too well at the moment," an aide remarked.

"It does not matter what happens in the Pacific," he replied. "Our eyes and ears do not face south, toward the Pacific. Our duty is to face north, toward Russia."

After the Marianas fell in the summer of 1944, putting the Japanese homeland within range of American bombers, many knew the war had moved into a deadly new phase, best summarized by the four words Fleet Adm. Osami Nagano muttered.

"Hell is on us."

America's capture of the Marianas triggered Tojo's ouster. With his exit, Yamashita's exile came to an end. The general was out inspecting his troops on September 23, 1944, when he received word of an urgent message. He rushed back to his headquarters to find a signal announcing his appointment as commander in the Philippines.

Yamashita's time on the bench was over.

"So it's come at last, has it?" he told his chief of staff, General Yotsuide. "Well, everything will be the same, even if I go there."

The general, who understood better than anyone that Japan was destined for defeat, assumed the demeanor of a doomed man. He met with the Manchurian puppet emperor Henry Pu Yi, who remembered how proud and even arrogant Yamashita had been when he first arrived in China. The general stood before him now, a somber soldier. "This is our final parting," Yamashita said. "I shall never come back."

The general was the same with his wife. Before he left Manchuria, he presented Hisako with a package wrapped in oilskin. When she finally opened it after the war's end, she discovered his diaries of the campaign in Malaya and Singapore, along with a copy of the speech he had planned to read to the emperor. Fellow officers in Manchuria urged Yamashita to leave his wife in China where she would be safe, but he disagreed, instructing her to return to Japan, to the land of her ancestors.

"You'd better die with your parents at home," he told her.

Hisako sensed this was different. "When he went to Singapore, I felt nothing," she later said. "This time I felt an ill omen. I felt I would never see him again."

In Tokyo, Yamashita attended a conference, where the chief of war plans outlined the Philippines defense strategy. Yamashita closed his eyes and began to snore. "Perhaps you are tired, General," the irritated chief said. "Would you like to take a rest?"

Yamashita opened his eyes. "Please continue," he replied. "I was just considering your plan. How many islands, for example, are there in the Philippines?"

More than seven thousand.

Yamashita was floored. "How do you expect me to draw up a defense plan?" he countered. "The enemy can make an unexpected attack on several of them at once. I must have the guaranteed help of the Air Force and Navy to enable me to defend this territory."

The general had other concerns as well. "How have you been treating the Catholic population?" he asked.

Individual Japanese commanders, he learned, were responsible for relations with the locals, an answer that drew Yamashita's scorn. "I do not agree that the Army on the spot should have been allowed to deal with the very large number of Catholics there," he said. "I think we should have been at great pains to give them leadership. If we have not done so, how can you expect these people to support us?"

Yamashita used his time in Tokyo to call on officers, including Gen. Yoshijiro Umezu, chief of the army general staff, who warned him of the difficult fight ahead. In consolation, Umezu reminded Yamashita that he was Japan's greatest soldier. Umezu predicted that the main battle for the Philippines would be fought on the island of Luzon; Yamashita agreed.

Yamashita then asked, given America's continued advance toward Japan along the flanks, how long he was expected to fight.

"If you can crush the Americans on Luzon, we can still win," Umezu told him, "even if they keep launching hooks to the south and the north."

Yamashita knew such a victory was impossible, but like a good soldier, he vowed to fight his hardest. He met the next day with Emperor Hirohito and Empress Nagako, enjoying the formal ceremony Tojo had denied him three years earlier. He saluted Hirohito, describing the moment to an aide-de-camp as the happiest of his life. He then prayed at the Yasukuni Shrine dedicated to Japan's war dead before calling on Adm. Mitsumasa Yonai, the navy minister.

Yonai could do little more than bow his head in sorrow.

"Do your best," he repeatedly told him. "Do your best."

To all, it seemed, Yamashita was cursed.

One of his final social stops was an October 3 visit to his wife's father in Kamakura, a seaside resort an hour south of Tokyo where the family had relocated to avoid air raids. A few days later he boarded a plane for the Philippines. "As he caught a final glimpse of the coast of Japan," one biographer later wrote, "there were tears in his eyes."

American planes had already begun bombing targets in the Philippines when Yamashita's plane touched down on October 9, 1944. The general settled into a dormitory at Fort William McKinley, the former U.S. Army base just outside Manila. He summoned his officers the following evening for a meeting in a hall blacked out against air raids. There he leveled with them. "I have been told by our Emperor that the crisis will develop first on this battlefield. This gives us all a heavy responsibility," he said. "I expect you to fight bravely, bearing in mind that victories are won only by resolute and united men. If we remember this, the Japanese Army must win in the end."

Yamashita met with the press afterward. He was alarmed to learn how badly relations had devolved between the Japanese and the Filipinos, an issue he had raised back in Tokyo. Guerrilla attacks had increased to the point where Japanese troops discovered dynamite in the basement underneath the officers' recreation room. As soon as American forces landed on Luzon, Yamashita knew, more Filipinos would turn against them. He had to keep the Filipinos out of the fight. His only solution, this late in the game, was to threaten them, which he did in the press. "Anyone who fights against Japan is our enemy, even if he is a Filipino," he told reporters. "In war we have to eat or be eaten, and if we do not stamp out the guerrillas we shall certainly be eaten."

Lt. Gen. Akira Muto, Yamashita's new chief of staff, arrived on October 20. The fifty-one-year-old Muto had previously served with Yamashita in Manchuria in the late 1930s. Like his new boss, Muto understood the reality of his mission. "There is no general I would rather serve with than Yamashita," he recalled, "but I knew this appointment was a death sentence." Muto's journey from Sumatra, in fact, had nearly killed him. During a refueling stop at Puerto Princesa on the Philippine island of Palawan, he had been caught in an American air raid. He dove into a muddy ditch for cover just as the rear gunner of a B-24 strafed his plane, setting it ablaze and burning up most of his luggage. Exhausted and filthy, he pressed on to Manila.

"It is a good thing that you have come," a relieved Yamashita told Muto when he reported to headquarters. "I have been waiting for you. Everything is bad." He sized up his new chief of staff, who stood before him still covered in mud. "Have a bath first," he told him. "Everything can wait till then."

The bespectacled Muto confided in his new commander that he had lost his uniforms in the air raid, including his underwear.

"Don't worry," Yamashita reassured him. "I'll lend you some of mine."

The arrival of Yamashita—the conqueror of Singapore—excited many of the officers. But Yamashita understood that he had inherited a disaster, a fiasco far larger than any one commander could remedy. He had arrived six months too late to make needed preparations in advance of a fight against MacArthur's superior forces. Of the fifteen officers on his staff, only three had ever served in the islands. Furthermore, outside of Muto, he did not know any of his new staff and had no time to learn their strengths and weaknesses. "We were all extremely troubled," Muto recalled, "by our lack of knowledge of conditions in the Philippines."

Japan's years of defeats, coupled with the army's lowered physical standards and the exhausting heat of the tropics, showed in the poor physical condition and depressed morale of many of his troops. Yamashita witnessed that when he visited the Manila piers to find lean and lethargic soldiers unloading ships. "You have far too many troops here," he told the supply officer. "They should be sent to fighting units and not be employed as stevedores. You had better start recruiting civilian labor."

As the officer explained, given the civilian contempt of the Japanese combined with the guerrilla menace, local labor was scarce and largely unreliable.

Yamashita likewise battled gasoline, vehicle, and rice shortages, the latter a paramount problem considering American submarines and bombers had destroyed as much as 85 percent of the rice shipments from Bangkok and Saigon. He drilled his supply officers on the desperate need for food. "Rice," he harped. "It is rice that we want."

To others, he was even more blunt, arguing that absent rice, America would have no trouble seizing Luzon. "They will accomplish it by hunger, not bullets."

The general's problems soon magnified. Nine days after he arrived, American troops sloshed ashore on Leyte, some four hundred miles southeast of Manila. Upon learning of the invasion, Muto asked a single question that best captured how ill-prepared the Japanese were to fight.

"Where is Leyte?"

Yamashita himself had never set foot on the island—nor would he ever—ultimately managing the battle with the aid of only a map. He had, however, studied MacArthur, viewing his opponent as "a precise, steady and relentless commander, whose campaigns had been almost without flaw." That understanding convinced Yamashita that Leyte—a rugged island dominated by mountains and jungle—was not MacArthur's goal but merely a prelude to the main fight on Luzon, the political and cultural heart of the Philippines. Yamashita was loath to siphon off his forces to defend Leyte, but he was ordered to do so by Field Marshal Count Hisaichi Terauchi, commander of the Southern Army, which was responsible for an area that ranged from Malaya and Burma to French Indochina and the Philippines.

In a heated two-hour meeting, Yamashita fought back.

"This is an order from our Emperor," Terauchi finally instructed him.

"If our Emperor has consented to this plan," Yamashita replied, "there is nothing else to do but proceed with it stubbornly."

Just as Yamashita feared, Leyte proved a disaster. The epic sea battle that opened the campaign cost the Japanese Navy a third of its surface ships, including four aircraft carriers, three battleships, nine cruisers, and nine destroyers. Of the fifty thousand troops Yamashita sent to Leyte, barely half ever made it to the island as American bombers and submarines obliterated the transports en route. "The waters of the sea around us," recalled one Japanese officer, "were tinted with blood."

The fight on shore proved equally calamitous. Starving Japanese troops were forced to hunt for coconuts, bananas, and bamboo shoots. A letter later retrieved from the pocket of a dead Japanese soldier captured the horror Yamashita's troops suffered. "I am exhausted. We have no food. The enemy are now within 500 meters from us. Mother, my dear wife and son, I am writing this letter to you by dim candle light. Our end is near," the soldier wrote. "Hundreds of pale soldiers of Japan are awaiting our glorious end and nothing else."

One month into the fight, Yamashita again pressed Terauchi to let Leyte fall. Few reinforcements would reach the Philippines, and each transport loaded with troops that departed Luzon for Leyte only jeopardized Japan's ability to make a final fight for Luzon. But Terauchi stood firm, urging Yamashita to persevere in the defense of Leyte.

"I fully understand your intention," Yamashita reluctantly concluded. "I will try and carry the campaign out to a successful end."

Yamashita's chief of staff was more cynical.

"The old man expects a miracle victory," Muto griped as the two officers departed the meeting. "He believes he will get help from Heaven."

But Heaven never delivered.

Yamashita learned on December 13 that MacArthur's forces had landed on the island of Mindoro, a little more than one hundred miles southwest of Manila, confirming what he suspected all along about his adversary's intention. He had no option but to abandon Leyte and prepare for battle on Luzon. Terauchi initially resisted, but eventually agreed.

On Christmas Day 1944, Yamashita sent a final message to Lt. Gen. Sosaku Suzuki, his commander on Leyte, leveling with him. No more help would come; Suzuki was on his own. The message was no doubt painful. Suzuki had served as the general's chief of staff in Singapore, sharing in that incredible victory. Now Yamashita implored him and his men to make a final stand and die honorably. "We shall seek and destroy our enemy on Luzon Island, thereby doing our part in the heroic struggle of the army and avenging many a valiant warrior who fell," Yamashita wrote. "I cannot keep back tears of remorse for tens and thousands of our officers and men fighting on Leyte Island. Nevertheless I must impose a still harder task on you. Please try to understand my intentions. They say it is harder to live than to die. You, officers and men, be patient enough to endure the hardships of life, and help guard and maintain the prosperity of the Imperial Throne through eternal resistance to the enemy, and be prepared to meet your death calmly for our beloved country."

The fight for Leyte resulted in 15,500 American casualties, including 3,500 killed. The Japanese paid a far heavier price, with an estimated 60,000 killed either in fighting or from disease and starvation. "After our losses in Leyte," Yamashita later said, "I realized that I could no longer fight a decisive battle for the Philippines." The debacle would reverberate up the chain of command. "Our defeat at Leyte," recalled Navy Minister Admiral Yonai, "was tantamount to the loss of the Philippines." That realization was not lost on MacArthur, who crowed over his victory in a Christmas Day communiqué. "The completeness of this destruction has seldom been paralleled in the history of warfare," he boasted. "General Yamashita has sustained perhaps the greatest defeat in the military annals of the Japanese army."

But Yamashita refused to give up. If he could not win a decisive battle, he would fight a delaying action; he would tie MacArthur down and make him regret ever setting foot on the sandy shores of the Philippines. "I was absorbed day and night," he later said, "in planning for the defense of Luzon."

The general anticipated MacArthur's forces would land at Lingayen Gulf, the same beaches where Japanese troops had invaded three years earlier. Yamashita decided not to defend the beaches or the more than one hundred miles of central plains that separated Lingayen from Manila, recognizing that the sea of rice fields offered no protection for his troops. The navy and air force wanted to try to hold Manila, but Yamashita disagreed. The city's strategic value lay in its harbor and airfields, both of which could be rendered useless by blowing up piers, fuel depots, and scuttling ships.

Manila's liabilities, by contrast, loomed large in a fight. Many of the capital's concrete buildings were inflammable. The city's flat, low-lying terrain made tunneling difficult and guaranteed it would take far more troops to defend than he could spare. What would Yamashita do about the city's nearly one million residents, many on the verge of starvation? Evacuating them was impossible, and he likewise did not want to be responsible for them in battle, particularly since the population's hostility toward the Japanese meant that many civilians would likely turn on his troops when MacArthur's forces arrived. Lastly, American carrier planes crowded the skies over Manila, hindering any battle preparations. "Persistent fighter attacks," Muto griped, "met every vehicle moving during daylight hours, continuing until the target burst into flames."

Just as he had in Malaya and Singapore, Yamashita planned to use the land to his advantage in what promised to be a titanic battle over an island roughly the size of Virginia. He decided to divide his more than 260,000 troops into three groups, dispatching them throughout the island to mountain strongholds. Lt. Gen. Shizuo Yokoyama would lead the eighty thousand men of the Shimbu Group to defend southern Luzon, including the mountains east of the capital as well as the volcanic Bicol Peninsula, a terrain so rugged that roads at times were little more than one-lane dirt paths, often left impassable from washouts and landslides. A small contingent of Yokoyama's forces would remain in Manila to maintain order, oversee the evacuation of food, ammunition, and artillery, and then blow up the harbor installations and water supply along with the roads and bridges over the Pasig River. Such moves would not only impede the advance of MacArthur's forces into the city, but hopefully rob the Americans of a deep-water port for future operations. Maj. Gen. Rikichi Tsukada would command the Kembu Group's thirty thousand troops, covering the area from Clark Field, just north of Manila, west through Bataan, and including Corregidor, where MacArthur's men had made a final stand. Yamashita would lead the 152,000 men of the Shobu Group into the mountains of northern Luzon around the city of Baguio. For the general, the pending battle represented a return to his youth, an opportunity for the Great Cedar to wield his experience in the mountains and forests to bleed MacArthur's army.

The battle for Leyte, however, had exacerbated Yamashita's earlier problems. "Supply shortages had reached unexpected proportions," Muto wrote. "With the weapons and ammunition destined for the Leyte campaign lying useless at the bottom of the sea, only meager shares of either were available for the equipment of newly organized forces." Faced with gasoline, oil, and vehicle shortages, Yamashita could hardly move the few supplies he did have. He counted barely five hundred vehicles per infantry division, a quarter of the more than two thousand America allotted. Throughout the three-year occupation, Japanese forces had allowed the island's railroads to rot. Beyond that he could find just three working locomotives, a figure he would later raise to a dozen, but still far too few. Logistics struggles forced Yamashita to scale down the 70,000 tons of supplies he initially ordered shipped out of Manila to just 13,000 tons. Even then, on the eve of MacArthur's invasion, troops proved able to move only around 4,000 tons.

Yamashita ordered all Japanese women and children to return to the homeland, which resulted in pushback from officials in Tokyo, who feared such an exodus would dampen morale. But he remained firm. He understood the horror of war and that Luzon would soon be no place for women and children.

"I know the real state of the battle," Yamashita said. "It is a very grave moment and I will take responsibility for their reparation."

Muto watched the women and children file aboard a troopship at the pier, delivering a message to them from Yamashita. "When you return to Japan," he instructed, "you must become good wives and mothers."

Yamashita faced another challenge over what to do with the estimated 1,300 prisoners of war and 7,000 civilian internees on Luzon, most crowded in camps around Manila. He wanted no responsibility for them. As soon as MacArthur landed, he informed Field Marshal Terauchi, he planned to turn the prisoners and internees over to a neutral nation, a decision that again drew a rebuke and a demand that he hold on to them unless it was an emergency.

"When the Americans land," he countered, "there will be an emergency."

The general prepared to depart, planning to move his headquarters from Fort McKinley briefly to Ipo, just north of Manila, before pressing on to Baguio. Following custom, he hosted a farewell dinner for the navy on December 23. Midway through the evening the power failed, but fortunately a young officer produced candles. The navy reciprocated a couple days later, throwing a party for Yamashita. During an earlier demonstration of a homemade antitank lunge mine, the general had been injured in the thigh.

"Our general has been wounded," Muto told the hosts. "So I hope you won't give him too much wine to drink."

"Don't be a damn fool," Yamashita erupted, no doubt showing the stress that had been building upon him. "I'll drink what I want."

The general's outburst stunned many of his junior officers, though he later apologized to his chief of staff that he had, in fact, had too much to drink. He departed Fort McKinley along with about half of his staff on December 26, almost three years to the day after MacArthur evacuated the Philippine capital. The group reached Ipo, setting up temporary headquarters in the superintendent's hut at the Manila waterworks dam. The general shared a small room at night with Muto.

"Your Excellency snored so loudly last night I couldn't sleep," Muto complained the next morning.

"Your snores," Yamashita countered, "were louder than the noise of the dam."

The general set off again on January 4 for Baguio. Along the way he met briefly with Shimbu Group commander Yokoyama, whose men were tasked with completing the evacuation of supplies from Manila. In bidding farewell, Yamashita reminded Yokoyama of the importance of the fight ahead, instructing him not to deliberately seek death.

"Your orders," Yamashita said, "are to fight a protracted battle."

CHAPTER 3

"It is cheaper to buy a child than a hog in the city of Manila today."

—JAIME H. MANZANO,
INTELLIGENCE SUMMARY, AUGUST 31, 1944

FORTY-TWO-YEAR-OLD MARCIAL LICHAUCO COUNTED THE days until MacArthur's return. The bespectacled Manila lawyer was the first Filipino to graduate from Harvard in 1923. Three years later he had earned his law degree on the banks of the Charles River in Cambridge. Slender and with neatly parted hair, Lichauco rarely went without a tie and sport coat, reflecting his studious nature. On top of practicing law, the married father of two toddlers had long advocated for his nation's independence, even coauthoring a history on the American conquest of the Philippines. He had since turned his focus to the Japanese occupation, chronicling the downward spiral of his beloved homeland. "Hunger, privation and want are becoming more and more acute," Lichauco wrote in his diary. "Every morning scores of emaciated corpses are found on the streets of the city."

Residents in Manila—caught in a vise between two of the world's most powerful generals—anxiously awaited liberation. Three years of enemy occupation had reduced life in the Pearl of the Orient to a desperate fight for survival. The Japanese had descended upon the Philippines, armed only with empty promises of Asian prosperity while looting the nation's warehouses, stores, and crops. In the city MacArthur had once called home, men, women, and children starved to death each day by the hundreds. Others turned to thievery, prostitution, and even grave robbing to survive. Manila had devolved into a

humanitarian catastrophe; the fate of an entire city and all its inhabitants was at stake. Hungry residents recalled MacArthur's pledge to
return and hoped for an end to the misery. "Three words," one resident wrote in her diary, "but, oh, so full of promise."

The crisis highlighted just how far Manila had come in the nearly
half-century since MacArthur's father had helped liberate the Philippine capital—and how much it had fallen since. Policy makers realized
after the Spanish-American War that Manila, which would serve as
the nation's front door to the business markets of China, India, and
Malaya, needed a face-lift to help attract industry and reflect America's growing global status. To spearhead that transformation, William Taft had recruited famed architect and municipal planner Daniel
Burnham, who over the course of his career helped cities such as Chicago, San Francisco, and Cleveland. He designed the famous triangu-
lar Flatiron Building in New York and Union Station in Washington
and later worked with the celebrated landscape architect Frederick
Law Olmsted, Jr., to redesign the National Mall. Burnham spent six
weeks in Manila in 1904–5, including Christmas in Baguio. "The dive
into the Orient," he wrote in a letter, "has been like a dream."

Burnham saw great potential in Manila with its vast natural
resources. He likewise was drawn to the old Spanish churches and
the ancient walled city of Intramuros, the 160-acre historic heart of
Manila, built soon after the city's founding in 1571 on the muddy
banks where the Pasig River emptied into the bay. "The fortress-city
was a veritable museum of Spanish architecture," one report later
noted. "Statues of medieval greats Magellan, the pioneer world nav-
igator, and Legaspi, the founder and first governor, graced the many
churches, convents and colleges founded by a watchful Catholicism."
In his nine-page plan for the city, Burnham recommended a radial
street pattern, similar to Washington's, emanating out from Intramuros, coupled with an investment in grand public buildings, social
clubs, ball fields, and parks. He proposed a bay-front parkway—an
idea he would parrot in his 1909 plan for Chicago's famed Lake Shore
Drive—as well as shaded streets along the river. "Possessing the bay
of Naples, the winding river of Paris, and the canals of Venice," Burn-

ham wrote, "Manila has before it an opportunity unique in the history of modern times, the opportunity to create a unified city equal to the greatest of the Western World with the unparalleled and priceless addition of a tropical setting."

In the four decades since Burnham drafted his plan, Manila had blossomed into a fourteen-square-mile modern city, one whose population had tripled to 623,000 residents by the eve of the war. The Pasig River bisected the city: business and retail districts perched on the northern banks, while government centers and older residential neighborhoods were located to the south. Beautiful neoclassical public buildings, many featuring towering columns, adorned the city, ranging from the Legislature and Post Office to the Agricultural and Finance buildings. Workers likewise had built the modern Philippine General Hospital, though in California Mission-style architecture, which opened its doors in 1910 with a dispensary, two operating amphitheaters, and 476 beds. "Manila is by far the most beautiful of all cities in the Orient," declared *New York Times* reporter Russell Owens in 1932. "From the top of the University Club it seems half hidden in a canopy of trees, green everywhere, a city within a park."

City life revolved around the luxurious Manila Hotel, which over the years hosted celebrities ranging from silent film star Douglas Fairbanks and novelist Ernest Hemingway to world heavyweight boxing champ Jack Dempsey, not to mention permanent resident Douglas MacArthur. Built in a style similar to the Philippine General Hospital—only with green roof tiles instead of red—the bayfront hotel proved synonymous with elegance, down to the Philippine mahogany ceilings and the silver, crystal, and chinaware imported from Great Britain. To guarantee fresh eggs, vegetables, and poultry, the hotel ran its own farm, while an on-site ice plant kept dishes chilled. Each of the 149 guest suites boasted intercoms and push-button room service, the first hotel in Asia to offer such amenities. When the hotel opened on Independence Day 1912—with fireworks, a concert, and glasses of French champagne—the newspaper headline captured the significance: "Manila Hotel—Monument to Americanism."

Streetcars operated by the Manila Electric Railway and Light Company shuttled commuters around the city on fifty-five miles of track complemented by 125 buses. A fleet of yellow cabs competed for fares with more traditional horse-drawn carriages. Policemen directed traffic through major intersections atop pedestals. American executives with companies ranging from General Electric to B.F. Goodrich thumbed through English-language newspapers or tuned in to radio broadcasts. Residents shopped along the Escolta—dubbed the Fifth Avenue of Manila—lined with theaters, restaurants, and shops. One of the finest was the seven-story H.E. Heacock Company's department store, completed in 1939 and finished in elegant Philippine Dao wood and sporting photoelectrically operated front doors. "Air conditioned from basement to roof," wrote the journal of the American Chamber of Commerce, "the spacious tasteful interior is a dream of comfort, refinement, and inviting shopping."

Recreation proved plentiful. Burnham's vision of a bay-front parkway had materialized in the form of Dewey Boulevard, named in honor of the Spanish-American War hero. Women with colorful parasols strolled along the tree-lined promenade where yellow carts sold Magnolia Ice Cream to children, many of whom played bicycle polo with cut-down mallets. Others sought refuge from the tropical heat in city swimming pools or played tennis and golf on one of Manila's four courses. Residents likewise could enjoy bowling, visit the aquarium, and even take tours of the four-thousand-inmate Bilibid Prison, which opened its doors to curious visitors each afternoon at four for a small fee. Manila had a robust nightlife as well. Residents dined at luxury hotels and social halls, like the Elks and Army and Navy Club, many with rooftop gardens to allow evening concerts. Others took in the latest Hollywood films, including *Gone with the Wind* and *The Wizard of Oz*, at the Avenue, Capitol, and Lyric theaters, all air-conditioned.

Despite the amenities, the same racial prejudices common in the United States dominated Manila social life, where Americans often treated locals as second class-citizens. No Filipino names graced the special guest list for the inaugural ball at the Manila Hotel. Many of the social halls, including the Manila Golf Club, the Polo Club, and the Army and Navy Club, refused to allow Filipino members.

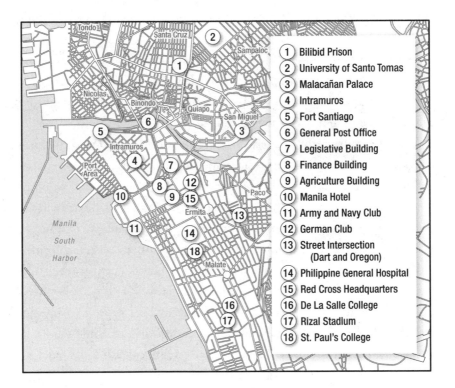

①	Bilibid Prison
②	University of Santo Tomas
③	Malacañan Palace
④	Intramuros
⑤	Fort Santiago
⑥	General Post Office
⑦	Legislative Building
⑧	Finance Building
⑨	Agriculture Building
⑩	Manila Hotel
⑪	Army and Navy Club
⑫	German Club
⑬	Street Intersection (Dart and Oregon)
⑭	Philippine General Hospital
⑮	Red Cross Headquarters
⑯	De La Salle College
⑰	Rizal Stadium
⑱	St. Paul's College

Manila in 1945.

The Wack Wack Golf and Country Club—a favorite of Dwight Eisenhower—was created, in fact, just so Filipinos would have a course to play. Restaurant and cabaret owners reserved the best tables for white customers—typically those closest to the dance floor—while Filipino patrons were forced to crowd in the back. Interracial relationships proved another taboo; Americans who married local women were derogatorily dubbed "squaw men."

No one was immune. Visayan congressman Jose Romero, during lunch at the Manila Hotel with a wealthy sugar planter, noticed a young boy at a neighboring table staring at them. "What are those Filipinos doing in here?" the youth asked his mother.

Life in Manila prior to the war could be arduous for the thousands of American soldiers, businessmen, and families in an era before widespread air-conditioning. Eisenhower and his wife, who lived in an un-air-conditioned suite at the Manila Hotel, often would eat in their underwear just to keep cool. Not only was the climate sultry, but the rainy season stretched from June through October. "It rains continually in a way that would have made Noah marvel," one officer complained. As fast as it was developing, Manila was still a city of gross disparities, with high-rises standing alongside huts roofed with palm fronds. "The city was a curious combination of East and West, old and new," recalled artillery officer Steve Mellnik. "While its modern buildings and wide boulevards proclaimed kinship with the twentieth century, exotically dressed aborigines and carabao-drawn carts suggested close ties with a primitive past. And its peculiar odor—a pungent mixture of Jasmine, burning incense, garbage and sewage—made us gasp."

The tradeoff came in the low cost of living, which allowed Americans to enjoy far more luxurious lifestyles than many might have afforded at home, complete with gardeners, housekeepers, drivers, and cooks. The afternoon siestas likewise helped guarantee a slower pace than at home. "To live in Manila in 1941 was to experience the good life," remembered CBS news correspondent William Dunn. "Who could visualize the horrors of war while living such a life under benign tropical skies."

The good life ended on December 8, 1941.

The Japanese Army seized Manila just nine days after MacArthur abandoned the city for Corregidor. American civilians and Filipinos stood shoulder to shoulder on street corners, eyes aimed north as the first enemy troops roared into the city late in the afternoon of January 2, 1942. Over Manila hung the specter of the Rape of Nanking, the 1937–38 capture of the Chinese capital that led to the slaughter of an estimated 350,000 men, women, and children. The dead proved so numerous that corpses piled along the banks of Yangtze turned the mighty river red. Twenty-five-year-old Pacita Pestaño-Jacinto, a journalist and graduate of the University of the Philippines, shared her fears in her diary, which would become one of the best chronicles of life in the Philippines under the Japanese occupation. "Now danger will not come from the skies," she wrote. "Now danger will be living among us. With us."

"Oh, God," one woman said as she watched. "Let's hope they're decent."

Throughout the evening and in the early morning hours of the next day, columns of Japanese troops poured into Manila. *Life* magazine photographer Carl Mydans was among the many who observed. "They came up the boulevards," he wrote, "in the predawn glow from the bay, riding on bicycles and on tiny motorcycles, their little flags with the one red ball looking like children's pennants. They came without talk and in good order, the ridiculous pop-popping of their one-cylinder cycles sounding loud in the silent city." Pestaño-Jacinto captured the animosity felt by many: "Grim yellow faces. Ugly fixed bayonets. Dirt on their clothes and in their souls."

Residents stared in silence as the Rising Sun rose up the flagpole over the U.S. High Commissioner's Office, signifying the start of a new era. News of Japan's capture of the Philippine capital reverberated around the world. "Manila, for forty-three years a symbol of American democracy in the Far East, fell to the Japanese invader today," United Press declared. "Thus a major American city fell to a foreign power for the first time since the British stormed and fired Washington in the War of 1812."

Troops immediately began rounding up American civilians—bankers, business executives, and secretaries—hauling them to the University of Santo Tomas, just north of the Pasig River, which would become one of the largest internment camps in Asia. No sooner had the Japanese arrived than the plunder of Manila began. Officers commandeered beautiful houses and apartments overlooking the bay. "Mere lieutenants took over palatial homes. The owners were merely ejected immediately, without fuss," recalled Manuel Buenafe, a twenty-five-year-old law graduate and writer when the occupation began. "Some were allowed to take along a bag or two." Pestaño-Jacinto witnessed the same. "They live like princes," she wrote. "They sink contentedly into upholstered chairs, gorging themselves on good food and American wines."

In addition to homes, troops seized cars and trucks. "The favorite procedure was for a Japanese—any Jap—to stand on the curb," Buenafe wrote. "When a car to his taste drove along, it was stopped and the riders advised to hoof it the rest of the way, with a curtsey and a bow." Soldiers likewise looted warehouses and confiscated stores of rice, sugar, and canned foods. Not content to grab just food and vehicles, the Japanese went so far as to pillage luxury department stores, including Heacock's. "It has been picked clean," Pestaño-Jacinto wrote. "Not by looters but by the Japanese themselves. Thick rugs, beautiful lamps, tableware of exquisite cut glass, clothes, beauty aids." Such selfish seizures only exacerbated the cynicism of the Filipinos, a sentiment best captured by Felipe Buencamino, a law student and soldier who quipped in his diary: "What kind of an Army is this that fights a war with pianos and nice residences?"

The Japanese set out to strip the Philippines of almost a half-century of American influences. Dewey Boulevard and Taft Avenue became Heiwa Boulevard and Daitoa Avenue, which translated respectively as Peace and Greater East Asia. Schools trashed Americanized textbooks. The Japanese even banned the color combination of red, white, and blue. One little girl with a pin of semiprecious stones designed like the American flag threw it into the bay while her nine-year-old brother burned his Superman, Buck Rogers, and Mutt and Jeff comics. "But the Japanese cannot read," the boy protested. "They do not know what it is all about!" Still, one could not be too careful: "Everybody knows by now," Pestaño-Jacinto wrote, "that caution is the better part of valor."

The military administration disbanded the legislature, abolished political parties, and installed a puppet government. Radio stations broadcast propaganda; so, too, did newspapers. The Japanese ordered clocks moved one hour ahead—the same as Tokyo—and replaced the peso. "The new currency was quickly dubbed Mickey Mouse money," recalled Jack Garcia, the son of a Spanish tobacco merchant who was seven years old when the occupation began. "It was no better than play Monopoly Money." Schools required students at both public and private institutions to learn Japanese and sing the national anthem, while all residents were ordered to bow to sentries. Posters plastered on city walls as well as in newspapers carried illustrations of proper etiquette. "Failure to do so means just one thing—a severe slap on the face," Lichauco wrote. "Many of us walk or ride several blocks out of our way to avoid having to pass a sentry."

A Japanese colonel addressed the public in March 1942 as part of the rebranding process. The bespectacled attorney Marcial Lichauco recorded the colonel's comments. Like Pestaño-Jacinto's, his diary, too, would prove an invaluable window into this time. "I have summoned you to this meeting because I want to find out what are your grievances, if any," he began, "and because I want to assure you that we are your friends."

The colonel held up his arms before the crowd.

"Look at the color of my skin," he continued. "It is exactly like yours. You and I are closely akin to each other. We belong to the same corner of the world. We have common interests and there is every reason why we should be friends and try to help each other. Our mutual enemies are the people of the white race who have tried to exploit you and our brothers living in Malaya and nearby lands."

Japanese Gen. Masaharu Homma, who had captured Bataan and Corregidor, often parroted that idea. "As the leopard cannot change its spots, you cannot alter the fact that you are Orientals." This messaging was not lost on locals. "Such is the kind of propaganda with which the Japanese are flooding the country," Lichauco noted. "Their theme is always the same—the white against the brown and yellow races."

Despite the ostensible ties between the two nations, the Japanese did not trust the Filipinos, many of whom resented the occupiers. "I think every Japanese soldier feels it, the hatred seething underneath our surrender," Pestaño-Jacinto wrote. "It is a hatred that he must match with the might, arrogance and cruelty of a conqueror."

The Japanese ordered residents to surrender all guns and later knives, including kitchen blades. Drugstores relinquished selling poisons such as arsenic, and authorities confiscated former police dogs from the public. To prevent residents from listening to overseas broadcasts, the Japanese forced citizens to take down rooftop antennas and turn over all radios—some eighty thousand total—so technicians could remove the short-wave components. When anti-Japanese leaflets appeared, authorities demanded residents register all typewriters along with samples of individual keys. The same applied for mimeograph machines and printing presses. The Japanese instituted neighborhood associations, forcing block leaders to keep tabs on area residents. Military authorities went so far as to bar families from traditional gatherings in cemeteries. "War changes everything for everyone," Pestaño-Jacinto observed, "even for the dead."

Along with the crackdown, the Japanese launched a propaganda blitz to demonstrate that America had been vanquished. Theaters played films on Pearl Harbor and later the fall of Bataan and Corregidor. "It is a very good propaganda," Lichauco wrote in May 1942, "but the entire film, I am happy to report, was witnessed by a large Filipino audience in absolute silence." He noted the same when he returned six months later. "Not a single handclap interrupted the picture," Lichauco wrote. "The Propaganda Bureau may be working hard but they are just wasting a lot of film."

To end any hope that MacArthur might soon deliver on his promise to return, the Japanese devised a spectacle far more powerful than a black and white film. Around noon on the sweltering Sunday of May

24, 1942—as heat waves radiated off the asphalt—Japanese troops paraded thousands of American prisoners of war through the streets of Manila en route to Bilibid. Exhausted and filthy after months of fighting, many collapsed only to be whipped by the accompanying Japanese troops. Horrified Filipinos watched in tears. Many threw fried chicken, bananas, and cigarettes; prisoners in exchange tossed money into the crowd. "It was an unforgettable sight," Lichauco wrote. "Although the streets were lined with thousands, there was a deathly silence."

Amid the prisoners of war, thirteen-year-old Fernando Mañalac spotted his older brother Alfredo, a twenty-two-year-old Philippine soldier who was captured with the Americans. Mañalac's mother let out a lone wail at the sight of her emaciated son, who would die two months later of dysentery and malaria at Camp O'Donnell. "Save for the sound of marching army shoes," Mañalac wrote, "there was such a deep sepulchral quietude that one could hear a pin drop." Philippine journalist Nick Joaquin observed that the parade accomplished its goal. "Filipinos stood and watched in an agony of embarrassment. These were the God-blessed Americans, the supposedly invincible," he later wrote. "Now here they were: mighty giants being herded rudely by little Jap soldiers. We would never recover from that loss of innocence."

Unlike the investment the enemy made in suppressing the populace, the Japanese exercised no real effort to manage the Philippine economy, as the weeks turned to months and then years. Troops seized crops of rice and cotton while imports dried up, leaving store shelves bare and prompting some shopkeepers to display empty boxes. Businesses closed, and the Japanese disbanded many government jobs, including slashing 35,000 public school teachers down to just nine hundred. Those lucky enough to remain employed suffered huge pay cuts. People from the provinces meanwhile poured into Manila looking for work, a trend described by Spanish priest Juan Labrador, who served as rector of Letran College in Intramuros. "City life has become polluted by a swarm of parasites: doctors without patients, lawyers without clients, teachers without schools, pharmacists with-out drugstores, and a host of unemployed applicants," he wrote in his diary. "The rush for employment in the city is a plague that is causing so much dysfunction."

The Japanese grew increasingly cruel, abandoning early efforts to win over locals. Troops slapped both men and women over minor traf-fic violations or failure to bow. Others tied residents to posts in the streets or public plazas and beat them, leaving the victims as bloody reminders to others. In one case, a sentry yanked the cigar from a city engineer's mouth and ground it out on the back of his hand. "No one is being spared," Lichauco wrote. "Some of our most prominent citizens are among the victims." Labrador described similar depravity. "The repertoire of exquisite torments is inexhaustible," the priest wrote in his diary. "Each day new forms of cruelty are being invented or imported." Women lived in fear of sexual assault. "My mother had to repeatedly put charcoal all over my face and to fix my hair short so that I would look like a man," remembered Josefina Reyes. "She had to do all of these things to protect me from tipsy Japanese soldiers roaming around in the dark streets who simply wanted to satisfy their sexual drive."

The rise in violence coincided with guerrilla attacks not only on troops but also on collaborators, later called Makapilis, a Tagalog abbreviation for the pro-Japanese group known as the Patriotic Asso-ciation of Filipinos. Those targeted included prominent officials, from bankers and newspaper owners to policemen and even a provincial governor. "The lot of traitors was particularly hard," wrote Forbes Monaghan, a Jesuit priest. "Their tongues were cut out and they were terribly tortured before being killed. In another suburb of the capi-tal the cutting off of one ear was part of the ritual; this told every-body the motive for the killing." In the wake of such violence, the Japanese declared any person found with a gun would be executed, a punishment that would include anyone caught with them at the time of arrest. "A few innocent individuals may have to be sacrificed," the Japanese warned, "but that is a necessary evil in times like these."

Yet guerrilla assassinations continued. "The number of killings in and around Manila is increasing so rapidly that I am afraid I shall have to omit giving further accounts of them," Lichauco wrote on July 17, 1943, "unless I am willing to turn this diary into an obituary column."

Pinched by the waning economy and climbing violence, ordinary residents simply wanted to survive. One of those was Nicanor "Nick" Reyes, founder and president of Far Eastern University. Armed with a business degree from New York University as well as a master's in business administration and doctorate in accounting from Columbia, the dapper educator liked to dress in a white suit. He had given up a career as the head of the economics department at the University of the Philippines to start his own school, convinced that upon independence, the Philippines would need professional accountants. In 1928, when the university opened its doors, enrollment had stood at seventeen students, but by the outbreak of the war, it had swelled to more than eleven thousand. The Japanese Army seized the campus, converting it into barracks and a prison. Reyes had no choice but to close the university. To support his family, he liquidated assets and tutored students.

But the Japanese took more than just his school. The Mitsui Mining Company seized his beautiful three-story home off Taft Avenue, forcing the family to move into a rental in Paco. As Reyes struggled to support his family, his daughter Lourdes, like so many other children caught in the grip of a war few understood, dreamed each day of returning to her backyard playhouse with red Spanish roof tiles. In the days before Japanese planes darkened the skies, she and her younger sister Teresita often competed at twilight to be the first one to spot the glow of a star. Teresita won most of the contests, her youthful voice wafting across the lush garden as she sang:

S-t-a-r-light, S-t-a-r bright
First star I see tonight
I wish I may, I wish I might
Have the wish I wish tonight!

Another who suffered as a child was Joaquin "Jack" Garcia, who missed his friend and playmate Arthur MacArthur. Before the war, his Chinese nanny had been friends with Ah Cheu, who cared for Arthur. A black Buick driven by a soldier would retrieve Jack and his nanny from his home on Callejon Rubio near Taft Avenue. The boys would drink Magnolia chocolate milk and eat biscuits in the MacArthur home atop the Manila Hotel. On the floor of the penthouse playroom—as the two boys assembled a truck from an Erector Set—Garcia met Douglas MacArthur. "The door opened," Garcia recalled, "and in came this tall, broad-shouldered man in khaki. It was the General himself." To his surprise, MacArthur sat down on the playroom floor and helped the boys build the truck. "As far as I was concerned, he just happened to be my friend's father. Nothing more than that," Garcia said. "Now they had all gone away. It was very sad."

As conditions in Manila deteriorated, basic goods dwindled, forcing residents to resort to creative solutions. Roasted rice and corn doubled as coffee, while dried papaya leaves wrapped in old newsprint or pages ripped out of books replaced Camels and Lucky Strikes. "So common was this kind of cigarette," remembered historian Teodoro Agoncillo, "that wags boasted that they were smoking the *Encyclopedia Britannica*, the *Tribune* or the Paris edition of D. H. Lawrence's *Lady Chatterley's Lover*." Children shuffled around in wooden clogs, and crafty seamstresses turned old bedsheets into shirts. Carmen Berlanga Brady yanked down the yellow-and-orange-plaid kitchen curtains, transforming them into underwear for her daughter Joyce, who was six when the occupation began. Hospitals likewise felt the loss, requiring the sick to supply towels and bed linens as well as bandages, cotton, and adhesive tape. Some dispensaries even demanded patients wash bandages and bring them back to be reused. Absent medicines, many turned to herbal remedies, using banana, guava, and tobacco leaves to treat ulcers and sores that resulted from worsening malnutrition. Journalist Joan Orendain summarized it best: "War, the ultimate leveler, made us all poor."

Fuel shortages left ambulances and police cars parked. Unable to drive prisoners to the courthouse, officers roped them together and marched them. The Japanese tore down gas stations just to salvage the rebar from the walls. Throughout Manila, horses and bicycles replaced cars. "Our next door neighbor tells me that he has just made a wonderful bargain. He has swapped his bicycle for a car," Pestaño-Jacinto wrote. "This incident is a typical example of how disproportionate values have become." She wasn't the only one to report such a seemingly lopsided deal. "I know of persons who exchanged their magnificent Buicks for one bicycle," Labrador wrote in his diary. "It was also amusing to see men, women, and priests practicing how to pedal the bicycle, bumping into one another, breaking their noses or colliding with frightened pedestrians." The Japanese, who had once commandeered cars, now snatched up all the bicycles, prompting Buencamino to quip in his diary: "They might take our legs, too."

Residents sold off anything to survive, from family heirlooms to jewelry. Marcial Lichauco hawked his camera, darkroom equipment, and binoculars, as well as his Carrier air-conditioning unit and his stock of whiskey. Nick Reyes liquidated his family's summer home in Baguio, which looters already had stripped of furniture, doors, windows, and even wiring. Firemen sold city hoses, while health inspectors condemned meat in order to confiscate and resell it. Those without salable goods often resorted to thievery. Chickens disappeared from coops. Someone pried up the two toilets from the mechanics shop where teenager Fernando Mañalac worked as a watchman. Others sawed down the iron fence that protected Lichauco's home. Manhole covers vanished along with fire hydrant lids, park benches, and even light bulbs. "One couldn't hang any clothes in his own backyard," Mañalac recalled. "In a matter of minutes, these would disappear mysteriously, including the line. Even rags disappeared."

Thieves grew increasingly brazen. One swiped a Japanese officer's sword during the middle of a movie, while another nabbed the mounted machine gun off of a truck. Others robbed people at gunpoint, including the daring holdup of an entire streetcar. "The women were allowed to keep their dresses on, but the men had to give up all except the barest minimum," Pestaño-Jacinto wrote. "Everybody's shoes were taken." Residents had to be vigilant against theft at all times. "If I happened to fall into an afternoon snooze in the driveway on a chair leaning against the wall and suddenly wake up," Mañalac later wrote, "it was a reflexive act for me to check whether my shoes were still on my feet, or if my belt or any piece of my clothing were still on my body."

Even the dead were not safe as thieves dug up thousands of graves to pluck rings from fingers and pry out gold teeth. Cemetery neighbors complained of the nightly pounding of sledgehammers coupled with putrid smells that wafted from opened graves. Pestaño-Jacinto recalled how a friend with scissors sliced up his deceased mother's clothes before the coffin left the house, explaining that this would hopefully deter grave robbers from touching her body. "This has never happened in the Philippines before. But happens very often today," Pestaño-Jacinto wrote. "The dead are being robbed by the living that the living may continue to live. Clothes, jewels, even dental plates can be sold. One must sell something to buy the food that one must eat."

The stolen goods often ended up on the black market around Rizal Avenue, a sprawling and desperate bazaar where residents and dealers haggled over everything from flour and sulfa drugs to used eyeglasses and scrap iron. After an American bomber crashed following a raid, one of its black rubber tires ended up for sale on the market. Another time a friend of Mañalac's father discovered his lost upper dentures, but at a price ten times what he originally paid, though the vendor tossed in a T-shirt to sweeten the deal. "Here was the last-chance haven for those dying of starvation," Mañalac wrote, "where goods and comestibles were bought and sold without questions asked." More than a market, the bazaar was a reflection of humanity, both good and bad. "In such places," Agoncillo wrote, "man's nature was laid bare for all to see. One would witness man's inhumanity to man, his nobility, his ruthlessness, his kindness."

As salable goods vanished, Filipinos faced widespread hunger, prompting Jose Laurel, maligned as a puppet president of the Japanese, to declare a national state of emergency on February 24, 1944. Laurel's decree mandated all able-bodied men and women between the ages of sixteen and sixty dedicate to the nation one day a week for the production of food.

"This is necessary," the president announced, "to forestall famine and starvation and to maintain our national existence."

Pamphlets, radio announcements, and billboards trumpeted the same theme: "Plant in order to live." City plazas, amusement parks, and even the edges of sidewalks teemed with sweet potatoes, corn, and cassava. "The farm," observed reporter Rodolfo Tupas, "came to the city." Journalist Jean Pope reiterated that idea. "The backyard plot," she wrote, "transformed white-collar folks into farmers overnight."

But such efforts proved too little, too late.

Those with the strength to walk often chose to escape Manila, hoping to find food in the provinces. "In pushcarts, they piled their miserable belongings: a small table, a chair or two, a bundle of clothes," Pestaño-Jacinto wrote in her diary in October 1944. "On foot, under the sun, a long endless caravan of pitiable humanity." Juan Labrador described the same tragic parade of poverty in his diary: "Manila is suffering more than the most punished Sodom of this war."

New mothers proved too malnourished to produce milk. Children waddled around with distended bellies, while toddlers resembled infants. "Food prices have reached undreamed of heights," Lichauco wrote. "Horse meat is a luxury."

Families abandoned children on the doorsteps of the wealthy or handed them over to asylums. Others sold them, a fact highlighted in an August 1944 American intelligence report. "It is a common sight nowadays in the crowded streets of Manila that a mother, with tears in her eyes, sells her child to whoever may pay her the agreed upon amount in cash," the report stated. "They are selling their loved ones not because of the money they may get out of it, but to be sure that their children, whom now it is impossible for them to maintain, may at least have two meals a day at the charity of others."

Nick Reyes brought home an orphaned girl named Milagros—Spanish for "Miracles"—after the Settlement House could no longer support children. Swarming with lice and with a swollen belly from malnutrition, Milagros appeared to be about six years old and desperately needed a bath, a job Reyes assigned to his daughters. "Milagros's bloated stomach was even more repulsive without her clothes on, and her skinny limbs looked slighter by comparison. Her skin was shriveled and hairy," Lourdes later wrote. "It felt slimy, and no amount of scrubbing could remove the fishy smell."

Santo Tomas internees with Filipino families in Manila begged officials to allow wives, sons, and daughters to move into the camp. "We have sold everything possible and have borrowed up to the limit," Edward Bennett wrote to the commandant. "My wife is not strong and the stresses of the last two years have already taxed her beyond her strength. I beg that you will take favorable action immediately."

American air raids, which began on September 21, 1944, increased the stress on the beleaguered population, prompting many residents to build dugouts, which for some seemed to foreshadow a violent end for the city. "The shelters," remembered journalist Joan Orendain, "were exactly like the graves dug for the dead." One American raid destroyed La Insular Cigar & Cigarette Factory, a landmark building dating back to the nineteenth century, where Jack Garcia's father worked. "Dad was a shattered man," Garcia later wrote. "A good part of his life had revolved around that factory. His second home had been destroyed." Children, oblivious to the danger, listened to the bullet casings and shrapnel rain down on the corrugated iron roofs, then charged afterward to collect metal shards, many still too hot to touch. "We traded it," recalled Joyce Brady Velde, "like baseball cards."

An army of beggars besieged Manila, including scores of malnourished children who crowded outside the handful of operating restaurants, holding up coconut shell halves for food. "There was a sickening contrast between the scene outside and inside restaurants," Agoncillo wrote. "Inside, there was gaiety, wine, rich food, and laughter; outside, there was the hustle and bustle of all kinds of people, arms outstretched to receive the munificence of the lucky ones." Mañalac could not help but note the poor health of the needy, often suffering disease and infection. "Many of these had hideous-looking gigantic leg ulcers that stank atrociously, with maggots creeping out of the rotten flesh," he wrote. "Joining their ranks were the lepers who were disbanded from a leper colony, the syphilitics, and the blood-coughing tuberculous."

Doctors at San Lazaro Hospital estimated in late December 1944 that as many as five hundred people starved to death each day. "Along the vast stretches of dust-covered streets, the dead could hardly be counted," Agoncillo wrote. "Some were covered with newspapers, others, less fortunate, were with the rubbish, almost naked, eyes staring at the skies." Lichauco saw a dead man on Taft Avenue within full view of the City Hall. Two days later the body remained, only covered in flies. "Every morning scores of emaciated corpses are found on the streets of the city," he noted in his diary. "More gruesome than these ghastly sights however, are the many old men and young children whom we often see lying around not quite dead yet, but soon to die, with no one able to do anything about it." Many would not make it. "Today," Lichauco wrote, "we are living under conditions in which only the fittest among us can hope to survive."

MacArthur was not oblivious to the horrible conditions and Japanese maltreatment of the population, which guerrillas dutifully radioed.

"Food problem very acute," one message warned. "Dying on sidewalks daily caused by hunger."

"Japs in Manila going house to house confiscating clothing and things they like," read another.

"Mortality from starvation in city mounting."

The misery only increased the hatred many felt for the occupiers. "No Japanese looks starved. No Japanese is allowed to starve. That is the irony of it," Pestaño-Jacinto wrote. "The host has shrunk to nothingness and the parasite blooms."

Nick Reyes's family witnessed the desperation after he learned the Japanese mining company had abandoned his home off Taft Avenue. He walked back from Paco to reclaim his property. "By dawn, a sullen crowd of people, more menacing in their silence, hovered like vultures outside our locked iron gate," daughter Lourdes later wrote. "They were eager to help themselves to whatever food the Japanese might have left."

Reyes explained that the Japanese had not left any food, but the crowd remained. To avoid any violence, he decided to let them inside. "Take anything you want," he said, "but please just leave the heavy furniture and the lights." He unlocked the gate.

Lourdes watched as strangers plundered her home. "A strange parade of people left our house carrying bottles of catsup and soy sauce, plates, glasses, pails, basins, used-up brooms, rags, even the garden hose, a wheelbarrow, a crowbar," she later wrote. "Children carried paper and odds and ends."

The Bradys experienced a similar horror one afternoon when the father was at work: several men armed with handguns forced their way into the family's Taft Avenue home. The bandits tied up and gagged the children, stuffing a rag soaked in shoe polish into then-eight-year-old Joyce's mouth, a smell that would haunt her for life. The bandits then ransacked the house. One started to stroke young Joyce's head, saying how pretty she was. Her mother yelled at the man to stop, but he continued.

"Don't touch her," her mother cried out. "I'll go with you."

To protect her daughter, Carmen Brady sacrificed herself.

The bandits led her to another room. "We heard her yells and screams," Joyce Brady Velde later recalled. "She was raped by at least two of the men." Her older brother, William Brady, who was seven when the war started, also recalled his mother's assault. "When she was brought back upstairs, she was white and nearly fainting," he later wrote of that horrific day. "My mother never recovered."

In the three-year wait for MacArthur's return, the nation's collective sense of morality collapsed. Doctors hawked bogus drugs, lawyers committed forgery and fraud, and police resorted to burglary and extortion. While desperate families sold children, loving wives sold themselves, all to survive. "Morality cowered before the relentless onslaught of economic forces that the war had marshaled and unleashed," Agoncillo wrote. "One witnessed everywhere graft and corruption, mayhem, armed robbery with assault, burglary, petty thievery, prostitution, selling of children, rape, embezzling and blackmailing." Journalist Carmen Guerrero Nakpil echoed the point. "We survived by means of savage and ardent cunning," she later wrote. "We became a race of spies, thieves, saboteurs, informers and looters, callous and miserly."

Amid the suffering and agony, many still waited and prayed that MacArthur would, in fact, return, that he would deliver on his promise.

"The end is near. It won't be long now," Ramon Garcia assured his son Jack, who in November 1944 celebrated his tenth birthday. "The Americans will free us real soon."

CHAPTER 4

"The Japanese were like madmen knowing that the Americans were coming."

—Erlinda Querubin,
testimony, June 30, 1945

THE FAINT LIGHT OF DAWN BROKE ON THE MORNING OF January 9, 1945, signaling the arrival of the moment Douglas MacArthur had long awaited: his return to Luzon and the completion of the promise he made almost three years earlier. His task force of 818 ships crowded Lingayen Gulf and the waters just beyond, having survived days of kamikaze attacks that would kill 738 sailors and leave almost fourteen hundred others wounded. MacArthur could not have been more pleased, as conditions for the landing this Tuesday were almost perfect: scattered clouds coupled with a gentle southeastern wind of just seven knots. Visibility stretched six miles, more than enough to reveal the awesome power of America's forces, a scene best described by CBS correspondent Bill Dunn. "On the dark purple water, as far as the eye could carry," he wrote, "hundreds of ships of every type completely surrounded us—transports and cruisers, cargo vessels and battleships, landing craft and destroyers."

MacArthur had selected Lingayen Gulf as the front door for his return to Manila for its strong geographical advantages, including little current and only a slight rise and fall of the tide during the dry season. Lingayen counted more than twenty miles of wide sandy beaches with a gentle slope, making it easy for landing craft and troops to hit the shore. The absence of bordering jungles, so common throughout the tropics, would allow ample room to maneuver during the offloading of thousands of vehicles, fuel drums, and crates of canned food, ammunition, toilet paper, and even carrier pigeons—a backup communication system in the event of wire failure. Furthermore, Lingayen offered easy access to major highways and railways that would allow troops to speed across the 110 miles that stood between MacArthur and his home. Radio Tokyo had promised the general the "hottest reception in the history of warfare," but MacArthur was optimistic his superior firepower would overwhelm the enemy, a feeling shared by his aides. "The Luzon campaign in my opinion will be rapid and deadly," General Fellers wrote to his wife. "The Nip can't take what is awaiting him."

MacArthur's invasion plan was two-pronged. The Sixth Army, led by Lt. Gen. Walter Krueger, would land first at Lingayen Gulf. That would include the I Corps under the command of Lt. Gen. Innis Swift and the XIV Corps led by Lt. Gen. Oscar Griswold. On the first day, a total of four divisions would charge ashore abreast of one another, followed by thousands more troops in subsequent days. This would cut off any hope Yamashita might hold out for resupply from the north. As the Sixth Army raced south toward Clark Field and Manila, forces with the Eighth Army under Lt. Gen. Robert Eichelberger would hit the beaches at Nasugbu, about fifty-five miles southwest of the capital. Other units under Eichelberger's command would land on the western shores of Luzon and then drive across the Bataan Peninsula. "Both forces ashore," MacArthur wrote, "we would then close like a vise on the enemy deprived of supplies and destroy him."

The planned speed of the operation stemmed in part from MacArthur's increased worry over the fate of thousands of American prisoners of war and civilian internees who awaited rescue on Luzon. The Japanese had locked up almost 3,700 men, women, and children behind the iron gates of the University of Santo Tomas in the heart of Manila. Another 1,275 internees and prisoners suffered just a few blocks away at the worn-out city jail of Bilibid, whose central guard tower Burnham had used decades earlier in his survey of the city. On the outskirts of Manila, the Japanese starved 2,600 more in filthy

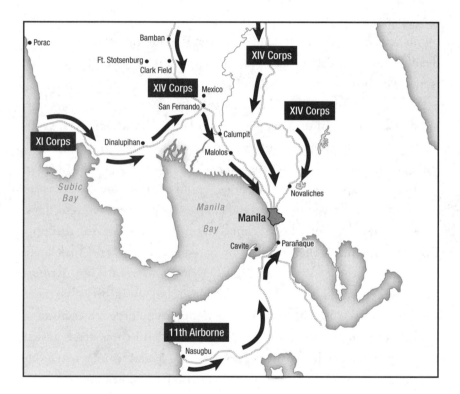

As U.S. forces advanced on Manila, the XIV Corps, which included the First Cavalry and the Thirty-Seventh Infantry divisions, came down from Lingayen Gulf, the XI Corps advanced across Bataan, and the Eleventh Airborne trekked up from Nasugbu.

camps at Los Baños and Cabanatuan. MacArthur knew that every day meager rations dwindled and guards grew more sadistic. He feared the Japanese might simply murder them all before his forces could liberate them. "I knew that many of these half-starved and ill-treated people would die unless we rescued them promptly," MacArthur later wrote. "The thought of their destruction with deliverance so near was deeply repellent to me."

MacArthur's worst fears had materialized just twenty-six days earlier at a prisoner of war camp on the island of Palawan, which held 150 Americans captured on Bataan and Corregidor. The Japanese Army Air Corps High Command, afraid that an American convoy spotted at sea was bound for Palawan, ordered guards to kill all the captives. An air raid alarm sounded in the Puerto Princesa camp around two p.m. on December 14, prompting guards to prod prisoners into several underground bunkers that resembled trenches. The Americans noted the extra armed guards hovering just outside the fence. Navy enlisted man Charles Smith from Alabama loitered around the opening of his shelter. A few feet away Lt. Masahiko Sato, who was the camp's second-in-command, began swinging his sword above his head like an exercise. A second later he brought the saber down atop Smith's skull. Army prisoner Eugene Nielsen of Utah watched in disbelief. "He just split his head open," Nielsen recalled. "He was killed instantly."

Before Nielsen could grasp what happened, Japanese troops armed with machine guns and rifles attacked. Soldiers hurled a bucket of gasoline and a lighted bamboo torch inside the first shelter. Douglas Bogue, a California marine perched in a nearby shelter, heard a dull explosion. He peered out and saw a black pillar of smoke rising above the shelter. So, too, did fellow marine Glenn McDole of Iowa.

"My God!" McDole exclaimed. "They're murdering everybody!"

Prisoners poured from the shelter, many on fire. "You could see these guys—human torches—coming out of these trenches," McDole recalled.

"Shoot them," one of the Japanese officers barked. "Shoot them."

Guards did as ordered. "As the men were forced to come out on fire, they were bayonetted, or shot, or clubbed, or stabbed," Bogue said. "I saw several of these men tumbling about, still on fire, and falling from being shot."

Army Dr. Carl Mango of Pennsylvania emerged with hands raised, pleading with the Japanese. "Dozo! Dozo!" he screamed. "Please! Wait a minute!"

Troops shot him, doused him in gasoline, and set him ablaze. Other prisoners charged the Japanese. One managed to wrestle a rifle away from a soldier and shoot him just before a second Japanese serviceman ran a bayonet through him.

The orgy of violence escalated as the Japanese attacked the other shelters, the slaughter set to the soundtrack of laughter. Nielsen ducked down only seconds later to smell gasoline. "There was an explosion," he remembered, "and flame shot through the shelter where I was." McDole and other prisoners in his trench dug a hole out of the back just as the Japanese tossed in a bucket of gasoline, turning the shelter into an inferno. "We could feel the heat from the fire as we got out of the hole."

Scores more were not so fortunate, a fact later gruesomely described in an American war crimes report: "Many of the men were cooked alive."

Amid the chaos about three dozen captives crawled under the prison's fence or tore through the barbed wire with bare hands, jumping down a bluff more than forty feet to the beach below. But the slaughter was not over. Japanese patrols hunted the escapees, many of whom ran out into the surf only to be picked off by soldiers on the beach. "The water," Nielsen recalled, "was red with the blood from those guys."

Soldiers found others hiding in the rocks and caves along the shore, dragged them out, and killed them. "I took refuge in a small crack among the rocks where I remained, all the time hearing the butchery," Bogue recalled. "The stench of burning flesh was strong." McDole hid in a rubbish pile, where he could see down the beach as the Japanese soldiers encircled an escaped prisoner. "The American knew his fate and began begging to be shot and not burnt, in such a high voice that I could hear," McDole later testified. "Then I could see them pour gasoline on one foot and burn it, then the other until he collapsed. Then they poured gasoline over his body and set it off."

Like McDole, Nielsen wriggled under a garbage dump, covering himself with coconut husks swarming with worms. He, too, witnessed troops capture a dozen escapees. Before killing them, the soldiers tortured the men, stabbing them in the stomach and groin with bayonets amid shouts of "banzai." "The Japanese were cheering," Nielsen recalled, "just like Americans at a real interesting football or basketball game."

Only at nightfall did the carnage finally end. Out of 150 prisoners, a mere eleven managed to escape and survive. American forces would later recover the remains of seventy-nine, many buried five deep at the opposite ends of the torched shelters where the trapped men had fled the flames. "In two dugouts," one report noted, "bodies were in a prone position, arms extended with small conical holes at the fingertips showing that these men were trying to dig their way to freedom." American forces likewise recovered the diary of an unknown Japanese soldier, who witnessed the carnage. "Although they were prisoners of war," he wrote, "they truly died a pitiful death."

The same day MacArthur prepared to land at Lingayen—almost four weeks after the massacre—that Japanese diarist put pen to paper again. "The prisoners of war," he wrote, "are now just white bones on the beach washed by waves."

MacArthur hoped to avoid another such slaughter in Manila.

Only the day before, he had shared his concerns with *Life* magazine photographer Carl Mydans as the two paced the deck of the *Boise*. "We must move fast," MacArthur said, his hands buried in his hip pockets. "We must fight hard and fast. As soon as we have a foothold on those shores my aim is to push south before they know what's hitting them. I want to save as many of those prisoners as we can."

Before he could rescue them, MacArthur had to first safely land his troops. Around six-forty-five, the gray morning light illuminated the eastern and western shores of the crescent-shaped gulf, where low-hanging clouds draped across the silhouetted mountains of the Zambales and Ilocos ranges. Dead ahead of the American warships stretched the gulf's wide flat beaches, a view punctuated only by the handful of tall buildings in the towns of Lingayen and San Fabian that bookended the planned invasion zone. The gulf resembled a parking lot this morning as the last of the warships maneuvered into assigned positions, all part of the pending fight's intricate choreography. "You could almost," one sailor recalled, "step from ship to ship."

This morning's invasion served as the climax of one of the greatest logistical operations of the Pacific War, all designed to bring MacArthur home. In addition to the hundreds of transports and landing craft now in the gulf, the assembled armada included no less than seven battleships, twelve cruisers, eighteen escort carriers, and sixty-six destroyers. Buried in the bowels and strapped down on the decks of the ships sat thousands of tanks, trucks, and bulldozers, slathered in Cosmoline and waterproofed, including a few jeeps handy soldiers low on supplies had been forced to seal against seawater with plasma and enema tubes. To guarantee a successful landing, MacArthur's forces had gone so far as to practice storming the beaches of New Guinea in December. "In point of the number of ships involved and the distance traveled from the bases to the attack area," one report noted, "this was the greatest amphibious operation undertaken during the entire course of the war in either hemisphere."

Reveille this morning had signaled the end of a forty-day voyage for many of MacArthur's troops in conditions few would recall fondly, with the possible exception of two artillerymen on the destroyer *Allen M. Summer*, who stowed away in a couple of empty officer state-rooms. Otherwise troops had bunked as many as five high in suffocating transports or slept above deck using ponchos to battle rain squalls. Crafty soldiers had scavenged packing boxes to defend against the elements, creating the look, one report observed, of a shantytown. Troops aboard the landing ships suffered the worst as amphibious tractors crammed the cavernous holds, while ambulances and trucks lined the top decks, loaded with everything from ammunition and engines to antiaircraft guns and drums of gasoline. Exhausted soldiers had no choice but to hunt for a few square feet of empty space, which often meant curling up inside or even under a vehicle.

The men had passed the long days reading books, watching movies, and playing poker. A few had tasted the illicit shipboard booze—known as raisin jack—distilled from the dried fruit swiped from the mess hall. "It was potent stuff too," one army report stated, "if your stomach could take it." Curious soldiers had practiced astronomy—the Southern Cross faded as the Big Dipper returned—while more dutiful ones cleaned rifles, bazookas, and mortars. Vehicle drivers occasionally fired up engines, and officers pored over maps and terrain studies. Christmas had provided a needed break from the monotony of long days at sea, complete with a turkey dinner and dressing. On board a few ships, soldiers enjoyed Christmas trees made out of palm fronds and decorated with real ornaments. "These little trees were somehow appropriate for Christmas in the South Pacific," one report stated, "palms instead of hemlocks, a blazing sun on a coral reef instead of the White Christmas every man would have preferred."

The tensions had increased as the troops reached the Philippines and the kamikazes swarmed each day at sunrise and sunset, terrorizing sailors and soldiers alike, who on a ship at sea had nowhere to take cover. General Griswold confessed in his diary that he felt it would be worse to drown after an attack than be killed on a battlefield. "It is one of the most spectacular things I have seen in this war," the XIV Corps commander wrote. "You've got to hand it to the Jap—he has guts!" The kamikazes had even unnerved MacArthur. "It has been an anxious four days," he wrote his wife only the night before. "I will be glad to come to battle grips on land."

The crashes of Japanese fighters and bombers loaded with fuel and bombs proved so violent that at times entire planes were reduced to fragments no bigger than a few square inches. The propeller off one kamikaze ripped through the *New Mexico*'s forecastle, sliced through a steel I-beam, and came to rest on the main deck. Such attacks hurled men overboard and tore off fingers and hands. Others suffered crushed eye sockets, compound jaw fractures, and burned faces and corneas. An orange-sized piece of aluminum engine casing embedded in one sailor's hamstring muscle. Another poor soul suffered a hit in the genitals. "The penis was found stripped of its skin pocketed in the left scrotal tissues," the ship's report noted. "The right testicle had been torn from its bed and badly mangled."

Officers had distracted the troops with lectures on what to expect in the Philippines, where soldiers would trade the sweltering jungles for cosmopolitan cities with trollies, restaurants, and bars. "Men were most interested in the descriptions of the towns and the women," one report noted, "a preview of the first civilization many of them had seen for over two years." The accompanying journalists likewise salivated over the idea of reaching the Philippine capital. "Everybody's dreaming," one exclaimed, "of that drink at the bar of the Manila Hotel." Troops drilled on debarkation methods and practiced first aid on one another, including splinting injured limbs, tying bandages, and administering morphine. On the eve of the invasion, soldiers drew ammunition, fired off last letters to family, and stole final showers. Throughout the ships, chaplains offered religious services. "As the sun sank in the west causing the color to fade wearily out of a radiant sky," one Thirty-Seventh Infantry report stated, "men lay down fully clothed in an effort to catch a few hours of sleep before breakfast and the beachhead."

The navy in recent days had finalized preparations for the invasion, much of them accomplished despite constant attacks by kamikazes. Sixty-five minesweepers had scoured the dark waters of the gulf on January 6. Intelligence reports had indicated five minefields, but six weeks earlier Filipino guerrillas had cut them free, towed them ashore, and pilfered the explosives, leaving only a handful of floaters for the navy gunners to destroy. The following day underwater demolition teams combed the surf for barbed wire that might snare troops. "As I swam into shore, the ships were firing over our heads—you could hear the shells hit the sand dunes, palm trees, and small native houses," Joseph Moretti wrote in his diary of the experience. "One house near my beach caught fire and burned to the ground."

A lack of charts had handicapped war planners, who were forced to consult a 1903 U.S. Coast and Geodetic Survey report to determine beach gradients. To supplement that dated information, hydrographic ships in recent days had taken depth readings and marked shoals that might strand landing craft, while reconnaissance flights snapped more than eighteen thousand photos. American warships meanwhile pounded the beaches, firing a staggering 16,795 armor-piercing and high-capacity rounds. Navy fighters and bombers joined the fight, flying 788 sorties, aided by guerrilla drawings of nearby arms and fuel depots. Gone now were any coastal defense guns, pillboxes, or even buildings within three thousand yards of the landing beaches that might offer mortar teams or snipers a place to hide. "These sketches," one report noted, "were remarkable in their accuracy and were put to good use by supporting aircraft throughout the operation."

At seven a.m. the massive guns opened fire again, in what the Sixth Army's report described as "a naval bombardment previously unequalled in southwest Pacific warfare." Across the battleships, cruisers, and destroyers, the guns barked one after the other, a rising crescendo in this symphony of destruction. In sickbays chaplains plugged the ears of convalescing kamikaze victims with cotton to guard against the thunder. The violent shudder of the ships filled the air with tiny particles of glass wool insulation that normally coated the bulkheads but now irritated the eyes, noses, and throats of fighting sailors. "At the height of the din," recalled James Patric, a sight-setter onboard the high-speed transport *George E. Badger,* "all that was visible shoreward was a huge cloud of smoke and dust, in which it seems impossible any living creature could have survived." The XIV Corp's report expounded on Patric's assessment. "The sun came up over Baguio Hills to witness the greatest flotilla ever assembled, in the west, its guns roaring, its airplanes droning and the landing troops poised for the Luzon Victory."

The kamikazes that had menaced MacArthur's forces for days once again pounced. A twin-engine bomber from Nichols Field clipped the foremast and radio antennas of the destroyer escort *Hodges* before crashing into the water. At seven-forty-five a.m., another dove on the light cruiser *Columbia,* just four thousand yards from shore, but boxed in by landing craft, she proved unable to make evasive maneuvers. The cruiser's 20 and 40 mm guns opened up—nineteen total— throwing up a thousand rounds. The *Boise,* moored nearby with

MacArthur onboard, fired another fifteen hundred. None stopped the suicidal pilot, who plummeted down at four hundred knots and crashed into the port side. The third such hit in as many days killed twenty-four men and injured ninety-seven.

Chaplain Arthur Anderson, who had survived the sinking of the escort carrier *Ommaney Bay* five days earlier, rushed to the *Columbia*'s ward room to find one officer's hand gone. He spied another sailor whose arm was nearly severed above the elbow. "Most of the wounded were bleeding profusely, and I used every rag, handkerchief, and piece of tubing I could find to make tourniquets," the chaplain recalled. "Another man had many chest wounds from which blood spurted. He was out of his head and thrashed about wildly. I pinned him down to the deck with all my weight and endeavored to plug the wounds with gauze until the doctor could take care of him."

The few desperate attacks, however, could not stop the invasion.

"Now hear this," loudspeakers crackled. "First wave man your boats!"

"Well, here we go again," one soldier muttered.

Assault troops slung carbines over shoulders and climbed down nets into the bobbing boats even as the bombardment continued, a scene recalled by infantryman Larry Buckland: "It sounded like railroad trains going over your head." Included this morning were fourteen surgically staffed landing craft, armed with plasma, whole blood, and gas gangrene antitoxin, and capable of carrying eighty-five stretcher cases plus another two hundred ambulatory patients. Despite the precautions, tensions ran high. "Our troops did not sleep very good last night," James Fahey, a gunner on the light cruiser *Montpellier*, wrote in his diary. "This will be the last day on earth for a lot of them. They are so young and healthy now and in a few hours many of them will be dead or wounded or crippled for life. Some will not even reach the beach."

MacArthur's aides shared similar fears following the ferocity of the kamikaze attacks. Brig. Gen. Courtney Whitney, tasked to oversee Philippines Civil Affairs, wrote his wife on the eve of the invasion that he expected a bloody battle. "It is one of the most audacious of the general's many audacious moves against the enemy," he wrote. "We are of course bound to take heavy losses in such an operation which will go down in history as one of America's decisive battles. But we are ready for it." General Griswold felt the risk acutely. "My heart was sad," he wrote in his diary. "I know that some of my boys who are on these ships will, by this time tomorrow, have laid down their lives."

Sgt. Ozzie St. George, a reporter with *Yank* magazine who was on board one of the patrol boats, stared ahead this morning at the wall of smoke, searching for the beach he knew was only five thousand yards away. "Only the tops of the 2,500-foot purple hills on the eastern side of the gulf were visible above the smoke," he wrote. "Spotting planes, looking like moving fly specks, dipped in circles above the hills."

At 9:10 a.m. landing craft opened fire with rockets at the beaches, which had been color-coded blue, red, white, and crimson, among others. Overhead buzzed navy fighters, strafing the shores in advance of the landing. The cocker spaniel Salty, the mascot on St. George's boat, began barking. "Shells whirred and whispered steadily over-head," the reporter wrote. "The concussions slapped at our faces. Even the tops of the hills were disappearing behind the smoke." St. George shot a glance on deck to find Salty spread-eagled. "He had given up competing with the bombardment."

The minutes ticked past as the boats sliced through the waves. "Gun fire on beach very heavy," noted the Luzon attack commander's log at 9:25 a.m. "All ships firing; rockets keeping up steady stream of fire." Air observers overhead dropped white flares when the first assault wave closed to within eight hundred yards of the beaches. "The bombardment ceased at zero hour," recalled Patric. "The silence was uncanny."

The commanders now anxiously awaited word of America's reception on shore, news that arrived first from a battleship *Colorado* float-plane overhead.

"Boys are on the beach," the radio announced. "No opposition."

The flagship *Wasatch*, which carried senior navy commander Vice Adm. Thomas Kinkaid and General Krueger of the Sixth Army, broadcast the news.

"The first wave has landed!"

Troops charged ashore first on the beaches near San Fabian at nine-thirty a.m., followed three minutes later by the arrival of soldiers at Lingayen. The massive naval guns began firing again, aiming at the flanks of the invasion beaches and inland targets. Similar reports of a lack of enemy troops poured in from the other beaches.

"No apparent opposition," one said.

"There is no encounter of enemy fire," parroted another.

"No enemy movement on the roads leading to the beaches."

All the leading assault troops stood on dry land by 9:40 a.m., much to the amazement of many who had expected a fierce battle. "When I came ashore," army chaplain Russell Stroup wrote in a letter, "my heart was in my mouth and there was that queer empty feeling in my stomach, but it was all premature. Our prayers were answered more surely than we had hoped. The trial by fire did not come."

Even Krueger, the stern sixty-three-year-old commander of Prussian descent, couldn't help but crack a slight smile over the invasion's ease. MacArthur, of course, beamed. "He left Luzon furtively in the dead of night aboard a small torpedo boat," wrote Associated Press reporter Yates McDaniel. "He returned today proudly and jubilantly, standing at the rail of an American warship in broad daylight."

Troops continued to charge ashore unimpeded. By eleven a.m., the first vehicles and cargo had landed. A little more than an hour later, soldiers captured San Fabian. The beaches that many feared only hours earlier would be soaked with blood now bustled as troops filled sandbags to make piers out to the landing ships. Others rolled barrels of oil up dunes and formed human trains, passing crates of rations and ammunition hand to hand. Amphibious bulldozers motored along the shore, helping to push stranded landing craft off sandbars and tow jeeps and trucks from the four-foot surf. The I Corps lost only one tank during the invasion, not to enemy fire but to the eight feet of surf that swamped it. "Many 2½-ton trucks came ashore in water which was higher than the driver's seat," the I Corps report stated. "Tanks waded through six feet of water."

Kamikazes returned at 1:03 p.m., zooming low over San Fabian and giving naval gunners little time to react. One plane crashed into the port side of the battleship *Mississippi*, killing twenty-six sailors and wounding seventy others. Seconds later another sheared the top of the funnel off the *Australia*. The Allied cruiser's fifth such hit seemed to confirm what one battleship division commander wrote in his war diary after a previous attack: "The *Australia* appears to be a marked ship."

A little more than four hours after the first troops slogged ashore, MacArthur climbed into a landing craft to join them. The general dressed this warm afternoon in a khaki uniform and wore his trademark Ray Ban sunglasses to guard against the tropical sun. Chief of Staff Lt. Gen. Dick Sutherland, Brig. Gen. Bonner Fellers, Col. Roger Egeberg, and a few other aides joined MacArthur in the boat, which departed the *Boise* at 2:07 p.m. Egeberg, who served as MacArthur's personal physician and sometimes confidant, later described the scene. "On our way toward the broad sandy beach, we looked at palm trees and a few buildings that looked unhurt, no great rubble or destruction. It seemed anticlimatic [sic]. We must have seen the worst the day before," the doctor wrote. "There was no enemy, nor did we hear any rifle or machine gun fire."

MacArthur appeared to read Egeberg's mind. "We won't be seeing or hearing any Japanese today," he told his physician.

Navy Seabees had built an earthen ramp to accommodate MacArthur's landing near San Fabian, but the general waved the skipper off. The boat instead aimed straight for the beach where the front yawned open, disgorging the general and his staff into the ankle-deep surf in front of the news cameras. Once on shore, MacArthur surveyed the crush of landing craft, tanks, trucks, and personnel carriers. "All of these vehicles and more were about the sands of Lingayen Gulf in the pulsing fever of a successful beachhead," he recalled. "Now and then a Zero would whine down over the beach, but this time we had the wherewithal to handle them. Almost a solid wall of fire would go up, and swarms of American fighters from the carriers offshore would dive in to take care of the intruder. It warmed my heart to finally see the weight on our side."

Newspaper correspondents buzzed around MacArthur, one of whom noted that the general clutched a new corncob pipe between his teeth and appeared tanned and well rested despite the constant kamikaze attacks. "I slept well last night," he quipped, "in spite of some little disturbance created by the Japanese during the night."

The reporters asked him about the progress of the landings.

"The Jap was apparently taken completely by surprise," MacArthur declared. "He apparently expected us from the south, and when we came in behind him he was caught off base. The entire operation so far has been a complete success."

Krueger later made his own comments to the press. "Our troops are like a tiger who has tasted blood," he said. "Our superb men are rearing to go."

CBS reporter Bill Dunn watched as MacArthur trotted down the beach that afternoon. "Ignoring the fine white sand that made walking difficult, the general strode from one command post to another, observing, asking questions, and making an occasional suggestion," Dunn later recalled. "Unlike the Leyte landing, however, there were no signs of the enemy, no bodies to inspect, no Jap unit insignia to be identified. There just wasn't any enemy to be found." In his first report from Luzon, Dunn elaborated on the ease of the invasion. "I've taken part in four major amphibious landings out here in the Pacific during the past year but yesterday's assault on the beaches of Lingayen Gulf was, at once, the dullest and the most thrilling of my experience."

As troops hurried to unload cargo, planes dropped thousands of leaflets over the Philippines, carrying a message from President Sergio Osmeña: "In a series of brilliantly conceived blows, General MacArthur's forces of liberation have successfully, in but a short span of time, destroyed the enemy army defending Leyte, seized firm control of Mindoro, and now stand defiantly on the soil of Luzon at the very threshold to our capital city. Thus are answered our prayers of many long months." In the days ahead, locals crowded the streets to celebrate MacArthur's return. "We'll bury him in Manila, right beside President Quezon," one gentleman professed to Dunn. "We'll build him the biggest monument in the world. He belongs to the Philippines."

MacArthur climbed back aboard *Boise* at 5:23 p.m., pleased with the day's success. The cruiser pulled anchor and moved five miles off Lingayen. By the time the sun dropped below the western horizon at 6:42, MacArthur counted 65,000 troops ashore, including the commanding generals of all four of his assault divisions. In addition to Lingayen and San Fabian, his forces had captured Dagupan. MacArthur couldn't resist taking a swipe at his rival Yamashita in the communiqué his headquarters released that day. "His back door is closed," he declared. "The decisive battle for the liberation of the Philippines and control of the Southwest Pacific is at hand."

The general's top aides onboard the *Boise* shared his enthusiasm, including Bonner Fellers, who wrote about it in a letter to his wife. "It is Mac's greatest play and the pay off! It will speed our entry into Manila," he wrote. "Tonight after we returned from a tour of the lines Mac sat down slick in his room and ate a quart of ice cream— just like a kid at a circus. He is very happy tonight for he was playing high stakes and again he was right and out thought Yamashita. It is a brilliant operation."

○   ○   ○   ○

GENERAL YAMASHITA WATCHED the American landings from atop the 7,400-foot Santo Tomas Mountain near Baguio, on the eastern side of the gulf. He had suspected all along that MacArthur would come ashore at Lingayen, but the landings occurred several weeks earlier than he anticipated, so much so that he initially mistook the American convoys for a much-needed resupply for his own forces. "We expected rice," his chief of staff Muto complained. "We got the American Army instead."

Yamashita ordered a messenger to depart for Tokyo with the news, slipping him a letter to deliver to his wife in Kamakura. "The American Army has landed and is already at my knee but everyone is in good spirits," Yamashita wrote her. "We are brave enough to deal them a heavy blow but our main difficulty is ammunition. I may be silent for some time as I am very busy."

The Japanese press corps sensed from the burly general's demeanor how dire the situation had become. The Americans had landed; the final fight had begun. "He has the air of a man about to fight his last battle," one wrote. "Here on these islands in the vast Pacific Ocean," reported another, "a great tragedy is about to occur."

Yamashita issued his final orders to his commanders. MacArthur's invasion had—just as the American general announced to the world—sealed the Philippines. No more help would come; the mission now was to slow the American drive. "It is easy to die with honor but it is much more difficult to hold up the enemy advance when you are short of ammunition and food," Yamashita told his men. "Those of you in the front line will be doing your duty if you hold them up for a day—or even half a day."

○ ○ ○ ○

JAPANESE REAR ADM. SANJI IWABUCHI planned to do everything in his power to stop MacArthur—even if it demanded he destroy Manila. The forty-nine-year-old Niigata native commanded the Manila Naval Defense Force, charged with blowing up piers, warehouses, and bridges in advance of MacArthur's arrival. Though Yamashita had ordered his forces to abandon the city once that work was done, Iwabuchi had no plans to leave, instructing his troops instead to fortify Manila. The navy admiral, in essence, was everything Yamashita was not. Unlike the tall and portly general, Iwabuchi stood just five feet three inches and weighed barely 130 pounds. He was dapper compared to the often rumpled Yamashita and sported a pencil-thin moustache, trimmed so that it curled around his upper lip, much like the one worn by famed Hollywood actor Clark Gable. More important, compared to Yamashita, who had proven himself a dogged leader on the battlefield, Iwabuchi's earlier time in command had ended in disaster.

A 1915 graduate of Japan's naval academy at Eta Jima, Iwabuchi had climbed the peacetime ranks as an aviator and gunner, then landed in April 1942 as the skipper of the *Kirishima*, a World War I battle cruiser that engineers later converted into a battleship. He was dispatched to the Solomon Islands later that year during the slugfest for Guadalcanal. During the late night and early morning of November 14–15, Admiral Iwabuchi's *Kirishima*, accompanied by four cruisers and nine destroyers, steamed to shell an airfield in advance of troop landings. En route the Japanese ran into a scrappy American task force of just four destroyers trailed by two battleships. In the ensuing fight, the Japanese blasted three of the four American destroyers. The glow from the burning warships silhouetted the battlewagon *South Dakota*, prompting the *Kirishima* to flip on its searchlight. The massive guns thundered, pounding the American warship twenty-six times, killing thirty-eight sailors, and wounding another sixty.

With all eyes trained on the battered *South Dakota*, Japanese lookouts failed to spot the battleship *Washington*, which, armed with radar, stalked the *Kirishima* in the dark waters, closing to just 8,400 yards, or less than five miles. For a battlewagon capable of hurling a 2,700-pound projectile some twenty miles, this short distance equated point-blank range. At one a.m.—two minutes after the moon set— *Washington*'s massive sixteen-inch guns roared again and again, firing a total of seventy-five projectiles. As many as twenty tore into Iwabuchi's ship, while dozens of smaller rounds raked the *Kirishima* from stem to stern, leaving holes as large as thirty feet in the battleship's deck. Fires erupted, making the engine rooms uninhabitable and threatening the magazines. The rudder was jammed to starboard, forcing the injured battlewagon to limp in a circle. In just seven minutes, the barrage reduced the *Kirishima* to ruins, while Iwabuchi had gone from victory to defeat.

Iwabuchi had no choice but to order his ship abandoned, which listed so far to starboard that sailors struggled to stand. Crewmen pulled down the ensign amid three shouts of banzai, along with the portrait of Emperor Hirohito, transferring them to the destroyer *Asagumo*. Engineers opened the Kingston valves on the bottom of the fuel tanks. The flood of cold seawater prompted the *Kirishima* to capsize. Iwabuchi was rescued, though in a culture that demanded a skipper go down with his ship, his survival proved an immense shame. The navy later packed Iwabuchi off to New Georgia, then parked him behind a desk in the personnel office at Tsuchiura Naval Base in Japan, an insult to any seafaring officer during wartime. Only through Japan's worsening fortunes—and the death of so many more capable officers—had Iwabuchi been given a second chance. Just as MacArthur saw Manila as his redemption, so, too, did Iwabuchi. This time, however, he had no intention of abandoning his ship.

He would go down with it.

Until late December 1944, Iwabuchi had commanded the 31st Naval Special Base Force, a small outfit comprising several battalions. Vice Adm. Denshichi Okochi, the Southwestern Area Fleet commander and supreme naval officer in the Philippines, planned to evacuate to Baguio with Yamashita. Before he departed, he placed Iwabuchi in charge of the newly formed Manila Naval Defense Force, ordering him to wreck the city's waterfront so as to rob American forces of the strategic asset. To streamline command in preparation for the coming battle, Okochi likewise surrendered tactical control of his ground forces to Yamashita, who would be in charge of all army and naval troops on land. That included Iwabuchi, who now fell under the command of General Yokoyama, head of the Shimbu Group.

Despite the army's plan to withdraw from Manila, Iwabuchi had other ideas. So, too, did some of his staff officers, who favored a stubborn defense of the capital, pointing to the urban bloodlettings in Stalingrad and Shanghai as examples of how Japanese forces might ensnare the invading Americans. During two January conferences, General Yokoyama had stressed that the Shimbu Group would not fight to the death in Manila but would rather retreat into the mountains east of the city. But Iwabuchi pushed back, just as MacArthur had done with Roosevelt in Hawaii. He argued that he could not abandon Manila until he had completed Admiral Okochi's orders to destroy the port, harbor, and bridges. Yokoyama, afraid of creating interservice friction, relented. He even agreed to place the army's remaining forces in Manila under Iwabuchi's command. The general's only demands were that Iwabuchi strengthen Fort McKinley and the eastern suburb of San Juan del Monte, move his headquarters to Fort McKinley, and promise to evacuate the city once he had executed Okochi's orders.

Iwabuchi agreed.

In addition to Manila, Iwabuchi controlled the capital's suburbs stretching twelve miles south, six miles north, and east to the Marikina River and Laguna de Bay, a sizable area of about 250 square miles. To defend it, Iwabuchi counted about seventeen thousand troops, not all of whom would fight in the city. The 12,500 sailors and 4,500 soldiers under his command were a motley crew of marines and naval guard units as well as hospital patients and even freshly inducted civilians. More than a few had been shanghaied off damaged or sunken ships, including the crew of the gunboat *Karatsu*, which was in port after the submarine *Narwhal* torpedoed it. "The repair work on the *Karatsu* will cease, and the personnel and weapons aboard will be diverted to land combat," Iwabuchi ordered. "The necessary weapons for land combat will be quickly removed, and in accordance with separate instructions, their disposition for land combat will be completed. Orders will be given later as to the disposal of the hull and engines."

Iwabuchi divided his forces into three combat commands. Col. Katsuzo Noguchi would be in charge of the Northern Force, comprising one naval and two infantry battalions. These 4,500 troops would hold the Walled City and all of Manila north of the Pasig River, east to San Juan del Monte. Upon the arrival of the Americans, Noguchi's forces would blow the bridges across the Pasig. Naval Capt. Takesue Furuse's Southern Force—made up of more than five thousand troops from one infantry and two naval battalions—would hold Nichols Field and Fort McKinley and block any effort by the Americans to break into the city from the south. Iwabuchi would command the Central Force of three naval battalions, totaling another five thousand men. To the admiral fell the job of guarding the heart of the capital, including the government buildings and the residential districts of Paco, Ermita, and Malate. "Hold Manila City and surrounding essential areas," he ordered on January 21. "Destroy enemy strength."

Iwabuchi's battle plan called for a defense centered on Intramuros, the ancient citadel guarded by towering walls from ten to forty feet thick. Around the Walled City, Iwabuchi planned a perimeter of large concrete buildings designed to withstand typhoons and earthquakes. Among those, troops grabbed the Legislature, Finance, and Agricul-

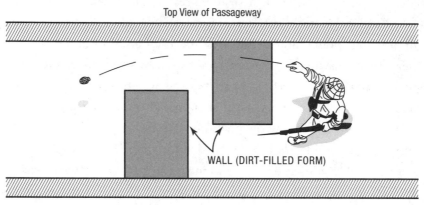

Top View of Passageway

WALL (DIRT-FILLED FORM)

Plan

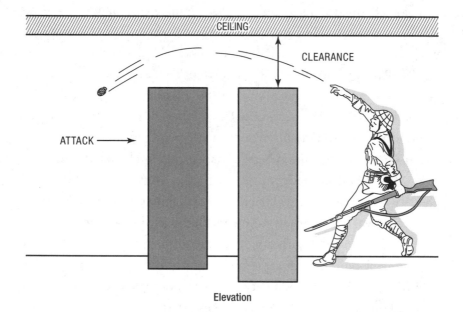

CEILING

CLEARANCE

ATTACK

Elevation

The Japanese fortified the insides of buildings, particularly passageways.

ture buildings along with the Post Office and City Hall. Like Intramuros, each of these would serve as a small fortress, around which marines buried ammunition and food needed to make a final stand. The Japanese dragged culvert pipes inside, covering them with half-inch steel plates and stacked sandbags to serve as bomb shelters. Others barricaded rooms with desks, chairs, and bookcases. To further slow any enemy advance through the corridors, troops built staggered walls filled with dirt four feet thick and seven high, leaving just enough clearance over which to toss hand grenades. The Japanese filled windows with reinforced concrete, knocked gun slits in walls, and dug trenches connecting the buildings to outlying bunkers.

Burnham's wide boulevards and parks, which had once transformed Manila into a welcoming city, promised to make it hell for advancing American soldiers, forcing them out into the open in any assault on these strongholds. Japanese troops further complicated the challenge by burying land mines along nearby roads, bridges, and vacant lots and stringing barbed wire so as to route Americans into the line of fire. To slow MacArthur's drive into the heart of Manila, Iwabuchi's forces set up outer strongholds and barricaded streets and intersections—no less than fifty just in Paco, Ermita, and Intramuros—securing them with machine guns and antitank weapons. Troops likewise scrambled to build pillboxes made of concrete, metal, wood, and sandbags, often using debris from buildings destroyed in American air raids to camouflage positions. In La Loma Cemetery, north of the Pasig River and on the highway coming into the city, crafty soldiers hid three 25 mm automatic cannons in pillboxes designed to look like fresh burial mounds, complete with sod, flowers, statues, and crosses.

Low on supplies, creativity proved a must, down to the use of satchels of rice in place of sandbags. Troops overturned trucks and cars and rolled heavy factory machinery out into the streets. Others sank railroad car axles upright in the pavement and even embedded coconut tree logs in concrete. Iwabuchi's forces trucked in aviation fuel from nearby airfields to burn buildings, while sailors stripped guns from ships sunk in the harbor and airplanes destroyed during American raids. Secret ordnance shops set up in underground tunnels churned

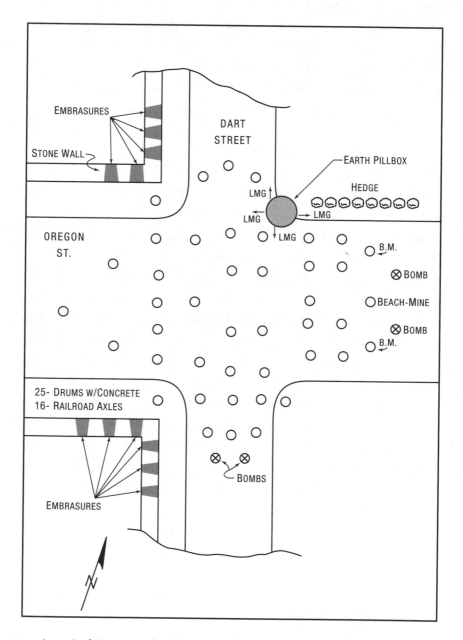

A typical Japanese fortification of a street corner, using pillboxes, railroad axles, and land mines. This intersection is of Oregon and Dart streets.

out ground mounts for aircraft machine guns, hollow charge lunge mines, and grenades. The Japanese likewise converted artillery shells, mortars, aerial bombs, naval beach mines, and even depth charges into improvised explosives that could be detonated using impact fuses and trip wires. Others made Molotov cocktails using red phosphorous. To slow the American advance, Iwabuchi's forces began blowing up bridges. Of the 101 bridges in Manila, the Japanese ultimately destroyed thirty-nine, including the six most vital ones spanning the Pasig River.

As men, women, and children in Manila watched the fortification of the city with fear, guerrillas radioed to MacArthur's forces. "All Manila highways barricaded," one report stated. "Japs erect pillboxes, trenches and road blocks on main streets."

"All main bridges across Pasig River are prepared by Nips for destruction," read another.

"Defensive preparation of civilian homes."

Residents who for years had anxiously awaited the return of MacArthur now worried over the hell that liberation might bring— and with good reason. Emperor Hirohito's forces sported an abysmal record in abiding by internationally recognized laws of war, like those spelled out in the 1907 Hague Convention and the 1929 Geneva Convention, both of which Japan signed, though the government failed to ratify the latter. Those treaties mandated the protection of prisoners of war, forbade poisonous weapons, and outlawed the unnecessary destruction and pillaging of towns and cities. But *manileños* needed only to look at the Rape of Nanking or the murder of thousands of Chinese civilians during Yamashita's campaign in Malaya and Singapore to see how little value Japanese forces placed on protecting civilians and property.

Many wondered: Would this be Manila's fate?

American air raids had triggered many out-of-work constables and other young men to abandon the Philippine capital to join the guerrillas, a move that prompted the Japanese to post sentries day and night at checkpoints on roads leading out of the capital. Even inside the city, ramped-up security coupled with excessive guards and patrols discouraged residents from venturing far outside their homes. Those who did were often conscripted by Japanese troops to fill sandbags, dig trenches, and haul war materials. "People began to disappear," Jack Garcia recalled. "Many left home early in the morning in search for work or food. Many never came back." The fear was set against the chaos of exploding warehouses and port facilities that shook the city. "It looks as though the remaining Japanese forces here are determined to fight to a finish," Marcial Lichauco wrote in his diary on January 18, "and, if necessary, to follow a scorched-earth policy rather than surrender Manila to General MacArthur."

The Japanese commandeered the White Dove Café at the corner of Taft Avenue and Vito Cruz, transforming the ice cream parlor and soda fountain fifty yards from the Garcia family home into a gun embankment surrounded by sandbags. Two more concrete bunkers soon followed, these just twenty-five yards from the home. Brother Egbert Xavier, director of nearby De La Salle College on Taft Avenue, phoned the house, asking if the family would feel safer relocating to the school a couple blocks away. Ida Garcia had a premonition about moving, though she took the precaution of dropping off folding cots and clothes. She demanded Jack and his older brother Ramon remain indoors and away from windows. At night the family said the rosary. Aided by a flickering oil lamp, Ida led the children in prayers from *Luz y Consuelo del Alma*, an old Spanish worship book. "The Japanese were digging in," Jack recalled. "There was no escaping the fact they were not going to give up without a fight. We prayed for a miracle."

Some Japanese troops friendly with locals warned them. "Big fighting coming," a soldier alerted Ida Garcia. "You no go out to street. Much danger. Better stay home!" A Japanese officer shared similar news with Spanish priest Juan Labrador, hinting that the end would be bloody. "I know," he said, "I shall die with Manila."

Others were far more pessimistic about the fate of the citizenry. "We shall fight to the last man," Jesuit priest Forbes Monaghan recalled one soldier saying, "and that means the last Filipino." Soldiers stockpiling gasoline drums voiced a sinister warning to other residents. "Very few of you," troops snickered, "will live to see the Americans."

These threats only amplified the lessons residents had learned of the cruel temperament of Japanese troops during the three-year occupation. That experience led Pacita Pestaño-Jacinto to make an ominous prediction when MacArthur's forces landed on Leyte. "Defeat is a bitter pill that the Japanese will not swallow," she wrote in her diary. "Defeat is the one thing that can make them turn into beasts."

CHAPTER 5

"Hunger had become a living thing, like cancer. It ate into our bodies and minds. We thought of nothing else but food and hate."

—Tressa Roka,
diary entry, January 26, 1945

ABRAM HARTENDORP WASN'T SURE HOW MUCH LONGER HE and other internees could survive at the University of Santo Tomas. Food stores were largely gone. So, too, were the pigeons, rats, and weeds that had sustained the nearly 3,700 men, women, and children during the long wait for MacArthur to return. Internees now starved at a rate of several a day; their skeletal bodies were wheeled from the camp in pushcarts for all to see, a grim reminder that anyone could be next. The fifty-one-year-old had witnessed a lot in a life that stretched across three continents, from his childhood in Holland, to his adolescence on a farm in the shadow of the Rocky Mountains, to his adulthood in the Philippines. Along the way Hartendorp had marveled at the 1910 passing of Halley's Comet, whose tail brushed so close to the earth as to spark panic. He nearly lost his hands to frostbite and had been fired once for teaching evolution to schoolchildren in Colorado.

But nothing in his half-century of world travel compared to what Hartendorp had seen on the roughly fifty-acre campus of Santo Tomas, where he had shed a third of his body weight as he watched humanity unravel. The once-stocky former journalist, poet, and magazine owner, whose bald head and freckled skin appeared out of place in the tropics, had parlayed his reporting skills into the role of camp historian, chronicling the more than eleven hundred days the civilians lived behind the iron gates of one of the largest Japanese-controlled internment camps in Asia. His chronology, which over the years dutifully covered committee meetings, camp personalities, and holidays, had devolved in recent weeks into a tabulation of calories and a scorecard of the starved:

"Three deaths."

"Four deaths in one day."

"There were again four deaths during the day, all of American men."

Hartendorp's tally promised to grow exponentially if MacArthur's forces did not soon reach Manila. Conditions at Santo Tomas had come full circle in the three years since the Japanese seized the university, on Calle España just north of the Pasig River. Founded in 1611 and originally located in Intramuros, the Dominican school had welcomed its first students twenty-five years before Harvard, making it the oldest university under an American flag. Set amid a wide grassy lawn, the university boasted an Education Building, annex, and gymnasium, all of which flanked the four-story Main Building, capped with a clock tower, that stood dead center of campus. The three hundred internees who rolled through the gates on January 4, 1942, grew within days to several thousand, a number that would reach its wartime peak later that year of 4,200. "Santo Tomas was never a residence university. It had no dormitories at all," recalled Eunice Young, a nurse. "The Japs segregated men and women, and jammed them into classrooms, halls, basements and offices."

Santo Tomas proved not only crowded but a melting pot. Americans comprised about 70 percent of the internees; the rest were a mix of British, Dutch, Polish, and Spanish, among others. Age, sex, and internee health likewise ran the gamut. The only commonality was that most were civilians, imprisoned simply because of their nationality. "You had bankers and community leaders mixed in with prostitutes and thieves," said Terry Myers, a nurse. "You learned to judge people not by their title as such but who they actually were." Along those lines, there existed a huge disparity in wealth, which made a difference in how comfortable life could be behind bars. "The rich were rich and the poor were poor, just as in the outside world," recalled Young. "Some internees had moved in with spring mattresses, plush chairs, and had arranged with Filipino houseboys to deliver more food regularly. Some of the women brought evening dresses. Another, with more sense, had brought a sewing machine. Some came with money, others without. Many arrived with only what they were wearing."

The one constant for everyone: escape was not an option. The Japanese made that clear in early February 1942, when three internees went over the wall. Within hours troops recaptured the men—two Brits and one Australian—beating them so violently that one's face resembled hamburger. Guards then hauled them out to La Loma Cemetery along with several additional internees to serve as witnesses. The Japanese prodded the escapees out to freshly dug graves and blindfolded them, though one of the internees refused to wear his. "I'll die like a man," he protested, "not a rat." Moments later three shots rang out, and the men collapsed. "Then the Japs stood over them, firing down into the grave," recalled witness Earl Carroll, who counted a total of thirteen shots. "Groans still were coming from that grave when the Japs began to shovel dirt into it." The executions horrified the rest of the internees. "The lesson has had the desired effect," Elizabeth Vaughan wrote in her diary. "No one speaks of escape."

Shut off from the outside world, internees mobilized to build what resembled a small city. Many had been business and industry leaders in Manila, while others had worked as carpenters, engineers, and schoolteachers. "Two things we did have in abundance: time and know-how," recalled *Life* magazine's Carl Mydans, who was interned for nine months at the start of the war, before the Japanese repatriated him. "There was never anything that had to be done for which there could not be found an expert." A nine-person executive committee oversaw sixteen department heads, who managed everything from the camp's medical and sanitation needs to work assignments, recreation, and education. The internees went so far as to appoint floor and room monitors and even designated Hartendorp as the camp historian. "We had offices and were keeping minutes," Carroll wrote, "just like a city council."

Food was the main priority. The Japanese did not provide meals but contributed seventy centavos per diem into a fund that the internees' Finance and Supply Committee could use to buy food for the camp. A central kitchen inside the Main Building fed three thousand adults two meals a day, including cracked-wheat porridge for breakfast and stew and a banana for dinner. In addition, Filipinos on the outside lined up every day to pass food and laundry through the gates in what became known simply as the "package line." This allowed internees with money to buy extra food. William Hoffman spent $13,000 during his time in Santo Tomas on food to keep himself, his wife, and two children alive, while others queued up for the camp's chow line. "Leading members of Manila society and some of the city's best known gourmets stood in those lines, week after week, month after month, tin plate in hand," Hartendorp noted. "Everybody ate what was offered, there being no alternative but hunger."

Medical care proved another necessity, particularly since the camp's internees ranged from infants to the elderly. Internees converted the Santa Catalina Convent, across the street from the university, into a 115-bed hospital, complete with specialized annexes dedicated to convalescent and children's care as well as an isolation unit for communicable diseases. Staffed by internee doctors and nurses, the hospital had an operating room, dental clinic, outpatient department, and physiotherapy room as well as a minor surgery and dressing station. The Japanese allowed the camp's doctors to send critical patients to Manila hospitals, while local hospitals, pharmacies, and the Red Cross supplied much of the food and medicine. The medical staff vaccinated internees against typhoid, cholera, and dysentery and even screened for venereal diseases, uncovering three cases of syphilis and nineteen of gonorrhea.

An army of six hundred internees built additional toilets and more than fifty showers. Workers likewise drained open sewers into the underground system, sank oil drums in the dirt to make outdoor latrines, and tapped new inlets into the city's water lines. Afraid that Manila's utilities might one day fail, internees filled the Main Building's six roof tanks with 72,785 gallons of water as well as the university's 680,000-gallon swimming pool. Carpenters built beds, benches, and a butcher shop, while seamstresses mended torn work clothes and stitched everything from mosquito nets and aprons to sheets and pillowcases for the hospital. "The cluttered rooms were swept twice a day, and once a week everything was moved out and the floors were scrubbed," recalled Hartendorp. "The toilets were scrubbed and disinfected twice a day. The University premises had never before been so clean despite the crowded, day-and-night occupation."

Much of the work required ingenuity. Internees planted thirty acres of gardens to grow yams, tomatoes, and pechay beans, while others made disinfectants and soap, using the oil from coconut milk. A camp laboratory churned out other necessities, from alcohol and caustic soda to Epsom salt and hydrochloric acid. On a more personal level, internees devised a system to provide sanitary napkins for menstruating women, each made from small flannel cloth and embroidered with the internee's name and room number. "A bucket of disinfectant was kept in the bathroom," said Margaret Sams. "Each and every cloth went into this bucket and was carted away every day, and a certain detail laundered the napkins and returned them to their respective owners." Internee leaders required every man to work three hours a day and every woman two. Outside that time, many performed individual services for a small fee, from cutting hair to laundry to shoe repair. A few even told fortunes. "One could have his teeth pulled, his hair cut, his shirt mended, his fever soothed," Mydans wrote. "We even had a police force."

To relieve crowding, internees constructed some six hundred shanties on the university's grounds, many from old lumber and bamboo and roofed with nipa palm leaves. Residents nicknamed these areas Glamourville, Jungletown, and Froggy Bottom, among others. The footpaths that wound between them were likewise colorfully called Fifth Avenue, Hollywood Boulevard, and MacArthur Drive. A mayor presided over each area, and shanty owners paid a one-peso monthly tax, which went into a fund for camp welfare purposes. "Though such a shanty to all appearance presented the utmost in squalor," recalled Hartendorp, "to the people crouching within, it was home." The primitive dwellings offered an escape from the otherwise crowded camp. "The shanties were private places where we could take our ease with a book," wrote nurse Denny Williams. "They were places for quiet conversations with friends, pretending we weren't at war, we weren't hungry or bored or uncertain of our future."

The adults set out to guarantee that internment did not rob the camp's children of an education. Using partitions, internees converted two large former laboratories on the fourth floor into fifteen class-rooms. Other spaces allowed for six additional rooms. Twenty-three former teachers from the Bordner School and American schools taught classes from kindergarten through college, in subjects as diverse as Latin, chemistry, and free-hand sketching. In addition to providing pencils, crayons, chalk, and blackboards, the education department cobbled together enough books to build a study hall, a reference library, and a children's library, which offered a total of some 2,500 volumes, including twenty-two dictionaries and seven sets of encyclopedias. Students even received typed report cards, including fifth-grader Caroline Bailey, who earned A's in both English and arithmetic and B's in science and history for the 1942–43 school year. "While every pupil has not had an individual text to use," one education department memo stated, "through a well-directed study hall, conducted in the morning, afternoon and evening, texts have been put to extensive use and in most cases one text was used through the study hall by 2–5 students."

The fall of Corregidor in May 1942 ended any hope that internment might be brief. "Previous to that," Hartendorp wrote, "the dullness of camp life had at times been relieved by distant bombing and cannon fire, by smoke clouds on the horizon and by flashes in the sky at night which proved to the internees that fighting was going on not far from Manila and that the invaders still did not have everything their own way. The cessation of such evidence of warlike activities had a depressing effect on the camp." Most found it vital to remain busy, but internees still struggled as weeks turned to months and then years. One of the biggest challenges was the lack of any space. "If you want privacy," a sign in the bathroom read, "close your eyes." American Red Cross nurse Marie Adams, who shared a room with forty women, found the constant chaos rattling. "There seemed to be no moment of the entire day that was free from noise," she recalled. "I was sure that I would crack up in a week."

To distract internees, the recreation department organized volleyball, basketball, and softball teams. The captives went so far as to recreate the National and American baseball leagues, with teams ranging from the Giants and Braves to the Yankees and Red Sox. The printed schedule even listed individual players' batting averages—captive Joe Yette had the highest at .522. Internee Archie Taylor likewise organized a boxing league, teaching more than seventy young men aged four to twenty. Army nurse Helen Cassiani learned to play golf from one of two interned pros. To prevent losing precious balls as she worked on her swing, Cassiani crocheted a small sack filled with cotton that functioned like a whiffle ball. "Once in a while he would let us take a swing at a real golf ball," she recalled of her instructor. "But if we had a bad hook and the ball went over the wall, then we had a terrible time trying to get the Japs to go out into the streets there and look for the ball because balls were at a premium."

Teachers hosted an evening story hour for children and dances for teenagers. The youths even put on a Christmas pageant. "Santa Claus came through the front gate," remembered Madeline Ullom. "The Christmas tree was a Baguio pine on the front lawn." Adults enjoyed vaudeville shows that featured comic songs and dances and even accordion and trumpet solos on an outdoor stage dubbed "The Little Theater Under the Stars." Internees interested in more quiet pursuits could check out any one of some seven thousand titles in the camp's makeshift libraries or catch up on the headlines in the twice-weekly newspaper, *Internews*, later replaced by the *STIC Gazette** with the slogan "Independent, Curt, Concise." *Life* magazine's Mydans, before he was repatriated, gave photography lessons. Many others played games of chess, poker, and bridge. A few crafty internees brewed bootleg liquor from cornmeal, cracked wheat mush, and fruit juices. Others gambled. One successful card player ended up owning four shanties, including a restaurant, while even prostitutes offered up their services.

Despite the wealth of activities, internment exacted a toll on everyone. "We lived in the past. Completely in the past. We told things that

* STIC = Santo Tomas Internment Camp

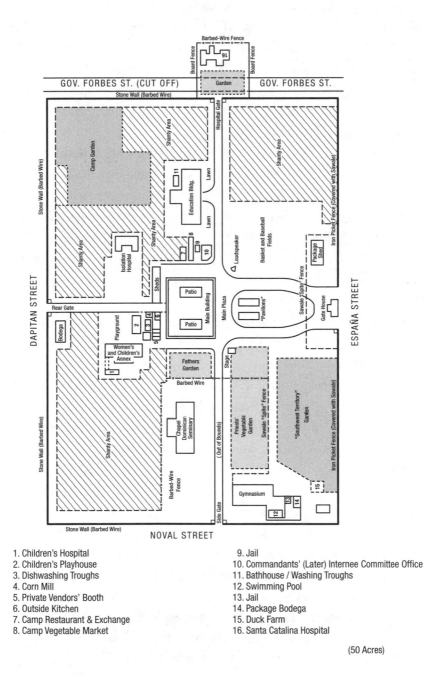

Barbed-Wire Fence

16

GOV. FORBES ST. (CUT OFF)　　Garden　　GOV. FORBES ST.

Stone Wall (Barbed Wire)

Hospital Gate

Board Fence　　Board Fence

Shanty Area

Camp Garden

Shanty Area

Iron Picket Fence (Covered with Sawale)

Stone Wall (Barbed Wire)

DAPITAN STREET

Shanty Area

11

Education Bldg.

Lawn

Lawn

Shanty Area

Basket and Baseball Fields

Package Shed

Shanty Area

8

Isolation Hospital

9

10

Loudspeaker

Sheds

Rear Gate

Sawale "Spite" Fence

Gate House

Patio

Bodega

Playground

Main Building

Main Plaza

"Pavilions"

Patio

ESPAÑA STREET

2

3　4

5

Women's and Children's Annex

Fathers Garden

1

Stage

Barbed Wire

Priests' Vegetable Garden

"Southwest Territory" Garden

Chapel Dominican Seminary

Sawale "Spite" Fence

Iron Picket Fence (Covered with Sawale)

(Out of Bounds)

Shanty Area

Barbed-Wire Fence

15

Stone Wall (Barbed Wire)

Gymnasium

13

14

Side Gate

12

Stone Wall (Barbed Wire)

NOVAL STREET

1. Children's Hospital
2. Children's Playhouse
3. Dishwashing Troughs
4. Corn Mill
5. Private Vendors' Booth
6. Outside Kitchen
7. Camp Restaurant & Exchange
8. Camp Vegetable Market

9. Jail
10. Commandants' (Later) Internee Committee Office
11. Bathhouse / Washing Troughs
12. Swimming Pool
13. Jail
14. Package Bodega
15. Duck Farm
16. Santa Catalina Hospital

(50 Acres)

The grounds of the University of Santo Tomas, showing the various buildings, gardens, and shanty areas. Replica of a hand-drawn map by an internee; scale is not exact.

we did as a child," Inez Moore recalled. "You couldn't look forward to anything." The poor diet likewise proved problematic. "Beer-bellies had disappeared long before, but now thighs and shanks and shoulders and arms showed their leanness," Hartendorp observed. "Many of the men—not at all that way inclined—were beginning to look like intellectuals, poets, divines!" Much to the heartache of parents, the children were not immune. Many had no concept of what life was like outside the walls. Others had never worn anything other than wooden shoes or even tasted fresh milk. Unlike American children, the youths inside Santo Tomas didn't dream of one day serving as policemen, firemen, or doctors but instead talked of becoming room monitors and mush cooks. "To many of these young children, the Japanese soldier was the hero, the top man," wrote Tressa Roka, a forty-one-year-old nurse who was interned with her fiancé on the day the couple had planned to marry. "I saw eight American kids fall in line with twelve marching Nips. They imitated their swinging arms and exaggerated goose steps with considerable enthusiasm and hilarity."

The barriers at Santo Tomas consisted of far more than just the concrete walls and iron gates. The inequality that had existed before the war grew more extreme as the months passed and conditions inside the camp began to deteriorate. Wealthier captives went so far as to pay poorer ones to perform daily jobs, like the neurotic internee with manicured nails who hired the wife of an American soldier to do her duties. "She worked to earn money for extra food for herself, an ailing mother, and two teen-age sisters," Roka wrote. "My prescription to cure the pampered darling's neurotic aches and pains was simple and practical. Dig in and do her own work, and donate the money she was paying now to the overworked soldier's wife. She could well afford it." Food was another source of inequity as rich internees feasted on fine meals delivered through the gates. "It used to aggravate a lot of us," recalled mining engineer Robert Wygle, interned with his wife and son, "to smell their pork chops frying while our tin can 'dishes' held nothing but musty, moldy, and bug-peppered 'line chow.'"

Others internees suffered the agony of separation from their families. That was the case for Hartendorp, a father of three sons and two daughters. Though he was an American citizen, his children were Filipino, leaving them safe from internment, free to go about their young lives while he sat locked up in Santo Tomas. His only interaction with them was through the periodic visits at the camp gates or smuggled letters, where he tried his best to offer advice. It was through such a letter that his oldest son Eddy confessed that he had fallen in love with the neighbor's daughter. "I am in very bad need for some one I can turn to for advice," he wrote. "You seem so far away." Such words pained Hartendorp, who felt powerless. "I want only the happiness of my children, but the one thing now," he replied, "is *to stay alive.* Put up with everything necessary, but *stay alive.* As long as you *remain alive*, you can be happy again, some time. But there is nothing left for the dead or for those whose loved ones are dead."

Hartendorp's torment reached a crescendo when he was forced to miss the young couple's seven p.m. wedding at San Miguel Church on July 27, 1942. In his diary that evening, he imagined the wedding, almost minute by minute. "I have been picturing to myself Eddy dressing and getting ready," he wrote. "I suppose he is wearing his black dress trousers and his white mess jacket. I wonder what Lourdes looks like." On his bed in his crowded room at Santo Tomas, Hartendorp kept his eye on the clock and fought back tears. "It is 7:20 now," he wrote. "If the service was on time, perhaps it will be over now. I wonder who is there, whether they sent out announcements and invitations." Ten minutes later Hartendorp concluded the wedding must finally be over. "I have never hated this place as much as now," he wrote. "I want to be home with my children, where I belong, where I ought to be. I should have been there all along. But, of course, this is war. I ought to be glad we are all still alive."

Hartendorp was, in fact, one of the lucky ones—his family was still alive. Georgia native Elizabeth Vaughan was interned with her two young children, Beth and Clay. Her husband, Jim, was an American soldier. Captured on Bataan, he was on the Death March and imprisoned at Cabanatuan. On July 10, 1943, while Vaughan mopped the floor of her room at Santo Tomas, a friend and fellow internee slipped her a sheet of notebook paper, folded into a two-inch square and sealed with adhesive tape. Vaughan read her name written on the outside. "The typed note wrapped tightly, almost wadded," she wrote that day in her diary, "gave the definite and heartbreaking news." Her husband had died in prison of dysentery. She was crushed. "Oh, Jim, Jim, why did this have to happen?" she begged in her diary. "You to die alone and suffering two days before our fourth wedding anniversary. Why couldn't I have come to you, to give you medicine, to answer your feverish calls for water?"

Internees followed the progress of the war via the information that trickled into the camp. Popular Manila radio commentator Don Bell, who as an internee went by his real name Clarence Beliel to avoid detection by the camp's commandant over his prewar anti-Japanese broadcasts, ran the camp's internal broadcast system, playing phonograph records each morning at reveille and again at night just before camp announcements and taps. Bell used the system—specifically his choice in music—to disseminate important news. "When the Americans entered Paris, he played 'Midnight in Paris' several times," remembered nurse Young, who was captured after the fall of Corregidor. "When MacArthur landed on Mindoro, he featured 'Better Get Out of Town Before It's Too Late.' For the Luzon landing, it was 'Hail, Hail, the Gang's All Here.' About the time of the Leyte landing, he described the arrival in camp of a delivery of rice, concluding with the cryptic, 'Better Leyte than never.'"

The Japanese Army took over Santo Tomas in February 1944, eliminating the package line that had been the single contributing factor to the camp's survival. In 1944 the community garden produced 124 tons of produce—most of it talinum, a leafy green similar to spinach—but that proved to be only a fraction of the food needed to sustain nearly 3,700 internees. After more than two years in lockup, most internees had already lost all excess body fat. Weight loss now increased dramatically. "Our ration decreased at first month by month, then week by week, and finally day by day," recalled Marie Adams. "We could see each other lose weight almost before our eyes." Nowhere was that more obvious than in the bathrooms. "Paunches, of course, had long since disappeared, but now men were losing their buttocks, strange as it may seem," Hartendorp observed. "In eight out of ten, these finely rounded features had flattened out in a most unsightly way, and in some of the older men the skin sagged down in flaps."

One hundred eighty five internees had died in the period between the camp's opening and January 31, 1944. That number soon escalated—and at a much faster pace. From February to September, another fifty-four perished, many so weakened that their bodies struggled to fight off infection. Starvation sapped energy, even among the children who enjoyed a better diet than the adults. Robin Prising, the eleven-year-old son of a wealthy Manila tobacco merchant, later described his exhaustion in a memoir about Santo Tomas. "Each day as I climbed the stairs I could feel my strength draining from me; I was growing weaker," he recalled. "I had not learnt much in the past weeks. It was easier to sit and let my mind drift from my arithmetic, to gaze over the trees in the front grounds, beyond the matted barrier of iron bars and out over the city. The view of church towers, the jumble of streets beneath the corrugated iron roofs of houses and the red-tiled roofs of buildings lent me an illusion of freedom as I sat hungry and constrained, muffling some vague feeling of anger. On a fair day I could see as far as the piers and stare at the grey Japanese warships in the bay."

Men and women grew testy with one another. "There was a tension among the internees that is almost indescribable," Adams wrote. "Irritability is one of the first symptoms of starvation, and certainly that symptom was marked among us. We were all cross, irritable, and edgy; we argued about things that were utterly insignificant. We were ready to claw each other's eyes out—over nothing at all. We were hungry; we were starved." Many developed beriberi, a disease caused by malnourishment that dimpled muscles in some and caused elbows, knees, and joints to swell in others. "Each day, we examined our faces, hands and legs for the telltale signs," Roka wrote in her diary on August 2, 1944. "Most of us had some symptoms, but what we feared most were the edematous legs that resembled useless and dead stumps of wood. Worse still were the distorted and large faces that resembled grinning Halloween pumpkins."

"If MacArthur doesn't soon come," went a common refrain around camp, "he'll get here in time to bury the last internee."

There was little doubt that the Japanese used food as a weapon—a form of punishment. "It seemed every time that our forces took over another island, they would cut our food," recalled American Frank Long, who worked in the camp's kitchen until beriberi left him unable to walk. "They were methodically and systematically starving us to death." The physical effects horrified Prising, who queued up hours before each meal, watching as internees fought over places in line. "As I waited in the queues from day to day I could watch the other prisoners shrink," he wrote. "From one day to the next their eyes sank further into their sockets, cheek bones jutted out of paper-thin flesh, knees became gigantic swollen joints attached to the sticks of their legs. The elderly wasted rapidly and, as their slack skin shriveled and began to crack, they grew into walking corpses. Their staring eyes, once troubled, took on a haunted look; then a milky film crept over the cornea and iris—the signal of approaching death."

Internees received a welcome distraction on the morning of September 21, 1944. Two days earlier the Japanese had announced in the press their plans to conduct antiaircraft gun practice. The weapons began firing at five a.m. Around nine-thirty internees spotted a plane in the skies overhead towing a target, while south of the city others spied as many as a half-dozen fighters that appeared to dogfight. "That's a rather dangerous practice," one internee remarked.

The captives watched as dark puffs of smoke peppered the sky. "That's a real fight!" someone cried. "That plane is on fire!"

To the amazement of the internees, dozens of carrier-based fighters and bombers from Adm. William "Bull" Halsey's Third Fleet swarmed out of the clouds and broke off for attacks on Nichols, Nielson, and Zablan airfields. The internees realized that this was no drill—it was an American air raid on Manila, the first since the fall of the Philippines two and a half years earlier. "Men, women, and children ran out of buildings and shacks shouting like maniacs," Roka wrote. "Others, with eyes cast heavenward, stood rooted to the ground. They could not believe their eyes! A few of the bombers flew low enough to give us the thrill of a lifetime! We saw, not the familiar and hated orange circle, but a flash of blue and a white star. It was like a beautiful dream!"

"This is a raid!" barked the camp's loudspeaker. "Take cover!"

Air raid sirens finally sounded, and antiaircraft fire thundered. Many of the internees ran for shelter, crowding the lobby of the Main Building. Smiles spread across faces. Some people cried; others embraced one another. A few even sang. "They're here!" internees shouted. "They've come back!"

A few narrated the progress of the battle overhead. "Look at that one dive!" someone yelled. "See that bomb dropping! Now listen! Just like clockwork! Isn't it beautiful?"

A Japanese machine-gun bullet tore into the asphalt near the lobby door, while shrapnel rained down around the camp, injuring several internees, including one hiding under a bed in a shanty. Those minor wounds did little to dampen the euphoria. "We pounded each other until we were black and blue," Roka wrote, "and we shouted until we were hoarse." Elizabeth Vaughan celebrated by giving her children the two lollipops she had saved for just such an occasion. "For an hour or more," Roka wrote, "we saw a show that could not be duplicated on Broadway."

American bombers reappeared in the skies in the days and weeks ahead, buoying the spirits of the internees. "Blood plasma and vitamin shots couldn't have done as much for the morale of the camp as the spectacular bombings we had witnessed in the last two days," Roka wrote in her diary. "We talked of nothing else." New Jersey native Albert Holland, a sugar executive before the war, observed the apparent medicinal power of America's air campaign. "We have no deaths on air-raid days," he wrote in his diary. "Perhaps they help in the struggle for survival."

The Japanese guards fumed, forcing anyone caught watching the aerial fights to stand for six hours and stare into the sun. It was a risk worth taking. "We reached a point where we weren't scared anymore," recalled American internee Margaret Gillooly, "because the only alternative was death, and what was that after what we'd been through?" Internees woke the next morning to the song "Pennies from

Heaven," while a few days later the loudspeakers played "Lover, Come Back to Me."

The American bombings proved a potent tonic for the spirits of the internees, but it did nothing to stall the progressive march of starvation. "The body, as long as it is living and breathing, consumes itself," Gillooly recalled. "As you were walking around and breathing, you were dying." Bodies often shrank in bizarre and disfiguring ways. Starvation carved deep pits on the inside of the internees' thighs near the groin. Hair and fillings in teeth dropped out, and fingernails turned brittle. "Many people complained of a growing hardness of hearing. Others suffered from blind spots on the retina," Hartendorp wrote. "It was a grisly thing to note such symptoms develop in one's own body."

To survive, desperate internees ate anything and everything, from tins of Pard brand dog food to the pigeons that once perched along the roof of the university. Caroline Bailey's parents even harvested the beans out of her prized stuffed animals. Children picked through the trash left behind by the Japanese guards for rotten potato peelings and stole the slop dumped in the troughs for the pigs. Internees not only ate such waste but were grateful for it. British internee Elsa Colquhoun feasted on a special birthday dinner comprised exclusively of rubbish. "Such a wonderful meal," she wrote in a thank you card, "all gathered from the Japanese garbage dump!"

Medical officer Maj. Samuel Bloom roasted his pet guinea pigs, while many others choked down everything from stray dogs and cats to snails. Even rats could fetch as much as eight pesos apiece on the camp's black market. "One man," Eva Anna Nixon wrote in her diary, "pioneered in rat cooking and others followed."

Roka recounted how a friend announced he had feasted on feline. "How was it?" she asked.

"A bit gamey," he replied. "I've been to several dog parties, too. It's much more tasty than cat!"

The best meal of all, Robin Prising's family discovered, were puppies. "Dogs or old tomcats could only be simmered for broth, but puppies were tender," Prising wrote. "Poached toad was the one delicacy

I could provide, but mother strictly insisted that toads caught in the latrines must be thoroughly washed." Even among children the pain of hunger surpassed the love for prized pets. "I was fond of Whiskers, but when the time came, I simply picked him up and presented him for slaughter," Robert Colquhoun, who was six at the time, recalled of his cat. "He tasted very good—rather like chicken." To the sadness of many, some culprit even ate the camp's mascot, a mauve-gray Persian raised since a kitten. "The poor splendid beast had gone into the pot," Hartendorp wrote, "like many a more common member of his genus, of some one without either conscience or an appreciation of the rarest of feline beauty."

Internees likewise ate wild plants, including pigweed, cassava root, and hibiscus leaves, though the latter was a purgative that often made people sick. So, too, did canna lily bulbs, which poisoned six internees in November. One of those was nurse Anne Louise Goldthorpe, who wrote in her diary that the sickness and nausea at least temporarily replaced the gnawing pain of her hunger. The rampant foraging prompted the camp's medical staff to broadcast a list of edible and poisonous plants. "It must again be emphasized and repeated that the use of condemned vegetables and garbage must be discontinued," the message cautioned. "While it is realized that everyone is hungry, we must not become panicky." Such warnings did little to ease the suffering. "Our hunger at this time was a living thing, like a torturing pain," Roka wrote in her diary on December 15, 1944. "It was with us day and night."

The Japanese, in contrast, ate like kings. Portly guards with apple cheeks roamed around camp with filthy cummerbunds that struggled to restrain bulging bellies. The Japanese further inflamed tensions by slaughtering pigs and carabaos in front of hundreds of starving internees. "Just as soon as the Nips disappeared with their freshly quartered meat," Roka wrote after the butchering of a carabao, "men, women and children rushed to the spot and, like voracious dogs, they clawed around the blood, entrails, dust and grit, searching for tail, ears, hooves, or anything that resembled food."

Another forty-three internees died between October 1 and the end of December. Food theft skyrocketed along with the black market prices. A kilo of sugar went for as much as $105, a kilo of rice $60, and a twelve-ounce can of corned beef $40. Even a pack of thirty cigarettes went for $18—prices few could afford. San Francisco native Jean Crichton wrote that desperate wives hawked their diamond rings just for rice. "The money lenders, usurers, profiteers and bloodsuckers," she wrote, "I have no illusions left about human nature." A rash of food thefts provoked a similar response from Albert Holland. "There is as much community spirit in this camp as among a pack of jackals."

"I weighed 92 lbs today," nurse Goldthorpe wrote in her diary on December 23. "I am losing almost a pound a day." Others experienced similar drastic losses. "I weigh 110 today—down 18 pounds in 17 days," Holland wrote. "81 pounds below my pre-war weight."

"I'm hungry," children up and down the halls cried each night, much to the frustration of parents powerless to provide. More painful than the cries was the obvious physical toll starvation took on the children, all of whom were innocent victims in an unending war. "The tremendously active kids that used to tear around the campus like savages were now little old men and women," Roka observed. "Hollow eyed, skinny and listless, they sat around and talked about food."

Robin Prising discovered in late 1944 that he could no longer run, not from a lack of energy but because his youthful knees could no longer support even his tiny frame. "Starvation is taking its slow toll," he wrote. "I can count my bones from the collarbone down—each joint, each jutting rib." To trick his body, Prising vomited his meager rations back up in his mouth, allowing him the sensation of swallowing them again. "Even the vomit tastes good," he wrote. "I go to the latrine as seldom as possible, trying to hold everything inside me, stingily preserving it for two or three days."

By the end of 1944, camp officials canceled all school. Neither the students nor the teachers had the strength to climb the four flights of stairs to the classrooms. "It is hard for me to realize," one woman said, "that I was a tennis champion just 3 years ago." Adult lectures likewise ceased as internees struggled to concentrate and battled memory loss. Others abandoned the games of chess and bridge that had helped pass the years. "When I went to bed at night, I felt just on the verge of screaming. I ached to the ends of my fingers and toes, with the most horrible ache that I have ever experienced," Adams wrote. "We were so thoroughly depleted that frequently I would sit on my bed and stare at the sink in the corner of the room, wondering whether it was worth while to make the effort to get up and go over to it to wash my hands, or whether it wouldn't be better to wait until lunch-time to do it, because it would save that much energy."

The average caloric intake for the internees in 1944 was 1,323 a day. By December that figured plummeted to 898, only to fall again the next month to just 567. A medical survey conducted by the camp doctors in January 1945 revealed that the average male had lost fifty-one pounds and the average female thirty-two. More than half of that weight was lost just since August 1944. "I was worried about a lump in my stomach," Goldthorpe, the nurse, confided in her diary on January 5, 1945. "Then I found it was my backbone. I never expected to feel that from the front."

As much as 90 percent of the camp's population suffered from edema, accompanied by either constipation or loose stools. Others battled bleeding gums, vision loss, and frequent urination. Army nurse Gwendolyn Henshaw ultimately lost all her teeth. Many women, who had long since stopped menstruating, discovered their bladder muscles were too weak to hold in urine. "When I'd stand up, I'd start urinating," recalled Sally Blaine, another army nurse. "It was terrible. It was absolutely embarrassing. Some of the girls really flooded themselves in front of other people." The agony of starvation struck most internees as intentional. "Many of us believed that the Japanese planned to kill us by slow starvation. If their plan was to make us suffer, they had succeeded," Roka wrote. "A bullet would have been more merciful."

In the absence of food, many resorted to fantasy. A mass mania swept the camp as starving internees copied and traded recipes, from baked Indian pudding and Boston-style fish chowder to clam pie and French dressing. "People would be sitting with their legs all edematous from vitamin deficiencies, talking recipes," recalled army nurse Anna Williams. "It was only a banquet of words." Roka could not help but note the tragedy of the craze. "What made the mania so pathetic and futile was that they copied and concentrated on recipes that called for hard-to-obtain ingredients even in a normal world," she wrote in her diary. "It stimulated their desire for food, and it used up energy that they could ill afford. It seemed like the cruelest form of torture."

Several internees attempted suicide, while others suffered breakdowns. "Many prisoners are losing their minds and furtively devour imaginary meals, slurping and eating the air," Prising wrote. "Men suck their thumbs, gnaw at their hands."

Prising noted with alarm how hunger had hollowed out his parents. His fifty-seven-year-old mother Marie had once been a stage actress in London and on Broadway. Her dark hair and eyes had captivated his father, Frederick, who happened to take in a show of the opera *Thaïs* while in New York in 1911. "That's the woman I shall marry," he declared when he first saw her.

Her beauty likewise had captured the attention of famed illustrator Harrison Fisher, whose work regularly appeared on covers of *The Saturday Evening Post* and *Cosmopolitan*. Harrison's drawing of Marie had graced the cover of the centennial edition of *Ladies Home Journal*. But the loss of so much tissue and muscle deformed her beauty. "Mother is so thin that her eyes and ears are enormous, the flesh of her arms hangs on her bones like a sleeve," he wrote. "Her hands are knucklebone."

Prising's sixty-six-year-old father, who had once advised William Taft, was in far worse shape. His beard had stopped growing, and he showed the telltale signs of death's approach. "When he undresses, I can see how his skin drips on his skeleton; the cavities are deep at his thigh and buttocks. Only his hands, his ankles and his feet are fattening—swollen from beriberi," the youth observed. "Father's eyes are growing a milky film; from day to day he becomes more quiet, more abstracted and gentler than ever. As he lies on his bed, unless his breathing is labored, I have to glance over at him to make certain he is still alive. If he notices me looking at him, he can scarcely smile."

The once-thriving camp—a testament to the collective will of the internees—began to crumble. "Every waking hour," nurse Bertha

Dworsky recalled, "was a struggle just to exist." Emaciated internees fainted and collapsed during roll call. "Food is getting much
shorter," nurse Goldthorpe noted with alarm in her diary. "The dogs
and cats have all been eaten. Nor is there a pigeon on the place." All
nonessential work ceased. Some eighteen hundred women, many with
dysentery and diarrhea, lined up to use only two serviceable toilets.
"Some stayed on their beds and cots to stare at the ceiling all day,"
Roka wrote. "They had lost all hope and faith that our forces would
return." Few had the strength to do much else. "This place is a living
graveyard," British internee Elsa Colquhoun wrote on New Year's Day
1945. "People in it are nothing more than spectres, grey ghosts. Their
minds, as well as their stomachs, are void."

The exhausted doctors and nurses, who each day manned the front
lines in the camp's battle against starvation, resorted to using blood
plasma as a food substitute. Even then desperate internees went so far
as to steal the precious bags from one another. "I saw many cases of
beriberi come into the hospital so bloated that the patient was unrecognizable," wrote Adams, who personally dropped fifty pounds. "The
patients lost all control of their normal functions. We were unable to
get laundry done; consequently a patient would sometimes have to lie
on the same sheet for a week. The situation in the hospital was horrible. The wards were in an awful condition."

Starvation brought out the worst in people, even Episcopal missionary Raymond Abbitt, who worked in the camp's isolation hospital.
Abbitt went so far one day, as he walked a tray of food to an eighty-
year-old patient, to contemplate murdering the man just so he could
eat his plate of watery rice. "What bothered me was that it entered my
mind that I could very easily just have bumped him off and killed him
to get that tray of food," Abbitt recalled. "You were that hungry at
that point. It always bothered me after I got food to eat that I would
ever have such a thought."

The camp's doctors battled incredible ethical dilemmas, including
who was entitled to more food, children or pregnant women. Hartendorp witnessed an elderly veteran of the Spanish-American War
pleading with a doctor for milk. "If there were any milk, I'd prefer to

give it the children," the doctor leveled with him. "We can't be senti-mental about this."

Three to four internees died on average each day in late January. "The aged and infirm died first, most from complications set in force from weakness," Earl Carroll recalled. "Then the late middle aged group started to go." Roka and her fiancé played a macabre game of guessing who would be next. "In the last year, we could pick out who would die," she remembered. "You didn't say anything, but you knew." Holland likewise learned to spot it when he landed in the camp hospital with beriberi, surrounded by men swollen like balloons, most of whom succumbed in the early morning hours. "Day in, day out the struggle goes on—against disease and against starvation: against death."

The Japanese often left the bodies in the rooms for hours, where rats nibbled the fingers and toes. The motor hearse that once had been used to haul the dead with dignity was replaced by a steady stream of small and shabby *carretelas* or horse-drawn wagons. "As I watched the carretela carrying today's dead out of the camp, I saw that there was not only a scarcity of food but everything else," Roka wrote. "One of the coffins was far too short, and the corpse's feet stuck out of the coffin in a grotesque manner."

Funerals also proved primitive affairs. Goldthorpe attended the memorial for Henry Umstad, who had died after suffering a high fever for several days. "What a pitiful group we were. All hungry, emaci-ated, threadbare in patched rags. I thought of this as we stood there in the mud floored Nipa shack singing 'Lead Kindly Light,'" she wrote in her diary. "I hope the fever burned the hunger out of him."

The January 21 passing of John Shaw, the seventy-three-year-old former head of the Canadian-Pacific Steamship Company in the Phil-ippines, stunned many in the camp. One of Manila's leading business executives, he had been a wealthy and prominent figure with a siz-able physical stature to match. Internees gathered at ten-thirty a.m. to watch two Filipino boys push his shrunken remains out of Santo Tomas in a handcart normally used to haul a few five-gallon water cans. One of those who watched was Robin Prising, whose parents had been close friends with Shaw. "Uncle John Shaw, the magnificent gourmet, lost over a hundred and fifty pounds as a prisoner of war," Prising later wrote. "The fattest man I have ever known died of starvation."

Chairman of the internee medical staff Dr. Ted Stevenson dutifully logged each passing as either "malnutrition" or "starvation," a fact that outraged the Japanese, who demanded he change the certificates so as not to embarrass the camp administration. Stevenson refused, prompting the commandant on January 30 to order him locked up in the camp jail. "He was," Carroll said, "too stubborn and too honest to yield on a matter of principle." Incarcerating Stevenson proved a futile gesture. "There were twenty-three deaths in December and thirty-two in January," Adams recalled. "We were dying at such a rate that we were afraid that our troops might not find any of us alive."

Internees struggled to hold on as the war inched ever closer to Manila. "For the last week, we heard heavy blast and earth-shaking rumbles," Roka wrote. "North, east, south and west—everywhere we looked we saw smoke and flames." Frank Cary likewise studied the horizon. "Still here, still waiting," he wrote in a February 1 letter. "It is clear that our forces are making progress as the battle sounds are coming this way. Fires blaze each day—some set by our bombs, some the result of demolition bombing. A great black column of smoke is rearing its head nearby. It smells like oil and rubber."

Despite the excitement, inside the camp the hours crawled past, a slow-motion blur of hunger, anxiety, and suffering. "In the anguish of waiting," Prising wrote, "freedom appears like some grotesque mirage." The question on everyone's mind, of course, was how much longer the internees could persevere. "We survived on hope," recalled Carroll, "hope that the American forces would arrive."

But hope might not be enough.

PART II

*"The stage was now set for the Battle of Manila,
a battle distinguished for ferocity and destruction."*

—SIXTH ARMY,
REPORT OF THE LUZON CAMPAIGN

The dark smoke from artillery fire wafts across the ruins of southern
Manila on the morning of February 23, 1945, as American troops
prepare to assault the Walled City. Pictured on the right are the battered General Post Office and the remains of the Santa Cruz Bridge.

CHAPTER 6

"No one will ever know the complete story of what happened in Manila in those bloody days of February, 1945."

—CAPT. MILTON SANDBERG,
DECEMBER 5, 1945

M AJ. GEN. VERNE MUDGE SUMMONED A SELECT FEW NEWS reporters to his tent on January 31, 1945. The forty-six-year-old commander of the First Cavalry Division—a South Dakota native and 1920 graduate of West Point—was about to spearhead one of the most daring missions of the Pacific War. Mudge's forces had wrapped up sixty-six days of fierce combat on Leyte and had barely had enough time to rest and reequip before embarking for Lingayen, landing on January 27. In that time, the cavalry had driven thirty-five miles south to the town of Guimba. Earlier that day in his tented command post, Mudge had met with an agitated Douglas MacArthur, who was frustrated over the slow progress of the American forces. The time to retake the Philippine capital had arrived—and MacArthur wanted Mudge to do it. "Go to Manila! Go around the Nips, bounce off the Nips, but go to Manila!" he had demanded. "Free the internees at Santo Tomas! Take Malacañan Palace! Take the Legislative Building."

MacArthur's blunt orders stemmed from his frustration with the Sixth Army commander, General Krueger, who had spent the past three weeks crawling down the central plains at a rate of only four miles a day. Krueger believed the lack of enemy opposition was a ruse, part of a plot that involved dangling Manila, like bait, to lure him too far ahead and trap him. Some of Krueger's fellow officers—including the Eighth Army commander, General Eichelberger—likewise questioned the enemy's motivations. "I still cannot make up my mind," he wrote, "whether the Japanese are being stupid or rather bright." MacArthur, however, disagreed, boasting to General Griswold that the battle for the Philippines had already been won—on Leyte. "I do not," Griswold confided in his diary, "have his optimism."

Not only was MacArthur certain that his forces would face little opposition, but he distrusted intelligence estimates that countered his own gut instinct, a fact he had revealed during a briefing over enemy troop strength on Luzon. At that meeting, Brig. Gen. Clyde Eddleman, Krueger's chief of staff, ran through the estimated Japanese numbers, while MacArthur fidgeted with his corncob pipe.

"Bunk!" he repeatedly interrupted.

"General," Eddleman finally said, "apparently you don't like our intelligence briefing."

"I don't," MacArthur replied. "It's too strong. There aren't that many Japanese there."

"Well," Eddleman said, "most of this information came from your headquarters."

Gen. Charles Willoughby, MacArthur's intelligence chief, jumped out of his chair. "Didn't come from me!" he hollered. "Didn't come from me!"

After the briefing, MacArthur pulled Eddleman aside. "I want to give you my ideas on intelligence officers," he said. "There are only three great ones in the history of warfare and mine is not one of them."

MacArthur was convinced the Japanese would abandon Manila, just as he had three years earlier, a confidence that infected some of his closest aides. "Mac has made a sucker out of Yamashita," General Fellers wrote to his wife. "The Nip cannot stage a comeback—we shall have Manila." To spur Krueger, MacArthur moved his headquarters ahead of his commander's, yet the cautious officer still plodded south toward the capital. Chief of Staff Dick Sutherland urged MacArthur to fire him. "If I were commanding the Sixth Army," he griped, "we'd be in Manila by now."

The general's impatience was triggered in part by the rescue only the day before of starving American prisoners of war at a camp near

Cabanatuan, some sixty miles north of Manila. In a daring nighttime raid, Army Rangers had sliced the phone lines, shot up the guard towers, and stormed the camp. "The next twenty minutes were pandemonium," recalled Lt. Col. Henry Mucci, who led the raid. "We killed about 225 Japs in all." Mucci's men liberated more than five hundred captives, many so emaciated that Army Rangers could carry them out two at a time. The horrible condition of the prisoners fueled MacArthur's fear over what he might find at Santo Tomas and Bilibid—camps that housed ten times as many people. Furthermore, unlike Cabanatuan, which had held soldiers, Santo Tomas housed civilian women and children. "What a barbaric gang the Japanese military are!" Fellers wrote his wife after Cabanatuan's liberation. "We hope the civilians in Manila will be spared."

So, too, did MacArthur.

Despite his optimism, the general had begun to prepare the public for the worst, a message delivered days earlier by CBS reporter Bill Dunn. "I know there are thousands of Americans living for the day when we re-enter Manila and, in theory at least, release these people," Dunn told his listeners. "As much as I hate to do it, I must repeat again the warning that this is definitely no time for optimism. General MacArthur has announced he will hold General Yamashita personally responsible."

On top of rescuing prisoners of war and internees, MacArthur had selfish reasons for wanting to move faster. Not only did he still feel the sting of his earlier defeat, but he had grown jealous of his former subordinate, Dwight Eisenhower, who over the course of the war had eclipsed him, winning great acclaim as the commander of American forces in Europe. MacArthur fumed when a proposed war bond advertisement listed Eisenhower's name above his. "I presume this is merely a clerical mistake," he fired back, "but if it is intentional I do not care to have my name included." MacArthur went so far as to derogatorily label his former chief of staff the "best clerk I ever had." He seemed to take pleasure, too, in his mentee's fumbles. After Eisenhower's great success with the D-Day invasion of France, the general had struggled to repel the Germans in the Battle of the Bulge. "Eisenhower's curve had gone down," MacArthur gloated. "He is not now considered the great leader he formerly was."

MacArthur saw in Manila an opportunity to once again seize the limelight. He understood better than anyone the power of narrative, having served as the army's first public relations officer during World War I. MacArthur had demonstrated his media savvy back on Corregidor, where he managed, despite his ultimate defeat, to construct a public image of himself as the lone general standing up to the Japanese. He did so through carefully crafted communiqués—many of them erroneous—that he personally labored over for up to two hours each day. Out of the 142 issued during his time on the Rock, 109 spotlighted a single soldier: MacArthur. America loved it—and him. In a sign of his media campaign's great success, cities across the nation had named roads, schools, and stadiums in his honor. Couples had danced the "The MacArthur Glide," and women had shown off a popular new hairstyle called the General MacArthur Wave. Parents from Oregon to Arkansas had christened newborn children Douglas.

Unlike Corregidor, however, Manila offered MacArthur the chance for a real victory, both on the battlefield and in newsprint and on the airwaves. So confident was the general that he would retake Manila without any trouble that his staff had begun to organize a victory parade, down to picking jeep assignments and selecting a route into the city along Rizal Avenue, which looped around Taft Avenue and Dewey Boulevard, past his old home atop the Manila Hotel. The plan called for the parade to end at eleven a.m. at the Legislature Building, where MacArthur would deliver a speech followed by President Sergio Osmeña. Afterward a band would play "The Star-Spangled Banner," and then the Philippine anthem, as each nation's respective flag rose up the pole. "It would be," as one historian later noted, "the liberation of Paris in the Pacific." For MacArthur, such a ceremony in Manila would serve as the redemptive final chapter to his earlier story of defeat. "He is," General Griswold noted in his diary, "insane on this subject!"

General Mudge's job was to deliver Manila to MacArthur.

The major general gathered in his tent around seven p.m. with a small group of some of the war's most seasoned journalists, all with previous ties to the Philippines. These men would be among the first into Manila, riding with Mudge's cavalrymen at the tip of the spear. Among those in the tent stood Carl Mydans, the thirty-seven-year-old *Life* photographer who had experienced firsthand the struggle behind bars at Santo Tomas.

Along with Mydans, the group this evening included CBS's Bill Dunn, United Press reporter Frank Hewlett, and Dean Schedler of the Associated Press. Hewlett and Schedler had earned the distinction of being the last two reporters to escape Corregidor before it fell to the Japanese. Hewlett, in fact, had penned the ditty that would become the theme song of the fighters on that rugged peninsula:

We're the battling bastards of Bataan:
No momma, no poppa, no Uncle Sam,
No aunts, no uncles, no cousins, no nieces,
No rifles, no guns or artillery pieces,
And nobody gives a damn.

Of the four, Hewlett had the most at stake in the success of the pending mission. He prayed that his wife Virginia was still alive inside Santo Tomas. He had last seen her on New Year's Eve in 1941, when he left for Bataan with General MacArthur. "She insisted," he later wrote, "on staying behind in Manila as a nurse in Santa Catalina Hospital."

After the fall of Manila, the Japanese had interned her along with thousands of other Americans. The State Department later informed Hewlett that the Japanese planned to repatriate Virginia, sending her aboard a crowded passenger ship to Goa, the same one that had ferried Mydans and his wife out of the Philippines. Thrilled, Hewlett rushed to India to meet the ship as it lumbered into port.

Perched at the rail, Mydans spotted his fellow reporter on the quay below. His heart sank; all the excitement over his own liberation vanished. "Under the stress of war and separation from Frank, whose fate she never learned, she lost her mind," Mydans wrote. "At the last minute the Japanese had ruled she was too sick to travel. She had been left behind in prison."

Hewlett had traveled to India for nothing.

"Virginia?" he shouted up through cupped hands. "Where's Virginia?"

Mydans knew he could not deliver such horrible news with a shout from the ship's rail, so he pretended not to hear him, but Hewlett continued to holler. "Please," the reporter cried. "Where is Virginia?"

Neither Mydans nor his wife could stand it any longer. "We'll come down as soon as we can," Shelley replied.

"Better wait for me," interrupted Dr. Hugh Robinson, a missionary and former internee. "I was her doctor. It will be better if I tell him first."

The Mydanses remained aboard ship as the doctor broke the news; the duo appeared small in the distance. "We could see the little motions of Dr. Robinson's hands as he talked," Carl Mydans remembered. "It was as painful as though we were there."

In the years since, Hewlett had heard no word from Virginia. Had she recovered from her breakdown or had she, like so many others, died behind the camp's iron gates? Now, traveling with Mudge's forces on the road to Manila, Hewlett would soon have an answer. "Santo Tomas was his last hope," his friend Bill Dunn recalled. "I could tell that those last few miles were to him maddeningly slow."

General Mudge advised the reporters of the danger of the operation. To seize Manila, he had organized three mobile units, which would later be known as "the flying columns." Two of the three included a cavalry squadron, tank company, artillery, engineers, and medical squadron. The third unit was largely a reconnaissance squadron. "Everything will be stripped down. No cots, tents, kitchens, barracks bags or lockers to be taken," orders mandated. "Carry all you need." To travel fast, troops packed little more than gasoline, arms, ammo, water, and four days of rations. These bare-bones forces would charge sixty miles through enemy-controlled territory and then break into a city of more than one million. To lead them, Mudge selected Brig.

Gen. William Chase, a forty-nine-year-old Brown University graduate who had grown up attending the Boston Symphony and Metropolitan Opera with his mother. "Mudge's plan," the moustached Chase later wrote, "was bold and dashing in true cavalry style."

But Mudge's plan wasn't without challenges, the largest being conflicting intelligence over the enemy's intentions for the capital. Would Japanese forces abandon Manila? Or not?

Guerrilla reports reflected the competing activities of both General Yamashita's and Admiral Iwabuchi's forces. Messages from late December and early January spotlighted the evacuation of president Jose Laurel, his family, and cabinet to Baguio. Others chronicled Yamashita's public debate and ultimate refusal to declare Manila an open city—as MacArthur had done prior to his departure in December 1941—arguing that such a move would make Japan look weak. Yamashita did agree, however, to withdraw most of his troops from the capital, an exodus that guerrillas dutifully reported. "Nips moving out of Manila," one report stated. "Movement done day and night."

But by mid-January, the intelligence changed. These latter reports described the fortification of the city in accordance with Iwabuchi's plan to fight for Manila, noting that much of the work was being executed by Japanese marines who made up the majority of the admiral's forces. "Nips bored holes in walls low enough for sniping in prone position," stated one report. "Evacuations in Luneta are believed for mines."

"Barricades constructed along main thoroughfares in the city," read another.

These reports that the enemy might try to hold the city failed to convince MacArthur, who as recently as January 23 chewed out his own intelligence officer for overestimating Japanese strength. "I don't see how," MacArthur huffed, "I have gotten as far as I have with the staff I have been surrounded with." Other commanders, however, proved far more cautious. In a letter to his wife on January 29, 1945, General Eichelberger zeroed in on the critical question: "We still do not know whether the Japanese are going to put up any resistance to the capture of Manila."

Mudge would know soon enough.

Absent concrete intelligence on the enemy's plans, the major general could at least bank on the ferocity of his foe, should his troops encounter him. American forces had experienced that on Leyte, where the Japanese had raped women, mutilated dead American troops, and even sliced off souvenir body parts; several Caucasian fingers were found wrapped in a white cloth in the pack of a dead Japanese soldier. Just three weeks earlier, an American who was gathering bamboo stumbled across the remains of a fellow soldier. "The head, arms, and legs had been severed from the body and the torso had been cut in half with the two portions lying several yards apart," reported Technician Fifth Grade Burdett Andrews. "I searched the area for the head and limbs but could not find them."

As the briefing concluded, one of Mudge's aides entered the tent with a tray of turkey sandwiches. The reporters were hungry, having not eaten all day after meeting with the liberated prisoners of war from Cabanatuan.

Mudge encouraged them to eat up. "I don't know when you'll eat again," he warned.

The journalists arrived around dusk in a dry rice field several miles south of Mudge's command post with instructions to report to Lt. Col. Haskett "Hack" Conner, Jr., who commanded one of the mobile units. Cigarettes glowed like fireflies over the field flattened by trucks, tanks, and jeeps. Above it all, the reporters heard the grunt and cough of engines. "It was impossible to size up the entire squadron, but what we could see was not too reassuring," Dunn recalled. "This was the team that was going to strike Manila? Was it smart to place our faith in such a limited force?"

A second lieutenant approached the journalists. "Your jeep will be the fourth vehicle after the tanks," he told them. "The colonel thinks you'll see more up there. Just pull in as near as you can to that jeep and fall in behind it when it moves out."

The reporters found Colonel Conner, dressed in jungle camouflage, with the insignia stripped from his uniform. The twenty-nine-year-old

West Point graduate's command post consisted of a patch of stubbled rice in the corner of the field. Conner hovered over a pile of maps, outlining the mission's objective by the faint light of a lantern. He asked the same question as Mudge: Were the reporters prepared for the hazards of the mission? "Again we insisted we were, actually stretching the truth a bit," Dunn recalled. "We really had no solid idea of what lay ahead, but we were not about to admit it."

"We're traveling light," Conner said. "When we hit the enemy, we're going to cut right through him and get into Manila before he knows what's happening."

The reporters listened.

"The rest of the division will be coming along after us," the officer continued, "and we'll let them worry about what we leave behind."

Conner concluded by advising the journalists to get some rest before the unit departed around midnight. The men spread out shelter-halves on the ground and lay down. "It had been a strenuous and an emotional day, and I was both tired and tense," Dunn recalled, "but fatigue won and I fell asleep almost instantly."

An officer woke the reporters before midnight, who climbed into the jeep that would carry them south to Manila. Hewlett and Mydans settled into the seat behind Dunn as the forces moved out at one minute past midnight on the morning of February 1, 1945. The jeep's windshield framed a view of the tanks ahead that rumbled down the rural roads, trailed by exhaust. "Behind stretched the rest of the column," Mydans observed, "all bulging with men and weapons and all black except for a faint glint on helmets and guns from a cloud-dimmed moon and the glow of burning cigarettes."

The column roared through empty villages, but as the hours passed, Filipinos began to appear in the darkened streets, cheering the troops who zoomed past. "Morning came and we kept rolling," Mydans recalled. "Sometimes we rode on highways and sometimes we bounced and trundled along in fields and carabao trails." When troops found the road blocked, bulldozers cleared the way. "Almost all of the bridges were out and we forded the rivers, the men holding their weapons high and often wading up to their chests in the water," Mydans recalled, "while the trucks and the lumbering tanks pushed and pulled each other with engines screaming and water flying."

In the city of Baliuag, euphoric Filipinos actually brought the column to a halt in what Dunn later described in a broadcast as "the greatest ovation these islands ever witnessed." An elderly woman wept amid the crowd as she waved the victory sign, while overhead church bells rang as young boys in a nearby steeple banged them with rocks. "Thousands of people thronged the streets, screaming, singing, and dancing about our armored column," Dunn wrote. "Women threw flowers at us and literally fought to touch our hands." Others ran alongside and begged for autographs and pressed eggs into the hands of troops. Dean Schedler feasted on hot sweet corn and Dunn on roasted camotes. General Chase relished fresh papayas and avocados. "The whole column," he said, "seemed to be eating its way to Manila."

"*Mabuhay*," many Filipinos yelled. "Welcome."

"God bless you," others cried.

The outpouring of emotion affected the reporters as much as the cavalrymen. "I was more moved by these people welcoming us than by the victory marches I have been on as we liberated southern France," recalled Mydans. Dunn felt the same. "Any member of the column, cavalryman or correspondent, who didn't get a kiss from one of the happy señoritas who stormed the loaded vehicles had only himself to blame."

Opposition proved sporadic even though Japanese troops occupied the area. At one point, General Chase broke for the night in a home that the owner professed Yamashita had once occupied. Whenever possible, troops took the Japanese under fire without stopping, including one such fight described in the Fifth Cavalry's report: "As our column approached a cross road, four Jap trucks loaded with men and equipment started to turn onto the main road. They were waved back by our leading elements and then received the surprise of their life as each passing truck load of American soldiers placed burst after burst into the trucks and Japs. All trucks were set on fire and several Japs killed and the rest scattered." The units that followed Conner's outfit often witnessed the carnage the colonel's men left behind: "Evidence all along the road revealed the running fight the group ahead of us had had to make."

At times Japanese attacks forced the cavalrymen to halt. The reporters dove for cover, while the soldiers charged into battle. "No football team moved with more coordination and cooperation," Mydans observed. "In the midst of the fight and with pinging bullets all around, I found myself watching, fascinated at the squadron's fighting skill." As soon as the enemy fell back, a clenched fist jerked up and down sent the column off again. "Our pauses were momentary and necessary but in no way an acknowledgement of enemy strength," Dunn remembered. "Bridgeless rivers gave us more pause than Yamashita's entire disorganized army."

On the night of February 2—after a day and half of travel—the column braked some twenty miles from Manila. Mydans and Schedler walked back to chat with the troops, leaving Dunn and Hewlett perched on the jeep's hood. "Suddenly," Dunn recalled, "Frank grabbed my knee in a vise-like grip that almost made me wince."

"Bill, this has *got* to be it," he said. "Virginia has to be there!"

Dunn wrapped his arm around his friend's shoulder, promising him it would be fine. "I had no information to back my words," he said, "but I, too, was praying that the Almighty was about to give a grand person his first real break in three years."

The cavalrymen closed in on Manila the following afternoon, but still not fast enough to satisfy Conner. Mydans spotted the unit's commander barking orders atop an embankment as the column climbed out of a river. "Let's go," he yelled. "Let's go. We've got to be in Manila today."

The cavalrymen reached Novaliches—about eight miles northeast of the capital—after five p.m. that Saturday, February 3. The column paused in front of the bridge over the Tuliahan River. Maj. James Gerhart surveyed the scene, then called for Lt. Jr. Grade James Sutton, a navy demolition expert attached to the cavalry. Time was suddenly critical. The Japanese had mined the bridge—and lit the fuse.

Under heavy fire, Sutton charged onto the bridge to find four hundred pounds of TNT and three thousand pounds of picric acid, more than enough explosives to drop the concrete and metal span into the river below. With just fourteen minutes until detonation, Sutton snipped the fuse and saved the bridge.

The soldiers pressed on toward the capital, wary of what other traps the Japanese had planned. Columns of black smoke rose skyward over the city, while to the west a blood-red sun sank on the horizon, an ominous welcome for the incoming troops. "Many Japs," a guerrilla report warned that day, "garrisoning Manila."

"Be alert," troops reminded one another.

The cavalry rolled past abandoned Japanese trucks, loaded with supplies. Enemy troops scattered in the distance, but the column did not stop. At Grace Park airfield on the edge of the city, the hangars burned. "There was not a rifle or machine gun in the column," Mydans said, "which was not pointing outward, trigger fingered."

The first troops crossed into the city at 6:35 p.m., passing the Balintawak Monument, a towering obelisk that honored the 1896 uprising against Spain. "We were entering Manila," one cavalry report noted, "and all weariness dropped off the shoulders of the men in anticipation of what we were going to have to do."

The column charged down Rizal Avenue, greeted in the dusk by celebrating Filipinos, including a group of children who sang "God Bless America." The troops pressed on toward Santo Tomas before enemy fire brought the column to a halt. The journalists jumped to the ground for cover, where Hewlett suddenly grabbed Mydans's arm. The reporter would soon have an answer over the fate of his wife.

"Tell me you think she's there," Hewlett begged.

Before Mydans could respond, Conner ordered the column to move out. The men climbed back into the jeep. Up ahead, Capt. Manuel Colayco, a thirty-nine-year-old Philippine guerrilla with the Allied Intelligence Bureau, flagged down the lead vehicle, offering to guide the column through the dark streets to Santo Tomas. Only the day before, Colayco had confided in his adjutant Lt. Carlos Paulino his prediction for the coming fight: "I think I will have the fortune of receiving the greatest honor that can be given to a soldier, that of dying for his country."

Mydans recognized his surroundings as the column closed to within a few blocks of the university. "We're there," he whispered to Hewlett. "We're almost there."

Hewlett rode in silence.

The column swung onto Calle España and charged toward the university's main entrance. The towering fence of Santo Tomas, covered in woven bamboo mats, slipped past the side of the jeep. Mydans tightened his grip around his friend's arm. "I felt a flush of illness," he wrote. "This was the moment I'd been living for for three years."

The column slowed, and soldiers dismounted, moving forward in crouched columns alongside the vehicles. The lead tank rolled right up to the university's main gate and stopped. The rest of the infantrymen and the reporters hopped down. "Fires were burning over much of the city," Mydans recalled, "and the red-lighted sky and stealth of the scene and pitch of emotion had me shaking so that my camera bag pounded against me." He ran along the fence and crouched. The front gate stood partially open, revealing only darkness. An officer shouted inside, but no one answered. Two of the tanks trained powerful spotlights on the university, prompting Mydans to poke a hole in the fence with his knife and peer inside. The grounds stood empty.

"Maybe they've gone," someone said. "Maybe they've taken them all away."

Hewlett finally spoke up, his voice barely more than a whisper. "No," he muttered. "They're in there. It's only the Japs are gone."

The men listened in silence.

"I'm sure the Japs have gone," Mydans finally said. "Let's slip in."

The reporters ducked through the gate and approached the camp's guardhouse. A Japanese sentry suddenly jumped out and fired at them from point-blank range. The blue flame that leapt from the gun's muzzle blinded the Americans, who dropped to the ground, relieved to discover the bullet had whizzed between them. "We lay there for a moment," Mydans wrote, "then dragged ourselves on our stomachs along the side of the fence, breathing hard."

"You all right?" Hewlett whispered to Mydans

"O.K.," he replied. "You O.K.?"

"I want two men to go in and get that son-of-a-bitch," one of the officers shouted as Mydans and Hewlett crawled back.

"Grenade!" someone cried. An explosion detonated and men fell to the ground, including Colayco, who would die from his wounds seven days later, his prophecy fulfilled.

Mydans crawled over and found Colonel Conner, wounded in the leg by shrapnel. "Run that tank in through the fence," Conner ordered. "Keep the flares going up as she goes in."

Flares tore into the night sky as the Sherman tank named *Battlin' Basic* pushed ahead, a scene described best by reporter Dean Schedler in his Associated Press dispatch about that night. "The snorting tank pushed against the gate," Schedler wrote. "The engine clattered. The gate groaned, cracked and crashed under the treads."

Mydans stared as the gate that for almost a year had separated him from his freedom crumpled. In the distance, illuminated by the flares in the sky overhead, he could see the university's Main Building, where he had lived during his time as a captive.

Cavalrymen charged in behind the tank with the newsmen in tow. More troops followed, fanning out around them as flares continued to fire up into the night sky.

"Any Americans in there?" Mydans shouted.

Silence greeted him.

A single internee finally emerged from behind a tree, dressed in a long coat. Troops aimed at him. "I'm an American," he exclaimed. "You Americans?"

"Yes," replied a chorus of soldiers, lowering their rifles.

"Good," he answered. "I'll lead you in."

The soldiers moved forward. "There's a Jap machine-gun nest on the left side of the building," the internee said.

"Thanks, Mac," a soldier replied.

The tank and troops turned to take on the machine gun. Mydans decided not to wait any longer. "That's the Main Building," he said, grabbing Hewlett and pointing straight ahead. "I'm going in across the lawn."

Mydans charged ahead with Hewlett in tow, the men guided only by a distant flickering light. As they neared the building, the photographer could see that the big doors stood open. "I tripped once, recovered myself and pushed into an hysterical mob of internees waving, shouting, screaming, some weeping," Mydans wrote. "The feeble, shadowy light from several candles only partly lighted the large lobby."

Once inside Mydans could just barely make out the balustrade of the Main Building's grand staircase. Even in the faint light, the photographer could see dozens of internees, many of whom parted to allow Mydans and Hewlett to pass. "Thank God you are here," one shouted. "It's been so long."

"Crowds pressed in on me so closely that I could not move and then suddenly the crowd picked me up, 40-pound camera kit and all, and passed me from hand to hand overhead," Mydans wrote. "I was helpless, nor was I able to talk above the din."

"Who are you?" someone called out in a stern voice.

The crowd returned Mydans to his feet.

"Americans," the two journalists answered in unison.

"If you *are* Americans, put that flashlight on yourself."

The photographer did as asked. "I'm Carl Mydans," he announced.

The lobby fell silent.

"Carl Mydans," one woman finally shouted. "My God! It's Carl Mydans."

He looked up to see Betty Welborn, who had shared a room in Santo Tomas with his wife, emerge from the crowd in front of him. The fifty-nine-pound Welborn wrapped her arms around his neck and wept. Other internees again rushed him, pushing Mydans up on the stairs and demanding a speech. Overwhelmed by the scene, the photographer froze. "I was unable to talk. I mumbled something about I never knew how good it could feel to be back here in Santo Tomas," he said. "Then I made my way out of the building, everyone feeling me, holding on to me as I struggled through the crowd."

"No, darling, no. He's an American," Mydans heard a woman say as he passed. "They have come for us, darling. Don't be afraid."

Mydans emerged to find American soldiers pointing rifles at three Japanese officers. Above in the windows, he saw more internees, starving yet cheering.

"God Bless America," someone shouted.

"What a sight for sore eyes," another said.

"Oh how long we have waited."

Throughout it all, Hewlett had stood at Mydans's side, but he could not wait any longer. "I found a little girl who could answer the question which was foremost in my mind," he later wrote. "She told me where I could find my wife and kindly offered to accompany me to the hospital where Mrs. Hewlett was held."

The three years of war had been unkind to Virginia Hewlett, who like others had nearly starved to death in Santo Tomas. In the wake of her nervous breakdown, she refused to bathe or even eat, picking her nails and face with a blank stare.

"He's gone, he's gone," she mumbled. "I didn't know."

In recent months, Virginia Hewlett had improved, but she often remained in a wheelchair. That night, amid the shouts and commotion, she rallied, standing in a windowsill. Virginia told her friend Rita Palmer she wished Frank could be with her to witness the liberation. She had no idea he was now just steps away.

Hewlett burst into the men's ward of the camp hospital. "Where's my wife?" the reporter demanded.

Nurse Eunice Young escorted the anxious reporter to the women's ward. There for the first time in 1,128 days Frank Hewlett saw his wife. "I found her there today, recovering from a nervous breakdown. Doctors said she would have fully recovered now if she had had sufficient good food. Though never a big girl, her weight has dropped to 80 pounds, but I found her in excellent spirits," he wrote in his first dispatch from the camp. "It was a reunion after years about which I do not want to think."

Soon after, Hewlett approached Dunn. "I found her!" he shouted. "I *found* her!"

"Frank grabbed me in a rugged bear-hug, then literally danced away to break the news to the others," Dunn recalled. "We were in the midst of thousands of deliriously happy people, but not one could top the happiness of Frank Hewlett."

○ ○ ○ ○

THE ARRIVAL OF THE CAVALRYMEN capped off a day of anticipation for nineteen-year-old internee Margaret Gillooly, a native of San Francisco who had moved with her parents to the Philippines in 1938, where her father worked as a manager with the H. E. Heacock Company's department store. It was obvious to Gillooly that the war was closing in on Manila, as evidenced by the daily explosions, bombings, and thunder of antiaircraft fire. Despite that, Gillooly sensed that this day was somehow different. "Your skin prickled. You couldn't go anywhere that you didn't feel this electricity running through your body," she recalled. "You just knew something was going to happen."

That afternoon Gillooly walked along the fence that for so long had defined her young life. She listened to Filipinos talking on the other side. "The Americans are coming!" she heard someone shout. "The Americans are coming!"

As if to confirm her suspicions, more than a half-dozen bombers buzzed the camp just as the sun set, a scene best captured by Tressa Roka in her diary. "They came so close that we thought they'd scrape their paint on the high tower of our building," she wrote. "While screaming adults and children waved and cheered, the goggled and grinning pilots dipped their wings, and one of them threw an object into the east patio. It was a pair of goggles, to which was attached a note with this ringing message: 'Roll out the barrel, Christmas will be either today or tomorrow!'"

The excitement spread like an epidemic through the camp, reminding American nurse Minnie Breese of an ongoing bet among internees over which outfit would be the first to reach Santo Tomas—the First Cavalry, the Marines, or the vultures. "We always thought," she later said, "the vultures were going to win." The flyover triggered other thoughts of what liberation might mean, like the ones internee Frank

Cary dashed off in a letter, moments after the planes vanished over the horizon: "Each day may prove the last day—and, oh how we long for that day! Food, food, food, is on everyone's mind. People dream of it, talk of it, think of it."

Eleven-year-old Robin Prising was another who stood in awe at the late-day flyover. The fighters buzzed so slow over Santo Tomas that he swore he could see the toothy grin of an American pilot. Momentarily forgetting his hunger, he ran as fast as his buckling knees would carry him and found his mother to share the news. "Not bombers," he exclaimed. "Pursuit planes—P-38's. One of the pilots smiled!"

To his father, whose feet had swollen like balloons from beriberi, the youth was adamant. "They'll be here by dawn!" he declared.

"No, not tomorrow," Frederick Prising cautioned his son. "Tomorrow is Sunday. They wouldn't come on a Sunday."

The loudspeaker crackled to life. "All internees, all internees, go inside the buildings. Keep away from windows."

The captives who moments earlier had been celebrating the thought of possible liberation and freedom marched back inside the university buildings, preparing once again to bed down under the yoke of the Japanese.

"Well, I guess it's time to turn in," Frederick Prising told Robin as the two sat on the porch that graced the Annex's side entrance.

"I want to watch!" the youth protested.

"You'll do nothing of the kind," his father admonished him. "Nearly time for roll call. Time for bed."

The Prisings returned to their room and climbed in bed. Power died at 7:20 p.m. "Guerrilla sabotage!" someone shouted.

His father soon fell asleep, but Robin lay awake in the dark, too excited by the late-afternoon flyover. "Inside my mosquito net I lie listening in the rumbling blackout," he wrote. "Machinegun fire, the reply of rifle shots. Hunger. I vomit back a mouthful of stew. Go dizzy. The suspense tightens over me."

Throughout the camp, that same tension seized others, many of whom stared at the horizon, painted with the telltale signs of the approaching war. "From our windows," an internee later wrote, "we could see the orange and red sky caused by fires and the black billows of smoke coming from the north of Manila."

For the internees, insomnia momentarily surpassed hunger. "Many stayed up beyond their usual bedtime," Hartendorp wrote. "Some said they would not take their shoes off yet, and others who had done so put them on again."

Many of those unable to sleep congregated in the corridors, gossiping and waiting for something, anything to happen.

A guttural growl—distant at first, but growing louder—filled the night air, as American tanks turned down Calle España and closed in on the iron gates of Santo Tomas. It captivated the internees, who could smell the gasoline exhaust, a scent long absent in the fuel-starved Philippines. Rifle shots roared outside, followed by the rattle of machine guns. Flares lit up the night sky. "We watched, waited, prayed, and listened with trembling excitement," Roka wrote. "We dared not believe! Not just yet! We have been fooled so many times!"

The internees could hear the frantic shouts of Japanese guards interspersed with the deep nasal voices of American soldiers yelling directions to tank drivers: "Turn right, turn right, watch that ditch."

"Honey, they're here!" Tressa Roka's fiancé shouted, pulling her close. "Let's go to the front of the building and see what's going on!"

Others remained cautious, even afraid. "Well, this is it," missionary Raymond Abbitt thought. "The Japanese have come to finish us off."

Nurse Goldthorpe sat with fellow internee Margaret Garrett in a passageway. Garrett's son Glidden ran up to them. "Mama, Mama," the boy announced, "the Japanese guards are very mad. They are going to all the rooms telling people to stay away from the windows. They say they will shoot us if we look out."

"Yes, Glidden," she answered flatly. "Stay out of the room then."

"But Mama," the youth interrupted. "Do you know why they are so mad? It's because the Americans are coming! Really, they are! I saw them from the window coming up the road by the back gate."

The boy now had his mother's full attention.

Internees suddenly began running down the hallways. "The Americans!" someone shouted. "They're coming in the front gate!"

Roka and her fiancé elbowed a spot in front of a crowded window, offering a view of the plaza as the tanks punched through the gate. "As in a dream, we watched the armored monster, the lead tank, with powerful searchlights, coming up the familiar road toward the Big House. We saw soldiers, tall and bronzed, in peculiar-looking uniforms, walking between and on the side of the tanks. All of them walked cautiously with guns in readiness. Like hypnotized subjects, we watched the tanks and the men come closer," she wrote in her diary. "Some of us were still dubious that they were Americans. Not until we saw the American flag draped over the lead tank did we really believe that, at last, the realization of a beautiful dream had materialized. We saw the lovely Stars and Stripes, our throats constricted and our eyes were blinded with tears."

"Over here!" one internee shouted.

"This way!" called another.

Roka watched as the lead tank slowed to a stop in the plaza below, where she could read the name painted in white on the side: *Georgia Peach*. "It was then that we went berserk with joy and excitement!" Roka wrote. "We clapped, cried, shouted, screamed, and cheered. A few fainted, while still others were completely bewildered. They were unable to comprehend what their eyes were witnessing."

Margaret Gillooly, who had sensed that this would be the day of liberation, peered down from a third-floor window. "There was a sea of women's faces. We had three heads high in every window," she recalled. "We were kind of hanging over each other to look out to see what was going on in the plaza below us."

She watched a towering American soldier below pull off his helmet, exposing a shock of red hair. The soldier turned his freckled face up to the windows crowded with women. "Hell," he exclaimed with a Texas accent, "this must be the place!"

"The minute we heard this drawl," Gillooly remembered, "everybody started screaming and shrieking, because we knew they were Americans."

Euphoria seized the internees, who charged the soldiers. "Like the last day of school, we poured out of the buildings shrieking like

Internees constructed some six hundred shanties, like the ones pictured here, to provide relief from the overcrowding at the University of Santo Tomas.

Trapped behind the university's towering walls, several thousand internees used ingenuity to turn the roughly fifty-acre campus into a functioning small city, including converting an old bathtub into a sink.

An anguished Filipino father brings his wounded child to American medics after the youth was injured during shelling of the beaches in preparation for the Luzon invasion.

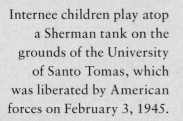

The story of starvation at Santo Tomas is written on the emaciated bodies of former internees (left to right) Arehugo Winkler, Thomas Loft, Arthur Williamson, Harold Leney, and David Norvell. The five men lost a combined total of 273 pounds.

Internee children play atop a Sherman tank on the grounds of the University of Santo Tomas, which was liberated by American forces on February 3, 1945.

After three years of suffering under the Japanese, Filipinos pour out into the streets to greet American troops on February 4, 1945.

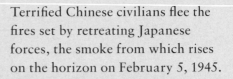

Terrified Chinese civilians flee the fires set by retreating Japanese forces, the smoke from which rises on the horizon on February 5, 1945.

Brig. Gen. Bonner Fellers shakes hands with civilian internees at the newly liberated Bilibid Prison on February 5, 1945.

Eighth Army Commander Lt. Gen. Robert Eichelberger, whose forces were ordered to close Manila's southern door, takes cover as a Japanese garrison opens fire on American troops at the village of Imus, en route to the Philippine capital on February 4, 1945.

Throngs of internees encircle Gen. Douglas MacArthur as he exits his staff car for a visit to Santo Tomas on the morning of February 7, 1945.

A half-starved Filipina girl clings to a box of army rations while the city burns in the background on February 7, 1945.

An American soldier watches Manila burn from the beach at Parañaque on February 8, 1945.

Troops with the First Cavalry Division advance past a dead Japanese soldier sprawled out in the street in the district of Paco on February 12, 1945.

Hungry Filipino children, after years of starvation, mob Technician Fifth Grade David Kind of Detroit for food on February 12, 1945.

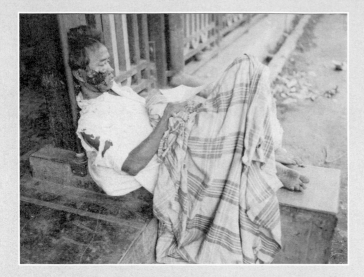

The hordes of wounded crowding San Lazaro Hospital have forced this refugee, with half of his right cheek ripped away by shrapnel from a Japanese hand grenade, to lean against a wall by the steps on February 13, 1945.

An American soldier carries a wounded girl to a boat landing in preparation to evacuate the ruins of the Walled City on February 23, 1945.

A resident of Manila, wounded during the fighting for the Philippine capital, is placed in a basket by neighbors for transportation to a first aid station.

An American machine gun crew covers the advance of an assault team en route to take a Japanese-held building during the bloody fight for the University of the Philippines.

American troops storm the south bank of the Pasig River during the assault on the Walled City on February 23, 1945.

Filipino refugees, many barefoot, pick through the wreckage of northern Manila, having just crossed the Pasig River following the fight for the Walled City. The nun carries a motherless infant born just three days earlier.

A platoon of American troops moves in to take the Walled City on
February 23, 1945.

delighted kids. We wanted to get near the tanks and those wonderful men! We wanted to shake their hands! We wanted to touch them!" Roka wrote. "Before the men in the tanks knew what was going on, they were pulled out of them and lifted on the shoulders of our scrawny fellow internees. It was impossible to hold back the worshipping and joyous internees, and it never occurred to any of us that our men still had to clean up on a hundred and forty Japanese garrisoned in the camp. We shook hands with our soldiers, we hugged and kissed them."

Bill Dunn soaked up the jubilation—the laughter mixed with tears and prayers—later describing it in his first broadcast from the camp. "This was liberation," he told CBS listeners. "The culmination of thirty-seven months of never dying hope!"

Some of the soldiers, knowing that Japanese forces were still camped inside, tried to press past the throngs of internees. "Come on, now, move!" troops demanded. "You're hampering us, damn it! Go on now, get back inside."

Others, however, broke down, horrified by the pitiful sight of emaciated men, women, and children. Wiping away tears, cavalrymen offered up their personal rations of tinned fruit and fished candy bars from their pockets. Starving internees refused to wait but dropped in place and began to tear away the packaging.

"It makes me sick to watch them," one soldier exclaimed, his cheeks moist with tears. "They're damn near starved to death."

Army nurse Denny Williams, captured on Corregidor in 1942, obeyed orders and turned to walk back inside the Main Building. As she passed a newly arrived soldier guarding the entrance, she reached out for him, wanting to touch his rough khaki uniform, to feel that he was real and confirm that her liberation was certain. "I only wanted to say thanks, soldier," she told him. "We waited—so long and—and God bless you, and thank you, thank you."

"Aw, that's okay," he assured her. "Now the GI's are here, you just take it easy."

"GI's?" she asked. "What outfit are they?"

The soldier laughed. "Government Issue," he said. "That's what they call ordinary soldiers now."

"I'm an Army nurse, and soldiers are never ordinary to me," she replied. "They're all heroes."

Robin Prising could not contain his excitement any longer. The youth slipped out of bed. Even from inside, he could see the bright lights of the flares and hear the crack of rifle shots. Shouts of internees echoed down the corridor, along with the cries of babies, now awake. He abandoned his sleeping father and made his way toward the entrance of the Main Building, lured by the boisterous mix of laughter, cheers, and sobs.

"They're here!" someone shouted. "They *are* here!"

Prising looked up at the towering troops. Women hugged them as the male internees pounded their backs. One of the soldiers reached down and grabbed Prising, hoisting him above the crowd. "Want to see what's going on, sonny?"

The soldier returned him to the ground, but Prising refused to let go, pulling him by the hand to find his mother, hoping to offer him up to her, "like some incredible human present." In a crowded corridor, Prising found his mother Marie, who stared at the soldier and froze.

She reached her hands up and seized his face. "It is all—over, then?" she asked.

Former editor of the *Manila Tribune* David Boguslav did the same, picking out the tallest soldier he could find to accompany him to the camp hospital as proof the moment of liberation had arrived. His wife Peggy, whose weight had plummeted to just seventy-five pounds, sat up in her bed.

"Look what I found," Boguslav announced.

"Where have you guys been all my life?" she exclaimed.

A grin stretched across the captain's face. "We've been a-comin'."

But Boguslav wasn't finished with the lanky soldier. "Piloted by Peggy in a wheelchair, and with my lantern as sole illumination, we went from bed to bed," he wrote. "Then they all believed. The Americans were here."

The internees had kept company with skeletons for so long that the young and healthy soldiers resembled giants.

"My land," one internee exclaimed. "How come you fellows are so big?"

Adding to the confusion, American uniforms had changed since the outbreak of the war; so, too, had the style of helmets. The faces of the troops glowed bright yellow, a side effect of the antimalarial drug Atabrine. More than anything, however, the internees marveled at the rounded cheeks, thick muscles, and white teeth, all long since absent from Santo Tomas. "My God," thought Gwendolyn Henshaw, an army nurse captured after the fall of Corregidor, "these people are sure fat."

Fellow nurse Bertha Henderson drew comfort simply from the presence of her fellow countrymen. "It was just the most wonderful feeling. It was just indescribable," she said. "The feeling of joy and relief to see an American after all that time."

Despite the internee celebrations, the soldiers still had a job to do— clear out the enemy forces. "Where are the Japs?" one of the officers demanded.

"In the Education Building!" a chorus shouted back.

○   ○   ○   ○

LT. CDR. TOSHIO HAYASHI, the commandant of Santo Tomas, holed up inside his office on the ground floor of the Education Building. The Japanese occupied the first and most of the second floor, while internees crowded inside the third, many of them young boys. Japanese sentries guarded the stairwells, preventing them from escaping. Internees instead hung out the windows, shouting to the troops below. "Let us out! The Japs won't let us out! They're holding us in here! Let us out!"

When he heard the approach of tanks, Hayashi had summoned Internee Committee leaders Earl Carroll and Sam Lloyd, along with interpreters Frank Cary and Ernest Stanley. Gathered by lamplight in his office, listening as the internees celebrated outside, Hayashi ordered Carroll and Stanley to retrieve the senior American officer so he could negotiate the possible surrender of the camp. The men set off for the Main Building, accompanied by civilians Shizuo Ohashi and his assistant Toshio Hirose as well as a Japanese lieutenant. The group wove through the throngs of joyous internees.

"Kill them!" some shouted. "Kill them!"

The group reached the Americans, where soldiers immediately stripped the lieutenant of his sword, pistol, map case, canteen, and flag. Troops likewise confiscated swords from Ohashi and Hiroshi, who protested that they were civilians.

"Why do you wear swords then?" the Americans countered.

The most hated of the Japanese guards, Lt. Nanakazu Abiko, appeared moments later. Abiko had prided himself on humiliating the internees. He had slapped them, forced them to stare for hours at the sun, and to bow even when starvation had left them so weak that many could no longer climb stairs or stand through daily roll call without fainting. Now this despicable guard stood before armed American soldiers. The troops ordered him to raise his hands, but instead he reached into a pouch strung over his shoulder. Maj. James Gerhart grabbed a rifle from a soldier and fired from his hip. A bullet tore into Abiko's chest, dropping the Japanese officer to the ground. He writhed in pain. Many internees, who only hours earlier had suffered under his command, swarmed the wounded enemy. "When I got over to where Abiko was, there was already a small crowd around him," recalled Peter Wygle. "He had been shot in the chest, but was still barely alive and breathing with a blood-froth in his mouth. The crowd began kicking him, and I'm ashamed to say, now, that I joined in."

"Here, take that, you bastard!" an internee shouted.

"Kick him for me!" cried another.

"I ain't ever gonna bow to you again, Shitface!"

Robin Prising peered through the crowd, noting that someone had nearly sliced off one of Abiko's ears. As the youth watched, a woman reached down and stubbed out a burning cigarette on his face. Another internee cut the buttons off his uniform for souvenirs. "Abiko howls and struggles, his body wracked by sudden jolts," Prising later wrote. "Drenched in thick blood, Abiko thrashes there, half dead. Animal noises and jerks are all that is left of him. The timid or the squeamish simply spit on him while he wriggles in their spit and his own blood, stinking of urine."

The melee stunned the young boy, who couldn't help but feel for the guard under attack, a sentiment that overwhelmed him with guilt. "This morning or this afternoon it might have been one of us who lay shot and squirming," he wrote. "But tonight it is Abiko. And as the Japanese officer sprawls on the cement floor, blood frothing from his mouth, his legs encased in military boots, the gargling rasps that come from his throat are softer than the curses of those who were once his prisoners. For my own part I am revolted by the sight of him thrashing there and by the rabble spewing abuse at this dying animal. At the same time I feel partly aloof from the zone of his dying, although I keep watching because death, like birth, is something boys of my age rarely see."

Dr. Ted Stevenson, who had been placed in the camp jail days earlier for refusing to alter internee death certificates, was now free. The doctor rushed over to the Main Building's clinic, much to the excitement of the nurses. "Enough, ladies, enough," he protested. "The camp jail isn't all that bad, and anyway, I was only there three days. Let's see what we can do for our new patients."

An internee burst into the room. "Hey, you people hear about Lieutenant Abiko? He's been shot. Maybe he's dead already, I hope!" He gleefully related the story of Abiko's refusal to surrender, his shooting, and the attack by internees.

Many of those in the clinic sounded off on Abiko.

"I can't say I'm sorry," someone said.

"Got what he deserved," added another.

"I hope he suffers."

Stevenson listened to the stream of vitriol from his colleagues. "War makes animals out of any of us," the doctor finally muttered.

Internee nurse Denny Williams listened to the debate. "I couldn't blame the people in the plaza. To us, this one man symbolized everything ugly and treacherous and vicious about the whole war," she later wrote. "Recalling the faces of the old men in the Gym, the man who had lost 45 pounds in 30 days, or the children searching the garbage can for anything at all to eat, I could find no pity for him."

"Seems wicked to waste band aids on these bastards," someone said.

In preparation to receive the wounded Japanese lieutenant, Stevenson asked Williams to wipe down a surgical table's dirty rubber sheet. "Put him up here, fellows," he instructed. "We don't want him bleeding on our floor."

Orderlies hoisted Abiko onto the table, and the doctor leaned over and pulled open his eyelid.

"Hey, look out!" a soldier yelled.

Everyone looked up just as a grenade tumbled out.

"What'd we tell you?" a soldier said, snatching up the grenade. "It rolled from the dirty bugger's clothing."

The doctor returned to his job, cutting off Abiko's uniform to reveal a broken arm among many other injuries. "One of the Lieutenant's ears was nearly severed and one cheek was gashed to the bone," Williams recalled. "Dr. Stevenson did the best he could, and when the bleeding was stopped and the wounds dusted with sulfa and covered, he ordered Lieutenant Abiko put to bed in the next room."

The internee who normally slept there objected, yanking up the sheet so that the wounded lieutenant rolled off. "I don't want this pig in my bed!"

"Her husband's a hostage in the Education Building," someone explained.

The orderlies instead placed Abiko on the floor. He lay there bleeding and suffering for four hours before he finally died. Orderlies hauled his body to Camp Jail No. 2 beneath the building's rear stairs, where it would rest until he could be buried the next day. Even among those who had tried to help save Abiko there was no affection or mourning the dead Japanese officer. "I for one," nurse Williams said, "hoped that his honorable ancestors would disown him when he showed up to join them."

Throughout the night men, women, and even children queued up for a final view of Abiko's bloodied corpse, including nurse Sally Blaine. "I went and looked at him but it made me sick at my stomach. I couldn't gloat. I didn't feel like gloating," she recalled. "No, that was to me nothing to gloat about; he was dead."

Robin Prising's mother voiced a similar sentiment when she learned of his demise. "Dead?" she asked. "Then that's best for him."

Others felt differently. "To us, he was more than one dead Japanese officer. He personified the entire Japanese Empire, defeated and cowed," Roka wrote. "With him lying dead, we had become human beings once more!" She scanned the faces of others in line. "What did I see in the stony expressions of my fellow internees as they slowly passed his body? Bitterness? Triumph? Satisfaction?" she wrote. "Following the example of some of their elders, I saw four- and five-year-old American kids spitting on the dead man. This, too, the war had done to young children."

CHAPTER 7

"Food and freedom are like heaven on earth."

—Vernon Newland,
Santo Tomas survivor, February 5, 1945

Japanese troops hustled to fortify the Education Building, blocking windows with mattresses and pillows and piling everything from beds and tables to chairs and broken bottles into the stairwells. Soldiers stood ready with rifles and bayonets. Internees who moments earlier had celebrated the arrival of the cavalrymen suddenly understood that the hasty blockades were designed to do more than just stall American soldiers. "We forced ourselves to realize the truth," said Robert Robb, the thirty-eight-year-old former editor of the *Philippines Free Press* huddled inside Room 216. "We were the hostages of the jittery Japs who had barricaded themselves in the north wing."

Robb surveyed his quarters. "Forty-three people packed into a room that at best accommodated 21," he recalled, "three terrified women, one whimpering little boy, and 39 frightened men." He heard the clamor of Sherman tanks outside as the mechanized monsters motored toward the Education Building, a three-story stucco structure.

"There are three tanks down there," internee Ed Price whispered.

"Vacate the shacks around the Education Building at once!" the internees heard an officer below holler. "You're in danger. There'll be shooting."

The grumbling grew louder as the thirty-ton tanks maneuvered into position, each armed with a 75 mm main gun that could hurl a twenty-pound projectile up to eight miles.

"They're putting a tank on each wing of the building," Price continued to narrate. "The boss man's tank is right in front of the center door."

From the windows up above, the internees watched as cavalrymen moved in behind the tanks, crouching low and out of the line of enemy fire.

"Those are big fellows, those tanks," someone in the room whispered. "They got a mighty wicked-looking cannon sticking out of the front end."

Japanese soldiers prodded internees to stand in front of the windows as shields, a bayonet at their back, while a second soldier peered over a captive's shoulder or through the narrow gap between the arm and body. A few took shots at the Americans on the ground below. "The only reason that the hostages were not killed or injured was because the American soldiers refrained from shooting," recalled Percy Ripka. "We suffered extreme mental agony during the entire time we stood in the windows."

The Americans meanwhile continued to negotiate with Commander Hayashi, whose forces inside the Education Building numbered about sixty five; the hostages more than two hundred. Major Gerhart rejected the commandant's request that he and his men be allowed to leave Santo Tomas, demanding instead that the Japanese capitulate. "The Commandant was given ten minutes in which to surrender under promise of fair treatment with all the honor of war," interpreter Frank Cary wrote in a letter. "He stalled for time, busying himself burning a military map of Manila."

Negotiations proved futile, triggering more drastic actions. The commander of the tank facing the building's center door popped his head up through the turret. "We'll give you Japs just three minutes to come out with your hands in the air," he shouted. "If you don't come out walking, we'll blast you out."

Panic seized many of the internees. "Hey, you," one shouted from the second floor. "We're up here on the second and third floors. We're Americans!"

"The Japs got us cornered here!" another added.

"You guys hit the deck, lie flat on the floor, face down, and get behind any shelter you have. Use your beds and mattresses as shields. Keep away from the balcony. Get as far back from the windows as you can. Get back in the rear corridor."

"Take it easy," an internee from the neighboring Room 215 shouted. "We got women and children up here!"

Robb hugged the wooden floor, his shoulders pressed tight against internees on either side in the crowded room. "I closed my eyes and measured off the distance between us and the road where the tanks were preparing to fire into the building," he said. "Just twenty-five feet away, they were. Just a hop, skip and jump to freedom. Just twenty-five feet in space, but in time an eternity away from us."

"You Japs in there—this is your last chance!" the commander below barked.

Hayashi crawled into Room 216, binoculars draped around his neck and his head covered by a helmet adorned with green twigs. Robb saw the commander's hands shaking. "At that moment he was undoubtedly the most frightened man in the world. And the thought hit me like a blow—in his fear he would do anything. He'd be a madman when the Americans shelled the building," Robb wrote. "My hands grew clammy."

"Okay, men," the tank commander shouted as he dropped down in the turret, the metal door clanging shut behind him. "Let 'em have it!"

Hayashi scurried back out into the corridor, putting another wall between himself and the tank fire. The internees braced themselves. Robb watched a mother in his room pull her young son close against her body. Another internee squeezed his wife's hand, while a woman nearby lowered her head her atop her husband's shoulder. Up on the third floor, eight-year-old Rupert Wilkinson climbed under a bed with his friend Nick Balfour, the two of them huddled under blankets. All now awaited the assault.

Gunfire erupted below, blasting the building's first floor. In Room 216, Robb felt the wooden floor suddenly vibrate against his face. "The machine-gun fire was deafening: a giant pounding on a colossal typewriter. Tracers flashed outside and occasionally across the ceiling," Wilkinson wrote. "I was frightened enough—and not frightened enough—to tell myself my life was charmed; I would not die."

Others were not so confident. "Mommy," the boy in Room 216 cried out in a high-pitched voice Robb could hear over the shooting below. "Are the Americans going to kill us too?"

The gunfire continued.

"I'm afraid, Mommy," the child whimpered. "Hold me tighter."

The youth's desperate cries moved Robb, who tried to reassure him, an impossible feat over the thunder of the guns. "Don't be scared."

Machine gun rounds tore through the building's facade, blurring time for the panicked internees. "The shelling continued," Robb said. "When had it started? Ten minutes ago? An hour? Two hours? Time didn't register."

The attack injured several Japanese troops. Others charged into the rooms with the internees, seeking shelter. "A very little thing at that moment—a word, a noise, or of all these things, a laugh—would have precipitated a tragedy," recalled William Weidmann. "Luckily, the internees kept strict silence."

The shelling finally stopped.

The tank commander stuck his head out again, demanding the Japanese surrender, but no one emerged. American forces opened fire again, filling the air inside the Education Building with dust that choked the internees. Many of the Japanese retreated to the third floor, taking refuge in the corridor behind Wilkinson's room. "American machine-gun fire killed one guard and wounded another," he later wrote. "Stray slugs and splinters struck several of our companions. When one elderly internee's bedding caught fire, the man dropped dead, apparently of a heart attack."

The guns again fell silent. The internees anxiously awaited the next move: would the Japanese surrender, or would the bombardment resume?

"Take it easy up there!" one of the commanders on the ground below finally hollered to them. "We'll figure some way to get you out."

○ ○ ○ ○

THAT NIGHT MANY OF the internees carried on, oblivious to the standoff in the Education Building. Fueled by excitement and adrenaline, few dared retreat indoors and climb in bed, no doubt afraid to wake in the morning and discover that the long-awaited prayer of liberation had somehow been just a dream. "No sleep tonight," Robert Wygle wrote in his diary. "Too much fighting. Too many huge fires and explosions. Too much excitement. THIS, my friends, after 37 months, IS IT!"

Internees who had saved a few cans of food popped them open, offering them up to the soldiers, like a meager reward for liberating them. "Blackout regulations were forgotten, and hundreds of fires were started with chairs, tables and benches," Roka wrote. "As we shared our miserable food with the soldiers, we laughed, talked, and listened to their experiences. How desperately we tried to catch up on the years we had lost! How wonderful those boys looked to us! Their presence acted as a heady wine and we couldn't seem to get our fill. We wanted them by our side all the time."

The soldiers handed out cigarettes to the adults and candy bars and chewing gum to the children. "One of the unforgettable things was the slow smile of wonderment on the pale tense face of a little girl of four tasting chocolate for the first time, her entranced eyes filled with tears of gratitude," International News Service reporter Frank Robertson wrote at five that morning in his first dispatch filed from Santo Tomas. "The misery of the internees and the gratitude, too, are almost indescribable."

A small boy with bright shining eyes stared up at Robertson. "Will we have food now? Real food?" he asked. "Tomorrow morning, too?"

Another little girl, whom Robertson estimated weighed half of what a child her age should, grabbed his attention. "My name is Louise," she said, her voice little more than a soft whisper. "You came on my birthday."

Bitterness over the years of misery was evident, Robertson observed, even among the children, including nine-year-old Kenneth Roberts. "I am going to America," the youth told Robertson, "to learn to be a soldier and kill Japs."

Dunn watched one little girl pocket a candy bar she had been given rather than tear into it, like the other children. "Don't you know what it is?" someone asked.

"Yes," the girl replied. "It's candy."

"Aren't you going to eat it?"

"No," she said. "My daddy needs it worse than I do. He has beriberi."

After months of surviving off of pigeons, rats, and weeds, the internees feasted that night on military rations and hardtack crackers. "The old army chow that G.I.s loathed," Emily Van Sickle said, "tasted to us like ambrosia."

Nurse Rose Rieper, whose weight had plummeted to just seventy pounds, stopped some soldiers who were about to discard unfinished army K-rations.

"Oh, can I have it?" Rieper asked. "Don't throw it away."

"You're hungry if you eat that."

Many of the internees, whose stomachs were accustomed to little more than watery gruel, found it difficult to digest solid foods. That was the case for Robert Wygle. "Sat up all night because a full stomach is too much of a discomfort and a joy to waste in sleeping," he wrote in his diary. "A full stomach is such an amazing thing. It hurts and is really misery—but the grandest sensation I will ever experience."

The rich treats sickened others. "I remember the first food we had. It was a cherry pie with evaporated milk on it," recalled nurse Rita James. "We were all awfully sick after we ate it. But it tasted good. Better going down than coming up."

The troops and the reporters understood the emaciated internees' obsession with food, a point hammered home for Robertson that night when he visited a cell-like room that forty internees called home. The reporter let his eyes wander over walls plastered with pictures of T-bone steaks. "The fascination which the starved inhabitants showed for the army food last night was not surprising after we heard stories of children running their finger-nails along the grooves in the kitchen table to pick out minute particles, or stories of banana stem leaves and roots being eaten," he wrote. "One woman said she and her husband had eaten three whole banana plants."

The troops, many of whom had been away from home for months and even years, likewise enjoyed the camaraderie of fellow Americans. "It sure is good to see kids again," one soldier told Emily Van Sickle. "And American women. It makes me feel almost like I'm home."

The feeling was mutual, recalled internee Margaret Bayer. "We kept the poor exhausted soldiers talking and answering questions," she wrote in her diary. "One soldier would be surrounded by 20 or 30 internees all asking the same questions."

"Which way did you come in?"

"What about Bilibid?"

"What about Los Baños?"

In between chatting with internees, soldiers went to work, fortifying the camp. "What in the world are you doing?" Lowell Cates, Roka's fiancé, asked one.

"Digging a fox-hole," he replied.

"What's a fox-hole?"

"Watch me, and I'll show you!"

The soldier finished digging his hole and spread out his poncho so he could lie down on it. "Catch on?" he said with a grin.

Roka stared in wonderment. "This is a new world!" she wrote in her diary. "So much to learn and so much to forget."

Despite the celebration, General Chase faced an immediate humanitarian crisis. Though the army would rush him ten thousand additional K-rations the next day, in the short term he did not have enough food to feed the nearly 3,700 starving internees the next morning for breakfast. He dispatched his supply officer to see the Catholic bishop of Manila, who resided next door to Santo Tomas. That night the bishop miraculously produced enough vegetables, rice, and fish to feed the internees. To Chase's amazement, he even sent over a bottle of Old Parr scotch. "The internees are practically skin and bone," Chase wrote in his first message to Mudge. "It would break your heart to see them."

The doctors and nurses meanwhile toiled throughout the night. "We had civilians killed. We had civilians wounded," recalled nurse Helen Cassiani. "It was a very bad scene. It was almost like being in Bataan again."

Dr. Stevenson collapsed twice. Others likewise passed out and suffered dizzy spells, a by-product of the starvation that plagued them all.

"What's wrong? They're all fainting," one of the newly arrived doctors said. "How long is it since you've had anything to eat?"

"Breakfast," one of the nurses replied.

The doctor ordered each to have a can of condensed milk. "We worked that night. We worked all night," recalled nurse Minnie Breese. "The doctors did too."

Finally amid a lull around two a.m., Dr. Stevenson instructed some of the nurses to rest. "You may be needed in the morning," he said, "if hostilities reopen."

Nurse Eleanor Garen tried to sleep downstairs, but the chaos made it impossible. "The heck with it!" she decided, retreating upstairs to her room. No sooner had her head hit the pillow than a soldier entered the room and woke her up.

"You're not supposed to be up here," he told her.

"I'm so tired, I'm going to sleep!" she protested. "I don't care *what* happens."

The soldier left her in peace.

Nurse Sally Blaine likewise knocked off work in the middle of the night. She made her way down the center aisle, where just eighteen inches separated two beds. "I walked up to the first American guy who was a big burly redheaded sergeant," she recalled. "I reached down and touched him on the shoulder."

"You have no idea how good you look to me," she told him, feeling, like many others, a sense of disbelief that American soldiers had arrived.

"You don't look so bad yourself, kid," he replied.

Nurse Denny Williams went to her room and stretched out, overwhelmed by exhaustion. "I'm free," she thought as she drifted to sleep. "We're all free."

o o o o

BUT NOT EVERYONE WAS SO LUCKY.

For those south of the Pasig River, news of MacArthur's return arrived not by tank but by telephone. That was the case when Jack Garcia picked up the receiver to hear his uncle Carl Loewinsohn in the northern suburb of Blumentritt on the line.

"Call your Mother or Father, quickly!" his uncle demanded.

The ten-year-old handed the phone off to his mother, listening to his uncle's animated voice even as he stood a few feet away.

"What's happening?" his mother asked. "What's going on?"

Her eyes suddenly grew large. "The Americans are there?" she cried. Excitement filled the room. "Cali," she continued, using his nickname. "Cali, I can't hear you."

The phone went dead.

MacArthur's forces had liberated the American internees at Santo Tomas, but the rest of the sprawling city—filled with more than one million Filipino men, women, and children—remained under Japanese control, and no one knew what the trapped enemy might do. That fear tempered the excitement felt by many, particularly as the sounds of war thundered across the capital. "From every section of the city we hear the detonations of tremendous explosions and the skies around us are aglow with fire," Marcial Lichauco wrote in his diary at eleven p.m. "For the past two hours, therefore, my entire household has been busy packing up food, clothing, medicine and a few other important belongings just in case we are forced to leave our house on short notice."

The scenes of the coming fight mesmerized sixteen-year-old Lourdes Reyes, who had climbed to the third-floor tower of her home to watch the brilliant sunset that afternoon. The room that topped her family's stately residence—with its commanding views of the high-rises along Dewey Boulevard—was where she often retreated to read books, assemble jigsaw puzzles, and play chess. As a fifth-grader, she had spent months there, quarantined with diphtheria, while her mother fed her medicine and sponged her clean. In an effort to make her not miss Christmas that year, her father had set up a small tree, which the family had decorated and encircled with gifts. Her only escape from the room during her months-long illness came on those mornings when her father smuggled her out for dawn walks along Dewey Boulevard.

Lourdes watched from the room that had once been her hospital ward the bloodred sunset over the bay, an image she would never forget. "By evening," she recalled, "towards the north where the sounds came from, the sky glowed the same vermilion. Thick clouds of smoke blew up against the clear night—higher and higher."

The horror of war approached, a hurricane on the horizon.

"The fires seem so near," her grandmother said that night, shivering.

"It is only because it is night time," Lourdes assured her. "They must be far off."

But not for much longer.

○ ○ ○ ○

Dawn rose over Santo Tomas on February 4, accompanied, as Prising noted, "by the rich odor of bacon and ham." He found a group of black soldiers.

"Skin and bones," one of them said.

The troops sized up his shriveled body, feeling his toothpick arms and legs as though in disbelief that that an eleven-year-old boy could be so slight.

"You hungry?" one asked.

Prising said he was. "They fed me, frying tinned ham and eggs over their fire," he recalled. "But warm food is too much for the starving. I was going to be sick as hell and didn't want the soldiers to know. So I managed to get away and in a moment retched and gagged, vomiting worms, bile and a mouthful of food."

As the sun climbed in the sky, troops shaved and washed, while others nursed mugs of hot coffee. General Chase cracked open the bottle of Old Parr, pouring himself a scotch and water with no ice to wash down his breakfast of a hard-boiled duck egg. The transformation of Santo Tomas from internment camp to military base continued. The worn grass where internees had paced away the years was now a parking lot of jeeps, trucks, and tanks. "Steadily through the night," Prising recalled, "soldiers had pitched tents and dug trenches and fox-holes: now, surrounded by bazookas, howitzers and machine guns, they were building fires, heating their rations and oiling their gun mountings. Meantime, more tanks and truckloads of soldiers were coming through the Main Gate. The encampment smelt of sweat, fried food and machinery."

Nurse Denny Williams opened her eyes in search of confirmation that it was all real. "On Sunday when I woke and I looked out the windows," she remembered, "I knew I had not dreamed of freedom." Others did the same, including former NBC correspondent Bert Silen. "With the dawn," he said, "we could see for the first time in three years the color of American tanks and our brave American soldiers. I can't begin to tell you what that sight meant to us." David Boguslav watched two soldiers take a break, strip down to the waist, and pick up a baseball. "Complete with fielders' gloves and ball, they were play-ing catch," the former journalist wrote. "They had come back, and everything was all right again."

In the Education Building—surrounded still by tanks and riflemen—the standoff continued. More than a dozen internees had escaped during the night, using knotted sheets to climb down. Par-ents, wives, and friends loitered outside, anxious for a safe resolution, while prisoners shouted messages down to others from the windows. A steady stream of buckets, hoisted up and down on ropes, delivered food, water, and hot coffee. "Hey Prising," one of the youth's friends yelled down, "get me out of here."

Over at the clinic, nurse Sally Blaine chatted with Lt. Col. Haskett Conner, who had been injured at the front gate by grenade shrapnel. "You had sort of a rough time last night, didn't you?" she asked.

"I slept like a baby," the officer replied. "I don't remember a thing after I laid down here last night."

Others treated wounded soldiers, internees, and even a few of the Japanese guards, including one who had the fingers on one hand blown off.

"Say, you nurses have had a rough time," one of the newly arrived doctors told Denny Williams. "Why don't you slack off? We'll take it from now on."

"We're too keyed up, too happy," she said, shaking her head no. "Why, we wouldn't know what to do with ourselves."

Additional forces arrived Sunday, albeit some of them tardy after the Japanese blew up the bridge in Novaliches. "To a certain extent this delay was appreciated," noted the Thirty-Seventh Infantry Division's artillery report. "A brewery at the river crossing was full of good cold beer and all that was necessary was to turn on the spigot and carry it away. Many a tired soldier refreshed himself at this point and considered the hardship of the advance on Manila well paid." Maj. Gen. Robert Beightler, the division's commander, saw no reason to stop his troops, some of whom filled five-gallon cans with cold beer. "In a few hours all the bottled beer and two vats of mature beer were gone," he wrote in his report. "What a picnic." One of those soldiers was Pvt. First Class Daniel Catale of New York, who for months had tasted nothing but chlorinated water and army coffee. Catale raised his glass. "This," he declared as he blew the foam off the top, "is like a shot in the arm. Now I'll be able to walk into Manila like I was fresh."

Just as villagers en route had celebrated America's arrival, thousands of *manileños* crowded the roads leading into the capital, waving, cheering, and crying. "Manila," one tank soldier wrote in his diary, "looked more like a parade than a bloody war." The crowds at times proved so thick that Capt. Bob Brown lost sight of his men. "A few Filipinos were still removing their hats and bowing low," Beightler observed, "just as they had had to do when the Japanese soldiers passed by."

Excited internees swarmed each vehicle that rolled through the gates of Santo Tomas. "Every time an army truck tore into the camp we rushed to the doors and windows to see if they had brought us food," Roka wrote. "Our camp ration of rice was increased and we had lima beans for lunch, but, unfortunately, hundreds became ill."

Internees still marveled over the meals, including Howard Hick, a former superintendent with General Foods in New York, who sat down to a table with his wife, Maybell. "If ever I've prayed," he announced. "I'm going to pray now."

"When he took his hand from his eyes," Maybell recalled, "he was crying."

The healthy young soldiers proved popular. "I can't resist touching them," one woman told Carl Mydans. "I'd forgotten that men looked this way."

Roka noted the same in her diary. "Our camp was buzzing with handsome officers and soldiers," she wrote. "The girls in the camp were besieged by dates and they were starting to primp and pay more attention to their appearances."

Santo Tomas had become a beachhead, a toehold that American forces held in Manila. The Japanese had grossly miscalculated, allowing a small advance force to penetrate the city without much of a fight, capturing both Santo Tomas and Malacañan Palace, the home of the Philippine president. But the Americans had gambled as well. General Chase's troops were not only far outnumbered, but now faced the added burden of caring for almost 3,700 men, women, and children, many on the verge of starvation. If Noguchi's Northern Force retaliated, Chase faced two options, both of which were terrible. He could abandon the thousands of civilians and battle his way out, or he could hunker down and face a siege until reinforcements arrived. Both scenarios shared a tragic commonality—the promise of heavy casualties. "We were short of food and ammunition, and would have been hard pressed to hold the compound," Chase recalled. "Again—we were lucky."

The intelligence picture likewise remained murky, as evidenced by a report that morning: "Enemy strength is not known, identifications are uncertain, and contact is mainly with small arms sniping from buildings and street barricades."

Throughout the day, troops labored to repair the camp's battered front gate—flattened by tanks the night before—while foot patrols roamed several blocks in all directions. Soldiers established an observation point atop the Main Building, offering views over the city. Several large fires spotted in the business district grew to seventy-eight by late afternoon. "The Japs were starting a systematic destruction of the business and Port Area districts," noted the Fifth Cavalry's report. "All bridges over the Pasig River were reported blown with the exception of the Quezon Bridge."

Chase ordered a small task force to roll out immediately and secure the vital span, which was about a mile southwest of the university. That same day, unbeknownst to Chase, Admiral Iwabuchi had demanded his Northern Force blow both the Ayala and Quezon bridges, the first of which now sat on the muddy bottom of the Pasig.

It was now a race for the latter.

A convoy of American tanks and trucks aimed south down Quezon Boulevard, heading deeper into Japanese-held Manila and navigating around several enemy roadblocks. The objective loomed ahead, the last span connecting north and south Manila. One block from the bridge, the convoy ran into a large tank trap made of mines, abandoned truck bodies, and steel rails hammered into the roadbed. Maj. Frank Mayfield and one of the tank drivers dismounted to investigate. It was impossible, Mayfield realized, to bypass it. Furthermore, all other routes to the bridge appeared impassable. He radioed the bad news to Chase, who ordered the men to return. "Numerous wrecked cars lined both sides of the street," noted the cavalry's report, "leaving only a narrow passage through which the convoy had to pass."

Just as Major Mayfield ordered his convoy to turn back, Japanese machine guns and even antiaircraft cannons opened fire. Projectiles rained down from the first and second floors of adjacent buildings. The Americans had driven into a shooting gallery. Drivers struggled to maneuver in streets crowded with wrecked vehicles. "All the men dismounted and found what cover they could," stated the cavalry's report. "The trucks were turned around and the men mounted up with several wounded and killed."

No sooner had the task force pulled out than Noguchi's forces blew the arched steel span. "All bridges across the Pasig River were now out," lamented the cavalry's report, "and we would have to ferry across or build a bridge."

Inside Santo Tomas, Prising approached the troops who manned the camp's gates. "Yesterday's guards had been Japanese," he observed. "Today's were American." The youth convinced one of the cavalrymen to let him outside the front gate, on condition he stay close and return within ten minutes. Outside the walls, Prising met several Filipinos, who were waiting for news of interned friends, family, and former employers. Many urged Prising to return to the camp where he would be safer.

"All the streets are mined," one warned.

Prising felt eager to taste freedom after years of being locked behind a wall, but the world that awaited him proved foreign. He saw burning buildings, including an entire block of leveled homes. Water mains had burst, leaving mud thick in the streets. American soldiers charged inside a nearby house, followed by an explosion and smoke. He waited, but no one came out. "My spirits sagged like my knees. I was afraid. It was as if the sun had been suddenly covered, a blackout in daylight," he wrote. "What I expected was an experience of total freedom; I wanted to be one of the first prisoners to leave the camp, but now as I stood in the street I realized that I was still a prisoner of war. Rubble blocked my way; a stuttering machine gun punctuated my despair; I turned back."

Back inside Santo Tomas, the ugly reality of war was likewise evident. Laborers buried nine Americans—three internees and six soldiers—in a plot separate from the graves dug for the despised Abiko and two dead Japanese soldiers.

Carl Mydans meanwhile explored the campus, snapping photographs that would populate the pages of *Life*. He spotted an emaciated couple under a tree, observing how beriberi had swollen their ankles. Adjoining them sat two healthy young army lieutenants. "The man held an unopened carton of cigarettes in one hand and in the other a K-ration chocolate bar which he was eating," Mydans wrote. "The woman sat sewing the fatigue shirt of one of the officers who was bare and brown to the waist."

"Tell me honestly," the man said. "What's it like out there?"

"Oh, it's going to be all right," one of the officers replied. "Our outfit got across the Novaliches this morning and they're fighting on the outskirts of the city right now. Don't you worry. They'll be in here today, and it won't be long before we have this city."

Mydans noted that the internee didn't respond. His female companion lowered her sewing and looked up at him.

"I didn't really mean Manila," the internee continued.

"He means the outside," his companion added.

The officers realized what weighed upon them. "It's going to be fine out there," the other lieutenant assured the couple. "Don't concern yourself with that. All you've got to do is to get your strength back. That's what you need now, food and strength."

The internee fell silent again, a bewildered look settling over his face, reminding Mydans of a child. "It's hard," the internee finally said slowly. "It's awfully hard after all this while—to explain what I mean."

Mydans spotted Spike Heyward, who before the war had served as the managing director of the largest sugar company in the Philippines. Mydans had known him during his own brief time at Santo Tomas, where he had admired Heyward as a thoughtful leader. "He was distinctly familiar but I was not at all certain who he was. He was so wasted and feeble that when, at last, I was sure it was he, my stomach tightened," Mydans recalled. "His arms were thinned to the bone, his chest was a skeleton stretched with skin, and like so many others I saw around me, his legs and ankles had swollen with beriberi into clublike appendages. When he walked he was clearly in pain."

Despite his physical condition, Heyward chatted with soldiers.

"Spike," Mydans interrupted.

"Well, indeed!" he exclaimed when he turned and saw the photographer. "I see you came in with more this time than you did the last."

Heyward sat down atop some ammunition boxes, and the two men chatted as Mydans worked up to the question foremost on his mind. "How was it, Spike, when you saw that tank and those troops coming in through the gate last night?" he finally asked. "Did it look like we always said it would?"

"You know," Heyward said, "I didn't see any of it last night. After all those years of waiting, I never left my shanty."

Heyward fell silent.

"It seems odd this morning, now that I've felt the strength to move around and have a look," he continued. "But last night I just lay there and listened to it."

Mydans concentrated on his old friend.

"It wasn't till this morning I felt I could walk out here and have a look," Heyward continued. "And you know, Carl, it looks just as I thought it would when I pictured it last night—and all those other nights."

Journalists filed the first news reports from Santo Tomas, announcing the camp's liberation and telling the world of the cruel starvation the internees had suffered. News stories spared little of the horror, describing how on the eve of liberation internees were forced to eat the raw hide of a carabao that Japanese guards had slaughtered for themselves. "Almost everyone has beriberi, pellagra or malnutrition," wrote Frank Robertson. "At least 70 percent of the children are underweight—many kiddies of six or seven have gained no weight since internment three years ago." Bill Dunn of CBS speculated on the probable fate of the internees had American forces waited any longer to break into Manila. "If our arrival had delayed another thirty days," he reported in his first broadcast, "the results might have been completely tragic."

Around dusk General Chase rolled up outside the Education Building in a jeep. His goal was to peacefully end the standoff, which had dragged on for almost twenty-four hours. The positive news story of the rescue of almost 3,700 internees did not need a bloody postscript about the murder of a few hundred.

"We're going to let those Japs go," Chase announced. "Our mission is to save these prisoners, not get them killed. And it's a good trade, two hundred Americans for less than half that number of Japs. Good—if we can make it."

His officers listened.

"There's a Jap lieutenant colonel in there, named Hayashi," he continued. "We know enough about him not to trust him very much. But we've got to try it. We're going to offer him and his men safe conduct out of this prison into an area somewhere out there in the city near their own lines. That means we're not going to have to take them very far. Somebody's got to go in there and talk to him."

Chase shot a glance at Lt. Col. Charles "Todd" Brady, executive officer of the First Cavalry Brigade. The wiry Brady's most distinguished feature was his moustache, the ends of which he fastidiously twirled into fine points.

"Todd," the general said. "You're the one who's going to do it."

Officers ordered the men to hold fire as Brady approached and entered the building. Mydans kept his eye on his watch the entire time, feeling the minutes drag past. After a quarter of an hour, Brady emerged from the shell-scarred building.

"How did it go?" Chase asked.

"Pretty well, sir," he replied. "Hayashi wants safe conduct with honor—and he says to a Japanese that means full arms and ammunition. I agreed to side arms and rifles, but no grenades or machine guns. He finally accepted. I told him to come out at dawn with rifles on the shoulder and form up into a column of threes and we would see him into an area between the lines. And I think he'll do it."

"Good," Chase answered. "You take him out in the morning."

Mydans had listened to the entire exchange. "What was he like, this Hayashi?" the photographer piped up.

"He's big for a Jap; about my height. And a rough customer. He came up to me wearing two pistols on his hips and stood with his feet apart and his hands on his guns, raising them up out of the holsters and dropping them back in while I talked."

"What did you do?" Mydans pressed.

"My hand twitched so, watching that son-of-a-bitch that I had to twirl my mustache to keep it steady."

CHAPTER 8

"We never believed that they would kill us."

—Celedonia de Arquillo,
testimony, July 23, 1945

Just a few blocks southwest of Santo Tomas, prisoners at Bilibid woke up that Sunday morning still under the dreaded control of the Japanese. The 1,275 men, women, and children had passed a long night in the crumbling old Spanish prison, watching the fighting in the streets outside and praying for liberation. The excitement had begun earlier that afternoon when prisoners had spied American planes swoop low over Santo Tomas. That was followed a few hours later by a subtle tremble of the buildings. Mining engineer James Thompson had gazed up Quezon Boulevard, where he spotted what appeared to be an endless column of tanks, personnel carriers, and jeeps rolling into Manila. Others had joined him to watch. "We were transfixed and utterly dumbstruck at the sight of such a powerful armed force," he recalled.

"It's the boys I tell you," Thompson shouted. "It's the boys."

"American tanks!" others hooted. "They're here, they're here!"

Fern Harrington had refused to believe the news, convinced starvation had made her fellow captives hallucinate. To be safe, the missionary climbed the stairs to see for herself. To her surprise, two American tanks, separated from the others, clanked to a stop behind Bilibid's back wall.

A head popped out. "Hell, Harvey," she heard one of the soldiers shout. "We're on the wrong street!"

That confirmed it for Harrington. "Never had profanity sounded so beautiful," she later wrote. "Everyone went wild, momentarily forgetting that we were still prisoners of the Japanese. I stood impassive, too stunned to comprehend what was happening as others cheered, laughed, cried, jumped and embraced one another."

The battle beyond the gates had escalated as the hours ticked past. "Manila was in flames, and as the city crackled with gunfire, the prisoners in Bilibid crouched near the windows of their cell blocks to watch the battle," recalled Charles Brown, an army doctor who had survived the Bataan Death March. "The masonry and steel of the prison trembled with every salvo of heavy artillery shells that fell perilously close to the walls."

Forty-six-year-old American Natalie Crouter, interned with her husband Jerry and two teenage children, could not look away. "I was so excited all night that I almost burst," she wrote in her diary. "I was up most of the night, going from one end of the building to the other to watch new fires that leapt into the sky."

Her husband, bedridden with beriberi, scolded her. "You damn fool, go to bed," he demanded. "You'll be dead tomorrow if you don't stop running around."

"I don't care if I am," Crouter shot back. "This is the biggest night of my life and I'm not going to miss any of it."

Dawn had brought little relief from the excitement. But as the morning wore on, the earlier euphoria gave way to fear, summed up by a single question: Where were the Americans?

MacArthur's forces had charged right past the prison the night before, liberating nearby Santo Tomas. Internees at the university woke up free that morning, where the lucky ones, like Robin Prising, feasted on fried ham and eggs. But their fellow prisoners, several blocks away at Bilibid, still starved under the frightful yoke of the Japanese.

The enemy had fortified the prison, shoveling dugouts and stacking sandbags to make machine-gun nests. The element of surprise had vanished. Japanese troops stood alert, scanning all approaches to the octagon-shaped prison from the rooftop. Many wondered if Bilibid's liberation would end in a bloody battle. Internee Donald Mansell glimpsed what such violence might look like when a fellow captive told him about a dead Japanese soldier sprawled out in the intersection of Quezon Boulevard and Calle España, a sight the curious internee could not pass up. He climbed the stairs and looked in the direction of where he saw the tanks the night before. "The dead man had been stripped of his clothes and shoes and was beginning to bloat," Mansell wrote. "It was macabre."

Around ten-thirty a.m., the Japanese summoned Maj. Warren Wilson and his civilian counterpart, Rev. Carl Eschbach. As Bilibid's senior medical officer, Wilson oversaw the 810 military prisoners of war who occupied half of the seventeen-acre compound, many of whom the Japanese had deemed too sick or lame to evacuate to the home islands in late 1944 to work in mines, shipyards, and factories. Eschbach represented the 465 civilian internees, whom the Japanese had transferred to the prison from Baguio in December and now kept segregated from the captured troops. Guards forced the duo to wait twenty minutes before ushering them into the office of the camp commandant, Major Ebiko. The enemy officer rose to his feet and read aloud a proclamation in Japanese. An interpreter then read it in English before giving Wilson the handwritten cursive message bearing Ebiko's name:

1. *The Japanese Army is now going to release all the prisoners of war and internees here on its own accord.*
2. *We are assigned to another duty and will be here no more.*
3. *You are at liberty to act and live as free persons, but you must be aware of probable dangers if you go out.*
4. *We shall leave here foodstuffs, medicines and other necessities of which you may avail yourselves for the time being.*
5. *We have arranged to put up sign-board at the front gate, bearing the following contents:*

Lawfully released prisoners of war and internees are quartered here. Please do not molest them unless they make positive resistance.

Unlike Santo Tomas, where a standoff had ensued in the Education Building, the Japanese guards at Bilibid prepared this Sunday to simply walk away. There would be no massacre of prisoners and internees, no final firefight with American liberators.

A dumbfounded Wilson thanked the major, signed a receipt for the number of prisoners at Bilibid, saluted, and departed. He immediately shared the news with fellow prisoner Carlton Vanderboget, an army surgeon.

"I don't get it," Vanderboget said.

Neither did Wilson. He gathered with his staff officers and organized a plan to guard the prison until the Americans arrived. "A number of baseball bats had been stashed away," he recalled. "These were brought out and issued to the guards who were assigned to cover all gates, doors, and other points of ingress into the Bilibid compound."

Eschbach likewise summoned all the civilian internees into the main corridor, where the men, women, and children crowded around him. Others spilled out the front door and down into the courtyard. "Gangway," someone shouted.

The internees turned to see eight Japanese soldiers march down from the prison's roof, their hobnail boots clicking on the steps and then the floor. The departure of Bilibid's rooftop guards symbolized that the promised liberation was real. "A hush swept over the crowd as we stepped aside to make a pathway for them," Harrington recalled. "They walked resolutely forward, looking neither right nor left." Tensions still soared. "I just held my breath for fear a hand grenade or two might be dropped," Ethel Herold wrote in her diary. Crouter studied the faces of the enemy, the guards who like so many others had for years stood between her and her freedom. "They filed through the narrow lane we left, they and we silent, their faces looking sunk and trapped," she wrote. "The corporal's fat face was sullen and defeated." The troops gathered at the gate, while others loaded weapons and equipment onto trucks. Not to be forgotten were the camp ducks and pigs, which the guards took with them. "They all went out without a backward look and the gate stood open behind them," Crouter wrote. "We were alone."

Many prisoners accustomed to Japanese brutality stood stunned by the anticlimactic departure. "Not a shot was fired," Vanderboget recalled. "We thought there would be a battle to defend the place, but there wasn't. Everything was calm, except our own personal emotions." Harrington, in contrast, felt torn. "I could never describe the emotion I felt as I watched them leave—a feeling of tremendous relief but also pity for them," she wrote. "I feared they were walking out to certain death."

Back inside the main corridor, all eyes turned back to Eschbach, who clutched Major Ebiko's message, his exciting announcement superseded by events. "I have our official release from the Japanese," he announced.

Eschbach read aloud the proclamation Ebiko had shared with him and Wilson. Upon conclusion, internees erupted in cheers as Eschbach held up a homemade American flag, prompting the newly liberated to sing "God Bless America" and "The Star Spangled Banner." "Here we are," Mansell wrote in his diary, "free after one thousand one hundred and thirty-four days." Crouter ducked out to find her husband Jerry and the couple's daughter, June. The family's three-and-a-half-year ordeal was now over. "I put my arm around his shoulder," Crouter wrote in her diary, "and the three of us sat there with tears running down our cheeks for quite a long while, not saying anything."

The prisoners and internees were technically free, but in all reality the men, women, and children remained hostages of the battle that raged just beyond the camp's walls. To venture outside into a city filled with enemy troops was suicide. Prisoners and internees settled down to wait for American forces to rescue them.

Wilson organized a detail to ransack the Japanese storeroom, while others climbed to the third-floor roof to watch the battle. Around three p.m., internees spotted American troops in the streets below, darting for cover amid enemy fire. "We waved," Thompson recalled. "We dared not shout for fear of attracting sniper fire to them or to ourselves, but they did not see us." Crouter witnessed the fighting as well. "I began to feel horribly sick in my soul as I watched war hour after hour—snipers picking off men; men cornering snipers, creeping down alleys; hunting; cornering; killing," she wrote in her diary. "There was plenty to watch, hour after hour, our own men and the enemy."

○ ○ ○ ○

UNBEKNOWNST TO CROUTER, Sgt. Rayford Anderson and a squad of nine American soldiers crept just outside Bilibid. Twenty-six-year-old Anderson, whose bald and wrinkled head made him resemble famed war correspondent Ernie Pyle, was on a patrol, searching for an overdue platoon that had failed to return.

As the soldiers approached the prison's main entrance, Anderson noted that the cheering crowds of Filipinos who had greeted American forces had vanished, a sign he feared meant the enemy was close. The soldiers spotted two Japanese sentries near the prison's gate. All ten took aim and fired, dropping them in the street. A Japanese machine-gunner up ahead opened fire, the bullets tearing into several lampposts. The sergeant offered his men the chance to abort the mission, but the soldiers refused.

"We didn't want to be chicken," Anderson later said.

The sergeant ordered his men to pull back and work around toward the prison's rear, hugging the walls and keeping in the shadows. The soldiers checked the surrounding houses and alleyways for snipers and then climbed to the second floor of an adjacent home, offering a view over Bilibid's towering stone walls.

The sergeant was stunned. He had expected the prison to be empty, but inside he spotted scores of Caucasian men, women, and even children. He waved, and the prisoners waved back.

The other infantrymen in his squad worried that it could be a Japanese ruse designed to draw them out.

The sergeant weighed his options. "All right, boys," he announced. "We'll advance till we draw fire."

The infantrymen darted across the street, pausing alongside a building attached to the outside of Bilibid's stone wall. Anderson ordered three of his men to provide cover while he and the other six forced the door. Sgt. Billy Fox tried the handle, but it wouldn't budge. He raised his rifle and fired two shots from his M1 into the lock. He then rammed his rifle butt into the door, busting it open. He slipped inside, followed by the others. "The windows of the room we got into were all boarded up," Anderson recalled. "It was mighty scary, sneaking into a room and poking around in the dark."

The room contained a few dusty chairs and desks littered with old papers. The soldiers spied a lone rat and a pile of feces that the men surmised had been left at some point by a Japanese sentry. They pressed on into an adjacent room, only to find a similar scene complete with boarded-up windows. At the far end of the room, Anderson spotted a ray of light shining through a crack in a board. "I stuck my eye up against it," he said. "At first I saw just a yard. Then I saw a bunch of men in blue denim trousers standing around right beside the window. It seemed hard to believe, but there they were. I rammed my gun against one of the wooden planks covering the window and broke it."

"Hey!" Anderson whispered. "We're Yanks. Come over here."

To his surprise, the men froze.

One of the infantrymen sang a few bars of "God Bless America," hoping to assure them the soldiers were Americans, but still no one moved. Another infantryman then tossed in a pack of Philip Morris cigarettes.

The soldiers watched and waited.

One of the prisoners retrieved the package and inspected it.

"By Jesus," he exclaimed. "It's the Yanks!"

Other prisoners approached and inspected the cigarettes before one of the captives finally summoned his courage and trotted over to the wall. Anderson shoved his hand through the broken board. The prisoner grabbed and shook it.

"I'm Sergeant Anderson," he told him. "I'm here with some American soldiers. We're all around you. You got nothing to worry about."

Word spread, and excited captives appeared, thrusting hands through the opening in the boarded window. Major Wilson soon arrived and dispersed many, but not before several prisoners hoisted up a stretcher that held an elderly man.

Anderson waved.

"I just wanted to see a Yank," the relieved prisoner said.

Major Wilson gave Anderson the tally of prisoners and internees, whereupon the sergeant and his men huffed it back to the battalion with the news.

Before long other troops reached the prison. Army doctor Theodore Winship was cooking corn and rice when he looked up and saw an infantryman at the gate. "Who are you?" he asked.

"I am an American soldier of the Thirty-Seventh Division," the young man replied. "We've come to free you."

"Where the hell have you been," the doctor barked. "We've been waiting three years for you."

Throughout Bilibid, prisoners and internees celebrated the arrival of the army, an excitement best captured by Robert Kentner in his diary. "The camp was more than elated—words cannot express the emotions of all prisoners," wrote the navy pharmacist's mate. "This day will be the most unforgettable day of all our lives."

Internee Natalie Crouter had just dozed off when she heard the cries of excitement followed by the arrival of a boy hollering the news: "Mummie, come, come!" he shouted. "They are here!"

After a long night and day of uncertainty, Crouter chose to stay on her bed. "I was too worn down to go out and join the crowd, so I just rested there letting the tears run down and listening to the American boys' voices—Southern, Western, Eastern accents—with bursts of laughter from our internees—laughter free and joyous with a note in it not heard in three years," she wrote. "I drifted into peaceful oblivion."

○ ○ ○ ○

ADMIRAL IWABUCHI KNEW the time to fight had arrived.

The same day American cavalrymen liberated Santo Tomas, he ordered the final destruction of Manila. Japanese forces had already begun to demolish the port, arsenals, and motor pools that might help the reoccupying American forces, but those earlier efforts now evolved into a deliberate strategy to torch the city's commercial and financial districts north of the Pasig, a move designed to slow the cavalry's advance while Noguchi's Northern Force retreated across the river to form a second line of defense. "The demolition of such installations within the city limits will be carried out secretly for the time being," Iwabuchi ordered, "so that such actions will not disturb the tranquility of the civil population nor be used by the enemy for counter-propaganda."

A special order would follow, the admiral noted, for the destruction of the city's water system and electric utilities. "As large a quantity as possible of aviation gasoline and bombs," Iwabuchi instructed, "will be transported from the storage areas in the suburbs to suitable places within the city and to the vicinity of various key points, and will be made use of as weapons of attack." He also ordered troops to blow up all the bridges in the suburbs. "The demolition must be done completely and thoroughly," he mandated. "In order to prevent the guerrillas from action to construct bridges, and to prevent speedy transmission of intelligence and passage across, several guard personnel will be posted at the completely demolished principal bridges." Iwabuchi likewise warned his forces to be vigilant about maintaining radio security. "The enemy may use our passwords, but the fact that he is not a Japanese can be detected by his pronunciation," he cautioned. "If you suspect him, talk to him in fluent Japanese."

North of the Pasig River, incendiary squads fanned out through Santa Cruz, Binondo, and the city's downtown retail and business districts. At nine a.m. on February 4, Dominador Santos, a Manila police captain en route back to the station, saw six Japanese troops slip inside the three-story Singer Building at the northwestern corner of Soler and Reina Regente streets, both carrying what looked like dynamite. Santos ducked into a nearby building to observe. Ten minutes passed before he witnessed the troops leave. "A few minutes later I heard a terrific explosion in the Singer Building and a fire broke out," he recalled. "I felt the shock and concussion of the explosion where I was hiding." Later that same day Angel Dionzon saw four troops with a five-gallon drum of gasoline in front of the Banco Hipotecario. The soldiers soaked gunnysacks in the fuel and hurled them inside the China Bank Building on Dasmarinas Street before lobbing a lone grenade. "The whole ground floor," Dionzon later said, "was burned out."

The chaos had only begun.

The following morning around nine-thirty, a large truck with eight Japanese troops rolled to a stop on San Vicente Street behind the Yucan Seh Drug Building. Yu Cheng Pho, the thirty-four-year-old employee of the Yutivo Hardware Company, looked out a mezzanine window into the truck bed and spotted what appeared to be a dozen airplane bombs, each about four feet long with blue noses and fins on the tails. One of the soldiers lugged a half-dozen inside the rear entrance of the Crystal Arcade, the four-story art deco building that fronted Escolta. One of Manila's finest commercial centers, the Crystal Arcade, so named for its intricate glasswork, housed the Manila stock exchange, cafés, and other luxury stores. The truck then motored down to the Yutivo Hardware Building on Dasmarinas Street, where Japanese sentries unloaded more bombs. Then it continued on to the corner of Rosario Street. Troops again hauled the weapons inside nearby buildings, targeting the modern concrete structures. That evening at seven p.m. the inferno began. Pho watched as the bombs gutted the once-grand Crystal Arcade. "There were explosions all over this area by this time and fires reached all around me," he recalled. "I ran to a Japanese air-raid shelter located behind the Capitol Theater Building on San Vicente Street. That is how I saved my life and the lives of my family."

The destruction intensified, prompting residents and merchants to flee. Japanese troops at times used rifle butts to smash glass doors, unloading more airplane bombs, including some hauled in the back of a horse-drawn cart. Others resorted to sloshing gasoline and using long bamboo poles to ignite it or tossing Molotov cocktails into lobbies. Building after building soon exploded. The Romanch Music Store went up in flames. So did the Philippine National Bank, the Roces Building, and Bank of the Philippine Islands. Black clouds billowed skyward as the flames marched down the Escolta, reducing Manila's Fifth Avenue to scorched rubble. Sixty-five-year-old real estate manager Vicente Arias was close enough to see Molotov cocktails explode. He held out as long as possible before fleeing with his family toward the American lines. "By this time," he recalled, "all of the surrounding buildings were ablaze."

○ ○ ○ ○

AT THE SAME TIME that Japanese troops began to torch Manila, soldiers under Colonel Noguchi swept through the working class district
of Tondo, rounding up suspected guerrillas on the north side of the
river who might help the Americans, a net that would snare scores of
women and children. One of those the Japanese grabbed was twenty-
five-year-old Ricardo San Juan, a married father of three who worked
in the city slaughterhouse killing pigs. Eight Japanese soldiers broke
into his house at eleven on the night of February 2 and tied him up
along with his wife Virginia. The Japanese marched San Juan and
his family, including his father-in-law and three children ages one,
three, and five, to the Isabelo Delos Reyes Elementary School on Sande
Street, which the soldiers used as a garrison. There the Japanese held
the family, along with dozens of others, overnight in the back near the
school's kitchen.

At six p.m. on February 3, troops prodded the captives to a nearby
house owned by Dr. Santiago Barcelona. The Japanese segregated
the men, forcing them into one room and the women and children
into another. Two hours later—as American forces closed in on Santo
Tomas—nearly two dozen Japanese troops pulled out a group of male
captives and led them across Juan Luna Street to the Dy Pac Lumberyard, which the Japanese had seized during the occupation to manu-
facture wood. "When we reached the place we were lined up in one
straight line beside a canal," San Juan recalled. "Our hands were tied
behind our backs and I was the last man in the line."

Via the beams from Japanese flashlights, San Juan counted twenty
other men in front of him. A few of the men, like San Juan, had fought
as guerrillas, but many others had not. At the head of the line stood
thirty-two-year-old Fructuoso Viri, who also worked at the city
slaughterhouse. Like San Juan, two Japanese soldiers had rustled Viri
out of bed in the middle of the night, binding his hands behind his
back and then dragging him off, leaving behind his pregnant wife and
children.

The Japanese untied Viri's hands this evening and prodded him about twenty-five feet away from the group. Guards then forced him to kneel. One of the soldiers, whom San Juan estimated to be about five feet six inches tall, clutched a sabre. Illuminated by the flashlight, the soldier raised the blade above his head and brought it down on Viri's neck. "His head," San Juan recalled, "was completely cut off."

The Japanese moved on to the second man in line. Then the third, fourth, and fifth, each one suffering a similar fate.

Twenty-three-year-old Ricardo Trinidad, who earned a living working as kitchen help, stood sixth in line. The Japanese had grabbed him, like the others, in the predawn hours of February 3, rousing him from bed by pressing a Luger against his head. Guards this evening untied Trinidad's hands and led him out in the field. A moment later a soldier bayoneted him in the right side of his back. To Trinidad's horror, the blade passed through his torso and popped out the front of his chest between his ninth and tenth ribs. "I fell forward on my face and while I was on the ground, I was again bayonetted on my right arm between my shoulder and elbow," he would later tell American war crimes investigators. "I did not say anything or cry. I pretended to be dead. The two Japanese soldiers left me and returned to the main group."

The slaughter continued.

In some cases the victim's head rolled off, but other times it did not. That was the case for Venancio Pimentel, the fourteenth man in line. The Japanese struck Pimentel once on the neck. He moaned. The soldier hit him a second time, but again Pimentel did not die. Finally one of the soldiers crushed his skull with the butt of his rifle.

San Juan's father-in-law, sixty-three-year-old Twan Yap, suffered a similar fate. "Oh!" Yap cried after the first blow. "How painful."

San Juan could only listen to his father-in-law, powerless to intervene. "When the Japanese heard him groan he was struck for the second time," San Juan recalled. "When he groaned again the Japanese hit him the third time till he died."

The soldiers continued down the line, eventually reaching the twentieth man, Dominador Antonio, who had lost his right hand the previous September in an American air raid. Like the others, the thirty-five-year-old Antonio did not fight or struggle. In the flickering beams of a flashlight, San Juan watched as the Japanese forced him to kneel and chopped his neck. "His head," he said, "was not separated from his body."

Then it was San Juan's turn. "When the executioner came to me," he later testified, "I was struck on the back of my neck by a saber. I fell forward and pretended to be dead."

As with several before him, the soldiers had failed to sever San Juan's head, striking him in the thick muscle just below his neck. The doctor who treated him seven days later would tell investigators that the saber ripped a gash thirteen inches long, three inches wide, and one and a half inches deep in the base of his neck.

Convinced he was dead, the Japanese abandoned San Juan. Moments later he pulled himself about two meters away into the towering weeds.

But the night's terror had only begun.

The Japanese returned to the same spot with a second group of captives. On his belly in the brush, San Juan counted nineteen women and twenty-seven children. Among them, he saw his twenty-five-year-old wife Virginia and the couple's three children. Four months pregnant at the time, Virginia held the couple's youngest child in her arms, one-year-old Jose. The Japanese had tied the adults together with a long strand of rope looped around the upper left arm of each woman. Guards herded the women into a circle around the children. The Japanese then formed a perimeter around them.

To San Juan's horror, the soldiers began to bayonet the children and even the infants, including two-month-old Celia Fajardo, wrapped in a gray flannel sleep suit. "Some of the babies were grabbed from the arms of their mothers and were held by their two hands in mid air by one of the Japanese soldiers," he later told investigators. "At that instant the executioner would stab them in that position."

The orgy of violence escalated. Hidden in the dark thicket barely eight feet away, San Juan watched a soldier plunge his bayonet into the chest of his five-year-old son, Cresencio. He heard the boy cry out before he collapsed and died. The same soldier then snatched up his infant son Jose. "That baby of mine," San Juan recalled, "was thrown into the air and then caught with the point of a bayonet."

Soldiers likewise killed his three-year-old daughter Corazon—her name Spanish for Heart—but San Juan did not see it; that was the only mercy he experienced that night.

With the children littered on the ground dead, the Japanese pounced on the mothers with blood-soaked bayonets. The same soldier who had tried to cut off his head ran his blade through the belly of San Juan's pregnant wife.

"Oh, how painful!" she cried, her final words echoing those of her father.

Then she, too, died.

And before the night was over, so would dozens more.

CHAPTER 9

"The American flag floats once more over the campus of Santo Tomas University, where 3,700 internees have been liberated."

—William Dunn,
CBS News, February 5, 1945

Colonel Brady gathered with his troops outside the Education Building before daybreak on the morning of February 5, 1945. After more than thirty-six hours, the time had arrived to escort the remaining sixty-five Japanese out of Santo Tomas and officially conclude the standoff. The moustached Brady outlined the morning's plan, noting that the Japanese would only be allowed to depart with side arms and rifles. All machine guns and grenades would be left behind. The cavalrymen would march in two parallel columns, sandwiching the enemy between them.

Brady's troops, lined up before him in an area that only hours earlier had been a no-go zone, listened attentively.

Each cavalryman, the colonel continued, would cover one enemy soldier, a cartridge in the chamber at all times. When the column reached the front line, the Americans would halt and the Japanese would continue alone. "Under no condition is any man to be trigger happy," Brady demanded. "We hope to get away with it without anyone being hurt."

The colonel concluded with a pragmatic warning.

"But if they fire—give them hell."

One of those waiting to capture the spectacle was *Life* magazine's Carl Mydans. "It was still dark," the journalist wrote. "Most of the camp was asleep, and the sounds of fighting in the city had lapsed into a few intermittent explosions."

Promptly at six-thirty a.m., Commander Hayashi and his men emerged from the Education Building in the cool predawn darkness, rifles slung over their shoulders as instructed. "As they appeared our men tensed up and fingers played with triggers," Mydans observed. "These Americans had seen many Japs before but they had always shot at them or were shot at. There was nervousness all around."

American soldiers armed with rifles and automatic weapons fell in along either side of the Japanese. Brady stepped to the front of the procession, trailed by Hayashi and civilian internee Ernest Stanley, who served as an interpreter.

"Let's go," Brady shouted over his shoulder. Stanley translated for Hayashi, who barked the order to his troops.

The column of American and Japanese troops marched toward the university's front gate. "Two limped because of wounds," wrote reporter Frank Hewlett in his news dispatch filed that day. "One rode a litter, in a two-wheeled cart." Like moths to a flame, internees crowded around to watch, while others hung out of building windows. "All arrangements had been made under cover of secrecy," noted the Fifth Cavalry's report, "but the entire populace of Santo Tomas hurriedly assembled to witness the reluctant release of the Japs and to happily congratulate the newly freed internees."

Denny Williams spotted the departing troops from her upper-floor window, then hollered to the other nurses sleeping in her room. "Hey, Shack, Josie, Frances," she shouted. "You'll miss something big if you don't wake up right now."

Williams watched the Japanese depart, final proof that her torturous ordeal was over. "Our former captors, in baggy pants with helmeted heads hanging and rifles on their shoulders, looked sloppy and ill-kempt beside the trim GI's," she wrote. "The long agony of doubt and uncertainty and pain and deprivation and near-death marched out of Santo Tomas Internment Camp with them. I felt like cheering."

One of the nurses did squeal.

"Be quiet!" warned another.

On the ground below, as the Japanese marched past, internee children shouted at them. "Make them bow," the youths demanded. "Make them bow."

American soldiers tried to distract them, no doubt afraid that any disruption might trigger violence. "Who would like a nice ice cream cone?" one soldier asked.

"What's that?" the children replied.

Such efforts proved futile, as Robin Prising, who was up early that morning scavenging for breakfast, observed. Just like spitting on the dead body of Abiko, insulting the outgunned Japanese was too much a temptation. "Small bands of men and women followed them through the encampment jeering and hooting—the women loudest of all—until the Japanese plodded out of the camp and the gates clanged shut."

The Eighth Cavalry's report noted how bizarre the morning's procession must have appeared. "This, the first parley or truce in the Asiatic war, was indeed a strange sight," the report stated. "The spectacle of live Japanese walking unscathed through lines of Cavalrymen is not one ever to be forgotten by the participants."

The scene triggered bitterness in some. "They got off too easy," more than a few muttered.

As soon as the Japanese departed, internees focused on what mattered most, a sentiment echoed in shouts from second- and third-floor windows: "How about chow!"

Once outside the university gates, Brady led the column east. Mydans ran ahead of the procession, snapping pictures that would soon run in *Life* magazine. "The Japanese marched confidently, singing cadence, heads erect, seemingly without thought of fear," he wrote. "In the silent, empty streets the column moved swiftly through the brightening dawn. Here and there a few Filipinos peering out of their houses in the besieged town witnessed the incredible sight and either ducked to safety or stood transfixed and silent. Several I noticed started to make the V-for-Victory sign but then, seeing armed Japanese as part of the column, froze in their motion."

American soldier Delphino Peña marched alongside the Japanese column when one of the enemy troops elbowed him. "Well, I just elbowed back a good two times," Peña recalled. "He didn't do anything like that anymore."

After a few blocks, Brady ordered his men to halt, and then addressed Stanley, the interpreter. "Tell the colonel that this is as far as we take them."

Hayashi shook his head no. "He asks you to conduct him farther," Stanley translated. "He says we are still within American lines."

Brady agreed with a nod, and the column continued. The morning sky brightened, and more locals appeared in doorways to watch. Mydans could hear distant gunfire. The column soon reached the large intersection of Legarda and Aviles.

"This is as far we go," Brady told Hayashi. "This is the front line. You are on your own."

Mydans noted Hayashi appeared nervous. The former commandant huddled with two of his officers, sending them ahead a block to survey the area. The men trotted back and conferred with Hayashi, who again asked Brady to escort them farther.

"This is where we leave you," Brady said, shaking his head no.

Filipinos continued to emerge from nearby buildings to witness the bizarre spectacle. "V for Victory! Americans!" some hollered. "*Mabuhay!*"

Such shouts only seemed to encourage other curious locals to venture outside, many of whom began to cheer and wave at the Americans. "Brady raised his arms toward them for silence," Mydans recalled. "He was misunderstood. The shouts of welcome increased and more people came running toward the street corner."

Colonel Brady ordered his men to step back, a cue for Hayashi that this was the end. The former commandant of Santo Tomas raised his sword and barked an order. Hayashi then faced Brady and saluted the American officer. "Brady returned it as the Japanese fell in step and began to move forward," Mydans observed. "As they passed out of our column, each officer and each man either saluted or bowed to Brady."

Mydans watched the Japanese set off down Legarda Street, where a large group of Filipinos had gathered to watch. "Stand back and keep quiet," Brady ordered.

The cheering Filipinos fell silent as the armed Japanese troops marched straight toward them. A second later terror befell them. Locals raced to get out of the way, tripping over one another and shouting in fright. "Under orders to make a show of bravery, the Japanese could not look back," Mydans wrote. "They could see only the terrified Filipinos scrambling for cover in front of them; and they knew only that the Americans stood behind them with guns at the ready."

Brady, Mydans, and the other cavalrymen watched to see what the spooked Japanese would do. Many of the enemy troops, overcome by fear, suddenly darted for nearby doorways. Others dove into the gutters, leaving only a few officers in line. "Behind them, screaming like a madman, ran Hayashi, grabbing at them, shoving them, beating them over the shoulders and rumps in a futile effort to re-form them into a dignified unit of soldiers," Mydans recalled. "And all the while Colonel Brady stood before his men, one hand supporting his elbow while the other gently twirled his mustache, until the last of the running Japanese had disappeared down the street."

○ ○ ○ ○

SANTO TOMAS WAS NOW truly liberated—free at last of all Japanese forces. American troops swept the Education Building for bombs as wives, mothers, and friends raced to greet the former hostages. Manila businessman Sam Wilson, who had served two years as a colonel of the guerrillas in Mindanao, arrived amid the morning excitement, anxious to see his wife and two sons. He brought with him a large American flag. "Bill Chase was ecstatic at the prospect of a formal review of his troops and a ceremonial flag-raising, but Sam overruled him," CBS reporter Bill Dunn recalled. "This flag, he insisted, was for the *internees*. They must be allowed to raise it themselves."

Even with the loudspeaker out, word spread that the American flag would be raised over Santo Tomas, and internees migrated toward the front entrance of the Main Building. Others leaned out of second- and third-floor windows, craning their necks for a glimpse. News reporters and army photographers jockeyed for spots to watch, some even climbing atop tanks and trucks to capture the historic moment.

"Many prisoners put on the best clothes they had left," Prising wrote. "The men hid their arms in long-sleeved shirts and each woman wore her most respectable dress. Few wished to look like prisoners of war— that would have been an admission of defeat."

Dunn joined the crowd out front for the nine-thirty a.m. ceremony, describing it in his news report later that day. "It was simple but unforgettable," he reported. "A few of the men emerged from a second story window to the roof of the building entrance, unfurled the flag to the sight of thousands of milling internees in the courtyard before them, then slowly hauled it to its proud position once again. As it caught the breeze—still tinted with the smoke of a hundred fires—the hungry thousands, without signal, began to sing 'God Bless America' in voices choked with obvious emotion."

Many of the internees lifted their arms over their heads as the words wafted through the crowd. An American bomber, as though on cue, buzzed the camp. "We nearly all broke down," recalled nurse Denny Williams, "but if our voices failed, our faith in our country and its fighting men was stronger than ever."

New York Times correspondent Ford Wilkins, whose weight had plummeted to ninety-nine pounds during his years as an internee, reflected on the ceremony's importance in an article that day. "For three years these people had not been permitted to express their loyalty to their country or to demonstrate their feelings," he wrote. "They had not seen an American flag, the symbol of their hopes and certainty of eventual liberation. This was the first display of the American flag in Manila since the Japanese invasion lowered the one in front of the High Commissioner's Residence on January 2, 1942, trampled it underfoot and raised in its place the red circle on a white field."

Amid the celebration, Dunn glanced over at Col. Fred Hamilton, who stood beside him. The cavalryman wept; so, too, Dunn noted, did other soldiers around him. The simple ceremony moved all who witnessed it. "No fanfare, no shouting," Dunn reported that day. "Just a song that was more than a prayer."

With the cavalry and the infantry now in Manila, General Griswold split responsibility for the city's north. The Manila Railroad, which ran just a few blocks east of Santo Tomas, would serve as the dividing line. The Thirty-Seventh Infantry would cover the sector from the railroad west to the bay, while the First Cavalry would take the eastern sector. The Sixth Army commander, General Krueger, meanwhile ordered Griswold to protect the city's electrical supply and secure the Novaliches Dam, Balara Water Filters, San Juan Reservoir, and the associated pipelines that formed the heart of the city's pressurized water system. "Intelligence reports indicated that the enemy intended to destroy or possibly pollute the source of water for the Manila area," observed the Sixth Army's report. "Early seizure of these sources of water supply was therefore vital to the health and even to the existence of the city's population."

The Eighth Army forces commanded by General Eichelberger raced to close Manila's back door. On January 31, the Eleventh Airborne Division had sloshed ashore at Nasugbu, fifty-five miles south of the capital in a move heralded by MacArthur. "This operation places the Eighth Army on the south side of Manila, which is now the center of the converging columns of the Sixth and Eighth armies," he announced to the press. "It largely seals off the possibility of the enemy troops south of Manila joining those in the north." Three days later the 511th Parachute Infantry landed atop Tagaytay Ridge. The two forces then charged north up Highway 17, a paved two-lane road. Just that morning Eichelberger had crossed the partially destroyed bridge over the Parañaque River, alerting MacArthur afterward that he had entered southern Manila. The general's vise around the capital tightened.

Early Monday afternoon fourteen food trucks from Lingayen roared through the gates of Santo Tomas, each one greeted by throngs of internees. "Food, Food, Food," Margaret Bayer wrote in her diary that day. "Each of us got a package of cigarettes and a box of matches today." Internees still struggled with the rich new foods. "We had good army chow today!" Roka wrote. "Wonderful army slum-gum, canned fruit, and coffee with all the sugar and milk we wanted! No food had ever tasted this good! No food had ever made people more ill! A few hours later, hundreds of us were seized with cramps and diarrhea, and many of us were too ill and weak to reach the toilets."

The American Red Cross likewise delivered 4,400 letters, triggering long lines of eager internees, some of whom had heard no word from home in three years. "As they tore open the envelopes," Hartendorp wrote, "it was easy to see on their faces whether the news was good or bad or a mixture of them." Hartendorp was one of the recipients of sad news. "There were several for me and from one of them, dated November 21, 1944, I learned that my father had died on June 17, aged a few months short of 78," he wrote. "The last time I had seen my dear father was when he was waving me good-bye in the Denver railway station in April, 1917, twenty-eight years before."

Even though American forces had arrived, armed with lifesaving food and medicine, starvation continued to claim victims. Some of the internees were beyond saving. Two had died the day of liberation. Two more had passed Sunday, and three on Monday. "Paul Whitaker died," Margaret Bayer noted in her diary on February 5. "He said he was ready since he had seen the Americans come in."

Internees and liberators alike struggled to adjust. As Carl Mydans wandered the grounds of Santo Tomas, spotting familiar faces in the hallways and lining up for food alongside former captives, he found that he could not shed his own experiences as an internee. "It was when I used the showers," he later wrote, "that I most had the uncanny feeling that nothing at all had changed and that I was still a prisoner, for there we were, crowded under the same shower heads, placing our soap and towels in the same little personal niches chosen years ago, and bumping and crawling over each other with a kind of reptilian unawareness of the bodies next to us. The voices, even the points of view, seemed the same. And so did the rumors."

"You know those sixty-five Japs they took out of the Education Building?" someone asked. "I just heard that they walked them right into an America-led Filipino ambush and killed every God-damn one of them right there on the street."

Mydans just listened, even though he had been there that morning and seen the release executed without a single shot fired. "Nothing had changed," the photographer later wrote. "Even some of my own prison self remained, for I knew enough not to inject fact into prison fancy and went right on showering."

Several of MacArthur's top aides visited Santo Tomas on Monday, including General Fellers and colonels Sidney Huff and Courtney Whitney. The sixty-five-mile trip from MacArthur's headquarters at a sugar refinery in San Miguel should have taken about an hour, but on this day the journey through pockets of fighting took twelve. Like the cavalrymen who had arrived forty-eight hours earlier, MacArthur's aides were shocked by the tragic condition of the internees who greeted them. "I don't know just what I had expected to find at Santo Tomas, but the scene was far different from anything I could have imagined," Huff later wrote. "We stopped in horrified silence when we saw, coming toward us, emaciated men and women dressed in torn, limp clothes. Hoarse cries came from their mouths. Tears flowed down their cheeks. I thought I had never seen such an unhappy sight, until I realized it was not a demonstration of sorrow; it was an outburst of pure, unalloyed joy!"

Before Huff could object, one internee wrapped his arms around him. What stranger would be so brazen? he wondered. Then he realized the man was no stranger but British engineer Sam Howard, who before the war had worked on the Philippine torpedo boat program. Huff, who assisted MacArthur on naval affairs, had considered him a brother. "I had to look again to be sure that this living skeleton of about 100 pounds was the same man who, when last I saw him, weighed 190 pounds," he recalled. "His thin arms cut into my flesh as we embraced. Other faces began to emerge from the strange crowd; faces that had a shadowy familiarity. Hands grasped mine in tight embrace—and I had to ask an old friend who he was!"

The colonel spotted his friend Myrtle Castle from Washington State in the crowd. When last Huff saw her, the day before he left Manila in 1941 for Corregidor, she had given him four diamond rings: "Take care of these for me, Sid."

Huff had wrapped them in chamois and placed them in his watch pocket, keeping them until he reached Australia, where he placed them in a safe deposit box. He had brought them back to the Philippines now, hoping to find her.

"I've got something for you!" he announced.

"I pulled them out of my pocket and held them out to her," he recalled, "four big, shining diamonds and worth plenty."

"Thanks," she said.

Her attitude of indifference irritated, even angered Huff, who felt he had done her a great service in safeguarding her jewelry for three years. "Don't you want them?"

"Oh, yes," she replied. "I want them."

"Look," he pressed, "if you're not interested in the diamonds, what do you want?"

"Why," she said, her eyes growing large, "I'd give anything in the world for a piece of bread and butter."

For Huff and many of MacArthur's other senior aides, the pain of seeing such suffering was exacerbated by the fact that many were old friends. The officers struggled to match up these hollowed-out souls with their prewar memories of the suited bankers, business executives, and socialites who now swarmed around them. In a letter that afternoon to his wife, General Fellers singled out internee Margaret Seals, the spouse of Brig. Gen. Carl Seals, who had served on Corregidor. The Japanese had captured the couple on the island of Mindanao after the navy seaplane that had evacuated them from the Rock suffered a ruptured hull during a stopover. General Seals eventually landed in a Manchurian prison camp, while the Japanese marched his wife off to Santo Tomas with other civilians. "Mrs. Seals weighs about 70 pounds," Fellers wrote, "her arms are about as large around as a half dollar." Fellers closed his letter with a simple statement that summed up his disgust: "The Japanese are fiends."

In a letter to his wife twelve days earlier, Colonel Whitney had imagined the postliberation social scene, a return to the gaiety many had known in Manila before the war. He now realized how wrong he had been. "The condition of these people was so pitiful dear," he wrote in his first letter after visiting the camp. "Had we delayed their liberation one week longer many more would have died." He couldn't shake the experience when he put pen to paper again the following day. "My visit to Santo Tomas was really very depressing—to see so many who had for years lived in the lap of luxury reduced to a livelihood like rats was pathetic," he wrote. "To see once proud aristocrats in a bread line with old rusty tin cans and then gobbling up the chow as tho their lives depended on it—as they did—was a terrible sight. I couldn't eat the whole time I was there in the realization that so many need it so much more than I."

The trauma of Santo Tomas weighed upon everyone—officers, soldiers, and even journalists. CBS's Bill Dunn was exhausted, opting to leave camp and travel to MacArthur's headquarters. "Never have I undergone such emotional extremes in such a short time, and I wanted a break, quickly," he later wrote. "Seeing so many old friends in various stages of malnutrition from bad to critical, listening to their stories of those thirty-seven months of trying to keep their spirits alive and their faith in their distant nation unwavering, was something I wasn't designed by nature to handle."

Despite the shock, the officers had important work to do. An inventory General Fellers compiled that day for MacArthur showed there were 3,677 civilian internees, including 480 children under age ten. Americans and British accounted for most of the internees, with 2,708 and 696 respectively. The rest came from Australia, Canada, New Zealand, and France, among other nations. Of the internees, 295 remained bedridden. The Japanese had pilfered all the rice but left a fifteen-day supply of food, including seven tons of corn, most of it in poor quality. American forces likewise discovered 2.5 tons of cassava, which is similar to a camote, and 1.5 tons of soybeans. "The Japanese tried to break the spirit of our internees and prisoners of war. They failed," Fellers wrote. "Sheer determination to survive probably sustained and saved those who survived. The majority need rest and food. A surprisingly few will require hospitalization."

Food proved only one of the concerns.

Fires devoured the districts north of the Pasig River, darkening the skies with acrid smoke and burning the pavement under the heels of American troops. "Manila is now a blazing inferno," Bilibid prisoner Robert Kentner wrote in his diary. "The fires are spreading and also coming towards the camp." Fellow captive Alan McCracken described the conflagration as a "holocaust." "Several times," he wrote, "I was conscious of definite whiffs that smelled exactly like beefsteak frying in your kitchenette—only it wasn't beefsteak." Soldiers stood on alert. "Japanese troops, caught in the flames they and their fellows had set, started running, screaming in fear, toward the American lines around the prison," a United Press reporter wrote. "They were silhouetted by the flames and the doughboys of the Thirty-seventh mowed them down."

At 9:11 p.m. on February 5, as fires raged on three sides of the prison, American forces ordered the former captives to evacuate Bilibid for the Ang Tibay Shoe Factory a few miles away, where soldiers rounded up cots and blankets, dug toilets, swept floors, and readied meals. Around the same time, troops gathered all available demolitions in Manila in preparation for blowing a firebreak. The job of moving 1,275 people from the prison proved enormous, requiring all of the Thirty-Seventh Infantry's vehicles and many commandeered from the cavalry. Jeeps, trucks, and weapons carriers rolled up to the prison's gate that night. "Stretcher cases went first," a reporter wrote, "then the walking casualties, a pitiful procession of wounded, paralysis and beriberi sufferers, some lacking an arm or a leg, all emaciated by long starvation, many staggering."

Despite the danger of enemy snipers and fire, the taste of freedom excited the former captives. "It was a thrill to get outside that wall and to ride in a wonderful jeep," Ethel Herold wrote in her diary. "The driver gave us crackers and gum."

General Beightler, commander of the Thirty-Seventh Infantry Division, watched as the vehicles pulled up outside the shoe factory.

"You guys sure have made monkeys out of those blasted Nips!" one former prisoner of war hollered to an American military policeman.

The prisoner then appeared to turn self-conscious.

"But I guess they kind of made monkeys out of us," he added.

The fires, the glow of which could be seen as far away as Los Baños internment camp some forty miles southeast of the city, set off alarms among senior officers:

"Japs going thru Tondo district setting fires," one intelligence report noted.

"Alert all your personnel to be especially careful tonight," warned another.

"These fires may be used as a cover by the Japs attempting a breakthrough."

The sudden scramble stood in marked contrast to the slow realization of some American commanders of the threat posed by Japanese demolitions, which was likely attributable to the weeks of conflicting intelligence reports over whether the enemy planned to evacuate or fight for Manila. The same day Colonel Noguchi's Northern Force began detonating buildings north of the river—and American forces rolled into the capital—Eichelberger had scoffed at the initial news of the fires. "The guerrilla reports make me laugh," he wrote to his wife on February 3 from a position just south of the capital. "The report tonight is that Manila is being burned by the Japanese, and yet I can look right down into the town and see lights and one little fire." Two days later the Eighth Army commander realized the error of his earlier assumption. "The fires in Manila," he wrote, "were bright enough so that we did not need a flashlight."

Compounding the challenges troops now faced were the swarms of eager civilians, anxious to greet the Americans and force gifts upon them even as the city around them burned. The flames meanwhile grew by the hour, radiating so much heat as to block one company of infantrymen from reaching the Pasig River. "The smoke and the dust were so intense, and the heat from burning structures so terrible, that little progress could be made," noted the XIV Corps report. In the skies overhead, MacArthur's personal pilot Weldon "Dusty" Rhoades watched Manila burn. "The spectacle was an appalling sight. The entire downtown section of the city was a mass of flames," he wrote in his diary. "Flames were rising 200 feet in the air from the center of the city."

Beightler, who was on the front lines of the inferno, could only vent over what he now realized was a deliberate plan to destroy Manila. "We were powerless to stop it—we had no way of knowing in which of the thousands of places the demolitions were being controlled," he wrote. "Imagine the major portion of the downtown shopping and business sections of Columbus or Cleveland or Cincinnati suddenly erupting in smoke and flames. Big, modern, reinforced concrete and steel office buildings were literally blown from their foundations to settle crazily in twisted heaps."

Infantrymen caught in the conflagration had no choice but to turn back as flames jumped from one building to the next, threatening to trap and incinerate them. But fire was only one of the hazards. Many of Colonel Noguchi's soldiers who had set off the explosions now retreated south toward the Pasig River. The fires corralled opposing forces onto the same few safe streets—the Americans charging north, the Japanese south. The two sides collided. "Japs popped out of alleys and buildings trying to escape the fire," recalled Capt. Labin Knipp. "We were ready and shot first. Most of the men in the lead threw grenades and charged shooting from the hip." Troops armed with Browning automatic rifles moved to the front. "We made quite a hole killing every Jap we saw," added First Sgt. Roy "Bus" McMurray. "At one place the fire had nearly choked off our street. We had to charge through the opening in a rush. The blistering heat and the walls of fire closing in on us had me wonder if we would make it."

But the infantrymen did.

The soldiers rallied at Plaza Santa Cruz, just a few blocks south of Bilibid. First Lt. Neil Anderson marveled at the raging inferno he had just escaped. "It was the first time I had ever seen a firestorm," he said. "Looking into the fire was like looking into a blast furnace of a steel mill of my native Pennsylvania." Sergeant McMurray meanwhile tallied the survivors. "Every time I ran a count our losses got higher. My best count was that we had over a hundred men wounded or lost in the fire," he recalled. "Looking south all I could see was a solid wall of roaring flame."

Maj. Chuck Henne, executive officer of the Third Battalion, 148th Infantry Regiment, ducked into a nearby building, searching for cover, only to find that scores of armed Chinese filled the ground floor. An elegant Chinese woman who spoke flawless English appeared, introducing herself as the liaison for the neighborhood defense group. Henne asked if the infantrymen might rest inside. She responded with an invitation for tea and cakes on an upstairs balcony, an offer the major couldn't refuse. "It was a once in a lifetime experience for not many men were ever privileged to sit on a balcony with a beautiful woman, partake of tea and cakes, and look out upon a burning city."

The conflagration just blocks beyond the gates of Santo Tomas replaced food as the talk around the camp. Internees and soldiers stood ready to stomp out any fires that might arise from the burnt ash and debris that drifted down inside the camp. "The Nips are systematically destroying Manila," a friend told nurse Denny Williams. "The bridges are all gone, and they've dug in behind the walls of the old Spanish city. Trouble is, a mess of Filipinos are dug in with them, so we don't dare bomb it."

Nightfall only accentuated the chaos outside in Manila's streets, a scene best described in the Fifth Cavalry's report: "With the coming of darkness large explosions followed by streaks of flame lit the western part of the city like a huge candle. At the mercy of the Japs the once most beautiful city in the Orient would soon be nothing more than a blackened skeleton. Each hour saw one section after another burst into flames," the report stated. "To many a soldier this night would not be forgotten and a feeling of retaliation, if and when the opportunity presented itself, ran high."

"Well, boys," one soldier lamented as he watched the fires from one of the university's towers. "There goes our good time in Manila."

MacArthur's aides joined internees to watch the inferno, some of whom climbed up to the university's roof for a better view. "Last night was a night of horror in Manila," Whitney wrote in a letter. "Throughout the night the terrific explosions from the enemy demolitions shook the city and great flames belched up thousands of feet to make it appear that the whole city was aflame." Internee Anna Nixon found the burning city mesmerizing, a scene she described in her diary. "I hear the fire crackle and am wiping off perspiration from the heat of it. In fact, I am writing this by the light of it, and it's nearly midnight now. Someone down there under a tree is playing his ukulele. It reminds me of Rome and Nero. The Japanese said they would burn the city and they have kept their word," she wrote. "I'm bone weary, but I can't sleep. These rolling, golden billows of fire fascinate me. They are so awful, beautiful, and tragic!"

○ ○ ○ ○

THE JAPANESE CONTROLLED the city south of the Pasig River, the Americans the north. Across Manila residents began to flee for safety, searching out large concrete buildings that might offer protection from artillery shells and fire. Red Cross director Modesto Farolan opened the headquarters on Isaac Peral as a refugee center. Other residents escaped to the German Club—a social hall on the corner of San Marcelino and San Luis streets—and De La Salle College on Taft Avenue.

In the walled city of Intramuros, Japanese troops blocked exits on the afternoon of February 5, demanding that all residents report to the Manila Cathedral on the corner of Santo Tomas and General Luna streets or to the San Agustin Church just three blocks away. By early evening several thousand gathered, lining the pews and crowding the courtyards outside. Many carried satchels of rice and beans, while others pushed carts. That night under the glow of the fires, Japanese troops began to pull young women out of the masses in what would become a citywide pattern of rape as parents and families proved powerless to intervene.

"No, please," residents heard women beg.

"Mama," another cried, "don't let them take me."

Elsewhere in the city residents hunkered down at home. Power had failed; so, too, had the city's water system. Newspapers had ceased publication, and absent electricity, many residents could not tune in to radio broadcasts for news. Japanese troops scoured the south bank of the Pasig, armed with saws and axes, destroying any canoes or boats that *manileños* might use to escape across the river. Japanese detonations continued to shake the capital, prompting Marcial Lichauco to compare the explosions to a July Fourth celebration. "Today should have been bright and clear," he wrote in his diary, "but only occasionally have I been able to get a peek at the sun through the clouds of smoke which envelop the city." The bespectacled lawyer watched Japanese troops retreat past his home, carrying little more than rifles and ammunition. "Discouragement, despair and defeat," Lichauco observed, "were plainly written on their faces."

From the church steeple near his home, Lichauco could see the Stars and Stripes that floated in the smoke-filled air above Malacañan Palace. All that separated him from liberation and freedom was the muddy Pasig River, which in a city filled with enemy forces might as well have been an ocean. Lichauco had already come to understand the reality of that danger acutely after Japanese troops, without warning to nearby residents, set fire to several warehouses across the street, triggering an inferno punctuated by the exploding fuel drums that rocked the neighborhood. Lichauco's wife and children fled to a residence a quarter mile away while he remained to pack the necessary items. Every ten minutes he would crawl up to the front windows for a glimpse. "The heat was so intense that we could not look out of our front windows for more than a few seconds at a time," he wrote. "I shall probably never again have a chance to witness such a spectacle at close quarters."

The explosions and fire drove the Garcia family into the backyard bomb shelter of their home just off Taft Avenue near De La Salle College. Unlike others who built their shelters belowground, Ramon Garcia had converted his library adjacent to the garage into a shelter, carefully relocating his prized books into the main house. He then lined the single room with sheets of galvanized iron, leaving a one-foot gap behind them that he filled with dirt. Garcia installed beams overhead yet below the ceiling, atop of which he piled sandbags. Inside the family stored oil lamps and candles along with canned food and twenty-gallon cans of water. Ida Garcia loaded the shelter with towels, which could be soaked in water and used to combat smoke inhalation. Inside this cramped shelter the family slept dressed each night. "A big bang or the staccato of machine gun fire, which appeared to get closer and closer every day, often interrupted the little sleep we got," recalled Jack Garcia, who was then ten years old. "We didn't know what would happen next." The spreading fires proved one of the largest fears, particularly since there was no way to combat them. "There were no fire fighters. There was no water. There was only hope," Jack wrote. "Hope that the winds would turn the fire around and spare us."

A few blocks away Far Eastern University founder Nick Reyes likewise moved his family downstairs to the first floor, where the children distracted themselves with games of chess and pick-up sticks while the parents hovered over a battery-powered shortwave radio. Sixteen-year-old Lourdes watched her mother kneel in prayer before an altar in her bedroom. Other times her mother and aunts repeated the rosary together. Lourdes and her father climbed to the third-floor tower room with its view of the city, one that worsened by the hour as the fires closed in on the neighborhood and shrapnel rained down upon the roof. "The nights turned into days, and the days into nights as the skies turned brilliant red with the blazing fires of the burning city," Lourdes recalled. "From dawn to sunset the pall of smoke blocked the sun."

○ ○ ○ ○

MacArthur was anxious to get to Manila.

Each day the general had set off south to the capital only to be thwarted by delayed troops and destroyed bridges. Finally on February 6, without having set foot in the city, MacArthur decided he could wait no longer. That Tuesday his headquarters announced to the world at six-thirty a.m. the liberation of the Philippine capital. "Our forces are rapidly clearing the enemy from Manila," the communiqué read. "Their complete destruction is imminent." Just as his headquarters had begun planning his victory parade before the first shot was fired, so, too, had MacArthur prepared his remarks dated February 2, the day before troops actually reached the city. "The fall of Manila was the end of one great phase of the Pacific struggle and set the stage for another. We shall not rest until our enemy is completely overthrown," he declared. "With Australia saved, the Philippines liberated and the ultimate redemption of the East Indies and Malaya thereby made a certainty, our motto becomes 'On to Tokyo.'"

American newspapers and magazines trumpeted the general's victory—even if it was a fiction. "Manila fell to MacArthur like a ripened plum," declared *Newsweek*, while the *New York Times* hailed it as "a spectacular climax to a spectacular campaign." A columnist in the *Washington Post* called it "a masterpiece of military planning and execution." Some editorial writers expressed amazement at the ease of the capital's liberation. "Given the far-reaching psychological and strategic importance of Manila," Barnet Norver wrote in the *Washington Post*, "it is nothing less than astounding that the Japanese did not make more of a fight for it than they did." Others, including noted columnist Ernest Lindley, couldn't help but point to the powerful symbolism of MacArthur's return: "It completes a cycle as dramatic as any in legend."

Personal congratulations for MacArthur poured in from world leaders, ranging from Australian prime minister John Curtin to Mexican president Manuel Avila Camacho. "The lustre of your recapture of Manila gives unbounded cheer to the Chinese people," wrote Chiang Kai-shek. "My Government and people join me in sending the forces under your command our heartiest congratulations."

The news of Manila's fall electrified Washington. Franklin Roosevelt cabled his personal appreciation to MacArthur. "This is," the president wrote, "an historical moment in the reestablishment of freedom and decency in the Far East." Others in his administration likewise showered the general with praise, including War Secretary Henry Stimson, a former governor-general in the islands who described Manila's recapture as the "culmination of one of the most brilliant campaigns in all history." Acting Secretary of State Joseph Grew, who had served as ambassador to Japan for ten years leading up to the war, held a press conference, telling reporters that sharing the news of Manila's liberation gave him "more pleasure than any he had been called upon to make since he left Japan."

Congratulations went beyond just the administrative branch. The House of Representatives voted unanimously to commend MacArthur; so, too, did the Senate. The city of Philadelphia went so far as to announce plans to hold a civic celebration in Independence Hall to celebrate the victory. Many of MacArthur's fellow officers cabled him, from Army Air Force head Gen. Henry "Hap" Arnold to Lt. Gen. George Patton, commander of the Third Army in Europe. Even retired Gen. John Pershing, who had blasted MacArthur decades earlier for his oversize ego, cabled his congratulations. "Well done," Pershing wrote. "Your latest victory has thrilled all your countrymen and particularly those of us who served in the early days in the islands."

MacArthur's declaration of victory—now heralded worldwide—

stood in stark contrast to actual events on the ground. The internees had been liberated, but as the general's own senior aides witnessed, much of the city now burned.

The Battle of Manila, in fact, had not even truly begun.

The letters and diaries of MacArthur's top commanders not only confirmed the horror, but to most, the ruin of Manila appeared certain. General Eichelberger wrote his wife on February 6—the same day MacArthur bragged to the world of the capital's capture—that the inferno was visible from fifty miles away. "The view of Manila last night was a terrible thing as the whole part of one side of the city seemed to be on fire. Smoke and flames were going way up in the air," he wrote. "What a shame it is." Even for a battle veteran, the level of destruction proved a first. "It was something," Eichelberger concluded, "I shall never forget." General Beightler, commander of the Thirty-Seventh Infantry Division, likewise watched from the rooftop of his headquarters. "The sky was a copper-burnished dome of thick clouds," he wrote. "So great was the glare of the dying city that the streets, even back where we were, were alight as from the reflection of a reddish moon. Great sheets of flame swept across the roof-tops, sometimes spanning several city blocks in their consuming flight. The roar, even at that distance, was like a Bessemer converter, and the earth shook frequently as yet more powerful demolition charges exploded, sending fountains of flame and debris in a hot, swirling eruption to meet the dense clouds overhead. We saw the awful pyrotechnics of destruction, spreading ever faster to encompass and destroy the most beautiful city in the Far East."

General Griswold, commander of the XIV Corps, saw no hope for Manila. "MacArthur has visions of saving this beautiful city intact," he wrote in his diary on February 7. "He does not realize, as I do, that the skies burn red every night as they systematically sack the city. Nor does he know that enemy rifle, machine gun, mortar fire and artillery are steadily increasing in intensity. My private opinion is that the Japs will hold part of Manila south of the Pasig River until all are killed."

Even among the press, there existed a huge disparity in the accuracy of coverage, based on the reporter's location. *New York Times* correspondent Lindesay Parrott, filing a dispatch from MacArthur's headquarters outside the city, mimicked the general's cheery communiqué. "What fighting still remains to be done in the city," Parrott wrote, "may be in the nature of mopping up rather than combat with an organized enemy." That contrasted wildly from fellow *Times* reporter George Jones's dispatch filed from within Manila, which presented an apocalyptic view of the capital. The *New York Times* published both on the same day, but Parrott's ran on the front page while editors buried Jones's report inside. "Fires were spreading over the greater part of Manila. The columns of smoke have merged until one great pall hangs over the southern portion of the city," Jones wrote. "Last night a red glow covered the skyline south of the Pasig River, silhouetting the cathedral domes and the towers of public buildings."

MacArthur's premature announcement of victory in Manila followed a trend his headquarters had adopted throughout the Pacific, one that frustrated his senior commanders, including Griswold, who repeatedly griped about it in his diary. "Why does he do this?" he wrote after one such announcement. "The man is publicity crazy," he huffed another time. "When soldiers are dying and being wounded, it doesn't make for their morale to know that the thing they are doing has been officially announced as finished." Eichelberger agreed. "It seemed to me, as it did to many of the commanders and correspondents, ill advised to announce victories when a first phase has been accomplished," the lieutenant general wrote. "Too often as at Buna and Sanananda, as on Leyte, Mindanao, and Luzon, the struggle was to go on for a long time. Often these announcements produced bitterness among combat troops."

The general's press statements drew the ire not only of his senior commanders but also of reporters, including Robert Martin, a correspondent with *Stars and Stripes* and *Yank*. "Mop-up is a favorite communiqué word. It sounds like a postscript that doesn't count," he wrote. "The battle has been won, the campaign is over, the strategy decisions have been made. All that remains is a mop-up of men who are not afraid to die by men who don't want to die. Mop-up is a tragic word. And who wants to die for it?"

In the case of Manila, MacArthur had no real sense of what was happening inside the city. Even as his commanders privately lamented the looming loss of Manila, MacArthur's headquarters' aides typed up final preparations for the planned victory parade, organizing jeep assignments and requesting that senior commanders radio the names of officers who would participate. One such invite went to Eichelberger, who dodged a chance to alert MacArthur of the parade's impossibility. "I shall be honored," he replied, "to accompany you on occasion of your formal entry into Manila."

CBS correspondent Bill Dunn, who had left Manila for a respite, arrived at the general's headquarters in San Miguel, astonished to learn of a pending press conference to announce the parade. "All at once the emotions and tensions of the past few days broke the dam," Dunn wrote, "and I became almost hysterical."

The newsman interrupted MacArthur's spokesman, arguing a parade was impossible. The Japanese had destroyed all the bridges; the city was in flames. Then it hit Dunn, who knew that the general's aides had visited the city. "General MacArthur had declared Manila an open city in 1942 and believed the Japanese would do the same," he said. "None of his immediate staff wanted to tell him he was wrong."

Dunn took the floor.

"If this announcement is released the General is going to look ridiculous!" he protested. "There is *no* possibility, physically, of a parade. Get down on your knees if necessary, let *me* talk to him, do *anything*, but don't release this announcement!"

"Calm down, Bill," urged Col. LeGrande Diller, MacArthur's aide-de-camp and public relations officer. "You've been through a lot in the past few days, but you mustn't get hysterical. The General knows what he is doing."

But Dunn refused to relent. "Emotion has nothing to do with this," he countered. "This is plainly a case where the General has been given erroneous intelligence. This statement will only tell the world he doesn't have the facts."

CHAPTER 10

"They beat me and pulled out my fingernails."

—Ko King Hun,
testimony, October 5, 1945

Around eight-thirty on the morning of February 6— just two hours after MacArthur announced to the world the fall of Manila—Japanese troops under Colonel Noguchi's command ordered all males over the age of fourteen to line up in the aisles of the Manila Cathedral. Many of the refugees who crowded the cavernous sanctuary this Tuesday morning felt exhausted after a restless night atop pews or stretched out on the stone floor. Fear and uncertainty only added to the stress. Though the Americans had reached Manila, thousands of civilian refugees in Intramuros remained prisoners of the Japanese, who had sealed the gates to the Walled City. No one knew what the enemy planned. The men queued up two abreast. Women and children watched as the troops marched an estimated one thousand males out the wooden doors with one armed guard for every ten men. The refugees were headed to the one place no one in Manila ever wanted to go: Fort Santiago.

For almost four centuries, Fort Santiago had served as Manila's epicenter of evil. Originally constructed as a primitive palisade on the banks of the Pasig River, the twenty-acre citadel had long ago traded its palm and earthen defenses for more than two thousand feet of stone walls, towering more than twenty feet high. Over the years the triangular-shaped fortress that anchored the northwestern corner of Intramuros had grown to include a labyrinth of dungeons that had played a starring role in the Spanish Inquisition. Associated Press reporter Raymond Cronin toured the fort's ancient cells before the war. "The ceilings and the walls dripped, since they were below the river bed," the journalist wrote. "The clay floors were wet and slippery. From rocks in the walls hung rusty chains in which the victims of other years, manacled by neck, leg and arms, dangled without food or water until the spirit was crushed or life departed."

Workers sealed the dungeons during America's administration, transforming the fort into the staid offices of the Army's Philippine Department. But the fall of Manila saw the resurrection of Fort Santiago's frightful origins as the headquarters of the dreaded Kempeitai, a place the Japanese sent captured guerrillas and other suspected enemies of the empire. "It is alive again. Fort Santiago," Pacita Pestaño-Jacinto wrote in her diary in March 1942. "People don't say its name aloud. They whisper it." Over the course of the war, the Japanese expanded the prison, packing inmates, as one witness later attested, like "slaves in the Spanish galleons." The Japanese used starvation as a weapon, triggering beriberi in many of the captives and leaving others blind. "In a period of twenty-five days," recalled Frank Bacon, an American mining engineer, "I had only two bowel movements." Chinese prisoner Ko King Hun dropped from 118 pounds to just sixty-eight in two months in 1943. "I was so thin," he said, "that I could form a ring around my leg by putting my thumb and index finger together."

Starvation proved only part of the horror.

Fort Santiago served as an interrogation and torture center. Guards pummeled prisoners with everything from swords to shovels until most lost consciousness, vomited, or spat up blood. Teeth proved a common casualty. American prisoner Margaret Morgan saw interrogators beat a pregnant captive so severely that she later miscarried in her cell. Waterboarding was another frequent torture as guards tied victims down, forced a hose in their mouth, and turned on the spigot. Filipino Jose Lichauco endured three rounds. "Each time," he recalled, "I lost consciousness." If the fear of drowning failed to make captives talk, interrogators resorted to electricity, forcing victims to sit on an electrically wired chair in a basin filled with water. "The shock would be so terrific," remembered Filipino Generoso Provido, "that the victims would shout like mad men and plead to be killed." Chinese merchant Jose Syyonping personally experienced that agony. "I felt so bad," he later testified, "that I urinated and I was forced to defecate."

Interrogators grew increasingly cruel and creative as the war progressed. "I was given the nail treatment," recalled Swedish prisoner Erik Friman. "This consisted of hammering slivers of bamboo under the finger nails until the nails pulled up at the root so they could be pulled out with dirty pliers." Other tortures were sexually sadistic. The Japanese burned testicles and jammed matchsticks into men's penises and cigarettes into women's vaginas. Interrogators hung a Chinese prisoner upside down then ran a wire deep into his body via his anus. "When they put him down," one witness recalled, "he was already dead." The Japanese at times even tortured the wives of suspected guerrillas, forcing their husbands to watch. Provido recalled one such occasion when guards stripped the spouse of a captive naked, burned off her pubic hair, and probed her with a large stick until she begged her husband to admit guilt. "This was the most revolting torture imaginable," Provido said. "It made me sick in mind and body."

The Japanese liked to show prisoners the bodies of murdered captives to frighten them into cooperating, including Filipino Ladislao Joya, who was forced to view two headless corpses. "I saw men with intestines taken out while living," he later testified. Interrogators went so far as to force prisoners to hurt other captives. That was the case for American Richard Beck, to whom the Japanese handed a baseball bat and demanded he strike an elderly Filipino prisoner. Beck's half-hearted swing prompted the investigator to demand he either hit harder or be shot. "After that," Beck said, "I beat the old man." One of the worst such atrocities happened to Joya, whom guards marched outside with other prisoners. Guards made two of the prisoners kneel before fresh graves. An officer handed Joya a sabre and ordered him to decapitate them. One of the men began to cry. Joya felt he had no choice but obey if he wanted to live. He raised the sword and swung it at the first man, hitting him just below the neck but failing to decapitate him.

"Come on," the officer barked.

Joya swung the sabre again.

And again.

"It took me two strikes to behead each victim," Joya would later tell war crimes officials. "After beheading, my investigator took the sabre from me and wiped the blood off by drawing the sabre over the shoulder of my coat." The Japanese then ordered Joya to lower the bodies into the graves and go retrieve the heads, which had rolled off to the side. "It was horrible," Joya recalled, "to see the head."

The American airstrikes on Manila in late 1944—foreshadowing America's return to the Philippines—prompted Fort Santiago to evolve from a torture center into a slaughterhouse. The work of disposing of the bodies was so intense that gravediggers at the North Cemetery labored one day in December 1944 without breaks from eight a.m. until ten p.m., burying truckloads of the dead. Santiago Nadonga estimated that he helped bury seven hundred people that day, many covered in cuts and bruises. "Some of them had wires around their necks and their hands tied behind their backs," Nadonga recalled of the corpses. "Their bones stuck out very prominent, as if they had been starved."

The men who marched out of the Manila Cathedral this February 6, one after the other as wives and children watched, would share a similar fate. "Don't worry," one of guards assured the spouses, "men will come back in three days."

Few believed him.

Thirty-one-year-old Rosa Calalang saw her husband Jesus march north. He suddenly broke out of line and ran back, embracing her and the couple's children one last time. He slipped her his wallet with his picture. "We watched them as they filed away," she would later testify. "That was the last I've seen of him."

o o o o

MacArthur's staff car slowed to a stop at the Balintawak Monument on the northern edge of Manila on the morning of February 7. The general had finally returned to the Philippine capital, four days after American troops first entered the city. Dressed in a khaki uniform, hat, and Ray Bans, MacArthur was accompanied by General Fellers and colonels Lloyd Lehrbas, Roger Egeberg, and Andres Soriano. A circle of generals awaited him this morning at the monument, including XIV Corps commander Oscar Griswold, Robert Beightler of the Thirty-Seventh Infantry Division, the First Cavalry's Verne Mudge, and William Chase, who had led the flying columns into the city. Chase couldn't help but sense that Griswold and Beightler felt sour this morning that he had beat them into Manila, a fact likely exacerbated when MacArthur exited his staff car and strode straight over to Chase, placing his hands on his shoulders.

"Chase," MacArthur began. "Well done! I have recommended you for promotion to Major General and have ordered you over to take command of the 38th Infantry Division which is bogged down in the Zig-Zag Pass east of Subic Bay."

Chase had a present of his own for MacArthur. On the first night in Manila, Chase's aide, Capt. Henry Freidinger—known simply as Friday—had found a pristine black limousine. Chase had instructed Friday to drive the car over this morning, where he presented it to MacArthur. The general was stunned. "This is my old car," MacArthur declared. "Thank you! I am glad to have it back again." So excited was MacArthur that he noted the car's return in his diary: "Retrieved own Cadillac automobile left on Corregidor and since driven by Jap commanding officer in Manila."

MacArthur was eager to visit the liberated internees and prisoners of war. He loaded up in a caravan and stopped first at Bilibid Prison. The army had moved the internees, who were initially evacuated because of the threat of fire, back into the prison after the conflagration spared Bilibid, which was better set up to care for the nearly thirteen hundred men, women, and children.

Senior medical officer Maj. Warren Wilson greeted the general and his aides. Roger Egeberg, MacArthur's physician, thought Wilson was the thinnest man he had ever seen who was not bedridden. The former prisoner stood erect and saluted.

"Welcome to Bilibid, sir," Wilson said, his voice hoarse.

"I am glad to be back," MacArthur said, grabbing his hand.

The general entered the wards to find many of the men atop cots. "Some eyes remained vacant, others smiled, many wept, and the sitting tried to stand—many couldn't," Egeberg recalled. "Those lying tried to sit up, and most failed."

MacArthur could not escape the fact that these were some of the same men he had left behind 1,064 days earlier when he climbed into the torpedo boat and fled Corregidor; the robust and healthy young soldiers were now hollowed out by years of starvation. One of the veterans would later tell Associated Press reporter James Halsema, who recorded the conversation in his private diary, that before his capture he had watched several soldiers on the march down from Topside leap from Corregidor's cliffs, preferring death to prison. "If I'd known then what I know now," the soldier said, "I would've jumped too."

Those who were well enough climbed to their feet and stood at attention alongside their cots. "They remained silent, as though at inspection," MacArthur later wrote. "I looked down the lines of men bearded and soiled, with hair that often reached below their shoulders, with ripped and soiled shirts and trousers, with toes sticking out of such shoes as remained, with suffering and torture written on their gaunt faces. Here was all that was left of my men of Bataan and Corregidor. The only sound was the occasional sniffle of a grown man who could not fight back the tears."

The general shook hands with some and touched the shoulders of others.

"I never thought I'd see you, sir," one dark-haired young American said.

"Dear God," another said between sobs. "Dear God."

"You're back," others whispered. "You made it."

"I'm long overdue," MacArthur repeated, his voice gravelly from emotion. "I'm long overdue."

The general wandered from ward to ward, where Egeberg heard him mumbling. "My boys, my men—it's been so long—so long."

An officer who had fought on Bataan approached the general, dressed only in a torn undershirt and filthy long underwear.

"Awfully glad to see you, sir," he said. "Sorry I'm so unpresentable."

"Major," MacArthur said, shaking his hand, "you never looked so good to me."

Not all the former prisoners remembered the general's visit so kindly. For some, both at Bilibid and Santo Tomas, the anger over his escape from Corregidor years earlier still burned, a sentiment Elizabeth Vaughn confided in her diary. "To those in the P.I.," she wrote, "there is nothing glorious about MacArthur except the brass of his uniform."

The general struggled over the horrible condition of his troops. "I will never know how the 800 prisoners there survived for three long years," he later wrote. "The men who greeted me were scarcely more than skeletons." The affect it had on MacArthur was obvious to those around him. "The general walked up and down through the prison wards with tears in his eyes," Chase recalled. "I have never seen him so moved."

Internees on the civilian side had fared little better. Malnutrition had left Natalie Crouter exhausted and mentally strained, unable to comprehend the excitement MacArthur's visit sparked in others. She looked up at one point to find MacArthur standing in front of her bunk. "He grabbed my hand and shook it, over and over, up and down," she wrote in her diary. "I was utterly dumb. I felt and looked more miserable and wretched every second. I could not say a word and just looked back at him speechless as we pumped our arms up and down, up and down. All of the last three years was in my mind and face, and at this actual, concrete moment of release, this biggest moment of my life, I felt no joy or relief, only deep sadness which could not come into words."

MacArthur did not say anything either but simply shook Crouter's hand before moving on down the line. "He must have sensed that no active spark of any kind existed in me," she concluded. "The lights had almost gone out."

Another woman with tears in her eyes held up her son so MacArthur could touch him. "Hello, sonny," he said. "I've got a boy at home just your size."

After his brief tour, MacArthur prepared to leave. "Arrangements are being made for food, hospitalization, and whatever else these men need?" he asked.

"Yes sir," Wilson replied. "Medical care and food are on the way."

"Good—you have done well through these years. Goodbye, and thank you."

MacArthur and his aides departed, pausing for a final survey of Bilibid. "I passed on out of the barracks compound and looked around at the debris that was no longer important to those inside; the tin cans they had eaten from; the dirty old bottles they had drunk from," he wrote. "It made me ill just to look at them."

The general climbed into his car, confiding in Egeberg that the brief visit to Bilibid had emotionally exhausted him. The car pulled away and headed toward Santo Tomas, taking alleys to avoid fighting in front of Far Eastern University. The fires north of the river had largely died down, but homeless residents wandered about the flame-blackened streets, calling out to American troops: "Burn Tokyo!"

Conditions at Santo Tomas had improved in the four days since American forces first arrived. Barely twenty-four hours earlier, a convoy of fifteen trucks and nine trailers with the 893rd Medical Clearing Company tore through the front gates of the camp. The company's thirteen officers and ninety-eight enlisted men, who had dodged fires and mines in the dash to reach Santo Tomas, had immediately relieved the camp's exhausted medical personnel. The starved and lousy prisoners rescued at Cabanatuan had spurred medics to ramp up the company's supply of vitamins, calcium, and vermifuges. "Every available vitamin tablet and ampoule was procured," recalled Maj. Frederick Martin. The staff had since toiled to convert the first floor of the Education Building into a 287-bed temporary hospital. "The litter and rubble strewn lobby and corridors of the building were eloquent evidence of the recent fighting that had taken place there," the company's report noted. "Many hours and much hard labor were expended clearing up the mess but by noon we had the main floor cleared and were set up and had already passed 97 patients through Admission."

The medical company's doctors noted the rough shape of many of the internees, even after several days of improved food. Many suffered from edema in the lower extremities while foot and wrist drop plagued others. Few of the women had menstruated in months, and many of the internees struggled with frequent or uncontrollable urination. Some suffered rises and falls in body weight of as much as eight pounds in twenty-four hours, suggesting problems with water metabolism. "These pathetic people were gaunt, pallid, suffered from breathlessness and weakness, pains in the extremities and swollen bellies and ankles," the company's report noted. "These cases of severe nutritional deficiency were what we took care of the first few days but in spite of endeavors six or eight of the more serious ones died in half that number of days." On top of the internees, civilian battle casualties flooded the hospital. "The surgical theater," the report noted, "was in use day and nite almost without interruption for the first week."

In addition to medical care, troops worked to clear the camp, hauling away twenty-six 2.5-ton truckloads of garbage and debris from around the Education Building during the first three days. Others carried well water to help make the existing toilets flush and brought in box latrines. The clearing company likewise cooked food, serving 320 meals that first night. Even though it was designed to feed just the hospital, Red Cross workers, journalists, and others showed up for a bite, all handled by just eight kitchen workers. "For the first week our mere clearing company kitchen served an average of 1800 meals a day," the report noted. "The internees, starved for so long, had ravenous appetites and would get into the mess line for seconds and thirds and more if we would let them. Indigestion and diarrheas became rampant but the starvelings continued gorging themselves reinforcing their diet with soda, bismuth and paregoric."

Word had spread throughout Santo Tomas that MacArthur would visit. Even the Japanese shelling that morning, which hit the camp gardens, shanty area, and Education Building, failed to dampen the excitement. Internees crowded around the windows for a view, while others tried to secure a spot out on the main plaza.

The general's staff car pulled up in front of Santo Tomas at ten a.m.

MacArthur stepped out and saluted the honor guard before facing the flag-draped balcony.

"There's MacArthur," internees shouted. "He's back."

Reporter Frank Robertson captured the scene. "People ran from all directions as they caught sight of his famous gold-embroidered cap and the glistening five stars on his collar," he wrote. "With joyous eagerness they pressed close, to shake his hands or just to touch him, almost with reverence." Walter Simmons with the *Chicago Tribune* marveled at the excitement. "He received a riotous demonstration—one girl even kissed him."

The general made his way into the lobby of the Main Building, mobbed by old friends so emaciated he struggled to recognize them. "At nearly every step MacArthur was halted while internees reintroduced themselves and told him they knew he would come back," wrote Associated Press reporter Russell Brines. "Several women grasped the general's hand and reminded him of the former social days in Manila."

One of those MacArthur encountered was Margaret Seals, whom General Fellers had run into days earlier on his visit. "Oh, General, I'm so glad to see you and your troops," Seals declared. "You and they were magnificent."

"I'm glad to be here," MacArthur replied. "I'm a little late, but we finally came."

The general embraced her frail and emaciated body.

"Well, Margaret, you look fine," he said. "A little thin—but fine."

Seals was far from fine—she would die three months later in Walter Reed Hospital, just one week after her return to the United States.

MacArthur saw Eda Knowlting of Pennsylvania, who kissed him on the cheek. "General," she cried, "we can't tell you how glad we are to see you."

"Mrs. Knowlting, I can't tell you how glad I am to be here," the general replied. "I wish I could have made it sooner."

Another internee begged for his autograph, but MacArthur demurred. "I would have to sign hundreds," he told the woman. "Please send your paper to me at my headquarters and I'll see that it is returned to you with my signature."

Eleven-year-old Robin Prising, never one to miss out, elbowed his way up close to watch. So, too, did camp historian Hartendorp, who took pride in the fact that MacArthur remembered him. "In the lobby of the Main Building," Hartendorp later wrote, "surrounded by a press of wildly cheering people, he caught sight of me, called me by name, grasped my hand, and said he was glad to see me."

The internees pressed in tighter. A woman dressed in rags passed her son over the heads of others so MacArthur might hold him. The general grasped the boy, stunned to see how starvation had left a vacant look in his eyes. Another internee buried his face in MacArthur's chest and cried. Others, in contrast, laughed uncontrollably. "In their ragged, filthy clothes, with tears streaming down their faces they seemed to be using their last strength to fight their way close enough to grasp my hand," MacArthur later wrote. "I was grabbed by the jacket. I was kissed. I was hugged. It was a wonderful and never-to-be-forgotten moment—to be a life-saver, not a life-taker."

The general made his way to the foot of the main staircase. His aides hoped to usher him into the nearby broadcasting room so he could give a brief speech to the camp, but the throngs of internees blocked his passage. MacArthur instead cut through the library and out a side door. From there he reentered the rear of the building, but the crowed continued to follow him. He managed to make it up a rear staircase to the quarters of the army nurses from Bataan. There he nearly collided with Edith Shacklette, who described the scene in her diary. "I ran out in my robe nude as a jaybird," the nurse wrote. "I up & kissed the general (hadn't combed my hair or washed my teeth as water is off). Photographers flocked around me! Oh gosh. Always was impulsive."

MacArthur then returned to the main stairs, where the internees down below in the lobby again erupted in applause. "His five stars were quite in evidence," Margaret Bayer wrote in her diary. "He was given a good ovation. People are beginning to realize he is a great man—it was hard to see the forest and not the trees for a time."

MacArthur was overwhelmed by the experience, a sentiment he described in a personal letter he wrote later that day. "My visit with

those mistreated, starving comrades was something I shall never forget," he wrote. "It touched me deeply." Griswold noted in his diary
afterward the obvious impact the visit made on MacArthur. "He was
much affected by pitiful sights and utter thankfulness of our starved
people at Santo Tomas and Bilibid who were literally being starved to
death by the despicable Japs."

The general confided in Egeberg that he was ready to leave. "This
has been a bit too emotional for me," he told his doctor. "I want to get
out and I want to go forward until I am stopped by fire—and I don't
mean sniper fire."

MacArthur's aides ushered him back to the camp's gates, but before
he left, he slipped seven-year-old Elaine Solomon of California a chocolate bar.

"Chase," the general said as his staff car drove through the university's gates, "I want to go to Malacañan Palace and see your troops in
the front lines."

Several of MacArthur's senior officers immediately attempted to
talk him out of it, arguing that enemy troops and snipers still populated the streets.

General Chase sat in silence through the debate. When it ended,
MacArthur addressed him again directly. "Chase, you will take me
down, I am sure."

"Yes Sir," Chase replied. "Let's go."

Gunfire rattled in the distance, and smoke from the many fires hung
on the horizon. Egeberg stared out the window. "Turning a corner on
a broad street," he wrote, "we encountered a stationary open truck
full of Japanese soldiers—some with guns in their hands standing up
leaning over the sides, others sitting, all dead."

The convoy rolled through the front gate of the presidential palace,
a colonial Spanish mansion constructed two centuries earlier as the
summer home of a wealthy merchant. Over the years the two-story
white palace, where MacArthur's father had lived when he served as
governor general, had grown to include a social hall, chapel, and gardens. Chase had radioed ahead, and the troops were lined up. MacArthur complimented them before he strode through the front door,

welcomed by former servants whom he remembered from his days as field marshal of the Philippine Army. MacArthur embraced several and asked for a tour. Soriano, Chase, and the brigadier general's aide Friday—armed with a machine gun—accompanied MacArthur as he explored the lower floor, surprised to find it empty and in decent shape. The group climbed the stairs to former president Manuel Quezon's office. "Here he stopped, took off his hat, and lowered his head in what must have been a silent prayer," Chase recalled. "He then said that he had worked for several years in close association with the late president and wished to be alone in the room for a while. We left in respect of his wishes."

MacArthur had shared a long history with Quezon, who had invited him to the Philippines to help build the nation's army and later served as the godfather of his son, Arthur. Quezon had evacuated Manila for Corregidor on Christmas Eve 1941, spending eight weeks on the Rock with MacArthur before slipping out one night on the submarine *Swordfish*. MacArthur had embraced Quezon the evening he left.

"Manuel, you will see it through," MacArthur had told his friend. "You are the Father of your Country and God will preserve you."

At that time, before Roosevelt ordered MacArthur to evacuate Corregidor, the general had planned to stay on the Rock and fight to the end. Quezon understood, removing his signet ring and slipping it on MacArthur's finger. "When they find your body," he told him, "I want them to know you fought for my country."

Quezon had spent the war in exile, his goal always to return to home. But the Philippine president's long battle with tuberculosis had ended just six months earlier when he died in a Saranac Lake hospital in upstate New York. Until his death he had tracked MacArthur's progress back to the Philippines. "Aurora," Quezon had cried out to his wife moments before he died, "he is only 300 miles away!"

MacArthur emerged from Quezon's office a few moments later and walked out onto a porch that overlooked the Pasig. Chase grew nervous, as the river served as the front line. With the bridges destroyed, American troops had yet to cross but would do so later that afternoon. At this moment, MacArthur was barely a mile and a half from his old home atop the Manila Hotel, the house he had vacated in such a hurry three years earlier that his family did not have time to even take down the Christmas tree.

The general's eyes gazed south across the river, where tangles of green lily pads floated upon the muddy waters bound for the bay. Across the river he could see the palace gardens, and to the west, like giant chess pieces, sat the General Post Office, City Hall, and the Legislature, Finance, and Agricultural buildings—the grand public structures that had long symbolized America's influence in the Philippine capital. Even as MacArthur soaked up the view, Japanese marines rushed to fortify those buildings, all part of Admiral Iwabuchi's plan to turn Manila into an urban quagmire. MacArthur at this very moment stood on the sidelines of a coming fight that the Thirty-Seventh Infantry's report would later call "the bitterest and bloodiest battle that Jap fanaticism could conjure."

Yet at this moment MacArthur failed to grasp the magnitude of the battle ahead, even though he had seen first-hand the city's destroyed northern districts. As Beightler remembered, MacArthur said that it was so quiet that the XIV Corps could jump the river and seize the rest of the Philippine capital with just a single platoon. Griswold recalled the same. "He seemed to think the enemy had little force here," he wrote in his diary. "Was quite impatient that more rapid progress was not being made."

An American mortar platoon a block down the street opened fire on the Japanese positions south of the river, interrupting MacArthur's solemn moment.

"I want to visit your front line platoons in action," he told Chase.

Chase agreed, and the men departed the palace. Word had spread throughout the neighborhoods that MacArthur was in Manila, and local men, women and children, cheering and waving flags, now crowded the sidewalks and streets.

"Viva MacArthur!" many shouted.

The general soaked it up. "Obviously much pleased and entirely oblivious to the always present danger," Chase observed, "he walked down the middle of the street." Adjacent to the presidential palace stood the San Miguel Pale Pilsen Brewery, owned by Col. Andres Soriano. At Chase and Soriano's urging, MacArthur visited the brewery at eleven a.m. This would be the last stop on his visit to Manila this morning. Chase was particularly parched and wanted a cold drink. "My tongue was hanging out a foot," he recalled. "The general drank a bottle and I drank a large pitcher."

○ ○ ○ ○

SECOND LT. JOHN HANLEY reached the Dy Pac Lumberyard at about the same time MacArthur downed his bottle of beer with General Chase. The night before, American intelligence had received reports of a possible massacre of civilians at the site. Hanley's job that morning was to investigate. The seasoned infantrymen had grown accustomed to violence on the battlefield. But there amid the towering weeds, the troops found that the dead did not wear camouflage fatigues but rather flower-print dresses, nightgowns, and even infant sleep suits. Of the more than one hundred men, women, and children brought to the site in the middle of the night on February 3–4, only four are known to have survived, including Ricardo San Juan, who watched the Japanese kill his pregnant wife and three children. The horror the troops discovered in a field less than three miles from the presidential palace would prove only the first of dozens of atrocities that would befall the Philippine capital, a window into the days ahead as American forces fought street to street through southern Manila.

The reports of that morning filed by Hanley and his men not only captured the brutality but also made clear that the civilians had been executed.

"On the adult bodies," Hanley noted, "the hands were tied."

"These were the cut and mangled bodies of men, women, and children," Sgt. Paul Smith testified in his affidavit. "They were scattered through the area, lying singly and in piles."

"It appeared," added Pvt. First Class Claude Higdon, Jr., "whole families had been killed."

American troops set up a perimeter, blocking curious residents from straying too close. In reality, the soldiers were the last to arrive. Locals in the days before had already visited the lumberyard as word of the slaughter had spread. Many had come in search of relatives, who had been dragged off by the Japanese in the middle of the night. Others had wanted to recover cash and valuables from the dead. Mutilation of the bodies made identification difficult at times, including one woman found sliced open from her vagina to her chest. Tondo teenager Manuel Mendoza made the gruesome discovery of his twelve-year-old cousin Greta. "Her head," the youth later told American war crimes investigators, "was nearly cut off and was hanging by the skin." In other cases, the Japanese had lopped the hair off of women, leaving it in piles several meters away. "Many had wounds of the abdomen," observed an American medical officer who visited later that day, "through which the intestines were protruding."

The tropical sun only further hindered identification, helping balloon the bodies as an army of flies attacked the corpses. The stench turned away all but the most determined. "I saw eight piles of dead bodies, the largest pile had about 15 bodies, another pile had about 12 bodies in it and the remaining piles had five or six bodies in them," recalled teenager Antonio Lamotan, who came at the request of neighbor and survivor Ricardo Mendoza. "I also saw other bodies scattered in the tall weeds."

Daniel Simon picked through the tangle of bodies, searching for the valuables of the slain family members of Faustino Fajardo, his godfather. He removed the gold earrings, bracelet, and ring from Fajardo's wife, Lourdes, still dressed in the nightgown she wore when the Japanese seized her. From nine-year-old Florencia Fajardo, he took a pair of earrings along with the engagement ring from the left third finger of twenty-eight-year-old Leonora Fajardo Pimentel, dressed in a yellow dress with red flowers. Amid the dead Simon spotted two-month-old Celia Fajardo, still swaddled in a flannel baby suit. He struggled with four-year-old Melita Fajardo's earrings. "It was fastened through," he recalled, "and when I took it part of the flesh went with the earrings."

As decomposition disfigured the dead, residents looked for telltale ways to identify loved ones. Manuel Mendoza recognized his friend Manuel Calinog from his blue sharkskin polo shirt and long gray pants. He confirmed Calinog's identify when he fished his Japanese-issued residence certificate from his right pants pocket. Several noted the "FFF" monogram on the left pant leg of Faustino Fajardo. Others recognized Agapita Mendoza from her employer's name on her apron, Dalisay Theater. "Her neck," recalled friend Benjamin Chome, "was half cut." Other witnesses identified thirty-five-year-old Antonio Dominador—the twentieth man in line that night next to San Juan—from his amputated right hand. Dominador's twenty-five-year-old wife Cecilia, even in death, still clung to the couple's slain nine-month-old baby, Arturo.

Maj. David Binkley, the Thirty-Seventh Infantry Division's sanitary inspector, arrived at the lumberyard on the afternoon of February 7. In a city without running water and sewer, public health was a major concern—and dead bodies served as insect breeding grounds. Binkley swept the area with brothers Francisco and Mariano del Rosario, undertakers for the city of Manila. The men counted 115 bodies, including many women and children; the blood proved so voluminous that it had run off in streams. Amid the weeds, Mariano del Rosario spotted one woman whom he surmised to be seven or eight months pregnant. The inferno that swept through Tondo in the following days had burned several dozen bodies beyond recognition, but investigators would still identity fifty-one of the deceased; the other sixty-four would be buried unknown.

The undertakers arranged for trucks to haul the remains to the North Cemetery, where burial squads would use a bulldozer to dig a mass grave. The last lorry loaded with the dead rolled out of the lumberyard that evening around six. An American war crimes report would later attempt to summarize what happened at the Dy Pac Lumberyard. "Whole families were indiscriminately murdered on mere suspicion that some one member was a guerrilla," the report concluded. "No one was too old or too young to escape attention; babies of two or three months, pregnant women, and an old woman of eighty, all suffered the same fate."

○ ○ ○ ○

AMERICAN INFANTRYMEN PREPARED to cross the Pasig on the afternoon of February 7. In recent days, intelligence regarding Japanese plans in Manila had begun to solidify, debunking the earlier hopes that the enemy would abandon the capital and instead confirming the guerrilla reports that had detailed preparations for an urban siege. That same day, in fact, troops found stashed in a grave in the Chinese Cemetery several charred records, including a copy of Admiral Iwabuchi's January 21 operational orders. This intelligence windfall not only detailed the breakdown of the admiral's North, Central, and Southern forces but also spelled out his mandate that his men hold the city at all costs, even identifying designated fortresses, like the Paco Railroad Station and Fort McKinley. "In general," stated a First Cavalry Division intelligence report, "the defense plan appears to have projected a tenacious delaying action." Analysts were quick to seize on a critical omission in Iwabuchi's plan. "Neither the sketch nor the orders," the cavalry's report noted, "provide for an eventual withdrawal from Manila."

This would be a fight to the death.

Colonel Noguchi's forces had avoided a battle in northern Manila, instead torching the city's commercial and financial districts before falling back across the river and blowing up the bridges. Those soldiers who made it out of the inferno prepared for a final stand in the Walled City. Iwabuchi's marines, meanwhile, fortified the surrounding government buildings and residential areas while Capt. Takesue Furuse's Southern Force fought to repel General Eichelberger's Eighth Army. MacArthur's troops would now have to cross the river and hunt down the enemy in the capital's populous south side. To do so, American forces carved up the city. The Thirty-Seventh Infantry would cross the Pasig near Malacañan Palace and then turn west and drive toward Intramuros and the waterfront. The First Cavalry would envelop Manila from the east, crossing the river farther south before turning toward the bay, a thrust that would parallel the infantry. The Eleventh Airborne would close the city's southern door.

With the bridges all sitting on the bottom of the river, troops would

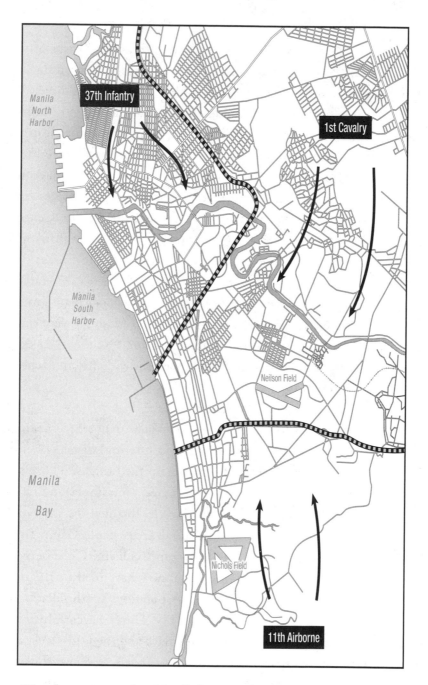

War planners carved up Manila between the Thirty-Seventh Infantry Division, the First Cavalry Division, and the Eleventh Airborne. The dividing boundaries between these forces illustrate how the Americans encircled the Japanese and drove them west toward Manila Bay.

have no choice but to cross the Pasig in assault boats, a slow and perilous feat that exposed them to attack by the more than eight hundred Japanese marines deployed in that area as part of Iwabuchi's Central Force. Plans called for the 148th Infantry to paddle across, secure the districts of Pandacan and Paco, and then drive southwest toward the Walled City and Manila Bay. The 129th Infantry would follow, hook immediately west, and seize Provisor Island, a roughly ten-acre island in the Pasig that housed a vital steam power plant. Officers had selected four departure points a few hundred yards east of Malacañan, a move that would allow them to float with the river's current and land in the palace's expansive gardens that ran along the river's south bank.

To shield the crossing locations from the enemy, infantrymen gathered that afternoon a couple blocks north of the river, awaiting the arrival of thirty assault boats and amphibious tractors, better known to the troops simply as alligators. Once the equipment arrived, platoons moved through the stacks of wooden boats, grabbing them and marching down to the Pasig to climb aboard. The first assault wave prepared to depart at three-fifteen p.m. Maj. Chuck Henne, who controlled the flow of infantrymen at the river's bank, joined the others to watch, all anxiously waiting for the enemy guns to open fire. "Quietly," Henne recalled, "the long line of boats pushed out beyond a jetty down stream into the main current which bent the formation into a long crescent."

Five minutes passed.

Then ten.

The infantrymen in the boats focused on the approaching riverbank, paddling amid the swift-moving brown water filled with clumps of lily pads.

The first wave hit the south bank at three-thirty p.m., just as the Japanese guns finally opened fire. The infantrymen scrambled up the bank and into the gardens. "Any idea of an unopposed landing," said Lt. Jimmy Falls, "was forgotten."

Henne summoned the other company commanders to instruct them how to cross. Tensions soared, as the Japanese were sure to target each subsequent wave. The major felt someone hovering over him as he studied the map on the ground. Irritated, he wheeled around to find General Krueger, commander of the Sixth Army. Henne politely asked if the general had any questions.

"No, Major," Krueger replied. "You're doing fine. Carry on."

The second wave pushed out into the river's current. No sooner had the first boats rounded the jetty than the Japanese opened fire with a mix of machine guns, mortars, and artillery. "The fire slashed down, blanketing the banks and churning the river to a brown froth," Henne remembered. "It built to a crescendo and clouded the river with dense smoke through which only the flash of exploding rounds could be seen."

The enemy machine guns and cannons proved the worst, shredding the wooden boats. "When we were hit we could only go forward," recalled Capt. Gus Hauser. "The current in the river was shoving us that way making the far bank closer, but minutes seemed hours." Reaching the south bank, troops poured over the sides, abandoning some of the wrecked craft to drift downriver toward the Walled City and the bay. Amphibious tractors meanwhile motored out into the water to retrieve boats for the next wave, drawing fierce enemy fire. Rounds ripped through the metal skin, leaving the wounded tractors to gasp as the air escaped, and the slain alligators sank to the muddy bottom. Henne marveled at the chaos of the combat before him. "Hollywood could not have staged the smoke, flash and bang more dramatically," he later wrote. "It was spellbinding to watch pieces of paddles and splintered chunks of boat plywood fly through the air while men paddled with shattered oars and rifles to work their boats to the far bank, seemingly oblivious to what was happening to them."

Over on the front lawn of Malacañan Palace, battalion surgeon Capt. Lew Mintz had set up his aid station to treat any casualties from the crossing when Japanese artillery suddenly rained down. "With only the rush of shells to warn us, the area around us erupted with high explosives," he said. "Many of the men were caught in the open and hit. By actual count eighteen men were on the ground requiring attention."

In the regimental headquarters inside the palace, Maj. Stanley Frankel worked with his assistant, Sayre Shulter, preparing orders for an assault the next day when the artillery blasted the lawn.

Moments later a soldier appeared at the door. "Lots of guys have been hit by Japanese shelling in the courtyard," he announced. "We need litter bearers to get them back to the aid station."

Shulter, a fastidious secretary who had spent much of the war shackled to his typewriter, darted outside with his boss reluctantly in tow. The shelling stopped, allowing the soldiers to retrieve the wounded. But the lull proved short-lived and the Japanese attacks resumed, one of which knocked Shulter to the ground. "I'm hit," he hollered.

Frankel charged over and pulled him to his feet. A quick inspection revealed no bleeding or obvious wounds. Frankel asked if he could walk.

"I can run," Shulter assured him.

The two trotted over to the aid station, where to Frankel's shock Shulter collapsed face down. The doctor grabbed him and rolled him over to check his pulse.

Frankel stared.

"This man is dead," the doctor announced.

"He can't be," the major cried.

The doctor turned back to Shulter. He opened his eyes and checked the pulse on both his wrist and neck. "Dead, dead, dead," he confirmed.

Frankel would later learn that the concussion blast felled him, adding the gentle secretary Sayre Shulter to the list of fourteen dead and 101 wounded that day. "He was," Frankel later lamented, "killed 200 yards from his typewriter."

○ ○ ○ ○

THE JAPANESE BEGAN SHELLING Santo Tomas again soon after MacArthur's departure that Wednesday morning. Many of the internees proved slow to grasp the danger; a few even hunted for pieces of shrapnel to keep as a souvenir.

Eva Anna Nixon was in her room when a fragment hit the window. "Look," one of her roommates said. "Our window has a shrapnel wound."

Everyone laughed.

Many of the internees migrated into the building corridors for protection. "While we sat in the hall exchanging stories that afternoon, there was a buzz over our heads, a loud crash, and then cement, glass, and dirt came tumbling down around us," Nixon wrote in her diary. "We ducked our heads and huddled close together. As soon as the dust settled, we looked out the window into the patio where water was pouring from the roof tanks through a shell hole over cracked and crumbled stones."

Evelyn Witthoff charged downstairs.

"Did you hear that?" she asked. "It buzzed right over our heads up there, and you should have seen us hit the floor! No siesta for me!"

"I don't have any shrapnel to take home, and I'm going to see if I can find some," one of the women announced. "There ought to be some around after that blast."

Another shell hit and exploded.

"Stay away from the windows," an American soldier shouted. "Get back against the wall and stay low. Don't go back into your rooms."

The women obeyed as the Japanese shellfire worsened. "We huddled against the wall and silently clung to each other. Another blast shook the building, and everything became hazy and dark. We covered our faces and braced ourselves," Nixon wrote. "A nurse, the color drained from her face, ran down the hall followed by two soldiers carrying a stretcher bearing two children dripping blood."

The reality of the attack now dawned on them.

"We huddled together like hunted animals, realizing that the next moment might bring death," Nixon wrote. "I was too stunned to pray."

Instead an old hymn came to mind:

Our God, our Help in ages past,
Our Hope for years to come,
Be Thou our Guide while life shall last,
And our eternal Home!

Internee Margaret Bayer suffered a similar experience that morning. She had stopped off in the lobby to retrieve message blanks while her sister Helen continued on upstairs at the moment one artillery attack began. "Immediately the first shell was followed by another in the plaza just outside the door where I was standing. I bit the dust under a table!" Bayer wrote in her diary. "Then they kept hitting and hitting. I could not get upstairs and Helen could not get down." Bayer grew frantic, picturing her sister trapped upstairs on her bed with shattered glass raining down on her. "Stretchers began coming down stairs bearing the most gruesome and bloody sights. No one looked like her!" she wrote. "Bodies were brought in from the front plaza and I hope I never see anything so awful. I finally raced for the stairs in a lull and to the second floor. Helen was there watching the stairs just as terrified and worried as I."

The experience traumatized Bayer. "The stairs and halls had lots of HOT shrapnel on the floor," she concluded, "but I was no longer interested in getting a souvenir."

The late morning attacks delayed the noon meal more than an hour. During a reprieve, the kitchen staff scrambled to prepare a lunch of bully beef and string beans, part of a posted menu that simply read: "Hot American chow—plenty for everybody." The break did not last as the Japanese began shelling the camp again in the afternoon, scoring several direct hits between three and four p.m. on the Main Building. At one point during that interval, troops recorded two bursts every three minutes.

One shell hit in Room 3 on the southwest corner of the Main Building's first floor. Teenager Terry Meyers was holding hands with fifteen-year-old Marjorie Ann Davis when the shell exploded. Disoriented, she crawled out of the destroyed room and ran into Paul Davis, who begged to know where his sister was.

"She should be right behind me," Meyers replied.

But she was not. Davis had been killed instantly. "I was holding her hand when one of the shells exploded," Meyers recalled. "I was just lucky."

"You're hit," someone told Meyers.

The teen looked down and saw blood coming out of her knee where shrapnel had torn into her leg. "I remember I was throwing up," she said. "All over myself."

Seconds before the shell hit Room 3, Mary Foley had ducked inside to retrieve some of her belongings accompanied by her husband, the Reverend Dr. Walter Foley, who before the war had served as pastor of Manila's Union Church. He had continued his work inside Santo Tomas, chairing the internee religious committee while his wife was known as one of the best singers in the camp. The two were well liked among the camp's medical department for volunteering to help. The explosion that afternoon killed the reverend and ripped the left arm off of his wife just below the shoulder.

Nurse Sally Blaine had heard about Dr. Foley's death when she reached the emergency room that afternoon. "There was a woman on a stretcher whose left arm was off," she remembered. "I didn't want to recognize her." Blaine approached her friend, but words suddenly failed her. "I was going to ask her could I do anything for her," she recalled. "I looked at her, I saw the arm was off, and I couldn't speak."

"Sally, you know me, I'm Mrs. Foley."

"Of course, I know you," Blaine replied, regaining her composure.

"Where's Frances Helen?" she asked, inquiring about the couple's twenty-year-old daughter.

"She's over there," Blaine replied.

"Could I speak to her?"

Blaine had not yet talked to the Foley's daughter and did not know if she was aware that her father had been killed.

The daughter came over. "How is daddy?" Mary Foley asked.

"Daddy is all right, don't you worry about daddy one minute, he is all right now," she assured her mother. "You just think about yourself and take care of yourself."

Frances Helen walked back over to Blaine, who estimated that she could not weigh more than ninety pounds. "Do you really know about your father?"

"Yes, I know," the daughter replied. "I know he's dead, but I didn't want mother to know it yet."

"I nearly died," Blaine recalled years later. "Oh God. The things that these little girls had to endure."

Another time that day, Blaine encountered her best friend, who was screaming. "Jane, Jane," she called out. "Get a hold of yourself. What's wrong?"

Between her sobs and shouts, Blaine learned that her friend had been walking with two others when a shell hit one of the women in the chest. "Jane was wild, hysterical and I tried to calm her down. I couldn't," Blaine recalled. "So I slapped her on each side of the face as hard as I could slap and then she stopped crying."

Frederick Stevens witnessed a similar scene after a shell hit Room 19.

"Where is she, where is she?" cried an older gentleman, stumbling over the debris in search of his wife.

Stevens knew what the panicked husband refused to accept; that she was gone. "He saw a high-explosive shell hit against human flesh and then dust, debris mixed with human arms, legs and bodies that were twisted and torn under. Where there were men and women, living and breathing, now only blood, bones, quivering flesh."

"Oh Lord," he cried. "Not my loved one, no, Oh Lord, not her."

A soldier seized the distraught gentleman and pulled him out of the room. "He came back as a stretcher-bearer," Stevens noted, "still looking, still hoping."

The afternoon shelling ended only to resume again around seven-thirty p.m. One round tore into the gymnasium, seriously wounding an internee who would die from his injuries the following day. Another shell destroyed a men's bathroom in the Main Building. Others continued to pound against the university's south facades, causing concrete to rain down and filling the air with dust as internees huddled in corridors. Doctors moved 150 patients from the hospital in the bottom of the Education Building to the yard out back. "The Educational Building suffered two direct hits and two officers and five enlisted men of this company were injured," the 893rd Medical Clearing Company's report noted. "There were many severe casualties among the civilian internees living in the Main Building of the University. These cases were immediately brought into our surgery and from this time on the surgical service was kept busy day and night."

The shelling prompted approximately eighty of the one hundred Filipino laborers the Civilian Affairs forces had hired to help clean the camp to vanish. Gone too were a dozen Filipino doctors. Tressa Roka gave up working in the children's hospital to volunteer to help the injured. "Stunned and weeping relatives walked through the narrow aisles to identify their dead and wounded, while doctors and nurses tried to do their work," she wrote in her diary that day. "I saw many of my fellow-members badly wounded. Many were dying. Moving from bed to bed in a daze, I did what I had to, and I was indifferent to the shells that whistled over the building."

Roka paused over the bed of an internee. Despite a horrific head wound, she recognized John McFie, Jr., a prominent Manila attorney and close friend. The fifty-five-year-old McFie was born in New Mexico, where his father had served as a justice on the New Mexico Territorial Supreme Court. The younger McFie had fought in World War I at Verdun. He had met his wife Dorothy in Hawaii, where she worked as a schoolteacher. The couple later married in 1928 in the Japanese city of Kobe.

"I knew a good thing when I saw it!" she told Roka one time.

Roka had grown close to the couple over the years of internment. She fondly referred to them in her diary as the Macks and had marveled at their obvious intimacy, which was reflected in simple gestures, like holding hands. "They seemed closer than ever," Roka wrote one day in May 1943 after chatting with the couple for an hour in the plaza. "Their devotion to each other was beautiful to see."

Roka had watched the way starvation had hollowed them out, turning John's hair bright white and sallowing Dorothy's skin. Despite the couple's failing health, the two remained forever upbeat. "They had never once lost their faith and optimism," Roka confided in her diary less than a year earlier. "From their cheerful manner, one gathered that the American forces were just outside the gates of the camp."

Now, just days after those forces tore down the camp's gate, she stood over John McFie, his head bloodied after a Japanese shell caught him unawares in the first-floor bathroom of the Main Building. "His breathing was stertorous, his pulse thready, and I knew that he had only a few minutes to live. But where was Mrs. Mack?" Roka wrote. "She must see him before he died. Bitterness overwhelmed me. It was not fair, not right that he should go like this! He above all, with his optimism and faith."

"Where's Mrs. Mack?" Roka asked one of the doctors.

"In Catalina Hospital with beri-beri," he replied. "Will you tell her?"

Roka's heart sank. There was no way she could deliver this awful news to her friend. "Please don't ask me to do that!" she begged, her voice a "frightened plea."

The doctor sensed Roka's distress. "All right," he said, patting her shoulder. "I'll do it."

Others witnessed similar tragedies as shrapnel tore open the bodies of men, women, and even children. "There was one beautiful girl, only 17, I'll never forget her," remembered nurse Beatrice Chambers. "Half her face was taken off."

Nurse Edith Shacklette, who only hours earlier had impulsively kissed MacArthur while wearing just a robe, vented her anguish in her diary. "We all worked all nite," she wrote. "War is hell." Roka echoed her. "This day had been a nightmare!" she added. "We were stunned and almost in a state of shock as we went about our work cleaning up the rubble and caring for the wounded and dying. What a pity! we kept thinking as we went about our duties. After surviving starvation, and then having to go like this!"

Those not working battled fear. "In bombing raids, you had time to run for shelter," recalled Frederick Stevens. "Being under shell fire was a new and terrible experience." That experience only further rattled the already fragile internees. "To be shelled when every internee had that feeling of exaltation of being freed, petrified the minds of all," Stevens wrote. "They were dazed, and absolutely helpless from physical or nervous shock. The horrors they had suffered in the past faded into insignificance and were beyond comprehension. Each shell had a sound all its own."

"Nobody is brave under shell fire, they just take it," said one internee who had served in the army in France during World War I.

That fear only intensified as the afternoon faded to evening. "Night shelling was especially exhausting and nerve-shattering," recalled Emily Van Sickle. "Straining ears in the darkness to catch sound rhythms of the next shell, we sometimes heard both sides fire simultaneously with a confusing irregularity of booms and swishes."

Internees dragged mattresses into the corridors, listening as American observation planes buzzed overhead, searching out the Japanese artillery. Others retreated outside. "We spent the entire night out under the stars," Bayer wrote in her diary. "The ground was hard and the night long and the mosquitos terrific, but with the help of some chocolate bars and crackers, we made it. We even slept a bit."

Dawn brought a much-needed reprieve from the fear and uncertainty that had gripped many. According to figures compiled by camp historian Hartendorp, the February 7 shelling killed twenty-two people, including twelve internees, eight Filipino and Chinese workers, and two American soldiers. Shrapnel seriously injured another twenty-seven internees, eleven workers, and one soldier.

Like many others who survived, Eva Anna Nixon reflected on the random nature of who lived and who died. "I picked up a piece of a Japanese shell, still hot which fell at my feet as I talked with Dr. Walter B. Foley that morning. Could I know I would never talk with him again?" she wrote in her diary. "I stood in lunch line with the intelligent lawyer, Mr. McFie, and we had discussed the future of the Philippines and China. A few hours later he was dying with his brains blown out. When I last saw Mildred Harper get into bed and heard her laughter ring through the blackout, I didn't know that shell fragments would put a stop forever to her merry laughter. And when Gladys Archer stopped me in the hall, I had no idea that in minutes her head would be severed from her body. And there was beautiful Veda—but they gave her blood plasma and she will live, even though her eye and ear are gone."

CHAPTER 11

"High and low, all are brought down in the great sieve of war."

—NATALIE CROUTER,
DIARY ENTRY, MARCH 8, 1945

SHORTLY AFTER BREAKFAST ON THE MORNING OF FEBRUARY 7—the same day MacArthur visited Santo Tomas and the infantry crossed the Pasig River—Japanese troops at San Agustin Church ordered males fourteen and older to gather in the front plaza, continuing the roundup of all military-aged men in the Walled City. Against the backdrop of artillery fire and explosions, the Japanese lined the men up in groups of four, marching an estimated fourteen hundred off to Fort Santiago, just as was done the day before with the men from the Manila Cathedral. "The only ones that they left behind," recalled thirty-five-year-old Lourdes Lecaroz, "were the old men and the home guards."

Three blocks north at the Manila Cathedral, which was still crowded with families whose husbands and fathers Noguchi's forces had seized the morning before, a soldier climbed up on a bench in front of the refugees. All eyes fell on him.

"Listen everybody, listen," he announced. "You can go home."

The women and children poured out of the cathedral's wooden doors just as the long column of men from San Agustin marched past. "We thought it was our men folk come back to us," recalled thirty-one-year-old Rosa Calalang, whose husband Jesus the Japanese grabbed the day before. "We were wrong." When the prisoners arrived at the citadel, troops ordered them to empty their pockets of pens, keys, cigarettes, and lighters. The Japanese then went down the line, stealing watches off the arms of the captives before marching the men inside and locking them into cells.

Around nine-thirty a.m., the Japanese stormed the San Juan de Dios Hospital on Calle Real in the Walled City, rivaled only in size by the Philippine General Hospital.

"Where is the director?" troops demanded.

The accuracy of America's artillery had convinced the Japanese that someone in the two-story hospital possessed a radio. Troops searched all the rooms but failed to find the offending transmitter. The Japanese demanded a list of all doctors, nurses, and patients before stationing guards at every exit to block anyone from leaving.

Elsewhere in Intramuros, Japanese troops armed with cans of gasoline, torches, and grenades began to systematically burn houses, shops, and offices. Calalang had barely arrived home from the cathedral when a neighbor ran past.

"Fire," she cried out. "Fire."

"Where?" Calalang asked.

"They are burning the houses," her neighbor replied. "The Japanese are throwing hand grenades at the houses. They threw one in our house."

Calalang rushed outside to see her neighbor's house enveloped in flames. She scanned the street and spotted Japanese troops hurling explosives into other homes. She darted back inside and grabbed her three children and seventy-year-old mother, Victoria: "We ran out of our home as fast as my children and my aged mother could make it." Two nuns likewise witnessed the Japanese sloshing liquid into the windows of the convent at San Agustin, mistakenly concluding that the troops were battling the fire. "This is not water," one of the nurses hollered after she smelled the fumes. "This is gasoline."

The Japanese had sealed all the gates and posted sentries, trapping residents inside the Walled City as explosions thundered. The flames threatened San Juan de Dios Hospital, triggering the Japanese to order the 160 doctors, nurses, and patients to evacuate to the nearby ruins of Santa Rosa College. Destroyed three years earlier during Japanese air strikes at the start of the war, the ruins now served as a firebreak. "We moved everyone except four of our bed patients who were too weak to walk out themselves," recalled nurse Sister Nelly de Jesus Virata. To the shock of the hospital staff, the Japanese refused to allow the attendants back inside to carry them out. Virata returned the next day after the fires died down to discover the bedridden patients had been burned alive. "We found them," she said, "all dark like charcoal."

The fires intensified as the afternoon turned to dusk and then evening. Block by block the Japanese methodically destroyed much of the 160-acre Walled City, erasing four centuries of history in an afternoon. Throughout the alleys and narrow cobblestone streets, terrified residents in the ancient city choked on the acrid smoke that billowed skyward. The Japanese had rigged explosives in the Manila Cathedral and surrounding buildings, detonating them early that evening. Thirty-seven-year-old Spaniard Miguel Blanco saw the cathedral's iconic dome explode, hurling debris and stones. Blanco dove for cover at a nearby fire station. The tall arched doors of the station framed the conflagration outside. The entire roof burned and collapsed into the sanctuary, littering the adjacent streets with twisted metal, brick, and blazing timbers. Thirty-five-year-old Mariano Agilada, perched at the window in the nearby Santa Clara Monastery, watched the cathedral burn until past midnight. "The breeze was very strong at that time," he said, "and we could see the fire getting bigger and bigger."

Rosa Calalang joined scores of her neighbors—along with the evacuated doctors and nurses—in the ruins of Santa Rosa College as the fires devoured Intramuros. "It was like broad daylight," Calalang recalled. "The heat was unbearable."

A similar scene unfolded inside San Agustin, where the burning of the adjoining convent forced the refugees to crowd into the sanctuary. "The fire became intense," recalled twenty-three-year-old Renee Pena. "It was like an oven where we were." Thirty-five-year-old Lourdes Lecaroz struggled just to breathe. "We were being suffocated," she said. "There were screaming and shouting almost continuously." Refugees begged the Japanese to let them out. Guards finally relented and opened the front door to reveal an apocalyptic scene. The clock tower overhead burned. "The bell was ringing," recalled twenty-five-year-old Remedio Huerta Beliso. "Cinders were falling everywhere."

Just blocks away inside the cells of Fort Santiago, the Japanese began the slaughter, a process that would run almost nightly for several days, no doubt part of a plan to eradicate males in the ancient citadel who might pose a threat when the walls finally came down. Troops marched into the cellblocks armed with drums of gasoline, tipping them over and letting the fuel flood the floors. Another marine tossed a torch. Prisoners trapped inside yanked on the cell bars. The Japanese machine-gunned those few who managed to escape. A captured Japanese diary dispassionately described the fates of the thousands of men imprisoned in Fort Santiago. "150 guerrillas were disposed of tonight," the unknown diarist wrote on February 7. "I personally stabbed and killed 10." Two days later he put pen to paper again: "Burned 1,000 guerrillas to death tonight." He concluded his diary on February 13. "While I was on duty, 10 guerrillas tried to escape. They were stabbed to death," he wrote. "At 1600, all guerrillas were burned to death."

o o o o

AMERICAN INFANTRYMEN HUNKERED DOWN in the palace gardens on the night of February 7, an area dotted with trees and stables and encircled by a brick wall. Beyond the perimeter, troops could see an open expanse of rice paddies, while to the east rose an earthen dike that protected the Estero de Pandacan. After the perilous river crossing, the exhausted soldiers welcomed a few hours of rest that night in the soft grass, the sky aglow as the Walled City burned just a mile and a half south.

Two battalions had made it across the river during the afternoon and early evening. Orders on the morning of February 8 called for expanding the American bridgehead about a mile through Pandacan and Paco to Harrison Boulevard, which would serve as the Thirty-Seventh Infantry's southern boundary. That job fell to Maj. Chuck Henne and others with the 148th Infantry. Meanwhile the 129th Infantry would cross the Pasig that day and hook west to capture Provisor Island, followed by the New Police Station, City Hall, and the General Post Office.

Little was known of Admiral Iwabuchi's immediate plans other than to repel the Americans and try to hold central Manila. Japanese snipers proved a powerful reminder of the enemy's wily defense. When Sgt. Tank Stauffer stepped in front of a gate to talk with Major Henne and Capt. Bob Brown, inadvertently exposing himself before Brown or Henne could grab him, a bullet thudded into his chest.

"I've been hit," Stauffer said.

Dazed yet still standing, the sergeant turned to walk off, when Brown stopped him and pulled up his shirt to examine Stauffer's wound. "The bullet hit center of his chest and exited the center back," Brown recalled. "Nice clean holes; the bullet apparently passing through his body not touching a bone."

Stauffer would survive.

At nine a.m. the Second and Third Battalions drove south side by side through the district of Pandacan to seize the Paco Railroad Station, which marked the infantry's southern border. The soldiers swept through the open rice fields, hustled along by Japanese mortar and artillery fire, toward the edge of the barrio. Infantrymen lined up and moved block by block through Pandacan without a single shot fired.

But the ease of the advance ended as troops closed in on the railroad station, a neoclassical structure fronted by a facade featuring four columns. Some three hundred Japanese marines had turned the elegant 1915 train station into a fortress protected by a series of pillboxes, 20 mm cannons, mortars, and a 37 mm gun. American troops probed the outer defenses for weakness, but the Japanese proved fierce fighters. "Very limited progress was made and in no part of the sector was an advance of over a few yards made," recorded the 148th Infantry's report. "Very stubborn resistance consisting of machine guns, light and heavy mortars, rocket and artillery was encountered."

February 8 rolled into the ninth.

And the standoff continued.

Artillery pounded the station, but even the monsoon of shells that would later reduce much of the building to rubble failed to dislodge the defenders. Some one hundred yards—roughly the length of a football field—separated the American infantrymen and the Japanese marines. But those yards might as well have been miles, except in the eyes of twenty-one-year-old Pvt. Cleto "Chico" Rodriquez. Raised by an aunt and uncle after his parents died, Rodriquez had fought just to survive as a youth in Texas, where he delivered copies of the *San Antonio Express* to earn money, sleeping most nights on a cot at the newspaper. During his down time, he flirted with street gangs. "At least during the war," he once said, "I knew the enemy was in front of me."

Rodriquez was joined by Pvt. John Reese, a Cherokee Indian who grew up on a reservation in Oklahoma. Despite the spray of enemy bullets, the two automatic riflemen crept forward, reaching a railroad shed about sixty yards from the station. Once inside, the infantrymen took up a position by the window that afforded them a view of the enemy. To their surprise, the Japanese charged. "It's either you or them," Rodriquez said, sighting the enemy and squeezing the trigger. "I just knocked them off."

One reloaded, while the other fired.

"A little bit more to the left, Johnny," Rodriquez hollered.

Reese swiveled and fired.

"You got him!"

The minutes ticked past. One after the other, the infantrymen sighted the enemy and fired, sighted and fired, with a pace reminiscent of a shooting gallery at a county fair. By the end of an hour, the two men had killed an estimated thirty-five Japanese.

Rodriquez spotted more enemy marines racing to reinforce several pillboxes, a move that promised to drag out the fight. The two men again unleashed their machine guns, killing forty more.

Rodriquez and Reece had come this far. Why not go farther?

The men darted out of the shed toward the railroad station, a direct charge straight into the enemy's line of fire. Sixty yards fell to fifty.

Then thirty.

And twenty.

The infantrymen dove for cover. Japanese guns roared and bullets zinged past as the men hunkered down. A few moments later, the enemy's guns quieted.

"Cover me, Johnny," Rodriquez yelled.

The Texan charged the entrance, pulled the pin, and lobbed a grenade inside the railroad station. Rodriquez yanked the pin from a second and tossed it, too. A hundred yards back, his fellow infantrymen watched in amazement as he hurled three, four, and then five grenades into the heart of the enemy's lair. The bombs exploded in succession, filling the air with hot shards of razor-sharp shrapnel that killed another seven Japanese marines and destroyed a 20 mm cannon that had menaced the infantry.

Rodriquez fell back with Reese twenty yards from the station's entrance, the danger far from finished. The two men raced to retrace their steps across the no-man's-land. Reese would dart ahead a few yards while Rodriquez covered him. The men would then flip-flop, each protecting the other.

The Japanese recovered and began firing again. The bullets whizzed past, but the men pressed ahead, each step carrying them closer and closer to safety. "Watch it, Johnny," Rodriquez hollered at one point. "That one nearly hit me in the nose."

"I got the S.O.B. sighted," Reese replied. "Don't worry."

The distance between the men and the station widened.

Safety was close at hand.

Another round zinged past, this one striking Reese in the forehead. He dropped to the ground. Rodriquez knew instantly his friend was dead.

He had no choice but charge those final yards alone.

Rodriquez and Reece, both of whom would later receive the Medal of Honor, broke the impasse that led to the capture of the railroad station the next day. Their heroic efforts were reflected in Reece's medal citation. "The intrepid team, in 2½ hours of fierce fighting, killed more than 82 Japanese, completely disorganized their defense and paved the way for the complete defeat of the enemy at this strong point."

○ ○ ○ ○

AT THE SAME TIME American soldiers battled Iwabuchi's Central Force for the Paco Railroad Station, the 129th Infantry prepared to capture Provisor Island. Bounded by the Pasig River on the north, the Estero de Tonque on the east, and the Estero Provisor on the south and west, the tiny island housed five buildings and multiple sheds, including the Manila Electric Company's power plant, the largest single unit provider of electricity for the Philippine capital. The Japanese recognized America's desire to protect the city's power system, setting up what promised to be a ferocious fight.

The island offered Iwabuchi's defenders clear lines of sight in all directions. The Japanese likewise controlled the only bridge, making it easy for them to reinforce the garrison, while the Americans would all have to come by boat.

But setting foot on the island proved only part of the challenge.

The reinforced concrete buildings were difficult to destroy from the outside, while the power plant's heavy machinery and equipment made for a mechanical labyrinth inside, one that the Japanese marines were not only familiar with but also had plenty of time to mine and booby-trap. Adding to the peril, Iwabuchi's forces had even constructed machine-gun nests inside many of the buildings. American infantrymen dubbed it "Battleship Island."

The first troops prepared to assault the power plant at eight a.m. on February 9; their objective, the boiler plant on the island's northeast corner. Under the cover provided by smoke pots, eight infantrymen slipped a boat into the water at the mouth of the Estero de Tonque. Everyone anxiously watched and waited as the troops stroked out into the canal. Ten more soldiers climbed into a second boat behind.

"I'll fire three bursts when we get across," one lieutenant said.

The boats closed in on the island when the wind wafted away the smoke. Then Japanese machine guns and 20 mm cannons opened fire. Troops in the first wave scrambled ashore, leaving the boat in the water to drift away. Japanese guns zeroed in on the second wave, killing two of the men and wounding several others. The survivors managed to haul the boat to shore and remove the wounded before the craft sank.

The infantrymen charged inside the boiler plant, repelling two attacks that morning before the Japanese drove them out at eleven a.m. The soldiers retreated behind a pile of coal twenty yards from the plant's entrance, a position that offered only limited cover as the Japanese gunners could shoot down on them from above and from the corners of the building. The Americans were trapped. As the hours ticked past, two of the infantrymen tried to swim the canal to retrieve help. Japanese snipers felled both. Obscured by the smoke from a burning oil tank, a third finally made it.

Not until nightfall could U.S. forces hope to recover the trapped men or send reinforcements across the canal. To stave off an attack, mortar teams targeted the far side of the boiler plant, forcing the Japanese to hunker down and preventing additional troops from joining them. Capt. George West finally swam across the Estero de Tonque, towing an assault boat behind him. He helped load the eight wounded survivors aboard. West attached the tow wire to his belt and began to swim back, planning to pull the troops across once he reached the far bank. Halfway there, the tow wire snagged on an underwater obstruction. West had no choice but to return the wounded men ashore, telling them to paddle as fast as possible. The men did, but the Japanese spotted them and opened fire with 20 mm cannons, killing three of the infantrymen.

At one-thirty a.m. five more assault boats set out in the darkness. The moon slid through the clouds, illuminating the small flotilla on the water just as the boats closed in on the island. The Japanese again let loose with machine guns, cannons, and mortars. The first two boats landed, but Iwabuchi's marines sank the last three, forcing the infantrymen to grab the wounded and wade ashore. Then Japanese set an oil tank ablaze, lighting up the island and forcing the infantrymen to take cover again behind the coal pile. Minutes turned to hours. Finally at five a.m. the flames died down, and the soldiers charged inside the boiler plant. The battle for the island resumed. "The dough-boys fought from panel to panel, from door to door, from inside and outside boilers, around turbines and from the rafters," wrote Royal Arch Gunnison of *Collier's* magazine. "It was a nerve-shattering battle, with the enemy ten or twenty feet away."

For American troops accustomed to battle in the jungles of New Guinea, the fight for the boiler plant proved dark and claustrophobic, a game of hide-and-seek with deadly consequences. The infantrymen paired off, wriggling through the machinery. At times, the troops could hear the enemy marines scurrying just a few feet away.

"Hey, Joe," some of the Japanese hollered in English, the echo bouncing off the walls and machinery, disguising the enemy's location. "I'm over here."

American troops resorted to similar tactics, dangling helmets so as to draw enemy fire, the muzzle flash illuminated in the darkness. "There was no escape for either outfit," Gunnison wrote. "This was kill or be killed. Food was short and there was no water. There was no outlasting the enemy. He had to be dug out."

One day turned to two.

Then three.

No one dared sleep in such close quarters with the enemy, who had placed machine guns inside boilers and hoisted them up in the rafters. The Americans resorted to using grenades and even bazookas inside the buildings. "Inch by inch," Gunnison wrote, "foot by foot, these Americans combed every hole, every fallen timber, and lifted and searched under every strip of galvanized-iron roofing, ducking, dodging, throwing back unexploded Jap grenades, patching wounds, swearing softly—since conversation would draw fire from the Japs five, ten, twenty feet away."

Finally, on February 11, the battle ended. The fight to take the ten-acre island resulted in 285 American casualties, including thirty-five killed and ten missing. In the end, as the Sixth Army's report lamented, it had all been for nothing. "The large steam turbine plant," the report stated, "was rendered completely useless by the destruction of all six of the generator units and some of the steam turbine ends."

For the soldiers, the fight had proven a terrifying ordeal. "It was the damnedest three-day nightmare I ever had," one infantryman later confided to Gunnison. "We had to take the chances. We had to come out in the open. The Nips were like termites in the woodwork. They'd have sat in those culverts and those boilers and behind those dynamos till they starved. We couldn't wait for that. So we just went in after 'em."

○ ○ ○ ○

ON THE CITY'S SOUTHERN BORDER, General Eichelberger's Eighth Army likewise faced tenacious resistance, braking the dash from Nasugbu to Manila. "We had almost begun to wonder what had happened to the Nips," quipped Edward Flanagan, the Eleventh Airborne Division's historian. "We knew they were around because we could see Manila burning. We soon found out where they were."

Eichelberger's army had collided with the formidable enemy defenses known as the Genko Line. The Japanese had originally anticipated an American invasion from the south, building a defensive line of reinforced concrete pillboxes, antiaircraft guns, and machine-gun nests that stretched from Nichols Field near Manila Bay northeast to Fort McKinley. American Intelligence estimated that reinforcements had swelled Capt. Takesue Furuse's Southern Force to more than six thousand soldiers and marines.

Those troops now manned twelve hundred pillboxes, many mutually supporting and some two and even three stories deep. Others were constructed of stone with domed roofs planted with sod and weeds that effectively camouflaged them. The Japanese arsenal counted forty-four heavy artillery pieces, including 120 mm coastal defense guns. Americans likewise encountered five- and six-inch naval guns, 150 mm mortars, and 20 mm, 40 mm and 90 mm antiaircraft cannons. Adding to the challenge, the Japanese converted almost three hundred depth charges and hundred-pound bombs into land mines. These complemented five-hundred-pound aerial bombs with low-pressure detonators the enemy buried in the highways leading into the city. Other rudimentary roadblocks included old tractors and steel rails sunk into the pavement. "From now on our advance was not measured in miles," Flanagan wrote. "It was measured in yards."

American artillery blazed a trail for the infantrymen, who battled house by house, assaulting pillboxes and bunkers with flamethrowers and demolitions. Japanese 90 mm antiaircraft shells exploded overhead, producing a rain of steel that pockmarked homes and stripped leaves and branches from trees. Troops saw leveled warehouses and even an apartment building with its walls ripped off, allowing infantrymen a glimpse of the homes inside. "Destruction and chaos marked the path of our drive into Manila," Flanagan wrote. "Houses and shops, flanking both sides of the highway which leads to the heart of the city, were torn up by both Jap and American artillery. Tin-roofed houses looked as though a giant can-opener had sliced through them, while once pretentious mansions, gauntly displayed charred chimneys and trash piles of rubble."

The fight for Nichols Field was fierce. The expansive open area gave the Japanese clear lines of sight on any advancing Americans. Marines had fortified airplane revetments, encircled the area with barbed wire, and dug tunnels linking gun emplacements and concrete pillboxes, one of which was three stories deep and found to have a mahogany bed. The defenders had lined the outer perimeter of the airfield with five-inch naval guns stripped off destroyed warships, prompting one company commander to fire off a note to his headquarters: "Tell Halsey to stop looking for the Jap Fleet," he said. "It's dug in on Nichols Field." The battle for the airfield would ultimately drag on until February 13. "The Japs," Flanagan wrote, "defended Nichols Field as if the Emperor's Palace itself were sitting in the center of the runway."

○ ○ ○ ○

ELSEWHERE IN MANILA FAMILIES grew frantic. Around the Garcia home off Taft Avenue, Japanese troops holed up in pillboxes and sniped civilians who dared trespass in public. Neighboring families, using breaches in backyard fences and walls, congregated in the Garcia backyard. "We were trapped within the parameters of our urban block," recalled Jack Garcia. "There was no way we could get out without being seen, stopped, or shot. The edict was very clear. No one was allowed onto the streets."

The fires made it impossible for the Garcia family to await the arrival of American forces. The family's vegetable garden provided the only firebreak, and it was far too small to protect them from the intense heat and rain of ash. Each family member packed clothes and food in bundles made from bedsheets, while Ramon Garcia prepared a black valise of jewelry, medicine, and important papers. The flames grew so intense that Jack could close his eyes and still see the fiery brilliance. "Every night the glow grew redder and appeared to cover more sky. The brightness of the blaze now stretched for miles and spread directly overhead," he recalled. "It was frightening."

Similar fears gripped the Lichauco family in the district of Santa Ana. On the morning of February 9, an American artillery round tore through the roof and lodged in the kitchen table. "Luckily it failed to explode," Lichauco wrote in his diary. "As my mother would undoubtedly say were she in our house today—only to the Holy Virgin Mary and the Blessed Saints in Heaven can we attribute this miracle." Japanese and American artillery fire shook the city day and night, forcing residents to shelter indoors. Absent electricity and running water, conditions throughout the city deteriorated. "Tomorrow it will be a week since American armored cars successfully entered the north side of the city," Lichauco wrote. "The Pasig is less than a hundred yards wide but we here on the south banks of the river have yet to see an American soldier."

Nick Reyes and his teenage daughter Lourdes likewise felt the crawling pace of the battle, watching from the third-floor tower as the fires closed in on the family's home near Taft Avenue. On the night of February 8, Lourdes spotted Japanese marines armed with torches emerge from a house in the nearby neighborhood of Leveriza. Moments later the home erupted in a blaze. The troops then entered another home and another, each one soon engulfed in flames. Over the crackling fires, she heard screams. Lourdes watched as the Japanese rounded up the men from each residence. She looked up at her father; the color suddenly drained from his face. Fire was no longer the only fear. "My knees turned to water," she later wrote, "and my heart throbbed in my head."

"It will be our turn soon," Nick Reyes whispered to his daughter. "Do not alarm your mother. It is only the men that they want."

○ ○ ○ ○

ADMIRAL IWABUCHI FACED A CRISIS.

The American infantry had crossed the Pasig River just four days after reaching the capital, penetrating the districts of southern Manila largely held by his Central Force. The cavalry now closed in from the east, while the Eighth Army charged up from the south, threatening to bust through his formidable Genko Line.

In response, Iwabuchi ordered his marines to strengthen the south bank of the Pasig. "Units must be especially watchful against enemy infiltration by boat." He likewise demanded Colonel Noguchi's Northern Force, the survivors of whom had fallen back to the Walled City, to penetrate and disrupt the American lines. To Capt. Takesue Furuse, he ordered the city's southern boundary secured. Despite the tenacious fighting of his troops on Provisor Island, at the Paco Railway Station, and on Nichols Field, it was clear to the admiral that Japan's defensive bulkheads threatened to collapse.

If that happened, Iwabuchi would be trapped.

On the morning of February 9, the admiral abandoned Manila for Fort McKinley just south of the city, afraid that retreat might prove impossible if he waited much longer. From there, if needed, he could orchestrate the withdrawal of his forces.

Just as he had done several years earlier in the dark waters off Guadalcanal, Iwabuchi elected at the last moment to forgo death and save himself.

The admiral had radioed daily battle reports to General Yokoyama, who was at the Shimbu Group headquarters near Montalban about ten miles east of the capital. Since American soldiers rolled into the city on February 3, Yokoyama had watched each day as dark smoke hovered over the capital.

The night of his arrival at Fort McKinley, Iwabuchi summoned naval staff officer Koichi Kayashima, instructing him to travel to Montalban and brief the Shimbu Group commander on the state of the fight.

Kayashima arrived the morning of February 10. Kenichiro Asano, chief of staff of the Shimbu Group, attended his briefing. "I sensed," Asano said, "that the Naval units were fighting against hopeless odds."

Those deteriorating odds coupled with the city's crumbling defenses had led Iwabuchi's forces in recent days to escalate attacks against civilians in Manila suspected of guerrilla ties, targeting former military officers, constables, and even a few priests known to be friendly with American internees. In each case, no trials were held nor evidence presented. Death was announced by a knock on the door. The lucky ones earned a bullet, the less fortunate a saber. The list of those attacked during those first few days of the battle read like a who's who of local law enforcement:

- ○ Constable Col. Jose Guido and his three teenage sons, the youngest fourteen;
- ○ Fellow constable Col. Alejo Valdes, his son, and his brother-in-law;
- ○ Manila police officer Jose Herman, his son, and nephew;
- ○ Father Patrick Kelly and three other Malate priests.

But those early, targeted assassinations paled compared to the tsunami of barbarity that would soon descend upon the Pearl of the Orient. Not only had troops begun killing the first of thousands of males trapped inside the Walled City, but marines now swept through neighborhoods south of the Pasig, seizing men and even teenagers, while setting entire blocks ablaze. Captured Japanese orders found on the smoldering battlefield—some mere fragments, others signed and dated—would later reveal that the atrocities were not random acts of unrelated violence but rather part of a systematic plan to destroy the city and annihilate all its inhabitants. "The Americans who have penetrated into Manila have about 1000 artillery troops, and there are several thousand Filipino guerrillas. Even women and children have become guerrillas," stated a February 13 order. "All people on the battlefield with the exception of Japanese military personnel, Japanese civilians, and special construction units will be put to death."

That battlefield, of course, was the city.

But Japanese commanders went farther, issuing precise instructions on how best to eliminate civilians. This was spelled out in an undated Manila Naval Defense Force battalion order. "When Filipinos are to be killed, they must be gathered into one place and disposed of with the consideration that ammunition and man power must not be used to excess," the order mandated. "Because the disposal of dead bodies is a troublesome task, they should be gathered into houses which are scheduled to be burned or demolished. They should also be thrown into the river."

What had started as a fight between two armies over one of Asia's great cities devolved on February 9 into one of the worst human catastrophes of World War II. An examination of the timeline of the dozens of atrocities that occurred in Manila point to that date as the fulcrum on which the violence shifted from individual attacks against suspected guerrillas to organized mass extermination. That was the day Iwabuchi chose to abandon the city; that was the day he realized the fight was hopeless.

And that was the day the true evil began.

PART III

"Everyone who escaped can tell a tale of horror."

—Col. James T. Walsh,
April 5, 1945

Filipino refugees make their way through the ruined capital on February 12, 1945.

CHAPTER 12

"The screams of my wife continued for some time and finally died out."

—Engracio Losa,
testimony, September 12, 1945

Japanese marines fanned out the morning of February 9 through Malate, rounding up men, women, and children and marching them to St. Paul's College, where troops assured residents they would protect them at the Catholic school.

One of those seized was fifty-nine-year-old Spaniard Cayetano Barahona, who had prepared to sit down to an eleven-thirty a.m. lunch in his Wright Street home. Two marines banged on the outside gate, telling him that soldiers planned to blow up the nearby Bureau of Science Building. "You have to leave," marines demanded.

Barahona protested, prompting the Japanese to raise their bayonets.

"No use of arguing," Maria Barahona pleaded with her husband.

Cayetano Barahona asked if the family might instead go south to Pasay.

"No," troops barked. "You must obey."

A similar scene played out in the Herran Street home of twenty-nine-year-old Domingo Giocado, who was asleep when enemy troops encircled his house. "Wake up," his wife told him. "Plenty of Japanese around this building."

"Why?" he asked.

"I don't know," she replied.

Marines banged on his door moments later. "Filipinos go to St.

Paul's," they told him. "Much better there at St. Paul's so that you will not be killed."

The Japanese not only went house to house, but they also rustled residents from bomb shelters. That's where marines found forty-four-year-old Clara Rice.

"Ma'am," Rice's servant told her, "they want us to get out."

She climbed out.

"Go," marines barked in English.

"Where?" she asked.

"Just go."

Other times troops grabbed residents off the street, including Dr. Luis Vazquez and his brother Daniel, both of whom wore medical uniforms and were en route to work at the Philippine General Hospital. The duo protested without success.

"You can't get through," the Japanese insisted.

Throughout Malate, individuals and families wandered onto the grounds of the Catholic college, prodded along by bayonet-armed sentries.

"*Kura*," the Japanese barked, ordering them to move along. "*Kura*."

Marines searched the new arrivals, stealing money, jewelry, and watches before ordering them to sit in the garden. The Japanese directed a few, including thirty-two-year-old Gurmuksing Kanusing of India, to pray before a shrine.

"You go to see Christ," the troops admonished.

As morning turned to afternoon, the college's garden filled up. A few Japanese troops, in a juvenile effort to show off before the detainees, bayoneted banana trees. One officer brandished his saber before twelve-year-old Salvador Sepulveda. "This," the officer bragged, "is the one I will use for the Americans."

Rain began to fall, prompting the Japanese to herd the soaked captives inside. "Don't bring your packages," the marines demanded. "Don't bring anything."

The detainees followed orders, including twenty-eight-year-old Josefina Punzalan, who eyed the fixed bayonets and the hostile faces of the Japanese. Fear washed over her. "We said some prayers," Punzalan recalled. "We said the rosary."

Captives may have traded the rain for a roof, but the conditions inside proved cramped at best as the marines ushered scores into a single room with no ventilation. The Japanese refused pleas to open a window, fearing shrapnel. Many of the babies cried, while several women passed out. "All the people," recalled Serafin Sepulveda, "were screaming and shouting because there was no air in the room."

"In case we are led to another room," Cayetano Barahona told his family members, "try to place yourself near the windows."

The Japanese finally relented and shuffled the detainees into the school's kitchen and then into the college's cavernous dining hall, a rectangular room that measured sixty-six feet long and twenty-nine feet wide. Several large windows offered views out toward Florida Street. Refugees sat in chairs and climbed atop the half-dozen tables. Others leaned against the walls, and still more plopped down on the floor.

"Stay near the windows," Cayetano Barahona reminded his family.

The numbers continued to swell until several hundred detainees crowded inside the dining hall, including dozens of children and pregnant women. Nationalities ranged from Filipinos and Chinese to Spaniards, Russians, and Indians.

Around five-thirty p.m., an officer accompanied by four troops strode to the center of the room. "Wait and be quiet," the officer said. "We are going to give you food."

The refugees struggled to understand.

"Who knows how to speak Japanese?" the officer asked.

Two Indians volunteered to translate. The officer explained that the Japanese planned to burn the houses in the neighborhood, but that those inside the dining hall would be safe. The troops held up candy and drinks, going so far as to open a couple cans and take a few swigs. The Japanese then dumped the food on the floor.

"Get the candies," the officer said.

The troops filed out of the dining hall as the starved detainees dove toward the center of room, a massive huddle of humanity tussling over candy.

Josefina Punzalan felt her earlier fears return. "Do not stand up, any of you," she ordered her family.

Others in the dining hall shared her suspicion. "Maybe it's poison," Luisa Barahona said.

Cayetano Barahona echoed his daughter. "Don't stand," he warned his wife and children.

Overhead hung several chandeliers draped in blackout paper, including one over the center of the room where people scurried for candy. A few of the refugees spied wires running from the fixtures through the transom and into the corridor.

"Miss," Luisa Barahona's maid said to her. "The lights are moving."

Luisa looked up just as the chandelier over the center of the room dropped and exploded. The other booby-trapped fixtures fell and detonated almost simultaneously. Witnesses would later recall the bright—almost blinding—flash of light that preceded the thunder of explosions. The first blast was deafening, followed by others that to damaged ears seemed muffled, even far away. At the Assumption Convent across the street, Sister Anna de Jesus saw the roof blow off, ultimately landing about three blocks away. "The college was burning," she said, "flames in all directions."

Inside the dining hall, the successive explosions shattered the windows and punched a gaping hole in the western wall of the room large enough for a truck to pass through it. On the ground where children and adults alike only seconds earlier had scrambled for candy lay dozens of shredded bodies, many missing arms and legs. Blood flowed on the floor, while dust and smoke clouded the air, choking the survivors. Few could see more than a few feet in front of them, including twenty-nine-year-old Pacifico Benito, who looked down. "I saw my right foot bleeding and also the calf of my left leg," he said. "I could not remember what happened then. I felt my head grow big. I did not even remember my wife." Others suffered similar trauma, including twenty-five-year-old Eutiquio Antipolo. "I vomited blood," he said, "because of the shock."

In those first few seconds after the initial explosion, disoriented and bloodied survivors struggled to sit up or stand. Cayetano Barahona, who had warned his family to keep away from the center of the room, found that even at that distance the explosion had blown off all his clothes except for his shoes and pants. Others felt themselves wearing the blood of strangers. Thirty-two-year-old Virginia Sepulveda woke up to discover the blast had burned her hair. Dazed and disoriented, the survivors stumbled toward the exits, some of them oblivious to the carnage around them. "I could hear children crying, men shouting and people asking for help," remembered thirty-year-old Marcelino Punzalan. "Because of this panic, people were stepping on the bodies of the men who could not stand." Sixty-one-year-old Theodore Blendo did just that as he held tight to his wife's hand. "We walked," he said, "over dead children and mothers with children."

"Let's run," people began to shout in Tagalog.

Outside in the corridor the Japanese tossed grenades through the transoms, which exploded and caused more chaos. Marines then stormed the dining hall and opened fire. Others attacked survivors with bayonets. Those who were able poured through the hole in the wall and ran toward Florida Street, where troops there greeted them with the rattle of machine guns and bayonets. Angeles Barahona staggered to her feet in time to witness a Japanese marine yank a baby boy from his mother's grasp and toss him into the air just as one might throw a ball. "Another Japanese with a fixed bayonet came in and just stuck the baby right in the middle of his stomach," Barahona later testified. "I saw the baby dangling with the bayonet still in his stomach." Her father witnessed it, too, noting how the impaled baby did not immediately die. "I could see," Cayetano Barahona later told investigators, "how the baby dangled moving his hands."

Twenty-five-year-old housekeeper Rosario Fernandez saw survivors jumping out of one of the windows. She followed, but as she prepared to climb up, a heavyset woman on the ground grabbed her dress. "She was pleading to me to save her."

"I cannot carry you," Fernandez said.

The Japanese opened fire behind her; Fernandez could wait no longer. "I tore that part of my dress she was holding and I jumped out."

Thirteen-year-old Winfred Colma clung to his mother as the marines continued the slaughter. "She was holding my hand at that time when the Japanese machine-gunned her," Colma recalled. "After that her hands lost hold of me."

"My child," Concepcion Colma cried. "My child."

A grenade exploded, killing Colma's nine-year-old sister Violeta, fourteen-year-old brother Camilo, and fifteen-year-old sister Illuminada. Colma stared at the remains of his oldest sister. "Her right leg," he said, "was cut off by the explosion."

Thirty-two-year-old Camilo Diego woke up in the corridor outside the dining room, where the explosion had hurled him along with his four-year-old daughter Lydia and thirteen-year-old daughter Alicia. Inside the dining hall lay the remains of his wife, Cocha, their eight-year-old daughter Rosalinda, and twelve-year-old son Romeo. Diego watched Japanese troops toss grenades and charge into the dining hall.

"Father," his eldest daughter Alicia cried, "I am burning."

Diego patted out the flames with his hands, but she, too, succumbed to her wounds, leaving him alone in the corridor with his badly injured four-year-old; they were the last two alive of a family of five. Diego pretended to be dead as troops chased survivors out into the garden and shot them, leaving bodies sprawled atop the compound walls. Marines hunted others who fled into the yards of neighboring homes, grenading a bomb shelter where dozens hid and massacring others in a maniacal fury.

"Kill me," one mother pleaded, "but don't get my baby."

The Japanese ignored her pleas.

A marine seized the newborn, tossed it into the air, and skewered the baby on a bayonet. The mother screamed before a marine mercifully shot her.

Terrified survivors swarmed the yard of Dr. Herminio Velarde, who heard the excitement and rushed downstairs, expecting to welcome American liberators. Instead the physician watched the Japanese scale his wall and begin murdering civilians. One marine seized a teenage girl who tried to hide behind a banana tree. On her knees, she begged for mercy. "He got his knife, held her by the long hair, raised the little girl and started to strike at the neck," Velarde recalled, "but he paused at this moment to get the rest of his comrades and they laughed and giggled, then finished the act. The girl fell dead on the spot."

Inside the college's dining hall, the slaughter subsided. Troops rifled through the valuables of the dead, the tally of which war crimes investigators later reported as 360. Camilo Diego watched the Japanese then douse the bodies with gasoline and set them on fire, turning the room into an inferno. Amid the chaos, Diego slipped away, carrying his wounded daughter Lydia to the college's chapel. He wrapped her tiny body in a cloak and placed her on the altar before God. "That child of mine," he later said, "died right at the altar."

○ ○ ○ ○

AT THE SAME TIME Japanese troops rounded up residents at St. Paul's College, others went through the posh district of Ermita extracting families from homes and bomb shelters and marching them to the Plaza Fergusson. By five p.m. the Japanese had corralled about two thousand men, women, and children of all nationalities. Troops separated the men and boys, herding them to the Manila Hotel. Others led the women to the Bay View Hotel. The nine-story hotel on Dewey Boulevard, which sat just across the street from the waterfront, was a short walk south from the Manila Hotel. The luxurious lodging had served as Jean MacArthur's first home in the Philippine capital before she resettled at the Manila Hotel with the general. Troops this Friday evening marched the captive women into the lobby, which was filled with guns and ammunition. Injured marines sprawled out on the floor along with the bodies of a few dead. The Japanese prodded the young women and girls upstairs to the third floor, depositing a group of about two dozen in Room 211 with a single window that faced Dewey Boulevard and Manila Bay.

"Matte, matte," the marines ordered. "Sit, sit."

The women did as ordered, surveying the room that measured about fourteen by fourteen feet. "It was bare but had some mattresses on the floor. There was no light, no water, no bathroom, but just a small closest in one corner," recalled twenty-five-year-old Lucy Tani, a stenographer. "It was very dark and hot in the room."

The marines closed the door, but the women could hear them on the other side. "We tried to make ourselves comfortable, but everybody was nervous and praying," said Esther Moras. "There was hardly room enough to lie down."

The women barely had time to sit when the door opened again at ten-thirty p.m. and several marines entered, carrying flashlights and candles to illuminate the faces of the women. "We pulled our hair down over our eyes and turned our faces to the wall," Moras said, "and crouched into the corner attempting to avoid their scrutiny."

The marines left, only to return again moments later. One of the marines grabbed fourteen-year-old Evangeline Garcia. Another marine with gold teeth—and armed with a pistol and bayonet—grabbed her fifteen-year-old sister, Priscilla.

"You go," he demanded.

Priscilla refused, prompting the marine to kick and slap the terrified teenager. "What else could I do but go?" she later said. "He had a gun."

The marines dragged the two teens by the arms to an empty room on the hotel's fifth floor that overlooked Alhambra Street. One marine took Priscilla into an adjoining room, while the other attacked Evangeline. "He pulled my dress up and noticed at that time that I was having my menstrual period," she said. "When he saw this, he kicked me in the buttocks, pulled his revolver from the holster and pointed it at me."

"Kill," the marine barked. "Kill."

To her surprise, however, the marine didn't shoot, but instead dragged her back downstairs to the room with the others. She searched out her older sister Esther, collapsing in her arms. "She was crying like her heart would break," Esther recalled. "I tried to soothe her and ask her what had happened."

"Nothing happened to me because I am menstruating."

"Where is Pris?" Esther pressed. "Where is Pris?"

"Oh," Evangeline cried out, "they are doing things to her, Esther! They are doing things to her!"

Esther pulled her younger sister close and held her. "Everybody in the room," she later said, "knew what was going to happen to us."

Evangeline's respite did not last. Three Japanese barged into the room minutes later and began searching out girls by candlelight. One grabbed Evangeline, prying her from her sister's grip. "I was not strong enough," Esther later said. "Everyone in the room was crying and trying to hide under mattresses and nets."

The marine dragged her back to one of the hotel's upper floors. She again protested that she was menstruating. He did not believe her, so he took a piece of cotton on the end of his finger, inserted it inside her, and pulled it out.

"I leave you here," he said.

Priscilla Garcia, meanwhile, was helpless at the hands of the marine who dragged her up to the fifth-floor room, empty except for a mattress on the floor and pillows. "He took me to the window and told me that there were many Americans on the other side of the river and that neither of us would get to see them as we would be dead shortly."

The marine grabbed her blouse and tore it off of her. He ordered her to remove her skirt, but Priscilla refused, prompting him to threaten her with his pistol. She relented. "He told me to lie down on the floor and seeing that I could not do anything, I obeyed him," she said. "I was crying and very much frightened." The marine slapped her and barked at her in Japanese. "He placed his pistol on one side of me and the bayonet on the other and then removed all of his clothes," Priscilla testified. "After removing his clothes he got on top of me." But the marine proved unable to force himself inside the fifteen-year-old. "He took his knife, cut me open, and then he finally succeeded."

When the marine finished, he ordered Priscilla to get dressed. She pulled on her clothes, which were soon soaked in blood, before he led her back downstairs.

"You will have Japanese baby," he told her, "not American baby."

Priscilla found her sister, Esther. "She was perspiring," Esther recalled. "Her hair was all messed up; her dress was turned around, and she was bleeding all over."

"Esther," Priscilla cried, "they did something to me! I want to die! I want to die!"

Pacita Tapia sat nearby and saw Priscilla return. "She seemed to be so dazed that she looked like she had seen something unspeakable," she said. "Her eyes just seemed to stare out into space and she acted as though she were in a trance."

Half an hour later, at about eleven-thirty p.m., another marine came for Priscilla.

"Get up," he ordered.

"No, no," she protested. "I am finished."

She was not.

The Japanese raped Priscilla two more times that night.

Her older sister's trauma was only beginning. Three marines grabbed Esther, dragging her to a room down the hall, where one of the troops ripped off her pants while the other two laughed. "I was struggling, kicking, and striking out with my arms, but the one who was holding me down slapped me all about my face with his bare hands," she recalled. "I became dazed from the slapping and when I finally got exhausted, I lay on the floor like a log." The marine then mounted her, finishing in less than three minutes. "He stood up, and one of the others got down on me. He had his trousers unbuttoned and his organ was out and he forced it into me," she said. "I tried to resist him but I knew all was over and I was lost." Esther covered her face. "When he finished, he got up and the third one attacked me in the same manner. "

The rape by three marines lasted less than twenty minutes. The troops then left her hurt and disoriented on the floor. "I crawled on my hands and knees, struggled to my feet, and somehow managed to get back to the room where I had been taken from the other girls," she recalled. "I just fell on the floor and sobbed."

But Esther's reprieve proved short-lived.

Another marine grabbed her moments later.

Then another.

And another.

Time and again marines dragged the twenty-four-year-old out and raped her, so many times, in fact, Esther lost count. "I was raped between 12 and 15 times during that night. I cannot remember exactly how many times," she later testified. "I was so tired and horror stricken that it became a living nightmare." At times, the Japanese grabbed her singly, other times in groups, often only moments after she had collapsed to the floor of the room from a preceding attack. "On each occasion I did my best to prevent the attacks, but as I grew weaker and weaker and my private parts became more inflamed and painful, I gave up all hope of living and expected them to continue until they killed me." Her horror finally ended about four a.m. "I was raped by a marine whose organ was so large that it tore my insides and I bled from my private parts," she said. "Only then did they leave me alone utterly exhausted, in great pain and bleeding badly."

The Garcia sisters were not the only ones marines attacked. Over the next several nights, troops returned to that room and others throughout the hotel again and again, often targeting the teenage girls and the young women, particular those with lighter skin. Similar abuse occurred at the nearby Alhambra and Miramar apartments. "They were like mad, wild dogs," recalled Paquita Coastas Garcia. Pacita Tapia echoed her. "They were not even human beings—they acted like animals."

Many of the girls fought back only to be dragged away by the hair, arms, and legs, kicking at the walls of hallways lit by candle and flashlight. In the upper-floor rooms where tourists once enjoyed the legendary sunsets over Manila Bay, troops slapped and punched women to force them to submit. Others wielded guns, bayonets, and swords. "I wanted to die," recalled Fanny Gadol. "Everything seemed lost."

The women returned to the downstairs rooms with bloodstained dresses. Others wore blank stares. A few shared their stories to warn the others.

"My God!" one woman howled. "The dirty bastards. They have raped me."

"I want to die," cried another. "I want to die."

"These Japanese beasts have evil designs on all of us."

Women cowered in fear in the darkened rooms, while the thunder of artillery at times shook the hotel, and a red glow rose from the dying city. "The girls were all crying, sobbing and screaming," recalled Vicky Gadol. "Everything was in confusion," added Margarita Salado Ghezzi. "Each time we heard the sound of the boots in the hallway, we would start praying."

Drunken marines with bloodshot eyes and red cheeks stumbled down the corridors, armed with whiskey bottles. Others opened the doors, their penises already dangling out of the front of their trousers. "We could smell the liquor from their breath when they came into the room," remembered Erlinda Querubin. "The Japanese were dirty, unshaven and smelled like pigs." A few of the troops attempted in a juvenile manner to demonstrate their bravado, including one inebriated marine who barged in and brandished his bayonet. "He showed the girls how sharp his bayonet was by cutting a big gash on the door," Ghezzi recalled. "He took that same bayonet and ripped open the skirt of a girl from the bottom hem up to her hips."

To deter attack, the women tried to make themselves appear unattractive, pulling their hair over their eyes and smearing their faces with mud from their shoes. One woman stuffed her mouth with rags to make her cheeks look swollen. "I took out my artificial teeth and told them I was very old," recalled Rebecca Habibi. Julia Ghezzi feigned illness. "I stuck my finger down my throat," she said, "pretending to be vomiting." Pilar Garcia Viuda de Castaner told a marine her daughter suffered from tuberculosis. "No good, no good, she is sick," Castaner protested. "She has blood in the mouth." Other women resorted to bribery, including twenty-four-year-old Carmencita Ballesteros, who offered a marine her wedding and engagement rings along with her husband's watches that she had in her purse. "When he saw the watches, which I was offering," she said, "he grabbed them and put them in his breast pocket and offered to pay me for them."

Conditions inside the once-luxurious hotel meanwhile deteriorated by the hour. Absent electricity, there were no elevators, lights, or fans to circulate the stifling air. Temperatures in packed rooms soared.

Without running water to flush filthy toilets or to even drink, sanitation proved another nightmare. The few pails of water the Japanese provided were hauled from the nearby swimming pool of the Army and Navy Club. Many captives suffered from a brutal thirst, which the Japanese cruelly exploited, tormenting women with buckets of undrinkable salt water and even water mixed with kerosene. Others resorted to choking down the stagnant green water from the toilet tanks. Querubin described the desperation in her room that followed the time the Japanese brought in a bucket of water. "We grabbed the pail and started to drink the water like animals," she recalled. "Some water was spilled on the floor and some of the girls licked up the water on the floor."

Over the women hung the uncertainty of who would be next. "Every night was the same—the Japanese would take girls all night long," said Luisa Guevara. "I lost track of what was going on—I thought we were all going to be killed." The captives tried to protect the young girls in each room, crowding them in the center surrounded by a wall of older women. The few prostitutes likewise offered themselves. Paquita Coastas Garcia recounted the agony of hearing her own daughter being abused down the hall, screaming for her. "I was so upset," Garcia said, "that I could not think straight." The days of terror turned Rebecca Habibi's hair white. "I could hear screams and cries and pleadings and prayers every night in our room and in the rooms around us," said Raymunda Guevara. "All of us," added Pilar Miranda, "were praying incessantly throughout the night." The fear wore down everyone. "It was so terrible," Querubin said, "none of us expected to escape with our lives."

The strain of the battle showed on the Japanese, who rather than rest spent each night drunk. A sense of doom had set in among the troops, who seemed to realize after only one week of fighting that MacArthur's larger forces, with superior firepower, would in the end win. It was only a matter of time, maybe even days. Some of the Japanese troops sought emotional comfort from the kidnapped women. One marine put Trinidad Llamas de Garcia and her daughter Teresita up in his private room, spoiling them with canned food and orange juice while professing his love for her daughter. "He told me," Garcia said, "that before he left to go forth and die he wished to have intercourse with my daughter as his last worldly pleasure." Other troops begged Filipino women to marry them, including Isabel Caro, imprisoned in the nearby Miramar Apartments. "He had a pistol," she said. "He told me that he was going to kill me if I did not marry him."

Finally on February 13, American artillery discovered the Bay View. Shells hurled from north of the river pummeled the once-grand hotel. Fires erupted that afternoon on the upper floors, while flames from the neighboring Coffee Pot restaurant reached through the windows of the ground-floor ballroom. "The place was in bedlam," Paquita Coastas Garcia said. "The women and children were screaming." The Japanese initially turned the bayonets on the women, refusing to let them leave, but later relented. The former captives flooded out the Bay View's main entrance onto Dewey Boulevard and into the middle of the battle. "The hotel was burning fiercely," said Trinidad Llamas de Garcia. "We barely escaped being burned to death."

○ ○ ○ ○

INSIDE SANTO TOMAS, many of the internees, who only days earlier had celebrated liberation, now struggled as the euphoria waned and the battle worsened. Not only did the barrage of artillery rattle nerves, but many wrestled with cramps and diarrhea sparked by the rich new foods. Adding to the misery, the lack of running water meant that the only means of flushing toilets was with buckets of water hauled in from outside. The challenge exacerbated the emotional strain for internees, including Roka. "No matter how hard I tried to chew my food slowly and tried to remain calm, nothing seemed to help. I wished desperately that I could have sat down to one meal without starting to bawl. I was beginning to dread mealtime," she wrote in her diary. "How I despised my weakness!"

Parents attempted to teach children, who had spent years eating little more than a watery gruel known simply as mush, about all the tasty new foods that awaited them. Bill Dunn captured one mother's efforts in a radio broadcast. "She tried," Dunn reported, "to describe cornflakes with fresh fruit and cream—ice cream, cakes and cookies—all the things which mean so much to the average child."

"Yes, mother," the boy replied, "but will I get plenty of mush?"

Six-year-old British internee Robert Colquhoun later recalled a similar experience when he spotted a strange elongated object. "It was a loaf of bread," he remembered. "The first I had ever seen." Colquhoun was enamored of a new product called Klim—milk spelled backwards—which was an evaporated dairy product. "I particularly loved eating the milk powder as it was," he wrote. "It stuck to the roof of the mouth, where it had to be dislodged with the tongue, and tasted delicious."

Despite that, he, too, struggled with the foods, landing in the camp hospital, where during lulls in the battle, American troops took time to visit the sick children. "One gave me a bullet case," Colquhoun recalled, "which I especially prized."

A February 11 report to MacArthur showed that the average internee gained more than one pound per day. Despite the improvements, MacArthur's staff noted with alarm that some internees had begun to sell Red Cross medical supplies to outside hospitals, pharmacies, and private practitioners. Furthermore, his staff was outraged by the sale of necessary goods at usurious prices before the camp's liberation. The report went so far as to list nineteen internees believed to have been the worst offenders. MacArthur put out a notice to all internees that he considered any such debts void. "I cannot bring myself to believe that there are American citizens who would so debase the cause of our country to seek to profit from the misfortune and tragedy that has been the common lot of all American and Allied civilians imprisoned by the enemy," MacArthur wrote. "I have directed the appropriate agencies of this headquarters to make thorough investigation thereof with a view of affording all protection within my power to any who have been wronged and bringing to justice all persons responsible therefor."

Internees meanwhile watched the haunting glow that hung over Manila as the city burned. "The nights are pretty hellish, with red sky and the sighing of shells over us," Robert Wygle wrote in his diary.

"Manila is still burning, but what there is left to burn after six months of fire is hard to imagine." Even for veteran journalists, who had seen some of the war's worst over the years, the destruction proved surreal. "There's something unreal about watching a great city go up in flames," Dunn wrote. "You know it's happening because it's right there before your eyes, but still there's a feeling that your senses must be playing you false."

Despite the struggles, fear, and uncertainty, a few internees found new happiness, including nurse Bertha Dworsky, who married John Henderson in the Main Building museum on the same day the Japanese artillery attack killed so many. "A few days ago we couldn't have thrown rice at them," Eunice Young wrote in her diary. "We needed it too badly to eat, but to-nite we could throw all we wanted."

○   ○   ○   ○

DURING THE JAPANESE OCCUPATION, Nick Reyes had run into a former employee of his from Far Eastern University. She had asked his thoughts on the war.

"The worst," he confided in her, "is yet to come."

That prophecy materialized on the afternoon of February 9 as the Reyes family now contemplated escape. Only the night before, Reyes and his daughter Lourdes had watched troops round up males and torch nearby homes.

One of the survivors of that horror visited the Reyeses' home that Friday, exhausted and with bloodshot eyes, asking for food. A former employee of Far Eastern University, he dropped to his knees and pleaded with Reyes to flee.

"It is your turn to be attacked tonight," the employee said. "You have grilled windows. How will you jump out when they burn your house?"

For Reyes, escape proved a painful proposition. He had built his elegant three-story mansion only a few years before the war with the help of one of Manila's finest architects, Pablo Antonio. The home featured a library, grand staircase, gardens, and stables, not to mention a matching playhouse. Like so many others, the war had cost Reyes dearly. He had shuttered the university he had labored so hard to build and sold his home in Baguio. In the final weeks of the occupation, the

Japanese, in a failed effort to steal his beloved Arabian horse, had flogged Kublai Khan so mercilessly that Reyes had to euthanize the animal. "There was a shocked silence in our house for days," Lourdes recalled. "Somehow, Kublai Khan's loss was like a loss of innocence— our rudest awakening to the cruelty of our oppressors and the inhumanity of men."

Only recently had the Reyes family, whose home a Japanese mining company had commandeered for much of the war, been allowed to finally return. Now the family once again faced the possibility of evacuation and loss.

The bigger challenge confronting Reyes and thousands of others across Manila was where to go. The Japanese controlled the southern part of the capital, much of which troops had begun to burn. Iwabuchi's marines had mined the streets and now sniped at civilians from pillboxes. Few even knew in what direction to flee to find the American lines. Beyond that, Reyes family members ranged from small children to the elderly; many of them wouldn't be able to make a miles-long trek across a war-torn city.

The only nearby place to seek refuge was De La Salle College, but Reyes found the gates locked. Rather than flee, he decided the family would instead hide in the three large bomb shelters in the garden, each cavernous and with camouflaged entrances. Enemy troops finding the house empty would assume the residents had fled and likely not search the gardens. "Safe in there," Lourdes recalled, "we could even survive the burning of our houses." Reyes instructed members of his extended family who lived nearby to return home and pack enough food and clothing to endure a long siege. Reyes likewise told his wife and children to pack knapsacks with food and to dress in dark clothes. He and his son Luis slipped on khaki trousers and long-sleeved shirts. His wife Amparing Reyes wore a dark dress, while daughter Lourdes put on a navy blue one with stripes. The couple's youngest daughter Teresita wore a dark blue dress with white polka dots. Reyes then asked each family member to bring him any prized valuables to lock in the safe. Lourdes handed over her stamp collection and the watch her father had given her for graduation.

The family prepared to sit down at four p.m. for an early supper before heading to the garden shelter. The table was set, knapsacks readied, and shoes laced tight. Upstairs Amparing Reyes finished up as the others gravitated toward the table.

Outside a rifle shot shattered the late afternoon, followed by the howl of a dog and then the stomp of boots. The family's cook Delfin charged into the room.

"They're here, señorito," he cried. "They're here!"

Amparing Reyes had seen the Japanese troops shoot the dog from her balcony above and charged down the stairs to the living room, where her husband gathered the family around him. Lourdes scanned the faces. Along with her father and mother, she spotted her sister Teresita, brother Luis, and the orphaned Milagros. Lourdes counted her uncle Maximo, aunt Purita, and her six-year-old cousin Edgar along with the family's laundress Vicenta, her son Atanacio, and the servants Paula and Liling. The footfalls of the troops approached. The Japanese began to pound on the door.

"Be brave," Nick Reyes told his family.

Japanese marines filed one after the other into the home and fanned out in the room. Lourdes counted ten, each armed with a rifle and fixed bayonet.

"We're only civilians," her mother pleaded.

One of the troops banged on the family's piano with the butt of his rifle. "The strange sounds," Lourdes recalled, "eerily rang like a death knell."

Marines seized Luis, Milagros, Edgar, and Atanacio, pulling the four children toward the garden. Purita charged after them, clutching a can of biscuits for her only son. "Candy," she pleaded. "Candy for the baby."

One of the troops hit her with his rifle.

The Japanese corralled the rest of the family. Marines grabbed Lourdes and Teresita, marching the siblings to the third-floor tower. Lourdes held tight to her little sister's hand. "Side by side," she recalled, "our little fingers linked."

"Pray," Lourdes whispered to Teresita.

One of the marines led Lourdes back downstairs to her bedroom, searching for a rope to bind them. He shredded a bedsheet and then blindfolded her and tied her hands. Lourdes spread her hands so that the binds were not too tight. The marine stepped outside of the room, presumably to take the bindings to the other troops. Lourdes seized the moment to slip her ties and lock the door. The marine returned and tried the door. He raised his rifle and fired, but the dense Philippine Narra wood held. Lourdes retreated into the bathroom and locked the inner door. She climbed behind a dresser—her rosary held tight in her fist—and recited the popular Catholic prayer, Memorare: "Remember, O most gracious Virgin Mary, that never was it known that anyone who fled to thy protection, implored they help, or sought thy intercession, was left unaided."

Lourdes finished her prayer but remained hidden as the minutes ticked past. Only when she smelled smoke did she climb out from behind the dresser and unlock the door. The Japanese had doused the ground floor of her home with gasoline, setting it on fire. The smoke rose like a specter up the grand staircase as she set out to find her family. "No words," she recalled, "can describe the horror I found in each room."

Lourdes first encountered her mother. The Japanese had bound and bayoneted her along with her aunt Purita, Vincenta, and maids Paula and Liling. Of the five, Lourdes discovered, the maids were dead. She hurried to untie her mother.

"Go look for your father," her mother told her.

Lourdes set off again through the smoke-filled home. In another room she found her father badly wounded and her uncle Maximo dead.

"Look for Ching," Reyes pleaded with his daughter, using the nickname for Lourdes' sister Teresita.

Lourdes placed her rosary in her father's hand and started for the stairs to the tower, the room where she and her father days earlier had watched the faraway battle, a storm on the horizon that had finally found them. Lourdes reached the top of the stairs. Teresita was unresponsive. She tried to shake her awake but realized she was gone. "In her white dress," Lourdes recalled, "she looked like a sleeping angel."

She descended the stairs to find her mother giving water to her father. The heat from the flames rose up through the home. Nick Reyes instructed them all to climb to the tower. Lourdes helped her father, while her mother and aunt crawled up the stairs. The flames and smoke increased. On the third-floor Purita pleaded with Amparing to let Lourdes escape and then begged the teenager to care for her son Edgar.

Nick Reyes slipped into unconsciousness. The others decided to flee. Reyes and Purita crawled down to the second floor, while Lourdes struggled to lift her father. The teenager heard her mother down below beg the family's laundress, Vicenta. "Help her! Help her bring señorito down!" she pleaded. "Haven't I always been good to you?"

Lourdes wrapped her father's left arm around her shoulder and slipped her right arm around his waist and lifted. "His lifeless body weighed heavily on me," she later wrote. "Dusk had set in. Smoke from the fire in the lower floors reached the entry to the top floor, making my steps precarious in the dark stairway."

The teen collapsed halfway down the stairs. Vicenta suddenly appeared, and the duo struggled together to lift Reyes before the laundress finally quit.

"It's useless—useless!" Vicenta cried. "He is dead! He is dead!"

The fires closed in on them. Overcome by shock and fear, Vicenta fled in search of her son Atanacio. Lourdes remained on the steps alongside her father's lifeless body. She could not lift him alone, but if she stayed on the stairs, she was guaranteed to die alongside him. Lourdes had no choice but to abandon him.

Flames feasted on the grand staircase, forcing Lourdes to follow her aunt and mother and escape down the circular back stairs. She reached the backyard and climbed over a wall behind the family's stables into a neighboring field. She found her mother, aunt, and grandmother, the latter of whom had returned to her own home next door before the massacre occurred. Lourdes joined about a dozen others under a makeshift lean-to made from salvaged metal sheets. Amparing lay on the ground next to her mother, who in shock sat in silence atop a stool. "Night came," Lourdes recalled. "The burst of artilleries and the rain of rockets intensified."

Vicenta had found her eight-year-old son Atanacio in the living room of the burning home, bayoneted along with Chito, Edgar, and Milagros. The only one still alive was Milagros. Vicenta dragged Milagros outside to the playhouse where the Reyes children had enjoyed untold evenings, watching the stars come out each night. Together the two hid there in the miniature home with its red Spanish roof tiles as the flames roared in the night sky and the embers and ash drifted down on the yard like snowflakes.

Over in the field behind the family home, Amparing fell into despair, unable to grasp why her own mother sat in silence on the stool. "Is Nanay mad at me?" she pleaded. "Why is she not talking to me? Please talk to me, Nanay."

Lourdes listened to her mother cry, while the others sat in silence, the only interruption being the thunder of artillery. "Night had descended, but one would not have been able to tell," she wrote. "The sun had been banished for days by the heavy pall of smoke that hung over the city." Bright flashes of gunfire pierced the acrid fog; so, too, did the flames that had at last engulfed the third-floor tower, where she had spent countless hours with her beloved father. The grand home that for so long had been the epicenter of her family and of her childhood had been transformed into a funeral pyre that now incinerated the bodies of her brother, sister, father, uncle, and cousin.

On the ground nearby, her mother continued to bleed, her life slowly ebbing away. "Don't leave me, please don't leave me," Lourdes repeatedly whispered in her mother's ear. "I love you very much."

"Stay with your aunt, Angelica," her mother urged her. "She has many good things to teach you."

Lourdes watched her mother grow delirious, murmuring as her mind wandered. At one point, Lourdes sensed that her mother dreamed of her brother.

"Stop it, you naughty boy," she said playfully, "stop it!"

Another time Amparing cried out to her eldest son, who had joined the army air force and was at that moment in a German prisoner of war camp.

"Avenge us," she hollered. "Avenge us!"

Throughout it all, Lourdes kept watch over her grandmother, occasionally silhouetted by the shellfire. "She was not cringing, nor covering her ears at all from the maddening sounds," Lourdes recalled. "I realized that she was shell-shocked."

Amparing calmed down and appeared at peace with those who had slaughtered her family. "It is all right. It is all right," she said. "I forgive them."

Despite her drift into incoherence, Amparing at times pulled her daughter close when the shells whistled overhead. "Sagrado Corazon de Jesus—"

Amparing interrupted her prayer to pull Lourdes down, wrapping her arm around her just as an incoming artillery shell tore into the shelter. The explosion ripped her grandmother in half and killed her mother and more than a dozen others.

In a crater filled with the dead, Lourdes flirted with consciousness. Hands reached into the dirt, grabbed Lourdes, and lifted her out, like a body from the grave.

"She's alive," someone shouted.

○ ○ ○ ○

TO CAPTURE SOUTHERN MANILA, war planners carved up the city. The Thirty-Seventh Infantry would clear the area from the Pasig River south to Harrison Boulevard and then turn west and drive toward Manila Bay, seizing the districts of Pandacan, Paco, Ermita, the Walled City, and the port. The First Cavalry, having secured the Novaliches Dam, the Balara Water Filters, and San Juan Reservoir, would cross the Pasig near the Philippine Racing Club and enter Manila from the east. Bound on the north by Harrison Boulevard and to the south by Libertad Avenue and Route 57, the cavalrymen would charge toward the waterfront paralleling the infantry and capture the districts of Santa Ana, Pasay, and Malate. The Eleventh Airborne would race up from the south, closing the door on any exit.

The bloody battles for the Paco Railroad Station and Provisor Island had proven an initiation for the infantry in the challenges of urban warfare, demonstrating that with a little creativity, the enemy could turn a benign power plant or rail station into a death trap. The ferocity of the fight hammered home a new realization for commanders, one spelled out in the 148th Infantry's report. "It was now evident that we had reached the point where the enemy elected to make his final stand," the report concluded. "From now on until the final day of the battle for Manila we were to encounter an unbroken succession of heavily fortified buildings, mutually supporting pillboxes at all street intersections, thickly sown mine fields, mined buildings, an abundance of all types of weapons, innumerable snipers, and an enemy who elected death over surrender."

Major Henne understood that reality firsthand, as the infantry's pace south of the river slowed to a crawl. Iwabuchi's Central Force had constructed pairs of supporting pillboxes at most intersections en route to the bay. Each one would have to be eradicated before soldiers could advance to the next block. A headlong approach, Henne realized, proved perilous, forcing his men into the enemy's line of fire. Troops could zigzag north or south to work around a pillbox, but often that would lead them into the crosshairs of Japanese marines holed up in the adjacent block's fortifications. The only way to advance was through the buildings, a fearsome experience as troops had to enter darkened stores, homes, and offices expecting, at every turn, to encounter the enemy.

Once inside, troops cleared every floor of the building and then blew a hole through the western wall and charged into the neighboring property.

Then the next.

And the next.

Each building or backyard taken proved a milestone in the long slog down a block. "Surely they heard us coming, blasting our way through walls of buildings," marveled Sgt. Mike Campbell, "but they stayed put in their pillboxes."

Infantrymen closed in and finally charged the rear of each pillbox, hurling satchel bombs and grenades at the Japanese marines. "Gains were measured," Henne noted, "more by street intersections cleared rather than city blocks secured."

The slow progress frustrated American commanders, including General Griswold of XIV Corps. "The fighting in South Manila is very bitter," he wrote in his diary on February 10. "Japs organize each big reinforced concrete building into a fortress, and fight to the death in the basement, on each floor, and even to the roof. This is rough. I'm getting a lot of unavoidable casualties." General Beightler of the Thirty-Seventh Infantry Division agreed. "The fighting," he wrote in his report, "was building by building, floor by floor and room by room."

CHAPTER 13

*"The Japanese caught some of the women, poured
gasoline on their heads and set their hair on fire."*

—Esperanza Esteban,
testimony, September 24, 1945

Francisco Lopez hid in the crawlspace underneath the German Club at the corner of San Luis and San Marcelino streets in the district of Ermita. The slender thirty-five-year-old film executive, who worked as the Philippines representative for Metro-Goldwyn-Mayer Pictures, joined more than five hundred of his neighbors and family members seeking refuge from the storm of American artillery and prowling Japanese troops. The morning of February 10 marked three days since Lopez had traded in the comfort of his nearby home for a dusty spot beneath the social club, where only four feet separated the ground from the overhead beams. Amid the darkness, no one dared light a match. "We had to stoop down," Lopez recalled. "We couldn't stand up."

Japanese troops had harassed anyone who dared venture out, even swiping Lopez's watch when he left once in search of food. Most refugees found it safer to stay underneath. Truckloads of additional troops rolled up around ten a.m. that morning and surrounded the club, forbidding anyone from climbing out of the crawlspace openings. Up above marines piled all the rugs, chairs, and tables in the center of the club, drenching them with gasoline and setting them on fire. The smell of fuel followed by smoke wafted into the crawlspace. Troops did the same outside, gathering the suitcases, parcels of canned food, and bundles of clothes refugees had brought with them, heaping them in front of the crawlspace openings before soaking them with gasoline. "You can just imagine the commotion and fright it caused," Lopez later testified. "Women and the kids lost their heads and started screaming."

"*Tomodachi!*" people yelled. "Friends! We are friends!"

German Club member Martin Ohaus, who had invited many of the neighbors to seek shelter at the facility, went out to reason with the Japanese officer. Ohaus explained that it was a social club filled with civilians who had taken refuge. Many of them were Germans, he added, allies of the Japanese. But the officer shoved him back and kicked him. Some of the women who were still nursing infants then volunteered to go beg for mercy. Lopez and others watched as several of the mothers with infant boys and girls cradled in their arms approached the Japanese and climbed down on their knees. To Lopez's horror, the marines plunged their steel bayonets into the infants, skewering their tiny bodies like kebabs before hurling them to the ground. Troops then seized some of women by the hair, tore off their clothes, and began to rape them.

"*Tomodachi!*" people screamed. "*Tomodachi!*"

The Japanese repeatedly raped one young girl, whom Lopez estimated to be no older than thirteen. One marine would climb off as another mounted her. No fewer than twenty soldiers attacked the girl. Lopez struggled to comprehend what he was seeing. Moments earlier he and his family had simply sought shelter at the club; now Japanese troops had set fire to the building and begun an orgy of rape against the women. The violence only escalated. The marines sliced off the young girl's breasts. One of the Japanese then scooped up a severed organ in his hand and placed it on his chest as though it were his own. "The others," Lopez recalled, "laughed!"

The film executive witnessed Japanese troops rape several other women. When the marines finished, two of the women appeared to be dead, but Lopez saw the chest of the third victim still rise and fall as she breathed. Troops drenched all three of the women's hair in gasoline and set them ablaze. Amid the chaos, Lopez spotted twenty-eight-year-old Bernardino Calub, one of his servants. Calub leaped through the flames, clutching his two-year-old son and namesake tight in his arms. The Japanese chased him down with a bamboo spear and stabbed the toddler. Calub turned on the murderer, beating him in the seconds before other troops pounced. The Japanese dragged Calub over to the ruins of the Lopez home and bound him to one of the concrete pillars of the garage. Troops tore down Calub's pants and sliced off his genitals. "I saw the Japanese," Lopez later told war crimes investigators, "stuff his severed penis in his mouth."

The fire inside the German Club raged, devouring the tables and rattan chairs. Acrid smoke flooded the crawlspace. Lopez could hear the crackle of the flames as the hardwood floors overhead began to burn. His sixty-five-year-old mother reached out and embraced him along with his brothers and sisters. "We might as well stay in here," she told them, "because you see what they are doing outside."

Refugees choked on the smoke, and the temperature soared.

"Don't go out, because it will be worse," Carmen Lopez continued to assure her children. "If we have to die, let's die all together in here."

Francisco Lopez debated what to do. The Japanese would not rape him; the worst he could expect was to be shot or possibly bayoneted, both of which promised a more merciful death than the one he faced if he remained under the German Club. Lopez decided to try to escape. "I prefer to go out and get it over with once and for all," he told his mother. "I don't have the courage to be roasted alive in here."

"If you decide that, go ahead," she finally told him. "You have my blessing."

Lopez wriggled out of the crawlspace and hurdled the burning barricade. His younger brother Jose followed, along with a neighbor, Joaquin Navarro, Jr. Troops sighted the trio and fired. Lopez glanced back to see a bullet rip through his brother's chest. His neighbor fell next, a round through his temple. Lopez kept running, even after his trousers caught fire. The Japanese continued to shoot. A bullet tore into his left foot, and he collapsed. "I half-way fainted from the pain and the shock, all the time thinking that that was a bad dream, that it was a nightmare, that I had to wake from it."

The wounded film executive lay flat, pretending to be dead as the conflagration swirled around him. Women continued to flood out of the crawlspace, only to be grabbed and raped by the Japanese. Lopez listened to the victims call on the saints in heaven for help and even beg the pilot of an American plane that buzzed overhead to bomb the club and end their misery. Amid the carnage, Lopez spotted his forty-year-old sister Maria, who tried to escape over the piles of blazing suitcases only to catch fire and burn to death. He likewise witnessed Japanese troops rape his twenty-eight-year-old sister-in-law Julia Lopez before slicing off her breasts, soaking her hair with gasoline, and setting her alight. Just steps away another woman Lopez knew fought off her attacker until a second marine came up behind her and swung his sword. "She fell to the ground practically decapitated," Lopez recalled. "Her head was attached by only a very little flesh." Even in death, the attack on the woman was not over. "This fellow right away jumped on her," Lopez later testified. "He raped her, although she was already dead."

Clouds of dark smoke climbed skyward as fire fully engulfed the German Club, turning the once-grand social hall into a death chamber for more than five hundred men, women, and children. The flames devoured the club's walls, reducing the clocks and artwork to ash. So, too, went the ceilings and the hardwood floors where business executives once dined and couples danced. The burning timbers collapsed atop those who remained underneath the club. On the ground outside, bathed by the heat, Lopez had no choice but to feign being dead, even as the remainder of his family broiled just steps away from him. "I heard my brother and my mother," he said, "screaming inside."

○ ○ ○ ○

TWENTY-ONE-YEAR-OLD HELENA RODRIGUEZ likewise heard the cries as she huddled inside the German Club's bomb shelter with her mother and two of her four brothers. The Rodriguez family had lived just a few blocks away, at 278 Zobel Street, until the Japanese began to torch the neighborhood. The family had sought shelter with friends who lived across the street from the club, but an artillery shell tore through the dining room ceiling, killing four people. "I survived,"

Rodriguez recalled, "by changing places with a housemaid a minute before a huge piece of shrapnel hit her in the chest."

The survivors had moved across the street to the club where Helena's brothers Alvaro and Alfonso slithered under the crawlspace. Helena, her mother Remedios, and brothers Vicente and Augusto climbed down into the U-shaped trench. In recent days, as the Japanese continued to burn surrounding houses, other neighbors joined them in the dugout, pushing the total up to around fifty men, women, and children.

Rodriguez heard the screams of the victims outside, but before she could grasp the slaughter, Japanese troops tossed several grenades into the shelter's entrance. Seconds later the bombs exploded, toppling two refugees. Smoke flooded the dark shelter, and people began to cough. "It was almost impossible to breathe," Rodriguez recalled. "Everybody was crying; children were running about in confusion."

"Let the children go out!" a few people hollered, hoping that the Japanese troops would show mercy on the young.

Rodriguez's eleven-year-old brother Augusto joined four others who climbed out of the shelter. Japanese marines didn't hesitate to squeeze the triggers. Forty-seven-year-old Remedios Rodriguez burst into tears. "Your youngest brother," she cried to Helena. "He is out there on the ground. He is dead. They have shot him."

Troops followed the gunfire with more grenades. Each explosion filled the air with smoke and dust, choking the refugees. Remedios Rodriguez could tolerate it no longer. She rose to leave, planning to plead with the troops. Helena saw the Japanese toss another grenade. Her mother recoiled but did not have time to dive for shelter. The bomb exploded, shredding her mother with a clap of thunder. "I just sat there and stared at her," Rodriguez testified. "I couldn't believe what I saw."

Rodriguez retreated deep into the shelter, fanning herself with a piece of cardboard. The explosions stopped. A marine climbed down into the dugout, holding up a candle. He asked if the survivors had any firearms. "We told him that we had nothing, that we were civilians," Rodriguez recalled. "You should have heard the children pleading before the Japanese, asking to have mercy on them." The marine left, and the shelter fell quiet. A moment later refugees heard a crackling noise, like the burning of grass. Rodriguez crawled toward one of the entrances and peered outside. The Japanese had poured gasoline and set fire to the entrances, trapping the refugees. "Everybody began screaming," Rodriguez said. "My sudden impulse was to jump out."

Rodriguez darted through the wall of flames, burning her arms, legs, and face and singeing her hair. She stumbled into a nearby foxhole, which was covered by a piece of corrugated metal with a mattress on top. Others joined her, including her friend, twenty-one-year-old Inez Streegan, forty-year-old Emil Streegan, and thirty-two-year-old French national Rene Levy. The foursome pretended to be dead as Japanese troops hunted the grounds for any escapees. "After a while we heard screams," Rodriguez recalled. "It was people who remained in the shelter who were being burned alive."

One of those, she realized, was her brother, Vicente.

The Japanese discovered the survivors. Levy panicked and sprang to his feet. He ran, only to be brought down by a bullet. Rodriguez and Inez Streegan remained still, but Emil Streegan moved. The marines reached down, grabbed him, and yanked him up. One of the marines plunged the bayonet into his chest, pulled it out, and drove it in again. Face down in the dirt, Rodriguez listened to the butchery. "I heard the slashes he received," she recalled. "The man kept screaming and asking for help."

The Japanese dropped Streegan back into the foxhole, who, still alive, began to moan. His warm blood soaked Rodriguez. She felt certain she would be next and began to pray. To her surprise, the Japanese walked away, but the reprieve proved temporary. The marines returned with gasoline, pouring it atop the mattress and metal sheet that covered the foxhole. The fuel trickled inside and doused Rodriguez. The troops set the mattress ablaze and left, no doubt convinced Rodriguez and her companions would burn to death, like the hundreds of others crowded under the club. The Japanese had blown up her mother with a grenade, gunned down her baby brother, and burned to death her three other brothers, but Helena Rodriguez would survive even as the flames roared just inches overhead and that heat became unbearable. "It felt like being inside an overheated oven," she recalled. "It was a miracle that our clothes didn't catch fire."

○ ○ ○ ○

SATURDAY AFTERNOON FADED to dusk and then evening, while Francisco Lopez pretended to be dead. The inferno had finally brought down the roof of the club, leaving only the concrete bones of the building that had once been the epicenter of German life in Manila. The screams of Lopez's mother, brother, and the hundreds of others had died out; so, too, had the howls of the violated women on the grounds around him.

Under cover of darkness, Lopez crawled to an air raid shelter in the yard of a neighboring home. That evening nine other men and women—all burned, bayoneted, or shot—joined him in the dugout that could comfortably hold half that many.

"Look out for my wound, my burns," someone would cry when bumped.

The group cowered inside for almost three days. No one dared talk or even cough as Japanese troops patrolled outside, at times even walking atop the shelter. On the second day one of the refugees, armed with a piece of iron, dug a well in the earthen floor of the shelter. "That muddy water," Lopez said, "we drank to keep alive."

A shell ripped a hole in the shelter on February 13, revealing the occupants hidden inside. The refugees had no choice but escape. Lopez's blasted foot had ballooned, making it impossible for him to walk. Sixty-year-old Joaquin Navarro, whose son and namesake had followed Lopez as he charged out of the crawlspace, grabbed one of the film executive's arms. Navarro's daughter-in-law Adela held the other.

Japanese troops occupied many of the nearby buildings, giving the survivors few options. The haggard bunch limped toward the nearby St. Teresa Academy. As the refugees approached the main entrance, which was blocked with sandbags, several Japanese troops popped up. The marines opened fire. Bullets blasted seven of the ten refugees, killing them. Navarro and his daughter-in-law, neither of whom were hit, instinctively dropped to the ground, pulling Lopez down with them.

"This is worse than death itself," one of them muttered.

Lopez listened as his two surviving companions debated what to do.

"Let's kneel before them and just plead for mercy," one suggested.

"If they kill us, that is better than living this way," added the other. "Anyway, we die of hunger or thirst, because it looks as if the Americans will take a little longer than we expected for them to cross the river and rescue us."

"If both of you are of that opinion," Lopez interjected, "let's do it."

Adela volunteered to untie the handkerchief that covered her burned left hand and wave it overhead to test whether the Japanese troops would fire. "As soon as I count to three," she continued, "the three of us get up and walk towards them."

"All right," Lopez agreed.

Adela untied her handkerchief and thrust it into the air. The Japanese did not fire. She then counted—one, two, three—and still no shots. Adela and her father-in-law climbed to their feet and then leaned down to lift Lopez. The Japanese rifles roared. Both collapsed onto the ground beside Lopez. "There was blood spurting out of the neck of the girl," he said. "The old man Navarro had been hit right in the kidneys."

The two begged for water, but there was nothing Lopez could do. He could not walk, much less run. Minutes later Adela died. Lopez lay in agony, debating whether it would be best to pull himself to his feet and let the Japanese finish him. "I don't want to live," he confessed to Navarro. "I have lost all my family, all my possessions, my home, everything I had in the world. What is the use of living without anybody?"

Navarro, too, had lost everything. The Japanese had slaughtered his wife Angela, his son Joaquin, and his three daughters, Pilar, Natividad, and Concepcion. The bullet that now festered inside Navarro's gut would soon end his misery.

"Don't do that," Navarro pleaded.

Lopez listened.

"When for the third time they haven't hit you," Navarro continued, "there must be a mission for you in this world—"

Before Navarro finished his sentence, Lopez knew he was right.

"—to tell the truth of what they have done to us."

○ ○ ○ ○

ONE HUNDRED AND FIFTY miles north of Manila, General Yamashita holed up in his headquarters near Baguio, far removed from the carnage in Manila. Since his withdrawal from the capital in late December, the Tiger of Malaya's mountain stronghold had come under increasing attacks from American bombers, including one raid that destroyed his residence, forcing him to relocate into a bunker.

The general would later claim that poor communications had left him ignorant of the battle for the Philippine capital, though his headquarters remained in wireless contact with Manila throughout much of the fight and General Yokoyama forwarded him daily reports with updates from Iwabuchi. Furthermore, Vice Adm. Denshichi Okochi, the supreme naval officer in the Philippines who was in Baguio with the general, would later tell American investigators that he and Yamashita received frequent reports on the battle's progress, from the ferocity of artillery to the dwindling ammunition. "With the information I received," Okochi testified, "I was able to picture the desperate situation of the Japanese units in Manila when the U.S. forces besieged the city."

But Yamashita's orders on the eve of the battle had been clear.

The general expected his troops to do everything possible to delay American forces, even if that meant holding them up for just half a day. The block-by-block fight showed Iwabuchi's forces were doing precisely as ordered.

Meanwhile General MacArthur remained about sixty miles north of Manila in San Miguel, where he had set up his headquarters on January 25 on a sprawling sugar plantation known as Hacienda Lusita. The peaceful, rural setting stood in sharp contrast to the violence and destruction in Manila and likewise proved far more luxurious and comfortable than what his adversary endured in Baguio. The general established his headquarters in a large building encircled by tropical cottages—each adorned with screen porches and nice furnishings— that housed President Sergio Osmeña, MacArthur, and many of his senior aides, some of whom, like General Fellers, made frequent trips into the city. American author John Dos Passos, who had come to the Philippines as a war correspondent, described the setting in his diary. "There are gardens with brick walls," he observed. "There's a swimming pool where, whenever the water is not full of tanned Americans diving and splashing and whooping, beautiful red and blue kingfishers skim saucily over the surface."

Since his visit to Bilibid and Santo Tomas on February 7, MacArthur had not returned to the Philippine capital. In fact, according to his diary, he would not set foot inside Manila again for twelve days. Throughout the twenty-nine-day fight for the city, MacArthur would visit the city only five times, and most of those occasions came long after the worst of the atrocities occurred and the heaviest fighting had ended. Like Yamashita, he left the fighting in the city to his subordinates, while his own diary records that much of the time he was engaged in "routine conferences."

MacArthur could not escape the fact that this was a battle he alone had set in motion back on Oahu, when he had lobbied against the navy's plan to take Formosa, berating Roosevelt over the need to return to Manila until his commander in chief needed aspirin. The general had sloshed ashore at Lingayen Gulf, convinced that the battle for the Philippines had already been won on Leyte. He had driven toward the capital, disregarding guerrilla reports on the city's fortification, while choosing instead to plan a liberation parade. He had then stood on the balcony at Malacañan Palace overlooking the Pasig River and declared that a single platoon could capture southern Manila.

In each case, he had been wrong.

Woefully so.

There was little doubt that in the end America would win. MacArthur had more soldiers and superior firepower. The question that now framed the battle was how much would victory cost? How many civilians would die by Japanese blade and American shellfire? How much of the Pearl of the Orient would be destroyed?

○ ○ ○ ○

AT THE SAME TIME as the German Club massacre, other troops went door to door through the district of Paco, just south of the Pasig River, rounding up hundreds of men. The Japanese did not target specific males but rather cast a large net, just as they had done days earlier in Intramuros. No one in this working-class neighborhood adjacent to the posh district of Ermita was spared. The Japanese grabbed men in their fifties and sixties alongside boys as young as fourteen. Victims likewise ranged from butchers and barbers to tinsmiths, kitchen helpers, and even priests.

One of those caught up in the sweep was Dr. Angel Enriquez, a thirty-five-year-old dentist. He was asleep inside his Dart Street home when marines banged on his door at two p.m., rousing the exhausted Enriquez, demanding he accompany them.

"Don't," his twenty-six-year-old wife Eva pleaded.

"No, no," the Japanese marine assured her. "He will come back at six o'clock."

Enriquez tried to comfort his wife. "Don't worry," he told her. "I will come back."

She watched as they marched her husband out the door.

Similar scenes played out in neighboring houses on that afternoon of February 10. A Japanese officer barged into the home of twenty-nine-year-old Francisco Aniban at 1188 Dart Street, climbing the stairs to find the family gathered. Troops seized Aniban and his sixty-five-year-old father-in-law Eugenio Balleta. "Forced labor," the officer announced. "You are going to work and I will give you sugar and rice."

In a city where starving families ate dogs and even rats to survive, the promise of food proved an intoxicating lure, one the Japanese used to entice dozens of others, including thirty-two-year-old Jesus Benitez. "You come along with us and work," troops assured the Dart Street resident, "and we will give you plenty of food."

Marines did not discriminate, grabbing Chinese immigrants alongside Filipinos, the healthy as well as the infirm. That was the case when several troops pounded on the door of forty-two-year-old Dr. Ambrosio Capili, who was bedridden.

"May I see him?" one of the marines asked his wife.

Celestina Capili showed the Japanese inside the home where one of the marines felt her husband's pulse. "He can work, he is not very sick," he declared. "Two hours only, then he will be back with plenty of food and medicine."

Ambrosio Capili refused to stand, insisting he was ill. One of the officers unsheathed his saber. "I looked at the face of the Japanese and saw him very serious," Celestina Capili remembered. "I called the attention of my husband."

The doctor relented.

"When he was at the door I gave him his hat," she said, watching as the Japanese led him up the street. "That was the last time I ever saw my husband."

In one of the more prophetic encounters, the Japanese grabbed Ricardo Esquerra, demanding that the owner of Victoria Funeral Home accompany them.

"Why?" the forty-one-year-old asked.

"You are an undertaker; you bury dead," one of the troops replied. "You better come with us and work with us to bury dead."

Japanese forces herded the men individually and in small groups toward an empty field on Remy Street. Terrified wives and mothers watched out of windows, while small children peered through fences. "I was so frightened," recalled Conrada Balleta, the wife of Francisco Aniban. "My children were crying and I was crying." Beneath the sweltering sun, captives waited throughout the afternoon as troops continued to arrive with additional prisoners. By five p.m. the Japanese had assembled more than four hundred men, corralling them into a long line. Marines searched the captives for valuables and weapons before binding the men's hands behind their backs, forcing them to squat.

When the Japanese tied Esquerra's hands, the undertaker protested. "Pass! Pass! *Tomodachi!*" he hollered to one of the officers, meaning he had travel papers. The officer fished Esquerra's pass from his pocket, read it, and then tossed it to the ground. "Why?" Esquerra pleaded. "That's a very good pass."

A second officer scooped the paper up and scanned the pass. He then unholstered his pistol and approached Esquerra. "You pass is good," the Japanese officer told him in broken English. "You very good man, but you die."

"Why?" the undertaker begged.

"Order," he replied. "Order from high officer."

Esquerra listened.

"Kill you," the officer continued. "All you."

Troops began seizing men in groups of ten from one end of the line, while marines at the opposite end marched captives off individually. Thirty-one-year-old Godofredo Rivera, an employee of the Asiatic Petroleum Corporation, watched as two marines grabbed his brother Arturo. Moments later he heard the crack of a rifle. They returned for Rivera, dragging him about twenty yards away from the line to the bank of the Estero Tripa de Gallina, a once-navigable waterway whose sinuous path had earned it the name Chicken Tripe. Rivera counted five marines, each armed with a rifle. The troops forced Rivera to his knees, where he faced the late-afternoon sun. Down below in the shallow water, he spotted the bodies of other victims, including his brother. Rivera knew he would soon share his sibling's fate. The Japanese behind him took aim and fired. "The bullet entered the back of my neck and came out the cheek on the right side of my face," Rivera later testified. "It fractured my jaw."

Troops returned to the line and grabbed another victim.

Then another.

And another.

Every few moments a rifle fired, and another husband, father, or son tumbled down the muddy bank, swelling the pile of bodies that floated amid the green lily pads. The marines marched some of the victims, not to the canal, but to the weedy edge of several small lagoons, where some traded rifles at times for swords. Rivera's seventeen-year-old nephew Aquilino suffered such a fate, though he, too, miraculously survived, despite a cut so deep in his neck that it exposed the vertebrae. Forty-one-year-old Jose Cabanero, who watched troops march his brother and cousin to their deaths, tried to run, zigzagging as rifles roared behind him. He almost escaped, but an officer finally brought him down with a sword. The marine slashed, stabbed, and kicked Cabanero, who rolled across the ground with each strike. "When I was facing upwards he gave me another blow right across the face, cutting my nose," the merchant later testified. "He gave me two blows right over my ear, and took off part of my ear."

Other victims tried to sway the killers, appealing to a sense of humanity that on this Saturday afternoon the Japanese lacked completely. Forty-two-year-old Federico Davantes, as he listened to the marine behind him work the bolt of his rifle, pleaded that he needed to live for the sake of his newborn son.

"*Tomodachi! Tomodachi!*" he cried. "*Kodomo takusan!*"

His pleas failed to sway the enemy.

The Japanese did more than just shoot and slash the civilians. Marines pulled seventeen-year-old Benjamin Urrutia and nine others from the line and led them toward Dart Street, pausing alongside a wall to blindfold each man. "Japanese and Philippines are good friends," the marine said as he cinched each blindfold. "*Tomodachi.*"

A marine grabbed Urrutia's arm and marched him through a gap in the wall. One of the troops hit the blindfolded Urrutia on the right side of his face and pushed him into a large hole. The teenager landed atop other men, only to have others topple down onto him. Guards then tossed several grenades into the pit. "When the hand grenades exploded blood began to flow out of my nose and mouth," Urrutia recalled. "Others were groaning and moaning and making sounds as if they were all choking."

The Japanese began to shoot those who had survived.

"We are all going to die together," one of the men cried out.

Urrutia pretended to be dead. The shooting stopped, and the marines shoveled sand in the hole, burying the men with each toss in what would prove one of four mass graves that war crimes investigators later uncovered, containing a total of one hundred bodies. Urrutia felt the earth fall on top of him, but he dared not move. "I could hardly breathe," recalled the youth, who later dug himself out, "because of the sand in my mouth."

Those who were killed by bullets and grenades were the lucky ones. For the rest, the Japanese devised a ruthless means of extermination, one that required imagination and forethought to turn an otherwise ordinary two-story home into a chamber of horrors. One of those paraded through the nearby residence at 1195 Singalong Street was twenty-one-year-old Eugene Bayot, a mechanic pulled out of the line as part of a group of ten men. The Japanese marched Bayot up the stairs to a second-floor balcony, where a marine tore off his shirt and fashioned it into a blindfold. Two troops then escorted him into a bedroom. Bayot managed to slip his blindfold down. One of the Japanese he observed wore an army helmet emblazoned with a star. The other stood shirtless, soaked in sweat, and sported a shaved head. In his hand, he clutched a saber. The afternoon light filtered through a single window, illuminating a large jagged hole cut in the center of the floor, the edges around it stained red with blood. The Japanese forced Bayot to his knees alongside the hole. "I then felt a hard blow on the back of my neck and someone kicked me at the back," he recalled. "I fell through a hole in the floor."

A pile of bodies broke his fall. The Japanese had failed to decapitate Bayot, burying the blade in the thick muscle at the base of his neck. The mechanic freed his hands and dragged himself to a corner. A guard just outside the ground-floor room occasionally peered in and shot any men who survived. Bayot pretended to be dead, watching as other unfortunate souls dropped through the ceiling. Throughout the afternoon, the Japanese marched in group after group of men, each of whom waited patiently outside the Singalong Street home for his turn to die. During that time, twenty-six-year-old Chinese immigrant Sy Chia heard the groans from a few survivors. Others remembered that the executioners stank of wine. Julio Ramirez would later tell investigators that as soon as he stepped into the execution chamber, he smelled blood, an unmistakably metallic scent attributed to iron-rich red blood cells.

Terror seized twenty-six-year-old Virginio Suarez as he waited on the balcony alongside Father Jose Tanquilot, while the Japanese blind-folded the men.

"Perhaps this is our last on earth," he cried out to the priest.

"Just pray to God," Father Tanquilot told him.

With brutal efficiency, the Japanese led teenagers and even grandfa-thers into the kill room, like sheep to the slaughter. The executioners worked with the competence of an assembly line—kneel, chop, fall; kneel, chop, fall. The sweat Bayot noted that soaked the executioner testified to the physical stamina required to decapitate so many men, to wield a sword over and over again with the power to cut bone. Down below in the dark, the handful of survivors moaned in agony; others gurgled and choked. "This is my house," one of the victims cried out, "and this is the place my head was cut."

Twenty-seven-year-old Pablo Martinez called out for his cousins Ubaldo Magtal and Pedro Cruz, both of whom were in his same group of ten men.

"I am here," Magtal replied.

But Cruz did not answer.

Ricardo Esquerra, the undertaker, spotted his friend Teodoro Val-dez. "Teodoro!" he cried.

His friend remained silent.

Esquerra reached over and grabbed Valdez's foot, pulling him toward him. Only then did he realize that his friend's head was sep-arated from his body. Twenty-five-year-old Felix Plata experienced a similar horror as the dead dropped around him. "I saw one head roll away," he said. "That was the head of one of my neighbors."

The executioners interrupted their murderous rhythm to swig wine or howl with laughter. "Banzai!" the survivors heard them shout amid chops. "Banzai!"

More bodies fell.

And the pile grew, a tangled pyramid of arms, legs, torsos, and heads, some attached, others not. Those who survived had to roll out of the way or risk burial beneath the dead. "I placed my hand and arm on the floor," Suarez recalled. "I could feel several inches of blood."

Dentist Angel Enriquez, who later succumbed to his wounds, remembered even more. "I saw," he said, "blood as deep as my ankles."

The slaughter continued as the afternoon faded to dusk and then nightfall. By then, as survivor Fidel Merino later testified, the jumble of dead reached almost to the second floor. Fellow survivor Eustaquio Batoctoy concurred. "The pile was about eight feet high."

That night, after the Japanese departed, the few survivors managed to escape, some via a board kicked out of one wall. Undertaker Ricardo Esquerra chose a different route. Like a mountain climber, he ascended the peak of bodies, pulling himself up via the arms and legs of the dead until he reached the hole through which he had fallen. "Within two or three days," neighbor Bessie Chase recalled, "the stench and odor emanating from this house was so terrible that one can hardly stand it."

The home burned like so many others in Paco. War Crimes investigators, who later tallied two hundred dead along the banks of the canal, lagoons, and pits, plowed through the ashes, attempting to determine the number of men who died in the house on Singalong. "We counted the skulls," recalled Francisco del Rosario, the undertaker hired by the army. "There were approximately two hundred skulls at that location." The investigative report into the slaughter of more than four hundred men that Saturday afternoon in Paco reads like the script of a horror movie. "The evidence clearly establishes a deliberate plan to exterminate all male civilians residing in the area," it concluded. "A more brutal and cold blooded series of murders can hardly be imagined."

○ ○ ○ ○

MANY OF MANILA'S WOUNDED staggered through the gates of Santo Tomas—some carried in the arms of loved ones, others wheeled in pushcarts—all drawn to the promise of aid from American doctors. The swelling numbers forced medics to convert the Education Building into a hospital. Internees living on the third floor and in the gymnasium moved outside, camping in army tents. Other uninjured refugees poured into the camp as well, believing it to be one of the few safe places in the city even as the Japanese continued to shell the university almost daily. "There were so many clamoring for admittance to the camp," Hartendorp recalled, "that measures had to be taken to prevent a greater influx than could be dealt with."

Twenty more doctors and one hundred nurses flew in from Leyte on February 9. "Their arrival," the company's report noted, "was most timely as their services were so urgently needed. Our men and officers had begun to show the effects of the strain of working under constant fire with no sleep." Internee nurses viewed the replacements as a godsend. "How strong, healthy, and beautiful they appeared to us!" Roka wrote. "Since most of the Santo Tomas nurses were ill and weak, we were glad to relinquish our work to the healthy and fresh nurses. Most of us were completely worn out from dodging shells, caring for the sick and wounded, and witnessing joy and anguished grief."

On February 11 the hospital evacuated most internee patients to the Quezon Institute, a little more than two miles away on the city's outskirts, wrapping up that evening at dark. The 287 beds available, however, were soon filled with civilians wounded by artillery shrapnel and gunfire. Once able, doctors transferred them to San Lazaro and the Children's Maternity Hospital, both set up to care for locals. The horror in Manila was reflected in the figures compiled by the 893rd Clearing Company. From February 6 to 23, the hospital admitted 925 patients. Doctors performed 352 surgeries—an average of twenty a day—including nine amputations. Thirty-eight patients died. "The civilians were mostly serious surgical cases, many of them with wounds already two and three days old," the company's report noted. "Many already had tetanus."

Through the wounded who poured in each day, internees learned of the slaughter beyond the camp's iron gates. "They were in a pitiful state, and their stories were all the same," Roka wrote in her diary. "The retreating and enraged enemy had gone on an orgy of massacre, rape, burning and destruction." Robert Wygle echoed Roka in his diary, noting the mutilated condition of many survivors. "They are so far beyond recognition that, in many cases, one can't tell whether they are men or women, boys or girls, dead or alive. Bloated, purple, twisted, matted and plastered with blood and dirt—apparently dead," he wrote. "Oh, Japs, if only the folks back in the USA could only know you as you are. I've hated your insidious ways for many years, but I loathe, detest and despise you with a murderous hate now. Let's take no prisoners."

Robin Prising watched a Filipino push a makeshift wheelbarrow through the gate, carrying the slumped body of a woman, her thick black hair matted with dried blood. "In a sweat of anguish, the Filipino kept wringing his hands; he begged on his knees; he shrieked and stammered at the medic in broken English."

"No, you go make her good. Make her alive. Please!" he begged. "Americans can do anything. Kill all Japs; win war. You can make her live, yes?"

"The woman's face had been blown off," Prising recalled. "While the man continued to rave, we washed his wounds and dressed them. Then the medic had to send him away. It was helpless agony to have to watch the man wheel the barrow back towards the Main Gate, to have to hear him whimpering crazily at every jolt, not knowing what he could do with his precious bundle of flesh that had once been a living woman with a face." The cost of his freedom, Prising realized, had been paid by others. "The armless, the legless, the blood-spattered, an endless river of Filipinos flooded towards Santo Tomas, one of the few places of refuge—the prison camp where we white prisoners of war had been saved at the expense of a whole city of Orientals."

Fellow internee John Osborn recounted in a letter the story of a mortally wounded Filipina woman who arrived in the camp's hospital. "I know I am going to die," she said, "but I shall die under the American flag, and that makes me happy." One of the nurses affixed a miniature flag just above the woman's bed. "Often, during the two days that she lived," Osborn wrote, "her eyes rested on the small flag and she smiled, and when she passed peacefully into her last sleep, the smile still rested on her lips." In another letter a few days later, Osborn was far more grim. "Refugees," he wrote, "say they could have walked along the streets by stepping from one body to another."

It wasn't just the internees at Santo Tomas who witnessed the bloodshed. Terrified evacuees flooded the American battle lines on the city's south side in such large numbers that troops had to stop fighting. "The whole street," recalled Maj. Henry Burgess, "became choked with pitiful human beings as thousands moved south to escape the holocaust of Manila." As Burgess and others soon learned, more than a few bore the wounds from Japanese barbarity. "Many nursing women had been bayoneted in their breasts, some had the tendons in the back of their necks severed by sabers and could no longer hold their necks up. Small children and babies had been bayoneted," Burgess said. "We had been admonished to keep our medical supplies for ourselves, and not to help others. Of course, we couldn't, and didn't refuse them assistance."

MacArthur's declaration of the fall of Manila angered the American troops, who each day fought the Japanese, while folks back home believed the battle had been won. Many of the soldiers told internees that the urban fight proved far bloodier than the battles on New Guinea, in the Marianas, or on Leyte. CBS reporter Bill Dunn captured the views of the soldiers in one of his broadcasts, reporting on the fanatical enemy troops entrenched in the buildings and rubble. "It is now a question," he reported, "of how long it will take to root each remaining Nip out of his hole and dispose of him."

"Manila was secured!" one soldier scoffed as he spoke to Roka near the lean-to where she resided. "Why, I'm the only man left in my platoon!"

"Most of the officers and soldiers who returned to camp said very little," she wrote in her diary, "but all were exhausted and grim-looking,"

Internee Emily Van Sickle encountered a similar response when she asked one of the soldiers she knew where his fellow troops were.

"They won't be coming back," the soldier replied. "We really got into it today. They sent us out to take a bridge—said everything was clear on the way. Before we reached the bridge, we ran into an ambush—Japs hiding in buildings that were supposed to be empty. They started pouring machine gun fire on us."

Eleven-year-old Prising, who often led troops up to the top of Main Building for views of the city, befriended an American soldier named Stan, a twenty-two-year-old from Illinois who carried a worn copy of poems by Hart Crane. "I had never heard anyone talk as Stan did," he recalled. "To him this war was part of the never-ending chaos of human misery, mankind's untold, unmeasured suffering that would persist through the ages while each civilization rose and fell. All personal grief and experience would be lost in that enduring chaos. And to the generations that replaced our own, it would be as though we had never lived." The soldier even shared a pint of beer with the boy, albeit with the warning not to get drunk. Prising looked forward to his time with him, spotting his fellow soldiers one afternoon without him. He asked where he could find Stan. None of the troops would look him in the eyes.

"Well," one finally admitted. "He walked into a booby trap."

The sacrifice of the troops was not lost on the civilians, who watched each day as wooden crosses mushroomed in the camp's three temporary cemeteries, each affixed with a dog tag and covered by flowers grown in the meager gardens of internees.

The Japanese, meanwhile, continued to shell Santo Tomas, prompting shanty dwellers to lug mattresses inside and join other internees who moved out of rooms and into the corridors, hopeful that the thick internal walls would provide extra protection. A captured Japanese diary later detailed one such attack on the camp. Enemy forces opened fire from the third floor of a building inside the Walled City at eight-thirty a.m. on February 10, aiming at the upper right corner of the Main Building from a range of about two miles. "Thereafter we fired fifty to sixty rounds continuously; fell in the vicinity of the target."

The attack that Saturday morning—just one week after American troops liberated Santo Tomas—killed six people, including a hospital patient recovering in his bed on the second floor of the Education Building. "A grim morning," Robert Wygle noted in his diary. "No one is fooled into thinking our war is over. We realize that tomorrow may see more of us dead and mangled. Faces are getting more haggard and many are more serious—but the thumbs-up spirit is untouched."

Such unexpected attacks rattled the already fragile internees, as evidenced by Roka's diary entry. "Still no sleep, no baths, and no rest!" she wrote. "The shells screaming through the air over our heads had unnerved us, and we wondered if we'd ever see our homes again."

Wygle's fourteen-year-old son Peter narrowly survived one attack that sprayed him with shattered glass and concrete. The youth later recalled other scenes of horror, including how shrapnel ripped off one internee's right arm. "She was wandering down the hall," he recalled, "carrying her arm in her left hand." Another time he scooped up a field hat in the camp's front yard. "Part of a skull," Wygle said, "fell out."

After one late-night Japanese artillery attack, Prising rushed to find his mother in the blasted Main Building. She was seated on the floor of her room, eyes distant and cradling a woman in her lap. With the help of another, Prising lifted the woman off his mother and helped her to her feet. "Still she did not recognize me," he later wrote. "She did not hear my voice; her eyes, unseeing and white, gazed past my light."

The youth led his mother by the hand out of the building and back to his father where Frederick Prising used a jug of water to gently rinse her head.

"No," she finally said. "No more now. I don't want any, any more."

The constant fear of death from the skies drained the internees, most of whom still struggled physically from starvation and emotionally from the shock of liberation.

Anna Nixon, who taught Sunday school in Santo Tomas, recounted in her diary a conversation she overheard in the food line. "You know, we're not out of danger yet," one internee remarked, "but I'd rather be shot than to starve to death."

The comment prompted a French woman in front to break down. "Who wants to die at all?" she cried out. "I don't want to die of starvation, nor do I want to die in the shelling. We've come through all this. I love life. I've learned to appreciate it more now. Why do I have to die? Oh, God, I don't want to die!" The internees around her fell silent. "We stood with bowed heads," Nixon wrote in her diary, "partly because we respected her in the depth of her tender feelings, and partly because we knew she had expressed the desire of every soldier on the battlefield, and every single one of us."

An American officer approached nurse Sally Blaine in the wake of the February 10 shelling. "Are you one of our nurses that's helped us?" he asked.

"Yes, I am," she replied.

He wrapped his arm around her.

"Wouldn't you like to go home?" the officer asked.

Blaine broke down crying, the first time she had wept in years.

At MacArthur's headquarters in San Miguel, army censors blocked all efforts by journalists to report on the shelling of the university, an act that drew scorn from the newsmen. American author John Dos Passos recounted in his diary the conversation of several reporters soon afterward in a run-down hotel, while swigging pink rum that tasted like chewing gum. "The shelling of Santo Tomas is the biggest story in the whole war and they won't let you write about it," one journalist complained.

"Why the hell couldn't they have gotten those people out of Santo Tomas instead of leaving them there to be blown to pieces with shells?" another asked.

"Might as well pull out and go back to the States if you can't write the news."

CHAPTER 14

"They liquidated everybody."

—Agustin Garcia,
testimony, August 17, 1945

M ODESTO FAROLAN HAD HUSTLED NONSTOP SINCE THE
Americans first arrived in Manila to turn the Red Cross headquarters into a refugee center and emergency hospital. The forty-
five-year-old Farolan, who once worked as a newspaper reporter
and editor, was appointed to serve as the agency's acting manager in
December 1944. Since then he had prepared for the worst-case scenario, a battle between two of the world's most powerful armies in
the heart of Manila. Located at the intersection of Isaac Peral and
General Luna streets near Taft Avenue, the two-story concrete structure displayed large Red Cross emblems on its walls, its roof, and all
its windows. Farolan and his staff had set up a makeshift operating
room, prepared meals, and tended to the scores of refugees whose
homes had burned. "From February 4 until February 10, I never left
the building except for short hours," Farolan recalled. "I stayed there
night and day."

Refugees continued to pour into the Red Cross, so many that the
staff stopped registering new arrivals at fifty, but more continued to
bang on the door by the hour. By some estimates, as many as one hundred men, women, and children crowded the passageways, rooms,
and small backyard. Included among them was the family of forty-
six-year-old Juan P. Juan, who lived next door at 1312 General Luna
Street, his property separated by a six-foot-tall stucco wall. A for-

mer schoolteacher and principal, Juan published educational materials for elementary schools. His eldest daughter, twenty-four-year-old Paulina Zabala, had given birth just ten days earlier to a boy, Rene. She had since hemorrhaged, requiring her to move from the family's home into the Red Cross clinic. Juan's forty-eight-year-old wife Lucia had accompanied Paulina to help care for the couple's daughter and grandson. Since the Battle of Manila began, artillery shells had pounded the Juan home and yard, prompting Farolan to invite the entire family of fifteen to seek shelter in the Red Cross. That morning around nine a.m. the remaining children and grandchildren carted mattresses next door.

Other refugees included nine German Jews, among them George and Bertha Kohnke, Waldemar and Martha Graetz, and Martin and Margaret Boss. The Kohnkes' twenty-three-year-old daughter Irene joined them, along with her fiancé John Lewy, who had fled Nazi Germany for the Philippines in late 1939. The twenty-seven-year-old Lewy had since worked in a photography studio and later as a restaurant supervisor. When the battle began, Lewy, his fiancée and future in-laws, and the Boss family had sought refuge in the Kohnke home at 189 Concepcion Street, next to the YMCA. After the Japanese began torching houses along the street on February 5, the families escaped to the Graetz home at the corner of at San Marcelino and San Luis. The artillery forced them to flee again three days later, but Japanese sentries refused to let them cross any streets, leaving them no choice but to bang on the door of the Red Cross.

"Nothing will happen here," one of the nurses assured them.

The star of the show was Patrocinio Abad, the twenty-six-year-old film actress who answered to the stage name Corazon Noble, or Noble Heart. The dark-haired beauty with a shapely figure had starred in eighteen films before the war, including Filipino hits like the 1938 *Dugong Hinugasan* and *Gunita* two years later. A trench mortar had killed Noble's husband, prompting her to seek refugee at the Red Cross at ten a.m. that morning with her ten-month-old daughter, Maria Lourdes Vera. Noble's two teenage brothers Vicente and Ramon accompanied her, along with her cousin Teresita Durango, also an actress, who performed under the name Tita Duran. Sixteen-year-old Duran, who had appeared in more than twenty-five movies, was the biggest child star of the Philippines, often compared to Shirley Temple.

A Japanese noncommissioned officer and a half-dozen troops visited the Red Cross around noon on February 10, not long after the Japanese had set fire to the German Club, just one block away. Farolan tapped staffer Corazon Abellera, who could speak some Japanese, to help translate, a job that devolved at times into sign language.

"How many refugees do you have?" the Japanese demanded. "How many came in today? Who are they? Where are their baggages?"

The Japanese appeared alarmed by the Germans, who amid the crowded headquarters had bedded down in the ladies' restroom. Troops thumbed through the passports and asked if the Germans supported the Americans or the Japanese.

"Japanese, *tomodachi*. Japanese friend," one said. "Heil Hitler."

Farolan escorted the troops on a brief tour of the Red Cross headquarters, showing them the operating room and his office. Amid the tour, Farolan directed a volunteer to replace two Red Cross flags that had blown down, but the Japanese objected.

"No good," one said in broken English. "Americans very bad, no like Red Cross. Japanese okay."

Troops spotted a cardboard sign atop Farolan's desk that read, "Philippine Red Cross Emergency Hospital" and "Refugee House." The Japanese refused to allow him to hang the sign. To emphasize the point, one of the troops used his bayonet to spear and then toss the sign to the floor. "I explained the purpose of the place," Farolan said, "that it was a refugee house, that we could not refuse people that were homeless and injured and we just had to take them in and that unless we closed the doors the people would continue coming in. They were wagging their heads and seemed to be displeased."

The troops left after twenty minutes.

Throughout the afternoon, staff cared for the sick and comforted the frightened as dusk settled over the city. In the emergency room around six p.m., Dr. German de Venecia, who earlier that day had amputated a woman's leg, prepared to operate on two boys who had been injured by shrapnel. While nurses prepped the patients, the doctor chatted with Farolan at his desk. On a bed nearby, Paulina Zabala cared for her ten-day-old son, Rene. Close at hand perched her mother, while steps away the German refugees relaxed in the ladies' restroom under the stairs. Elsewhere in the building, others prepared to sit down for dinner, thankful to be out of harm's way.

No one noticed the Japanese marines who appeared at the back gate. Seconds later gunfire erupted outside in the garden. Those inside paused. "We heard shots," Corazon Noble recalled. "We thought it was the beginning of a street fight."

The Japanese blasted the back door, which flew open. A child perched in front of the door collapsed right next to her grandmother. "Doctor, doctor," the woman began to shriek. "My granddaughter has been hit. I have been hit also."

Four Japanese marines filed one after the other through the back door, each armed with a rifle and fixed bayonet. Refugees began to scream as the Japanese opened fire. Some dropped to the floor; others dove behind desks and chairs. A bullet zinged through the legs of German refugee John Lewy, who turned and darted toward the women's restroom to alert the others. One of the marines raised his rifle at Noble, who clutched her infant daughter in her arms. The film star ducked behind a medicine cabinet, only to find it was not large enough to shelter her. The marine's rifle roared, and a bullet shattered her right elbow. Noble collapsed to the floor. "I lay prone," the actress recalled, "and I placed my ten-month-old baby under me but the Jap was not satisfied."

The marine approached, towering over her with his bayonet. He plunged the blade into her chest just below her right breast. He pulled the bayonet out and stabbed her again and again, slicing her upper left arm, left leg, ribs, abdomen, and back. Only later would Noble realize that in the marine's maniacal fury to stab her nine times, his steel blade had gone all the way through her and into her ten-month-old daughter. "She was," Noble later testified, "bayoneted through and through three times."

The Japanese moved on in search of other victims.

Thirty-two-year-old registered nurse Gliceria Andaya heard the gunshots and the screams of the grandmother who barged into the emergency room. Andaya instructed fellow staffer Corazon Abellera, who earlier that day had dealt with the Japanese, to go speak to the marines. Andaya followed her out of the clinic, yelling at everyone she passed to lie down, take cover, and remain quiet. She spotted several young children who would not lie flat. One of them, whom Andaya estimated was no more than three years old, sat up, about to cry. "When she started to open her mouth," Andaya recalled, "the Japanese just put three bullets in her mouth until the child fell dead."

Abellera bravely approached the Japanese and began to speak. One of the marines answered her by raising his rifle and pointing it at her chest. Abellera ducked behind Andaya, who was dressed in a white nurse's uniform with a badge on her left arm and Red Cross cap atop her head.

Andaya rose to the challenge. "Wait a moment," the nurse pleaded.

She dropped to her knees before the marine and raised her hands over her head.

"Wait a moment."

Andaya explained that that she was a nurse and that this was a Red Cross building filled only with refugees. The marine turned to his commander behind him. Andaya waited. The marine then turned back toward her and drove his bayonet into the left side of her chest, perforating the lung and nicking the top of her kidney. The nurse toppled to the ground still conscious. She watched as the marines headed for the clinic.

Inside the clinic, where Farolan had moments earlier chatted with the doctor, the Red Cross manager heard the rifle shots coupled with the screams of women and children. He recognized nurse Andaya's shrill cry seconds later, followed by the thud as her body hit the floor. Hobnail boots signaled the approaching enemy. Farolan dropped to the floor and crawled under his desk as the first of two marines burst through the door. Thirty-two-year-old nurse Florita Loveriza covered a patient on a cot and dove under a table, while Dr. German de Venecia tried to hide behind a steel cabinet along with a female attendant. The marine spotted the doctor and raised his rifle.

"He is our doctor," the attendant pleaded. "Please save him."

The marine paused for a second before he twice squeezed the trigger.

"*Aruy!*" the doctor cried out, a Tagalog expression of pain.

The Japanese then turned and fired at the attendant but missed. She collapsed and pretended to be dead. The marine paused to reload his rifle before he approached two empty cots near Farolan's desk that moments earlier held patients. The Red Cross manager peered out from his hiding place as the slaughter continued. The marine lowered his rifle and with the tip of his bayonet overturned the cots, revealing two crouching people. "One bayonet thrust," Farolan recalled, "finished each one of them."

The marine then turned toward Farolan's desk. He jammed his bayonet under the table where Farolan remained silent, sitting atop his steel Red Cross helmet. The blade dinged the helmet. The marine then fired his rifle twice, but the bullets passed between his feet and scraped the bottom rim of the helmet. The Japanese gave up on Farolan and turned to the other four patients still in cots. A marine bayoneted Lucia Santos de Juan, who had been caring for her eldest daughter Paulina and baby grandson Rene. He plunged his steel blade into the right side of Paulina's abdomen and again through her mouth. The marine then stabbed the ten-day-old infant boy, Rene. On the ground just outside the clinic, the bayoneted nurse Andaya watched the massacre unfold. "The wounded were lying on cots," she recalled. "I saw them jab the bayonet on each patient followed by a revolver shot by the Japanese who was following the other one."

The marines walked to the other side of a screen that divided the clinic from the improvised operating room, bayoneting the two teenagers who had awaited surgery before the slaughter began. Troops moved on throughout the building, killing six more of Juan P. Juan's grandchildren, including four-year-old Edward Santos and his two-year-old sister Amelia, four-year-old Armando Marcelo and his twin three-year-old brothers Carlos and Ernesto, and their two-year-old sister Ana Maria Marcelo. "From where we were we could hear victims in their death agony, the shrill cries of children and the sobs of dying mothers and girls," Farolan recalled. "We did not dare move."

When the Japanese shot at John Lewy, the German refugee turned and charged back to the women's restroom to warn the others as several marines gave chase. Pandemonium broke out in the restroom. Lewy's fiancée Irene Kohnke crammed into the first toilet stall along with Martin Boss and his wife Margaret. Lewy raced for the second stall along with George Kohnke, his wife Bertha, and Isabel Tabaque, a Filipino servant for Waldemar and Martha Graetz, both of whom were out in the open.

"Americans," the marines barked. "Americans."

"*Escusi*," one of the Germans replied. "*Escusi*."

The marines opened fire. A bullet tore into Bertha Kohnke's abdomen. Another round struck George Kohnke in the throat, knocking him to the ground. Lewy dove onto the floor next to him in the toilet stall, using his body for cover.

"Please have mercy on us," Waldemar Graetz cried.

But there was none.

The Japanese shot Graetz in the stomach. He collapsed and tried to get back up, but the marine drove his bayonet into him and killed him. The Japanese shot Martha Graetz in the right forearm. The marine stepped on her, and she cried out, prompting him to bayonet her to death. The Japanese then went after Martin and Margaret Boss in the first stall. On the floor of the neighboring stall, Lewy listened to Margaret beg for her life, seconds before the marine plunged his bayonet into her with such force, the steel blade repeatedly hit the floor beneath her. "I was laying there inside the toilet and had to listen to all that terrible groaning and screaming outside, my people killed brutally next to me," he said. "I didn't hear Irene being killed—that was fortunate in a way."

Isabel Tabaque, the twenty-three-year-old housemaid for the Graetz family, cowered inside the stall with him. Eight months pregnant, she wanted to run. "I told her to stay right there and keep quiet," Lewy said. "The only chance was to play dead." Lewy lay flat, his chest and head sandwiched between the toilet and the wall. From his position, he saw the Japanese enter the stall. Lewy held his breath. The marine raised his rifle with the bayonet, pointed it at Lewy, then drove the blade into him just below his right hip. He pulled it out and plunged the bayonet into him again, so deep that the blade lodged in the board beneath him. Pain shot through his body. The marine moved the blade back and forth, back and forth, working it free. "I didn't give a sound," Lewy said, "but bit my lips until they bled."

Moments before the slaughter began, Juan P. Juan had returned to his home next door to help a couple of his children and some neighbors prepare dinner for the others inside the Red Cross. Juan heard the report of rifles, followed by the screams and cries of women. He ordered everyone to hide in the family bomb shelter, demanding that no one leave for fear the Japanese might spot them, cross the wall, and continue the carnage. Ramon Abad in fact spied a Japanese marine atop the Red Cross garage, scanning the surrounding area. "We were all electrified with fear because we thought that the Japanese were looking for us and more people to kill," Juan later said. "We all stayed inside the air raid shelter almost breathless waiting what would be our fate."

The minutes dragged past before the shooting stopped and the marines departed. The Japanese had converted the Red Cross into a charnel house, with the passageways, clinic, and restroom crowded with the bodies of women and children. Despite her own wounds, Corazon Noble fought to save her infant daughter. "After they left, I tried to put her intestines back in her stomach," she said. "I did not know what to do."

Juan ventured outside the shelter. His twelve-year-old niece Leticia Alba staggered out of the Red Cross, having survived the slaughter by hiding in a storeroom. "She was pale," Juan remembered, "and looked very much afraid and could hardly talk."

"What happened?" he begged her.

"Finally she broke and informed me that all of them inside the Red Cross building, including my wife, my daughter, daughter-in-law and all the seven grandchildren, were massacred by the Japanese," Juan recalled. "I myself could not utter a word as I felt almost unconscious with the shocking news."

Corazon Noble's brothers Vicente and Ramon climbed out of the shelter and started for the Red Cross.

Juan intercepted the youths. "Boys," he warned, "don't go inside."

The young men stared at him.

"All the people inside the Red Cross are dead."

Ramon Abad broke down crying.

A few other survivors did, in fact, trickle out in the hours and even days ahead. German refugee John Lewy survived, though his fiancée did not, dying with little dignity on the bathroom floor alongside her mother and father, a tragic end to the story of refugees who had tried to escape the horror of war half a world away. "When I came to my senses again I thought it was a dream," Lewy later said, "but everybody was dead." Modesto Farolan lived; so, too, did child actress Tita Duran and nurse Gliceria Andaya, who would lie for four days on the floor of the Red Cross until the building finally caught fire and burned. American investigators would later surmise that the Japanese, in the span of less than half an hour, murdered more than fifty people.

Later that Saturday, Corazon Noble, the beautiful actress who for years before the war had enraptured the nation, emerged from the Red Cross, her elbow shattered and suffering nine stab wounds. In her arm, she clutched her daughter.

Her brother Vicente went to her.

"Take the baby to the doctor," she said, handing him her daughter.

Vicente looked down at his tiny niece and saw three bloody bayonet wounds. "The baby said nothing," he noted, "only she was murmuring."

Though he ran to find a doctor, the effort proved futile. Maria would survive for only four hours. The Juan family buried the ten-month-old in the backyard alongside ten-day-old Rene. A single white cross marked the resting place of the massacre's two youngest victims. "I just lay on the ground," Noble recalled. "I was exhausted."

o o o o

ADMIRAL IWABUCHI HAD ABANDONED Manila for Fort McKinley on February 9, dispatching a staff officer to brief Shimbu Group headquarters on the deteriorating state of the battle. Two days later, having received no word from General Yokoyama, Iwabuchi changed his mind. He would return to Manila.

He would return to the fight.

And the slaughter.

Staff officer Koichi Kayashima later speculated about Iwabuchi's rationale, suggesting the admiral may have believed that Fort McKinley might fall before Manila. But there were other personal motivations, he noted, that had nothing to do with tactics. "He could not stand by and see his subordinates being seized and killed," Kayashima suggested. "In line with the traditional belief of Japanese warriors of olden times, that is, to choose one's place of death and die bravely, it seems that he, as Commanding Officer of the Manila Naval Defense Force, decided to meet his death in Manila."

The city Iwabuchi returned to had descended into pandemonium as his forces continued the roundup and execution of thousands of civilians. The four days spanning February 9 through 12 witnessed some of the worst atrocities in the Battle of Manila. In addition to the extermination of residents at the German Club, the Red Cross, and throughout Paco, marines machine-gunned and bayoneted thirty-six men in front of the Philippine General Hospital, among them former Supreme Court justice Anacleto Diaz. Troops killed another forty-three men, women, and children in the yard of the Tabacalera Cigar and Cigarette Factory and across the street at the Shell Service Station. Fifteen more were slain in the yard of a home on Kansas Street, including twenty-day-old Sylvia Brugger, whom one survivor baptized with garden water moments before she died. Each day, each hour, the deaths mounted, in homes, schools, and even churches.

The horror, as Iwabuchi now made sure, was far from over.

CHAPTER 15

"This is a doomed and tragic city."

—ROBERT SHAPLEN,
NEWSWEEK, FEBRUARY 26, 1945

AMERICAN FORCES RUSHED TO OPEN MORE HOSPITALS ON the city's outskirts to treat the growing roster of wounded soldiers and civilians. The 29th Evacuation Hospital, made up of twelve officers and eighty-seven enlisted men, had rolled into Manila on February 5, taking over the Washington Elementary School near the San Lazaro racetrack in Santa Cruz. The hospital opened the next day and within twelve hours admitted 157 patients, including 115 battle casualties that required surgery. The lack of space prompted the hospital to relocate on February 7—the same day MacArthur toured Santo Tomas—to the former Legarda Elementary School in Sampaloc, providing enough room for 650 beds. All told, from the middle of January through the end of March, medical staff treated 5,558 patients, many suffering from wounds of the upper extremities. "The types of casualties received required more surgery than in any other campaign this hospital participated in," the hospital's report stated. "This no doubt was caused by the larger number of artillery, mortar and rocket bombs employed by the enemy."

The 71st Evacuation Hospital had set up on February 6 in a former slaughterhouse and tannery, made up of a single building and three large sheds. "It had been used," the hospital's report noted, "as a Japanese Ordnance Repair Shop and was littered with vehicles, motor parts and a captured American tank." Not only had the complex once housed enemy forces, but for the first thirty-six hours, medics shared the space with troops from the 140th Field Artillery, who rained shells down on targets inside Manila. Medics used one shed for administrative work, pre-op, X-ray, and surgery. The other two served as surgical wards, each able to house one hundred patients. The rest of the hospital was spread out under tents. Casualties soon soared. Thirty-two patients arrived on February 7, a figure that jumped to 525 in three days. By February 14, just one week after opening, the hospital counted 1,046 patients. From February 7 through March 14, the hospital averaged 122 admissions each day, a figure that spiked to 293 on the afternoon American forces crossed the Pasig. During those five weeks doctors completed 916 surgeries, including twenty-two amputations and twenty-two craniotomies, and treated 107 compound fractures. Sixty-three patients died, all but four in surgery.

The 54th Evacuation Hospital was the newest to open, accepting its first patient at three p.m. on February 11 at the Quezon Institute, including many internees transferred from Santo Tomas. Troops converted the ground floor into officer quarters, a mess hall, and storage. Medics used the second floor for surgery, X-rays, a laboratory and pharmacy, and wards. The third-floor rooms, which had not been burned or destroyed, became additional wards and housed a dental clinic. Nurses set up quarters in the fourth-floor day room, while enlisted men pitched tents behind the hospital. Generators provided power, and pit latrines served as toilets since there was no running water. The eight-hundred-bed hospital even boasted an outdoor movie theater and a recreation room that enlisted men used to hold dances. The fierce Battle of Manila, however, kept the doctors and medics busy, as evidenced by the hospital's records. From January through March, medics exposed 6,546 X-ray films, performed 960 surgeries, and treated 346 fractures.

As doctors raced to treat the thousands of wounded, intelligence forces focused on deciphering the enemy's battle plans, including determining what units Japan employed and assembling the names and backgrounds of senior officers. To do so, soldiers sifted through abandoned Japanese supply dumps. Troops learned of one enemy unit after discovering it painted on the side of a destroyed truck. Another time soldiers read it off the helmet of a dead tank crew member. Captured enemy documents revealed a combined Japanese fighting force of around seventeen thousand, a ragtag gang that included stevedores, torpedo assembly teams, and sailors shanghaied from sunken ships. American intelligence reports characterized the enemy as "polyglot," "puny opponents," and a "potpourri" infantry. "It is a hastily organized group," one report observed, "including personnel drawn from the hospitals, and ordered to be sparing of its short supply of ammo."

American forces seized records from the homes of the Japanese consulate and president Jose Laurel, who evacuated to Baguio before MacArthur's arrival. Major Henne marveled at how untouched Laurel's house was in the otherwise ransacked city. It was as though the president had left just moments before the infantry arrived. "All of the essentials of living were present including dishes, flatware, pots and pans, and linens," Henne said. "One deep closet was boarded shut but quickly opened to reveal a hoard of food stuff. The house was rich in souvenirs but the food, excepting some canned salmon, was given to the Filipinos in the neighborhood." After battling through the fires that ravaged the districts north of the Pasig and then crossing the river, Henne enjoyed a real treat that evening. "I spent the night in Jose Laurel's house sleeping in one of the beds which may have belonged to the man himself, but I doubt that he slept there fully clothed with his boots on."

Soldiers interrogated Manila police chief Col. Antonio Torres, singled out in a 1944 intelligence report as the "only official to welcome the Japanese occupation army." Valuable records turned up in unlikely places, including naval codes found in a Manila theater. In a seminary, soldiers discovered an order from Admiral Iwabuchi demanding that his forces conduct suicide attacks. Troops rifled through the pockets of dead Japanese soldiers and marines, recovering dog tags, address books, ration cards, notebooks, photo albums, postal savings books, and postcards. On a suicide squad soldier killed on February 11, troops found his final letter home, dated the day of his death. "This life of mine has been previously presented to the Imperial Highness and to avoid disgrace I shall not return alive without accomplishing my mission," he wrote. "To the family remaining, it is very regrettable to have caused anxiety. Be joyful even if I should die in battle as I have only died for loyalty to the Emperor and filial piety."

On the battlefield, American soldiers had almost encircled the Japanese, who in their retreat left behind not only valuable intelligence but massive amounts of weapons and ammunition, from tanks and airplane engines to thousands of rolls of barbed wire, machine guns, and eighteen cases of hand grenades. The Thirty-Seventh Infantry had come from the north, crossing the Pasig near Malacañan Palace and turning toward the Walled City. The First Cavalry, meanwhile, had enveloped the city from the east before crossing the river using native *bancas* or skiffs that could hold only three to five men at a time. The Eleventh Airborne charged up from the south. The Japanese troops battling inside southern Manila risked entrapment as American forces tightened the noose. To help in the fight, tanks on the north bank of the Pasig blasted enemy barges and targets in the city. "The platoons were alternated every four hours throughout the day and night," noted the 754th Tank Battalion's report, "in order to keep a continuous rate of fire."

The Japanese put up a ferocious fight. "Massed artillery south of the Pasig River has harassed our installations north of the river, destroyed pontoon bridges and hindered the advance of our troops," a February 14 intelligence report stated. "This artillery has been skillfully emplaced in buildings and behind walls." Enemy troops proved just as fierce in direct combat, at one point dragging two wounded Americans off the battlefield. "Unable to restrain himself any longer, Sgt. Templeton, shouting for the platoon to follow him, rushed forward, firing his M1 from the hip as he moved," the cavalry report noted. "Two Japs dropped dead, the third, no doubt believing a devil was after him, started to run. His retreat was quickly ended with a bayonet thrust delivered by Templeton." A few lucky troops enjoyed a brief reprieve on February 9 when soldiers camped for the night at the Wack Wack Golf and Country Club. "In the peaceful setting of this once beautiful club the rigors of war seemed far away until work on the following day's mission began."

The lack of air support exacerbated the challenges faced by the cavalry and infantry. Despite requests from his senior officers, MacArthur ruled out bombing, fearing it would endanger too many civilians, who, he argued, "will not understand liberation if accomplished by indiscriminate destruction of their homes, their possessions, their civilization, and their own lives." The general later relented and allowed artillery, but only after troops suffered heavy casualties crossing the Pasig River. "From then on, putting it crudely," recalled General Beightler of the Thirty-Seventh Infantry Division, "we really went to town." In the end, artillery would prove equally destructive. Over the course of the battle, American forces would fire more than 42,000 mortar and artillery rounds, including 27,680 shells from 105 mm and 155 mm big guns. Errant projectiles at times crashed through the roofs of homes, churches, and bomb shelters. "Some districts of the city," the Sixth Army commander General Krueger later wrote, "were completely destroyed."

Residents south of the Pasig were trapped day and night in the crossfire of American and Japanese artillery. "It was like a bowling alley over our heads," wrote John Dos Passos, "guns shooting first from one side then from another." Between Japanese demolitions and American artillery, Manila was being destroyed from the inside and out. Men, women, and children retreated belowground, like rats, where conditions inside cramped air raid shelters devolved as the hours turned to days. Bunkers built to house a single family at times held multiple families, leaving little room for anyone to lie down, sit, or even stand. With so many bodies pressed together, the air inside stagnated and the heat soared. Austrian Hans Steiner, in a letter to his mother, recounted his experience. "We lived like dogs," he wrote. "All around us there were fires and explosions; it was the best imagination of hell one could get." William Brady recalled his family's struggle. "The shelter was filled with refugees. Everyone was crying and praying," he wrote. "One or two persons had vomited. Somebody was squatting and defecating from fright or dysentery just outside. Kids were urinating inside."

Artillery set fire to a home on General Luna Street in Paco, where members of the Kishinchand family had sought refuge, trapping ten-year-old Mira, thirteen-year-old Pari, and three-year-old Radhi. "I came out with my brother and my mother," recalled nineteen-year-old Sundri Kishinchand. "My three sisters were burned by the fire." A similar tragedy occurred in the yard at the Malate Catholic School, which at the time served as an emergency hospital. Francisco Ramis dove across his two nephews as artillery rained down. "When the shelling stopped there was wailing all over the place," recalled his nephew Benjamin Ramis. "I tried to get up and felt the heaviness of my uncle. He was dead. Hit by shrapnel on the left temple." Another projectile exploded atop a shelter in Intramuros where Sancho Enriquez's children hid. His wife had stepped out moments earlier to fetch water from a well. "When she came back," Enriquez said, "she found the mutilated bodies of our four children almost beyond recognition."

Japanese troops compounded the challenge, holing up in schools, cathedrals, and government buildings. Col. Lawrence White, regimental commander of the 148th Infantry, seized a church, only to discover machine guns hidden under the altar. The Japanese likewise planted big guns and snipers in commercial towers and hotels, forcing the Americans to hammer them with artillery before sending in troops. "I can see little hope of saving many of Manila's famous buildings," White told a reporter. "This is a full-scale artillery battle and you know what that does to a city." Assaulting such strongholds proved equally as perilous for the infantry. "The reduction of each large building was a small battle in itself," noted the 112th Medical Battalion's report. "Progress for a single 24 hour period was sometimes not more than 300 yards." American soldiers couldn't help but marvel at the enemy's willingness to die. "The only Japs to yield ground," noted the First Cavalry's report, "were dead Japs."

The enemy had effectively turned the urban landscape against advancing American soldiers, who were more accustomed to fighting in the jungle than battling house by house and building by building across a major city. Japanese troops dropped Molotov cocktails and even aerial bombs from upper-floor windows and barricaded interior stairwells with broken glass and barbed wire. Their creativity went beyond just obstacles. "A double-barrel shot gun equipped with bayonet," a 145th Infantry report stated, "is a very dangerous weapon in hallways and room to room fighting." American forces resorted to twelve-man assault teams armed with bazookas, explosives, and flamethrowers, the latter of which was extremely effective but could ricochet in tight spaces and even suck up all the oxygen in a room. "The heat had glued the Japs to the wall," one soldier bragged. "They looked like wall paper."

Each block American forces gained revealed more of the enemy's cunning. On Gilmore Street troops counted 182 mines, including several dozen made from five-hundred-pound depth charges. Electric mine detectors proved worthless given all the metal in the rubble, slowing America's advance. "Tanks attempting to negotiate this sector were hard put to find a road, five being destroyed and many crew killed," noted the Eighth Cavalry's report. Pvt. First Class Deane Marks witnessed a tank hit a mine that, from the size of blast and subsequent thirty-foot crater, he suspected was either a buried aerial bomb or depth charge. "For a split second I saw the tank upside down as high as the telephone wires," Marks said. "Debris started landing, mostly dirt, asphalt, and equipment from the tank. When the dust cleared, there it was, all thirty tons lying on its back." Lt. William Swan came upon a similar scene soon after several tanks hit mines, including one that was totally destroyed. "The turret was off on one side of the road and the tracks off on the other side," he remembered. "At my feet lay an American steel helmet absolutely flattened with a crushed head inside."

In another case, troops found a dead Japanese soldier, whose body had been rigged with an incendiary bomb. The enemy likewise filled pickle, pear, and peach cans with explosives, careful not to remove the labels. Other times the Japanese booby-trapped woven figurines on store shelves and even religious relics. Even condoms were used to secure blasting caps shoved inside bamboo sticks. Soldiers discovered similar creativity at La Loma Cemetery, where the Japanese booby-trapped the chapel and stashed ammunition, mines, and grenades in mausoleums. Troops planted 120 depth charges in rows among the graves and dug in pillboxes. "Outwardly these pillboxes resembled large mounds of earth covering tombs," one report stated. "They were sodded completely with flowers growing over them and crosses mounted above them."

Between the National Psychopathic Hospital in the eastern suburbs and the Pasig River, American troops discovered a network of eight caves connected by tunnels. Inside, soldiers found an underground munitions factory—powered by generators and equipped with American drill presses—that included workshops to build booby traps, bombs, and mines. The Japanese likewise navigated the city's water mains for attacks. Elsewhere troops discovered enemy forces disguised in civilian clothes and even dressed as women. "In his physical resemblance to the Filipino," one intelligence report noted, "the enemy possesses a powerful weapon of deception." Other signs, however, pointed to difficulties the Japanese faced. Near Fort McKinley, Americans found an abandoned aid station filled with blood-soaked blankets, while the bodies of dead enemy soldiers and marines often sported homemade bandages, indicating a shortage of even basic medical supplies. "Enemy morale," one intelligence report speculated, "is apparently low."

The torching of Manila, meanwhile, continued, much to the frustration of officers who had hoped to spare the Pearl of the Orient. The fires north of the Pasig had largely subsided, leaving the smoldering ruins of some of Manila's great buildings, including the city's Opera House, the Ideal, Avenue, and State theaters, and Heacock's department store. "The old Escolta—Manila's Fifth Avenue—is gone—completely gone. There are blocks where not even a stone stands atop another," Bill Dunn reported. "The bank which used to handle CBS business in the Far East has been gutted by flames so fierce that window panes hang like icicles." General Griswold vented his hostility to reporters. "A lot of this destruction is wanton and of no military purpose," the XIV Corps commander said. "We are doing all we can to stop it, but we are up against a needle in a haystack job." General Fellers wrote to his wife of MacArthur's misery. "Mac," he explained, "is very depressed over the destruction."

American troops on the front lines not only battled the enemy but treated hordes of starved and wounded civilians, many with infected gunshot and bayonet wounds. "Day after day the destruction of the city went on and the stream of casualties was ceaseless," observed a 112th Medical Battalion report. "The Battalion drove itself to the limit to keep pace with the pitiful human traffic." Displaced residents, having suffered for years under the Japanese, swarmed mobile kitchens set up to feed the advancing troops. Other refugees resorted to looting to survive. "Not only furniture," observed Filipino journalist Felipe Buencamino, "but even walls and floors are being carted away."

"They killed my father and they killed my mother," one rescued boy told troops. "I want to get these wounds fixed; then give me a gun and a lot of bullets."

The promise of safety forced desperate residents, like thirty-four-year-old Elsie Hamburger, on an odyssey across an apocalyptic wasteland toward American lines, her path illuminated by the fiery red glow. Along the way the German immigrant had seen her husband killed by shrapnel, a toddler speared on the end of a bayonet, and more than a dozen bound men pushed into an inferno. "The Japanese seemed to be absolutely wild," she recalled. "I could hear the screams and moans of those being burned."

Finally she reached the dividing line between the two forces. On one side she spied two Japanese troops, who opened fire on her with a machine gun. Across the street she saw an American soldier—and the hope of rescue. "I arose on my hands and knees, tore off my clothes, and crawled across the street," Hamburger testified. "Before I passed out I took this American soldier in my arms and kissed him."

"God bless America," she said.

○ ○ ○ ○

IN SANTA ANA, Marcial Lichauco and his wife Jessie welcomed the appearance of American cavalrymen south of the Pasig on February 10, an arrival broadcast by the tolling of church bells, long forbidden by the Japanese. "We ran up the street and met a platoon of soldiers,"

Lichauco wrote in his diary. "Jessie had a hard time suppressing her tears as she greeted the men, and so, for that matter, did most of the women around us." The family returned home, where Lichauco scooped up his two-year-old daughter Cornelia. Unable to resist the historic moment, he carried her back to introduce her to the Americans, who he noted all hailed from Texas. "They gave Cornelia some chewing gum and I have been having quite a time since then explaining to her how to enjoy it."

The excitement proved short-lived. Battered refugees began arriving that afternoon, fleeing the district of Malate, some crawling on hands and knees. By the morning of February 11, thousands clogged the streets, overwhelming the nearby convent and school. "From their incoherent account of what they had seen and experienced," Lichauco wrote, "it was apparent that the entire district was being razed to the ground by the Japanese." Aided by two household servants, Lichauco set off to find his relatives, threading his way amid the parade of refugees. "I met thousands of them painfully making their way towards Santa Ana," he wrote. "Many were wounded, and nearly all were dazed from fatigue and lack of sleep." He ran into a friend, whose daughter had been shot through the leg by a Japanese sniper. Lichauco pressed on with his search. "Farther up the road," he wrote, "I saw my mother who could walk no more but as I had taken the precaution to bring a pushcart we were able to carry her safely home."

Absent any relief agencies, Lichauco and his wife converted their home and an adjacent property into a makeshift aid station, where, over the course of the battle, the family would ultimately help more than twelve hundred people. "I never realized," he wrote, "how much punishment the human body could endure." A local doctor volunteered to assist along with several women who could wash wounds and offer first aid. With no electricity, running water, food, or even fuel for cooking, the challenge proved daunting. The wounded patients sprawled out on the bare cement floor without pillows, mattresses, or mosquito nets. Not only did the makeshift aid station lack toilets, but Lichauco had no bedpans, soap, or towels; the only water came from wells. Those unfortunate souls who passed away were simply wrapped in old paper or cardboard and buried in a nearby churchyard. "The stench of blood is sickening and as nearly all the patients we have accommodated were able to get away with only the clothes they had on their backs you can well imagine the odors that permeate the infirmary," Lichauco wrote. "The suffering of the men, women and children quartered here is indescribable."

CHAPTER 16

*"The Western mind cannot grasp the realities of this
awful crime. One must grope into the shadows of
history to find a parallel. Genghis Khan, the Mongol
Horde blazing a trail of utter destruction."*

—GENERAL HEADQUARTERS,
SOUTH WEST PACIFIC AREA,
MILITARY INTELLIGENCE SECTION, GENERAL STAFF

HUNDREDS OF REFUGEES HUDDLED IN THE RUINS OF SANTA
Rosa College in the Walled City. Included among them were the
doctors, nurses, and patients from San Juan de Dios Hospital as well
as families forced out of the Manila Cathedral. The ruins resembled
a squatters community with makeshift tents constructed from corrugated metal tucked amid the scorched and crumbling brick walls
of the school. Artillery shells whistled continually overhead even as
refugees boiled rice over outdoor fires. Tensions soared, as Japanese
marines periodically showed up to drag off groups of men.

Around seven p.m. on February 11, the Japanese again visited the
refugees. This Sunday evening, however, marines came for the women
and children. Troops rounded up fifty, including eleven-year-old Rosalinda Andoy and her mother Adelaida, ordering them to march across
Solana Street to the ruins of Santo Domingo Church. At the front of
the church, the marines stopped them, demanding that the refugees
enter three at a time. Rosalinda walked in next to her mother, where
three troops greeted them. One of the marines raised his rifle and
drove his bayonet into Adelaida's breast. She dropped to the ground
in a seated position. Another plunged his blade into her back. "My
mother caught me by the arm and pulled me down on my back," Rosalinda said. "A Japanese stepped on my head while I lay on the ground

and bayonetted me several times. I turned my body facing the ground and the Japanese bayonetted me in the back."

But the marine refused to quit.

As Rosalinda squirmed beneath his boot, the marine plunged his bayonet into her again and again and again, puncturing her chest, back, arms, and legs.

Her intestines popped out.

Yet the steel blade continued to rise and fall, rise and fall.

The marine finally stopped, pulling his blade out after the thirty-eighth blow. Rosalinda pretended to be dead, her blood draining onto the church floor.

The marines ushered in another group of three victims. The sounds of the slaughter mixed with the moans of the victims, many of them children.

"Mother," Rosalinda heard one child cry, "I am dying."

Sixteen-year-old Rosario Nieves entered the church following her mother Balbina. Her twelve-year-old sister Isabel had gone in moments earlier behind Rosalinda and now lay on the ground bleeding. Balbina realized what was about to happen and pushed her daughter to the ground. Rosario looked up just as the marine attacked her mother. "She received seven bayonet thrusts," she said. "After my mother had been bayonetted the Japanese stepped on my head and bayonetted me twice at the right side, twice near the center of my back, once in the left shoulder and once in the left neck."

Finally the Japanese left.

The scorched church, where before the war families had celebrated baptisms, communions, and weddings, had devolved into a slaughter-house. Rosario regained consciousness about an hour later. Her sister Isabel was alive, though she would succumb to her wounds within hours. "I went to my mother and tried to wake her up," Rosario said, "but she was already dead. So I slept by her side till morning."

Rosalinda likewise crawled over to her mother and curled up next to her in the dark, no doubt feeling the warmth of her body as she lay amid the rubble of this once holy place. Despite her own wounds, Adelaida tried to comfort her daughter and prepare her for the inevitable. The Japanese had killed Rosalinda's father, and soon Adelaida would join him. "My mother brushed my hair and said she was dying and that I must be a good girl." Rosalinda said. "My mother died and I slept beside her."

o ɔ o ɔ

FIRES CLOSED IN ON the Garcia family home off Taft Avenue on February 12. Ten-year-old Jack could hear the screams of his neighbors fleeing the conflagration, adding to the soundtrack of war that included the rattle of machine guns and the explosions of artillery. That afternoon Furuda-san visited the home to deliver a warning. Ida Garcia had met the stocky young Japanese soldier in the latter days of the occupation, when he knocked on the front gate and asked to draw water from the family's well. Through that one-time act of kindness, an unlikely friendship had formed. Furuda-san had visited often, helping to repair the chicken coop gates and tussling with the family's two dogs, Rex and Tiger. The enemy soldier even managed to score a twenty-five-kilogram bag of sugar for the family, worth a small fortune in the latter days of the occupation.

But today was not a social visit. "You must leave now," he warned. "All of you must go away now."

His words frightened the family.

"Very dangerous," the Japanese soldier continued. "Soldiers burn house. Americans coming, shooting, shooting, please go now."

The neighbors who sheltered at the Garcias' home listened to Furuda-san's warning. Several begged to go to De La Salle, which was right around the corner. The Garcias' emergency plan all along, in fact, had been to seek refuge at De La Salle, where Jack and his older brother Ramon attended school. Brother Xavier had called in the latter days of the occupation, inviting the family to preemptively move into the school. Ida Garcia's sister Helen Vasquez-Prada was already there with her husband and four sons after troops commandeered their home in January. The Garcia family had decided to wait, but just in case, Ida had dropped off food, clothing, and folding cots.

But Furuda-san balked at De La Salle.

The soldier told them his commanding officer would not allow any residents on Taft Avenue, which ruled out the school. "Was it Japanese officialdom that didn't want us to go? Or was it Furuda who thought it best that we give De La Salle a miss?" Jack Garcia would later speculate. "Did he know something we didn't?"

American artillery aimed at enemy troops in Rizal Memorial Stadium continued to fall short of the sports complex, shaking the ground and showering residents in the Garcias' yard with dirt and debris. One such errant projectile two days earlier had likely killed more than a dozen people in the makeshift shelter behind the home of Nick Reyes, which was just a few blocks from the Garcia home. His daughter Lourdes at this very moment lay amid the rubble of her family's home, waiting for rescue. Japanese troops, meanwhile, had turned over several orange trams, blocking Pennsylvania Avenue and Vito Cruz Street. Marines had piled sandbags alongside and created machine-gun nests. Rifle fire greeted any resident who dared venture onto the street.

Despite the danger, the Garcia family had no choice but to try to escape, a challenge made all the more perilous as artillery fire increased through the afternoon. With De La Salle no longer an option, the family decided to try for St. Scholastica's College, a Catholic institution that occupied an entire city block and was ringed by a high adobe wall that would offer protection from shrapnel and gunfire. To go there, however, meant the family had to cross Pennsylvania Avenue, right in the line of fire.

Furuda-san reluctantly approved of the plan.

"Quick, go now," he told them. "Take everything, you have only short time to move your things. Quick, maybe later you no can cross street anymore."

The family grabbed the prepared bundles of clothes and gathered with four other families in the vacant lot next door, which fronted Pennsylvania Avenue. A glance in either direction revealed Japan's fortifications. "There were," Jack recalled, "more machine guns than we envisaged and there were mortar emplacements everywhere, strategically positioned and hidden behind heavy sandbags."

It was time to go.

The families charged across Pennsylvania Avenue. Miraculously the Japanese guns remained silent, but the family's good fortune ran out. The gates at St. Scholastica were locked. Ida banged on the metal gates, but no one answered.

Artillery shells whistled overhead. She banged again and again.

"Who is it?" one of the nuns inside finally asked.

Ida explained that five families needed shelter, but the nun refused to open the gates. "We are full and cannot take in any more people."

Out on the street—and in the line of fire—the families grew desperate. At any second troops might open fire. Ida detected the nun's German accent and switched languages, appealing to her in her native tongue. "We bring food. We carry rice, tinned meat, and sacks of beans," she pleaded. "For the love of God, let us in before the Japanese start firing at us or one of those bombs kills us all!"

The families waited. Finally the gate yawned open to reveal a young nun, who hugged Ida and ushered the families inside. Ramon Garcia and other neighbors ferried in the food. No sooner had the family arrived than Jack Garcia looked back to see an artillery shell blast the family's home, destroying the back. "There goes my bedroom, the kitchen, and part of the dining room," the youth said to himself.

The nun's claim that the school was full proved accurate. Refugees crowded the rooms and even passageways, many of them neighbors and friends. The Garcia family finally found a spot in a second-floor room, where Jack collapsed atop some cushions, while his father set up folding chairs he found. Artillery shells continued to buzz through the air, one of which hit the school and shrouded the room with smoke. The family relocated to the ground floor, settling down in a crowded corridor.

"Help me," someone down the hall cried. "I've been hit in both legs."

Several refugees had ferried rice across Pennsylvania Avenue—the same spot where the Garcia family had moments earlier crossed—when the Japanese opened fire with machine guns. Bullets had shredded one man's legs. Jack Garcia went to see the commotion, staring at the wounded man's slacks, bright red with blood.

"Where's the doctor?" someone shouted.

The image haunted the ten-year-old, who listened to the injured man moan as the afternoon turned to evening. "What next?" the youth wondered. "I was scared. It was an uneasy and emotional apprehension that was building up within me and I couldn't help but dread that something frightful was about to happen."

○ ○ ○ ○

JUST ONE BLOCK AWAY at De La Salle College, sixty-eight men, women, and children, including some of Manila's most prominent families, listened to the thunder of artillery as American soldiers closed in on the Japanese. The Catholic educational school, which enrolled twelve hundred students before the war, served as one of the safest shelters south of the Pasig River. Set back off Taft Avenue with a wide lawn and circular drive, the three-story concrete structure was built in the shape of the letter H with a northern and southern wing. Beyond its sturdy construction, the school—widely recognized as one of the finest in the Philippines—was an elegant building with a white neo-classical facade adorned with four Corinthian columns and topped by statues of children gazing up at Saint John Baptist de La Salle. Arched windows and doors opened onto the garden, while second-floor balconies offered views from above. Classrooms occupied most of the first and second floors, each one crowded with rows of wooden desks.

The Japanese had commandeered the school during the occupation, converting it at one point into a hospital. They had interned the nine American brothers but allowed the seventeen German missionaries to stay, albeit confining them to the south wing. There brothers had attempted to continue the school's mission throughout the occupation in the limited space, which consisted of a large ground-floor assembly room. A wide staircase led to the second-floor chapel, while the area underneath it functioned as a wine cellar and now doubled as a bomb shelter. The third floor housed the offices and private rooms of the brothers. The chapel served as the spiritual heart, providing a graceful space for daily mass, baptisms, and communions. An arched entrance opened onto the green-and-white-tiled floors with a long center aisle that divided the rows of wooden pews, each carved with the school's emblem. Chandeliers dangled from the barreled ceiling, while behind the polished communion rails rose the altar.

On the eve of battle, Japanese troops had seized nearby homes, prompting Brother Xavier to open the school as a refugee center. Four families—three Filipino and one Spanish—had jumped at the offer. Included among them were the wives, children, and servants of Judge Jose Carlos, Dr. Antonio Cojuangco, Dr. Clemente Uychuico, and Enrique Vasquez-Prada, a Spanish businessman. The fifty-nine-year-old Vasquez-Prada was joined by his wife Helen, who at forty-one was eight years younger than her sister Ida Garcia. The couple's four sons ranged in age from five to twenty-one, all of whom attended De La Salle. The family was well liked in Manila. Enrique Vasquez-Prada was known for his great sense of humor, though he had suffered recently from pleurisy that left him weak. Helen was "tall and slim, with a pale complexion," remembered one friend. "She had blue eyes and golden hair, like that of the fairies in children's stories."

The forty-three civilians joined the seventeen brothers, seven school employees, and refugee priest Father Francis Cosgrave, a forty-eight-year-old Australian who had come to De La Salle after the Japanese seized his church and home in the Manila suburb of Baclaran. Servants outnumbered the family members, helping to draw water from the well, prepare meals from canned goods, and care for the children, the youngest of whom was three. The refugees mostly congregated on the ground floor sleeping atop mattresses and blankets scattered around the base of the stairs with the exception of sixteen-year-old Antonio Cojuangco, Jr. The teen spent most days in bed in a small room beside the chapel entrance, where he battled typhoid under the anxious care of his father and a male nurse, Filomeno Inolin. "That boy looked forward to the coming of the Americans," recalled his brother-in-law Servillano Aquino. "He prayed and prayed."

"If I die, I should like to see the Americans first," the youth repeatedly said, "because we have suffered much under these people."

The refugees had passed the nine days since the Battle of Manila began waiting for the Americans to appear on Taft Avenue, monitoring the progress of MacArthur's forces via a shortwave radio hidden on the third floor. Dr. Uychuico saw firsthand the results of the fighting, summoned by the Japanese to perform surgery on wounded marines. Father Cosgrave meanwhile said mass each day, and Brother Lambert Romanus held classes for the children. During lulls in the shelling, refugees climbed to the rooftop to watch the march of fires across the city, while five-year-old Fernando Vasquez-Prada was thrilled at the sight of the American observation planes that buzzed in the skies. Like so many others caught in the gauntlet between American and Japanese forces, fear remained a constant burden on everyone, especially Helen Vasquez-Prada. She could not shake a fortune-teller's long-ago warning that she would one day die by the sword.

The fear of violence had only escalated in recent days as the tenuous peace long maintained by the brothers and the Japanese began to break down. Japanese troops stormed the south wing on February 7 allegedly hunting for weapons. Marines forced all the refugees up to the second floor and searched them, using it as a chance to molest the women. "They were pretty rough and nasty," recalled Brother Antonius von Jesus. Aquino echoed him. "I don't think you could hide a gun in the pocket where a dime couldn't be hidden." The Japanese bound Brother Xavier and Judge Carlos and marched them out the door, neither of whom was seen again. Before leaving, troops ordered the rest of the refugees to remain inside at all times, to stay off the balconies, keep away from the windows, and even refrain from singing in the chapel. "From then on," Cosgrave recalled, "we were virtual prisoners."

Artillery fire escalated as the Americans targeted Japanese forces dug in at the sports stadium that backed up to the school. On February 10, a shell tore through the second-floor dining room, peppering Dr. Cojuangco with shrapnel. "Everybody got scared at that time," called Aquino. "It was getting very close." Aquino helped his sick brother-in-law downstairs as a precaution. Cosgrave likewise moved his daily mass to the chapel's windowless entryway, the same place he later chose to baptize the Cojuangco's adopted three-year-old son Ricardo. During intense shelling the refugees gathered at the base of the stairs or crowded in the wine cellar, praying the rosary, while Father Cosgrave gave absolution. The heat and lack of air only increased the stress. "We could hear these shells exploding against the building," Cosgrave said. "The fighting seemed to be coming closer and closer."

The morning of February 12—the same day Furuda-san warned Ida Garcia to take her family and escape—Cosgrave canceled mass. Shells buzzed the church and machine guns rattled on the street. The refugees huddled in prayer. By mid-morning, the fighting had let up enough that Aquino helped his brother-in-law back up to his room on the second floor, which offered better ventilation. Aquino remained, eating his lunch with the teenager and his nurse, Inolin. Aquino's wife, Trinidad, and father-in-law, Dr. Cojuangco, joined them. Others climbed to the second floor, including several of the brothers, a few servants, and three of the Carlos children: Rosario, Asela, and Tony.

Around noon a Japanese officer accompanied by about twenty enlisted marines arrived, claiming to hunt for three guerrillas believed to have been firing from the second floor. Troops searched the premises and seized several servants.

"You can't do this," one of the brothers protested.

The Japanese officer hit him.

The marines marched the servants out the door, a departure followed seconds later by gunfire. The Japanese returned after a few minutes, hurling the battered servants back inside the building. The refugees at this moment remained scattered throughout the premises. A few hovered around the stairs, while others hid inside the wine cellar and still more were up near the chapel. Brother Flavius Leo, who had just sat down with Cosgrave next to the wine cellar, heard the officer bark an order.

"They're going to kill us," cried Leo, who understood Japanese.

The missionary turned to Cosgrave. "Father," he pleaded, "give us absolution!"

Before anyone could respond, the marines lunged, aiming their steel bayonets at the refugees. "I raised my hand to give him an absolution," Cosgrave later testified, "and the bayonet of the Jap passed under my arm into his heart."

Leo collapsed on top of the priest's knees, pinning him in place. The marine stabbed Cosgrave through the left side of his chest, pulled the blade out, and drove it into his shoulder. The Japanese next attacked the Vasquez-Prada family, bayoneting twenty-two-year-old Enrique followed seconds later by twenty-one-year-old Herman. "They were hit in the throat," recalled youngest brother Fernando, "and killed instantly."

The toppled siblings could no longer shield Fernando from the attackers. One of the marines plunged his blade into the five-year-old's chest. He yanked it out and rammed it in again. "My mother seeing the Japanese soldier going for a third blow sprang up and scooped me off the floor," he recalled. "Like an enraged tigress she fought back, she kicked, she bit, she swung her fists." Her efforts did little. "My mother was slashed across the shoulder. A big piece of flesh was hacked out of one thigh," Fernando said. "My poor mother tried to protect herself with her hands. The fingers of both hands were sliced away. She was stabbed in the abdomen and fell to the floor."

"Let her take time to die," the officer sneered.

The marines then butchered fourteen-year-old Alfonso before plunging the bayonet twice into the chest of the elder Enrique Vasquez-Prada. The attacks on the missionaries and the Vasquez-Prada family sent other refugees diving into the wine cellar and fleeing up the stairs toward the chapel. Antonio Madrileno, who worked for the Vasquez-Prada family, joined others inside the shelter. Refugees lay on the floor and covered themselves, listening to the shouts and screams outside. "Some of the women and children," Madrileno recalled, "were crying and the brothers were praying."

The Japanese split up to pursue the refugees. Some entered the darkened wine cellar armed with a light, motioning everyone outside. One after the other the men and women filed out, each one struck by the butt of a rifle. The Japanese then ordered them to turn and face the wall. Seconds later the marines began to shoot and stab them. The unfortunate souls who cried or moaned received additional jabs. "When the Japanese had finished bayoneting us they pulled and dragged the bodies and threw them in a heap at the foot of the stairs, the dead being thrown upon the living," recalled Cosgrave, who wound up near the bottom of the pile. "Not many were killed outright by the bayonetting, a few died within one or two hours, the rest slowly bled to death."

Other troops bounded up the stairs, hunting the rest of the refugees. Marines caught thirty-two-year-old Juanita Tamayo, who worked as the cook for the Cojuangco family, on the second landing along with Juanita Carlos and her twelve-year-old daughter, Cecilia. "I raised my hands," remembered Tamayo, who opted not to watch. "I tried to cover my face and a bullet came through my hand."

The round blew off the little finger on her right hand. Marines killed Juanita Carlos and shot her daughter in the stomach. Cecelia lived long enough to later crawl up the last few stairs and collapse at the chapel entrance where she died.

Twenty-one-year-old Rosario Carlos, her twenty-year-old sister Asela, and fourteen-year-old Fortunata Salonga, who worked as a maid for the Aquino family, were also on the second floor. Each one fell moments after being discovered, the victim of a bullet or a blade. Rosario Carlos, who preferred to be shot rather than stabbed, positioned herself in front of the one marine whose rifle did not have a bayonet. The attacker stood face to face when he squeezed the trigger. The bullet ripped through the left side of her chest just below her collarbone and exited her back.

Steps away Aquino huddled inside the small room to the right of the chapel with his brother-in-law, wife, father-in-law, and the nurse, Inolin. When the massacre began, he had started to go down to investigate, but others below motioned for him to retreat and hide. He had slipped back in the room and closed the door. The five refugees waited and listened as Japanese marines with hobnail boots climbed the stairs. "We heard four rapid shots," recalled Inolin, "followed by the wail of women."

Aquino cracked the door open for a peek. The Japanese fired a single shot into the room, the bullet digging into the wall. Aquino slammed the door again, but the Japanese ordered them to come out. The trapped refugees had no other option.

The nurse opened the door to reveal a Japanese officer clutching a pistol and two marines armed with fixed bayonets. The troops motioned again for the five of them to exit. Inolin departed first, followed by Dr. Cojuangco and then Aquino. As soon as he emerged, Aquino surveyed the scene, spotting his maid sprawled on the floor, soaked in blood. A few feet away lay Rosario Carlos and her sister Asela, whom he had heard scream. "She was sitting down and bleeding. Her arm was shot and it was dangling, hardly connected to her body," he recalled. "Blood was all over her."

The Japanese ordered Inolin to turn around and face the wall. "When the nurse obeyed," Aquino said, "the Japanese stabbed him with the bayonet."

"Oh!" he cried.

The Japanese pulled out the blade and drove it into him again and again. "I received four thrusts," Inolin later testified, "two in the back, one in my right arm and one in the right side of my neck." Dr. Cojuangco saw the nurse drop and darted for the chapel, but the Japanese caught him seconds later. "He was stabbed," Aquino recalled. "He was able to get inside a few more steps before he collapsed."

Aquino chose to fight. The twenty-four-year-old lunged at the closest marine but missed. The Japanese drove his bayonet into Aquino's chest just below his left nipple. The blade popped out his back. Aquino tumbled to the ground, and the marine stabbed him again on the right side of his chest. Blood spilled out of him, making the tile floor slippery, but Aquino refused to quit, crawling toward the marine, hoping to grab his legs. "He let me come close to him," Aquino said. "When I was about a foot away from him, he stabbed me on the right shoulder near the base of my neck." The marine crouched down so as to draw more strength from his legs. "He decided to push me just like a broom from the wall toward the other end of the corridor."

With each step, Aquino felt the blade drive deeper into his body until the rifle barrel penetrated his shoulder. His wife Trinidad, who had come out of the room behind him, watched in horror. She wrested free from the marine who held her and ran toward her husband. A rifle cracked. Aquino watched her lose her balance, stumble, and collapse on her hands and knees near the chapel entrance, a bullet in her back. The marine followed and stood over her. He raised his bayonet and plunged it into her back. Aquino watched, powerless to intervene. The marine pulled his blade out and rammed it into her back again and again before returning to Aquino and bayoneting him twice more. "At that instant," he later said, "I turned my head wishing I was dead."

One of the marines then entered the room and seized his sick brother-in-law, dragging the sixteen-year-old out to the center of the corridor. The youth who had prayed to see American troops before he died instead looked up into the face of a Japanese marine, who raised his bayonet and drove it into him, killing him.

The Japanese turned to the chapel, where more than a half-dozen refugees and brothers hid among the wooden pews. Near the entrance, troops found brothers Alemond Lucian, Lambert Romanus, and Hartmann Hubert. Marines butchered the latter two, but Lucian tried to defend himself, only to be sliced in half by a sword.

The Japanese then split up. Two moved down each of the outer aisles, while a single marine walked down the center of the chapel. Amid the pews in the middle of the sanctuary, the Japanese slashed brothers Adolf Gebhard and Paternus Paul. Next to fall were brothers Victor Konrad and Mutwald William, crouched on the right side in front of the first pew. Troops then discovered seventeen-year-old Regina Acuna, a servant for the Uychuico family, bayoneting her nine times, including stabs through the right cheek and two through her throat. Six-year-old Tony Carlos, who had hidden in the confessional, burst out and ran toward the brothers. One of the marines drove his bayonet in the boy's back, raised him in the air, and hurled him to the floor dead.

The Japanese closed in on the last two missionaries, Brother Antonius von Jesus and Brother Maximin Maria. When the massacre began, Brother Antonius had heard the gunshots and started for the stairs to investigate. En route he ran into Brother Maximin, bloodied from a bayonet wound and fleeing the Japanese.

"It is all over," Brother Maximin had cried. "They are going to kill us all!"

The two had retreated to the front left of the chapel, where Brother Antonius had tried to tend to his fellow missionary's wounds until the marines found them.

"I am a German," Antonius pleaded. "You can't kill me."

The Japanese ignored his protest. One of the marines drove his blade into Antonius's chest, piercing his lung. The missionary fell back against the wall. The marine put his boot on his chest to make it easier to pull out the blade. The other marine meanwhile rammed him twice in the belly with his bayonet. The two then stuck him five more times in the arm, before finishing off Brother Maximin.

The slaughter ended.

The assault on the brothers and refugees at De La Salle had lasted barely twenty minutes yet in that time Japanese marines had killed or mortally wounded forty-one men, women, and children, turning this once holy place into a hellhole. Blood not only stained the green-and-white-tiled floors of the chapel but splattered the walls. The dead littered the pews and corridor outside, while a heap of bodies lay at the bottom of the stairs. The Japanese had to step over and around them to ransack the premises, opening cupboards and trunks, stealing food, medicine, and personal belongings off the dead and dying. Troops retreated outside to drink, returning at times to laugh and mock the suffering of their victims. "We remained there all the afternoon," Cosgrave recalled, "during which time many who had been wounded had already died."

For the survivors, the misery had only begun. With the Japanese encamped around the building, no one dared leave in search of help. The only option was to pretend to be dead and wait for the Americans to arrive, which could be days or even a week. The Japanese knew that some of the victims feigned death, going so far as to place a glass of water beside each body so that the troops could check if the person had sipped it.

"Don't drink from your glass," Fernando Vasquez-Prada's father warned him. "Drink from someone else's whom you are sure is dead."

The shelling and machine-gun fire outside continued as the afternoon gave way to dusk and then evening. Helen Vasquez-Prada, surrounded by the bodies of three of her four children, howled in pain. "My father and I had to crawl to the chapel to get her some water," recalled Fernando, who was careful each time to return to his original position, where coagulated blood left an outline of his tiny body. "She felt cold and asked for some blankets, saying she could feel my brother's cold head underneath her body."

Brother Antonius climbed to his feet and staggered downstairs begging for anyone who could provide first aid, but the few survivors proved too weak. He found a bottle of whiskey in the rector's room, downed the brown liquor, and stumbled to his bed, where he attempted to dress his wounds with iodine before he passed out. Cosgrave wriggled out of a pile of bodies around ten p.m. to find he was soaked in blood. He spotted Brother Arcadius Maria. The bespectacled missionary vomited blood, while a hole in his head leaked brain matter. Cosgrave administered last rites to him and the few others he found alive. "I was more than edified to see the patience and the resignation with which these people met their death," the priest testified, "some of them actually praying to God to forgive those who had put them to death."

Cosgrave climbed the stairs and crept through the chapel, inventorying the bodies of the brothers and refugees. The priest made his way into the sacristy and collapsed. "As far as I could see," Cosgrave noted, "everyone was dead."

Servillano Aquino awoke to find it dark in the hallway outside the chapel. He was exhausted and in pain from being swept across the floor at the point of a bayonet. He called out to his wife Trinidad, but she did not respond. "I could not lift my body up," he said, "so I crawled instead inch by inch to my wife and I found out she was dead." Rosario Carlos had heard him cry out and spoke up, confessing she was in such agony that she wished she were dead. Her sister Asela Carlos likewise clung to life, though neither could understand her murmuring.

Aquino's voice had rallied his father-in-law Dr. Antonio Cojuangco, who now stirred in the dark. "I am here," the doctor said. "Please send somebody here."

Juanita Tamayo, whose finger was blown off, responded. She

climbed up from the stairwell landing and pulled Cojuangco closer to his son-in-law. Aquino begged for water, and she gave him some, which he gulped despite his father-in-law's warning that it was dangerous to do so with chest wounds. "I preferred death," Aquino later said, "rather than suffer thirst." Asela asked for water, which she drank, and soon thereafter she died; so, too, did Aquino's maid, Fortunata. Aquino tried to sit up but fainted. He tried two more times and each time passed out. "I wanted to faint because I found out that one does not feel any pain when he faints," he said. "It was easier to die this way."

The Japanese returned the following morning. Those still alive pretended to be dead as troops moved through the first and second floors, kicking the bodies to see if anyone stirred. To Aquino's horror, the Japanese tried to rape his fourteen-year-old maid, who at this point had been dead for almost ten hours. Troops tore the dead teen's panties off but found rigor mortis prevented them from parting her legs. "She was dead. She was cold," Aquino later testified. "No sane man would do that."

The Japanese then tried to rape Rosario Carlos, who pretended to be dead. Marines moved her hands and then spread the twenty-one-year-old's legs. "I heard them talk and laugh," she said. "I felt them tearing the lower part of my underclothing, but I didn't move." Suddenly she heard a voice bark an order in Japanese. "I felt my dress pulled down, and a little while later I felt somebody step on my stomach."

Departing troops slipped off Aquino's ring, watch, and even shoes. Afterward Aquino tore the shirt off one of the brothers and plugged his wounds. His father-in-law's health declined throughout the day. Blood continued to seep out of his body, and his belly swelled like a balloon, forcing Tamayo to have to press on his stomach to force the air out until he finally died that night. "He was," Aquino reflected, "in agony."

Many of the wounded brothers scattered throughout the chapel died that day. Outside in the hallway, Aquino listened one by one as the groans fell silent. Each time a missionary expired, one of the others would call out his name.

"Let us pray for him," someone would announce.

Fernando Vasquez-Prada tried to comfort his mother but with little success. Her wounds proved too much, both physical and emotional. "As the hours passed my poor mother lay agonizing, her entire body mutilated, the cadavers of my brothers surrounding her," Fernando said. "I gave her water and tried to clean her wounds." Enrique Vasquez-Prada busied himself trying to care for Fernando, the lone survivor of his four sons. He escorted the five-year-old up to the second floor where he found a tin of adobo. Enrique opened it and fed the canned meat to his hungry son. No sooner had he pried open the top than Japanese troops returned. The youth watched one of the marines drive his bayonet into the top of his father's head. The steel blade popped out under his chin. "My father was killed in front of my eyes," Fernando recalled. "I crept back to my mother's side to perhaps seek warmth. She knew my father had died."

Helen Vasquez-Prada, who had long feared she would die by the sword, began to slip into madness, cursing the troops who had wiped out most of her family. "Bastards!" she wailed. "Son-of-a-bitch!"

Her painful cries carried all the way upstairs, where even Aquino could hear them on the ground just outside the chapel. Japanese troops, no doubt tired of her howls, finally silenced her with a bayonet. "My mother lasted three agonizing days," Fernando later said. "She screamed day and night from the pain of her wounds."

The survivors prayed that the increased shelling and machine-gun fire outside heralded the arrival of American troops. Shells at times struck the school. A piece of stone fell at one point and hit Aquino. The Japanese meanwhile attempted to set fire to the building but succeeded only in destroying the books and furniture inside the church gallery. For much of the time, Cosgrave hid behind the altar, subsisting on communion wafers and the water he found in the altar vases. Those refugees who were able to, joined him there or in the small room above the sacristy. Despite his own injuries, the priest continued to administer to those around him, making rounds among the wounded. "Father Cosgrave would come to us day and night to give us our last extreme-unction," Aquino said. "He gave us consolation that if we should also die, we would go to heaven. He came every day—sometimes twice."

The health of the survivors deteriorated as the days passed. "I had difficulty in breathing because my lungs were punctured by the bayonet," recalled Aquino. "We wished we were dead." Out on the street, survivors listened to the clatter of trucks rolling through the rubble. "Every minute we were expecting the Americans to come up," Aquino testified. "We could hear voices and then they would vanish. We did not know whether it was the Japanese, Americans or Filipinos."

Around noon on February 15—seventy-two hours after the massacre—the survivors heard voices outside of the school, this time speaking English.

"Father," Aquino said to Cosgrave, "I think they have come."

"When I see Americans, I will go out and wave at them," replied the priest, who kept watch out the windows. "But the Japs are still around."

The survivors had endured too much to risk being killed now. Rather than dart out, the refugees huddled and waited as minutes turned to hours. Around five p.m. that afternoon, American soldiers entered the bloodied downstairs of De La Salle.

"Anybody alive?" one shouted.

Up the same staircase where Helen Vasquez-Prada's painful cries had once echoed, now came the familiar twang of an American accent. For the exhausted survivors crouched behind the chapel altar, liberation had at long last arrived.

"Yes," Cosgrave shouted. "We are alive. We are here."

○ ○ ○ ○

MAJOR HENNE and his fellow troops with the Third Battalion, 148th Infantry Regiment, closed in on Taft Avenue on February 12, the prominent north-south boulevard about ten blocks inland from the bay. The soldiers formed the tip of the spear as the Thirty-Seventh Infantry and First Cavalry divisions continued the western drive across Manila, constricting the Japanese each day between America's advancing front line and the waterfront. In that time the infantrymen had watched the battlefield evolve. The more residential areas of Pandacan and Paco, where fortifications consisted of mined streets and pillboxes, had morphed into the populous and commercial district of

Ermita, crowded with multistory hotels, apartments, and government buildings.

Iwabuchi's Central Force had proven adept at using this vertical landscape against them, targeting the infantrymen from above. "The high buildings gave the Japs a bird's eye view of a wide area and coverage of the street grid for blocks so that on most streets no one moved without drawing fire," Major Henne recalled. "Screening smoke was used but even so the men were exposed and when exposed the Japs connected." The infantrymen had no choice but to hold up the advance and eliminate the threat. "The preferred solution was to use cannon to blast the upper floors to rubble and then move in," he said. "An equally favored alternative was to burn the building. When these alternatives wouldn't work riflemen moved in to take the building floor by floor."

The job had led to high numbers of Japanese dead, whose remains littered the streets, buildings, and pillboxes.

"Based on reports from the line companies, the numbers of Jap dead in positions being overrun were the highest of any count since crossing the Pasig River," announced Lt. Jimmy Falls, the battalion's intelligence officer.

To help the infantry this Monday morning, American artillery and mortars zeroed on the prominent buildings along Kansas, Marcelino, and Colorado streets. Sherman tanks and self-propelled 105 mm howitzers took over the fight.

The first of the infantrymen reached Taft Avenue that afternoon, a major milestone in the advance on Manila Bay. The troops stopped, waiting for the other companies and battalions to the north and south to catch up. The area remained dangerous. Japanese snipers still lurked, and scores of enemy land mines lay buried in the roadway. Despite that, throngs of civilians emerged, apparently anxious for life to return to normal. "It was astonishing," Henne recalled. "From out of nowhere they came and in minutes Taft Avenue south of Herran became a busy thoroughfare. The Filipinos using the street showed no concern about the noisy battle still going on in the area."

A reminder of that danger occurred the following afternoon when an explosion shook several blocks of the capital. "A Filipino and his donkey-drawn caretela hit a mine and in the blink of an eye, the man, his donkey, his cart and pedestrians within a wide area were atomized," Henne remembered. "A freakish feature of the incident was a caretela wheel left lying at the edge of the deep crater."

The explosion drew Henne out onto the sidewalk of Taft Avenue along with a guerrilla captain attached to the battalion. The men watched the flow of people, many of whom appeared oblivious to the explosion, before the guerrilla stepped out into the street to stop and question a passerby. The guerrilla allowed the man to continue.

The individual took only a few steps before the guerrilla raised his gun and shot him. Henne watched in astonishment as the man crumpled to the street, dead.

"Jap," the guerrilla announced.

The infantrymen began the push toward Manila Bay the afternoon of February 13. The final blocks promised to be a perilous battle as the soldiers drove west toward Dewey Boulevard, the wide bayfront parkway Daniel Burnham had envisioned almost a half-century earlier. Lined with tall hotels and apartments, the boulevard offered the enemy plenty of tactical advantages over the Americans. Mortarmen set out to clear a path. One platoon comprised of twelve 81 mm mortars set a record that night, firing more than four thousand rounds. To increase the punch, mortar teams used both high-explosive rounds with delayed fuses, so as to penetrate roofs and detonate on lower floors, and white phosphorous rounds, designed to start fires and raze buildings. Bazooka teams joined the fight, blasting buildings. The sky glowed from the fires that night. Sunrise revealed the extent of the damage as infantrymen navigated through a maze of debris. "Picking their way down narrow confined streets through the heaps of galvanized steel roofing and masonry they endured the peculiar, sickening odor of burned flash coming from the countless corpses strewn throughout the area," Henne recalled. "The fires which had swept the area made it difficult to distinguish the dead Filipino civilians from the Japanese."

CHAPTER 17

*"Cannibals in the lowest strata of life could have
pursued no crueler methods."*

—REPORT NO. 13,
JUNE 11, 1945, WAR CRIMES BRANCH,
OFFICE OF THE THEATER JUDGE ADVOCATE

IWABUCHI KNEW THE BATTLE WAS NEARING ITS CLIMAX.
The convergence of the Thirty-Seventh Infantry from the north,
the First Cavalry from the east, and the Eleventh Airborne from the
south had by February 12 sealed the city, trapping Iwabuchi and his
dwindling force of four naval and two army battalions. American
mortar and shells rained down, destroying much of his few remaining
artillery pieces. His hodgepodge troops were left with little more than
rifles, bayonets, and grenades.

General Yokoyama, who had been slow to grasp the situation in
Manila, finally realized how dire it truly was. If left inside the city,
Iwabuchi and his men faced certain annihilation. Shimbu Group headquarters radioed Iwabuchi with a plan. Five battalions east of the city
would depart the night of February 13 and charge the American lines
near Novaliches, Quezon, Marikina, Mandaluyong, and Pasig areas at
midnight on February 16 to create a diversion. "The Manila Defense
Force," orders mandated, "should then conduct a daring charge with
its entire complement to effect a breakthrough of the envelopment."

Conditions inside the city worsened as American troops closed
in on Iwabuchi's men. From his headquarters up in Baguio, General
Yamashita, until now silent on the battle, finally intervened, censuring
Yokoyama on February 15 for failing to rein in Iwabuchi and demanding the admiral immediately vacate Manila.

"Withdraw at once in accordance with our original plan," the Tiger ordered.

Yokoyama again demanded Iwabuchi retreat to Fort McKinley, alerting him that troops would conduct a surprise attack on American lines as initially planned. "Counterattacks in our area are making some progress," the Shimbu Group messaged. "The Manila Naval Defense headquarters hereafter will be located at McKinley. Maintain close liaison with Shimbu Group headquarters and strengthen and secure the defense of the vicinity."

The base staff officer at Fort McKinley followed up with a message to Iwabuchi. "Today, Shimbu Group headquarters has ordered your headquarters to move to McKinley," the officer radioed. "In view of the increasing difficulty to effect a break-through, it is urgent that you move immediately, tonight. Will the headquarters move?"

From Fort McKinley and the Shimbu Group headquarters to Yamashita's Baguio stronghold, everyone waited for Iwabuchi's answer. Would the admiral retreat and live to fight another day or would he choose to make a final stand in Manila?

"The headquarters," he radioed at last, "will not move."

For Iwabuchi, the time to die had arrived.

The admiral had fumbled his hopes of turning Manila into another Stalingrad, far outgunned by American artillery and overrun on all sides by Yank cavalry and infantrymen. What did it matter now if he disobeyed orders? Iwabuchi radioed Admiral Okochi, who had tapped him to lead the Manila Naval Defense Force, confessing his failure. "In anticipation of disruption in communications, I hereby submit this message to you," Iwabuchi began. "I am overwhelmed with shame for the many casualties among my subordinates and for being unable to discharge my duty because of my incompetence. The men have exerted their utmost efforts in the fighting. We are very glad and grateful for the opportunity of being able to serve our country in this epic battle. Now, with what strength remains, we will daringly engage the enemy. 'Banzai to the Emperor!' We are determined to fight to the last man."

Iwabuchi then sent a message to General Yokoyama.

"In view of the general situation, I consider it very important to hold the strategic positions within the city," he radioed. "The transfer of the headquarters will hinder the execution of operations. We have tried to make ground contact with Fort McKinley but failed. Escape is believed impossible. Will you please understand this situation?"

Yokoyama's headquarters continued to send desperate messages over the next few days to Iwabuchi, imploring him and his forces to try to escape.

"The night of the 18th will be the best time for your breakthrough," one read.

But Iwabuchi ruled out such an operation, appearing resigned to his fate. Rather than escape, he and his men would hunker down. The Americans would have to dig them out of the few remaining urban fortresses, from Rizal Memorial Stadium and the Philippine General Hospital to the concrete government buildings and the ancient Walled City. There would be no retreat and no surrender. Iwabuchi would make the end as bloody as possible—for everyone. "We can hold out another week if we remain entrenched as we are. What is vitally important now is to hold every position and inflict severe losses on the enemy by any means. Fixed positions are our strong advantage. If we move, we will be weak," he messaged Yokoyama. "Therefore, in conducting the main operation, please conduct your plan without considering us."

○ ○ ○ ○

JAPANESE TROOPS HUNTED the streets of southern Manila—the areas still beyond the bounds of the American's control—shooting anyone who dared stray outside. Large massacres, like the German Club, Red Cross, and St. Paul's went hand in hand with scores of small-scale atrocities as marauding troops attacked families in homes and pulled others out of bomb shelters and butchered them in the streets. The Japanese went so far as to lure victims into an open lot on Kansas Street by planting a Red Cross flag.

To escape the flames and artillery, refugees often congregated in the large compounds of some of the city's wealthiest, whose elegant concrete homes offered protection from flying shrapnel and gardens that served as firebreaks. These gatherings, however, proved easy targets for the enemy. Troops murdered approximately one hundred on February 10 at the home of Walter Price, an American businessman who had made his fortune as the founder of Leyte Transportation Company before the Japanese interned him at Los Baños. Two days later marines killed twenty-eight more at the residence of businessman Carlos Perez-Rubio. A similar atrocity played out the morning of February 13, when troops slaughtered one hundred men, women, and children at the home of the late Pedro Campos, the former president of the Bank of the Philippines. Thirty-five more civilians fell February 17 at the home of Dr. Rafael Moreta.

Throughout southern Manila, the Japanese not only targeted large gatherings but also seized refugees singly and in small groups. Russian immigrant Helen Kremleff could only watch as marines marched off her husband Eugene, never to be seen again. Fellow Russian native Eva Gurevich suffered a similar horror when troops grabbed her husband Boris and twenty-three-year-old son Leonid. Desperate to intervene, she presented the Japanese with passports for her family, but the marine threw them to the ground.

"Go," he barked at her, pushing her up the street.

"When I was about a half block away," she recalled, "I heard three shots."

The Japanese picked through the ruins of destroyed homes in search of victims. That's where troops found Alexander Bachrach, the former agent for the Studebaker Corporation of America. He had just enough time to say farewell to his wife.

"Goodbye, Darling," he called out. "This is it."

"I looked around," his wife would later tell war crimes investigators, "to see him shot in the forehead."

Refugees realized that nowhere was safe.

"Japanese patrols were going back and forth," recalled Dr. Augusto Besa, a surgeon. "If they saw anyone in the open, they would shoot him."

German native Max Hahn witnessed the same. "I heard them shooting," he later testified, "as they went from shelter to shelter up the street."

Such terror forced some to do the unimaginable.

"Many mothers," recalled British citizen Stella Mary Best, who hid for four days under a home with two dozen others, "had to smother their babies until they died in order to keep them from crying out and giving away all the people under that house."

o   o   o   o

NEWS REPORTERS FLOCKED each day to the sixth floor of the battered National City Bank of New York building on Calle Juan Luna, which American forces had converted into an artillery observation post. Just a few hundred yards north of the Pasig River—and seventy feet above the booby-trapped streets and blood-soaked gutters—journalists could relax in safety and chart the battle's progress. The view from atop Manila, glimpsed between the smoke from the fires, was unrivaled. Twenty-seven miles to the west, Corregidor climbed out of the dark waters of Manila Bay, while to the south reporters could see the radio towers of Cavite Naval Base. Down below spread the Walled City, its defensive moat that kept out invaders for centuries filled in to create an eighteen-hole golf course. Bomb craters and trenches carved up the fairways, greens, and tee boxes, while the once-lush grass was scorched black from fire.

American troops had seized the bank days after the start of the battle. Like so much else in Manila, the once-grand building had been reduced to a burned-out skeleton of concrete and steel. Ankle-deep rubble and crumbled plaster littered the lobby along with twisted metal filing cabinets and charred typewriters, artifacts of a once peaceful time. The Japanese had previously occupied the building as evidenced by straw mats, discarded grenade boxes, and ripped satchels of rice. A narrow path cleared of mines and traps led through the debris up the stairs to the third floor, where troops had stacked a double line of sandbags in the windows. Observers aimed field glasses down on the Walled City; a desk pushed lengthwise in front of the window supported a .30-caliber machine gun. "The gunner sat hunched behind the desk," observed *Yank* magazine reporter Ozzie St. George, "one hand on the tripod."

The sixth floor functioned as the nerve center for America's artillery attacks against the Japanese, offering unobstructed views not only of Intramuros but also of the port and Ermita. As they did below, observers covered the windows, while a soldier sat in the hall, a field phone pressed at all times to his ear. In offices where brokers once worked, officers hunched over maps of Manila twenty-four hours a day, each block numbered and marked with its range. From this perch, artillerymen called in targets and reported the outcomes of attacks. "Here I found a vantage point for photographing a whole continuous action unequaled elsewhere in the war," recalled Carl Mydans. "Almost every day of the siege I spent some time with the observers, covering the progress of the assault and enjoying, after I got there, ease and luxury I had not often experienced in battle, sitting there with a group spinning yarns."

The reporters who visited each day invariably came away with a story, a window into the horror residents south of the Pasig now endured. "A short distance outside the wall I watched a Filipino woman frenzied trying to round up her brood of children," wrote *Newsweek*'s Robert Shaplen. "Through the glasses I could see her looking with despair toward our side of the river, wondering how she could get across." *Time* magazine's Bill Gray, as shells soared overhead, shot a glance at Capt. Francis Shannon, Jr., of Cincinnati, sitting in a chair calmly reading a copy of *Margery Wilson's Pocket Book of Etiquette*. "There is," the journalist wrote, "no explaining war-time reading tastes." Bill Dunn of CBS marveled not only at the precision of the artillery fire but at the enemy's tenacity. "They are not trying to retreat, withdraw or reinforce," he noted. "They are just staying put until such time as we kill them off."

Enemy troops knew the Americans studied them from above, converting civilians into human shields. The Japanese packed women and children into the lower floors of buildings that housed artillery. Ira Rosenberg, a staff photographer with the *New York Herald Tribune*, observed the enemy one day preparing to transport cannons across an open park toward an apartment building. "Before moving the artillery pieces," he recalled, "they would encircle it with civilians." Another time Rosenberg watched enemy forces, trucking supplies through one of the gates of the Walled City, devise a devious means to fend off attack. "To facilitate this movement," the photographer said, "the Japanese seized a young Filipina girl, stripped and lashed her nude body to a doorway, using her as their shield."

For the reporters, safely removed from the hand-to-hand fighting in the streets, there was a theatrical experience watching death delivered from afar, one accentuated by the army's generosity in providing visitors with light refreshments.

"Just have a chair," one officer told Walter Simmons of the *Chicago Tribune*. "The show is about to start; the curtain will go up in just a minute."

Like other reporters, Simmons thrilled at the experience, describing how the shells rumbled through the skies overhead with a roar similar to a freight train. Each time he saw flying stone, concrete, and dust seconds before he heard the explosion.

"Just across the river is Jap territory," Lt. Joseph Gallaher of Youngstown, Ohio, told him. "You can see them moving around over there."

The artillerymen watched a group of enemy troops dart from behind one of the walls of Intramuros and run toward Taft Avenue.

"Twelve, thirteen, fourteen, fifteen," said Pvt. Leon West, ticking off the troops who dove to the ground, guns raised. "Now they're flopping."

The Japanese troops stood a moment later and crept forward. Then more troops emerged from behind the wall, falling in behind them.

"Just watch," one of the artillerymen advised Simmons.

Suddenly the area where the troops stood vanished in a cloud of black smoke. Other explosions followed. When the smoke cleared seconds later, two dead Japanese marines lay sprawled on the ground. The blast had likely vaporized the others.

"One of those babies hit just where a Jap was standing," hollered First Lt. John Robohm of Minneapolis.

The few survivors stumbled toward the Metropolitan Theater, leaving the dead. "The Japs seem to have got into the theatre building, sir," one sergeant said.

"That's all right," Robohm replied. "We'll put on a little matinee for them!"

Royal Arch Gunnison with *Collier's* magazine was in the observation post with *Yank's* St. George one day when about a dozen Japanese troops began tossing furniture off a third-floor balcony of the Manila Hotel, about fifteen hundred yards south of the bank. Troops began to hoist up what appeared to be boxes of ammunition.

"God," one of the artillerymen muttered. "What a target."

The commanding officer of a 155 mm howitzer battalion jumped on the phone, relaying the details and asking for permission to fire his so-called "Long Tom," capable of hurling a ninety-five-pound shell up to nine miles. "Each time the Long Toms shoot," John Dos Passos observed, "it's like being hit on the head with a baseball bat."

The officer gave his troops the go-ahead.

"Boy," one of the men announced, "this is going to be a beautiful sight."

Gunnison, who had lived in Manila before the war and knew the history of the hotel, felt his heart sink. "It was like smashing the Waldorf-Astoria in New York or the St. Francis in San Francisco," he wrote. "There it stood, its two red cupola towers across the river, half a mile away. There was MacArthur's old penthouse apartment. Beneath was the palm lobby and the once air-conditioned dining room where presidential parties and visiting American and Oriental dignitaries had dined for years."

To the artillerymen, none of that mattered. "The hotel," St. George noted, "was just another target, a long dreamed-of lush spot that had gone the way of the other lush spots—the Army and Navy Club, the Spanish Club, the University Club."

The sixth floor of the bank offered one of the best views of the pending attack. "This is like a $2.20 box seat," exclaimed Staff Sgt. Leroy Erwin.

"It'll take 'em a few minutes to line the guns," the lieutenant announced.

Reporters and soldiers waited, all eyes glued on the hotel.

"On the way," the artilleryman in the hallway called out.

The shell roared over the bank seconds later, just missing the hotel. "Five-zero left," the commanding officer corrected, "five-zero short."

"They have stopped throwing things," one of the observers called out.

Everyone focused on the hotel.

"No," the observer corrected, "the little sons of bitches are still on the porch."

"On the way," came the call again.

The freight trained rumbled overhead.

Another miss. Then another.

The observers and artillerymen rushed to correct the range as more shells roared through the skies. Suddenly smoke blanketed the top of the hotel.

A direct hit.

The wind wafted the smoke away moments later to reveal a hole in the red tile roof, an entry wound. The upper floors of the once-grand hotel now burned and would continue to do so throughout the night. The target had been eliminated. Dos Passos watched the barrage from a similar observation post at the Great Eastern Hotel with other correspondents, noting the smoke curling skyward.

"There goes our drink at the bar," one lamented.

○ ○ ○ ○

AMERICAN TROOPS on the ground saw a far different battle than the artillerymen perched atop the National City Bank of New York. The retreating Japanese had left a trail of massacres for the Americans to follow, like macabre breadcrumbs. Often lured by the rancid smell of the dead—or tipped off by survivors, family, and neighbors—troops cautiously entered the ruins of homes, schools, and churches only to discover hundreds of men, women, and children, slain by gunfire, bayonets, and swords.

In one such case, soldiers on San Antonio Street stopped at the home of Spanish businessman Bartolome Pons and his wife Rosario. The Japanese had brutally murdered most of the family and household staff. American forces tallied the dead—five women, two men, and an infant, the majority of whom had been shot. "The baby," noted Maj. Donald Forward, "had been bayoneted." Some of the deceased were dressed in pajamas. Around the neck of one woman dangled rosary beads. Another was pregnant. Several showed signs of abuse, including a victim whose head the Japanese had rammed into the coils of a rocking chair. "One of the persons was scalped," Technician Fourth Grade Stevens Loska testified. "There were hairs lying on the floor."

The soldiers explored the home, rescuing a dog that had refused to leave the bloated body of its master. The Japanese had eaten the food in the refrigerator and had stripped the residence of valuables before smashing the furniture and picture frames and even slashing cushions. Amid the scattered personal papers, troops found the Spanish and American passports of Bartolome Pons and his wife, Rosario. "There is no visible motive," one report noted, "other than the desire to kill."

The discovery of the dead in the Ponses' home proved all too common for advancing American troops, who functioned not just as soldiers but as crime scene investigators. Outraged over the slaughter, MacArthur ordered all massacres investigated. "Desire full details," the general cabled, "of all authenticated cases of atrocities committed by the enemy in the Manila area as soon as possible."

The Japanese frequently attempted to cover up such massacres, largely by using fire as a means to destroy the bodies and the evidence. As the pace of the battle accelerated, enemy troops more often simply left the dead behind.

Along with the bodies, American soldiers occasionally found survivors. Pvt. First Class Serifine Ruggio with the 129th Infantry was advancing through Paco when he discovered a group of wounded civilians. Staff Sgt. Harlow Clark sliced the bindings of the survivors, while Ruggio helped them back to an American aid station. "All four of the men," he noted in his affidavit, "were wounded and 2 of them had big, deep gashes in the back of their necks which looked as though they had been cut with sabers."

"Japanese," one said, imitating bayonet thrusts. "Stick, stick!"

Capt. William Kropf, a surgeon with the 129th Infantry, gave the survivors blood plasma and readied them for medical evacuation. He likewise treated a wounded mother and her six-year-old daughter, who also had survived the slaughter. "The woman had one bayonet wound in her chest and another in her thigh," the doctor later testified in an affidavit. "The little girl had 6 bayonet slashes in her back and side."

These few proved the fortunate ones.

Infantrymen found piles of bodies stacked several feet high behind the Shell Service Station and on the grounds of the nearby Tabacalera Cigar and Cigarette Factory. Troops counted a half-dozen babies—five males and one female—between the ages of six and eighteen months. "I examined the body of one of the babies," testified Capt. William Gardner, "and found it had been bayonetted through the left cheek." It was clear from Gardner's report that the captain had seen enough. "A short distance away, another group of dead civilians lay, but I did not go over to examine them."

Maj. David Binkley visited a few days later, one of many such sites the Thirty-Seventh Infantry Division's sanitary inspector witnessed as part of his job chronicling the dead and arranging burials, often in mass graves. In his report on the massacre, Binkley singled out the murder of a mother and her children, all of whom had suffered saber blows to the neck and head. "The woman lay face down with an arm around each child," he wrote. "One child had part of its skull sliced off."

o   o   o   o

ON FEBRUARY 13, the day after the Garcia family reached St. Scholastica, American shelling increased dramatically. "The building shook and chunks of concrete and timber started to drop around us," recalled Jack. "We huddled close to one another, pillows covering our heads in a vain attempt to protect us from the falling debris."

The school suffered a direct hit, rattling the building and filling the air with acrid smoke. Ramon Garcia jumped to his feet in the passageway.

"We're getting out of here right now," he hollered.

The family members did as ordered. Some of the other refugees told them to stay put, but others followed Ramon Garcia's lead. No sooner had the family vacated than an artillery shell exploded in the corridor behind them, filling the area with the thick dust of pulverized concrete. Ramon Garcia refused to stop, hustling his family toward the exit as panic seized the other refugees. Screams filled the air, and the school began to crumble. "Ceilings were collapsing and large chunks of concrete began to fall," Jack Garcia remembered. "Fires in various parts of the edifice were now threatening."

The panic magnified as the sudden throng of refugees bottlenecked the exits. Others tripped over the abandoned suitcases, bundles, and even pushcarts.

"Stick together," Ramon Garcia shouted.

Jack ran sandwiched between his mother and older brother, while his father led the family, elbowing a path through the crowd. A shell suddenly detonated in front of them in the corridor, knocking the entire family to the floor. Dazed, Jack climbed to his feet, relieved to find his brother and parents unhurt. The youth then spotted the youngest son of Enrique Montaner, the chief engineer of the city's water department. The Montaners had fled alongside the Garcia family when the shell exploded. Jack froze, staring at the youth's shirt, now soaked red with blood. The boy's mother howled and then collapsed upon her son, desperately trying to revive him. "Only a moment before he was running beside me," Jack said. "Now he lay there dead."

Another shell rocked the building. The blast wave again toppled the Garcia family members. Jack climbed back on his feet. The youth looked down and saw Mrs. Montaner still atop her dead son a few feet away, her arms wrapped tight around him. She did not move. Jack watched as a man lifted her off her son. "When he did, I saw blood flowing profusely from the back of her head," Jack recalled. "It was a gaping wound just behind the right ear. Her blouse was covered in blood."

Ida Garcia wailed at the sight.

Before Jack could move, someone grabbed his hand and pulled him down the corridor toward the exit, away from the dead mother and son. Shells continued to shake the building, and refugees choked on the dust and smoke that flooded the air. "Everyone was running, panic-stricken," he recalled. "People were screaming, some asking for help, others searching for a loved one they had lost in the pandemonium."

The family finally made it outside. Jack looked up to see that the normally blue afternoon sky was obscured by what he later described as cinnamon-colored clouds of smoke from surrounding fires. "It was an eerie sight. Manila's leafy southern suburb, home to so many thousands, was burning uncontrollably around us."

The thunder of artillery at times drowned out the screams of the wounded. The bloodied bodies of the dead and injured littered the grounds. Ida Garcia took a head count before the family moved under a large mango tree in the schoolyard. Darkness fell, and the family remained. Hundreds of others took up refuge around the campus, parking under trees or crawling into abandoned foxholes. Still others ambled out into the open, like zombies. Jack watched the building burn; the crackle of flames interrupted by the occasional crash of timbers. Machine guns rattled in the streets, while shells whistled overhead. Inside the schoolyard Jack listened to survivors call out the names of missing loved ones. Others whimpered in grief over the dead. "Most distressing of all," he noted, "were the moans of the terminally wounded and dying."

The night crawled past. Morning finally arrived, and the shelling subsided, at least until around nine a.m. when American howitzers opened fire again. Retreating Japanese troops added to the chaos, lobbing grenades over the wall into the schoolyard.

The family moved from under the mango tree into a shell crater, seeking better protection. Barely half an hour later, however, Ida Garcia suddenly demanded that everyone climb out. She had experienced a similar intuition about De La Salle. Even though she had taken clothes and food, she had balked at moving her family.

"Quickly," she barked. "Now."

"But we're safe here," Ramon protested.

"We are not!" she declared.

The rest of the family reluctantly followed her out of the crater, seeking shelter under a nearby tree. Two other families—one Filipino and one Chinese—climbed into the hole. Shells continued to zoom overhead. One detonated right over the crater, killing all five members of the Chinese family. "No more than ten minutes. That's all the time that transpired from the moment Mum leapt out of the trench until the shell exploded," Jack recalled. "This was no longer luck. We were truly blessed."

The shelling escalated throughout the morning, leaving terrified refugees caught in the crossfire. "There was no let-up," Jack said. "There was nowhere we could go. The shells were coming from all directions. There was no escaping."

High overhead an American observation plane circled, drawing the ire of the refugees. "Can't he see there are no Japanese here?" someone yelled. "Bastard!"

In a desperate effort, refugees climbed out from under trees and from foxholes to link hands and form the letters S-O-S. The shells continued to thunder overhead as the minutes felt like hours. "That's enough," someone finally shouted.

Refugees scurried back to safety, waiting to see if the makeshift message would have any effect. Shells continued to whistle and explode, but moments later the artillery miraculously stopped, replaced by a deafening silence. No sooner had the American guns fallen silent than Japanese troops again hurled grenades over the wall into the schoolyard. But a distinct new sound joined the chorus of explosions—a low and steady grumble, distant at first but coming closer. The high adobe walls blocked any view, prompting refugees to sit up and listen. "The sound was unmistakable," Jack recalled. "It was the metallic reverberating sound of metal cleats on the asphalt road."

Tanks.

But were the tanks American or Japanese?

No one knew. Many assumed that the armor must be Japanese, as enemy troops encamped at the nearby stadium and had constantly harassed the refugees. Were the Japanese coming to reinforce the others? What would happen to the refugees?

The clatter grew louder.

Grenades continued to land in the schoolyard, exploding amid the sea of civilians, many of whom darted for cover. "Fragments of red-hot shrapnel flew in all directions, inflicting further injury to many," Jack said. "Those already wounded and who could not move from where they lay were the worst affected. It was chaotic."

The wall suddenly crumbled, hurling shattered stone blocks and filling the air with dust. A lone tank rolled over the debris. The turret swiveled in front of the Garcia family. A second tank motored in behind it, followed by a third. Soldiers in odd uniforms surged into the schoolyard behind the armor, rifles drawn.

"The Japanese have come back to kill us," someone screamed. "Pray!"

The troops ran straight toward the Garcia family. Jack clung to his mother and closed his eyes, prepared to die.

His mother squeezed him. "Pray my son," she whispered in Spanish. "This is where they finish us off."

The troops closed the distance. The Garcias, who had survived so much, huddled together awaiting the rattle of gunfire and slashing of bayonets.

"Don't be afraid," someone shouted. "We're here to help you."

Jack Garcia opened his eyes.

A woman nearby fainted.

Others cheered and then swarmed the American liberators. "Don't move," one of the officers warned. "Stay where you are. There may be snipers out there."

The officer's orders did nothing to stifle the current of excitement that electrified the crowd of refugees who for eleven terrifying days had survived the burning and barbarity of the Japanese. They mobbed the troops. Soldiers secured the school and passed out hardtack biscuits to the children. "The sound of distant gunfire didn't matter anymore," Jack said. "We didn't care. Everything was going to be all right!"

Jack and his older brother Ramon met several troops, one of whom gave Jack a chocolate bar. The siblings perched on the edge of a crater, legs hanging over the side. The buzz of an incoming mortar interrupted the conversation. The troops dove for cover, but neither Jack nor Ramon moved. Jack heard the thud of the mortar hit and looked up to see it lodged in the ground just a few feet in front of him, close enough that he could see the bomb's rear fins. "My brother and I just sat there mesmerized by the sight of an unexploded shell," he said. "We had never seen a live bomb before. As I stared at it, I felt two hands grab me by the shoulder and pull me down from the crater's edge."

But the Americans had little time to celebrate. Troops prepared for a Japanese counterattack, and hundreds of civilians only complicated any such fight.

"You should go to Santa Ana where you'll be well cared for; fed and told where to seek temporary refuge," one of the officers instructed them. "So make a move."

The news shocked many of the refugees, who this afternoon had felt safe for the first time in years. Now American troops planned to send them back out into a chaotic city seared by fires, treacherous with booby traps, and full of marauding Japanese. It was late in the day. Darkness would soon fall. Many of the families had injured relatives or young children and elderly family members, promising to make a miles-long hike through the war-ravaged city all the more perilous. "There was no other way," Jack recalled. "We had to move."

○   ○   ○   ○

JUST A FEW BLOCKS from St. Scholastica, sixteen-year-old Lourdes Reyes struggled in her family's backyard bomb shelter. She had survived the direct hit on the makeshift lean-to, the night of February 9, that had killed her mother, grandmother, and a dozen others. Someone had pulled her from the crater moments after the explosion and placed her on the ground beside her wounded aunt Purita, who had moaned throughout the rest of the night until she, too, finally died the next day.

The Reyes family servants later helped Lourdes back over the fence, where she joined others in her family's shelter, waiting out the battle. "For four days more I miraculously survived, though all around me people were being killed by bombs and grenades, by hunger and thirst," she recalled. "It seems there is no limit to human endurance, however unbearable the loss of loved ones."

The horror of what she had seen would haunt her, an experience bookended by the final words of both of her parents. Her father, moments before the Japanese stormed the home, had implored her to remain strong. "Be brave," he told her.

Her mother, even after seeing her family murdered, absolved the killers. "I forgive them," she repeated seconds before her death. "I forgive them."

For four days, Lourdes waited underground in the darkness, plagued by fear, hunger, and thirst. Now after all she had suffered, she heard the rumble of tank motors and the distinct clank-clank-clank of steel treads on pavement.

The *Georgia Peach*, one of the Sherman tanks that had liberated Santo Tomas eleven days earlier, crashed through her family's gate and rolled up the driveway to find the once-grand home reduced to charred and smoldering ruins.

"What's the matter there, George?" she heard one of the soldiers say.

This was the picturesque moment of liberation Lourdes and her father had envisioned—American tanks and soldiers at last.

But none of it mattered now.

"There were no flags nor wild cheering from my family to greet them: Bob from Texas and Anthony from Louisiana bringing freedom. What did they mean to me now?" Lourdes later wrote. "We had waited and waited for the liberators but for many it was in vain, because the enemy went berserk in the face of defeat."

○ ○ ○ ○

MAJOR HENNE AND HIS fellow troops with the Third Battalion, 148th Infantry, closed in on Manila Bay late in the afternoon of February 15, the air filled with the salty smell of the sea. Since crossing the Pasig River eight days earlier, the infantrymen had fought through the districts of Pandacan, Paco, and Ermita one intersection, one building at a time. The battle had proven a slog, leaving troops wearied and nerves frazzled. "Relaxing is impossible for uncontrollably muscles tighten and teeth are clenched," Henne recounted. "The blast of a heavy shell is an unforgettable experience as is the dud that rings ears to go bouncing overhead down a cobble stone street. The close ones leave a chalky taste in one's mouth; probably from newly ground molars."

The block-by-block combat that had come to symbolize the Battle of Manila was best summarized by the First Cavalry Division's report. "As the noose tightened in the heart of Manila," it stated, "progress was measured in feet and yards." The fanatical Japanese defenders who reduced the pace of the battle to a crawl had not only worn out the frontline troops but also exhausted American commanders, including General Griswold, who took to his diary to vent his frustration over the fight. "The strain of this battle is very noticeable on us all," the XIV Corps commander wrote. "Very slow progress, with bitter fighting. We are constricting the enemy in a smaller space day by day."

Just as Iwabuchi realized that he was trapped, so, too, did American generals. Griswold had ordered the Eleventh Airborne, following its rapid drive north from Nasugbu, to halt at the city's southern border, so as not to intrude into the area assigned to the First Cavalry Division. American forces meanwhile held the city north of the Pasig, while Manila Bay blocked any Japanese escape to the west. The Thirty-Seventh Infantry and the First Cavalry now pushed side by side toward the waterfront. Adding to Iwabuchi's challenge, the Fifth and Twelfth Cavalry regiments had already reached the bay on the city's southern boundary and would soon turn north, driving up

Taft Avenue in a straight shot aimed at the Walled City barely three miles away.

American commanders knew that some of Iwabuchi's remaining forces had holed up in several strongholds along Taft Avenue and Dewey Boulevard, including the Rizal Memorial Stadium, the Philippine General Hospital, and the neighboring University of the Philippines. As the infantry and cavalry closed in on the bay, U.S. troops surrounded and isolated these fortresses. Each of these buildings would have to be taken in a series of battles that would begin with a pummeling of artillery followed by the charge of assault teams armed with rifles, bazookas, and flamethrowers. The capture of each structure, involving room-by-room fighting, would serve as a mile marker along the road to the Walled City, which promised to be the finale in the Battle of Manila. "Intramuros," Griswold lamented, "is a formidable obstacle."

Major Henne and his men, having crossed Dewey Boulevard that afternoon, stole glimpses of the bay's blue water ahead. Japanese marines on destroyed ships in the harbor targeted the advancing American troops with machine guns and auto-cannons, forcing the infantrymen to take cover until mortar teams could silence the enemy. Infantrymen then charged ahead, reaching the bay at five-thirty p.m. Along the seawall, riflemen killed several pockets of Japanese marines who failed to put up much of a fight. Everyone, both friend and foe, was exhausted. "The Japs offered little resistance," Henne observed. "They seemed resigned to being killed. They were."

Throughout the afternoon and evening, infantrymen secured the lines, from Herran Street south to Harrison Boulevard. Much fighting still remained, but the troops had achieved a major goal. The infantry had reached the bay and isolated the Japanese. Lt. Jimmy Falls, the popular battalion intelligence officer, wanted to glimpse the blue waters that he had fought so hard for since he reached the city. With his eyes glued on the horizon, Falls failed to spot a Japanese antitank and -personnel mine, known because of its circular shape as a "tape measure mine."

His foot stepped atop the bomb, which required as little as seven pounds of pressure to detonate. There along the city's waterfront, the last vision he would see was the dark blue of Manila Bay. "Jimmy, killed instantly, was badly mutilated," Henne recalled. "The small bundle of his remains returned to the Battalion command post was shocking to those close to him. He was only gone—gone somewhere."

CHAPTER 18

"South of the Pasig Manila was a city of death and of horror."

—SGT. OZZIE ST. GEORGE,
YANK, APRIL 27, 1945

THE GARCIA FAMILY SET OUT FOR SANTA ANA AT FIVE P.M. on February 14, climbing over the rubble of the wall U.S. tanks had toppled. The Japanese had made almost no effort to hold Santa Ana, one of Manila's more inland districts, sandwiched between Paco to the west and Pasig River to the east. The community had served as the welcome mat for the First Cavalry, who after enveloping the capital had crossed the river on February 10 to find hundreds of cheering *manileños*, including Marcial Lichauco and his family. Since then, as the field of battle had shrunk to the Walled City and a series of strongholds along Taft Avenue and around Intramuros, Santa Ana's location on the sidelines of the fight had made it a haven for the thousands of displaced refugees.

Ramon Garcia hoped his family might make it at least to Paco before nightfall, a distance of several miles to the east. No sooner had the family set out than everyone realized even that might be an ambitious goal. This was no simple walk but an arduous hike through the tangled debris of a wrecked city. "We encountered barbed wire barriers, burnt out vehicles, and upturned wooden carts," his son Jack recalled. "Twisted fragments of roofing sheets flew about and large trees blocked the streets."

The dead populated this urban wasteland with bodies and body parts littered along the streets, buried in the rubble, and even a few dangling in trees, victims of land mines. The family stumbled that Wednesday afternoon across four dead Japanese marines whose rotting remains blocked the path forward. "There was no way we could get around them. We had to step over them!" Jack recalled. "I tread carefully over the first corpse with great apprehension. With a handkerchief pressed hard over my nose and mouth, I struggled to hurdle over the others." Each block revealed more of the same, a mix of both enemy troops and civilians. Fires had blistered and blackened many of the dead. Other times the clustered corpses hinted that the deceased were members of a family.

No one spoke as the group trekked east, afraid of drawing the attention of any lurking Japanese troops. "We moved slowly through a heavy pall of smoke that engulfed the area," Jack said. "Only the crackling sound of fire curling circuitously around timber frames broke the silence." The afternoon began to fade as the family closed in on the Singalong Church, the twin spires of its belfry silhouetted against the red sky. "The stone building," Jack said, "stood out majestically amid the ruins of thousands of homes that once surrounded it." Closer inspection revealed the shell holes in the roof, shattered stained-glass windows, and pockmarked plaster, the remains of which covered the floor. Hundreds of refugees crowded inside. Ramon Garcia steered his family toward a side door only to be blocked by other refugees who claimed the church was full.

"We wouldn't want to go in there anyway," Garcia huffed, noting the battered ceiling. "It's not only packed, but the place is downright dangerous."

Garcia made his way across the yard toward the presbytery with his family in tow, climbing the steps to the porch and walking through the open doors. The day's waning sunlight filtered through the smashed windows to reveal an empty room, stripped by looters. Jack took a few steps inside when his father stopped him.

"Don't look!" he demanded. "Stay outside."

His father's admonition came too late.

Jack looked up in horror. Dangling by the neck from the rafters was a priest in a ripped brown robe. Two nuns in bloodied habits—and with hands still bound behind their backs—swayed nearby. Jack noted their cowls hung down on their shoulders, revealing the thick rope that dug into their throats. "I could not move. I wanted to run but my legs wouldn't budge. I tried to scream, but no sound was forthcoming. My jaw dropped and trembled. I attempted to close my eyes, but I couldn't do that either!"

His father ushered him out of the door, marching past the rest of the family. "No, not in there," he barked, making no mention of the dead. "Let's get out of here."

At the main gate Garcia stopped, rummaging in his pocket for the burnt butt of a cigarette. Night fast approached, and Garcia and his family were adrift in a sea of smoldering ruins. "Where the hell do we go from here?" he mumbled.

Jack saw what his father did not. Up ahead, sandwiched between the rubble of several large homes and hidden by avocado trees and banana plants, stood a traditional two-story nipa hut with walls made from woven palm and coconut fibers. Shells had torn holes in roof and shrapnel in the sides, but the hut had survived.

The family knocked on the door, but no one answered. Repeated rapping finally prompted a voice inside to demand in Tagalog what the family wanted.

Ida Garcia described the family's escape from Malate, begging for the owners to allow them inside just the night. The woman refused.

Garcia continued to plead until a gravelly voice from an upstairs window interrupted her: "Show them in."

An elderly gentleman came down the stairs. Ida again recounted her family's saga and asked permission to spend the night. The owner agreed. "But only for the night," he said. "It is important you move out early tomorrow morning."

The owner apologized for a lack of food, but he provided them an earthenware jug to draw water from a well in the yard. Japanese snipers, he warned, hunted at dawn and dusk. "Don't stand in front of open windows and keep well below window-sill level," he cautioned. "Please, don't light up any cigarettes in the dark."

Evening settled over the home. Ten-year-old Jack, who had once enjoyed carefree afternoons playing with his friend Arthur MacArthur, was distraught. He had seen his home destroyed, his friends killed, and clergy hanged. He cuddled up next to his father, while his mother prayed aloud the rosary. "The sound of rifle shots and short bursts of machine gun fire interrupted the moments of prayer, but Mum did not stop," he recalled. "She prayed on and we responded. There was nothing else we could do. We were again in God's hands."

The next morning the light filtered through the hundreds of holes that peppered the walls and ceiling of the home. Jack let his eyes follow the rays, noting the shrapnel and bullet fragments still dug into in the wooden beams and floor. The Garcia family set out on the morning of February 15, the same day American forces finally reached De La Salle and discovered the slaughter of Ida Garcia's sister, husband, and three sons, leaving five-year-old Fernando the sole survivor of his immediate family.

Ramon Garcia led his wife and sons east along San Andres Street, continuing inland and away from the bay. The family had to navigate roadways littered with metal sheets and timbers, circumventing unexploded shells. Broken glass and concrete crunched beneath their feet. "Block after block, the scene remained unchanged," Jack recalled. "Everywhere you looked, one saw ruins and more ruins, burnt-out vehicles and the harrowing sight of more dead people."

The dead both repulsed and fascinated Jack. "No two corpses lay the same way," he observed. "Each grotesque figure told a different story. A story that accentuated the last moments of their lives." Those moments were filled with terror, facing the razor-sharp blade of a Japanese bayonet or the muzzle of a rifle. He passed one charred body face down on all fours, killed while trying to crawl away. Others the youth noted had died alongside loved ones, the bodies locked in a final embrace with hands around one another's waists and necks. "A very poignant scene," Jack remembered, "was that of a person lying on his back with a stiff right arm pointing to the heavens."

The family pressed on through the rubble. The artillery that had whistled overhead for days fell farther behind with each block gained in the eastward journey out of the battle zone. The family reached

Paco late that morning. While ravaged, it was now occupied by American troops who patrolled the streets. Gone were the bodies that for two days had lined the family's route, like silent spectators in the marathon to safety. Alongside the removal of the dead, residents picked through the rubble of flattened homes and businesses. "Unlike the other areas that we had passed by in the previous days the streets of Paco were full of people moving around freely," Jack observed. "They no longer had to look over their shoulder, worried they'd meet a crazed Jap pointing a rifle with a fixed bayonet at them. Cold fear no longer showed in their faces."

The bridge across the Paco River—a narrow tributary of the Pasig that marked the start of Santa Ana—had been destroyed. A toppled coconut tree stood in its place, offering the only passage over the filthy black water. Ramon led the family followed by Ida. Halfway out she turned and motioned for her two sons. Jack and his older brother moved out on the log. The duo had not traveled more than a few paces when Jack heard a splash. He looked up to see his mother bobbing in the squalid stream. Furious, she waded ashore unhurt, where her anger gave way to relief at the realization that the family's arduous journey neared its end. Santa Ana had endured. Homes and shops still stood, spared the hurricane of destruction that leveled Paco, Ermita, and Malate.

In the plaza in front of the Church of Santa Ana, Ramon Garcia ran into his dear friend Jose Sansó Pedret, a fellow Spaniard. The owner of an ironworks business, Sansó Pedret's home had survived the battle. After learning of his friend's losses, he immediately invited the Garcia family to stay at his home.

"It's not the Ritz," he said, "but we'll make you as comfortable as possible."

His spacious home resembled a Spanish villa with a red tile roof, but he had sheltered so many refugees that the only accommodation left was a ground-floor room used to store hay for horses. For the exhausted Garcia family, it was perfect. The Garcias had lost everything, but unlike so many less fortunate souls, every member of the family had survived the battle and the perilous hike out of the war zone. The family had no sheets or blankets to lay over the hay, but would bed down that night under the cover of safety provided by the U.S. Army. "I was so weary," Jack remembered, "that I dropped on the bed of straw like a sack of potatoes."

○ ○ ○ ○

THE FIFTH AND TWELFTH CAVALRY regiments readied for the assault on Harrison Park and Rizal Memorial Stadium on the morning of February 16. No sooner had soldiers ushered the refugees out of St. Scholastica than the cavalry moved into the property, setting up a command post for what promised to be a fierce fight on one of the most unlikely of battlefields—a baseball diamond. The massive park and sports complex stretched from Taft Avenue some twelve hundred yards west to Manila Bay. It was bound on the south by Vito Cruz Street, which marked the edge of Manila's city limits. Harrison Boulevard served as the northern boundary, doubling as the dividing line between the Thirty-Seventh Infantry and the First Cavalry divisions. In addition to a baseball field, the sprawling sports complex housed a track and field stadium, coliseum, tennis courts, swimming pool, and the wide-open expanse of Harrison Park.

The day before, the cavalrymen had liberated the survivors of the massacre at neighboring De La Salle on Taft Avenue and cleared the school for use as an observation post for this morning's assault. Other cavalrymen meanwhile had advanced up the bay front, driving the Japanese defenders from Harrison Park east and into the stadium. Heavy sniper fire this morning signaled the looming fight. American mortars and artillery opened fire at seven-fifteen a.m., targeting the coliseum and baseball stadium, both made from reinforced concrete and offering ample places for Iwabuchi's marines to seek refuge from the shellfire. General Fellers watched the opening salvos from atop De La Salle, including a Long Tom strike on a group of Japanese marines on the baseball diamond. The 155 mm shells from the heavy field weapon obliterated the enemy. "When the smoke died down there was not the slightest sign of any of them," the general wrote his wife. "This may seem horrible, but in view of the atrocities these beasts have committed, it is impossible to sympathize with them."

Cavalrymen seized the coliseum in just fifteen minutes, which guarded the entrance to the more heavily fortified ball diamond. Sherman tanks punched a hole in the stadium's east wall and then climbed the rubble into the outfield. Japanese marines retreated into bunkers dug into the field, while snipers took aim at the American cavalrymen from the rafters above the stands. At one point, American troops held the outfield, while the Japanese occupied home plate. "During the lull in fighting, a Japanese officer, wearing a sword, blithely walked out into clear view to third base," an Associated Press reporter wrote. "When the firing started the Japanese officer made a dash for home. He was out—for keeps—by the proverbial mile." The battle dragged on for two hours before the few surviving Japanese marines retreated beneath the grandstand. American soldiers had little interest in a close-quarters fight in the dark. "Those Japs remaining in the heavy barricaded dungeons of the grandstand," the Fifth Cavalry report stated, "were quickly dispensed with by flame throwers and dynamite."

American troops expected more of the same in the assault on the Philippine General Hospital, where Japanese marines held an estimated seven thousand men, women, and children hostage, and the neighboring University of the Philippines. These two sprawling complexes—located on Taft Avenue just a mile and a half to the north—stood among the last major strongholds south of the Walled City and its defensive ring of fortified government buildings. Despite red crosses painted on the roofs of all of the hospital buildings as well as the front of the administrative building, the Japanese had fortified the hospital in violation of the Geneva Convention. Iwabuchi's troops had stacked sandbags in the windows and doors and built machine-gun nests along the foundations of various hospital buildings. The Japanese used the medical center as cover to fire artillery on American positions north of the Pasig, stashing ammunition among the shrubbery. The enemy had gone so far as to set up a cannon inside the building just a few yards from the office door of the hospital director.

Snipers dressed as doctors took aim on the streets from the windows of wards occupied by civilians.

For the thousands of refugees, conditions inside proved atrocious; most packed the first floor to avoid the artillery. "The halls of the hospital were so crowded that it was impossible to go through them," remembered American missionary Ann Keily. "Bombing and shelling went on continuously." None of the toilets worked, which left the air filled with the stench of human waste. The rotting bodies of dead patients and refugees—it was too dangerous to venture outside to bury them—only added to the misery. At night Japanese troops prowled the rooms and corridors with flashlights and matches, hunting young women to rape. Other times enemy forces took potshots at people who tried to draw water at the well. Refugees cowered in silence, listening to the hobnail boots in the corridors. "Every Japanese soldier or sergeant, any one with a sword, was giving orders and counter orders," recalled Dr. Antonio Sison, director of the hospital. "They would speak to me with bayonets pointed at my breast."

Sixteen-year-old Edgar Krohn, Jr., had seen just how dangerous it was both inside and outside the hospital. Along with his mother and father, the German youth, whose family ran a textile remnant importation business, had bounced around southern Manila for days before finally reaching the hospital on February 14. Even then, the family's arrival during a mortar attack was traumatic. "A man in front of us had been hit; a razor sharp piece of shrapnel had sliced open his abdomen, exposing his intestines," Krohn recalled. "As we ran past him, he was trying to stuff his intestines back into his body." But the carnage had only continued. During a lull in fighting, Krohn had gone to the artesian well in the yard, when a shell exploded steps away. A piece of shrapnel dug into his right temple, a minor wound compared to the refugee in front of him who absorbed most of the blast. "He turned around," Krohn said, "blood was flowing from his wounds and one of his eyeballs was hanging out of the socket."

Krohn's father rushed the teen to the emergency room, where doctors soaked in blood hovered over patients, hacking off infected limbs without anesthesia; the only bandages were made from shredded bedsheets and curtains. "In a corner I caught sight of a pail containing amputated arms and legs," Krohn recalled. "There was no place to dispose of them." After doctors bandaged his wounded temple, the family settled into a hallway off one of the wards, moving again each day throughout the hospital in search of a safer space. At one point during an artillery attack, his mother grew hysterical, prompting his father to slap her, the only time he had ever witnessed him strike her. Another time the family hunkered down in a white-tiled room when Japanese troops barged in and dragged a woman out; she was later found raped and murdered in the yard. "I have always looked back on this incident with anguish and I have always asked myself why no one among the many in the room interceded on her behalf."

The Krohns weren't the only ones desperate for safety. That quest had led eleven-year-old Jim Litton and his family into the anteroom of the hospital's elevator shaft. Like the Krohn family, the Littons had barely made it to the medical center alive. The family of five had approached via Florida Street on February 9, which was littered with debris from the wrecked buildings. Litton's mother had led the way, while to her left walked fifteen-year-old Narda Pangan, a part-time domestic helper from Bataan who lived with the family while she studied in Manila. Jim was daydreaming when the family came within a block of the hospital. An explosion rattled him. Ears ringing, he looked to his left and saw his older brother George, covering his face with both hands. Jim looked ahead and saw the legless body of a girl with long dark hair. Her left arm had been ripped off just below the shoulder. The dazed youth struggled for a moment before he realized it was Narda. "She lay moaning," he recalled, "blood flowing from the stump of her lower torso."

Jim spotted his mother unconscious on the ground nearby, her left arm riddled with shrapnel from the land mine explosion. His cousin Anselmo Salang scooped her up and the family fled to the hospital, where doctors went to work on her. Jim saw his mother again a few days later. "She was bandaged," he recalled, "her face blackened by burns. She was in pain and moaning. The whole ward smelled of rotting flesh and of death." Like the Krohns, the Litton family had roamed the hospital in search of a safe place to hide. At one point, Jim bedded down in a room filled with brains, hearts, and livers preserved in glass jars. The increased shelling finally drove the family into the anteroom of the elevator shaft in the hospital's basement. From there, Litton could climb into the crawlspace under the hospital. For five days he and his family survived in the dark below, waiting for American troops to liberate them. "From a peep hole in the crawl space," he said, "we could see American tanks on Taft Avenue."

The end of the struggle fast approached. On the morning of February 16, the Americans blasted the hospital and surrounding buildings with Sherman tanks and M10 tank destroyers after earlier efforts to drive out the Japanese with machine guns, rifle grenades, 3.2 inch rockets, and 37 mm cannons had failed. "This direct fire was employed as a last resort," the 148th Infantry's report noted, "and every caution possible was taken to prevent casualties among civilian prisoners." American infantrymen assaulted the neighboring Bureau of Science Building along with the Nurses Home and the Chemical Laboratory at ten-thirty a.m. "Fighting continued in these buildings through the day," the infantry's report stated. "A withdrawal was made from the Bureau of Science at dark, but the occupation of the others continued."

American forces resumed the fight the following morning with the successful assault of the Bureau of Science Building. The infantry's report logged the outcome: "All resistance was destroyed." Capture of the science building coupled with the Nurses Home allowed gunners to place both frontal and flanking fire on the hospital. Inside the battered medical center, refugees took cover. The Krohn family holed up in the crawlspace beneath one of the elevated walkways, while the Littons remained sheltered in the basement anteroom of the elevator shaft. Refugees could hear the click of hobnail boots on the floors overhead as the Japanese retreated through the hospital. "By midmorning, the barrages came in quick succession. Machine-gun fire from both sides suddenly opened up in a deafening duel," recalled Miguel Avanceña, another youth who hid in the elevator shaft with his family. "Showers of sparks from exploding shells and shrapnel so terrified us that prayers asking God to save us filled the basement."

The guns finally fell silent.

Edgar Krohn crawled out and popped his head up, peering over the edge of the walkway. Dead ahead he spotted a soldier crouched on one knee, his rifle pointed at him. "How many are you in there?" the infantryman barked, lowering his gun.

"Many," the teenager replied.

"Get out of there fast," he ordered. "You're covered."

What started as a whispered rumor among refugees in the darkened basement soon rose to a roar. "*Amerikano!*" people hollered in Tagalog. "*Amerikano!*"

Litton, who never thought he would live through the siege, felt a sudden relief wash over him. Not only had he survived, but so, too, had his family. "I am alive," he wanted to cry. "I am alive."

The eleven-year-old's euphoria was shared by the thousands of other men, women, and children who poured out of the blasted hospital, flooding the American lines. Thirteen-year-old fellow refugee Luis Esteban spotted a dead Japanese marine sprawled out in the driveway. As payment for all he had endured, Esteban spat on the marine. "Don't do that," his father gently admonished him. "He was a human being."

The torrent of patients and refugees not only hindered the assault but overwhelmed American medical services. An emergency assembly area east of Taft Avenue counted more than two thousand refugees by late that afternoon, with more streaming in by the hour. "Casualties ran into the thousands," stated a 112th Medical Battalion report. "The Battalion ambulances, jeeps and trucks formed an endless chain of evacuation through the debris-littered and shell-pocked streets. All hospital facilities in the city were used to receive the casualties but even these were inadequate." Convoys of trucks and ambulances hauled the wounded through battered blocks to a hospital just outside Manila. "The evacuation continued through the night," the Thirty-Seventh Infantry's report noted. "An estimated total of 7000 were eventually rescued."

But the Battle of Manila was far from over.

American forces turned next to the University of the Philippines, for a fight that would drag on for several days as troops battled to clear the various buildings. "The area we are moving into is a cauldron of complete wreckage," observed the Fifth Cavalry's report, "with the ever present litter of battle and the stench of enemy dead."

Each night as America's grip tightened, enemy troops attempted to slip through the lines and escape. A few Japanese conducted suicide charges, lured by the promise of a posthumous promotion to second lieutenant. Many others blundered into American outposts. U.S. soldiers shot sixty-four Japanese on the evening of February 20. "A fair bag for one night's work," bragged one cavalry report.

The Japanese managed to capture cavalryman Sgt. Henry Clark two nights later. His mutilated remains, found the next day, revealed that the enemy had sliced the first two fingers off of each hand. Coagulated blood around the wounds proved he was alive at the time. "Both of the deceased's ears were partially cut off," reported Capt. John Amesse, a surgeon. "Bayonet perforations of chest and abdomen were present. Lack of blood around these areas is consistent with post mortem mutilation."

The battle for Rizal Hall, the largest building on campus, proved typical of the ferocious fight American troops faced throughout Manila. Like much of the city's architecture, the three-story concrete building was designed in an elegant neoclassical style with towering columns and an open internal courtyard. Japanese marines had fortified the building, hacking gun slits in the walls, barricading windows and entrances, and mounting pillboxes on the roof with open lines of sight on all approaches. A small team of American cavalrymen stormed the building at eleven-thirty a.m. on February 20, fighting room to room. After two hours, troops had made it only to the second floor, the Fifth Cavalry's report noted, "with the rain of lead still heavy."

The Americans finally reached the third floor by five p.m., but they had little time to celebrate. "A terrific explosion rocked the building from one end to the other and gray clouds of pulverized cement and dust covered the entire structure," the report stated. "Those observing the scene could well imagine what had happened; as the dust slowly drifted away, they saw the entire center section had been blown." Tensions soared as everyone outside awaited word about the fate of the platoon. The radio soon crackled as the lieutenant relayed the news. The blast miraculously had killed only one American soldier; the rest, including a few wounded, prepared to evacuate for the night. "Their complete disregard for human life enabled them to attempt destruction of buildings housing our troops in spite of the presence therein of their own."

The next morning American forces blasted Rizal Hall for two hours with tanks, tank destroyers, and two self-propelled 105 mm howitzers borrowed from the Thirty-Seventh Infantry. "Numerous holes were opened in the sides of the building," according to the cavalry's report. "From external appearance it did not seem possible anything alive could remain within." The Americans assaulted the building at 2:35 p.m., securing part of the structure by nightfall before continuing the fight on February 22. The inside of Rizal Hall had been reduced to rubble and dust. Many of the stairs proved impassable, while others were a challenge to navigate. Troops likewise had to overcome primitive Japanese barriers, including spools of rope and boxes filled with asphalt. Cavalrymen inched from room to room, backs pressed up against the walls, hurling grenades ahead to drive out the enemy. "Looking through a crack of a door the platoon leader saw the heads and shoulders of four men and the hunched backs of several others," Master Sgt. Robert King, commander of the Second Platoon, Troop C, wrote in his report afterward. "A grenade was tossed into this group."

As dusk settled over Manila on February 22, the cavalrymen prepared to hunker down. Neither side wanted to surrender ground after such a battle, so the Americans and Japanese would share the wrecked building for the night. After several sleepless nights, American morale sagged. But the Japanese were not finished fighting. Iwabuchi's marines launched an eight p.m. assault on the Americans on the second floor, firing machine guns and tossing grenades. "The holding force was engaged in the fire fight for about thirty minutes, then the Japs let up for about ten minutes before launching a second attack," the cavalry's report noted. "This next attack was repulsed in twenty minutes, whereupon the Japs withdrew and no more fire was received from them."

The Americans remained on alert in the darkened building, expecting another assault as soon as the moon set and the light faded. The soldiers fell silent with nothing to do but wait, listen, and worry. There was little doubt that the battle for Rizal Hall was nearing its climax, a fight that had already claimed the lives of 166 Japanese.

Around one-thirty a.m., cavalrymen heard enemy voices at the far end of the building. Ears perked up, and the men listened to the Japanese. "At first they seemed to be conversational tones but gradually increased into a weird chant until there was a full chorus of singing," recorded the cavalry's report. "This commotion went on for about forty-five minutes culminating in a final burst of song and loud shouting, immediately followed by many reports of exploding grenades and dynamite charges."

The cavalrymen continued to listen.

More grenades exploded.

Then silence.

More detonations went off at half-hour intervals until around four a.m., at which time a lasting silence settled over the wrecked building until morning. No imagination was needed to envision what the doomed Japanese troops had done. An assault team moved in the next morning, clearing each room. In the first room, soldiers counted nineteen bodies, all dismembered by grenades in what the cavalry's report described as "an appalling sight." But the carnage did not stop there. "In the five adjoining rooms and at the foot of the staircase were more bodies showing the same manner of death," the report stated. "A total of 77 had completed the ritual which our troops had listened to during the early morning hours."

○ ○ ○ ○

THE FIGHT for the University of the Philippines set the stage for the last act in the Battle of Manila. MacArthur's forces, having encircled the city on February 12, had in the ten days since compressed the Japanese into a roughly one square-mile area in the heart of Manila. The remnants of Admiral Iwabuchi's Central Force defended the handful of government offices surrounding the Walled City—the Legislature, Finance, and Agriculture buildings, plus a few others—while Colonel Noguchi's Northern Force hunkered down behind the towering stone walls of Intramuros.

For the surviving civilians still trapped inside the Walled City, the days were apocalyptic. Fires had destroyed much of the ancient citadel, and artillery rained down on it. The dead bodies of Filipino men, some naked, dangled from lampposts. Sister Nelly de Jesus Virata watched the Japanese strip the clothes off two men and bind them to a post next to an engulfed building. "They were burned alive," she later told war crimes investigators. "Their bodies were just like charcoal." Rosa Calalang likewise witnessed the burning, noting how the smell of roasting meat had attracted a hungry audience. "The dogs," she recalled, "were already biting the cooked flesh."

Inside the Church of San Agustin—one of the Walled City's last refuges—misery prevailed. Women and children slept on benches, in corridors, and atop the stone floor. Absent running water and toilets—and with an outbreak of dysentery—feces littered the sanctuary. Starvation claimed others, whose withered bodies were buried in the orchard behind it. With most of the men killed at Fort Santiago, Japanese troops prowled at night in search of women. Twenty-four-year-old Pacita Siguenza plucked out her dentures to look less attractive. "We could never sleep," recalled twenty-eight-year-old Conchita Huerta, who was assaulted by the Japanese. "They came every night."

"Rape won't hurt," she was warned, "if you don't fight back."

Forty-five-year-old Andrea Lopez, whose husband and son were both marched off to Fort Santiago, ran out of food on February 12. To survive, she and others ate, not just the fruit from banana and papaya trees, but the leaves and even stalks. The wealthier Spanish families offered up pets to the hungry. "My family killed four dogs," Lopez said. "As the people were fighting to get a piece we had to eat it raw most of the time."

The anguish increased as American artillery targeted the towering walls of Intramuros along with potential sniper nests in preparation for the eventual assault. San Agustin's tower fell victim, leaving the hands of the clock frozen at seven-thirty p.m. "Sometimes, as twilight fell, there would be a pause in the barrage. Observation planes would be heard overhead," recalled Tony Trinidad, who was eleven years old. "Up in the sky, small parachutes with bright lights would be seen hovering. Immediately we would stuff our ears with cotton and place a piece of wood between our teeth. The deafening shelling would resume, to continue all night."

More than once, errant projectiles blasted the church, killing refugees. Trinidad recalled seeing a woman cooking over a large caldron when a shell exploded. "We found her torso in the cauldron," he said, "but the head was missing." Another time a shell hit the crowded room his family shared with others, filling the air with dust. "The two kapok mattresses we had set up as partitions had saved our lives; we found them spiky with shrapnel," he said. "The families to our left and right were all dead or dying."

Survivors could offer little more than prayers for the injured. "We tried to help the wounded," recalled Ester Aenille, "but there was no medicine, so we put wine on the wounded and made bandages of our clothing. The dead were everywhere."

The Japanese at one point forced all the refugees outside the church as a ploy to pilfer watches and other valuables refugees had brought with them—petty theft against the backdrop of doom. Dr. Antonio Gisbert experienced another surreal moment when a Japanese officer summoned him simply to practice his English. During the two-hour conversation, the officer asked whether Gisbert thought America would win the war. The doctor replied that he was too busy with patients to even think about it.

"I think Japan will win eventually," the marine replied.

It was clear to most others, however, that the end was near. A drunk Japanese officer played with a hand grenade one night, telling refugee Lourdes Godino that when the Americans came through the walls, he planned to pull the pin.

"We will all die," she responded.

"If I die, you also die."

Godino pleaded that the refugees were innocent civilians.

"I am innocent, too," he said.

"We want to die with our families," she begged.

"I, too, want to die with my family."

Colonel Noguchi's soldiers and marines continued to execute civilians who might prove problematic when the Americans breached the walls. On February 17 troops showed up in the ruins of Santa Rosa College, one of the only other places where the masses gathered, rustling Rosa Calalang awake in her makeshift shelter at three a.m.

"How many are you?' the Japanese demanded in Tagalog.

Troops had seized Calalang's husband Jesus from the Manila Cathedral on February 6. Now eleven days later marines had come for the rest of the family. The Japanese grabbed Calalang, her mother Victorinia, and her three children, along with four others, marching them across the street to Santo Domingo Church.

"What are they going to do to us?" Victorinia asked.

"Mother," Calalang replied, "we better pray."

"What are they going to do?" her mother pleaded.

"I do not know."

Calalang's daughters started to whimper. "Mammy," one cried, "why did you wake me up?"

In the ruins of Santo Domingo, the Japanese again attacked the civilians with bayonets, this time without any ruse of leading them inside the church. One of the marines stabbed Calalang's nine-year-old daughter Aurora in the hip.

"You've hit me," the girl cried and started to run.

The Japanese gave chase, but Calalang pounced, striking him. Another marine bayoneted her twice in the back, knocking her to the ground. Enraged troops stabbed her five more times in the breast, groin, abdomen, and thigh. Calalang watched helplessly as the Japanese marine caught up to her daughter and plunged his bayonet into her again and again until she died. Troops then killed her mother, Victorinia.

The Japanese returned to the ruins of Santa Rosa College and brought back a second group of civilians, followed by a third, each one suffering the same fate. In addition to women and children, Japanese targeted some of the medical staff from San Juan de Dios Hospital, who until now troops had spared.

"Doctor, doctor," one Japanese marine shouted amid the ruins, summoning the few surviving physicians before marching them across the street.

Troops then returned to the ruins. "All nurses come out," the Japanese ordered.

Calalang lay amid the debris, watching this parade of victims in the final hours before dawn. "I could see the people running," she said, "and the Japanese chasing them." Many of the women and children were friends and acquaintances. Calalang watched marines bring in a young woman she knew only by her first name Sally. In her arms Sally held her younger brother. "The Japanese bayonetted her and her brother, while she was pleading and pressing her brother close to her," Calalang later testified. "We found Sally the next morning dead, clutching her dead brother."

On the ground near Calalang, Dr. Leandro Coralles suffered from bayonet wounds. "Somebody please put up my head," he cried. "I can't breathe."

Calalang listened as he moaned.

"God," the dentist begged. "I can't breathe."

Finally his voice fell silent.

Those who were able crawled back to the ruins, where the few remaining nurses from San Juan de Dios Hospital tried to help them.

Calalang was rescued by friends who had come in search of her. Her wounds, however, proved so severe that the nurses summoned a priest, who administered confession. One of the nurses told her that her misery would soon be over.

"We don't know," the sister added, "if we will be next."

"Pray," Calalang replied, "that the Americans are coming."

In an effort to cover up the slaughter before the Americans arrived, the Japanese gathered some survivors, forcing them to bury the dozens of dead in the ruins of Santo Domingo Church. Many of the bodies, exposed for days to the hot tropical sun, had ballooned. The dresses of others were hiked up to the waist. The Japanese had gone so far as to bayonet one woman through her genitals. The survivors battled nausea to drag the remains into foxholes and bomb craters before shoveling dirt over the bodies. "One of the women that we saw," recalled Benita Lahoz, "was beheaded."

The Japanese hunted down the last few men alive inside the Walled City. On February 18 marines seized the remaining hospital patients from Santa Rosa College, marching more than fifty off to the ruins of the University of Manila.

"What are you doing?" one cried when the Japanese attacked them.

"We are only killing pigs."

That same day marines grabbed the last Filipino men out of San Agustin Church, including scores of sick and elderly along with thirty-four priests. The Japanese herded them into a warehouse for the night before prodding them the next evening to the Plaza McKinley, at the corner of Aduana and General Luna streets, in front of the ruins of the Manila Cathedral. There they forced seventy men into the larger of two underground bomb shelters and the remaining seventeen into the smaller.

"Don't sit down," one of the officers barked as troops fired a pistol in the air. "Just stand up and all will be able to go inside."

The smaller shelter measured roughly six feet wide and ten feet long. After the last man climbed inside the dark dugout, the marines rolled an oil drum in front and shoveled dirt along the sides. "There was no room we were packed in so tight," recalled Epifanio Gutierrez, Jr., an eighteen-year-old Spaniard. Troops paced atop the shelter seconds before several grenades rolled down the two ventilation shafts. One of the priests asked what it was. He began to repeat his question when the bombs exploded. "Those killed," recalled Father Jose Barullo, "were mutilated beyond recognition."

Seventeen-year-old Spaniard Emilio Carceller, who was crammed inside with his twenty-year-old brother Eduardo and forty-five-year-old father, kicked the oil drum away from the entrance. A marine outside opened fire into the dugout.

"I am hit in the eye," Emilio cried as he collapsed dead.

A bullet tore into his father, killing him, too.

The Japanese tossed in more grenades. The explosions deafened the few dazed survivors and filled the air with dust and the acrid smell of gunpowder. The marines departed. Throughout that night, the survivors listened to explosions and rifle shots as the Japanese attacked other shelters filled with refugees. "The worst part of it," recalled Father Barullo, "was that we could hear the Japanese laughing."

The next morning the marines returned, pouring sand down the ventilation holes to suffocate the survivors. Even after the captives dug small air holes, the men inside struggled to breathe, conditions made all the worse by the tropical heat and the press of bodies. The men guzzled bottles of Jerez wine that the Japanese had stashed inside the dugout, while a priest that afternoon took confession. Several of the refugees decided that the only hope was to slip out under the cover of darkness. "We made up our minds that night that if we were going to die we might as well die outside in the open," Barullo said, "breathing fresh air, where we could see the heaven and see the sky."

A similar horror unfolded nearby inside the larger bomb shelter, where the Japanese had crammed seventy men in a dugout that measured barely five feet wide and fifty feet long. The Japanese likewise dropped grenades inside and shot those who tried to escape. Marines then shoveled earth in front of the entrances to bury alive the few survivors. Father Belarmino de Celis, injured by shrapnel, tore his habit to make a bandage. The air inside was thick, and the thirty-seven-year-old Spanish priest feared he might suffocate. He pulled himself through the tangle of bodies toward the shelter entrance where he dug with his fingers. "I was able to make a small hole," he said, "and then I lay down there with my mouth near the hole for respiration."

The sun finally rose, but dawn brought no relief from the misery. "Many were still breathing and almost all of them were asking for water," Father Belarmino recalled. "Nobody was asking for food." Artillery shook the shelter, and dirt dropped inside through the overhead timbers. One by one the others began to die. Day turned to night and then day again. Conditions inside the dugout deteriorated as the bodies began to rot. "A profound silence prevailed," recalled Julio Rocamora, the only other survivor. "There were no other signs of life; nothing but darkness and flies and stench." The two survivors dug a hole out on the night of February 22, after enduring three days in the earthen tomb. The men crawled to the nearby ruins of the Department of Justice, where Father Belarmino set off to find food and water for them. "I did not find food, but I found water in the tank of a toilet," he said. "As I drank I could feel my strength coming back."

○ ○ ○ ○

INSIDE SANTO TOMAS, American troops set up a screen near the Main Building, where at night internees spread out on the lawn atop blankets and chairs and watched Donald Duck cartoons, newsreels, and movies as the Japanese slaughtered men, women, and children just a few miles beyond the camp's gate. The rattle of distant machine guns and artillery occasionally drowned out the dialogue and music, while the flash of flares obscured the images that paraded across the screen. Hartendorp marveled at the odd juxtaposition during *Rhapsody in Blue*, a film about the life of George Gershwin starring Robert Alda as the famous composer. "A representation of theatrical and musical life on Broadway, to the accompaniment of an avalanche of death thrown upon America's enemy on the other side of the world!" the camp historian wrote. "Surely, no picture of the kind was ever shown under more bizarre circumstances."

The newsreels proved a highlight for many of the internees, an opportunity to catch up on the hurried progress of the war that so many had missed.

"We won't be satisfied until Manila is taken!" one of the news commentators announced at the end of one such a reel.

"We cheered madly," Tressa Roka wrote. "The goose pimples that crept over my skin felt like heady wine coursing through my veins and capillaries."

Robin Prising befriended a young Filipino boy who sat near him on the lawn, the duo laughing at actor Al Jolson until the horror of war intruded. "I saw, under the army blanket thrown carelessly over his lap, the bandaged stumps of his knees," Prising recalled. "His laughter is the only full, free laughter I have ever heard."

Internees who only two weeks earlier had hovered near death continued to obsess over food. "We consumed vast quantities of coffee mixed with all the sugar and canned milk that we wanted," Roka wrote in her diary. "We wouldn't believe that it would last, so just as quickly as we had drunk the coffee we would rush back to the mobile coffee kitchen with our empty Lactogen cans for more."

"Give the poor bastards all they can drink at all hours of the day," Roka's fiancé Lowell Cates heard the sergeant in charge of coffee declare. "Pretty soon when they realize it's there for the asking, they won't be slopping it up all the time!"

"It was the same way with our food," Roka wrote. "We took more food than we could eat and we were always hoarding it."

Fellow internee John Osborn described in a letter a similar fascination with the parade of extravagant meals. "The food still seems wonderful. Fresh beef. Fresh pork, and big fresh eggs flown from the States. Bread cut into generous slices; a can of evaporated milk every day for each internee," Osborn wrote. "I have gained 16 lbs. Gradually the wrinkles in my abdomen are being smoothed."

Just as starvation had disfigured bodies in odd ways, so, too, did the sudden and uneven return of weight. Roka noted how one nine-year-old had packed on the pounds just around her abdomen, making her belly appear swollen atop her skinny legs. As the camp's children grew stronger, the youthful energy that had vanished in the months before the liberation returned. "The camp children had ceased to be the little old men and women," she wrote. "They were normal kids again, and they began to annoy us with their running, screaming, and general rowdiness. The soldiers were spoiling them horribly. When they weren't stuffing their mouths with candy, chewing gum, and chocolates, they were riding the jeeps and trucks in the camp with the soldiers."

To outsiders, however, the internees looked terrible. "They haven't any idea what poor condition they really are in," General Fellers, who visited the camp each day, wrote his family. "They are so happy they're in a daze, and nearly everyone has eaten so much and so fast he has suffered from upset stomach."

The cacophony of artillery fire day and night served as a reminder that the internees lived on the sidelines of the fight for Manila. "We had to shout to each other to be heard above the terrific noise of the detonating shells," Roka wrote. "We wanted to get away! We had had enough of killing and warfare!" Internee Robert Wygle echoed Roka in his diary. "The guns still crash and the shells still swish over our heads," he wrote. "We still get a Jap show now and then, but it seems they are about through now and are slowly being churned to hamburger in the old Walled City."

Roka and her fiancé climbed in a jeep on one afternoon for a tour of northern Manila, an area now cleared of all enemy forces. "The last time I had been out, I had seen many Japanese soldiers and civilians, and the business section of the city was still standing," she wrote in her diary. "Today it was completely leveled, and there were no Japs." Roka visited the Plaza Goiti near the Escolta, Manila's once-prominent shopping avenue. "We looked to the north, east, south and west, as far as the eye could see," she wrote. "There was nothing but crumbling walls, and in some blocks there was absolutely nothing—everything had been leveled off by dynamiting and shelling. We passed the devastated areas and came to crowded streets filled with hungry and ragged Filipinos who were lined up for blocks to receive their food rations."

Internees did not have to venture outside the walls to experience the horror of the fight, which still materialized even in the relatively safe enclave of Santo Tomas. Sgt. Ozzie St. George, a correspondent with *Yank*, described one such scene. "There was a soldier, half dazed by shellfire, who entered the main lobby of Santo Tomas University with a bundle of something wrapped up in a sheet," the reporter wrote. "He asked what he should do with it, and they asked him what it was, laundry? He said no and lifted the sheet and it was the upper half of his best friend's body."

St. George noted that a new lexicon arose among the troops to describe the fight now raging on the opposite side of the Pasig:

"Across the river."

"South of the River."

"The other side."

Refugees meanwhile continued to stream across the Pasig, a scene captured by CBS reporter Bill Dunn in one of his broadcasts. "The stories that come out of south Manila, borne on the drooping shoulders of homeless refugees, are both harrowing and unbelievable," he reported. "The Japanese, in his dying frenzy, seems determined to take as many innocent civilians with him as possible."

The bloodshed overwhelmed the veteran newsman, who finally vowed that he would no longer report on the atrocities. "But I do want to testify to the truthfulness of the stories you have already heard," he told listeners. "As unthinkable as many of them may appear, they have been completely verified by official army circles and by personal observations of the war correspondents. A friend of mine who spent nearly a quarter century in Japan sized up the situation perfectly. 'Just as we underestimated their preparedness,' he said, 'we over estimate their civilization.'"

Fellow reporter Henry Keys of the London *Daily Express* interviewed Dr. Josephina Bulatao, a physician from the Philippine General Hospital who was nearly killed in Paco. "I cannot understand why they are doing these terrible things to my people," she said as she broke down in tears. "They are not human beings at all." Bulatao could at least communicate. The horror had left others so shell-shocked that interviews with reporters proved impossible. "It was painful to probe into the shattered minds of the refugees who crept to safety," wrote *Newsweek*'s Robert Shaplen. "Most of them were so dazed that they were unable to speak. Several times when I started to ask a question, the only response I could draw was a stare and a torrent of tears. After a while it seemed wiser not to try."

Keys struggled to contain his outrage over what he witnessed. "At last the Japanese have matched the rape of Nanking," he wrote in one dispatch. "In Manila they have piled outrage on outrage, infamy on infamy, until it has become a city of nightmarish horror." MacArthur's aides likewise fumed over the destruction. "The Jap is a fiend.

He is burning and murdering indiscriminately," Fellers wrote his family. "It takes all one's strength to see the refugees. They haven't the slightest idea which way to go. Their homes are destroyed; many are wounded; most of them have not slept for days, and if they had slept it would be on the ground in dangerous areas. The suffering, the mental torment, and the losses which these people endure are indescribable."

Fellers related the story of a young mother he met, her clothes tattered and her beautiful face covered in filth. In her arms, she cradled a baby. "Thank you for saving us," the woman said to him.

"How she could be grateful for anything was beyond me," Fellers wrote. "I asked her if her home was gone and she said, yes, a direct hit had destroyed it immediately but it was most fortunate that she and her child were outside. Where this girl went and what happened to her I don't know, but I can never forget her face."

Life magazine photographer Carl Mydans experienced a similar encounter when he stumbled upon a wounded woman in the doorway of a torched shop, her dress shredded and a swollen and crusty black injury on her thigh. The reporter asked how long she had been in the doorway. "Since yesterday," she muttered.

"Has no one helped you?" Mydans asked. "Have you had any food?"

"No," she replied.

The photographer set off in search of help. Unable to locate a litter, he tore down a bamboo gate. Along with several Filipinos, Mydans hoisted her atop his jeep, carting her to a nearby aid station.

The medic sized up her injuries. "All right," he finally said, "put her into that ambulance."

The corpsman loaded the woman, but then the medic turned to Mydans. "No good," he told the photographer. "She's done for."

The medic closed the door of the ambulance. Mydans watched as he shook his head, too. The woman was one of countless victims. "All morning we had seen the long files of people walking mutely rearward past advancing infantry," Mydans said. "Some of them limped with improvised wound dressings. Many of them walked, heaven knows how, with open wounds. Some were empty-handed; some carried pitiful little bundles or struggled with little carts or staggered under loads on bamboo poles." To Mydans's surprise, none of the victims complained; few even asked for help. Most moved like zombies, one foot after the other—the pilgrimage of the damned, all headed away from the war zone. "Everything you ever had or hoped for is gone," Mydans recalled. "Your mother is dead, your father is dead, your son is dead, your baby is dead. There's black dust and ashes where your home was. There's no water and no food."

To American reporters, many were nameless faces. But to Filipino journalist Felipe Buencamino, the refugees were friends, colleagues, and prominent Manila citizens and socialites. Amid the ash-covered streets, he encountered doctors, lawyers, judges, and bankers. He saw former senator Elpidio Quirino, whose wife Alicia had been machine-gunned along with the couple's son Armando and two daughters, Norma and Fe. Three of Quirino's five children were gone. "He was not the same man I had seen so many times in the past, banging the gavel in the rostrum of the Senate," Buencamino wrote. "Senator Quirino had aged in ten days and his face had a lost expression."

The reporters learned that amid the fighting and chaos there was no time for proper burials or even to identity the dead, who were collected in piles and interred in mass graves, a scene witnessed by Walter Simmons of the *Chicago Daily Tribune*. "At a spot where bodies lie a bulldozer with an armored cab is scooping out a hole," the journalist wrote. "This done, it pushes the bodies in, backs up with a jerk, then surges ahead, leaving a gash of fresh, leveled earth in its wake."

American journalists accompanied by troops crossed the Pasig to pick through the worst of the city's ruins. Scattered amid the smoldering debris stood the occasional gutted office, lone facade, or even home miraculously untouched by the battle. Over it all hung the caustic smell of smoke mixed with the stench of rotting dead. At the pontoon bridges built by the army—covered with steel and wooden decks—military police sorted out the bottleneck of refugees, troops, and ambulances. *Newsweek*'s Shaplen watched the tragic parade one day. "Mothers and children were dripping with blood, their heads bandaged, broken limbs dangling," the reporter wrote. "And along the streets and in the grass, bodies of shot and bayoneted Filipinos lay unattended. A human foot was lying on the road."

"It's plenty hot up there today," a military policeman warned Simmons one day as the reporter prepared to cross. "Better get your tin hat on."

Bill Gray, the *Time* magazine journalist who replaced Bill Chickering after he was killed in a kamikaze attack en route to Lingayen Gulf, cabled his editors detailed notes of what he saw south of the Pasig. "Americans have formed only the meagerest image of the devastation and tragedy which the Japs have chosen to leave in Manila. The city's misery goes on and on," Gray wrote. "How many hundreds or thousands of civilians already have died by fire or shell outside the Intramuros nobody knows."

Gray visited the Singalong Church, the same one the Garcia family had passed a few days earlier en route to Santa Ana. The reporter found the inside crowded with about two hundred refugees, some stretched out atop benches, others lying on the floor between piles of salvaged household items, chicken cages, and tethered goats. A three-legged dog hobbled amid the wounded. The reporter let his eyes wander, noting how artillery shells had shattered the stained-glass windows. The occasional sparrow fluttered through the shell holes, while the shards of glass littered the marble floor. A cracked glass case stood in one corner, displaying a dusty wax figure of Jesus Christ. "A Filipino woman in a yellow-flowered dress lay in a wooden cart where the ambulances came to take away the wounded," Gray wrote. "Somebody had placed a gold crucifix beside her."

For the journalists who covered the battle, the realization crystallized that the fight would end only when the last Japanese marine died. "Progress is slow because of the necessity of prying the suicidal maniacs out of their every hiding place, one by one or group by group," reported Bill Dunn. "They are not trying to retreat, withdraw or reinforce. They are just staying put until such time as we kill them off." *New York Times* reporter George Jones noted that much of the death and destruction was punitive. "A beaten enemy is wrecking his vengeance on Manila and its people and we are obtaining a glimpse of the same wanton cruelty and pillage that the Japanese military visited upon other oriental cities," he wrote. "The evidence is not pretty to see."

Reporters at times experienced bizarre moments, including a discovery Simmons made one day of a street carpeted with Japanese occupation bills. "That bank's full of it," a soldier told him.

Simmons stepped through the doors of a nearby bank and confirmed. "The floor is covered ankle deep with worthless paper money," the reporter wrote. "Here is the elegy of dashed enemy hopes—peso notes for the Philippines, guilders for the Dutch East Indies, shilling and pounds for Australia, rupees for India, $5 and $10 bills—for what? Hawaii or Alaska, maybe. Or maybe for the United States."

Others who had lived in Manila before the war struggled to match up memories of the once-vibrant city with the new wrecked reality. "It was heartbreaking to inch along with one of the fighting outfits into buildings, hotels, offices, banks and homes in which you had stood freely and happily, meeting your friends, dining under slowly revolving fans," wrote Royal Arch Gunnison, a reporter with *Collier's*. "Today these places are either razed to the ground or they are so gutted by fire and so completely looted by the Japs that nothing but shattered memories and desolation remain."

Accompanied by John Dos Passos, Gunnison explored homes littered with torn dinner jackets and slashed family portraits, personal mementos of peaceful times and lives destroyed in the fury of battle. Inside one such residence, as troops searched out a hidden enemy machine-gunner, Gunnison pushed open a door, dropping to the floor in fear of what he found. "There," he wrote, "propped up in bed, on second glance, I saw a Jap soldier, dead—an automatic weapon across his lap, a hot-water bottle behind his head. A shell had burst against his window an hour or so before and had taken care of him."

Like Gunnison, George Jones of the *New York Times* explored one of the few standing apartment buildings south of the river that overlooked the bay and the Manila Hotel. Without power, the elevators did not work, so he climbed the stairs. Inside a third-floor apartment, Jones found the floors covered with Japanese envelopes and shattered teacups. Glass crunched beneath his feet as he climbed up to another apartment. "Here we saw oriental and western clothing strewn on the floor," he wrote, "drawers emptied, mattresses removed from beds, beautiful silverware and pewter thrown into a corner and phonograph records—strangely intact—scattered over the room. Farther up in another apartment we came across beautiful oriental furniture, richly carved and inlaid with mother-of-pearl. Here the departure had been violent, for table legs and chair legs were broken and a statue of Buddha had been smashed against the floor."

The windows framed a view of the bay, where Jones counted dozens of sunken ships, whose masts pointed like skeletal fingers at the smoky sky. To the north, he saw the Manila Hotel, still in enemy hands, as American forces crouched low and approached. "Block after ruined block marks the progress of the battle for Manila, and any building with intact walls stands defiantly alone in the midst of ashes and concrete rubble," he wrote. "Horrible charred bodies lie unheeded along the streets and sometimes only a blackened grinning skull remains. Looking at them, one knew that Manila as we once knew it is dead. No victory parade can bring back old Manila." MacArthur realized it, too, abandoning his celebratory plans. "I understand," General Eichelberger wrote to his wife, "the big parade has been called off."

MacArthur's premature announcement of the capital's liberation meant that news editors back in the United States had little interest in stories or broadcasts out of Manila. After all, according to the general, the battle had been won. That made stories out of Manila a tough sell for reporters in a busy war competing for precious airtime or front-page real estate. This de facto censorship infuriated journalists, prompting Bill Dunn to complain in vain about it to Eichelberger. MacArthur more actively censored the press after reading news accounts that described the death of Manila. The general ordered his press officer Col. LeGrande Diller to strike such phrases from any reporter's story. "MacArthur was shattered by the holocaust," headquarters staffer Paul Rogers recalled. "He had gone to great lengths in 1941 to prevent needless destruction of the city he loved. Now his own forces were killing it ruthlessly and methodically."

Other senior commanders privately lamented the erroneous assumption that the enemy would abandon the capital—even though guerrilla reports before the battle had pointed to just such a scenario. "I do not believe anybody expected the Japs to make a house-to-house defense of Manila," Eichelberger wrote to his wife. "They are raising hell up there." In a follow-up letter four days later, he returned to the subject. "I must say that I never heard anybody predict that any such fight would ever take place," he wrote. "We knew that a lot of defenses had been erected, but it was generally expected that the Japanese would declare Manila an open city or would evacuate." General Fellers wrote to his wife that the fight for the capital had been for naught. "The long drawn-out battle was caused by a rather futile effort to save Manila and the civilian population," he concluded. "If anything should happen to Tokyo, the Japanese have asked for it."

CHAPTER 19

"The old Walled City of Intramuros this morning was a man-made hell."

—George E. Jones,
New York Times, February 23, 1945

Aⁿ merican forces readied at dawn on February 23 for the assault on Intramuros. The ancient fortress that for more than three centuries had stood against Chinese, Dutch, and Portuguese invaders had become one of the last major strongholds for the Japanese in Manila. An estimated two thousand enemy troops occupied the 160-acre citadel, protected by two and a half miles of towering stone walls that rose in places as high as twenty-two feet. Japanese troops had all along prepared to make a final stand in the Walled City, eliminating an estimated four thousand male civilians in recent weeks who might pose a threat during the fight. MacArthur's generals understood the challenges that awaited them. "The entire area," one army report noted, "was medieval in structure and its defense combined the fortress of the Middle Ages with the fire power of modern weapons."

In an effort to secure the northeast approaches to the Walled City, American troops the day before had seized Manila's City Hall in what had proven a dogged fight as Japanese defenders repeatedly repelled the infantrymen. "Tremendous fire was placed on the target," noted the 716th Tank Battalion report, "until the entire northeast corner of the four-story building collapsed." Troops finally stormed City Hall with bazookas and flamethrowers, battling the enemy room by room before securing the municipal building at 2:50 p.m. and at a cost of 206 Japanese dead. A similar fight had played out nearby at the five-story General Post Office, where American forces trapped the last of the enemy in the basement. "The tedious process of eliminating this fanatical group with flame-throwers, burning oil, and demolition charges," the Thirty-Seventh Infantry Division's report noted, "continued throughout the rest of the day."

War planners expected another protracted fight for the Walled City. Civilian escapees had described elaborate tunnels the Japanese had dug to move troops throughout Intramuros and even within the stone walls. Escapees further relayed that most of the enemy's fortifications aimed toward the south and the east, including tank traps, mines, and barbed wire designed to snare infantrymen. Complicating any fight, war planners realized, were the hordes of women and children, some of whom the Japanese had shanghaied to serve as human shields. Furthermore, many of the civilians, who had faced starvation even before the battle began, now hovered near death. In the hope of preventing unnecessary bloodshed, General Griswold had attempted days earlier to convince the Japanese to release the residents of the Walled City.

"Your situation is hopeless—your defeat inevitable," the XIV Corps commander broadcast. "I offer you an honorable surrender."

Only silence, however, answered him.

"So," he wrote in his diary, "it is a fight to the death!"

To limit American casualties, the Sixth Army commander General Krueger again pleaded to use bombers, but MacArthur refused. "The use of air on a part of a city occupied by a friendly and allied population is unthinkable," the general said. "The inaccuracy of this type of bombardment would result beyond question in the death of thousands of innocent civilians." MacArthur's decision frustrated his commanders, including Griswold, who rationalized the potential civilian deaths because the Japanese were already burning, shooting, and bayoneting thousands. "Horrid as it seems," he wrote in his diary, "probably death from bombing would be more merciful." Despite that, Griswold was loath to risk his troops. "I understand how he feels about bombing people—but it is being done all over the world—Poland, China,

England, Germany, Italy—then why not here! War is never pretty," he wrote. "I am frank to say I would sacrifice civilian Filipino lives under such circumstances to save the lives of my men. I feel quite bitter about this tonight."

The plan for the seizure of Intramuros was multipronged, with assaults on two sides of the Walled City so as to throw the enemy off balance. Six days earlier on February 17, artillery had begun blasting openings in the north and northeastern walls, where Japanese fortifications were the weakest. The north proved particularly vulnerable; the enemy had concluded that the Pasig River would serve as a natural barrier to an invasion. The artillery attacks would build up to a ferocious hour-long bombardment shortly past daybreak on the morning of the assault that would be rivaled only by the pummeling of Lingayen Gulf six weeks earlier. Afterward troops with the 129th Infantry would paddle across the muddy river in boats, while soldiers with the 145th Infantry would charge overland from the General Post Office. The First Cavalry Brigade, meanwhile, would prevent any escape by the Japanese to the south or the west.

War planners had debated a nighttime assault but ultimately decided that in a dense urban environment, it would be easier and safer to coordinate the artillery and infantry during the daylight hours. The tides proved another concern. Crossing the river at high tide would have been ideal, making the off-loading of troops and equipment easier. But high tide that day would occur in the dark predawn hours and not again until the early afternoon. Commanders were reluctant to begin the assault so late in the day, leaving troops only a few hours of light. If Japanese defenses proved fierce and troops had to withdraw, doing so after dark could result in a disaster. "The element of surprise was not a factor of great importance in choosing the time of attack, for the ring about the Walled City was growing smaller day by day," noted the XIV Corps report. "Furthermore, the enemy had been told that the American troops were coming."

At seven-thirty a.m., as the sun inched skyward along the eastern horizon, American artillery opened fire on the Walled City. "The huge guns were jacked up on their supports to permit point-blank fire," wrote headquarters staffer Paul Rogers. "The first rounds used were high-explosive shells. Then smoke and white phosphorous shells were sent over." News reporters, many camped out in General Griswold's command post atop a burned-out hotel just north of the Pasig River, watched the opening salvos. "I have witnessed naval bombardments," reported Bill Dunn of CBS, "but nothing to match the concentrated fury of this barrage." George Jones of the *New York Times* focused on the walls. "Forty feet thick at the bottom and 20 feet at the top, this century-old wall dissolved in great geysers of black smoke, showering rubble and shrapnel," he wrote. "The air filled with smoke and dust and quickly Intramuros was obliterated from sight. The only thing to be seen through this curtain were flashes of exploding shells."

Ten minutes passed.

Then twenty.

The guns still thundered, one after the other, each of the 120 artillery pieces an instrument in this morning's symphony of destruction. In one hour, artillery would fire a staggering 7,896 rounds—a total of 185 tons of ordnance. That was combined with another nineteen hundred mortars. Every second of the bombardment saw an average of three shells fired, creating a continuous rolling thunder that rendered telephones worthless, forcing observers to fall back on visual communications. "The old soft stones," recalled Major Henne, "were no match for the gunpowder of modern artillery."

For the refugees held hostage inside the Walled City, the bombardment was pure terror, like being trapped underneath a roaring freight train. Shells pounded the ancient walls, pulverizing the stone and filling the air with thick dust, making it hard not only to see but to breathe. Inside the dark and smoky San Agustin, the Japanese forced refugees to drag all the furniture out of the corridors. Troops mounted a machine gun at the front door and passed out grenades, while Formosan guards attached bayonets to bamboo poles. Over in the ruins of Santa Rosa College, flying shrapnel wounded and killed several refugees. "We could not even see each other because of the smoke," said Benita Lahoz. "We thought that we were all going to die." Father Belarmino de Celis, who had escaped being buried alive, huddled inside the Department of Justice Building, choking on dust as the windows, walls, and doors began to collapse around him. "The firing became intense," he later said. "It seemed a very inferno."

At eight-thirty a.m. a cloud of red smoke rose over the south wall of Intramuros, the signal for the artillery attack to end and the ground assault to begin. "The ensuing silence," Dunn recalled, "seemed even louder than the bombardment."

"Now there's nothing more I can do but sweat," Griswold told Dunn. "I've given them all I've got and they're under a higher command."

Down below, the assault boats pushed away from the muddy bank to begin the crossing. All eyes focused on the troops, the sun reflecting off the wet paddles. "It was a breathless moment," Dunn recalled. "Not a shot was fired at them," remarked Jones of the *New York Times*. "The bombardment had been a tremendous success."

At the same time troops began to cross the river, artillerymen fired smoke mortars in front of the Legislature, Agriculture, and Finance buildings—all in Japanese hands—so as to prevent any counterattacks on the ground forces. Infantrymen charged from the General Post Office, Metropolitan Theater, and City Hall, darting across the burned and pockmarked golf course to reach the eastern wall at 8:33 a.m. Artillerymen laid down a heavy concentration of smoke across the middle of the Walled City, blocking any enemy view of where troops entered and preventing reinforcements.

At 8:36 a.m., troops debarked from the assault boats and scrambled up the bank and over the rubble into the Walled City. "A lone sniper under Jones Bridge opened up with a machine gun and was immediately silenced. It was the only opposition," Dunn reported. "As dazed, half crazed civilians moved out of the north wall toward the boats, our troops moved in and the fighting within the walls began."

Dunn watched Griswold, who stood beside him, wipe the sweat from his hands and face. "God bless them!" the general muttered. "God bless them!"

The Americans pushed into the Walled City, using flamethrowers, grenades, and bazookas to destroy enemy pillboxes. "Retaking the Intramuros," one report noted, "developed into a small-arms duel."

Jones witnessed the same. "A short rattle of machine guns and sharp clash of rifles," the reporter wrote, "told the story of the only opposition that had survived the bombardment—the greatest and heaviest seen and heard in Manila." Behind the walls, troops found a wasted city, whose narrow streets and alleys were now packed with the rubble of homes, shops, and churches, forcing the infantrymen to pick through the debris. Father Belarmino de Celis, who was nearby in the Department of Justice Building, heard the advancing troops.

"Come on, come out," one of the soldiers shouted.

"I knew by the voice and the manner of speaking that it was truly an American—and my joy knew no bounds," he later said.

The exhausted priest limped outside, leaning against one of the walls. He saw several nuns from the Santa Clara Convent emerge as well. Fires and artillery had reduced the convent to ruins, forcing nearly a dozen clergy to hide in the basement. Japanese patrols had missed the few stragglers, who had survived off rice and water, unsure in the dark underground of how much time had passed. Father Belarmino told the Americans where to find his companion Julio Rocamora, the only other survivor from the air raid shelter. The priest watched troops carry him out on a stretcher.

Infantrymen opened a can of meat for the refugees and gave them chocolate and water before loading them in assault boats and sending them across the river. Jones watched the first boats arrive, noting the bare feet and bloodstained habits of the nuns, who clutched photographs, rosaries, and crucifixes. The sisters stepped onto the north bank of the river and fell to their knees in prayer. "The soldiers," Jones wrote, "bared their heads in embarrassment, unable to face such a pathetic scene."

Other civilians arrived in later boats, including one man who clung to his wife with one arm and held his twelve-month-old daughter in the other. "I don't know where my sister is," he repeated.

Sporadic street fighting erupted as the Americans pressed deeper into the Walled City. Staff Sgt. Maynard Mahan ducked behind a concrete block, while Japanese rounds buzzed overhead. He lit a cigarette and waited, closing his eyes for a break as he inhaled. A mortar exploded nearby, raining stone down around him. He realized then that his cigarette had vanished, stolen by a piece of flying shrapnel. "Damn it," he shouted. "That was my last butt."

Around eleven a.m. troops reached the scorched ruins of Santa Rosa College. There among the makeshift shelters made of burned timbers and corrugated sheets of metal, soldiers discovered eleven-year-old Rosalinda Andoy, whom the Japanese had bayoneted thirty-eight times. Nurses in the ruins had bandaged her wounds, including the hole in her stomach that had exposed her intestines. Rosalinda had miraculously survived twelve days. Another unlikely survivor was Rosa Calalang. Convinced she would die, nurses had summoned a priest to hear her last confession, yet she, too, had lived. Soldiers this morning hustled those who could walk out to the foot of the Jones Bridge, while litter bearers came for the wounded, carrying them to waiting ambulances.

On a later sweep through the ruins, troops heard an unmistakable sound. "That sounds like a baby!" one announced.

The Americans began tearing apart the rubble. Underneath the ruins of a staircase, they found a recently deceased mother still clutching an infant girl to her breast. The soldiers pried the baby free and carried her to a battalion aid station, where medics administered blood plasma and warm broth. Others bathed her and swaddled her in fresh clothes made from an old pair of military fatigues. Medics turned her over to civilian authorities. "How do you like that?" Staff Sgt. Harry Bulfer complained. "We get a real souvenir and right away we have to give it up. What an army!"

A few blocks away at San Agustin Church, refugee leader Dr. Sebastian Siguenza told the others it was no longer safe. Not only had the Japanese fortified the church, but troops now fired mortars from the remains of the tower and the rear of the convent, making the entire property a potential target of American artillery. "We had better leave this place," he informed the others.

Refugees pleaded with the officers to allow them to leave. The Japanese finally relented, ordering those who were able to line up single file by a side door. The refugees gathered up small bundles of food and prepared to leave. Siguenza fastened a white flag to a pole. The Japanese opened the door just wide enough to allow one person out at a time. The doctor led the group, each step taking them farther away from the hellhole of San Agustin, where unburied bodies filled several wheelbarrows on the patio.

"Don't be afraid," Siguenza told the others. "Go peacefully."

The refugees navigated the debris-cluttered streets, while smoke and dust wafted through the air. Siguenza pushed ahead, flag gripped in his hand.

"We are Filipinos!" the refugees cried out.

A Japanese rifle roared.

Siguenza toppled over dead.

Some of the refugees wanted to turn back.

But back to what—a squalid church filled with dead Filipinos and doomed Japanese? Or should the group press ahead, hoping to reach the Americans?

"Go forward," someone shouted. "Walk straight ahead."

Isabelita Moreno reached down and grabbed the flag from the rubble beside Siguenza's body, leading the group. "She too, was shot," Lourdes Lecaroz later testified. "Other people were shot, both women and children. It was terrible."

Yet the refugees pressed on despite Japanese sniper fire, eventually reaching Letran College. Up ahead in the road rumbled a tank: safety at last. "American soldiers embraced us," Mary Tormey recalled. "We walked out from there."

American forces hurried to erect a rudimentary footbridge over the river made of pontoons and boards to help with the outward flow of refugees, a scene captured by Jones in his dispatch that day. "Over it streamed what was left of the civilian population of Intramuros. Those who weren't emaciated from starvation bore wounds and cuts from bullets," he wrote. "At intervals in this pitiful procession came Chinese carrying litters on which lay sick, wounded or dying men, women and children. But this apparently unending column was merely an indication of the horror of Intramuros."

Thirty-five-year-old Henry Keys, a correspondent with the *London*

Daily Express, would be one of the first reporters to experience the horror of the Walled City. "Come along," one lieutenant told him, "if you really want to see something."

Keys set off that afternoon with the officer and several litter bearers to visit San Agustin, navigating the narrow and mined streets. The only occupants left inside the church were the dead and those too wounded to escape. In one courtyard, around a battered statue, Keys saw shelters made of corrugated iron. "I knelt down and I looked inside and the first thing I saw was a dead girl," he said. "One of her feet was crushed to pulp and her mouth was broken and a lot of blood had come from it."

Keys followed the lieutenant, passing behind the statue and into the columned veranda of the convent. He looked to the right and saw the emaciated body of a kneeling boy, a bullet hole through the base of his skull. To his left, Keys noted a pile of bloodied bodies, a tangle of arms, legs and torsos, many showing stab and shrapnel wounds. A layer of gray ash had settled over everything, like a dusting of snow.

The reporter continued deeper into this death chamber, where he found another lieutenant kneeling next to a wounded young woman. Keys could see that her jaw had been shattered, likely smashed, he suspected, by a Japanese rifle butt. "She bore other wounds on her body and was barely breathing," Keys later testified. "The lieutenant gently patted her lips and was dropping water into her mouth."

In another nearby room an enlisted man hovered over a beautiful young woman, her legs covered up by a blanket. "Look at this!" the soldier said.

The enlisted man lifted the blanket. Keys let his eyes wander down, stunned to see two bloody stumps tied with what appeared to be handkerchiefs.

"She told us that a Jap hacked her feet off," the soldier said.

The scene made him feel sick. The reporter looked away, only to spot a dead Japanese soldier nearby on the ground. The enemy's remains, unlike all the rest, were not mutilated. "He was the only decent, whole piece of humanity in the place; the only clean piece of humanity," Keys said. "He was dressed in a white singlet on the shirt and some pants. He was lying there like an animal and I was told that he had been there some weeks, having been brought in when he was ill and cared for by the nuns."

Keys walked back out into the corridor.

"Come here!" the lieutenant called. "This is alive!"

On the ground amid the toppled bricks and crumbled mortar, he saw a girl so emaciated that she did not look human. She lay still as though dead, but every so often her entire body shuddered. "The flies were all over her as they were all over all these other wounded and dead," Keys said. "We brushed them away."

The reporter had seen more than enough. He returned to the footbridge, instructing a few litter bearers to go retrieve the young woman with the severed feet. A little while later, the men returned, carrying her. As she passed, Keys noted she held up her left hand and with two fingers flashed the victory sign.

The few remaining Japanese troops—some discovered dressed in American uniforms and sporting U.S. rifles—retreated behind the towering walls of Fort Santiago. American soldiers pursued them, battling them around the burning remnants of the ancient citadel. "Every building," said Capt. David Conner, "was completely gutted and destroyed by fire and bombing." Beyond the fires, troops found yet more scenes of horror, including a body hanging by the neck from a wire, a look of extreme pain and terror frozen on the face. "The hands," Conner said, "were clutching the wire."

The Americans found only three refugee survivors, all former patients from San Juan de Dios Hospital that the Japanese had grabbed from the ruins of Santa Rosa College. Two of them proved so badly injured that neither could speak, but the third related his story. "He said that he had a little rice two weeks ago," said Tech Sgt. Frank Pitchek. "Since that time he had been eating bugs and drinking his own urine."

The Japanese vanished underground into Fort Santiago's labyrinth of tunnels and damp dungeons, forcing the Americans to ferret them out. "Every thinkable method was employed including gasoline and oil," noted one Thirty-Seventh Infantry Division report. "It was effec-

Amid the fighting for the Walled City, MacArthur returns to the ruins of his home atop the once-luxurious Manila Hotel on February 23, 1945.

An American tank rumbles through the historic gate of Fort Santiago inside the Walled City on February 26, 1945.

American troops found dead women and children inside the Walled City on February 23, 1945.

A Filipino examines several dead bodies at the Philippine General Hospital for any sign of identification before the remains are hauled away for burial.

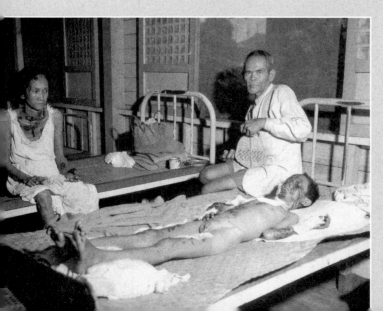

Isobela Mercado and her husband Angel Estandarte tend to their badly injured son Jose after the Japanese locked the family's home and set it on fire. The family escaped, only to be burned by Japanese flamethrowers.

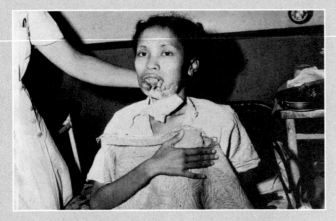

Lourdes Ental, pictured here in San Lazaro Hospital on March 2, 1945, was hit in the face by grenade shrapnel after she fought off Japanese troops who tried to assault her.

The torched ruins of the Red Cross Headquarters in Manila, where Japanese marines slaughtered more than fifty men, women, and children in a rampage on February 10, 1945.

Eugene Bayot, who survived Japanese efforts to decapitate him with a sword, later sketched for war crimes investigators the inside of the Singalong Street death house, where enemy troops beheaded approximately two hundred men on February 10, 1945.

Cheng Suy, one of the few survivors of the Singalong Street death house, shows war crimes investigators the deep divot in his neck that resulted from the failed Japanese effort to decapitate him.

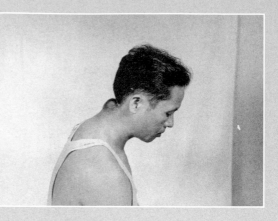

Gen. Douglas MacArthur, with President Sergio Osmeña at his side, salutes the color guard at Malacañan Palace during a ceremony to hand over power to the Philippine government on February 27, 1945.

MacArthur peers inside the wrecked Malinta Tunnel on his visit to newly captured Corregidor on March 2, 1945.

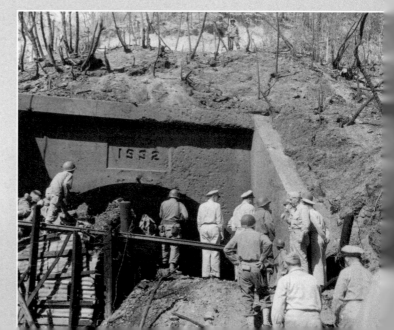

Residents stroll past the wrecked Cu-Unjieng Building on the Escolta, which was once known as Manila's Fifth Avenue.

Life goes on as Filipinos walk in front of the ruins of the Philippine Legislature in May 1945.

Sixth Army Commander Gen. Walter Krueger, right, confers with Maj. Gen. Charles Mullins, Jr., on April 7, 1945.

The elusive Tiger of Malaya, Gen. Tomoyuki Yamashita, hikes down out of the mountains to surrender to American forces on September 2, 1945.

Yamashita, pictured second on the right, surrenders his forces in Baguio on September 2, 1945. Seated directly across from him, with his hair parted and looking down, is British Lt. Gen. Arthur Percival, whom Yamashita defeated in Singapore at the start of the war.

Yamashita, flanked on the right by Lt. Gen. Akira Muto and on the left by interpreter Masakatsu Hamamoto, sits through the war crimes trial on October 29, 1945. In front of Yamashita, seated left to right, are defense lawyers Col. Harry Clarke, Capt. Milton Sandberg, and Capt. Frank Reel.

Ricardo Esquerra, who was nearly decapitated in the Singalong Street death house, shows the wounds on the back of his neck during the Yamashita trial on November 3, 1945.

Maj. Milton Herr talks to famed Filipina actress Corazon Noble, who was shot and bayoneted inside the Red Cross Headquarters, outside the Yamashita trial on November 29, 1945. Japanese forces killed Noble's ten-month-old daughter, Maria Lourdes Vera, during the massacre.

Gen. Tomoyuki Yamashita testifies in his defense in a packed Manila courtroom on November 28, 1945.

Jean MacArthur, pictured here with her husband in July 1946, returned to Manila soon after the battle ended.

tive for when things cooled and men entered these chambers, Japs were found piled high having suffered just as horrible a death as they inflicted on the thousands of innocent civilians they massacred."

The battle for Intramuros was finally over.

Four hundred enemy dead were counted just inside Fort Santiago. In recent weeks, American soldiers had grown accustomed to witnessing the barbarity of Japanese massacres. But even those could not prepare them for what they found inside Fort Santiago. "When the Japanese realized that Manila was lost," one report noted, "they engaged in a final orgy of mass murder by shooting, bayonetting and burning alive of all prisoners remaining inside the fort." As the buildings still smoldered, American soldiers swept the fort, where Japanese troops at the start of the battle had executed thousands of Filipino males. Infantrymen discovered one dungeon that appeared to have been used as a crematorium. "There were ashes and bones scattered on the floor," Conner recalled, "and the entrance to the dungeon was badly blackened and charred."

In the frenetic final days of the battle, the enemy had failed to torch all the evidence of war crimes. In a room that measured twelve by fifteen feet, U.S. soldiers found a warehouse of the dead. "These bodies were piled on each other, in some places four deep," recalled Maj. Frank Middelberg. "All of their feet pointed to the only doorway into the room. I noted that their hands were tied behind their backs." Staff Sgt. Jacob Klein likewise witnessed the scene. "The bodies, shriveled and bony, were at least partially clothed," Klein later testified in an affidavit. "They were blood-spattered and bullet-riddled and some showed signs of having been bayonetted."

Eleven more dead were found in a nearby room and hall, all shot in the back; thirty others were located in a stone building, many seared by fire. "Bodies in the rear part of the building appeared to have been placed side by side, some face up and some face down," stated one report. "Near the doorway the bodies were in a state of disorder, being strewn over each other in a grotesque mass. It appeared the bodies near the only doorway had been thrown inside indiscriminately and hurriedly."

None of this compared to what awaited troops underground.

A horrid stench of decay drew soldiers down the damp stone steps into the dungeons in the northwest corner of the fort near the Pasig River. There the troops faced a set of steel doors. "These double doors were bolted from the outside by means of an ancient-type one inch steel bar that was operated by means of a long steel handle," one report said. "It had been further secured by wrapping lengths of wire so that the bolt could not be moved." The concussions from the artillery had jammed the door. "Some enlisted men assisting me cut the wire to the boltlike latch," recalled Middelberg. "With considerable effort, we were able to slide the bolt and kick open the door. As the doors opened a terrific stench seemed to blast from the inside."

Several dozen bodies were piled near the front door, but those proved only a prelude to the horror. The darkened dungeon was filled with hundreds of dead, layered several deep. The decomposition of so many had heated the air inside the dungeon and filled it with the smell of ammonia. "So thick were the walls and roof that the room had not been disturbed on the inside by artillery or bombing," one report stated. "Those near the entrance were piled up and from their positions indicated they had died in an instinctive effort to go toward the only exit despite the fact it was closed."

The army's report noted that unlike the other rooms full of the dead, all of whom showed signs of being mercifully shot or bayoneted, evidence in the dungeon made this "a more diabolical, cruel and premeditated atrocity than the others." Middelberg summed it up in his affidavit. "All indications," he said, "pointed to the fact that the civilians were locked in the cell, the steel door bolted and left to die of starvation." The medical officer agreed; the bodies in effect had been mummified. "The starved and dehydrated condition of the people before death," the investigative report noted, "would account for the fact their bodies were not bloated and swelled when found."

The grim scene made it impossible for Americans to calculate a precise tally of the dead. The 129th Infantry report estimated the dungeon held about three hundred bodies. Major Binkley, the Thirty-Seventh

Infantry Division's sanitary inspector, put the tally at five hundred, while a Manila undertaker later estimated more than a thousand. In the end, no one would ever know for certain. "The total number of bodies could not have been ascertained because they were piled several deep," testified Col. John Frederick, commander of the 129th Infantry Regiment. "The stench from the bodies was virtually unbearable and the stage of decomposition precluded detailed investigation."

For General Griswold, who had watched the fight from a battered hotel north of the Pasig, the successful capture of the Walled City came at the relatively low cost of twenty-five Americans killed and 265 wounded. He could now focus on the few remaining government buildings that ringed the Walled City and housed Admiral Iwabuchi and the last of his men. "God has been good to me this day—and I am very grateful," the XIV Corps commander wrote in his diary. "I am sure that the battle for Manila will soon be history. It has been a great strain and responsibility."

○ ○ ○ ○

As American forces battled for the Walled City on February 23, MacArthur prepared to return to the Manila Hotel, where soldiers wrapped up the fight for the general's old home. It had been a hectic day for American forces. Not only had the infantry assaulted Intramuros, but forty miles south of Manila, soldiers had stormed the internment camp at Los Baños. In a daring seven a.m. raid timed to catch the Japanese during morning calisthenics, troops killed 243 guards and rescued 2,147 internees, liberating the last of the four Manila area prisoner of war and internment camps.

Throughout the fight for the capital, MacArthur had kept tabs on the fate of the Manila Hotel, information he dutifully cabled to his anxious wife back in Australia. The family had fled in such a hurry three years earlier that MacArthur had been forced to abandon almost forty boxes of medals, decorations, and insignias along with three shotguns, a dozen sets of cufflinks and watches, and his wardrobe of 216 linen and silk handkerchiefs. Jean had left behind five pearl necklaces, more than a dozen brooches, and a locket with hair. Even young Arthur had been forced to surrender his beloved toys, from drums and trumpets to his play tank, fire engine, and train set.

On February 14 the general had welcomed the news of the recovery of his father's silver, which the Japanese ambassador had planned to spirit out of Manila. One of the servants in the ambassador's home had recognized Arthur MacArthur's name engraved on the top of the silver chest. During the ambassador's hurried evacuation, the servant hid the chest, which included the original 1909 invoice from Tiffany.

U.S. soldiers later found another stash of the family's silver, which had been labeled as medical supplies. "House still unharmed but not yet in our hands," MacArthur cabled his wife on February 16. "Have recovered all of our silver which had been removed from the hotel to the Watson Building near Malacañan, apparently prepared for shipment to Japan." The general closed: "Be Patient."

Two days later, after artillery observers at the National City Bank of New York spotted the Japanese troops hoisting ammunition up to a third-floor balcony, the grand hotel had become a target. "I saw the Manila Hotel in flames," General Fellers wrote to his wife. "It was a tragic fight. Flames thousands of feet high."

MacArthur had relayed the news to Jean. "Do not—repeat not—be too distressed over the house," he cabled "It was a fitting end for our soldier home."

The general had prepared Jean for the worst though he had personally remained optimistic he might be able to salvage at least some of the many belongings the family had left behind when forced to escape to Corregidor at the start of the war.

At six a.m. on February 23, MacArthur departed his headquarters for the trip into Manila, accompanied by his aides colonels Roger Egeberg, Lloyd Lehrbas, and Andres Soriano. The general watched the fighting for the Walled City and visited the High Commissioner's Residence and the Army and Navy Club, both of which the Americans had secured just a few days earlier. By eleven-thirty a.m. that Friday, MacArthur looked across the wide-open Luneta Park at the Manila Hotel. At this distance, the damage appeared minimal. The facade around some of the upper windows was scorched, but the five-story hotel still stood intact, a prominent feature on the city's skyline.

Five hundred yards was all that separated the general from the home he had made with Jean and their young son Arthur, the place where for the first time in his life he had escaped the loneliness that had long plagued him. There in his penthouse he had surrounded himself with mementos of his rich family history and awards of a successful life, from his father's artifacts from the Civil War to his own medals earned on the muddy battlefields of France. He had spent evenings in his grand library surrounded by the works of William Shakespeare, Edgar Allan Poe, and Joseph Conrad, enjoyed Manila's famous sunsets over the bay from the terrace, and played with Erector Sets on the floor of his son's playroom. And now, after living in exile for three years, one month and thirty days, MacArthur was at last coming home.

American troops only the day before had fought a ferocious battle to retake the hotel as Japanese troops retreated into the basement. "300 lbs explosive plus flame throwers have failed to clear them out," one report noted. A few hours later, however, dogged American soldiers killed the last of the enemy and captured the famous landmark.

Fighting remained fierce throughout the morning around the hotel. Machine guns rattled, and mortars rained down. MacArthur's sedan could not make it across the Luneta, forcing him out on foot to make the last dash across the park accompanied by cavalrymen.

He was close.

So close now.

Suddenly his home erupted in flames. Japanese troops had likely reentered the hotel the night before—as had often proven the case throughout the battle—and torched his residence. "I watched," MacArthur wrote, "with indescribable feelings, the destruction of my fine military library, my souvenirs, my personal belongings of a lifetime."

Troops charged the hotel, climbing through the rubble and ash toward the penthouse with the general in tow, flanked by soldiers armed with submachine guns. Gunfire erupted as the Americans passed every floor, littering the landings with dead Japanese. "The higher the stairs, the warmer the bodies were," Egeberg recalled. "I was afraid one of them might be just wounded, or shamming."

Finally MacArthur reached his home. A dead Japanese colonel sprawled across the threshold, surrounded by the emperor's two shattered vases that Jean had placed by the door in hopes that the enemy might spare the home. She had sadly been wrong. "Nothing was left," MacArthur noted, "but ashes." Egeberg explored the ruins of the home. "The books were still on the bookshelves," he said. "You could read the titles on their spines, but when you touched them, they just disintegrated."

A young lieutenant stood over the dead Japanese colonel; smoke wafted from the barrel of the American's gun, and a smile stretched across his face.

"Nice going, Chief," he said to MacArthur.

"But there was nothing nice about it to me," the general later said. "I was tasting to the last acid dregs the bitterness of a devastated and beloved home."

CHAPTER 20

"The Japs have murdered wholesale and retail. To call them beasts would be to slander the beasts; to call them fiends would be to slander the fiends."

—JOHN OSBORN,
LETTER, FEBRUARY 25, 1945

GEN. DOUGLAS MACARTHUR DEPARTED HIS HEADQUARTERS at eight a.m. on February 27 for another trip down to Manila. This morning he planned to officially hand over power to Philippine president Sergio Osmeña in a ceremony at Malacañan Palace. The sixty-six-year-old Osmeña had served as the nation's vice president under Manuel Quezon when the war began. He had evacuated to Corregidor on Christmas Eve 1941, eventually escaped via submarine and plane to Australia, and later settled in Washington, home of the exiled Philippine government. Quezon's death had elevated Osmeña to president, who returned to the Philippines alongside MacArthur.

The windows of the dark sedan framed a view of the desolation where desperate residents hawked anything to survive, from bootleg whiskey to 1941 magazines, offering a nostalgic snapshot of life before the war. "As I passed through the streets with their burned-out piles of rubble," MacArthur recalled, "the air still filled with the stench of decaying unburied dead, the tall and stately trees that had been the mark of a gracious city were nothing but ugly scrubs pointing broken fingers at the sky. Once-famous buildings were now shells. The street signs and familiar landmarks were gone. One moved by sense of direction rather than by sight."

The Battle of Manila still dragged on, though the fury waned. American forces had isolated Admiral Iwabuchi and the last of his troops, committed to fight to the death in several buildings that rimmed Intramuros. In the wrecked city, Malacañan Palace stood in comparatively good shape. Much of the damage to the presidential home was the work of American troops, hunting hidden treasures of the president Jose Laurel. "It had scarcely been touched by the war and its carved woodwork, crystal chandeliers, paintings, furniture, rugs and hangings were all intact," recalled Lt. Gen. George Kenney, MacArthur's air commander. "It was a real oasis in the midst of desolation."

An American band kicked off the morning's ceremony with "Ruffles and Flourishes" before MacArthur entered the state reception room through the crimson-brocaded draperies and strode across the thick, flowered rug. With his hat off and hair slicked in a part, MacArthur stepped up to a lectern draped in blue velvet and adorned with reporter microphones. Camera floodlights illuminated him. Behind him stood colonels Roger Egeberg, Lloyd Lehrbas, Lt. Col. Andres Soriano, and Brig. Gen. Basilio Valdes, the Philippine Army's chief of staff whose own brother was murdered by the Japanese in the opening days of the battle. Steps away stood President Osmeña, members of his cabinet, and spouses, including the first lady, who wore a gauzy green dress and carried orange and yellow chrysanthemums.

In this palatial residence where MacArthur's father had governed almost a half-century earlier—and from whose windows he could see the smoldering ruins of his own home across the river—the general reflected on his deep personal ties to Manila. "For me it was a soul-wrenching moment. Nearly every surviving figure of the Philippines was there, but it was the ghosts of the past—the men who used to be—who filled my thoughts," MacArthur later wrote. "In this city, my mother had died, my wife had been courted, my son had been born; here, before just such a gathering as this, not so long ago, I had received the baton of a Field Marshal of the Philippine Army."

"Mr. President," he began, occasionally glancing at his notes, "more than three years have elapsed—years of bitterness, struggle and sacrifice—since I withdrew our forces and installation from this beautiful city that, open and undefended, its churches, monuments, and cultural centers might, in accordance with the rules of warfare, be spared the violence of military ravage. The enemy would not have it so, and much that I sought to preserve has been unnecessarily destroyed by his desperate action at bay—but by these ashes he has wantonly fixed the future pattern of his own doom."

MacArthur went on in his short speech, which totaled fewer than five hundred words, to praise America's allies who had helped battle the Japanese and make his long-awaited promise to return to the Philippines a reality. "On behalf of my government, I now solemnly declare, Mr. President, the full powers and responsibilities under the Constitution restored to the Commonwealth whose seat is here reestablished as provided by law," he said. "Your capital city, cruelly punished though it be—"

The general's voice broke, and he stopped. "His bronze features," recalled Brig. Gen. Courtney Whitney, "blanched and whitened." Whitney struggled to maintain his own composure. Tears filled MacArthur's eyes. "I could not go on," he later wrote. "To others it might have seemed my moment of victory and monumental personal acclaim, but to me it seemed only the culmination of a panorama of physical and spiritual disaster. It had killed something inside me to see my men die." That statement would later draw fire from some Filipinos, who criticized MacArthur for singling out American war dead but making no mention of the untold slain civilians.

MacArthur regained his composure and finished his remarks: "has regained its rightful place—citadel of democracy in the East."

The silver-haired Osmeña, dressed in military khaki, immediately remedied MacArthur's lapse. "We mourn the destruction of our once beautiful capital city of Manila and the murder of thousands of innocent people by the Japanese vandals," he said. "To General MacArthur, this campaign has been a crusade. Friend and defender of our race, he never lost faith in the spiritual strength of our people."

"As Osmeña began speaking," *Time* correspondent Bill Gray cabled his editors, "MacArthur seemingly sincerely embarrassed by tears, stepped out of the room and pulled himself together behind the drapes before returning."

After the ceremony, MacArthur, his earlier embarrassment replaced by a broad smile, kissed First Lady Esperanza Osmeña on her left cheek. "I am so glad," he told her, "you're home."

○ ○ ○ ○

MacArthur had abandoned his plans for a victory parade through Manila, but he refused to forgo the opportunity to return to Corregidor, going so far as to borrow four patrol-torpedo boats from the navy to complete his symbolic redemption. He was joined the morning of March 2 by eleven of the fifteen original staffers who had evacuated with him on that dark night three years earlier. With his trademark Ray Bans on and his officer's cap pulled low to block out the sun, MacArthur climbed aboard PT-373, christened "Hatches" after its canine mascot. "So this is the 373. I left on the 41," MacArthur told to the boat's skipper. "It has been a long time."

Lt. Joseph Roberts pulled away from Pier 2 with MacArthur perched at the bow. Around him on deck stood General Krueger, Chief of Staff Dick Sutherland, military aide Carlos Romulo, and Navy Vice Adm. Daniel Barbey. The other three boats ferrying the rest of MacArthur's aides fell in line astern. "We had departed in the darkness of a somber night," the general recalled. "We came back in the sunlight of a new day." Out in the bay, MacArthur settled into a deck chair. The last time he made the voyage from Manila to Corregidor was Christmas Eve 1941, the night he had buried his head in his hands as he evacuated the capital, the city on fire behind him. "Once the PTs were on their course," Barbey later wrote, "he hardly took his eyes off the blue silhouette of the island, lighter in color than the thirty miles of water ahead."

Some six thousand Japanese troops had holed up on Corregidor as the Battle of Manila raged just across the bay. MacArthur's air commander George Kenney had proposed the general pound Corregidor and then let paratroops seize it.

"Go ahead," MacArthur told him.

The 1,735-acre island suffered some of the most concentrated shelling and bombing of the Pacific War, first from the Japanese, then from the Americans. From January 23 through February 16, 1945, the Fifth Air Force flew 2,028 sorties against the Rock, pummeling it with 3,163 tons of bombs. MacArthur's forces had followed up the bombardment by dropping two thousand paratroopers atop Corregidor at eight-thirty a.m. on February 16. Another thousand troops assaulted the island by boat. "The fight for the small island," one army report noted, "was fast, vicious and bloody."

U.S. soldiers armed with white phosphorous grenades, satchel bombs, and flamethrowers had to destroy Japanese troops hiding in tunnels and caves. The violence was such that one rattled enemy soldier fled the cave, bleeding from his eyes, ears, nose, and mouth. Another time nine Japanese troops, all screaming and on fire, charged out of a cave. "In several instances," the Sixth Army's report noted, "the enemy resorted to mass self destruction." American troops were not immune to the horror. "I sat down on a rock and burst out crying," one medic said. "I couldn't stop myself and didn't even want to. I had seen more than a man could stand and still stay normal."

MacArthur stepped onto Corregidor's blasted cement dock around ten this March morning, pausing to let his eyes roam over the scorched rock. War had transformed this once-lush tropical island into a barren wasteland of rock, rubble, and rebar. All that remained of the verdant jungle and foliage that had blanketed the hills was the burned stubble of tree stumps. The bombing had managed even to eradicate color from the island, leaving only a pallet of brown, beige, and gray. "Corregidor," MacArthur told Kenney, "is living proof that the day of the fixed fortress is over."

The general made his way off the dock and into the front seat of a jeep for a tour of the Rock. "Malinta Hill, where the tunnels in which MacArthur and his staff worked during the early stages of the fighting on Bataan and Corregidor, was almost unrecognizable," wrote Associated Press reporter Dean Schedler. "The General walked from his jeep and peered into the entrance, while soldiers with machine guns kept the guns trained against possible enemy sniper fire." MacArthur stumbled at one point over the charred skull of a Japanese soldier. "They made it tough for us," the general said as he turned the skull over, "but it was a lot tougher for them."

MacArthur likewise visited Battery Wheeler and the destroyed Administration Building, wading through ankle-deep debris for a glimpse of his old office, now redecorated with a gaping shell hole over the area where his desk once sat. "The odor of long dead Japanese," wrote George Jones of the *New York Times*, "permeated the route of the general's itinerary." Just as bad as the smell were the large bluebottle flies that swarmed the island, flies that had grown fat feasting on a buffet of dead. "They were so thick," one lieutenant griped, "that they showed up in aerial photos." MacArthur returned to the cement ruins of one of the houses he had occupied years earlier.

"I am home again," reporters heard him murmur.

The jeeps began the final ascent up Corregidor to what was known as Topside, the highest point on the island that towered more than six hundred feet above sea level. "On the way up the hill we had passed details of soldiers who were disposing of the Japanese dead," recalled headquarters staffer Paul Rogers. "The bodies had been piled into square pyres. I watched as soldiers poured gasoline on the bodies and then threw a match. The bodies burned like logs. The stench of burning flesh was added to the stench of decaying flesh still lying in the brush and debris. There was no exhilaration, just revulsion."

At eleven-thirty a.m. MacArthur's entourage reached Topside. Bulldozers had cleared the rubble around the parade ground's flagpole made from an old ship's mast, which was bent and pockmarked from shrapnel. The blasted remains of the Topside Barracks loomed in the background, while the occasional rifle crack echoed in the distance. "Corregidor's dusty heights were festooned with red, white, blue, and the green and brown camouflaged parachutes of paratroopers who made the initial landing," *Time* magazine's Bill Gray observed. "Many chutes still hung on gaunt, broken limbs of trees or were snagged in dead foliage." Thirty-three-year-old Col. George Jones, the 1936 West Point graduate who commanded the Rock Force, stood in front of several hundred American troops, many exhausted and clad in bandages from the fight.

"Sir," Jones said, saluting, "I present to you Fortress Corregidor."

"The capture of Corregidor was one of the most brilliant operations in military history," MacArthur told Jones. "I see the old flag pole still stands. Have your troops hoist the colors to its peak and let no enemy ever haul them down again."

Buglers began to play as the flag rose up the pole.

"Colonel," MacArthur said afterward, "my heartiest congratulations."

○ ○ ○ ○

THE BATTLE OF MANILA was nearing its end. The seizure of the Walled City had left only three major strongpoints held by the Japanese—the Legislature, Agriculture, and Finance buildings, all just a few hundred yards east of Intramuros. The three neighboring structures formed a triangle, bound by San Luis and Padre Burgos streets and Taft Avenue. Not only had architects designed the concrete structures to withstand typhoons and even earthquakes, but the surrounding parks and wide streets promised to make a direct assault perilous. "The buildings had been laboriously converted by the Japanese into individual fortresses of the most formidable type with sandbagged gun emplacements and barricades in the doors and windows covering all approaches to each building as well as adjacent ones," according to a XIV Corps analysis. "Machine guns within the buildings themselves were sited to fire down corridors, stairways, and even inside rooms."

Unlike earlier battles, there were no civilians trapped inside, only an estimated seven hundred Japanese marines under the command of Iwabuchi: three hundred in the Finance Building and two hundred in each of the others, the last of the admiral's Central Force. War planners had debated starving Iwabuchi out but ultimately ruled against it. The enemy was well provisioned, meaning such a siege could stretch out for weeks or longer. Furthermore, the location of the buildings in the heart of Manila meant snipers could continue to be a menace, a reality that would force the United States to cordon off several blocks and hinder clean-up efforts. The army had no choice but to hammer the Japanese with artillery and send in troops. The 148th Infantry would take the Legislature and Finance buildings, while the Fifth Cavalry would seize the Agriculture Building. "The reduction of these buildings was effected concurrently," noted the XIV Corps report. "Each represented fierce floor to floor, room to room, and hand to hand fighting."

The assault kicked off with a ferocious artillery bombardment, sighting the powerful Long Toms on the elegant buildings that had stood as symbols of America's nearly half-century of influence on the islands. Of the three, the Legislature was the tallest, rising six stories above Padre Burgos Street and flanked by two four-story wings, while the Finance and Agriculture buildings were both five-story trapezoids, each built around internal courtyards. The heavy-caliber Long Toms packed a much greater punch than the smaller guns of tanks and tank destroyers, but artillerymen soon realized that when firing at point-blank range—at times as close as 150 yards—projectiles ricocheted or overshot the targets, landing among friendly troops. General Beightler of the Thirty-Seventh Infantry marveled at the destruction. "We made a churned-up pile of dust and scrap out of the imposing, classic government buildings."

At five p.m. on February 25, two days after the assault on Intramuros, U.S. forces paused to broadcast a message to the Japanese troops holed up inside, including Iwabuchi who planned to make his final stand in the Agriculture Building:

Your life is yours to take or to keep as you desire, but is it true loyalty to the Emperor to throw away your life for a cause that is now hopeless?

Fate has given you three choices:

1. You can commit suicide.
2. You can hold out a few minutes and then be blown to dust.

3. You may come to an honorable understanding with us
   and live to serve the new Japan when the war is over.

If you surrender to us you will not be humiliated or disgraced. Our troops will not fire for thirty minutes during which time you may come over to us.

All eyes focused on the buildings. "The ranks were strained and tense as the thirty minute period of grace ended," observed the Fifth Cavalry report. "None of the defenders gave up, and our troops were ready for any attempted treachery."

Infantrymen stormed the rear of the Legislature Building the following morning at nine a.m., securing the first floor of the north wing and the first and second floors of the main structure. Japanese marines hunkered down in pillboxes set up in corridors and rooms poured lead on the infantrymen, killing two and wounding another fifty-two. The battle ground to a halt after five hours. To fight on only guaranteed more casualties. Mortar teams laid down a smoke screen, allowing the men to retreat. Artillery picked up the fight, pounding the north and south wings, leaving a scene best described by the army's historian, Robert Ross Smith: "Only the battered central portion, roofless and gutted, still stood above its wings like a ghost arising from between toppled tombstones."

At two p.m. on February 27, American troops assaulted what was left of the Legislature Building. By six p.m. infantrymen secured all but a few tunnels and dugouts in the basement, a job that officially ended at noon the following day.

The cavalry meanwhile pummeled the nearby Agriculture Building, where Iwabuchi directed the last of his marines. Initially he implored his troops to fight to the death, as evidenced by his directive, which Lt. Hoichiro Miyazawa recorded in his diary. "If we run out of bullets we will use grenades," the admiral told his men. "If we run out of grenades, we will cut down the enemy with swords; if we break our swords, we will kill them by sinking our teeth in their throats."

But Iwabuchi's vigor withered under the onslaught of America's merciless guns, which pulverized the columns and ripped gaping wounds in the concrete walls around him, exposing the building's sinuous veins of rebar. To glimpse his own fate, Iwabuchi needed only to look west, where American artillery had reduced the ancient walls of Intramuros to gravel piles and killed Colonel Noguchi and the remnants of his Northern Force. The situation inside the Agriculture Building deteriorated by the hour. The well his troops had dug on the ground floor of the building was inadequate and ammunition ran low; in the Finance Building some of his troops were armed only with bamboo spears. Iwabuchi was outgunned, outmanned, and surrounded. The admiral knew he had reached the end. In the three weeks since MacArthur's forces had charged into Manila, Iwabuchi had presided over one of the most barbaric massacres of World War II. His troops had wantonly slaughtered tens of thousands of men, women, and children in some of the most cruel and horrible ways. Survival was not an option.

And he knew it.

Iwabuchi summoned his last remaining forces inside the battered Agriculture Building. He apologized for leading them to doom. "If anyone has the courage to escape, please do so," he instructed them. "If not please take your lives here."

The forty-nine-year-old admiral retreated to his quarters on the main floor in the northwest side of the building. Armed with a knife, Iwabuchi slit open his belly.

Japanese marines attempted to escape under the cover of darkness, only to fall prey to American guns; seventy-five were killed on the night of February 27. Seven managed to slip through the lines and tried to swim out to a sunken ship but were also killed. Artillery meanwhile continued to hammer the Agriculture Building, including a three-hour barrage that began at eight a.m. on February 28. "After the number of rounds fired into this building during the past few days, it did not seem possible that any soul could be living in such a mass of rubble and twisted steel," noted the Fifth Cavalry's report. "The entire northeast corner had been blown away leaving a gaping hole."

Troops firing bazookas and flamethrowers finally cleared it out on

March 1, leaving only a few underground bunkers. American patience, however, was over. "A last minute appeal to surrender was made," logged the cavalry's report. "After waiting a few minutes without an answer, drums of gas and oil were poured into the opening and set afire. This last opening was then blown shut with satchel charges."

Iwabuchi's remains would never be found.

The Finance Building was all that remained. The same day the Agriculture Building fell, American forces repeated the earlier broadcast to the Japanese troops inside the final stronghold, giving them just thirty minutes to surrender. During that time, at five-minute intervals, the announcer prodded the trapped enemy. "The man who stood beside you a few hours ago is now dead—what is your choice?" American forces broadcast in Japanese.

The time ticked away.

"You have ten minutes left, do you want this to be your lifetime?"

All eyes focused on the crippled Finance Building as five minutes wound down to three and then just ninety seconds. "At this point one Jap came literally tumbling down over the rubble in front of the building," one report noted. "He was followed almost immediately by twelve more who advanced to our lines and surrendered."

More emerged from a nearby pillbox and foxhole, bringing to twenty-two the total who surrendered. American forces continued to blast the building for two more days, wiping out the last of the enemy troops on the top floor on March 3. "At the end," concluded Robert Ross Smith, "the Finance Building was a shambles; the portions not knocked down seemed to be standing only from sheer force of habit."

The Battle of Manila was over.

CHAPTER 21

"It may never be possible to determine the complete human toll of the sack of Manila."

—War Department Release,
April 17, 1945

WITH THE GUNS FINALLY SILENT, SURVIVORS CRAWLED out of the rubble, seeking loved ones amid the city's wreckage. The twenty-nine-day Battle of Manila had claimed the lives of old and young, rich and poor. Artillery had vaporized many, while others died at the steel tip of a bayonet. Alongside thousands of Filipinos, the Japanese had slaughtered Russians, Spaniards, Germans, and Indians, as well as two Supreme Court justices, the family of a senator, and scores of priests. "The list of known dead that has come to my attention sounds like a Who's Who of the Philippines," Lichauco wrote in his diary. "Judges, lawyers, bank directors, doctors, engineers and many other well-known figures in public life now lie rotting in the ruins and ashes of what was once the exclusive residential districts of Malate and Ermita."

Survivors hunted through the debris for husbands and wives, parents and children, brothers and sisters. For some, like Jose Herman, that meant returning to the spot where the Japanese had tried to kill him. Marines had pulled the police lieutenant from his home on February 7 along with his son and nephew. Herman had survived only because he slipped off a bridge into the water seconds before a Japanese sword would have sliced through the bone in his neck. His son and nephew were not so fortunate. "My son's body had a watch in a pocket that I gave him," Herman recalled. "His watch stopped at

11:25." Others had to dig through mass graves, where starved dogs had often feasted on the top layer of bodies. That was the case for Juan Gonzalez, the godson of former Col. Jose Guido, who was killed along with his three teenage sons. "I just dug down," Gonzalez said, "and every body that I could not recognize I left it there."

Many had lost their entire families. Fred Canillas visited his family's home on Leveriza Street in Malate, where the Japanese had butchered his parents, five sisters, and two brothers. Amid the scorched ruins he found only a vertebra and a few other charred leg and finger bones—his entire family reduced to the contents of a small box. Prudencio Chicote Lalana, who survived the massacre at the Moreta home, returned after he was released from the hospital. He, too, found only a handful of small bones, so burnt that when he reached for them, the pieces crumbled to dust in his hands. Near the iron frame of a piano, he found his spouse's remains. "My wife was wearing a rosary around her neck," he said, "and some of the beads I found embedded in the collarbone."

Some survivors found loved ones whose bodies bore testimony to the torture endured in their final moments, victims with swollen and bruised faces or missing ears, noses, and eyes. The Japanese had gone so far as to pull out Eugene Kremleff's fingernails and burn his buttocks. "The skin was badly blistered," testified an American officer, "but had not fallen from his body." The horrific ways people died coupled with decomposition forced relatives in some cases to identify loved ones by clothes, cigarette cases, and key chains. That was true of the murders of former constable Col. Alejo Valdes and his son. "I was able to identify my brother Ramon's body by his belt buckle," recalled Armando Valdes, "and the body of my father by the cloth of his shirt and also by the hair left in the front part of his skull."

Those who found remains were the lucky ones. Others would have no resolution. Eva Gurevich searched in vain for her husband and son, who were grabbed by the Japanese. "There was no trace of them," she said. "They just vanished." Rita Losinas was so desperate that she hired a fortune-teller for help finding her husband, who was killed at De La Salle. "With a heavy heart full of pity, I have, during these recent days and weeks, observed the searchers—the seekers after lost loved ones," Santo Tomas internee John Osborn wrote in a letter. "Daily have they gone out the España Gate hoping to find some trace of relative or friend—to change the dreadful uncertainty to certainty, though it be the certainty of death. First they visit the site of the old home, now probably but a heap of ashes and broken walls. Then to the homes of relatives and friends for news of the lost. Finally they just walk the streets looking at the dead, who are today numerous on Isaac Peral and other thoroughfares in the Ermita and Malate districts."

Every day the thirty-thousand-circulation *Free Philippines* newspaper—published by the U.S. Army and distributed out of the back of an old Ford pickup truck—ran notices of missing persons, many of them children and even toddlers.

"Ana Mari Gomez, age 2. Jose del Prado, Age 9. Send information to Jose Gomez, 2158 Azcarraga."

"Isabelo de los Reyes, Jr., 7 yrs. Head wounded, Singalong Church of Malate District. Inform 1009 O'Donnell. Reward."

"Victor Vantchurin, 19, missing since February 10, 1945. Send information to his family at Santo Tomas."

Manila had become a city of the dead.

The fight to retake the Philippine capital had resulted in the deaths of 16,665 Japanese, the near total destruction of Admiral Iwabuchi's forces. In contrast, MacArthur's men suffered 1,010 killed and another 5,565 wounded. Filipino civilians, however, paid the largest price. An estimated 100,000 men, women, and children died either at the hands of the barbarous Japanese or under the rain of American shellfire. "There were graves everywhere," Hartendorp wrote, "bodies being buried where they had fallen; mounds large and small, rudely marked with crossed sticks or entirely unmarked, in the yards of what had once been homes or along the cracked sidewalks. For survivors to obtain death certificates and burial permits or to arrange the barest of funerals was impossible."

Families and neighbors often interred relatives in backyards. George Simmie, the business partner of Carlos Perez-Rubio, helped bury the bodies of his friend and his family in the garden of the home where the massacre occurred. The job proved arduous because of the hard soil and the advanced state of decomposition. "When we grabbed hold of a leg in an effort to pull them," Simmie testified, "the leg would come off and the body would disintegrate." Jose Guido's family chose to cremate the remains of the colonel and his three sons. "We used a spading fork to put the bones on a galvanized iron sheet," recalled Faustino Gonzalez, "then we placed gasoline on them and burned them." Hashmatrai Hotchand, who helped bury four fellow British Indians, followed his family's tradition. "As is our village custom," he said, "we threw them in the sea."

Like hundreds of others, Paciencia Montano in contrast had no money or help to bury her husband Manuel and her twenty-two-year-old son, Artemio, whose remains she found on the bank of the Estero Tripa de Gallina in Paco. "I left the bodies where they were," she said. "They were later burned by the American soldiers."

Few witnessed the full scope of the horror like Mariano del Rosario, the city's thirty-eight-year-old undertaker who was hired by the army to help dispose of the dead. It was a job that paid by the body. From February 3 until March 31, Rosario testified that his burial squads collected some eight thousand corpses, averaging at one point 150 a day. Workers buried some of the deceased in large shell holes. Others wound up in several mass graves dug with army bulldozers, including one in front of San Juan de Letran College in Intramuros and another in front of Jefferson Elementary School on Canonigo Street. One of the worst jobs was clearing the dead from the bowels of Fort Santiago, a job accomplished with a flamethrower. "Those in the dungeon," recalled Captain Conner, "we destroyed by pouring gasoline on them and burning them."

In contrast, few bothered to dispose of the enemy dead, whose bloated bodies littered the streets beneath swarms of fat bluebottle flies. Desperate residents had stripped such corpses of precious boots and even plundered valuable gold teeth. The family of twelve-year-old Rod Hall proved one of the exceptions, deciding to bury a dead Japanese soldier in a shallow grave in the family's garden on Dakota Street, though Hall's brother and a friend would later exhume the skeleton for use as a school biology project. "In the night," Bilibid internee Natalie Crouter wrote in her diary, "when the wind is from a certain direction over the Walled City, the air is laden with smell of charred wood, wet cement, gun powder, pungent chemicals, and over all that sickish sweetish odor which is rotting flesh and blood. Once in the nostrils, it is never forgotten." Headquarters staffer Paul Rogers noted the same. "There was an overpowering stench of death and decay. It pervaded the air, and there was no escape," he wrote. "This was not Manila. It was simply hell."

Ethel Herold stopped two military police one day, asking how the officers endured the fetor she described in her diary as "holy godawful."

"You get used to it," one replied.

Worse than the stench of death was its taste, which settled on the tongue. "No amount of spitting," recalled Major Henne, "could clear it away."

The city, meanwhile, overflowed with the wounded, who filled thirty-two hospitals, many of them little more than primitive aid stations set up in filthy schools, churches, and even race clubs. "I didn't sweep it out," one American medical officer complained, "I shoveled it out." Exhausted doctors and nurses struggled to treat 23,457 patients, while public dispensaries tended to an average of 87,540 people per day. The carnage shocked even battle veterans, like Maj. John Carlisle, who led a civil affairs unit tasked with rounding up medical supplies and food. "If I told you some of the things I have done and seen here in the last few days," Carlisle said to *New York Times* reporter George Jones, "you wouldn't believe me." Jones toured hospitals where doctors performed surgery by lamplight. He met the wounded wife of French consul Louis Rocque. A doctor's exam showed that her husband had died from two saber cuts to the head, one of which had penetrated his brain, while the other nearly decapitated the diplomat. "We never believed," she said, "people could be so cruel." Such viciousness was not lost on MacArthur's senior aides, including General Fellers, who summed up the enemy's behavior in three words: "It is beastly."

Overburdened physicians battled a scarcity of basic supplies. "Not only beds, but pallets and bare floors were used to make places for the civilian wounded," wrote Col. Maurice Pincoffs, who was to serve as the city's new health director. "They lacked instruments, dressings, drugs, linen, food, water and light and, since there was no transportation to carry away the dead, in the morgues the naked bodies were stacked like cordwood and filled the air with stench." Many suffered horrific injuries, from gunshot and shrapnel wounds to compound fractures. Others had survived bayonet attacks and even failed decapitations. Many more had endured sexual assaults and would later battle venereal diseases. "There are hideous wounds among innocent civilians," Crouter wrote in her diary. "It is a nightmare peopled with those we used to know, every name familiar. Total war spares no one, crushes all." Spanish priest Juan Labrador echoed her in his diary. "So many families of acquaintances and friends exterminated. So many mutilated," he wrote. "Manila is a picture of sadness impossible to describe." As heinous as the stories were, survivors couldn't help but note the redundancy of the Japanese barbarity. "The tales told by refugees are horrible and monotonously similar," James Halsema observed in his diary. "If you've heard one, you've heard all."

The wounds went beyond just physical. Starved, exhausted, and overwhelmed, Hartendorp had suffered a nervous breakdown soon after American tanks knocked down the gates of Santo Tomas. Throughout his years in captivity, he had missed the weddings of his children and the births of his grandchildren, losses that crystallized for him when he looked up one day to find a young man standing before him in the battledress of a Philippine Scout, a helmet atop his head and a rifle in his hands.

"Eddy!" Hartendorp cried, referring to his oldest son.

"I'm not Eddy, papa!" the young man replied.

"Who the hell are you?" he demanded.

"I'm Henry, papa."

Hartendorp had been locked up so long he had failed to recognize his youngest son, who had been only fourteen years old when the Japanese interned him. Over the course of the war—and in his absence—his son had become a man and a soldier. "I took him in my arms," Hartendorp wrote. "He had grown to be a very husky fellow."

Lourdes Reyes returned home to find few remains of her family life.

All that had survived, she noted, was her playhouse with its red Spanish roof tiles, where she and her sister used to compete to be the first one to see the stars in the evening sky. "That night, I wished hard by the stars, that it was Ching, standing there, instead of our playhouse or me," Lourdes later wrote, using her sister's nickname. "I wished and wished many nights afterwards, but Ching and my family, and my happy childhood days never came back again."

The damage extended far beyond human casualties. The combination of Japanese demolitions and burnings coupled with American artillery had flattened 613 city blocks, an area containing eleven thousand buildings, ranging from banks and schools to churches and houses. There was no electricity, no running water, and no sewage. At night the entire city was dark. The battle had left an estimated two hundred thousand homeless, dependent upon army civil affairs units for everything from rice, canned meats, and vegetables to soap, shoes, frying pans, and mosquito nets, all of which had to be trucked in from Lingayen Gulf. Desperate residents lined up daily starting at three a.m. outside army aid stations. "Men, women and children hold baskets or hats for their supplies," Jones wrote in the *Times*. "There are just as many inside the doors at 5 p.m. as at 5 a.m."

Sanitation proved an immediate concern, particularly as the rat population exploded. Some eight hundred thousand people depended on artesian wells for drinking water. Workers hustled to build hundreds of public pit latrines and haul away tens of thousands of pails of so-called night soil. There was no city garbage service so laborers put out 4,500 oil drums to serve as trash cans. "Sanitation had broken down to the point that it was miraculous that we hadn't seen epidemics of cholera ravaging the population," recalled army doctor George Sharpe. The battle likewise had robbed the city of streetcars, motor vehicles, and many horse-drawn carriages. Residents resorted to baby strollers to push goods. Gone, too, were the telephone system and the postal service, reducing communication to foot and bike messengers. "The morale of the firemen, which had dropped steadily during the underfed and underpaid days of Jap occupation, hit rock bottom when their engines were machine-gunned during the battle of Manila," one civil affairs report noted.

A postwar American survey by the War Damage Corporation—a government financial agency designed to handle losses not covered under regular insurance policies—calculated the damages to public, private, and church properties at $800 million, a figure that in contemporary dollars would run to more than $10 billion. In a city as old as Manila, questions arose over values, particularly relating to church possessions, whose library shelves once housed centuries-old texts and whose convents and cathedrals dated back three hundred and four hundred years. "There is some damage in all districts in Manila but the most valuable sections have been practically destroyed," the report stated. "The port area and the Santa Cruz district have suffered a 90-percent loss; Malate and Intramuros, 93 percent; Paco, Ermita, and Binondo, from 68 to 85 percent."

The total lack of transportation, homes, apartments, and hotels was reflected in the advertisements that appeared each day in the *Free Philippines.*

"Houses wanted," one notice stated.

"Wanted to buy ten good bicycles," read another.

"Loan wanted," pleaded another.

Many of the losses proved priceless. The battle had destroyed the Philippine National Library and Museum's collection of 550,000 books and pamphlets along with 2,500 paintings, carvings, and sculptures. Gone, too, were the Scientific Library's 320,000 texts and the 20,000 volumes in the Supreme Court Library. The battle had destroyed not only the Manila Observatory's collection of rare barometers and seismographs, but also its extensive historical records of typhoons and earthquakes that dated back to the early time of the Jesuits. The Philippine General Hospital had lost 12,500 volumes of clinical histories comprised of the records of almost three million patients. The city's once-lush botanical gardens, which had boasted Indian tigers and Russian bears, were scorched ruins. "Nothing is standing but the burnt stumps of century-old trees," one article noted. "Gone also are the birds and animals, their cages nothing but twisted steel."

Beyond municipal and cultural losses were those suffered by the business community, which was vital to jump-starting Manila's economy. In the short term, American civil affairs units put 27,239 people on the payroll at wages from 1.25 pesos to five pesos a day. The battle had wrecked Manila's piers and crowded the harbor with an estimated three hundred sunken ships. Warehouses had been looted and burned, equipment and machinery destroyed or shipped to Japan, crops laid barren, and soil depleted. "War damage to coconut trees alone is estimated at $15,200,000, which will require years to rehabilitate," noted a report by the U.S. Army Corps of Engineers. The American Chamber of Commerce offered a reward for ledgers, books, and stock cards seized by the Japanese from all American and European firms. The lack of raw materials promised to make it hard even for companies that survived the battle. "The manager of one of the Manila oil companies," Hartendorp wrote, "in speaking of the rebuilding of his plant, stated that he would have to begin again at the beginning—with a land survey."

Amid the smoldering ruins, it was hard to tell who had done more damage—the Japanese defenders or the American liberators. Some of MacArthur's commanders made clear afterward that protecting the city was not their priority. "To me the loss of a single American life to save a building was unthinkable," wrote General Beightler. "If I could have had those dive-bombers too, I might have made the big rubble into little rubble." As a result, American forces at times found themselves the subject of scorn as survivors emerged from the ruins and began to tally lost loved ones and property. "I spat on the very first American soldier I saw that unspeakable day in February 1945," recalled journalist Carmen Guerrero Nakpil, who saw her husband shot, home burned, and childhood friends raped. "Damn you!" she later wrote. "You did your best to kill us."

So vast was the destruction that it proved difficult to comprehend.

"I had no conception of it, could not picture it, until I saw it," Natalie Crouter wrote in her diary.

"For one who had not seen this," added Spanish priest Juan Labrador, "it is impossible to believe or imagine it."

The destruction prompted even larger questions for others, including former Bilibid internee Ethel Herold. "All this ruin, all this misery, all this death," she wrote in her diary. "Oh, God! I wonder is there a God?"

There was a realization expressed over and over again among those who wandered through the miles of wreckage, the smell of death heavy in the air, that even though the city could be rebuilt, it would never be the same. The destruction was simply too much, too complete. "I have seen the death of a whole city," Santo Tomas internee Robert Wygle wrote in his diary. "A new city may stand in its place some years from now, but it will bear little resemblance to its predecessor."

"There seemed nothing left even to mourn," Hartendorp wrote. "Manila was gone. It remained a name only."

Some of MacArthur's aides and commanders, who had expected the Japanese to abandon the capital and spare the Pearl of the Orient, felt the loss keenly. General Beightler was more callous than his colleagues. "So much for Manila. It is a ruined city," he wrote. "Let us thank God our cities have been spared such a fate."

MacArthur, who had once envisioned a grand entry parade into Manila, experienced an entirely different reception when he moved his headquarters to the Wilson Building, which was filled with debris, garbage, and dust. "There was no joy in our entrance," recalled headquarters staffer Paul Rogers. "I do not remember seeing a Filipino smile during the entire duration of our stay there." For the first meal in the city, the headquarters staff set up outdoors under a canvas roof. "The tables were covered with huge black flies which clung to everything and everybody. Half a dozen Filipino mess boys wielded paper fly whisks, in our faces and touching our faces, to drive off the pernicious pests. We all knew where they had bred and were breeding, but did not care to discuss the matter. We had brought death to the city, and perhaps we deserved to eat it."

Looters stole his jeep that night.

Santo Tomas internees who had sat ringside for the battle ventured south of the Pasig to check on old homes, family, and friends, greeted by a towering sign erected by American soldiers: "Warning: Mines & Booby Traps. Stay Out of Buildings and On Main Traveled Routes." Tressa Roka explored Malate and Ermita, two of the hardest-hit areas. "I wandered through rubble-torn streets that I could not recognize, as there were no landmarks, no trees, no buildings, houses, or signs to guide me," she wrote. "Yet I had lived in this section for four years." Natalie Crouter found the experience emotionally overwhelming. "I am appalled and feel beaten by all I have seen," she wrote. "I listened all those weeks to the guns. Now I see what they did. Everyone should *see* it and learn one lesson forever."

Like others, eleven-year-old Robin Prising could not resist surveying the damage, jumping in a jeep for a tour. He noted that bulldozers were already at work, clearing roads so that American trucks could pass. The half-naked survivors horrified him more than the destruction. "Manila had become a no-man's land of cripples crutching about on laths salvaged from tottering homes. A blinded man with a hideously disfigured face begged us for food. Stunted children raised fingers in V for Victory as we passed," he wrote. "Gouged with wounds, blistered by burns, everyone went scavenging in and out of the carcasses of houses for anything they could eat or sell or save."

At one point the troops stopped and began kicking a rusty can. "Suddenly someone shouted," Prising recalled. "A Yank had kicked the can into the severed arm and outstretched hand of a child that lay rotting in a ditch." Elsewhere the boy ran across the body of a dead Japanese soldier. "Flies swarmed the corpse, an enemy corpse which no one would bury," he said. "The eye sockets were alive, wriggling with maggots, and the mouth of the corpse, rigidly open, exposed a row of perfect teeth."

Despite the constant presence of death, there, too, returned the urgency of life. At Santo Tomas, female internees began relationships with American soldiers. "Sex, which I had known about only theoretically, took place behind every bush and tree," Prising recalled. "In the mornings, when the little tots came out to play, they found the ground littered with condoms and blew them up like balloons."

Brothels popped up across the street from the university. "Hey, you, Big Boy!" women called out. "You want to make pam-pam?"

Internees weren't the only ones interested in sex. American troops, who were exposed to urban civilization for the first time in two years, frequently visited Filipino prostitutes, sending the venereal disease rates, as noted in the Thirty-Seventh Infantry Division's report, soaring. Medical officers and chaplains gave morality talks, while the army began checking and treating known prostitutes. Doctors examined 105 prostitutes, of whom 25 percent tested positive for gonorrhea. Physicians administered syphilis tests to eighty, only to discover three out of every four were infected. During February, 254 soldiers tested positive for venereal disease, most for gonorrhea. "It is anticipated," one report noted, "that the syphilis rate will increase sharply as the incubation period of the disease is reached."

The problem proved so widespread that MacArthur's physician Roger Egeberg suggested that the general bar troops from going out inside the city.

"What?" MacArthur asked incredulously.

"There isn't very much V.D. in those troops that are stationed far away from Manila," he replied. "It's among those stationed in Manila or who come here when they have a day or two of furlough. You know, all those engaging kids who want you to have pom-pom with their big sister. Well, both syphilis and gonorrhea are way up."

"Declare Manila out of bounds to our troops?" the general countered. "Why, Doc, do you know what you're asking me to do?"

MacArthur told his physician that American forces provided one of Manila's few economic generators, propping up the handful of bars, restaurants, and shops.

"No, Doc, that's an insult to the soldiers and hard on the disrupted economy of this war-torn city," he declared. "You've got some pretty good medicines for those diseases now, haven't you?"

MacArthur's lax attitude differed from many of the frontline medical officers, who saw up close the awful reality of life on the streets of Manila. The city's social fabric had begun to unravel during the latter stages of the Japanese occupation, but post-battle it totally disintegrated. "Morals and convention had been completely set aside," recalled George Sharpe, a doctor. "When we drove through the streets, children of six and seven ran up to soldiers and openly pandered for prostitutes. They carried sacks of bootleg whiskey asking outlandish prices from many of our men. It was really appalling to even the most unthinking person as to what the effect of war had on these people."

○ ○ ○ ○

THOUGH THE BATTLE OF MANILA was over, the army's work was far from finished. General Yamashita remained elusive. Just as he had done after the seizure of Singapore, the Tiger of Malaya had seemingly vanished, his whereabouts unknown. "Yamashita is finished," Fellers wrote his wife. "Probably gone to Japan or dead." Some of MacArthur's top aides couldn't resist taking a swipe at the Japanese general, even though Yamashita's forces had executed what Robert Ross Smith later characterized as "a most effective delaying action." General Willoughby, MacArthur's intelligence chief, crowed: "The arrogant conqueror of Singapore, Yamashita, suffered the most humiliating defeat in the annals of Japanese history; his conduct of operations from Leyte to Luzon was inept, hysterical, second-rate."

The Japanese general remained in the mountains near Baguio, waiting for MacArthur's troops to come find him. Enough U.S. soldiers were left in Manila to maintain order and hunt down stray Japanese troops, but the remainder would require rest and relaxation before continuing the fight. Some of the troops savored a brief reprieve at the Wack Wack Golf and Country Club. "To breathe clean air again, air free of the stench of dead and burnt buildings, to swim in the club pool and relax were only a few of the many pleasures we were to enjoy," one report noted. "All men were free of the worry that had been companions with each and every one for over a month."

For weeks American patrols continued to discover rogue Japanese soldiers and marines hiding in the rubble, performing an exercise troops called "beating the tin," a reference to the sheets of metal roofing that littered the city. "It was not unusual to spot a Jap by seeing soles of the man's boots under the sheets of iron," Major Henne recalled. "Prisoners were taken in increasing numbers but a high proportion of the Japs clutched their weapons or a grenade inviting quick dispatch." The Americans killed seven on March 5, most near the intersection of Isaac Peral and Taft Avenue. Two days later troops found a wounded Japanese merchant marine—weak and hard of hearing—in the ruins of the Finance Building. The following day soldiers caught five more Japanese on a raft in Manila Bay.

Others worked to clear thousands of enemy land mines in what proved a race against time as booby traps claimed the lives of residents, including one killed inside the chapel at La Loma Cemetery. Troops collected thousands of artillery duds and hundreds of mines, piling more than fifty tons of unexploded ordnance in Burnham Green in front of the Manila Hotel. Army officials debated how best to dispose of it all when the heat from the sun prompted one of the bombs to detonate, which triggered a massive reaction. "This explosion, which caused no damage other than a large crater in the ground," noted the Thirty-Seventh Infantry's report, "relieved the battalion of the responsibility of moving the duds and mines from the city."

Bulldozers helped clear 2,038 city blocks and then came back and cleared more, upping that figure to 3,904. The city's sanitation section, along with malarial control units and the army and navy, hauled away 30,938 truckloads of debris, while planes in the skies overhead sprayed for mosquitos and flies. The army also looked for ways to entertain the troops, taking over a thousand-seat theater in Manila which after reconditioning was used to stage evening performances, often using professional Filipino entertainers. The premiere show after the city's liberation was Fernando Poe's *South Seas Caper*. "The theater," one infantry report noted, "was always packed to capacity."

The army likewise organized volleyball, basketball, and softball leagues, hosting the first baseball game at two p.m. on March 31 at Rizal Memorial Stadium, with General Beightler throwing out the first pitch. Famed composer Irving Berlin arrived in Manila, visiting Malacañan Palace to perform a new song he dedicated to General MacArthur titled "Heaven Watch the Philippines."

○ ○ ○ ○

THE BATTLE HAD BARELY ENDED before Jean MacArthur returned, like so many others, anxious to see Manila and visit the ruins of her home. She had spent the entire war in Australia with the couple's young son, Arthur, never once leaving Brisbane. On hearing the news that American forces had reached Santo Tomas, she dashed off a letter to a friend on February 5. "Manila is free," she exclaimed. "Oh you can't imagine what this means to me, I can't find words to express it—I am so thankful."

General MacArthur had sent for her as soon as the fighting slowed, preferring, just as he had done on Corregidor, to have his wife and closest confidante by his side, regardless of the danger and the private scorn it generated from officers who had to leave spouses behind. The sixty-four-year-old MacArthur justified it by telling his married aides that unlike them he had only a few years left to share with his wife and son.

"Doc," he once told Roger Egeberg, "you have a long life ahead of you, time to enjoy and appreciate each other. I can't count too many years."

Bonner Fellers flew to Australia to escort Jean and Arthur back to Manila aboard the refrigerator ship *Columbia Express*, which throughout the two-week journey observed strict blackout precautions for fear of enemy submarines. The ship steamed past Corregidor and into Manila Bay on the Tuesday morning of March 6, 1945. In the distance, Jean could see the outline of the Manila Hotel. "Now," she thought to herself, "that doesn't look so destroyed."

The freighter anchored in the bay surrounded by the wreckage of hundreds of sunken ships. General MacArthur had not seen his wife and son for five months, since he had departed Australia in October for the Leyte invasion. He climbed aboard a tender at eleven-thirty a.m. for the trip out, joined by his senior aides Egeberg, Lloyd Lehrbas, and Andres Soriano.

On deck, Jean held a borrowed set of navy bedsheets, unsure if she would find any in the wrecked city. Seven-year-old Arthur stood by her side.

MacArthur boarded the ship and grabbed them both, holding tight. His family had returned. Overhead flew a formation of fighters and bombers.

"Isn't it wonderful to see *our* planes?" Jean said to General Kenney. "The last time I was here, they were all Japs and instead of watching them we were running for cover. George, what have you done to Corregidor? I could hardly recognize it when we passed it this morning. It looks as though you had lowered it at least forty feet."

Kenney and MacArthur laughed.

With the couple's home destroyed, MacArthur had moved into an elegant two-story mansion in the Santa Mesa district not far from Malacañan Palace. The home, known locally as the Casa Blanca or White House, included a swimming pool and immaculate gardens. The property had belonged to Russian native Emil Bachrach, a wealthy car distributor who died before the war. His wife Mary had kept the residence, which the Japanese had seized. General Kenney originally claimed the home for himself but made the mistake of describing it to MacArthur. The next morning MacArthur skipped his normal breakfast with his air officer, returning later. "George, I did a kind of dirty trick on you," he confessed. "I stole your house."

Throughout the capital, lodging was at a premium as landlords demanded exorbitant rents, forcing families to double and triple up. While MacArthur lived in luxury, many of his aides bounced around between battered apartments and homes. General Fellers described the situation best in his response to a journalist who inquired about visiting. "Manila was practically destroyed," Fellers wrote. "There are absolutely no accommodations for the people here much less for an increase."

No sooner had Jean arrived than she went on a tour of Manila, paying a visit to former friends at Santo Tomas. The jeep rolled through the gates of the university where she was immediately struck by the emaciated internees. "Lord," she thought.

She had dressed that day in a hat and gloves, yet through her window she saw men and women shuffling around in rags, the remnants of shirts, trousers, and dresses many had worn for three years. "I had a horrible feeling about my own clothes. It just didn't seem right. I felt that I was embarrassingly overdressed," she said. "So I had the driver stop, and I quickly took off my hat and gloves, but there wasn't much else I could do about it." She exited the jeep and greeted old friends she had known before the war, some of whom had lost all their teeth. Jean saw the pathetic shanties many of them had lived in throughout the war and paused at the graves of those who died.

Her friends appreciated the visit, including Mary Fairchild, who dashed off a note to her afterward. "Your coming to Manila was the crowning touch to our miraculous deliverance." But the visit pained Jean. "It was just heartbreaking," she said. "These were people that I had known that had lived in the lap of luxury in the Philippines."

Jean likewise visited the internees still recovering a few blocks away at Bilibid, though her reception there was not as generous. "Well," Natalie Crouter wrote in her diary, "she looks as though she had her feet up in front of a fireplace for three years, keeping nice and warm." Many resented her visit, considering how bad most still felt and looked. "It may be a good thing for her to see our condition, the devastation, get a taste and smell and touch of it, closely."

The MacArthurs called on President Sergio Osmeña and the first lady at five-fifteen p.m. before returning to the Casa Blanca. The couple shared a bedroom on the second floor of the grand home, while downstairs Arthur slept in a room with his Chinese nanny, Ah Cheu, who had escaped from Corregidor with the family.

As she lay in bed, Jean heard the distant rattle of small arms followed by the roar of American artillery. "I think I'd better go down and check on Arthur," she said.

She slipped downstairs to his bedroom, finding her son sitting up in the middle of his bed, his nanny asleep a few feet away. "Do you hear those guns?" she asked.

"Yes, Mommy," he said. "I hear those guns."

"I just want you to know that they're our guns."

"Oh," he said, "that's all right."

Arthur lay back down and soon fell asleep. Jean returned to her husband's side. "He remembers," she told him, "when we were shelled on Corregidor."

A few days later General MacArthur took Jean to visit the couple's old home atop the Manila Hotel. The structure still stood, as she had seen from the deck of the *Columbia Express*, but the artillery and subsequent fires had gutted the insides of the once-luxurious hotel. The couple climbed the stairs around two p.m. on the afternoon of March 17 to the fifth-floor penthouse that had served as the family's first married home. It was here that they had brought young Arthur home after his birth at Sternberg Hospital near Intramuros and here where the family had christened him.

The roof was gone; so, too, were most of the walls, making it impossible for Jean to tell where one room ended and another began. Five inches of ashes blanketed the floor of the general's study, all that was left of his fine library. She paused to look at the remains of her baby grand piano, which the Japanese had destroyed with a bomb. Under her feet crunched the shards of her crystal glassware and china. The wrecked home appeared symbolic of what MacArthur once wrote: "I had learned a bitter lesson of life, never try to regain the past, the fire will have become ashes."

The total destruction of all her possessions, including Arthur's baby book, crushed Jean, who described it in a letter to a friend. "You wanted to know about my apartment at the hotel. Of that, as well as everything else almost that I know in Manila is gone," she wrote. "You can't possibly conceive of the destruction wrought by the enemy here. His brutality is something that, to me, isn't even paralleled in the darkest ages. He destroyed, killed, burned, massacred and looted. Entire families that I knew here were murdered. Others have completely disappeared from the face of the globe. Even as much as I had been told before I arrived, I couldn't grasp it until I got here."

PART IV

"In a way we were all massacred. Only, some of us were fortunate to have lived through it."

—Servillano Aquino,
testimony, January 27, 1949

A Filipina woman, wounded in the face and eye by shrapnel, waits with her child in front of the family's burned home in the district of Paco for help across the Pasig River.

CHAPTER 22

"What the Japanese did not steal, the fire devoured.
What the fire did not devour, the bombs pulverized."

—JUAN LABRADOR,
DIARY ENTRY, MARCH 17, 1945

SHORTLY BEFORE EIGHT A.M. ON SEPTEMBER 2, 1945—ON A
muddy hilltop outside the village of Kiangan, more than two thousand feet above sea level—American infantrymen gathered to await the arrival of a man many had come to think of as a ghost.

The Tiger of Malaya.

Barely three weeks earlier, on August 15, Emperor Hirohito in a radio broadcast to the Japanese people, had brought an end to the war that for the United States had begun 1,347 days earlier with the attack on Pearl Harbor. Those intervening years had witnessed some of the greatest destruction the world had ever seen, from the firebombing of Tokyo to the atomic attacks on Hiroshima and Nagasaki—and, of course, the leveling of Manila, MacArthur's beloved hometown and America's portal to Asia.

In the six months since the end of the battle for the Philippine capital, American troops had hunted Yamashita throughout the highlands of northern Luzon, forcing the Tiger to abandon Baguio and hike deeper into the Sierra Madre Mountains, at times clutching a golf club as a walking stick. His men had to grapple not only with the jungle but with dysentery, malaria, and starvation, forced to drink muddy water and eat grass, berries, and snakes. Lt. Gen. Akira Muto, Yamashita's bespectacled chief of staff, described the hardship in his diary. "One cannot imagine the jungles during the rainy season unless one has experienced it," he wrote. "The dampness of the putrid earth which had yet to see the rays of the sun. The odor of steaming fallen leaves. The cries of various dangerous insects at night. It was completely lacking in beauty."

The war's end had found Yamashita in command of 50,500 troops. He had heard via radio, albeit two days later, Hirohito's rescript announcing the cessation of hostilities, a scene Muto captured in his diary: "Tears flowed endlessly." The general likewise felt the agony, expressing himself in verse. "It knifed deep into my heart."

Muto had begged to stay with him in his hut that night, afraid the general might commit suicide. "Don't worry," Yamashita assured his senior aide. "I won't go alone to die. I have a great duty still to see all my troops go back to Japan."

Junior officers, fearful the Americans would humiliate Yamashita, had implored the general to do otherwise. "If I kill myself, someone else will have to take the blame instead of me," he countered. "I must take responsibility myself alone."

On August 24, an American fighter pilot appeared in the skies over Yamashita's mountain headquarters. Several weeks earlier the same airman had bailed out of a disabled P-38, only to be captured by the general's forces. Following news of Japan's surrender, soldiers had escorted the pilot back toward American lines, releasing him along with a letter from Yamashita, who congratulated the airman on his devotion to duty. That pilot now returned with a letter of his own sealed in a tube from Maj. Gen. William Gill of the Thirty-Second Infantry Division, opening a dialogue that led to Yamashita's decision to walk out of the mountains.

Before he departed for the two-day hike, the Great Cedar wrote a poem:

My men have been gathered from the mountains
Like wild flowers.
Now it is my turn to go
And I go gladly.

Yamashita had done what just a year earlier he had thought was impossible: he had survived the war. But a larger question remained.

Would he survive the peace?

That Sunday, as the sun climbed in the eastern sky, twenty-four American soldiers with the Thirty-Second Infantry anxiously awaited the Japanese general on a muddy trail. Tensions everywhere remained high, including nearly two thousand miles north, where that morning General MacArthur prepared to preside over Japan's official surrender ceremony aboard the battleship *Missouri* in Tokyo Bay.

Promptly at eight a.m., Yamashita emerged on the path, walking stick in his left hand and leading a party of twenty-one senior officers, aides, and orderlies.

Lt. Russell Bauman of Wisconsin stepped forward to greet the Japanese general. "I have been charged with bringing you and your party through our lines without hindrance, delay or molestation," he told Yamashita.

"I want to tell you how much I appreciate the courtesies and good treatment you have shown us," Yamashita replied through an interpreter.

The group set off again, hiking the last several miles down. "General Yamashita, whose weight had dropped from 200 to 165 pounds, appeared in good condition during the walk out of the mountains," an Associated Press reporter wrote. "He puffed only slightly, but stopped occasionally to wipe his closely shaven head."

The party arrived at a rural schoolhouse at ten-thirty a.m., where Col. Ernest Barlow of the Thirty-Second Infantry and Lt. Col. Alex Robinet with the 128th Infantry Regiment waited. All eyes studied the once-portly commander, dressed in worn jungle fatigues that hung on his gaunt frame. Yamashita sat atop a stool and pulled off his muddy footwear and leggings, swapping them for a pair of shined shoes his orderly handed him. Someone offered him a cigarette. He nodded his appreciation, slipped it between his lips, and lit up.

News photographs snapped pictures, though the pop of the flashbulbs rattled Muto. "The war is over," he said. "We've had enough of those mortars."

One of the interpreters translated his comments, and everyone laughed, easing the tension. Yamashita feasted on army K-rations, interrupted occasionally by soldiers armed with short-snorter bills* who pressed the general for an autograph.

A convoy of trucks rolled up to the school. Yamashita climbed into the front seat of a one-and a-half-ton truck, while his aides crowded behind him in the back. The men bounced down the wrecked mountain road. "We had nothing to complain about," Muto later wrote, "because we had ordered the destruction of this road ourselves." At one point the truck bogged down, forcing troops to pull it free with a bulldozer. Filipinos gathered around to watch, shouting insults at the Japanese and waving stones.

Yamashita stared ahead stoically.

"That is typical," one of the general's interpreters scoffed, "of the weaker nations. Cruelty to the vanquished."

"I guess Japan is one of the weaker nations," countered one of the Americans.

When road conditions improved, the Americans transferred the prisoners to sedans for the remainder of the trip to the First Battalion Command Post of the 128th Infantry Regiment near Kiangan.

After months of living in the sweltering jungles, the Japanese were amazed at the long and orderly rows of American tents. "This is like a cinema," one said.

Yamashita disembarked and came face to face with General Beightler, who had personally witnessed the destruction and bloodshed Yamashita's troops had inflicted upon men, women, and children in Manila. "As he walked toward me," Beightler wrote, "he proffered his hand. I refused to shake hands; he then stepped back, saluted, and bowed."

The convoy continued another hour south to Bagabag, where Yamashita and his aides dined in the officers club. "We were served cold canned beer," Muto wrote, "which tasted very good." Afterward guards escorted the prisoners to the airstrip, where Yamashita

---

* A short-snorter bill was a banknote often signed by people traveling together.

boarded a C-47 for the flight to Luna Airport at Lingayen Gulf. A convoy of jeeps drove them to Baguio, a route lined at times by angry locals. "The insults," Muto noted, "coming from Filipinos on the way were unbearable."

The convoy reached the High Commissioner's Summer Residence at two-thirty p.m., a white two-story concrete mansion often blanketed by mountain fog. Military police separated the officers and enlisted men and then searched them all. Yamashita and the other senior officers carried swords. The general presented his weapon—forged in the seventeenth century by the famous swordsmith, Kanenaga Fujiwara—to Lt. Col. Aubrey Saint Kenworthy, who commanded the military police entrusted to guard the prisoners. MacArthur would later donate the famous sword to his alma mater, West Point. Guards also relieved Yamashita of a small amount of Japanese money and a pair of U.S. Army Medical Corps scissors found among his toiletries.

Several of the Japanese officers carried American dollars, ranging from Muto who had several hundred to Maj. Gen. Naokata Utsunomiya who had a thousand. Muto likewise had eight thousand Philippine Victory one-peso notes, each in consecutive numerical order. Guards noted that all had American cigarettes.

A guard searching one of Yamashita's orderlies discovered a live hand grenade in the upper-right-hand pocket of his coat. "It's a heck of a thing to come to a peace conference with," quipped the officer who removed the grenade.

The Americans could not be too careful, even though it ruffled the Japanese. "Not only was our baggage examined, but we were given physical examinations," Muto griped. "Although we were aware that the inspections were being conducted as a precaution against suicides, we resented such a breach of etiquette."

Afterward guards led Yamashita, Muto, and a few of the senior officers to rooms on the second floor of the residence, while the others were locked up in the Thirty-Second Infantry Division's stockade. At seven p.m. the guards returned, escorting the officers to the auxiliary dining room for supper, where Yamashita enjoyed a bowl of vegetable soup along with mashed potatoes, peas, buttered bread, and a steak, prepared by Cpl. Edward Kapica. "He ordered it medium rare, and that's the way he got it. I kinda hoped he'd choke on it," Kapica later told reporters. "He asked for a beer to wash it down with and got a can of good American ale."

Yamashita was asked at one point if he planned to kill himself.

"No," he said jokingly. "No hara-kiri."

The following morning, September 3, 1945, guards came for the general and his senior officers and marched them downstairs to the dining room at 11:40 a.m., where Yamashita would formally surrender his forces.

Though the High Commissioner's Summer Residence had escaped bomb damage during the war, it had fallen prey to looters, who had stripped the elegant home of much of its fine furniture and its library. A long rectangular table stood in the center of the wood-paneled room, draped with a white cloth. The few surviving ornate wooden chairs with woven backs lined one side of the table; simple folding chairs and stools the other. A half-dozen microphones perched on the tabletop beneath bright bulbs that dangled from wires overhead. A few feet away on another table lay the swords seized the day before from the Japanese officers. Guerrilla leaders, senior officers, and news reporters crowded around the table, including one who stood atop a stepladder for a better view.

Muto stood behind the folding chair farthest from the door followed by Yamashita, Admiral Okochi, Rear Adm. Kaoru Arima, and lastly the interpreters. The Tiger of Malaya briefly sat down, before an officer reminded him to stand until the American delegation arrived. He climbed back to his feet, fidgeting with his hat. The scene this Monday morning was no doubt eerily familiar to Yamashita. Only three and a half years earlier he had sat across just such a table in the Ford Motor Company factory on the island of Singapore. That day, as he stared down Lt. Gen. Arthur Percival, Yamashita had casually kicked off his leather boots. When the buck-toothed British commander begged for more time, Yamashita had pounded the table with his open hand, demanding he surrender immediately. Percival had caved, his defeat destined to forever share the same date as his daughter's birthday.

At this table in the mountains of Luzon, Yamashita's war had come full circle. The victor had become the vanquished.

The American officers filed inside the room. Maj. Gen. Edmond Leavey, who would preside over Yamashita's surrender, sat facing the center of the table. Lt. Gen. William Styer sat to his right next to Lt. Gen. Jonathan Wainwright, who had surrendered on Bataan and suffered the rest of the war as a prisoner of the Japanese, losing forty pounds. He had passed through the Philippine capital when the war ended, stunned to see the handiwork of Yamashita's forces. "Manila was shockingly destroyed," he wrote. "The very contour of the city seemed changed."

To General Leavey's left sat none other than Arthur Percival, who like Wainwright had spent the war in captivity. MacArthur had wanted the British commander to attend Yamashita's surrender, to stand victorious across from his former adversary. Percival studied Yamashita. "I saw one eyebrow lifted and a look of surprise cross his face—but only for a moment," he recalled. "His face quickly resumed that sphinx-like mask common to all Japanese, and he showed no further interest." News reporters likewise were anxious to capture the dynamic between the two former foes. "Percival and Yamashita were reluctant to look at each other during the initial stages of ceremony," wrote Rodolfo Nazareno of the Manila *Star Reporter*. "Finally they caught each other's eyes and their glances seemed to reveal inward hostility."

Leavey began the ceremony at noon. "Please be seated," he said.

The general introduced himself and then asked Maj. Gen. Walter Wood, Jr., to read aloud in English the terms of Yamashita's surrender.

"You have heard read the instrument of surrender," Leavey said afterward to Yamashita. "Are you ready to sign the surrender documents?"

An interpreter leaned over Yamashita's shoulder and whispered to him what had just been read. "I am," Yamashita replied with a nod.

On the table sat four leather-bound copies in English and Japanese along with several fountain pens. Yamashita stepped forward at 12:04 p.m. "He was rigid," one reporter noted, "as he signed." Col.

George Bishop then passed the surrender documents to Leavey for the Americans to sign. Afterward Leavey presented the pens to Wainwright, Percival, and Styer, slipping the last one into his own pocket.

The Japanese officers awaited the next move.

"General Yamashita, Vice Admiral Okochi and the others shall be held as prisoners of war," Leavey announced in conclusion.

Colonel Kenworthy, head of the military police trusted to guard the Japanese prisoners, moved to take them into custody. "He walked up to Yamashita," Wainwright noted, "punched an extended index finger into the Jap general's shoulder, and motioned him out of the room like an umpire thumbing a player out of a ball game. He was to be taken to Bilibid Prison to await trial as a war criminal."

Wainwright watched Yamashita weep as he left.

The former prisoner of war rose and approached Styer. "General," he said, "this might seem a little strange, coming from me, but I hope Yamashita is shown the courtesy due his rank, in the matter of personal accommodations, housing and food."

"He'll be given everything he's entitled to, under the Geneva Convention," promised Styer, commanding general of American forces in the western Pacific. "We don't want to be guilty of treating anyone as the Japs treated you and your men."

At three p.m. military police loaded Yamashita and his compatriots into a convoy bound for the airport. "From our speeding jeep," Muto said, "I could see the blurred image of the pine-clad hills where we had once lived in caves." Guards later loaded the prisoners aboard two C-47s. The twin-engine military transports then roared down the runway and lifted off into the sky that afternoon, taking Yamashita back to Manila.

Back to the scene of the crime.

○ ○ ○ ○

WHILE TROOPS HUNTED YAMASHITA in the mountains, an army of American investigators spent the spring and summer months preparing for the eventual war crimes trials of the general and other Japanese commanders. Investigators interviewed victims, including many still confined to hospital beds, ultimately producing thousands of pages of sworn testimony. Others photographed wounds and walked massacre sites with survivors, sketching maps and diagrams of places such as De La Salle, Fort Santiago, and San Agustin that would later help in the re-creation of the horror.

The dogged work identified twenty-seven major atrocities just in Manila and another 276 that occurred throughout the Philippine islands. The list, of course, was by no means complete, despite the diligence of investigators. In some cases, entire families had been slain, leaving no one to report the massacre. Missing, for example, was any record of the murders of Far Eastern University founder Nick Reyes and his family. Investigators dedicated a report to each atrocity, recording the details of what occurred, logging witnesses, and tallying as best as possible the names of victims. Some of the reports totaled hundreds of pages. The investigation into the rapes at the Bay View Hotel, for example, ran 781 pages and included testimony from 106 witnesses.

At the same time investigators canvassed the field hospitals and ruins of Manila, teams of analysts with the Allied Translator and Interpreter Section deciphered thousands of captured Japanese orders, letters, and diaries. Many of these records documented brutality not just in Manila but in the rural provinces as well.

"Kill American troops cruelly," one commanding officer demanded. "Kill all those who oppose the Emperor, even women and children."

"Four prisoners were executed," read a Japanese soldier's diary. "With a stroke of the sword their souls went to Hell."

"All natives, both men and women, will be killed," ordered another.

A few of the diaries revealed remorse. "Taking advantage of darkness, we went out to kill the natives. It was hard for me to kill them because they seem to be good people," an infantryman wrote in March 1945. "Frightful cries of the children were horrible." Another recorded that he spent his days hunting natives. "I have already killed well over 100," he wrote. "Now I am a hardened killer and my sword is always stained with blood. Although it is for my country's sake, it is sheer brutality. May God forgive me! May my mother forgive me!"

The revelations contained in such records sparked outrage in MacArthur against his former adversary Yamashita. Col. Sidney Mashbir, who oversaw the Allied Translator and Interpreter Section, showed him an order from the Battle of Manila, instructing Japanese troops how best to kill women and children.

"He's not fit to die as a soldier," MacArthur said of Yamashita.

"That was that," Mashbir recalled. "He was a dead man."

As investigators realized, victims had come from all social and economic backgrounds. Some spoke fluent English, while Spanish, Chinese, and Tagalog translators had to be enlisted to interview others. More than a few were illiterate, signing their sworn statements with the letter "X." At times, victims broke down, which was dutifully noted in each statement. "The witness," one investigator observed, "appeared too grief-stricken to testify at more length."

In every interview, investigators made judgments about who might one day serve as a witness in a war crimes trial, a fact often highlighted in the reports. "They speak flawless English and have remarkably clear memories of the massacre," one investigator noted of German Club survivors Francisco Lopez and Helena Rodriguez. Other witnesses did not make the cut. "She does not speak English, is very nervous, and appears to have been badly frightened at the time of the incidents related."

The interviews about sexual assaults proved some of the hardest. Investigators in the Bay View case noted the "extreme reticence" of many victims to describe what happened to them. The interview with Father Belarmino de Celis, a priest in Intramuros, turned awkward when investigators pressed him to identify rape victims.

"Yes, I know their names," he admitted. "But I will not divulge them because it would dishonor them. Some are married and still living."

Other victims, like Remedios Huerta Beliso, who was assaulted at San Agustin, shared her story with investigators but no one else. "I didn't tell my husband," she said. "I never have told him."

Investigators interviewed children, who at times were among the few survivors of a particular massacre, including eight-year-old Ismael Sedro.

"Do you know what it means to take an oath?" the investigator asked.

"It means to tell the truth," he replied. "You get in trouble if you tell a lie."

"Then, you will tell us the truth?" the investigator pressed.

"Yes," the youth said. "I want to tell the truth."

Only a few hundred Japanese had survived the battle. Those few who did were often young enlisted men, many of whom had been badly wounded and left for dead. Most denied any knowledge of the slaughter of civilians, but a few admitted it, including thirty-year-old Ichiro Sato with the 86th Air Corps. The married father of two toddlers recounted his role in killing civilians in Suloc, about forty-five miles south of Manila.

"Many people were killed—men, women, and children," Sato said.

"Did you participate?" investigators asked.

"I furnished all the soldiers for the kills but I actually did not participate."

"How many people were killed each time you furnished the soldiers?"

"About six hundred women and children."

"What was the total amount killed?" investigators pressed.

"About fifteen hundred men, women and children."

"How were they killed?"

"They were all bayonetted."

Another soldier who confessed was Sohei Michishita, a twenty-five-year-old sergeant and assistant squad leader with a motor transportation supply company. Japanese forces rounded up about eleven hundred civilians, half of whom he estimated were women and children. At a primary school in Sulac, officers assigned Michishita and others groups of civilians to slay.

"I killed my 15 men near the school," Michishita said.

"How did you kill the 15 men assigned to you?" investigators asked.

"I bayonetted eight and chopped the heads of seven with my sword."

"Why did you kill those fifteen men?"

"I just took orders from the higher ups."

In each case, investigators probed survivors for physical attributes that might help identify the perpetrators. How tall was he? What kind of uniform did he wear? Did he have gold teeth, a moustache, or glasses? In many of the sworn statements, victims fell back on the same racial stereotype that all the Japanese looked the same.

"It is hard to distinguish one from the other," said Joaquin Maranon.

"They all look alike to me," added Elsie Hamburger.

"He had slit eyes like all the other Japanese," said Cayetano Lagdameo.

Page after page of testimony reveals the struggle many victims had comprehending why the Japanese had perpetrated such cruelty against them. Many who had lost loved ones proved understandably bitter and hostile.

"My future life is only for vengeance," declared Dr. Walter Frankel, who watched the Japanese shoot his wife in the neck and kill her.

"What the Japanese have done to us was a premeditated act," added Jose Yulo. "It is savagery and they don't deserve to be among civilized people."

"I honestly believe they had no reason whatever for murdering us; they just hated Filipinos," Maranon told investigators.

Even American investigators proved at a loss to comprehend the widespread butchery, exhausting the thesaurus for adjectives like "diabolical," "inhuman," and "savage." The numerous reports compiled on each atrocity often included commentary by investigators on how humans could commit such barbarities.

"This orgy of looting, raping, and murder defy credence, were it not for the mass of indisputable evidence establishing its commission," read one report.

"Such a cruel, heartless massacre is difficult to visualize," stated another.

"They were simply slaughtered without just cause."

Of all the interviews with prisoners of war, investigators zeroed in on one enemy serviceman who offered a motive, an explanation that dovetailed with what many Filipinos believed. The sack of Manila was payback for Filipino loyalty to America, exemplified not only by the organized guerrilla resistance throughout the islands but also by the passive resistance of the citizenry. "It is recommended," XIV Corps investigators wrote, "that information contained in this report which condemns the Japanese nation in their atrocious prosecution of war in the Philippines be given the widest publicity so that Japan may be properly exposed as a nation which is truly an enemy of the civilized world."

CHAPTER 23

"There can be no doubt that once again, as in Nanking and Shanghai, the Japanese Armed Forces have shown themselves to be absolutely ruthless, barbaric and brutal."

—LT. COL. EDMUND STONE,
REPORT, FEBRUARY 26, 1945

MILITARY STAFF CARS ROLLED UP OUTSIDE NEW BILIBID Prison some twenty-five miles south of Manila on October 5, 1945, carrying the American lawyers chosen to represent General Yamashita in his upcoming war crimes trial. The six-member defense team consisted of Col. Harry Clarke, Lt. Cols. Gordon Feldaus and Walter Hendrix, Maj. George Guy, and Capts. Frank Reel and Milton Sandberg. Few had wanted the assignment. The war had been over barely a month, and tensions remained high. The ruins of Manila served as a daily reminder of the horror that had unfolded in the Philippine capital eight months earlier. Furthermore, representing a defendant described by the *Washington Post* as "one of the most hated of all the Japanese" shined an unwanted spotlight on the families of the lawyers back home in America. "I feel sure he will do his best since defending Yamashita is his duty," Mary Hendrix told the *Atlanta Constitution*. "This is one case I am hoping my husband will lose."

A trigonometry teacher at Altoona High School in Pennsylvania went so far as to single out Colonel Clarke's niece Thelma one day in class. "How do you feel," he asked, "about your uncle being a traitor?"

The public hostility was not lost on the lawyers whose job was to fight for the life of a man who only weeks earlier had been their sworn enemy. But the rancor ran deeper. As the senior commander in the Philippines, Yamashita served as the face of the barbaric military that had raped and murdered tens of thousands and destroyed the Pearl of the Orient. Even his lawyers were not immune from such feelings. Colonel Feldhaus personally viewed Yamashita as a savage. "Our feelings towards our unwanted client were at first somewhat antagonistic," he wrote. "I personally was quite bitter about having been appointed counsel on his case." Major Guy felt the same. "We had all seen the ravages and destruction in Manila itself and many of us had seen similar sights out in the provinces and in other cities in the Philippines," he wrote. "We all knew that Yamashita was entitled to a defense, but we all wondered, 'Why does it have to be us?'"

The defense lawyers swallowed such personal views that Friday as they prepared to meet their infamous new client for the first time. Military police escorted them to the chapel, which would serve as the conference room. The lawyers requested Yamashita and his senior officers. "So you're the guys that have to defend these monkeys, are you?" one of the prison officers said as the men waited for the general's arrival.

Yamashita had spent the month since his surrender in a ten-by-fifteen-foot cell on the prison's death row, his only furnishings a cot, a table, and two chairs. American officials had interviewed him and his senior staff multiple times, and on each occasion the general had cooperated. Interrogators had found him to be strong, humble, and soldierly, rating him "as intelligent, but not profoundly so." The bespectacled Muto, in fact, was described as "the real brains of the combination." Furthermore, interrogators noted Yamashita had shown "an almost childish interest recounting his own campaigns and in finding out how much we had actually known of his movements and situation."

Lt. Samuel Stratton couldn't help but record another of the general's quirks. "He was a terrific cigarette moocher," he recalled. "Whenever I would question him, I would leave my pack of cigarettes on the table and invite him to have one. The pack usually was empty by the time the interview was concluded."

But the otherwise gabby general turned evasive when pressed to describe what had happened in Manila, stating that he had never planned to defend the capital; American forces had arrived before all the troops evacuated and forced a fight, a statement that failed to take into account Admiral Iwabuchi's extensive efforts to fortify Manila. He likewise claimed ignorance of any of the atrocities, blaming poor communications, even though, as other senior officers in Baguio would later attest, Yamashita maintained radio contact with Manila through at least the middle of February. By that time, Japanese forces had committed the worst of the massacres. Yamashita furthermore was in contact through June with the Shimbu Group commander General Yokoyama, who was Iwabuchi's superior officer. Beyond the Philippines, Yamashita received reports throughout the duration of the war from Tokyo and abroad. Through those broadcasts he would have learned that Spain—in news trumpeted worldwide—had severed ties with Japan in April over the slaughter of so many of its nationals in Manila, including the torching of its consulate and the murder of its diplomatic personnel.

Other senior Japanese leaders took the same approach. Everyone seemed to know just enough of the horror that unfolded in the capital to know it was safer not to be associated with it. The obfuscation clearly frustrated interrogators, as evidenced by one summary: "Neither Gen. Yamashita nor his Chief of Staff, nor for that matter, any of the officers interviewed, would accept any responsibility for the Battle of Manila."

"I don't know," interviewers noted, was the rote explanation.

Interrogators didn't buy it.

The death of the commanding officer in Manila made for an easy scapegoat, a rogue officer who had taken it upon himself to destroy a city and butcher its inhabitants. But would one field commander really be so brazen as to order the liquidation of tens of thousands of innocent civilians without at least tacit approval from his superiors? "Another explanation," one report suggested, "is that Yamashita was quite well aware of the progress of the entire battle but thought it best to let the responsibility fall on Admiral Iwabuchi, who was eventually killed in the Agriculture Building. It seems unlikely that their communications were as bad as they made them out to be."

Yamashita would now face a similar grilling from his lawyers, who would use his statements in the coming weeks to help build a defense before the start of the trial.

Military police escorted Yamashita, Chief of Staff Muto, Maj. Gen. Naokata Utunomiya, and interpreter Masakatsu Hamamoto across the prison courtyard and into the chapel. The Japanese bowed to the altar and then turned and bowed to the lawyers. "It must have been difficult for the conqueror of Malaya to bow as he did in the Japanese fashion to Lt. Colonels and Captains of the American army," Feldhaus wrote. "However, this he did, in a most respectful manner, with a complete lack of arrogance."

Colonel Clarke introduced the lawyers, who were all curious to meet the notorious general. Guy fixated on Yamashita. Though tall by Japanese standards, the general was still lean from his months in the mountains, making it appear that his loose Japanese field uniform swallowed him. "His head seemed to be unusually large, particularly so for a Japanese and the face was marked with heavy lines," Guy wrote. "His neck was thick and bull like and the back of his neck and head ran in almost a vertical line from the white shirt collar which was turned down over his tunic collar."

Hamamoto opened his mouth and surprised the lawyers with his perfect English, all of whom were curious to know where he had learned to speak the language. "Harvard," he answered. "Class of '27."

The lawyers explained that the United States planned to prosecute Yamashita for war crimes. Three days earlier the prosecution had served the general with a single sweeping charge, accusing him of failing to execute his duty as a commander and prevent his forces from committing brutal atrocities in Manila and elsewhere in the Philippines. Muto professed his shock at the news, which was disingenuous given his own sordid history with Japanese barbarity. Yamashita's chief of staff, in fact, had served as a senior officer in China during the Rape of Nanking—and was present in that city at the time of some of the worst atrocities. "To me the idea of General Yamashita's being indicted as a war criminal is something the like of which I have never seen in a dream," Muto said later. "I was absolutely astounded when I learned about it."

Yamashita likewise objected, claiming he had never heard of any such atrocities. "We cut him short," Reel recalled. "There was no doubt about it. The atrocities could certainly be proved. What we were concerned about was the question of any connection that the general might have had with them. What we wanted to know, first, was how in the world so many brutalities could be committed and he not know about them."

Yamashita walked them through Japan's disastrous campaign for the Philippines, from Leyte through MacArthur's invasion of Lingayen Gulf.

"Where did the city of Manila fit into this picture?" lawyers asked.

Yamashita largely stuck to the same story he had told army interrogators earlier. "I decided to put Manila outside of the battle area," the general said. "I ordered my troops out of Manila. I decided to abandon it without a battle."

The lawyers pressed him on the Battle of Manila. If he had ordered everyone to leave, then why was the city destroyed? Yamashita blamed the navy. "The Japanese army had moved out. There were only fifteen or sixteen hundred army troops left in the city, and their essential mission was to guard those military supplies that had not yet been removed," he said. "But there were approximately twenty thousand Japanese naval troops who did not move out, and they were the ones who fought the Americans."

The lawyers pressed him to explain why Iwabuchi had failed to follow repeated orders and withdraw from the city.

The general could not give an answer. "It was entirely contrary to my plans for Manila," he maintained.

Throughout the interview, the attorneys noted, Yamashita's answers remained consistent. "His forthright manner, his candor and his strength of character made a distinct impression on me that first interview and those qualities continued to impress me as time went on and as my contacts with him became more frequent," Guy wrote. "I am confident that my associates on the defense staff had the same impressions."

Before the conference concluded, the attorneys asked one final question: "When surrender was unavoidable, why hadn't the general committed suicide?"

Yamashita said such an action would have violated his orders, which mandated that he surrender and cooperate with the Americans.

But Tojo had attempted to kill himself, the lawyers pointed out.

"Yes," Yamashita replied. "Tojo disobeyed the order of his emperor."

○ ○ ○ ○

CROWDS QUEUED UP outside the High Commissioner's Residence on Dewey Boulevard on the afternoon of October 8, all awaiting a chance to watch the arraignment of General Yamashita. The impending trial of the Tiger of Malaya promised to be the main attraction in a city that still remained in such ruin that heavy rains prompted the dead to float up out of shallow graves. American engineers had restored limited power and water, though most residents depended on candles and coconut oil lamps. It was a similar story with Manila's roads. The army had repaired the ones needed to move troops and supplies, but the rest remained pock-marked with foot-deep holes and were often impassable in the heavy rains. The lack of housing proved another crisis, prompting primitive huts made of salvaged lumber and corrugated metal to mushroom in the ruins of once-grand buildings. "Manila was for the greater part a shack-town," Hartendorp had observed, "a sprawling, giant slum."

The city's broken economy had triggered a robust black market. A rash of bootleg liquor had killed dozens, including more than twenty American soldiers and left another six blind. The streets teemed with prostitutes and pimps and crime soared. "The fearsome Japs are gone," remarked an editorial in the *Manila Post*, "but the hoodlums and hold-up gangs infest the streets, waylaying peaceful, law-abiding citizens; break into homes, rendering it impossible for city residents to enjoy freedom from fear." Leftover land mines only added to the anguish, killing more than two hundred and injuring four times as many. Only a few weeks earlier a bulldozer ran over a buried five-hundred-pound aerial bomb off Dewey Boulevard, triggering a spectacular explosion that killed one, wounded two others, and left a crater five feet deep and twenty-two feet wide. The population, as Hartendorp wrote in a September op-ed, was shell-shocked. "This country has suffered not only widespread destruction, devastation, and death, but also the mental traumas which result from prolonged periods of misery, grief, fear, and hate."

Into this devastated city, Yamashita now returned, the man most held responsible for the despair and misery. Outside the High Commissioner's Residence—a few blocks south of the Manila Hotel and ground zero for some of the city's worst destruction—long lines formed this Monday, so many that vendors showed up to hawk ice cream, creating a carnival-like atmosphere. Workers inside had scrambled to transform the semicircular ballroom—its white plaster ceiling and pale blue walls still scarred by shrapnel—into a makeshift courtroom. Seven French doors offered views of the American ships anchored in Manila Bay; two crystal chandeliers that had survived dangled from the high domed ceilings. A rectangular table with leather chairs for the judges sat atop a plywood stage, while immediately in front of it stood a witness stand, interpreter station, and opposing desks for the prosecution and the defense.

MacArthur's staff had laid the groundwork for what would prove to be the first war crimes trial in the Pacific. Neither a court-martial nor a civilian trial, the proceedings would be a hybrid, best described by one journalist as an "Allied legal laboratory." MacArthur's staff had drafted twenty-two rules that would govern the trial, running to just seven pages. Those rules spelled out Yamashita's rights to defense counsel and indeed advance copies of all the charges against him and translated copies of all testimony and records. The defense could call and cross-examine witnesses, who would have to give testimony under oath. The regulations governing evidence, however, were loose at best, described simply as anything the commission deemed "would have probative value in the mind of a reasonable man." "The rule of evidence," noted *New York Times* reporter Robert Trumbull, "can be boiled down to two words: anything goes."

Maj. Gen. Russel Reynolds served as the presiding judge. The fifty-year-old Michigan native was joined by two other major generals and two brigadier generals. These five officers would decide Yamashita's fate. The defense was wary of the judges, who were all subordinate to MacArthur and unlikely to buck his wishes. Furthermore, none were combat soldiers, making it hard for them to appreciate the tactical mess Yamashita had inherited when he landed in the Philippines.

More important, not a single one had any legal training. "It was," Captain Reel later wrote, "far too much to expect laymen without legal assistance on the bench to understand the trial of a case of this type, a case that was to make fundamentally new law and that would necessarily involve hundreds of legal decisions on matters of evidence, international law, the construction of congressional statutes, and the interpretation of treaties."

Maj. Robert Kerr led the prosecution. A forty-one-year-old Oregonian and graduate of the University of Michigan law school, Kerr prided himself on the fact that he was not a member of the Judge Advocate General's Corps but was an infantryman, a "mere soldier," he liked to say. Four captains, all of whom had served as district attorneys in civilian life, assisted Kerr. Lastly Maj. Glicerio Opinion rounded out the prosecution, the only Filipino on the team. In comments to the reporters on the eve of the arraignment, Kerr announced that he would seek the death penalty for Yamashita. Over the course of the trial, he said he would introduce as many as one thousand exhibits, including captured Japanese orders, diaries, and victim statements. The crimes committed by the general's troops, he said, occurred not just in Manila but throughout the archipelago. "I'm amazed myself at the universal pattern of atrocities—of what the Philippine people went through," he said. "If we gave them all, this trial would go on for months."

The courtroom was packed that Monday afternoon, confirming the decision to hold a dress rehearsal the day before. Loudspeakers dangled from the ceiling overhead, while the bright klieg lights only drove up the heat and humidity. Officials reserved fifty seats for accredited journalists, including three motion picture cameramen from the Signal Corps perched in the balconies, plus a few extra seats in the first row for visiting dignitaries. The remaining three hundred spots were open to the public, though hundreds ultimately had to be turned away in the end for a lack of space. Seventy-five military police, wearing white helmets and gloves, stood guard. Officers frisked all spectators for weapons, aided by four Manila policewomen who searched the females.

Many dignitaries turned out, including General Styer and First Lady Esperanza Osmeña in a white mestiza dress. She was joined in the front row by her daughter Rosie, who wore a corsage in her dark hair, and her daughter-in-law, Mary, the widow of Osmeña's son, Emilio, who was executed by the Japanese. "The arraignment," one of Yamashita's lawyers said, "was a gala affair."

"Attention," the bailiff called out at two p.m.

Everyone stood.

The commission members filed in and sat on the dais. Military police then escorted Yamashita inside at 2:02 p.m. All eyes focused on the Japanese commander, whom Colonel Clarke had ordered to dress as sharply as possible. The general wore a green uniform with high cavalry boots and gold spurs. Four rows of campaign ribbons adorned his left breast. Prosecution trial assistant George Mountz described Yamashita's entry in a letter: "He hesitated, bowed slightly, with respect but not servitude & sat down." There was little doubt Yamashita was nervous this afternoon in a courtroom operated by his former enemy. "Sweat gleamed at the roots of his close-cropped graying hair, as he took his seat next to his American defense counsels," one journalist wrote. "He held his cap uncertainly, laid it on the table and then placed his hands on it."

News reporters proved anxious to glimpse the fabled commander, who had fallen from his lofty perch as a powerful general to prisoner of war. *Newsweek* called him the "Toothless Tiger," while the *Los Angeles Times* labeled him the "Gopher of the Philippines." Other media outlets, reflecting the racial hostility so prevalent during the war, fell back on other stereotypes, describing him as having "beady" and even "rat-like eyes." *Time* magazine characterized him as a primitive monster. "He looked like an ogre—a squat, shaven-headed, simian figure in a green uniform."

"They've fattened him up for butchering," one reporter quipped, noting that Yamashita had gained weight in the month since he surrendered.

Amid the illumination of floodlights and the pop of flashbulbs, Yamashita stood center stage as a symbol of the cruel Japanese regime that had slaughtered hundreds of thousands, not just in the Philippines but also in the cities and villages of China, Malaya, and elsewhere. The same day as the arraignment, Australian officials requested the

United States, if unable to convict Yamashita for any reason, hand him over so he could be tried for the atrocities his troops committed during the Malayan campaign. Prosecutor Kerr later described in a letter the raw emotions surrounding the trial. "It probably is impossible for anyone who was not on the scene to conceive of or understand the feeling of outrage, hatred and vengefulness of the people of the Philippines who had suffered long years of barbarous mistreatment by the forces under Yamashita's command." That was true outside in the streets, where American forces guarded Japanese prisoners of war, who worked from dawn to dusk cleaning up battle debris. "Guards keep their carbines pointed at the populace," reporter James Halsema observed, "not at their prisoners."

Reynolds began the afternoon's arraignment, stating that the commission would hear evidence from the prosecution and defense before determining the general's guilt or innocence. If convicted, the commission would decide his sentence.

"The proceedings," the judge said, "will be conducted in a fair and impartial manner, which is traditional American justice."

Kerr introduced for the record the orders establishing the basis for the commission. The prosecutor then noted that a certified copy of the charge against Yamashita was served on him on October 2 at New Bilibid Prison. "Whom does the Accused desire to introduce as Defense counsel?" Reynolds asked.

"I am happy to accept the choice of the Commission as to my counsel," Yamashita said through an interpreter. "I am highly honored to have been given such distinguished persons to represent me."

Yamashita requested to have his chief of staff Muto and his deputy chief of staff Naokata Utsunomiya serve as additional counsel. "There are a number of records and facts with which they alone are conversant. I need their advice and assistance."

The prosecutor objected, arguing that both men planned to testify on behalf of Yamashita, but Reynolds shot him down. "The Accused has stated his belief," he said. "It is the desire of this Commission to conduct a fair trial; accordingly, subject to objection by any member of the Commission, the request of the Defense is granted."

"Thank you," Yamashita said.

Kerr pointed out that both would later stand trial. Furthermore, the prosecution refused to recognize either by their former titles. "We maintain, sir, that the day when Yamashita had his Chief-of-Staff or Assistant-Chief-of-Staff is over."

Reynolds ordered the single charge against Yamashita read aloud. Afterward, the judge asked if the defense was ready to enter a plea.

Colonel Clarke challenged the charge, arguing that it failed to state a violation of war actually committed by Yamashita. There were no times, dates, places or specific actions, just the broad charge that he had failed to control his troops.

Kerr said the prosecution had compiled a Bill of Particulars, outlining individual accounts of atrocities. He added that the full list of atrocities was not yet complete and requested permission to file additional charges at a later date. "We have certain new information just recently received which we have not had an opportunity so far to incorporate in the Bill of Particulars," Kerr said. "If we may have assurance that later we may file a supplemental Bill of Particulars, we are willing to proceed."

The defense objected but was overruled.

The court recessed for fifteen minutes to allow prosecutors to present the defense with the Bill of Particulars, a nineteen-page list of sixty-four atrocities. The massacres outlined proved widespread, from murdering almost 150 American prisoners of war on the island of Palawan to killing 25,000 Filipinos in Batangas Province. Many others focused on the horror inside the Philippine capital, ranging from starving internees at Santo Tomas to slaughtering civilians at De La Salle, the Red Cross, and Fort Santiago. "The charges," *Newsweek* wrote, "read like a chamber-of-horrors indictment."

The court returned at 3:25 p.m., at which time commissioners set a trial date of October 29. "The Accused," Clarke said, "is ready to plead."

"General Tomoyuki Yamashita," Reynolds announced, "at this time the Commission will hear your plea to the Charge and specifications which have been read to you. You may plead either guilty or not guilty."

Flashbulbs exploded and movie cameras rolled as the judges, lawyers, and hundreds of spectators focused on the former Tiger of Malaya.

"My plea," Yamashita said, "is not guilty."

○   ○   ○   ○

YAMASHITA'S LAWYERS HAD THREE WEEKS to prepare the general's defense before the opening day of trial. Attorneys secured a battered two-story home with a high stone wall on Taft Avenue to serve as the team's legal command center, where guards could truck Yamashita in daily in the back of an ambulance to keep the populace unaware. Secrecy was paramount. "There were," George Guy noted, "thousands of Manilans who would have welcomed the chance to take the law into their own hands."

The job facing the defense was gargantuan. American investigators had spent months interviewing survivors, collecting evidence, and building a case. To follow up on those investigations—a job that would require interviews with hundreds of witnesses scattered across the Philippines—would take months at best, time the defense simply didn't have. Under such constraints, the lawyers decided it was impossible to put forth an alternative explanation for the carnage in Manila but chose rather to focus solely on defending Yamashita on the prosecutor's charges.

Guy hopped a plane to Japan to round up character witnesses, while the others worked with Yamashita to review the atrocities detailed in the Bill of Particulars. That included interviewing any Japanese prisoners of war who might provide insight into what happened. Lawyers likewise focused on the challenges Yamashita faced as a commander, from the byzantine chain of command to his poor communications, inferior troops, and lack of food. The general's only alibi, his lawyers determined, was that overwhelmed by superior American forces, he had left everything else in the hands of his subordinates. "We worked every day," Reel said, "every Sunday, every evening."

The lawyers faced additional struggles, including trying a case amid a hostile local populace in the center of devastated Manila. "By vir-

tue of this press buildup, Yamashita was already convicted in the eyes
of the world, and certainly in the eyes of the Filipinos, even before a
shred of evidence had been introduced against him," Guy wrote. "The
task confronting the defense seemed enormous indeed."

The defense's job soon became even tougher.

At four p.m. on October 26—the Friday before the Monday start
of the trial—a messenger arrived to serve Yamashita's team with a
supplemental Bill of Particulars. The prosecution had added fifty-
nine new atrocities. "We were dumbfounded," Reel recalled. "We
had expected that perhaps one or two or three new items might be
added; but here we were, just two days before trial, and the charges
that we would have to meet were almost doubled—from sixty-four to
one hundred and twenty-three, and practically all of them involving
new places, new persons, new witnesses." Going forward at this point
was impossible. The defense had no option but to request a continuance, a move Yamashita's lawyers knew the judges would resist given
the intense publicity. "The power behind the Commission was in a
hurry," Reel wrote. "But after we had worked day and night for three
weeks on sixty-four items of a Bill of Particulars, the Commission simply could not refuse us some time to prepare for fifty-nine new ones."

On the night before the trial opened, attorneys allowed Pat Robinson of the International News Service to interview Yamashita, whom
American servicemen had stopped calling the Tiger of Malaya in favor
of the Louse of Luzon. The general asked Robinson if he thought the
American press would be fair to him. Robinson said he did. "That's
very good," Yamashita replied. "I recognize more than ever the American spirit of fair play, which I had not previously realized would work
in my favor."

Robinson told Yamashita that if he was found guilty, he would
likely be hanged, a statement that made the general laugh as he
gripped his neck with both hands.

"I don't see how I can be convicted, any more than the United States
President or General MacArthur could be if American troops had
committed atrocities," Yamashita countered. "How can I be convicted
of crimes I didn't even know about?"

CHAPTER 24

"Nothing has seared the hatred against the Japanese in the Filipino heart more deeply than seeing our capital city converted into a funeral pyre."

—Brig. Gen. Carlos Romulo,
Free Philippines, February 22, 1945

On the morning of October 29, 1945, exactly three weeks to the day after the general's arraignment, spectators jockeyed for a spot in line outside the High Commissioner's Residence. "It was first come, first seated," noted the *Los Angeles Times*. "There was no favoritism." Adding to the excitement of the opening day of trial, military police only the night before had discovered a Japanese land mine buried near the residence's Dewey Boulevard gate; the detonator was exposed by the recent heavy rains.

In preparation for the trial, guards had moved Yamashita from New Bilibid Prison to a special cell on the second floor of the residence, which before the war had served as the bedroom of American high commissioner Francis Sayre's two stepsons. The trial that kicked off this Monday morning promised to be a logistical nightmare, requiring an army of translators to cover languages ranging from Japanese and Spanish to Chinese dialects of Mandarin, Amoy, and Cantonese as well as Tagalog, Visayan, and other obscure Filipino dialects. The 123 specific charges against Yamashita, according to a tally compiled by *Yank* magazine, accounted for 62,278 tortured and murdered civilians, 144 slain American officers and enlisted men, and 488 raped women and children. Even Great Britain, which had endured the brutal German bombings known as the Blitz, counted only 61,000 dead civilians throughout the entire war.

Many local newspapers published the charges verbatim: "repeatedly raping more than 40 women and female children"; "entire settlements were devastated and destroyed wantonly"; "killing approximately 200 men, women and children."

"The list goes on endlessly," one reporter observed. "If you can shake off the sense-dulling repetition of detail and realize that each of these thousands was a separate, breathing, life-loving human being, it becomes horrible reading."

Yamashita's odds, most agreed, seemed poor. "From the very beginning," *Yank* magazine claimed, "you couldn't find a sucker to bet two pesos to 200 on Yamashita's acquittal."

The defense began the proceeding pleading for two more weeks to prepare. Captain Reel told judges that the defense had anticipated prosecutors might add one or two additional charges but had never imagined facing fifty-nine new ones, filed at four p.m. on the Friday before the start of trial. Defense of those charges would require more time to investigate. "We believe that it is unconscionable in a case of this type to practically double in the last minute the list of offenses charged."

Judge Reynolds asked the prosecution's opinion. "Defense Counsel is much better prepared to judge the difficulties of preparing the defense than I am," said Major Kerr. "I can only say that the Prosecution is ready and anxious to go to trial."

After a brief discussion in chambers, judges denied Reel's request for a continuance, adding that at the end of the prosecution's case, if defense still felt it needed more time, the judges would again consider the motion.

"The case," Reynolds announced, "will proceed."

Kerr began with his opening arguments, warning of the gruesome details he would present in the days ahead. Guards would carry some witnesses into court atop stretchers; other victims would be "permanently mutilated, physically ruined for life." Even then, the trial would provide only a snapshot of the butchery that had unfolded in the Philippines, not a forensic accounting of every atrocity Japanese troops committed. "We Americans are a Christian nation; we are reared in the tradition of fair play and decency," Kerr told the panel of five judges. "If the Commission finds the evidence unpleasant, as I am sure it will in many instances, it is simply because those are the facts. That is the type of case we are trying, gentlemen; it is not a pleasant proceeding."

Despite the voluminous charges and gory details of individual massacres, he argued the case was really quite simple. Yamashita had failed in his duty to control his troops, who in turn slaughtered tens of thousands of men, women, and children.

"That is the charge," he said. "That is the case."

Kerr jumped into the horror right away, calling Corazon Noble as a witness at 11:08 a.m., the famed actress who was shot at the Red Cross headquarters. The twenty-six-year-old wore a black dress adorned with a single orchid. She cradled her bandaged right arm in a sling, forcing her to raise her left hand to take the oath.

"My name is Patrocinio Abad," she began. "My screen name is Corazon Noble."

Noble walked the court through her story, describing how her husband was killed by a trench mortar, prompting her to move into the Red Cross headquarters with her ten-month-old daughter Maria Lourdes Vera. Four Japanese troops had then barged into the building and opened fire, an account one reporter described as "hell on the loose."

"I saw them aiming at me," she testified, "so I hid behind a cabinet where they keep the medicines, but the cabinet was not enough to cover me, so that my elbow, my right arm was out, and the Japanese shot me through my right elbow."

"When you were hit by the bullet what did you do?"

"I started to lie down—I laid—"

"On the floor?" the prosecutor interrupted.

"Yes, sir; and a Japanese came near me and stabbed me with his bayonet."

"How many times did he stab you with his bayonet?" the prosecutor asked.

"Nine times."

The cavernous courtroom was silent as journalists and spectators alike hung on her every word, described by reporters as a "bloodbath," "a story of horror," and a "nightmare of doom." Not only did Noble tear up as she testified, but so, too, did First Lady Esperanza Osmeña. Reporters likewise studied the Japanese general who sat just steps away from the actress. "Yamashita appeared nervous and fidgety," wrote the reporter for the Manila *Courier*. "Every now and then he would remove his horn-rimmed spectacles, put them on the table and then clamp them on again."

"Can you tell the members of the Commission what happened to your infant child at that time?" the prosecutor pressed.

"I had her under me, and when the Japanese stabbed me I felt a pain in my arm, it was hurting me," she said, "so I didn't see how he bayonetted my baby, only I know that she was bayonetted through and through three times."

"Three times?"

"Yes, sir."

"As a result of that bayonetting, what happened to your infant child?"

"She died."

○ ○ ○ ○

NOBLE WAS THE FIRST of scores of similar victims who took the stand as the days turned to a week and then two weeks and then three. The bay breeze cooled the courtroom, though on afternoons when the wind was still, the air inside grew hot and sticky. Hundreds of onlookers packed the ballroom and its balconies, sitting shoulder to shoulder, anxious to experience the first war crimes trial in the Pacific. Beneath powerful klieg lights and with moving pictures rolling, a parade of widows and children, priests and gravediggers testified to the grim horror of what had happened in Manila.

The prosecution hurried to present its own case, torn by the directive to prove all 123 alleged atrocities, but also rushed by judges anxious to wrap up the trial as soon as possible, so much so that the commission worked a half day on Thanksgiving. On average half a dozen charges were covered each day, reducing massacres that at times killed hundreds to just a few pages of testimony. For those who had survived the Battle of Manila, the atrocities were well known—the Red Cross, German Club, De La Salle, and St. Paul's College, among scores more. Other witnesses recounted the massacres in the provinces, including an estimated 25,000 killed in Batangas.

In cases where many survived, the prosecution chose to put on just a few witnesses, enough to paint in broad brushstrokes the atrocity for the record before moving on to the next one. But even in its abbreviated form, the testimony was often so ghastly that the *New York Times* described the trial as "foul a tale of savagery as is recorded in all history." The *Chicago Tribune* agreed, comparing the testimony of one witness to *Dante's Inferno*. "Not even the wholesale butchery of the Belsen prison camp in Germany was more revolting than the testimony of Francisco Lopez."

Similar anecdotes filled the growing trial record:

"The Japanese soldier stabbed me in the back," testified Leoncio Tolentino. "The point of the bayonet came out my breast."

"One of my sisters is pregnant," added a weeping Justina Manlisik. "They slashed her stomach open and when the baby come out they cut its head off."

"They burned all parts of my body with the cigarettes, the vital parts of my body, too," Beatriz Sapinoso told the judges.

On the morning when women testified about the rapes inside the Bay View Hotel and Alhambra and Miramar apartments, judges closed the court to the general public to protect their privacy. Sixteen-year-old Priscilla Garcia broke down, describing how her attacker sliced her vagina open with a knife to make it easier to rape her.

"Oh my God!" she cried out on the stand.

Her twenty-four-year-old sister Esther testified she had been raped more than a dozen times. "I couldn't even think anymore," she recalled. "They just dragged me out of the room. They kept doing that the whole night. I couldn't resist."

One of the most dramatic witnesses was Rosalinda Andoy, the eleven-year-old girl the Japanese bayoneted thirty-eight times in the ruins of Santo Domingo Church in the Walled City. She told the judges she had lived in a refugee home since the Japanese had killed her mother and father. "The girl's feet," the *New York Times* noted, "were dangling in wooden Filipino slippers that kept slipping off as she sat in the witness chair." During the proceedings, Rosalinda raised her left arm to reveal ten scars; then she pointed out the four on her right arm. She then stood up and pulled her faded pink dress above her brown bloomers, revealing eighteen scars on her chest and stomach. Tears ran down her cheek, dropping, as a reporter for *Time* magazine noted, on her dress.

"Before your mother died did she tell you anything?"

"Yes, sir," Rosalinda replied.

"What did she tell you?" the prosecutor pressed.

"To be always good."

Many of the spectators wept. "Her simple honest narration moved the entire courtroom," observed the *Manila Chronicle*. "American generals on the trial board," added the *New York Times*, "wiped their eyes during the child's testimony."

Her powerful story inspired Navy Petty Officer Second Class Bernard Katz to write a poem titled simply "Rosalinda Andoy—Age 11."

Do not weep, little one
Your tears are burning hot
They sear the very sun
They scar the human lot.

But Rosalinda was not the only child witness.

Ten-year-old Ang Kim Ling, the son of a prominent Chinese merchant in Los Baños, approached the stand, clinging to the hand of his eight-year-old sister, Elisa Ang, a scene best described by Mac Johnson of the *New York Herald Tribune*. "Gripping the sides of the chair, he told his story, while his sister stood behind him, fascinated by the whirling motion-picture cameras and the popping of flash-bulbs," the reporter wrote. "Sometimes crying, sometimes biting his lips, Ang

Kim Ling, through his interpreter, described how four generations of his family were killed by the Japanese."

"After I was stabbed," the boy testified, "I closed my eyes."

"When you woke up did you see any of the other members of your family?"

"I saw a head, a few legs and arms laying on the ground."

Like Rosalinda, he showed the commission his scars; so, too, did his younger sister, raising her black dress to reveal sixteen bayonet wounds. "The audience of American soldiers gasped," Johnson wrote, "as every one wondered how the girl survived the wounds, nearly any one of which could have proved fatal."

Several of the witnesses aimed their anger directly at Yamashita, including Chinese native Ang Be. Japanese troops had bayoneted three of her children to death behind a Shell Service Station in Manila, including her three-year-old son, whom she cradled in her arms at the time. The distraught witness lunged at Yamashita as she left the stand. "Let me get at him," she screamed. "He is a bad man."

Military police pounced on her amid exploding flashbulbs. "As they led her out of the courtroom," wrote a reporter for the *Manila Times*, "she continued to rage and almost fainted in the arms of her attendants following the emotional struggle."

Seventeen-year-old Julieta Milanes, whose father and fourteen-year-old brother were killed during the Japanese roundup of males in Paco, likewise accosted him. "You still have face to look at me, Yamashita. If I could only get near you! You don't have shame!" she yelled. "You ought to be hung. You ought to be cut in pieces."

"On the chairman's order two prosecutors led her from the courtroom," the *New York Times* reported. "Yamashita showed no expression except puzzlement."

Another dramatic moment came during Ricardo Esquerra's testimony. The undertaker was one of the few who had survived the Singalong death house, where saber-wielding Japanese troops had decapitated two hundred victims. Esquerra had climbed the mountain of bodies to escape.

The prosecutor asked to see his wound. Esquerra stood up and, as Robert Cromie with the *Chicago Tribune* reported, glared at Yamashita. "You, first!" he shouted at the general. "See the scar!"

Military police on November 14 discovered that witness Fausta Espiritu of Batangas, who was assaulted by the Japanese and whose husband's tongue was cut out, had packed her handbag with rocks. She stammered for an excuse when pressed. "I just picked them up and put them in my purse," she said, "to throw at the dogs."

Even neutral observers, like *London Daily Express* reporter Henry Keys, who visited San Agustin hours after its liberation, struggled with their emotions. "I found it hard," he wrote of his time in court, "to tell of the hate that burned inside me."

Santo Tomas historian Abram Hartendorp provided one of the few moments of levity amid the tales of horror when defense lawyer Colonel Clarke drilled him on food. "Was the ration supplemented by any poultry within the compound?"

"We had some ducks—but they also starved to death."

The audience howled in laughter. "It really brought down the house," George Mountz wrote in a letter, "and that was the end of that line of questioning."

Each day the atrocities piled up. "The prosecution's map of Manila on the court room wall, where pins are put daily to show the places where the population of whole neighborhoods were lined up, shot down, bayonetted, tortured and raped, is becoming thickly dotted as the reckoning against the Japanese grows," observed Robert Trumbull of the *New York Times*. The parade of violence only desensitized spectators; some even dozed, Trumbull noted, while the massacres of entire families were recounted. "Revolting testimony of rape, mass murder, and obscene atrocities is becoming so common in the trial," wrote the *Chicago Tribune*'s Cromie, "that it has reached the point where even the most fantastic horrors fail to register in the minds of listeners."

Manila radio announcers read excerpts of the trial during dinner hour, while newspapers carried the blow-by-blow testimony of each witness, feeding the highlights to hungry readers unable to score one of the coveted courtroom tickets. Sensational headlines often trumpeted in bold the shocking details:

" 'Rape Pools' Described by City's Prettiest Women," one stated.

"Courtroom Tearful as Girl Speaks," read another.

"Defense Silent as Orgy of Murder, Rape Is Told."

Some editorials questioned how much barbarity was needed. "Perhaps enough testimony against Yamashita has already been heard," quipped the *Boston Globe*, "unless it is planned to hang him more than once."

Others pointed to the trial as evidence that Japan could not be trusted to rule itself in the future. "The Japanese soldiers in the Philippines have written a page of history as terrible as any the foulest mind could conceive," wrote the *Hartford Courant*. "It is a record so base that the whole human race should feel ashamed."

Yamashita's lawyers meanwhile could do little more than suffer through the testimony. "Day after day, tales of bestiality and horror were recounted by Filipinos, Chinese, and occasionally Americans, until the listener wondered whether he was living on this green earth or in a bloody gash on the corpse of hell. There had to be revenge," Reel wrote. "There had to be personal vengeance, somehow—on someone."

Lawyers and spectators alike often shot glances at Yamashita, who perched at the defense table, his personal interpreter Hamamoto providing him with a running translation of the proceedings. "Yamashita sits through it all," Mountz wrote in a letter, "with little or no expression on his face." *Newsweek* observed the same. "His reddish eyes barely flicker behind horn-rimmed glasses," the magazine reported. "Sometimes his head nodded drowsily as the first 200 prosecution witnesses told stories—many unprintable—of Japanese terror and orgy during the siege of Manila."

Yamashita's lawyers faced the challenge of how to confront witnesses who were often victims of such ghastly crimes. The lawyers in some instances simply chose not to cross-examine them. In other cases, the defense questioned the type of uniforms the perpetrators wore, trying to distinguish whether troops belonged to the Japanese army or navy. Another avenue lawyers probed was whether the victims had ties to the Filipino guerrillas, which, if so, might have given the Japanese a motive.

But the greatest challenge the defense faced centered on the incredibly loose rules of evidence. In addition to putting victims on the stand, prosecutors often submitted additional witness statements gathered during the postbattle investigations. Unlike a witness on the stand, defense lawyers could not cross examine or challenge such statements. The same proved true with captured Japanese records, some of which consisted of little more than fragments of diaries plucked from the pockets of dead enemy soldiers. How could the defense verify the information in them?

Another challenge for the defense was the allowance of hearsay testimony, which is when a witness relates what someone else told them. Such evidence is normally forbidden in American courtrooms. "Hearsay evidence was admitted. Not merely first degree hearsay from an identified source, but rumor and gossip from unidentified sources," Reel wrote. "Third and fourth degrees hearsay was admitted." At one point, in a moment that revealed the presiding judge's lack of legal knowledge, Reynolds asked Colonel Clarke if such testimony would be allowed in a stateside courtroom.

The judge's question floored members of the prosecution. "Imagine," Mountz wrote in a letter to his father, "the Judge asking the defense counsel what the law is."

The defense could only object, so often, in fact, that it prompted an unusual query one day from Yamashita's former chief of staff, Muto. "Who is this Mr. Jackson?" he asked.

The defense lawyers realized that he had mistaken the word "objection" for "Jackson." The lawyers joked that his last name was "Not sustained."

The defense lawyers were not the only ones bothered by the evidentiary elasticity. Capt. Norman James Sparnon, who worked with the Allied Translator and Interpreter Section, served as both a prosecution and a defense witness. "The trial stinks. A court that accepts hearsay evidence is a disgrace to the nation it represents," he confided in his diary. "Was told by a member of the war crimes commission that MacArthur had issued an order to the effect 'If the commissioners fail to bring a verdict of Guilty and the death penalty then they will have failed in their duty.' This is of course hearsay, but if such evidence can be used against Yamashita then why not against MacArthur."

Yamashita's defense likewise zeroed in on what the attorneys viewed as a major hole in the prosecution's case. Victim after victim testified to the horrific rapes, murders, and mutilations Japanese troops had committed, but none of the prosecution's more than two hundred witnesses were able to link Yamashita directly to those crimes. "There was not one word or one shred of credible evidence to show that General Yamashita ever ordered the commission of even one of the acts with which he was charged," defense lawyer George Guy later wrote, "or that he ever had any knowledge of the commission of any of these acts, either before they took place, or after their commission."

Many of the news reporters who covered the trial grew sympathetic with Yamashita and his defense lawyers, recognizing that the rules of evidence and proceedings appeared tilted in favor of the prosecution. "It's like a man being tried rightly or wrongly for rape, and finding the girl's father is the judge," one correspondent huffed.

Yank magazine's Robert Schwartz walked out of the courtroom one day and never came back. "I was convinced that he was a man of unusual caliber who was being railroaded," Schwartz wrote. "I left the trial after nine days because I felt as though I were watching a lynching." *Newsweek*'s Robert Shaplen agreed, noting how one of the judges spent each day doodling, while another stared out the window. "In the opinion of probably every correspondent covering the trial, the military commission came into the courtroom the first day with the decision already in its collective pocket."

These sentiments trickled out into the media. "There are wide differences of opinion here regarding the fairness of the hearing," noted an article in the *Los Angeles Times*. "The majority of G.I.'s and Filipinos here appear to think that Yamashita has gotten too many breaks, and some of the natives fear he will get off entirely. On the other hand, an amazing number of correspondents believe that the defense has received unfair treatment and even exhibit sympathy for the accused general." On both sides, passions ran deep. "Yamashita complains he isn't getting a fair trial," opined the *Boston Globe*, "and the complaint comes from the finest baby killer in Asia."

MacArthur, who was in Japan overseeing the occupation, monitored the progress of his former adversary's trial. He grew alarmed at reports that lawyers wanted more time to prepare Yamashita's defense. "Commander in Chief disturbed by reports of possible recess in Yamashita case," his staff cabled. "Doubts need of Defense for more time and desires proceedings completed earliest practicable date."

The prosecution rested its case after nineteen days, turning the trial over to Yamashita's lawyers. The defense called a string of witnesses, ranging from family friends and fellow officers to a member of the Japanese parliament, all of whom painted Yamashita as a moral officer who opposed his nation's military aggression. Some of these witnesses, however, had no firsthand knowledge of what he was like as a commander in the field.

"Among the people of Japan he was respected as one—as a man of highest character," testified Keichoku Yoshida, a Tokyo lawyer and friend.

"General Yamashita believed very greatly in righteousness," added Lt. Gen. Shigetaro Amakasu. "He is a humanitarian."

"Among the Army men, General Yamashita was known as a man of high virtue, and a man of the utmost integrity," said Shigemasa Sunada, a twenty-five-year veteran lawmaker who represented the Japanese city of Kobe.

During his time on the stand, Muto proved a fierce defender of his former commander, highlighting the myriad difficulties Yamashita faced.

"Did General Yamashita ever issue orders for the killing of non-combatant civilians?" prosecutors asked.

"Absolutely not," the bespectacled general fired back.

"Did your headquarters ever receive any reports that Japanese soldiers had killed non-combatant civilians?"

"I have never heard of such a thing."

Captain Sparnon testified that out of the several hundred thousand captured Japanese records, nowhere did his outfit discover an order from Yamashita to destroy Manila. "Have you ever seen an order of General Yamashita ordering the killing of non-combatant civilians in the Philippines Islands?" defense lawyers pressed.

"No, sir, I have not."

Prosecutors countered on cross-examination. "Your knowledge of captured Japanese documents or orders goes only to the written orders, is that not correct?"

Sparnon confirmed.

"You have no knowledge as to orders which may have been transmitted by wire or radio?" Kerr asked.

"No," he replied. "We would not have that."

Some of the testimony was clearly false, including witnesses who argued that the food ration for internees at Santo Tomas was comparable to what Japanese troops received. Lt. Gen. Shiyoku Kou, who was in charge of internment and prisoner of war camps, told commissioners that when he visited the camp in late 1944, internees all appeared healthy, eating fruits, vegetables, and even meat at a time when internees, in fact, survived on dog food, pigeons, and rats. Shizuo Ohashi, a civilian employee who worked at Santo Tomas from 1942 through the camp's liberation, echoed Kou. "There were no deaths from starvations," he told commissioners, "but there has been deaths of men over 60 years of age who died from natural causes."

One question hung over the proceedings as the procession of witnesses testified day after day: Would the Tiger of Malaya take the stand in his own defense?

Colonel Clarke put that mystery to rest at 11:05 a.m. on November 28 when he stood before the commission and announced his next witness.

"General Yamashita," the lawyer called out.

"The sleepy court, wearied by twenty-six days of evidence, awoke with a start," wrote the *Courier.* The *Manila Post* described the scene as "electrified," while the *Manila Chronicle* said the news threw the "courtroom into a mild turmoil."

Against the backdrop of this excitement, Yamashita rose from the chair he had occupied daily for almost a month. He dressed this morning as he had each day, in a green field uniform with his white shirt collar turned out. Four rows of ribbons decorated his left breast and he wore gold spurs on his shined boots. The general walked slowly across the courtroom, raised his right hand, and swore to tell the truth.

"Yamashita wants no mistakes about what he says," the general told his interpreter. "Listen carefully."

All eyes focused on the Japanese commander as he took his seat on the raised platform in front of the crowded courtroom. "The burly general filled the witness chair and tapped his leg with his fingers as he spoke," observed Robert Cromie of the *Chicago Tribune*. "He spoke in a clear, deep voice," added *Newsweek*'s Robert Shaplen. "Thrusting his large, shaven head forward and half-closing his eyes against the floodlights, he stared at the ceiling and at the five American officers on the bench."

During Clarke's examination, Yamashita testified about the struggles he faced, from the threat of Filipino guerrillas and MacArthur's superior forces to the lack of adequate troops, fuel, and rice, pressing issues that consumed him. "Did you ever issue any order directing that any of these atrocities be committed?"

"I definitely did not order these things," he replied.

"Did you ever receive any report, from any sources whatsoever, that any of these atrocities had been committed?" Clarke pressed.

"No," Yamashita said. "The first time that I heard about them was when I got the charges at New Bilibid Prison, and I was very surprised."

Asked if he had anything to add, the Tiger grew fierce in his defense. "I have never ordered such things, and I have never condoned such actions, nor have I ever recognized such actions; and if I had known of them in advance, I would have taken every possible means to have caused them to stop. And if I had found out about them afterwards, I would have punished them to the fullest extent of military law."

Kerr began his cross-examination of Yamashita on November 29. The prosecutor had, throughout his examination of the defense's other witnesses, tried to show that what happened in Manila and the Philippines was not an isolated occurrence, asking questions about Japanese atrocities in Singapore and the Rape of Nanking. He asked Yamashita to look at a large map of the Philippines spiked with pushpins.

"Each red pin or disc represents a major violation of the laws of war, which according to testimony in this case was committed by your troops," Kerr said. "According to the evidence, approximately 60,000 unarmed men, women and children were killed in the Philippine Islands by men under your command. Do you deny to this Commission that you knew or ever heard of any of those killings?"

"I never heard of nor did I know of these events."

"Can you explain to the Commission how all of those murders could have been committed from one end of the Philippine Islands to the other for a period of over seven months without your ever having heard of it?" the prosecutor pressed.

"I absolutely know nothing about it."

"This is your opportunity to explain to this Commission, if you care to do so, how you could have failed to know about those killings."

Yamashita reiterated that he was under attack day and night from American forces. Not only did he arrive in the Philippines unfamiliar with the conditions there, but he also suffered from bad communications and poorly trained troops. "I found myself completely out of touch with the situation. I believe that under the foregoing conditions I did the best possible job I could have done," he said. "If the present situation permits it, I will punish these people to the fullest extent of military law. Certain testimony has been given that I ordered the massacre of all the Filipinos, and I wish to say that I absolutely did not order this, nor did I receive the order to do this from any superior authority, nor did I ever permit such a thing, or if I had known of it would I have condoned such a thing, and I will swear to heaven and earth concerning these points."

Kerr refused to let up. "You have no explanation to make concerning that conduct by your troops; is that correct?" the prosecutor demanded.

"The matter of having combat in Manila is in direct opposition to my ideas and is tactically unsound," Yamashita countered.

"Then you desire to lay the blame and responsibility for these wrongs entirely upon subordinate officers and men; is that correct?"

"The persons who perpetrated these crimes should be punished and the immediate superior units should be subject to investigation and upon the findings they should receive either criminal or administrative punishment."

"You admit, do you, that you failed to control your troops in the Philippines?"

"I have put forth my maximum effort in order to control the troops, and if this was not sufficient, then somehow I should have done more," he said. "Other people might have been able to do more, but I feel that I have done my very best."

"Did you fail to control your troops?" Kerr pressed. "Please answer 'yes' or 'no.'"

"I believe," he fired back, "that I did control my troops."

The three days Yamashita spent on the stand—his testimony stretched more than fifteen hours—resonated with many of the spectators and journalists who covered the proceedings. "When the defense rested, the task of the trial commission no longer seemed simple," wrote *Time* magazine. "Yamashita's spirited defense had suddenly emphasized the lack of precedent for war crimes trials, the vagueness of the charges—violations of the rules of war. The commission had other problems. What was Yamashita—a consummate liar or a victim of circumstance? What was to be his fate? The rope or the firing squad? Prison? Freedom? Manila waited for the answer."

○ ○ ○ ○

AT EIGHT-THIRTY on the morning of December 5, spectators jammed the courtroom of the High Commissioner's Residence, all anxious to hear final arguments in the case of *United States v. Tomoyuki Yamashita*. There was little doubt that the defense's numerous procedural objections throughout the trial, coupled with the critical press accounts, weighed heavily upon the five jurists. That was evident in the statement President Judge Reynolds read aloud behind closed doors to the prosecution and defense. "It is directed that the final arguments be restricted entirely to the charge and bill of particulars, and the material which has been accepted by the Commission as evidence or probative material," Reynolds told the lawyers. "That is to say: the final argument will not be utilized as a means of re-arguing any ruling, decision or policy of the Commission, implied or otherwise. Further, there will be no discussion or criticism, implied or otherwise, as to the propriety of General Styer or General MacArthur's action in convening the commission or the regulations issued for its guidance."

After thirty-two days and hundreds of witnesses, the trial boiled down to the question of whether a commander could be held responsible for the actions of his troops. The defense went first this Wednesday morning. Four of Yamashita's lawyers each tackled a part of his story, from the general's military background and the conditions he inherited in the Philippines to his struggles against Filipino guerrillas and America's superior forces. "The prosecution contends that there was a plan in the Manila atrocities. We do not see any," Milton Sandberg declared. "We see only wild, unaccountable looting, murder and rape. If there be an explanation of the Manila story, we believe it lies in this: Trapped in the doomed city, knowing that they had only a few days at best to live, the Japanese went berserk, unloosed their pent-up fears and passions in one last orgy of abandon." Did the prosecution believe, Sandberg pressed, Yamashita ordered all of the rapes and massacres? "If General Yamashita is not charged with ordering the Manila atrocities, what is the charge?" the lawyer continued. "Is he charged with having failed to punish the 20,000 dead Japanese left in the city after the battle?"

Outside of orders to destroy factories, warehouses, and matériel—legitimate wartime targets—the defense argued most of the destruction in Manila resulted from the twenty-nine-day battle. Sandberg pointed out that American artillerymen fired 155 mm howitzers at point-blank range until buildings collapsed. "The battle of the south side of Manila was a house-to-house, room-to-room battle, and it was a battle of Japanese small arms against American artillery, mortar fire and flame throwers," Sandberg said. "If the Japanese had wanted to destroy the city, why did they not do so in January, after the American landing of Lingayen? Why did they not put to the torch the vast populous sections of Manila, Quiapo, Santa Cruz, Sampaloc, San Juan, Santa Mesa—all highly inflammable, yet left virtually untouched and unharmed?"

Frank Reel argued that many of the atrocities were directed against Filipino guerrillas. "To us the guerrillas were patriots and heroes, and rightly so; but to the Japanese forces they were war criminals," Reel argued. "They were the most dangerous form of war criminal: treacherous, ruthless, and effective." But Yamashita's challenges went beyond battling guerrillas. The general suffered from poor communications—cut landlines and spotty wireless—as well as a fragmented command and scattered forces. "We don't say that these atrocities did not occur," Reel said. "We tried through this trial to show that General Yamashita had no connection with them."

Prosecutor Kerr in his closing statements countered that the slaughter and destruction were far too organized and widespread to have been just a few battle-crazed troops. He added that witness after witness testified to the participation of officers in atrocities. "They were led; they were commanded; they were acting as military units in a military operation," Kerr said. "These were not wild, drunken orgies by individual soldiers on their own! Not at all!" The prosecutor likewise challenged the defense's assertion that guerrillas goaded the Japanese to commit such crimes. How then did that explain the butchery of thousands of women and children—even babies in the arms of mothers? "The whole length of the Philippines was blanketed with one horrible atrocity after another over a period of seven months," he argued. "Tens of thousands of innocent men, women and children were massacred under the most horrible, heartrending conditions, or subjected to the most inhuman tortures and indignities."

Kerr read a sampling of captured Japanese orders and diaries, which detailed the slaughter of civilians: "All natives, both men and women, will be killed."

"Burned 1,000 guerrillas to death tonight," Kerr read from another.

"Kill even women and children who oppose the Emperor."

"Is this warfare?" the prosecutor asked. "We have another explanation for it. We say they are the victims of Yamashita! They are the victims of the type of warfare that was conducted by Yamashita; by the troops under him." Kerr attacked the defense's claim that Yamashita lacked communications, pointing out testimony that had revealed he was in contact with forces in Manila throughout the battle. Along similar lines, he challenged the general's claim that he was too busy fighting to monitor his troops. Yamashita made time for social visits in Manila, Kerr argued, yet never visited internees at Santo Tomas or prisoners in Fort Santiago.

The prosecutor likewise zeroed in on the assertion that the general was a strict disciplinarian. "If we accept that, it makes it all the more unlikely that his subordinates would have violated, as obviously they did in these many, many ways—flagrantly violated—not only the regulations of the Japanese army but the regulations and the principles of mankind, unless they had felt and had known that their conduct was approved and permitted by the accused."

A theme Kerr wove throughout his nearly three-hour closing was that Yamashita had a responsibility, as a commander, to control the actions of all his forces, no different than the way a sea captain is liable for the fate of his ship. "It was his duty to know what was being done by his troops, under his orders, under his commands," Kerr argued. "He failed in his mission in the Philippines; not merely to hold the Philippines for the Japanese, but he failed in his mission here to protect the Philippine people who were in his custody." In closing, Kerr argued that if the commissioners found Yamashita guilty of failure to perform his duty, then the Tiger of Malaya should be executed. "Anything less than the death sentence would be a mockery!" he concluded. "In view of the aggravated nature of the crimes, in view of the measure of the crimes, we recommend that the sentence in the case of death be carried out by hanging."

○ ○ ○ ○

EARLY ON DECEMBER 7, Colonel Kenworthy, who commanded the military police assigned to guard Yamashita, visited the Japanese general in his second-floor cell at the High Commissioner's Residence. As

Yamashita polished off his breakfast, Kenworthy asked if the general was prepared to hear the verdict.

"I am ready," Yamashita answered.

Did the general have an opinion on what decision awaited him?

"There can be only one verdict," he said. "It was decided upon long ago."

Spectators turned out by the hundreds that cloudy afternoon—exactly four years to the day after the Japanese attack on Pearl Harbor—to learn the fate of the Tiger of Malaya, each one passing through a security checkpoint before filing inside where, as a precaution, military police had doubled the normal daily detail. The air was tense this muggy Friday, punctuated in the cavernous ballroom by the occasional cough or shuffle of feet. "Every inch of the court space was packed," observed the Manila *Courier*. "Even the balconies overlooking the court were filled to capacity."

The reporters, many of whom had grown sympathetic to Yamashita, participated in a collegial poll. Of the ten journalists who had covered the trial from gavel to gavel, eight felt Yamashita should be spared the noose. "The verdict will be not guilty," predicted Pat Robinson of International News Service. Robert Stewart of United Press echoed him. "Hanging would be a violation of every law ever written," he said. Anatolio Litonjua of the *Philippine Press* and Lowell Limpus of the *New York Daily News* proved the lone dissenters. "It is inconceivable that Yamashita did not know about the atrocities," Litonjua argued. "He should get the death penalty."

Even James Halsema, who had suffered as an internee and now worked as a stringer for the Associated Press, believed the general should go free. "The prosecution," he wrote in his diary, "has never been able to show that Yamashita issued orders calling for the destruction of Manila or the killing of civilians or POWs."

Reporters weren't the only ones who felt Yamashita might survive. "The Defense were quite wonderful," Captain Sparnon, who served with the Allied Translator and Interpreter Section and was a witness in the case, wrote in his diary after closing arguments. "There is no doubt they have done a magnificent job and I am sure Yamashita has been more than impressed by the effort made on his behalf by men of an enemy country." Armando Malay, a Filipino reporter with the *Manila Chronicle*, agreed. "They have discharged such duty as diligently and as passionately as if they were defending a brother American officer." Even members of the prosecution team were anxious. "Rumor has it," George Mountz confided in a letter, "that they will acquit him."

Regardless of the verdict, the news would be explosive. This was, after all, the first war crimes trial in Asia, a bellwether case that would foreshadow the fate of Japan's leaders. The reporters all wanted to be first with the news, none more than the Associated Press. To beat the competition, reporters devised a system to speed the news. Dean Schedler, who had been one of the first reporters into Santo Tomas, took a seat in the audience. Al Valencia stood just outside the courtroom with a view of Schedler. As soon as the judge announced the verdict, Schedler would flash the news via a finger code. Valencia would relay the outcome to Halsema, who was parked at a phone with an open line connected to a fellow reporter at the wire service's Manila office.

Yamashita entered the courtroom, as always, dressed in a green field uniform, the collar of his white shirt folded out. Campaign ribbons still adorned his left breast. "He carefully laid the envelope in which he kept notes and papers on the table, greeted his lawyers with a slight smile, and sat down," Reel recalled. "He betrayed no sign of nervousness or apprehension. To all appearances, this was just another day of trial."

Kenworthy made his way to the center of the room, turned, and faced the crowd to deliver a stern warning. "There will be no demonstrations," he ordered. "When the judgment is pronounced, you will not utter any sound or make any display, either of pleasure or of dissatisfaction. I know there is a natural impulse to react to so dramatic an event, but in the interests of decorum, you will restrain yourselves."

Yamashita at times stole glimpses at the throngs of spectators. Over the course of the thirty-two-day trial, an estimated sixteen thousand people had attended.

But today was different—today the world would learn whether

one of Japan's most famous generals would die for the destruction of Manila.

"Attention!" Kenworthy hollered at two p.m.

The five judges filed into the courtroom and took their seats behind the bench amid the whir of motion picture cameras and exploding flashbulbs. For a case as high-profile as this, the judges, in their final meeting, had made an unusual pact. "We agreed with one another never to discuss publicly or in public writing anything about the trial of General Yamashita," Presiding Judge Reynolds wrote decades later in a private letter. "We decided this course of action because we believed the very voluminous record would be sufficient for future research, and should stand on its own feet."

"The Commission is in session," Reynolds announced.

The presiding judge, reading from prepared remarks, outlined the charges against Yamashita, noting that the atrocities took place throughout the entirety of his time in command. "The crimes extended throughout the Philippine Archipelago, although by far the most incredible acts occurred on Luzon," Reynolds said. "It is note-worthy that the Accused made no attempt to deny that the crimes were committed."

Over the course of the trial, Reynolds stated, the commission had heard testimony from 286 witnesses in eleven languages, a parade of doctors, lawyers, teachers, and nurses, most of whom had described what happened to them and their loved ones. That testimony was complemented by 423 exhibits, ranging from captured enemy orders and photographs to victim statements. "Many of the witnesses displayed incredible scars of wounds which they testified were inflicted by Japanese from whom they made spectacular escapes followed by remarkable physical recovery," he said. "For the most part, we have been impressed by the candor, honesty and sincerity of the witnesses whose testimony is contained in 4055 pages in the record of the trial."

Reynolds acknowledged the hard-fought arguments on both sides, stating that the prosecution had shown that the crimes were so exten-sive and widespread that such violence must have been either ordered or permitted. He likewise said the defense had successfully portrayed the incredible challenges Yamashita inherited when he took command in the Philippines, from shortages of food, fuel, and equipment to the struggle against an overpowering enemy. Reynolds added that Yamashita and his senior staff all maintained that any such atrocities ran contrary to the general's policies and orders. "Taken at full face value," the judge said, "the testimony indicates that Japanese senior commanders operate in a vacuum, almost in another world with respect to their troops, compared with standards American Generals take for granted."

Spectators hung on every word. "An unearthly silence came over the courtroom as the General continued to read," Mountz wrote in a letter. "I know personally the perspiration began to drop off me as the suspense continued to mount."

Reynolds prepared to wrap up his comments, pointing out that Yamashita was an experienced commander and as such understood the authority and responsibility entrusted to him. "It is absurd," he said, "to consider a commander a murderer or rapist because one of his soldiers commits a murder or rape. Nonetheless, where murder and rape and vicious, revengeful actions are widespread offenses, and there is no effective attempt by a commander to discover and control the criminal acts, such a commander may be held responsible, even criminally liable, for the lawless acts of his troops."

Reynolds paused.

"The Accused, his Senior Counsel and personal interpreter will take position before the commission," the judge ordered.

Yamashita and his legal team approached the bench. The general had prepared a statement, which Hamamoto read aloud. Yamashita said he had at all times, in his battle against MacArthur, conducted himself in accordance with principles of fairness and justice. "I have been arraigned and tried before this Honorable Commission as a war criminal," he said. "I wish to state that I stand here today with the same clear conscience as on the first day of my arraignment and I swear before my Creator and everything sacred to me that I am innocent of the charges made against me."

Reynolds prepared to deliver the verdict.

"The room was deathly still," Kenworthy recalled. "It seemed that all persons therein were holding their breath, not making the slightest noise."

The judge began to read from his prepared remarks in a slow and calm voice. Overhead the bright klieg lights illuminated the room like a Broadway stage. "It was as though the spectators had been splashed in the face with ice water," wrote the reporter for the Manila *Courier*. "Spectators stiffened, eyes glued to Yamashita."

Reynolds said that the commission concluded that the atrocities committed by Yamashita's troops were not sporadic but rather were methodically supervised by Japanese officers. During that time, he had failed to control his forces. "Accordingly upon secret ballot, two-thirds or more of the members concurring, the Commission finds you guilty as charged and sentences you to death by hanging."

Everyone in the courtroom focused on Yamashita as the interpreter whispered the decision to him. "I feel that he must have known what was coming," recalled George Guy, one of his lawyers. "When the final words were translated, there was scarcely a change of expression on his quiet and solemn face." Others observed the same. "Not a muscle moved in his broad face as he took in the import of the verdict," wrote the reporter for the *Manila Times*. "The silence in the courtroom was disturbed only by the whir of movie cameras taking a record of the momentous event."

The general made a curt bow to the commission members before Kenworthy motioned for him to follow him out at two-fifteen p.m. "As the convicted war criminal started leaving the courtroom, the tension broke and people started filing out," the reporter with the *Courier* wrote. "There were no smiles; there were no grimaces."

Newsweek reporter Robert Shaplen, who had seen the worst of the Battle of Manila, cabled his thoughts to his editors. "He maintained to the end, and said so in his final statement, that his conscience was clear and that he was innocent of the charges. I believe he really thought so," the reporter wrote. "What's more I think his legal counsel thought so, too, because after the decision was announced they maintained this conviction privately. I never saw a defense staff take a decision any harder." Others agreed, including Halsema, who wrote of his admiration for Frank Reel: "If I ever were being tried, I'd certainly hope to have him as my lawyer." The former internee, who had more reason than most to want to see the Japanese punished, felt the conviction was a mistake. "I still don't think justice was done," he wrote in his diary, "and think executing Yamashita will be a first-class blunder with unpleasant repercussions in the future."

"C'mon," Colonel Clarke finally said to Reel. "I hate like hell to do this but we better go up and see him."

Outside on the streets word spread quickly of the verdict. "Yamashita will die," crowds chanted in Tagalog.

Filipino newspapers likewise celebrated the news. "Yamashita gets justice," declared the *Manila Chronicle*. "The death sentence," added the *Star Reporter*, "came as an answer to the prayers of the thousands of war widows and orphans."

President Osmeña released a statement. "The Filipino people who have suffered so much at the hands of the cruel enemy feel that justice has been done." Manila councilor Elvira Montenegro filed a resolution with the municipal board, requesting General MacArthur hang Yamashita in the Walled City. "Manila has suffered the brunt of Japanese bestialities and it seems fair that its people should be given the privilege to see Yamashita atone here for all the atrocities committed by his men."

Reporters even tracked down Yamashita's wife in Japan. "The American method of justice is admirably fair," she said. "I am pleased with it."

Back in his cell at the High Commissioner's Residence, Yamashita smoked a cigarette when his defense lawyers came up to visit him. Muto was distraught. "Why must they hang us?" he asked. "Why can't they shoot us like true soldiers."

Yamashita shot him a stern look and then softened. The general shook hands with his lawyers. As a token of his appreciation, he gave to each of them his few belongings. To Harry Clarke, he gave a silver watch, ribbons, and a field tea set he had used from his time in Malaya through Manchuria and now the Philippines. He gave Gordon Feldhaus a three-star gold general's insignia and his general staff *fourragere* cord. To Guy, Yamashita presented his gold-plated presentation spurs because he was a cavalry officer. Frank Reel and Milton Sandberg each received watches, gold good-luck coins, and calligraphy brushes.

Yamashita gave his leather belt to Walter Hendrix. "You're the only man," he said, "fat enough to wear this."

The general had a request for his former chief of staff. That night in the mountains when Yamashita had learned of Japan's surrender, he had told Muto that he planned to stay alive long enough to make sure his troops returned home, a job that now fell to Muto. "That is my last wish," he told him. "That is my last command."

Military police transferred Yamashita that day to Luzon Prisoner of War Camp No. 1, where he was stripped of his belt, pocketknife, and all other items he might use to harm himself. Now that the general had been sentenced to die, America wanted to make sure he lived long enough to suffer that fate. Guards locked Yamashita in a makeshift cell consisting of a concrete floor surrounded on all sides and above by wire mesh. That evening two officers from the Judge Advocate's Office drove out to check on him at ten p.m. "General was lying on a GI cot, dressed in underwear, with most of his person exposed, with a blanket over him. He was sleeping. A guard armed with a rifle, was stationed immediately outside the door of the cell," according to a memo of the visit. "General Yamashita was adequately, carefully and securely confined and it would be almost impossible for him to escape or to successfully attempt suicide."

CHAPTER 25

*"An uncurbed spirit of revenge and retribution,
masked in formal legal procedure for purposes of
dealing with a fallen enemy commander, can do more
lasting harm than all of the atrocities giving rise to
that spirit."*

—SUPREME COURT JUSTICE FRANK MURPHY,
FEBRUARY 4, 1946

YAMASHITA'S LAWYERS MOBILIZED TO PREVENT THE GEN-
eral's execution.

More than three weeks before his conviction in a Manila courtroom, the defense team had filed a petition for writ of habeas corpus and another for prohibition to the Philippine Supreme Court. The
lawyers had argued that the overall charge against Yamashita was too
vague, that the trial against him was unfair, and that the U.S. Army
had no jurisdiction over him. The move had outraged MacArthur.
"Under no circumstances will anyone appear in the Supreme Court
of the Philippines," the general had ordered on November 19, 1945.
"No outside interference will be countenanced and any order by the
Philippine Supreme Court will be ignored."

The Philippine Supreme Court in Intramuros had been destroyed
during the Battle of Manila, so oral arguments were held in an annex
of Malacañan Palace on November 23. Reporters crowded the small
room, fascinated by the concept of Yamashita seeking help in the highest court of the country his forces had destroyed.

Lt. Col. Walter Hendrix exploded during the proceedings that Friday, accusing MacArthur of using the court to railroad his former
adversary. "We contend," Hendrix told the nine black-robed judges
in his Atlanta drawl, "that General MacArthur has taken the law into

his own hands and has disregarded the laws of the United States and the Constitution. He has no authority to act on this case either from Congress or the President of the United States. He is a great soldier and general but not a great lawyer. The orders from General MacArthur regarding this case are illegal."

Hendrix compared Yamashita's trial to the prosecutions of Germans at Nuremburg. "Europe is one world, and there the rules are set up by the United Nations. The other world is in the Pacific and in this world the crimes are being tried by the rules of General MacArthur," he said. "They have ignored every law of the world. They have taken every law and thrown it out the window on Dewey Boulevard."

Hendrix likewise blasted the tribunal. "As far as the commission is concerned, its members have violated every law in the world and have made General MacArthur's orders the law. The members of the commission are not lawyers or justices, such as you and I are, yet they are trying one of the greatest cases," he said. "If you heard the decisions of the court, you would be shocked and amazed."

"Why don't you appeal to General MacArthur?" one of the judges asked.

Spectators erupted in laughter, considering Hendrix had just excoriated the general. "Well, sir," the lawyer replied, "I don't believe I'd do that."

Hendrix then pointed out that the Philippine Constitution gave any person the right to due process under the law, a statement that drew a rebuke from Justice Ramon Ozaeta. "I don't think the makers of our constitution had in mind a person like Yamashita," he said, "who came to our country as an invader."

Hendrix's passion ultimately failed to sway the Philippine Supreme Court, which five days later denied the defense's motions, arguing that the commission was properly formed and that Philippine civil courts lacked jurisdiction.

The defense had expected the denial, but needed the adverse ruling of a local court in order to appeal to the U.S. Supreme Court. But even then, lawyers could not be sure the Supreme Court would hear the case. Another fear centered on whether MacArthur would order Yamashita executed before the Supreme Court decided whether to intervene. The general's lawyers cabled a desperate plea to the clerk of the Supreme Court. "General Tomoyuki Yamashita sentenced to hang. It is feared sentence will be executed before court can act on petition for writ habeas corpus now before court and on petition for writ certiorari now en route to you. We urgently request court to order secretary of war to stay execution until court can act on both petitions."

At the urging of Chief Justice Harlan Fiske Stone, the War Department suggested that MacArthur await the decision of the Supreme Court. The general refused. "It is believed," he wrote on December 8, "that the Supreme Court has no jurisdiction and the military authorities propose to proceed in normal military jurisprudence with the case." MacArthur's extraordinary position, placing himself above the Supreme Court, prompted War Secretary Robert Patterson to intervene. "Secretary of War directs final action in Yamashita case be withheld pending disposal by Supreme Court," Washington cabled the next day. "You will be promptly advised of action taken by Supreme Court."

The defense counsel was jubilant. "The Supreme Court had still not decided to grant us a hearing, but at least Yamashita's life was spared while the problem was under consideration," Reel wrote. The Supreme Court went further; before recessing for Christmas on December 17; it issued an order staying Yamashita's execution until it decided whether to hear the case, a move that prevented the war secretary from changing his mind. "Court requested Secretary of War to advise proper military authorities of this action," Washington wrote. "Secretary of War herewith advises you officially of Court's action and directs you not to take further action in Yamashita case."

The justices of the Supreme Court debated whether to even take up the controversial case. The court's members, no doubt reflecting the diversity of public opinion, were at odds. In a letter earlier that same month, Chief Justice Stone in fact had singled out fellow jurist Robert Jackson, who had taken a leave of absence from the court to work on the Nuremburg trial, describing the prosecution of German war criminals as a "high-grade lynching party." "I don't mind what he does to the Nazis, but I hate to see the pretense that he is running a court or proceedings according to common law," Stone wrote. "That is a little too sanctimonious a fraud to meet my old-fashioned ideas."

On the side of hearing the case stood Justice Hugo Black, who went so far as to draft a proposed statement that he planned to release to the press if his colleagues voted against hearing the case. Black was joined by Justice Wiley Rutledge. "It was a battle royal all the way," he wrote in a private letter to a friend. "It was only after three days of debate in conference and by the narrowest margins that we succeeded in getting a hearing." So controversial was that decision that Justice William Douglas initially demanded the order for oral arguments state he had voted against it, before Stone and several other justices convinced him such a move would only "emphasize the dissension."

The final chapter of one of the ugliest battles of the Pacific War would be written by America's highest court. The War Department agreed to allow three of Yamashita's six lawyers—Clarke, Sandberg, and Reel—to travel from Manila to Washington to present the general's case. The argument would be narrow. The lawyers would not be able to argue Yamashita's guilt or innocence, but only the questions of the lawfulness of the commission, the charges against Yamashita, and the fairness of the evidence. Furthermore, the lawyers operated under no illusion that the Supreme Court would prove friendly ground. After all, this was the same court that only a year earlier had upheld President Franklin Roosevelt's controversial decision to intern Japanese Americans.

In a sign of the times, citizens across the country fired off letters to the justices in Washington, complaining about the court's decision to intervene. "I fail to see why this Supreme Court had to butt into this," wrote J. K. Roach of New York City. "I hope it stays out of the other cases or we will never get the damn criminals hung."

"A dead snake and a dead Jap are both good," griped J. W. Smith from New Orleans. "Alive—both are destructive."

The defense team, barred from seeing Yamashita since his conviction, was granted permission to visit the general on December 23. That

Sunday the lawyers drove out to the prisoner of war camp. Guards had stripped the former Tiger of Malaya of his uniform, forcing him to wear old army fatigues. "I realize that the matters you will discuss before the American court do not concern my guilt or innocence," he said. "I know that there are important legal questions, judicial questions that should be decided, and some of them should be decided for the peace of the world."

Yamashita paused so Hamamoto could interpret. "That is not to say," he continued, "that I don't realize I have a personal stake in the outcome."

The three attorneys flew out of Manila on Christmas Day, touching down four days later at National Airport in Washington. The defense spent the following week preparing to go to battle again before the high court. Promptly at noon on January 7—almost a year to the day when American forces stormed the beaches at Lingayen Gulf—the clerk of court rose. "The Honorable, the Chief Justice and the Associate Justice of the Supreme Court of the United States!" he announced. "Oyez! Oyez! Oyez!"*

Chief Justice Stone entered the courtroom followed by his fellow jurists, all in black robes. "I glanced around the room," Reel wrote. "Every seat was filled. There were lawyers, members of the Department of Justice, officers from our own Judge Advocate's Department, throngs of spectators—the curious who had been drawn by the newspaper headlines." Throughout six hours of oral arguments spread over two days, defense lawyers not only challenged the legality of the commission but also raised important questions of what Yamashita's conviction might one day mean for American leaders. "The case at bar involves more than a precedent to brandish before a defeated enemy," Clarke argued. "It involves a precedent which we must also be ready to apply within our own forces and to acknowledge in all cases of friend and foe alike."

Then it was all over—and the world began the wait to learn whether the Supreme Court would spare Yamashita's life. In Tokyo, MacAr-

---

* This is the traditional call used to open proceedings before the Supreme Court.

thur received periodic updates by cable as the days ticked past. "No decision Yamashita case today."

On February 5 the high court finally handed down its answer, siding 6–2 against Yamashita. Chief Justice Stone, who just two months earlier had compared the German war trials to a lynching, wrote the majority opinion, reiterating that the court had no concern over the guilt or innocence of the Tiger of Malaya but focused instead on the lawful power of the commission to prosecute Yamashita. Stone not only affirmed that the commission that tried Yamashita was legal but also noted that military tribunals as sanctioned by Congress were outside the bounds of the high court to review. "Corrections of their errors of decision is not for the courts," the justice wrote, "but for the military authorities which are alone authorized to review their decisions." Stone took a similar dodge on the admission of objectionable evidence such as affidavits and hearsay testimony. "For reasons already stated," he wrote, "we hold that the commission's rulings on evidence and on the mode of conducting these proceedings against petitioner are not reviewable by the courts, but only by the reviewing military authorities."

On the key question of whether Yamashita could be held liable for the actions of his troops, the court noted that the laws of war presupposed that a commander's duty included making sure his troops did not commit crimes. Failure of an officer to restrain his forces only invited the commission of such atrocities, while stripping a commander of that liability promised to further undermine laws designed to protect civilians. "Those provisions," Stone wrote, "plainly imposed on petitioner, who at the time specified was military governor of the Philippines, as well as commander of the Japanese forces, an affirmative duty to take such measures as were within his power and appropriate in the circumstances to protect prisoners of war and the civilian population."

Justices Wiley Rutledge and Frank Murphy both wrote sharp dissenting opinions. Rutledge's spanned thirty-two-pages—totaling nearly fourteen thousand words, nearly double the length of the court's majority opinion. "More is at stake than General Yamashita's fate," the justice began. "Never before have we tried and convicted an enemy general for action taken during hostilities or otherwise in the course of military operation or duty. Much less have we condemned one for failing to take action." Rutledge went on to attack the proceedings, from the ill-defined charges and the admission of affidavits to the lack of adequate time given to Yamashita's lawyers to prepare a defense. He acknowledged that the defense had talented attorneys, but that was canceled out by the denial of reasonable opportunity for them to perform their jobs, particularly when the charges were doubled on the eve of trial. "I can't believe in the face of this record," he concluded, "that the petitioner has had the fair trial our Constitution and laws command."

Justice Frank Murphy echoed Rutledge in his own thirteen-page opinion, though in far more eloquent prose. Murphy had once served as the governor general of the Philippines and was no doubt sensitive to the emotional impact of the atrocities. Still, the justice argued that the trial was not only procedurally flawed but on a larger level a threat to American values. "That there were brutal atrocities inflicted upon helpless Filipino people, to whom tyranny is no stranger, is undeniable," Murphy wrote. "That just punishment should be meted out to those responsible is also beyond dispute. But these factors do not answer the problem in this case. They do not justify the abandonment of our devotion to justice in dealing with a fallen enemy commander. To conclude otherwise is to admit that the enemy has lost the battle but has destroyed our ideals."

The Fifth Amendment right to due process, Murphy argued, applied to any person accused by the federal government or any of its agencies, with no exception made for enemy belligerents or accused war criminals. Likewise the immutable rights of an individual were not reserved solely for those who win on the battlefield. "They belong to every person in the world, victor or vanquished, whatever may be his race, color or beliefs," he wrote. "They rise above any status of belligerency or outlawry. They survive any popular passion or frenzy of the moment. No court or legislature or executive, not even the mightiest army in the world, can ever destroy them."

Similar to Rutledge, he attacked the limited time given to the defense, the loose rules of evidence, and the charges, highlighting that Yamashita was not actually accused of participating in any of the atrocities or even ordering them. Furthermore, Murphy warned that American generals and civilian leaders needed to be prepared that the court's ruling might one day boomerang on them. "The high feelings of the moment doubtless will be satisfied. But in the sober afterglow will come the realization of the boundless and dangerous implication of the procedure sanctioned today," he wrote. "No one in a position of command in any army, from sergeant to general, can escape those implications. Indeed, the fate of some future President of the United States and his chiefs of staff and military advisers may well have been sealed by this decision."

There was no doubt about Murphy's passion in the case, prompting his receipt of a note from fellow justice Felix Frankfurter, who wrote that he disagreed with his colleague's opinion, but with a caveat. "I wholly respect the utterance of your conscience taking a contrary view." Rutledge felt the same, though the verbiage of opinion had been more academic than passionate. In a letter to a friend, Rutledge wrote that the *Yamashita* case would one day outrank *Dred Scott* in the court's history, the controversial 1857 decision that upheld slavery. "These trials cannot be glorified now and the time will come when they will be generally condemned," he wrote. "American justice just isn't done this way, whoever the accused may be, except that is in a time of war fever."

American news outlets delivered mixed reviews of the Supreme Court's decision. "The Yamashita case sets a precedent. We believe it is a good one," wrote the *New York Times*. "It is that high officers are responsible for the acts of men under their command when the acts are as wanton and widespread as were those of Yamashita's troops in the Philippines." The *Los Angeles Times*, while complimenting the zeal of the dissenting justices, argued military commissions are a more expeditious means of justice. "The decision of the court is clear-cut and dooms Yamashita to the noose."

Others papers, like the *Washington Post*, proved more critical, arguing that Yamashita never would have been convicted had he been afforded a judicial trial: "We shall not make progress in establishing a regime of law and justice in the world by ignoring the basic elements of fair play—not even in the trial of war criminals." A few noted there was more at stake than just Yamashita's neck. "This case rises far beyond the fate of one Japanese commander," argued the *St. Louis Star-Times*. "What is really at issue is the respect of American law for the rights of all men."

Letters and telegrams meanwhile cluttered the inboxes of the two dissenting justices. "Thank God for six sane men against two Jap coddlers in the Supreme Court," cabled Mrs. D. C. Cowles of California. "Shame. Shame. Shame."

Rutledge confided in a friend that he expected his dissent would whip up a "tornado," but he was stunned by how many people wrote in support and to commiserate over the majority's decision. "I never thought that I should live to be ashamed of my country, and yet such is the case today," wrote Willard Fraser of Texas.

"The effect of the majority decision was, in my opinion, to find American justice guilty," added Fred Dewey of Washington.

"May it be to your everlasting glory that you have responded to this call of conscience," wrote Robert Burch of California.

The Supreme Court had cleared the way for the army to execute General Yamashita. Only one step remained—Douglas MacArthur's review and approval of the sentence. The two men had only a year before faced off in one of the greatest battles of World War II. Now Yamashita's fate rested in the hands of his former foe. Would MacArthur approve of his sentence, or would he show mercy?

The general wrote out his answer by hand. "It is not easy for me to pass penal judgment upon a defeated adversary in a major campaign," he began. "I have reviewed the proceedings in vain search for some mitigating circumstance on his behalf. I can find none." MacArthur noted that a soldier's duty included the protection of the weak and unarmed, a duty Yamashita violated. "This officer," he wrote, "of proven field merit, entrusted with high command involving authority adequate to responsibility, has failed this irrevocable standard; has failed his duty to his troops, to his country, to his enemy, to mankind;

has failed utterly his soldier faith. The transgressions resulting there-from as revealed by the trial are a blot upon the military profession, a stain upon civilization and constitute a memory of shame and dis-honor that can never be forgotten."

MacArthur not only approved the findings and sentence but ordered Yamashita to be hanged "stripped of uniform, decorations and other appurtenances signifying membership in the Military Pro-fession." The review, described by the *Los Angeles Times* as a "chill, scathing denunciation," left little doubt of the hostility he harbored for the general whose forces had destroyed his beloved Manila.

Yamashita's lawyers made one final effort to save him, appealing to President Harry Truman to commute his sentence to life in prison, earning a second stay of execution. Allied occupation forces in Tokyo meanwhile clamped down on the Japanese press, barring any unfavor-able commentary on MacArthur's decision, even as a petition drive gathered eighty-six thousand signatures in the hopes of convincing American authorities to allow him an honorable death. "I thought and prayed that the sentence would be lessened or at least Yamashita would be given a soldier's death," said Lt. Gen. Yoshio Kozuki, who served as vice minister of demobilization. "This is brutal."

Lt. Gen. Mamoru Hara, who also worked in the demobilization ministry, predicted possible public demonstrations in Japan in oppo-sition to Yamashita's hanging like a common criminal. Both Kozuki and Hara complained about MacArthur's order to strip the former Tiger of Malaya of his uniform and decorations. "We are heirs to the samurai tradition," Kozuki said. "In those days even the robe which a soldier wore at his death had special significance, and a man was allowed to die honorably."

Reporters tracked down Yamashita's wife, who was more stoic. "I have been prepared for the decision," she told Japanese journalists.

In the end, President Truman refused to intervene. As the Asso-ciated Press noted, the president "did not even accord the dignity of formal rejection." He instead sent a secretary to deliver the news to reporters, while the Pentagon released a statement. "The War Department has been advised that the President will take no action on the petition for clemency filed by counsel for General Tomoyuki Yamashita," the notice read. "General MacArthur has been given this information." One reporter was more vivid in his characterization: "The doom of the despoiler of Manila was sealed."

Yamashita's lawyers, saddled with a defendant none had initially wanted, had taken the case of an enemy war criminal from a battered ballroom in Manila to the highest court in the United States and lastly to the desk of the American president.

But all involved knew there was no other play left to make. "It was indeed the end of our efforts," Reel recalled, "and our client's chance to live."

The Pentagon cabled the news to MacArthur: "The Secretary of War directs me to advise you that you have authority to take such action in the case as you deem advisable." MacArthur in turn relayed the news to General Styer. "You are authorized to proceed with the execution without further delay."

○ ○ ○ ○

IN THE PHILIPPINES, preparations for Yamashita's execution commenced. The municipal board of Manila passed a resolution, requesting the general be hanged in the Walled City where the Japanese had slaughtered thousands of innocent men, women, and children. "Intramuros," the resolution stated, "hallowed by the blood of our martyrs, consecrated by history, but destroyed and rendered desolate by the Japanese, should be made to rise again in its true light to command the admiration of the whole world, by making it the site for the public hanging of General Yamashita."

American authorities meanwhile planned to bar reporters and photographers from the execution, refusing to release even the time and date of the hanging, a move that led the *Manila Post* to later label it "the most closely guarded secret since the end of the war." "After the execution is accomplished," orders demanded, "the press will be furnished a simple factual statement generally limited to a statement of time and place, behavior of accused just prior to execution and any last words." On February 21, General Styer ordered the commanding officer of the Philippine Detention and Rehabilitation Center to execute Yamashita in two days "at an hour or hours to be fixed by you."

○ ○ ○ ○

IN THE EARLY MORNING hours of February 23, 1946, exactly one year after American troops stormed the Walled City, guards came for General Yamashita. In preparation for his execution, military police had transferred him from the prisoner of war camp to the Philippine Detention and Rehabilitation Center at Los Baños, placing him in a rudimentary cell with a tin roof and walls of meshed invasion matting.

Two days earlier Yamashita had written a final 120-word letter, reiterating what he told the judges who sentenced him. He had done his best to control his troops and would meet God unashamed. He closed by thanking his lawyers for his dogged defense. "I don't blame my executioners," he wrote. "I will pray God bless them."

On a more personal level, the Great Cedar, who began the war years earlier with a poem, prepared to meet his death the same way—in verse:

The world I knew is now a shameful place
There will never come a better time
For me to die.

For his final meal, Yamashita ate asparagus and bread, washing it down with a beer before he closed his eyes for a few hours of sleep, snoring loudly, as always, until the guards came for him. Per MacArthur's orders, he dressed in army-issued khaki shirt and trousers, stripped of all insignia of rank and medals. Guards then bound his hands and hurried him quietly from his cell, so as not to alarm the ten thousand incarcerated Japanese soldiers in nearby stockades, the remnants of his defeated army. "We were sorry for the General but we were too hungry, fed up, and war-weary to consider any form of protest," one later said. "All we wanted to do was to go home."

Guards escorted Yamashita that Saturday morning into a nearby sugarcane field where workers had constructed a primitive gallows painted black in a clearing surrounded by several trees, including a towering mango whose large canopy sheltered the gallows. Several huge floodlights illuminated the scene, encircled by an additional fence of wire mesh and green camouflage.

Lt. Charles Rexroad waited atop the gallows for Yamashita. The forty-two-year-old son of a traveling Methodist minister, Rexroad had served as a guard at San Quentin before the war, no doubt aided by his towering size; he stood six foot three inches tall and weighed 245 pounds. Rexroad would, during his time in the Philippines as an innocuously titled "theater technician," hang fifty-three war criminals, developing such a proficiency that he would later brag that he could fasten a man's ankles, secure his arms and hands, slip a noose over his neck, and adjust the knot in less than fourteen seconds. "Putting a rope around a man's neck is like pointing a gun at him," the moustached hangman often said. "Don't do it unless you mean to kill him."

The stars shone down on this warm morning, the only sound the rhythmic hum of the generator that powered the floodlights. The crunch of gravel signaled Yamashita's approach, flanked by an interpreter and a Buddhist priest. "One man catches all eyes," Rexroad wrote that night, "the central figure whose hands are bound in front." Four official witnesses watched as the Japanese general climbed the thirteen stairs, appearing calm and stoical. At the top he asked for permission to bow toward Tokyo, which was granted. Rexroad then went to work, positioning him between the two uprights. "There is no lost motion" he wrote, "straps are secured, the noose is placed over the condemned man's head; the bulging knot is pulled taut under the left ear."

The Buddhist priest began to chant in a high-pitched voice.

"Have you any last words to say?" the executioner asked.

The interpreter translated for Yamashita.

"I will pray for the Emperor's long life and his prosperity forever," he said.

Yamashita, who had defeated the British at Singapore, had landed in the Philippines convinced he would die. This morning that time arrived.

Rexroad wielded his knife, slicing the rope that held the counterweight. The trapdoor sprang open at 3:02 a.m., and Yamashita dropped six feet, coming to halt with a sudden, arresting jerk. The general bounced once and then swayed, his body turning in an arc as the priest's chant rose to a crescendo and then faded.

"I pronounce this man dead," the medical examiner declared at 3:27 a.m.

Undertakers transported Yamashita's remains to the morgue, where technicians stitched him inside a blanket. Attendants then lifted his body atop a canvas stretcher and hauled the general out to the Japanese cemetery at Luzon Prisoner of War Camp No. 1, about twenty five miles south of the capital. There, amid a sea of graves, his final resting place marked only by a white post from which hung his dog tags, Yamashita was buried, as one news report noted, "among soldiers whose misdeeds sealed his doom."

EPILOGUE

*"The Manila of 1941 was a unique Manila, a Manila
that had never existed before, a Manila that would
never exist again."*

—WILLIAM DUNN,
CBS NEWS CORRESPONDENT

THE PEARL OF THE ORIENT—THE STAR OF TOURISM BRO-
chures and steamship ads—today exists only in history books,
museum plaques, and fading memories. As former internee Natalie
Crouter noted in her diary one afternoon in March 1945, just days
after the guns fell silent: "The past is dead."

And nowhere was that more true than in Manila. The tropical city
whose sinuous canals, broad bay front, and ancient Walled City had
once inspired famed urban planner Daniel Burnham in his quest to
build the perfect American city in Asia had vanished in a battle unlike
any other in the Pacific War.

But the twenty-nine-day fight represented more than just the
destruction of roads, buildings, and sadly even lives. The battle served
as the violent end to America's colonial experiment in the Philippines,
symbolized by the pulverization of the grand neoclassical public structures that had long represented Washington's influence in the islands—
the General Post Office, City Hall, and the Legislature, Finance, and
Agriculture buildings. Much of the capital and its economy still lay
in ruins just sixteen months later, when the United States granted the
Philippines independence on July 4, 1946.

It proved an ironic twist that the bloody epilogue of America's
imperial story should have been written in part by Douglas MacArthur, whose father had helped capture Manila almost a half-century

earlier. Father and son not only bookended this American epoch but proved pivotal players in two of the most destructive periods of Philippine history, which in the end cost hundreds of thousands of lives.

Few cities in World War II suffered as much as Manila, which endured three years of Japanese occupation that ruined the economy, triggered widespread starvation, and shredded the social fabric. The battle to liberate the city proved an even greater nightmare. Not only did the war rob the Philippines of its capital, but it also destroyed generations of families, the effects of which still ripple through lives even today. "By the end of the war, we had nothing," recalled journalist Joan Orendain. "All we had was our memories—death's stench, the hunger, the blood, the terrible sounds of bombs, grenades, and bullets, the great fires, the odor of charred bodies and charred wood, and the eeriest sounds of all—the whistling of a bomb about to hit, and the keening over the slain, in its aftermath. We hear those sounds today as clearly as we heard them then."

Manila has never truly recovered from the battle. Though many of the landmark structures eventually were rebuilt—the Walled City lay in ruins and was filled with squatters for decades—much of the postwar investment was aimed at Makati, just south of the capital. There stand the steel and glass high-rises that house the banks, department stores, and international corporations—a shiny new city next to the old. There are still traces of Manila's prewar grandeur and history. Workers rebuilt the Legislature, which today houses the National Museum of Fine Arts. The Manila Hotel still draws thousands of tourists a year, including many Japanese, and MacArthur's former penthouse home has been turned into a guest suite. Tourists can explore the rebuilt Walled City in bike rickshaws and tour Fort Santiago, where plaques outside the dungeons memorialize the hundreds who died. In contrast, the site of the old German Club, where the Japanese burned hundreds to death, remains an empty field—hallowed ground.

Yamashita's wife later petitioned the American government for his remains, which eventually were transferred to Japan, where the conqueror of Malaya and Singapore is buried in the Tama Reien Cemetery in Tokyo. MacArthur, for all his efforts, vanquished his opponent not on a chaotic smoke-filled battlefield but in a staid courtroom in downtown Manila. Yamashita's loyal chief of staff Akira Muto, who was hanged in 1948 alongside the general's onetime rival Hideki Tojo, defended the Tiger of Malaya until the end, even though his spirited testimony and subsequent prison writings proved self-serving, considering he was convicted for his own role in the Rape of Nanking. "He was executed for the crimes which he knew nothing of, which his men committed regardless of what he said," Muto later wrote. "Yamashita did his best, as a Japanese warrior should, and I believe our General is innocent. I can only depend upon the judgments that will be made by future historians."

Muto was not the only one to follow Yamashita into court. The Shimbu Group commander and Iwabuchi's immediate superior, General Yokoyama, likewise was tried for war crimes in a case that mirrored the one against Yamashita, down to the testimony of many of the same witnesses. He, too, was sentenced to die. Troops likewise captured Takesue Furuse, who commanded the Southern Force and was the only senior leader under Admiral Iwabuchi to survive the battle for the Philippine capital. On March 21, 1949, in a Manila courtroom, Furuse pleaded guilty to six charges of ordering the massacre of civilians. Court member Col. Antonio Sayson asked if Furuse understood he was surrendering his rights to a trial.

"I am responsible as commander," he said, "and I still plead guilty."

The court, stating that he had shown leadership by taking responsibility for his actions, spared Furuse the rope, sentencing him instead to death by musketry.

"May God have mercy on your soul!" the court president concluded.

But it was not God who saved Furuse and Yokoyama.

Philippine president Elpidio Quirino, in one of his final acts in office in 1953, pardoned Furuse, Yokoyama, and scores more Japanese war criminals. What made the move all the more powerful was that Yokoyama had been convicted of the murders of Quirino's wife and three of his children, who were all gunned down during the Battle of Manila. "I am doing this," Quirino said, "because I do not want my children and my people to inherit from me hate for people who might yet be our friends."

Yamashita's trial and its unorthodox regulations occasionally invite debate among legal scholars and historians over the question of fairness. It was an argument his defense hammered throughout the trial and one his zealous attorney Frank Reel later expounded on in his own 1949 book, *The Case of General Yamashita*. Even decades later the trial rankled Yamashita's lawyers. "I think we made a hell of a mistake," George Guy said in 1967. "His case was a sad chapter in our military and judicial history."

Maj. Gen. Russel Reynolds, the presiding judge in the case, later regretted the pact the court members made to never speak publicly about the trial. In a private 1970 letter, he wrote that the court's silence allowed Reel, Guy, and others to shape the public narrative of the trial. For Reynolds and his fellow judges, who he revealed voted unanimously to convict and hang Yamashita, the voluminous trial transcript filled with page after page of eyewitness testimony was "damning." Furthermore, Reynolds refuted any suggestion that MacArthur had dictated the trial's outcome. "After weighing all the evidence with the utmost care, and after applying my own knowledge gained from experience of what a commanding general can and cannot do to control the actions of troops, I reached my own personal conclusion in which my conscience remains clear as a bell," Reynolds later wrote. "The accused was clearly guilty as charged."

What happened in Manila in February 1945 was not an isolated outbreak of barbarity but part of a pattern of Japanese brutality that played out across Asia, from the Rape of Nanking to the slaughter of an estimated 250,000 Chinese civilians in the aftermath of Jimmy Doolittle's April 1942 raid on Tokyo. Yamashita's own troops had committed similar atrocities earlier in the war in Malaya, and had America not hanged him, in all likelihood, either the British or Australians would have. Even now, more than seven decades after the Battle of Manila, it is hard not to read the thousands of pages of raw victim statements and sift through scores of photographs of the mutilated survivors and appreciate the context of that time and the sentiment of so many in the Philippines: someone had to be responsible, someone had to pay the ultimate price.

MacArthur is still a revered figure by many in the Philippines, more than a half-century after his death in 1964 at the age of eighty-four and despite the criticism of some that American artillery played a large role in the city's destruction, both in lives lost and in property ruined. "Douglas MacArthur bears as much responsibility as Sanji Iwabuchi for the cruel fate that was inflicted on Manila," concluded Filipino historian Alfonso Aluit, author of *By Sword and Fire*. American William Brady, who survived the Japanese occupation and the battle, agreed. "One side killed and destroyed us willfully," he wrote. "The other side killed and destroyed us willy-nilly."

A towering statue of MacArthur guards the dock on Corregidor from where the general made his nighttime escape in the early days of the war. Despite his close ties and affinity for the Philippines, MacArthur returned only twice more after the war: the first time to witness the nation's independence, and the second in 1961 to celebrate the fifteenth anniversary of that occasion, a trip he described as a "sentimental journey." Adoring crowds cheered that summer day as the feeble general emerged from the plane with a salute, dressed as always in a khaki uniform and cap. "My life has been interwoven with yours for nearly sixty years," MacArthur told those gathered. "Here I have lived my greatest moments. Here I have my greatest memories."

Yamashita's hanging did little to provide resolution for the victims, even as the rope that snapped his neck was cut up into six-inch pieces and passed out to some survivors of the Bataan Death March. Many victims would battle years of physical torment, including Cayetano Lagdameo, who survived Japanese efforts to decapitate him with a sword in the Singalong death house, forever tattooing his neck with a ten-inch scar. "During cold days," he said years later, "the scar still aches." Other victims wrestled with emotional wounds. American nun Sister Mary Trinita Logue, who was waterboarded at Fort Santiago, was so traumatized by the torture that she struggled just to take showers. Five-year-old Fernando Vasquez-Prada, who watched marines butcher his mother, father, and three brothers at De La Salle, refused to speak for two years. "I could not talk," he later said, "could not say a word." Scores more struggled to understand the level of barbarity inflicted upon them. "It was just total hatred and savagery," explained

Juan Jose P. Rocha, whose mother was killed by shrapnel. "You cannot explain it."

More than two decades ago, survivors of the battle formed an organization—the Memorare Manila 1945 Foundation—dedicated to preserving the story of the civilian sacrifices of the city's liberation. The foundation, led by the now-deceased Rocha, worked to compile a detailed accounting of those killed. The group published questionnaires in Manila newspapers, asking readers to submit names of family members killed. The response proved overwhelming. The organization's files, which are open to researchers at the Filipinas Heritage Library in Makati, are filled with painful tales of tragedy. More than a few list the cause of death as American shelling.

"Landmine explosion," one wrote. "Body blown to bits and was never found."

"Burned alive in her house," read another. "Her screams were unbearable."

"Raped and bayonetted."

Even a half-century later, many of the questionnaires revealed the grief and anguish that still haunted survivors. Loreto Franco Racho listed her father, two sisters—ages fourteen and fifteen—and maternal grandmother who were shot by Japanese troops in Ermita. "I saw them all die," she wrote, "all four of them."

Angie Abad Santos witnessed the bayoneting of her father by the Japanese and the decapitation of her brother. "On the morning of February 14th, the Americans came, but for what? For my mother and me, it was the end of our world," she wrote in her questionnaire. "The pain is still there, the nightmares are there, the dreams that they may suddenly come back alive and well—I have had those for the last 50 years."

To memorialize those killed, the organization recruited sculptor Peter de Guzman, who designed a statue of a weeping mother cradling a dead infant in her arms. Around her are the bodies of other victims. The powerful statue, which was dedicated at the fiftieth anniversary of the battle, stands in the Plazuela de Santa Isabel at the corner of General Luna and Anda streets, almost midway between San Agustin and the rebuilt Manila Cathedral—a fitting location, given the horror that unfolded inside the Walled City. The inscription on the statue provides an epitaph for the tens of thousands of men, women, and children who died during those three terrible weeks in February 1945. "This memorial is dedicated to all those innocent victims of war, many of whom went nameless and unknown to a common grave, or never even knew a grave at all, their bodies having been consumed by fire or crushed to dust beneath the rubble of ruins. Let this monument be the gravestone for each and every one," the statue reads. "May they rest in peace as part now of the sacred ground of this city: the Manila of our affections."

ACKNOWLEDGMENTS

Nonfiction books are like historical scavenger hunts, and as such, I owe a great thanks to the army of archivists and researchers who helped me hunt down the innumerable pieces of the narrative puzzle. At the National Archives in College Park, Maryland, I want to thank Nate Patch and Eric Van Slander, the two of whom have been an incredible assistance to me with this book as well as my previous ones. Likewise, Jim Zobel at the MacArthur Memorial Library and Archives was a great help, demonstrating time and again his unrivaled mastery of all things MacArthur. André Sobocinski, with the Navy's Bureau of Medicine and Surgery, went above and beyond to help me locate important records on the suffering endured by so many at Bilibid Prison. Down in the great state of Texas, I want to thank Lou Jurika, whose father was one of the first officers into Manila and who has an amazing family archive, which he graciously shared.

I am likewise indebted to many people in the Philippines who assisted me in my research. Thanks go to Maria Cecilia Ayson at the Filipinas Heritage Library in Makati. Likewise, the wonderful John Silva and Mike Henderson were so accommodating during my visit to the Ortigas Foundation Library in Pasig City. Through John, I had the opportunity to meet and visit with Battle of Manila survivor Alberto Montilla, who in his lovely home boasts quite possibly the greatest personal library of World War II literature related to the Philippines. Montilla generously gifted me a copy A.V.H. Hartendorp's comprehensive two-volume history *The Japanese Occupation of the Philippines*, an incredibly rare and important book that I treasure.

I owe thanks to Dr. Ricardo Trota "Rico" Jose at the University of the Philippines. He is not only one of the foremost experts on World

War II in the Philippines but an entertaining host who wasn't shy about demonstrating his handheld Japanese air raid siren, regardless of its affect on his nearby colleagues. I also want to thank Rico's brother, Regalado Trota Jose, who is the archivist at the University of Santo Tomas. It was an honor to spend time with famed economist and historian Dr. Benito Legarda, Jr., a wonderful storyteller who shared with me powerful anecdotes of life during the Japanese occupation. I also want to thank Karl-Wilhelm Welteke, a modern-day Indiana Jones who, armed with a handheld GPS, took me on a two-day adventure through the jungles of Corregidor.

Others I am indebted to include Battle of Manila survivors Rod Hall, Edgar Krohn, Joyce Velde, Juergen Goldhagen, and Lourdes Montinola, along with fellow historian Peter Parsons, who has produced several great documentaries on the Philippines during World War II. Paul Whitaker graciously shared photos from his excellent collection, and Nelly Fung helped enlighten me on the tremendous work of her parents, Jessie and Marcial Lichauco. Thanks as well go to Seth Mydans and the other family members of famed *Life* magazine photographer Carl Mydans, who was one of the first journalists in Manila. I also want to thank William Leo Coakley, heir to the wonderful writer, Robin Prising. I owe so much to my dear friend and *tokayo* Jim Litton, who repeatedly went out of his way to help me. Jim not only sat for a lengthy oral history about his family's ordeal during the battle, but he personally escorted me through the city, taking me inside the Philippine General Hospital, De La Salle College, and the Manila American Cemetery, not to mention treating me to a delicious lunch one afternoon at the landmark Manila Polo Club. Along similar lines, I owe a great debt to Jack Garcia, who now lives in Australia. That Jack and his family survived the battle was nothing short of miraculous, and it is an honor to share his story.

Closer to home, I owe a debt to the wonderful folks at the Citadel's Daniel Library, who have been so great to me over the years. Special thanks go to David Goble and Pamela Orme, who treat me like family each time I visit. The same is true for the great individuals at the Charleston County Public Library, including my friend Stephen Schwengel and Sonja Chapman, who helps me with my mountain of interlibrary loans. Several other writers provided me with records and leads, including Joseph McCallus, author of the excellent book *The MacArthur Highway and Other Relics of American Empire in the Philippines*. Nathaniel Helms graciously shared with me the diary of Yamashita's executioner, whom he met in Texas, while John Bruning, author of *Indestructible*, handed over his vast collection of photos. Thanks as well go to Michel Paradis, who provided me with the interrogation notes of Hidecki Tojo, and my good friend Steve Moore, who wrote the terrific book *As Good as Dead* about the Japanese massacre of American prisoners of war on the Philippine Island of Palawan.

Pulling together so many records from varying sources into a cohesive and accurate story is always a challenge. As the manuscript took shape, I was fortunate to have many volunteer readers in the United States and the Philippines, including several members of the wonderful Memorare Manila 1945 Foundation, an organization dedicated to preserving the memory of the Battle of Manila. For their gracious help, I want to thank Dr. Rico Jose, Lou Jurika, Jim Litton, Jack Garcia, Santo Tomas survivor Angus Lorenzen, Rod Hall, Joan Orendain, and Jose M. Cabarrus. I am indebted to my amazing editor at Norton, John Glusman, whose powerful book *Conduct Under Fire*, chronicling his father's ordeal as a prisoner of war, is a must-read for anyone interested in the Philippines. John spent countless hours going line by line through this manuscript, using his gift for language and storytelling at each step to help improve the narrative. I also want to thank his ever-patient assistant, Lydia Brents. Copyeditor Janet Biehl was an absolute wonder. Not only did she help make sure I didn't embarrass myself, but her edits and recommendations were tremendous. Thanks as well are due to Norton's marketing and publicity departments, both of which have proven invaluable over the years. I likewise want to thank my wise and terrific agent, Wendy Strothman, who has been a tireless advocate of my work for more than a decade. Last but not least, I owe a tremendous debt to my wonderful family. My amazing wife, Carmen Scott, must feel like she lives on the front lines as she not only listens daily to the stories of my research but also gives each chapter its first and no doubt painful read. Carmen's support is equaled by that of our two beautiful children, Isa and Grigs, with whom I love to share the wonder of history.

NOTE ON SOURCES

THE BATTLE OF MANILA LASTED JUST TWENTY-NINE DAYS YET produced tens of thousands of pages of records, from official military reports and victim statements to the individual diaries and letters of those who survived the horror in the Philippine capital.

The National Archives and Records Administration in College Park contains significant battle-related records, including the naval war diaries and action reports for the invasion of Lingayen Gulf. Likewise, it houses the voluminous army records on the urban fight, ranging from the field artillery and tank battalions to the medical clearing companies and prisoner of war interrogation reports.

In addition to military records, researchers can peruse thousands of pages of atrocity reports and sworn statements from survivors of the Japanese butchery, many taken bedside by investigators in field hospitals. The report on atrocities in the Walled City, for example, runs some four hundred pages, the rapes at the Bay View totaled almost eight hundred, and the materials on the torture and suffering endured at Fort Santiago topped out at over twelve hundred pages. These statements and the accompanying photographs of victim wounds offer a chilling and personal view of the horror that unfolded during those few weeks. Complementing those records are the trial transcripts for Gen. Tomoyuki Yamashita, who as commander of Japanese forces in the Philippines was convicted and executed for the atrocities in Manila, and other senior commanders, including Shizuo Yokoyama, Takesue Furuse, and Masatoshi Fujishige. Yamashita's transcript alone totaled 4,055 pages, a tally which did not include the more than seventeen hundred pages of exhibits.

Gen. Douglas MacArthur's extensive personal papers are divided between two archives. The National Personnel Records Center in St. Louis holds the general's official military file, totaling more than 4,200 pages and including everything from his efficiency reports, correspondence, and commendations to his medical records and even autopsy. The best place to study the general, however, is the MacArthur Memorial Archive and Library in Norfolk, Virginia. This great institution not only houses important papers and artifacts from MacArthur's life and years in uniform but many excellent collections of letters and diaries of his senior aides and internees at Santo Tomas. Two other vital institutions include the Library of Congress and the U.S. Army Heritage and Education Center, which hold the papers of some of the judges who presided over Yamashita's case in the Philippines and the Supreme Court justices who sealed his fate.

The Philippines naturally is home to several important archives. The Filipinas Heritage Library in Makati is a must-stop for anyone interested in the Battle of Manila. The library houses the extensive files of the Memorare Manila 1945 Foundation, an organization founded by battle survivors. These records include hundreds of completed questionnaires that, like the victim statements on file at the National Archives, provide a powerful window into the civilian deaths. In addition, the library is home to the Roderick Hall Collection, one of the best assemblages of books related to the war in the Philippines and the liberation of Manila. More important, the collection includes many unpublished manuscripts and diaries that cannot be found elsewhere.

The American Historical Collection in Quezon City is another invaluable resource, largely for its decades of back issues of the *Bulletin*, which published many important articles and diaries on life during the Japanese occupation and the subsequent liberation of Manila. The archives at the University of Santo Tomas, where several thousand civilians suffered internment for more than three years, also boasts fascinating artifacts, letters, and official records, including the war damage claim that tallies the destruction down to the number Bausch and Lomb microscopes lost. The Ortigas Foundation Library in Pasig City is another important stop; so, too, is the Manila Hotel archives, which include fascinating photos of this landmark property, including pictures of the inside of MacArthur's penthouse home before it was destroyed.

In addition to archival sources, I interviewed survivors in the United States and the Philippines and found it helpful to visit many of the battle and atrocity sites throughout Manila as well as on Corregidor. While many of the buildings were destroyed during the fight, a surprising number still exist, including the Philippine General Hospital, San Agustin Church, De La Salle University (formerly College), and Fort Santiago, which includes the dungeons where hundreds of dead were discovered. I found it particularly powerful to accompany survivor Jim Litton on a personal tour of Philippine General Hospital, where his family sought shelter in the anteroom of an elevator shaft. It likewise proved haunting to climb the steps at De La Salle and sit in the chapel where so many were slain.

There are some excellent published works that detail the Japanese occupation and the battle that were vital to my research. Many of those unfortunately were published only in the Philippines and can be difficult to find. Those include A.V.H. Hartendorp's comprehensive two-volume history *The Japanese Occupation of the Philippines*, Tressa Roka Cates's terrific *The Drainpipe Diary*, Marcial P. Lichauco's *"Dear Mother Putnam,"* Robin Prising's beautiful memoir of Santo Tomas, *Manila, Goodbye*, Pacita Pestaño-Jacinto's *Living with the Enemy*, and Joaquin "Jack" L. Garcia's *It Took Four Years for the Rising Sun to Set (1941–1945)*. Most of this book, however, is based on primary sources, like official reports, diaries, and sworn statements, which are detailed in the extensive endnotes. It would be impossible to list all the primary sources I consulted, a tally that would run into the tens of thousands. Even a list of the newspaper articles would run into the high hundreds. As such, I have chosen to include only a select bibliography of the books I consulted and found most useful.

The Battle of Manila was so gruesome that it's difficult to comprehend or even believe humans are capable of such barbarity. As a result, I have chosen to quote liberally throughout the book from the first-hand accounts of those who survived. I felt paraphrasing their stories would risk sacrificing the intimacy and authenticity of the terror and tragedy so many endured. Simply put: it's more powerful to hear someone's story directly than via a middleman. All quotes and dialogue in this book come from official military reports, captured Japanese records, victim statements, trial transcripts, memos, cables, letters, diaries, news stories, oral histories, and memoirs, both published and unpublished, and in some cases from the recollections of those involved.

ARCHIVES AND LIBRARIES

○ Air Force Historical Research Agency, Montgomery, Ala.
○ Allen Country Public Library, Fort Wayne, Ind.
○ American Historical Collection, Quezon City, Philippines
○ Archives of the Episcopal Church, Austin, Tex.
○ Australian War Memorial, Canberra, Australia
○ Charleston County Public Library, Charleston, S.C.
○ Daniel Library, The Citadel, Charleston, S.C.
○ Filipinas Heritage Library, Makati City, Philippines
○ Franklin D. Roosevelt President Library and Museum, Hyde Park, N.Y.
○ Hoover Institution Archives, Stanford University, Palo Alto, Calif.
○ Houghton Library, Harvard University, Cambridge, Mass.
○ J. Y. Joyner Library, East Carolina University, Greenville, N.C.
○ Library of Congress, Washington, D.C.
○ MacArthur Memorial Archives and Library, Norfolk, Va.
○ Manila Hotel Archives, Manila, Philippines
○ Marlene and Nathan Addlestone Library, College of Charleston, Charleston, S.C.
○ National Archives and Records Administration, College Park, Md.
○ National Museum of the Pacific War, Fredericksburg, Tex.
○ National Personnel Records Center, St. Louis, Mo.
○ Navy Bureau of Medicine and Surgery, Falls Church, Va.
○ Ortigas Foundation Library, Pasig City, Philippines
○ Thomas Cooper Library, University of South Carolina, Columbia, S.C.
○ University of Santo Tomas Archives, Manila, Philippines

- U.S. Army Heritage and Education Center, Carlisle, Pa.
- Watkinson Library, Trinity College, Hartford, Conn.
- William L. Clements Library, University of Michigan, Ann Arbor, Mich.
- Willis Library, University of North Texas, Denton, Tex.
- Wisconsin Historical Society, Madison, Wis.
- Wisconsin Veterans Museum, Madison, Wis.

NOTES

ABBREVIATIONS

ACPL	Allen County Public Library, Fort Wayne, Ind.
ADV ECH GHQ	Advanced Echelon, General Headquarters
AFWESPAC	U.S. Army Forces, Western Pacific
AGWAR	Adjutant General, War Department
AWM	Australian War Memorial, Canberra, Australia
FHL	Filipinas Heritage Library, Makati City, Philippines
HIA	Hoover Institution Archives, Stanford University, Palo Alto, Calif.
HL	Houghton Library, Harvard University, Cambridge, Mass.
HUMEDS	Historical Unit Medical Detachments
LOC	Library of Congress, Washington, D.C.
MIS	Military Intelligence Service
MMAL	MacArthur Memorial Archives and Library, Norfolk, Va.
NARA	National Archives and Records Administration, College Park, Md.
NPRC	National Personnel Records Center, St. Louis
OMPF	Official Military Personnel File
RG	Record Group
SCAP	Supreme Commander for the Allied Powers
SWPA	Southwest Pacific Area
UM	William L. Clements Library, University of Michigan, Ann Arbor

UNT	Willis Library, University of North Texas, Denton
USAHEC	U.S. Army Heritage and Education Center, Carlisle, Pa.
YTT	Yamashita Trial Transcript; trial transcript of *United States v. Tomoyuki Yamashita*, in Boxes 127–34, RG 153, Records of the Judge Advocate General (Army), War Crimes Branch, General and Administrative Records, NARA.

Prologue

1 **"I consider him":** Charles T. Menoher, efficiency report on Douglas MacArthur, August 28, 1919, OMPF of Douglas MacArthur, NPRC.

1 **Gen. Douglas MacArthur walked:** MacArthur, *Reminiscences*, pp. 141–43.

1 **The toll:** Ibid., p. 142; Romulo, *Fall of the Philippines*, p. 100.

1 **a pressed uniform:** Manchester, *American Caesar*, pp. 232–33.

2 **A patrol-torpedo boat:** Commandant, Sixteenth Naval District to Commander, Motor Torpedo Boat Squadron Three, Operation Order, March 10, 1942, PT Boat File, MMAL.

2 **Just as he had told:** Sayre, *Glad Adventure*, p. 241; Elizabeth E. Sayre, "Submarine Saga: Elizabeth Sayre Tells of Escape from Corregidor," *St. Petersburg Times*, September 17, 1942, p. 8.

2 **"I want you to":** Wainwright, *Wainwright's Story*, pp. 3–4.

3 **"Jean":** Douglas MacArthur, " 'They Died Hard—Those Savage Men,' " *Life*, July 10, 1974, p. 74.

3 **the capital's bank vaults:** "Sixth Annual Report of the United States High Commissioner to the Philippine Islands," February 15, 1943 (Washington, D.C.: U.S. Government Printing Office, 1943), pp. 49–57; Sayre, *Glad Adventure*, p. 227.

3 **luxurious home:** Huff and Morris, *My Fifteen Years*, pp. 37–38; Jean MacArthur, oral history transcript no. 5, Box 15, RG 13, Papers of Jean MacArthur, MMAL.

3 **"Malaria and malnutrition":** Frank Hewlett, "Inhuman Agony Finally Forces Heroes of Bataan to Surrender," *Pittsburgh Press*, April 12, 1945, p. 3B.

3 **"More frequently":** Mellnik, *Philippine Diary*, p. 78.

4 **"Victory":** Manchester, *American Caesar*, p. 237.

4 **"Sir, you are well":** MacArthur, *Reminiscences*, p. 129.

4 **"You're out on the end":** Mellnik, *Philippine Diary*, p. 92.

4 **"In the name of fair play":** Survey of Intelligence Materials no. 10, February 16, 1942, Microfilm Roll #23, President Franklin D. Roosevelt's Office Files, 1933–44, pt. 4: Subject Files, Thomas Cooper Library, University of South Carolina, Columbia, S.C.

4 **"Dugout Doug MacArthur":** Norman and Norman, *Tears in Darkness*, p. 121.

4 **"He removed his droopy":** Mellnik, *Philippine Diary*, p. 3.

5 **"Good-bye and God bless you":** Ibid., p. 4.

5 **"George":** Beck, *MacArthur and Wainwright*, p. 144.

5 **"Gone was the vivid":** MacArthur, *Reminiscences*, p. 142.

6 **"The smell of filth":** Ibid., p. 143.

6 **"He was just heart broken":** Jean MacArthur, oral history transcript no. 6, Box 15, RG 13, Papers of Jean MacArthur, MMAL.

6 **"What's his chance":** MacArthur, *Reminiscences*, p. 143.

6 **"You may cast off":** Ibid.

6 **"Aye, sir":** Sloan, *Undefeated*, p. 145.

6 **"I shall return":** MacArthur, *Reminiscences*, p. 145.

PART I

7   **"America's army"**: Entry for January 9, 1945, in Lichauco, *"Dear Mother Put-nam,"* p. 198.

CHAPTER 1

9   **"In conducting war"**: *Affairs in the Philippine Islands, Hearings before the Committee on the Philippines of the United States Senate*, 57th Cong., 1st sess., Senate Doc. no. 331, pt. 2 (Washington, D.C.: U.S. Government Printing Office, 1902), p. 871.

9   **paced the deck**: Entry for January 8, 1945, in W. M. Downes to Ernest King, "War Diary of U.S.S. *Boise* for January 1945," February 5, 1945; MacArthur, *Reminiscences*, pp. 239–41.

9   **In advance of the landings**: Potter, *Bull Halsey*, p. 324.

10   **threat from suicide planes**: Howard L. Young to Chief of the Bureau of Ships, "War Damage Report of U.S.S. *Ommaney Bay* (CVE 79)," February 3, 1945.

10   **"A tremendous explosion"**: Drury, *History of Chaplain Corps*, p. 2:196.

10   **"Intensity of fire"**: Young to Chief of the Bureau of Ships, "War Damage Report."

10   **pilots tore into**: Morison, *Liberation of Philippines*, pp. 104–11; Rielly, *Kamikaze Attacks*, p. 158.

10   **"The action was so fast"**: William Chickering to Audry Chickering, January 5, 1945, copy courtesy of Doral Chenoweth.

10   **The ferocious kamikazes**: Smith, *Triumph in Philippines*, p. 66.

11   **"If the Lord"**: Bonner Fellers to Dorothy Fellers, January 8, 1945, Box 2, RG 44a, Papers of Brig. Gen. Bonner F. Fellers, MMAL.

11   **"Always Bataan"**: Rogers, *MacArthur and Sutherland*, p. 1:218.

11   **"Bataan"**: Ibid.

11   **"Bataan is like a child"**: "MacArthur Marks Fall of Bataan by New Vow to Retake Philippines," *New York Times*, April 9, 1943, p. 1.

11   **"fleeing general"**: Manchester, *American Caesar*, p. 275.

11   **"coward"**: Ibid.

11   **"deserter"**: Ibid.

11   **"A foul trick"**: Brougher, *South to Bataan*, p. 32.

11   **"I am going"**: James, *Years of MacArthur*, p. 3:126.

12   **"This action was taken"**: Beck, *MacArthur and Wainwright*, p. 273.

12   **"because he knew of a man"**: Luvaas, *Dear Miss Em*, p. 76.

12   **had enlisted housewives**: Beatrice Oppenheim, "Grandmothers Take War Jobs," *New York Times*, June 6, 1943, p. X10; Herman, *Freedom's Forge*, p. 283.

12   **American B-29 bombers**: Warren Moscow, "51 Square Miles Burned Out in Six B-29 Attacks on Tokyo," *New York Times*, May 30, 1945, p. 1.

12   **"We must be careful"**: George Marshall to MacArthur, June 24, 1944, in Bland, *"Aggressive and Determined,"* p. 494.

13   **"Mr. President"**: "Political Point for a Politician," *Life*, August 15, 1955, p. 52.

13   **"In fact"**: Manchester, *American Caesar*, p. 369.

13   **"Every battle action"**: Willoughby and Chamberlain, *MacArthur*, p. 209.

13   **"both a refuge"**: Rogers, *MacArthur and Sutherland*, p. 1:135.

13   **"One by one"**: MacArthur, *Reminiscences*, p. 240.

14   **MacArthur drew confidence**: "Text of Morgenthau's Speech Here," *New York Times*, April 13, 1943, p. 18.

14   **A convoy**: "Life Aboard the Transports," undated public affairs narrative, Box 8605, RG 407, Records of the Adjutant General's Office, WWII Operations Reports, 1940–48, 37th Infantry Division, NARA.

14   **"They never come"**: MacArthur, *Reminiscences*, p. 240.

14   **"I had a warm"**: Ibid.

14   The son of a Wisconsin: Ibid., pp. 4–14; James, *Years of MacArthur*, pp. 1:8–16.
14   "Boy Colonel": MacArthur, *Reminiscences*, p. 14; Manchester, *American Caesar*, p. 16.
15   "It was here": MacArthur, *Reminiscences*, p. 15.
15   "Washington was different": Ibid., p. 16.
15   "Arthur MacArthur was": Manchester, *American Caesar*, p. 30.
15   "Your indomitable courage—": "MacArthur Drops Dead as He Talks," *Milwaukee Sentinel*, September 6, 1912, p. 1.
16   "Comrades": Ibid.
16   "Already his face": Ibid.
16   "Our commander": Ibid.
16   "Our father": Ibid.
16   "He died the death": "Widow Prostrated at Husband's Death," *Milwaukee Sentinel*, September 6, 1912, p. 2.
16   "My whole world": MacArthur, *Reminiscences*, p. 36.
16   Mary Pinkney Hardy: Ibid., pp. 13–14.
17   "Our teaching": Ibid., p. 15.
17   "You must grow up": Manchester, *American Caesar*, p. 41.
17   To help secure: James, *Years of MacArthur*, p. 1:63.
17   "Doug, you'll win": MacArthur, *Reminiscences*, p. 18.
17   MacArthur scored 93.3: James, *Years of MacArthur*, p. 1:66.
18   "The dead were so thick": MacArthur, *Reminiscences*, p. 60.
18   "On a field": C.A.F. Flagler to Commander in Chief, American Expeditionary Forces, Recommendation of Brig. Gen. Douglas MacArthur for the Award of Medal of Honor, December 18, 1918, OMPF of Douglas MacArthur, NPRC.
18   "He alone made victory": Reginald H. Weller, 1st Lt., Infantry, U.S.A., statement to Accompany Recommendation of Brig. Gen. Douglas MacArthur for Medal of Honor, December 12, 1918, ibid.
18   "Won't you be real good": James, *Years of MacArthur*, p. 1:304.
18   "I entered into matrimony": MacArthur, *Reminiscences*, p. 83.
18   "It was an interfering": James, *Years of MacArthur*, p. 1:323.
19   "My mother put too": Manchester, *American Caesar*, p. 702.
19   "A brilliant, young officer": G. W. Read, Efficiency Report on Brig. Gen. Douglas MacArthur, July 1, 1923, OMPF of Douglas MacArthur, NPRC.
19   "One of the most efficient": Chas. T. Menoher, Efficiency Report on Douglas MacArthur, August 28, 1919, ibid.
19   "Well fitted": Douglas MacArthur, "Summary of Efficiency Reports," 1915, ibid.
19   At thirty-eight: Donald Brannon, "Story of the Fighting MacArthurs," *St. Louis Post-Dispatch*, March 18, 1942, p. 1C.
19   "My first inclination": MacArthur, *Reminiscences*, p. 89.
19   "She said my father": Ibid.
20   "If only your father": Manchester, *American Caesar*, p. 144.
20   He prided himself: For background on MacArthur's personality and intellect, see the oral histories of Frederic S. Marquardt (September 5, 1971), Clovis E. Byers (June 24, 1971), John A. Elmore (June 25, 1971), Roger O. Egeberg (June 30, 1971, and September 23, 1982), Gaetano Faillace (August 31, 1971), George C. Kenney (July 16, 1971), Arthur D. Struble (June 22, 1971), Charles A. Willoughby (August 28, 1967), Dwight D. Eisenhower (August 29, 1967), and Armel Dyer (June 14, 1966), all on file at MMAL.
20   "His mind was": La Follette, *Adventure in Politics*, p. 269.
20   "He was a brilliant man": Richard J. Marshall, oral history by D. Clayton James, July 27, 1971, MMAL.
20   "He was a genius": Bonner F. Fellers, oral history by D. Clayton James, June 26, 1971, MMAL.
20   "I never in all my life": Jean MacArthur to Angie McCarthy, undated, Box 5, RG 13, Papers of Jean MacArthur, MMAL.
20   "The sensation": Eisenhower, *At Ease*, p. 214.

20   " 'Discuss' is hardly": Ibid.
20   "Always it was": Carl Mydans, *American Caesar*, master transcript, undated, MMAL.
20   "Has an exalted": John J. Pershing, Efficiency Report on Douglas MacArthur, July 1, 1922, OMPF of Douglas MacArthur, NPRC.
21   "MacArthur is the type": Entry for July 27, 1933, Ickes diary, Reel 1, Harold L. Ickes Papers, LOC.
21   "MacArthur could never see": D'Este, *Eisenhower*, pp. 226.
21   "He talks in a voice": Tugwell, *Brains Trust*, p. 434.
21   "My son": MacArthur, *Reminiscences*, p. 19.
22   "I could not have told": H.H. Kohlsaat, "From McKinley to Harding," *Saturday Evening Post*, June 24, 1922, p. 16.
22   "We have about": Karnow, *In Our Image*, p. 138.
22   "No imperial designs": MacArthur, *Reminiscences*, pp. 19–20.
22   "There was nothing": Dower, *Cultures of War*, p. 80.
22   "niggers": Storey and Codman, *Secretary Root's Record*, p. 67.
22   "injuns": Miller, *Benevolent Assimilation*, p. 179.
22   "savages": Storey and Codman, *Secretary Root's Record*, p. 57.
23   "The country won't": Miller, *Benevolent Assimilation*, p. 179.
23   "The only good Filipino": Ibid., p. 180.
23   "No cruelty": Anti-Imperialist League, *Soldiers' Letters: Being Materials for the History of a War of Criminal Aggression* (Boston: Anti-Imperialist League, 1899), p. 3.
23   "These people are": Robert Hughes testimony, February 28, 1902, *Affairs in the Philippine Islands, Hearings before the Committee on the Philippines of the United States Senate*, 57th Cong., 1st sess., Senate Doc. no. 331, pt. 1 (Washington, D.C.: U.S. Government Printing Office, 1902), p. 559.
23   "Millions of ants": Worcester, *Philippines*, p. 384.
23   Soldiers waterboarded: For various examples, see the testimonies of Robert Hughes (March 3, 1902), Charles S. Riley (April 14, 1902), William Lewis Smith (April 14, 1902), Edward J. Davis (April 17, 1902), Grover Flint (April 21, 1902), Richard T. O'Brien (May 19, 1902), Fred McDonald (May 26, 1902), and Arthur L. Wagner (May 29, 1902), all in *Affairs in the Philippine Islands, Hearings before the Committee on the Philippines of the United States Senate*, 57th Cong., 1st sess., Senate Doc. no. 331, pts. 1–3 (Washington, D.C.: U.S. Government Printing Office, 1902), pp. 558–59, 1529–41, 1727–28, 1765–68, 2544–45, 2752–54, 2847.
23   "You know what 'black paint' is": Stirling, *Sea Duty*, p. 76.
23   "After we finished": Ibid., p. 79.
23   "I want no prisoners": Karnow, *In Our Image*, p 191.
24   The fight dragged: *Life*, May 22, 1902, cover.
24   The conflict ultimately: Karnow, *In Our Image*, p. 194.
24   "The Filipino soldier": Arthur MacArthur testimony, April 8, 1902, in *Affairs in the Philippine Islands, Hearings before the Committee on the Philippines of the United States Senate*, pt. 2, p. 894.
24   "If old Dewey": Kohlsaat, "From McKinley to Harding," p. 16.
24   "The U.S. conquest": Karnow, *In Our Image*, p. 198.
24   "The educational work": MacArthur, *Reminiscences*, p. 24.
25   "almost stopped perspiring": Taft, *Recollections of Full Years*, p. 81.
25   "small man": William Taft to Elihu Root, January 9, 1901, in Rowland T. Berthoff, "Taft and MacArthur, 1900–1901: A Study in Civil-Military Relations," *World Politics* 5, no. 2 (1953): 206.
25   "military martinet": William Taft to C. P. Taft (ca. October) 1900, ibid., p. 204.
25   "When he died": Petillo, *Douglas MacArthur*, p. 95.
25   "The Philippines charmed": MacArthur, *Reminiscences*, p. 29.
25   "Like all frontiersmen": Ibid.
26   "The archipelago": Arthur MacArthur testimony, April 8, 1902, in *Affairs in*

the Philippine Islands, Hearings before the Committee on the Philippines of the United States Senate, pt. 2, p. 867.

26 **"color line"**: Ibid., p. 877; Manchester, *American Caesar*, p. 30.

26 **"I have never"**: Arthur MacArthur testimony, April 8, 1902, in *Affairs in the Philippine Islands, Hearings before the Committee on the Philippines of the United States Senate*, pt. 2, p. 877.

26 **"Attitudes die hard"**: MacArthur, *Reminiscences*, p. 84.

26 **"Daddy"**: Manchester, *American Caesar*, pp. 144–45; Perret, *Old Soldiers*, pp. 147–49.

27 **"For Douglas MacArthur"**: Petillo, *Douglas MacArthur*, p. xvii.

27 **"Do you think"**: Quezon, *Good Fight*, p. 153.

28 **"Mother's death"**: Petillo, *Douglas MacArthur*, p. 176.

28 **"My loss"**: Ibid.

28 **"This is going"**: Huff and Morris, *My Fifteen Years*, p. 23.

28 **"With my little family"**: MacArthur, *Reminiscences*, p. 107.

29 **"Maybe when"**: Huff and Morris, *My Fifteen Years*, p. 38.

30 **"Behind us Manila"**: Rogers, *MacArthur and Sutherland*, p. 1:120.

30 **"poor man's war"**: Willoughby and Chamberlain, *MacArthur*, p. 84.

30 **"Operation Shoe String"**: Ibid.

30 **"the Cinderella war"**: Ibid.

30 **"die on the vine"**: Ibid., p. 107. See also Clyde D. Eddleman, oral history by Lowell G. Smith and Murray G. Swindler, January 28, 1975, Box 2, Clyde D. Eddleman Papers, USAHEC.

30 **"The jungle"**: Manchester, *American Caesar*, p. 337.

30 **"road to Manila"**: Willoughby and Chamberlain, *MacArthur*, p. 87.

30 **"I'm going to meet"**: Clyde D. Eddleman, oral history by D. Clayton James, June 29, 1971, MMAL.

CHAPTER 2

31 **"There is no weapon"**: Entry for January 6, 1945, in Pestaño-Jacinto, *Living with the Enemy*, p. 270.

31 **Gen. Yamashita**: Background on Yamashita is drawn from three biographies: Potter, *Life and Death*; Swinson, *Four Samurai*; and Barker, *Yamashita*.

31 **Built like a bear**: Akashi Yoji, "General Tomoyuki Yamashita: Commander of the Twenty-Fifth Army," in Farrell and Hunter, *Sixty Years On*, p. 188.

31 **"Old Potato Face"**: Bob MacMillan, "Yamashita Gives Up," *Yank*, October 12, 1945, pp. 3.

31 **"a florid, pig-faced"**: Yamashita Interrogations, Box 7, RG 44a, Papers of Brig. Gen. Bonner F. Fellers, MMAL.

32 **The lack of oil**: U.S. Strategic Bombing Survey, *Oil in Japan's War* (Washington, D.C.: U.S. Government Printing Office, 1946), pp. 6, 86.

32 **Hungry residents**: Parillo, *Japanese Merchant Marine*, p. 219; U.S. Strategic Bombing Survey, Medical Division, *The Effects of Bombing on Health and Medical Services in Japan* (Washington, D.C.: U.S. Government Printing Office, 1947), pp. 75–77.

32 **"The fate"**: Yoji, "General Tomoyuki Yamashita: Commander of the Twenty-Fifth Army," in Farrell and Hunter, *Sixty Years On*, p. 201.

32 **"This was a guiding"**: Ibid., p. 205.

33 **"If I had only been"**: Potter, *Life and Death*, p. 16.

33 **"If Japan ever"**: Ibid., p. 21.

33 **"For a regular officer"**: Ibid., p. 22.

34 **"Before Vienna"**: Ibid.

34 **"When I was posted"**: Ibid., p. 30.

34 **"My life"**: Ibid., p. 39.

34   "ruthless and forceful": Hideki Tojo, interview notes by Edmund Bodine at Sugamo Prison, undated (ca. March 1946), copy courtesy Michel Paradis.

34   "I have nothing": Swinson, *Four Samurai*, p. 82.

35   "If you say anything": Potter, *The Life and Death*, p. 32.

35   "He may be": Ibid., p. 33.

35   "All our secrets": Ibid.

35   "There were several": Ibid.

35   "My country": Ibid.

35   "I visited my friend": Ibid., p. 36.

35   "You know the results": Ibid., p. 38.

36   The Malay Peninsula snakes: Leasor, *Singapore*, pp. 124–25.

36   Malaya produced: Swinson, *Defeat in Malaya*, p. 28.

36   "the bolt": Theodore H. White, "Singapore: City and Base," *Life*, March 17, 1941, p. 17.

36   Construction of the base: "Britain in the Pacific," *Glasgow Herald*, February 14, 1938, p. 10; "Singapore Stormed," *New York Times*, February 15, 1945, p. E1; Leasor, *Singapore*, pp. 122–23.

37   "The naval base": White, "Singapore: City and Base," p. 18.

37   "I pray": Potter, *Life and Death*, p. 45.

37   "On the day": "On Sailing for Hainan to Invade Malaya," December 4, 1941, in Potter, *Life and Death*, p. 183.

37   "Gibraltar of the Orient": "Britain Opens Asia Fortress," *Los Angeles Times*, February 15, 1938, p. 1.

37   "empty shell:" Peter Edsen, "Singapore Seen as 'Empty Shell,'" *Independent*, October 8, 1940, p. 9.

37   "Your American fleet": Ibid.

38   "With the infantry": Tsuji, *Singapore*, pp. 183–84.

38   "The majority": Chapman, *Jungle Is Neutral*, p. 21.

38   "Here come the tanks": Tsuji, *Singapore*, p. 182.

38   "Well": Swinson, *Defeat in Malaya*, p. 52.

39   "I don't want them": Yoji, "General Tomoyuki Yamashita," in Farrell and Hunter, *Sixty Years On*, p. 193.

39   "bicycle blitzkrieg": Bayly and Harper, *Forgotten Armies*, p. 116.

39   "Singapore's back door": "Invaders Pay Dearly," *Courier-Mail*, February 12, 1942, p. 1.

39   "The possibility": Churchill, *Second World War*, p. 4:49.

39   "The entire male": Prime Minister to General Ismay, for COS Committee, January 19, 1942, ibid., p. 4:51.

39   In barely eight weeks: Tsuji, *Singapore*, p. 213.

39   "The Singapore": Ibid., p. 221.

39   "It is a good": Toland, *Rising Sun*, p. 271.

39   Conditions inside: Leasor, *Singapore*, pp. 2, 231–33, 243–48; "Witness Describes Fort's Final Days," *New York Times*, February 16, 1942, p. 4.

39   "The whole island": Harold Guard, "Writer Escapes to Describe Blazing Hell of Singapore," *Tucson Daily Citizen*, February 16, 1942, p. 12.

40   "I am sure": C. Yates McDaniel, "Smoke Hides Sun in Singapore as War Waxes on City's Outskirts," *New York Times*, February 11, 1942, p. 4.

40   "There must": Prime Minister to General Wavell, February 10, 1942, in Churchill, *Second World War*, p. 4:100.

40   "It is unlikely": General Percival to General Wavell, February 13, 1942, ibid., p. 4:104.

40   "So long as you": General Wavell to General Percival, February 15, 1942, ibid., p. 4:106.

40   "Owing to losses": Ibid.

40   Shortly before six p.m.: Percival, *War in Malaya*, pp. 291–93; Leasor, *Singapore*, pp. 251–55; Tsuji, *Singapore*, pp. 267–68; Swinson, *Defeat in Malaya*, p. 149.

41   "Exhausted": "With White Flag," *Osaka Mainichi*, February 17, 1942, p. 3.

41 **"The faces"**: Tsuji, *Singapore*, p. 268.
41 **"Yamashita wanted"**: Leasor, *Singapore*, p. 4.
41 **"My attack"**: Potter, *Life and Death*, p. 80.
41 **"I want your replies"**: "Enemy Commander Unyielding in Interview with Defender, Tokyo's Version of the Final Conference Discloses," *New York Times*, February 17, 1942, p. 6. See also "Gen. Yamashita Dominates Percival in Dramatic Surrender Negotiations," *Osaka Mainichi*, February 17, 1942, p. 3.
42 **"We were"**: Entry for February 13, 1942, in Pownall, *Chief of Staff*, p. 2:85.
42 **"With the fall"**: "An Era of Empire Ends at Singapore," *Life*, February 23, 1942, p. 17.
42 **Yamashita's stunning**: Bayly and Harper, *Forgotten Armies*, p. 129; Smith, *Singapore Burning*, pp. 388–97, 536–39.
42 **"severe disposal"**: Bayly and Harper, *Forgotten Armies*, p. 211.
43 **Members of the House**: "Representatives Cheer Singapore Fall," *Japan Times and Advertiser*, February 17, 1942, p. 2; "Tokyo Celebrates Singapore Victory," *Japan Times and Advertiser*, February 17, 1942, p. 1; *Japan Times and Advertiser's* special twelve-page "Victory Supplement," published February 17, 1942.
43 **"Singapore has fallen"**: "The Historic Victory of Singapore," *Japan Times and Advertiser*, "Victory Supplement," February 17, 1942, p. 1.
43 **"The ruin"**: "Collapse of British Empire," *Chugai*, in "Today's Press Comments," ibid., p. 2.
43 **"The downfall"**: "Singapore's Doom and Its Worldwide Effect," *Osaka Mainichi*, February 15, 1942, p. 4.
43 **"I am not a Tiger"**: Yoji, "General Tomoyuki Yamashita: Commander of the Twenty-Fifth Army," in Farrell and Hunter, *Sixty Years On*, p. 205.
43 **"the worst disaster"**: Churchill, *Second World War*, p. 4:92.
43 **"fate of the English-speaking"**: "Foe Says City's Surrender Also Menaces India," *Chicago Daily Tribune*, February 16, 1942, p. 1.
43 **"There can now"**: Hanson W. Baldwin, "10 Weeks of Pacific War Show Japan Unchecked," *New York Times*, February 15, 1942, p. E4.
44 **"I know they want"**: Potter, *Life and Death*, p. 96.
44 **"I suspect things"**: Ibid., p. 98.
44 **"Hell is on us"**: Interrogation of Fleet Adm. Osami Nagano, November 20, 1946, in U.S. Strategic Bombing Survey [Pacific], Naval Analysis Division, *Interrogations of Japanese Officials* (Washington, D.C.: U.S. Government Printing Office, 1946), p. 2:356.
45 **"So it's come"**: Swinson, *Four Samurai*, p. 190.
45 **"This is our final"**: Pu Yi, *Last Manchu*, p. 200.
45 **"You'd better die"**: Swinson, *Four Samurai*, p. 191.
45 **"When he went"**: Potter, *Life and Death*, p. 100.
45 **"Perhaps you are tired"**: Ibid., pp. 102–3.
46 **"If you can crush"**: Swinson, *Four Samurai*, p. 191.
46 **"Do your best"**: Ibid., p. 192.
46 **"As he caught"**: Ibid.
46 **American planes**: Various dates are given for Yamashita's arrival in the Philippines. I have used the date he testified to under oath in his war crimes trial.
47 **"I have been told"**: Potter, *Life and Death*, p. 104.
47 **"Anyone who fights"**: Swinson, *Four Samurai*, p. 196.
47 **The fifty-one-year-old**: "Statement of Lt. Gen. Muto, Akira," December 27, 1945, Box 1907, RG 331, SCAP, Legal Section, Manila Branch, 201 File, 1945–49, WWII, NARA; Department of State, Interim Research and Intelligence Service, Research and Analysis Branch, Biographical Report, BR-J#42, October 4, 1945, ibid.
47 **"There is no general"**: Potter, *Life and Death*, p. 104.
47 **"It is a good thing"**: Akira Muto testimony, November 21, 1945, YTT, p. 2998.
48 **"Have a bath"**: Akira Muto, "The Truth of the Philippines Campaign: Unpublished Memoirs of Lt. Gen. Muto, Akira, Chief of Staff, Fourteenth Area Army,"

June 17, 1947, Box 59, RG 554, Records of General Headquarters, Far East Command, Supreme Commander Allied Powers, and United Nations Command, NARA.

48 "Don't worry": Swinson, *Four Samurai*, p. 199.

48 "We were all": Akira Muto testimony, November 21, 1945, YTT, p. 3000.

48 "You have far": Swinson, *Four Samurai*, p. 197.

48 "Rice": Akira Muto testimony, November 21, 1945, YTT, p. 3028.

48 "They will accomplish": Potter, *Life and Death*, p. 106.

49 "Where is Leyte": Ibid., p. 110.

49 "a precise, steady": Report of Interrogations of Tomoyuki Yamashita and Akira Muto, September 4–6, 1945, Box 7, RG 44a, Papers of Brig. Gen. Bonner F. Fellers, MMAL.

49 "This is an order": Potter, *Life and Death*, p. 110.

49 "The waters of the sea": Martin, *GI War*, p. 312.

49 "I am exhausted": *Biennial Reports of the Chief of Staff of the United States Army to the Secretary of War, 1 July 1939–30 June 1945* (Washington, D.C.: U.S. Army Center of Military History, 1996), p. 173.

50 "I fully understand": Potter, *Life and Death*, p. 113.

50 "The old man": Ibid.

50 "We shall seek": Swinson, *Four Samurai*, p. 203.

51 "After our losses": Potter, *Life and Death*, p. 124.

51 "Our defeat at Leyte": Mitsumasa Yonai interrogation, November 17, 1945 in U.S. Strategic Bombing Survey [Pacific], Naval Analysis Division, *Interrogations of Japanese Officials*, p. 2:331.

51 "The completeness": "The Texts of the Day's Communiqués on the Fighting in Various War Zones," *New York Times*, December 26, 1944, p. 2.

51 "I was absorbed": Tomoyuki Yamashita testimony, November 28, 1945, YTT, p. 3557.

51 The general anticipated: "Summary of Interrogations of General Yamashita and Other Responsible Commanders and Staff Officers," n.d., Box 8640, RG 407, Records of the Adjutant General's Office, WWII Operations Reports, 1940–48, NARA; Tomoyuki Yamashita testimony, November 28, 1945, YTT, pp. 3526–28; Muto, "Truth of the Philippines Campaign," pp. 8–22.

52 "Persistent fighter attacks": Muto, "Truth of the Philippines Campaign," p. 12.

52 "Supply shortages": Ibid., p. 11.

53 "I know the real state": Potter, *Life and Death*, p. 129.

53 "When you return": Ibid.

53 "When the Americans land": Swinson, *Four Samurai*, p. 207.

54 "Our general": Ibid, p. 205.

54 "Your Excellency snored": Muto, "Truth of the Philippines Campaign," p. 22.

54 "Your orders": Swinson, *Four Samurai*, p. 208.

CHAPTER 3

55 "It is cheaper": Jaime H. Manzano, Intelligence Summary NR-15, U.S. Philippine Island Forces, Headquarters Kalayaan Command, "General Conditions in Manila," August 31, 1944, copy courtesy of Lou Jurika.

55 "Hunger, privation": Entry for December 10, 1944, in Lichauco, *"Dear Mother Putnam,"* p. 193.

56 "Three words": Entry for May 10, 1942, in Pestaño-Jacinto, *Living with the Enemy*, p. 40.

56 "The dive": Daniel Burnham to Charles Moore, March 13, 1905, in Moore, *Daniel H. Burnham*, p. 1:245.

56 "The fortress-city": Stephen L. Garay, "The Breach of Intramuros," May 1, 1948, Instructor Training Division, General Instruction Department, Armored School, Fort Knox, Ky.

56   "Possessing the bay": D. H. Burnham, "Report on Proposed Improvements at Manila," June 28, 1905, in 59th Cong., 1st Session, December 4, 1905–June 30, 1906, *House Documents*, vol. 11 (Washington, D.C.: U.S. Government Printing Office, 1906), pp. 627–635.

57   In the four decades: Background on Manila is drawn from Terrain Handbook 41A, Manila City, December 6, 1944, Box 1344, RG 331, Supreme Commander for the Allied Powers, Legal Section, Administrative Division, Misc. File, 1939–49, NARA; "Map of Manila," YMCA, Manila Branch Army & Navy, 1940, Box 3, RG 112, MMAL; Roderick Hall, interview by author, February 25, 2015; James Litton, interview by author, September 17, 2015.

57   Workers likewise: Details on Philippine General Hospital come from John E. Snodgrass, comp., *History and Description of the Philippine General Hospital: Manila, Philippine Islands, 1900 to 1911* (Manila: Department of the Interior / Bureau of Health / Bureau of Printing, 1912), pp. 29–50.

57   "Manila is by far": Russell Owen, "East Is East," *New York Times*, October 16, 1932, p. SM8.

57   City life: Day, *Manila Hotel*, pp. 1–42.

57   "Manila Hotel": Ibid., p. 17.

57   Streetcars operated: Terrain Handbook 41A, Manila City, December 6, 1944, pp. 43–46.

58   "Air conditioned": "America Looks at Heacocks," *American Chamber of Commerce Journal* 20, no. 4 (1940): 31.

58   Recreation proved: "Map of Manila," YMCA, Manila Branch Army & Navy, 1940; Hall interview; Litton interview.

58   Despite the amenities: Day, *Manila Hotel*, pp. 18, 24–26.

60   "squaw men": Karnow, *In Our Image*, p. 214.

60   "What are those": Day, *Manila Hotel*, p. 25.

60   "It rains continually": Storey and Codman, *Secretary Root's Record*, p. 92.

60   "The city was": Mellnik, *Philippine Diary*, p. 5.

60   "To live in Manila": Dunn, *Pacific Microphone*, p. 20.

61   Over Manila hung: Chang, *The Rape of Nanking*, pp. 4–8.

61   "Now danger": Entry for December 31, 1941, in Pestaño-Jacinto, *Living with the Enemy*, p. 13.

61   "Oh, God": Russell Brines, "How the Japanese Took Over Manila," *Tuscaloosa News*, November 5, 1944, p. 4.

61   "They came": Mydans, *More Than Meets*, p. 68.

61   "Grim yellow faces": Entry for January 4, 1942, in Pestaño-Jacinto, *Living with the Enemy*, p. 14.

61   "Manila, for forty-three": "U.S. Forces Still Resisting Stubbornly from New Positions After Manila Falls," *Pittsburgh Post-Gazette*, January 3, 1942, p. 1.

62   "Mere lieutenants": Buenafe, *Wartime Philippines*, p. 84.

62   "They live like princes": Entry for January 20, 1942, in Pestaño-Jacinto, *Living with the Enemy*, pp. 17–18.

62   "The favorite procedure": Buenafe, *Wartime Philippines*, p. 84.

62   "It has been picked clean": Entry for February 2, 1942, in Pestaño-Jacinto, *Living with the Enemy*, p. 19.

62   "What kind of an Army": Entry for September 26, 1944, in Buencamino, *Memoirs and Diaries*, p. 149.

62   Dewey Boulevard and Taft: Entry for May 18, 1942, in Lichauco, *"Dear Mother Putnam,"* p. 42.

62   "But the Japanese": Entry for February 27, 1942, in Pestaño-Jacinto, *Living with the Enemy*, p. 24.

63   "Everybody knows": Ibid.

63   "The new currency": Garcia, *It Took Four Years*, p. 45.

63   "Failure to do so": Entry for February 1, 1942, in Lichauco, *"Dear Mother Putnam,"* p. 21.

63   "I have summoned": Entry for March 22, 1942, ibid., pp. 29–30.

63   "As the leopard": Karnow, *In Our Image*, p. 308.
64   "Such is the kind": Entry for March 22, 1942, in Lichauco, *"Dear Mother Putnam,"* p. 30.
64   "I think every Japanese": Entry for January 4, 1942, in Pestaño-Jacinto, *Living with the Enemy*, p. 15.
64   "War changes everything": Entry for November 1, 1943, ibid., p. 188.
64   "It is a very good propaganda": Entry for May 15, 1942, in Lichauco, *"Dear Mother Putnam,"* p. 42.
64   "Not a single handclap": Entry for December 21, 1942, ibid., p. 71.
65   "It was an unforgettable": Entry for May 24, 1942, ibid., p. 43.
65   "Save for the sound": Mañalac, *Manila*, p. 23.
65   "Filipinos stood": Joaquin, *Manila, My Manila*, pp. 291–92.
65   "City life has": Entry for June 2, 1942, in Labrador, *Diary of Japanese Occupation*, p. 106.
66   "No one is": Entry for February 28, 1942, in Lichauco, *"Dear Mother Putnam,"* p. 26.
66   "The repertoire": Entry for March 12, 1942, in Labrador, *Diary of Japanese Occupation*, pp. 76–77.
66   "My mother": Bernard L. M. Karganilla, "Witness," in Constantino, *Under Japanese Rule*, p. 222.
66   "The lot of traitors": Monaghan, *Under Red Sun*, p. 165.
66   "A few innocent": Entry for December 10, 1944, in Lichauco, *"Dear Mother Putnam,"* p. 110.
66   "The number of killings": Ibid., p. 109.
67   In 1928, when: Joaquin, *Mr. F.E.U.*, pp. 7–8.
67   "S-t-a-r-light, S-t-a-r bright": Montinola, *Breaking the Silence*, p. 25.
68   "The door opened": Garcia, *It Took Four Years*, p. 43.
68   Roasted rice: Agoncillo, *Fateful Years*, p. 2:581.
68   "So common": Ibid.
68   Carmen Berlanga Brady: Joyce Velde, interview by author, February 19, 2015.
68   Hospitals likewise: Entries for May 29, 1943, and August 31, 1944, in Lichauco, *"Dear Mother Putnam,"* pp. 98, 178.
68   Some dispensaries: Picornell, *Remedios Hospital*, p. 32.
68   "War, the ultimate leveler": Orendain, "Children of War," in Constantino, *Under Japanese Rule*, p. 66.
69   "Our next door neighbor": Entry for July 30, 1943, in Pestaño-Jacinto, *Living with the Enemy*, pp. 167–68.
69   "I know of persons": Entry for January 18, 1942, in Labrador, *Diary of Japanese Occupation*, p. 49.
69   "They might take": Entry for November 7, 1944, in Buencamino, *Memoirs and Diaries*, p. 168.
69   "One couldn't hang": Mañalac, *Manila*, p. 86.
69   "The women": Entry for May 30, 1944, in Pestaño-Jacinto, *Living with the Enemy*, p. 215.
69   "If I happened": Mañalac, *Manila*, p. 86.
70   Even the dead: Leon O. Ty, "Ghouls Desecrate Thousands of City Graves with Help of Jap Sentries," *Free Philippines*, May 31, 1945, p. 3.
70   "This has never happened": Entry for December 9, 1943, in Pestaño-Jacinto, *Living with the Enemy*, p. 195.
70   The stolen goods: F. M. Caliwag, "Buy and Sell," *Sunday Times Magazine* (Manila), April 16, 1967, p. 58.
70   "Here was the last-chance": Mañalac, *Manila*, p. 87.
70   "In such places": Agoncillo, *Fateful Years*, p. 2:578.
71   "This is necessary": Entry for February 25, 1944, in Lichauco, *"Dear Mother Putnam,"* p. 155.
71   "Plant in order to live": Agoncillo, *Fateful Years*, p. 2:550.

71   **"The farm"**: Rodolfo G. Tupas, "The Glory behind the Shame," *Sunday Times Magazine* (Manila), April 16, 1967, p. 14.

71   **"The backyard plot"**: Jean Pope, "A Time of Utter Dislocation," *Sunday Times Magazine* (Manila), April 16, 1967, p. 44.

71   **"In pushcarts"**: Entry for October 17, 1944, in Pestaño-Jacinto, *Living with the Enemy*, p. 237.

71   **"Manila"**: Entry for December 20, 1944, in Labrador, *Diary of Japanese Occupation*, p. 245.

71   **"Food prices"**: Entry for November 16, 1944, in Lichauco, *"Dear Mother Putnam,"* p. 192.

71   **"It is a common"**: Jaime H. Manzano, Intelligence Summary NR-15, U.S. Philippine Island Forces, Headquarters Kalayaan Command, "General Conditions in Manila," August 31, 1944.

71   **"Milagros's bloated"**: Montinola, *Breaking the Silence*, p. 10.

72   **"We have sold"**: Edward B. Bennett to the commandant, May 4, 1944, University of Santo Tomas Archives, Manila.

72   **"The shelters"**: Orendain, "Children of War," in Constantino, *Under Japanese Rule*, p. 67.

72   **"Dad was a shattered"**: Garcia, *It Took Four Years*, p. 84.

72   **"We traded it"**: Velde interview.

72   **"There was a sickening"**: Agoncillo, *Fateful Years*, p. 2:548.

72   **"Many of these"**: Mañalac, *Manila*, p. 83.

73   **Doctors at San Lazaro**: Entry for December 21, 1944, in Buencamino, Jr., *Memoirs and Diaries*, p. 186.

73   **"Along the vast stretches"**: Agoncillo, *Fateful Years*, p. 2:548.

73   **"Every morning"**: Entry for December 10, 1944, in Lichauco, *"Dear Mother Putnam,"* p. 193.

73   **"Today"**: Ibid.

73   **"Food problem very acute"**: Message no. 205, December 15, 1944, "Extracts from Daily Philippines Messages Sheets," Box 310, RG 496, Records of General Headquarters, Southwest Pacific Area and U.S. Army Forces, Pacific, MIS Administrative Section, General Correspondence, 1942–46, NARA.

73   **"Japs in Manila"**: Message no. 212, December 22, 1944, ibid.

73   **"Mortality from starvation"**: Message no. 221, January 1, 1945, ibid.

73   **"No Japanese looks starved"**: Entry for September 18, 1944, in Pestaño-Jacinto, *Living with the Enemy*, p. 226.

73   **"By dawn"**: Montinola, *Breaking the Silence*, p. 18.

74   **"Take anything"**: Joaquin, *Mr. F.E.U.*, p. 158.

74   **"A strange parade"**: Montinola, *Breaking the Silence*, pp. 18–19.

74   **"Don't touch her"**: Velde interview.

74   **"We heard her yells"**: Ibid.

74   **"When she was brought"**: William C. Brady, "War Is Hell," unpublished narrative, Memorare Manila 1945 Foundation Collection, FHL.

74   **"Morality cowered"**: Agoncillo, *Fateful Years*, p. 2:586.

74   **"We survived"**: Carmen Guerrero Nakpil, "The Watershed," *Sunday Times Magazine* (Manila), April 16, 1967, p. 11.

75   **"The end is near"**: Garcia, *It Took Four Years*, p. 95.

CHAPTER 4

76   **"The Japanese"**: Erlinda Querubin testimony, June 30, 1945, in Report no. 61, "Investigation of the Rape of Forty Civilian Women and the Attempted Rape of Thirty-Six Civilian Women, of Various Nationalities, in Ermita, Manila, Philippine Islands, During the Period 9–13 February 1945," Box 1113, RG 331, SCAP, Legal Section, Administrative Division, War Crimes File, 1946–50, NARA.

76 His task force: OPNS Narrative, Hist., M-1 OPN, Luzon Campaign, drafts, 37th Infantry Division, October 11–December 11, 1944, Box 8603, RG 407, Records of the Adjutant General's Office, WWII Operations Reports, 1940–48, 37th Infantry Division, NARA; Potter, *Nimitz*, p. 352.

76 MacArthur could not: "Aerology and Amphibious Warfare: Amphibious Landings in Lingayen Gulf," Chief of Naval Operations, Aerology Section, July 1945, NARA.

76 "On the dark": William Dunn, broadcast transcript, January 10, 1945, RG 52, Papers of William J. Dunn, MMAL.

76 Lingayen counted: Thomas C. Kinkaid to Commander in Chief, U.S. Fleet, "Action Report—Luzon Attack Force, Lingayen Gulf—Musketeer Mike One Operation," May 15, 1945; Terrain Study no. 93, Lingayen, October 4, 1944, Box 1930, RG 331, SCAP, Legal Section, Administrative Division, Manila Branch, Terrain Study, 1944–45, NARA; General Headquarters, SWPA, Military Intelligence Section, General Staff, G-2 Estimate of the Enemy Situation with Respect to an Operation against Lingayen Gulf and the Central Plain of Luzon, November 22, 1944, MMAL.

77 "hottest reception": Krueger, *From Down Under*, p. 224.

77 "The Luzon campaign": Bonner Fellers to Dorothy Fellers, January 8, 1945, Box 2, RG 44a, Papers of Brig. Gen. Bonner F. Fellers, MMAL.

77 "Both forces ashore": MacArthur, *Reminiscences*, p. 238.

79 "I knew that many": Ibid., p. 246.

79 MacArthur's worst fears: Report no. 49, "Investigation of the Alleged Atrocities Committed at Camp 10 A, Puerto Princesa, Palawan, Philippine Islands, against American Prisoners of War between 1 August and 14 December 1944," August 18, 1945, Box 1111, RG 331, SCAP, Legal Section, Administrative Division, War Crimes File, 1946–50, NARA; V. W. Dyer Jr., "Palawan Massacre," March 15, 1948, Box 1276, RG 331, SCAP, Legal Section, Administrative Division, Documents & Maps, 1945–48, NARA. All testimony and documents cited below, unless otherwise noted, come from Report no. 49.

79 "He just split": Eugene Nielsen, oral history by George Burlage, December 11, 1989, UNT.

79 "My God": Glenn McDole, oral history by William J. Alexander, October 10, 1996, UNT.

79 "You could see": Ibid.

79 "Shoot them": Tomisaburo Sawa testimony, July 31, 1947, Box 1276, RG 331, SCAP, Legal Section, Administrative Division, Documents & Maps, 1945–48, NARA.

79 "As the men": Douglas W. Bogue testimony before the International Military Tribunal for the Far East, excerpts of which are included in Dyer, "Palawan Massacre."

80 "Dozo": Glenn McDole, oral history by William J. Alexander, October 10, 1996.

80 "There was an explosion": Sworn Statement of William J. Bachus et al., March 16, 1945, copy courtesy of Stephen Moore.

80 "We could feel": Glenn Weddell McDole, statement, January 24, 1945.

80 "Many of the men": Agent 2257, "Interrogation of Escapees from Bataan and Corregidor," January 7, 1945.

80 "The water": Eugene Nielsen, oral history by George Burlage, December 11, 1989.

80 "I took refuge": Douglas W. Bogue, statement, January 23, 1945.

80 "The American knew": Glen Weddell McDole, statement, January 24, 1945.

81 "banzai": Nielsen oral history.

81 "The Japanese were cheering": Ibid.

81 "In two dugouts": Charles W. Simms, "Report on Re-Internment of American Prisoners of War, APOW #10, Puerto Princesa, Palawan, P.I.," n.d.

81 "Although they were": Entry for December 15, 1944, captured Japanese diary (neither owner nor unit listed).

81 "The prisoners of war": Entry for January 9, 1945, ibid.

81 "We must move fast": Mydans, *More Than Meets*, p. 183.

82 **"You could almost":** Langone, *Star in the Window*, p. 128.

82 **In addition:** OPNS Narrative, Hist., M-1 OPN, Luzon Campaign, drafts, 37th Infantry Division, October 11–December 22, 1944.

82 **Buried in the bowels:** Ibid.

82 **"In point of the number":** Ibid.

82 **Reveille this morning:** "Life Aboard the Transports," undated public affairs narrative.

83 **"It was potent":** Ibid.

83 **"These little trees":** Ibid.

83 **General Griswold confessed:** Entry for January 6, 1945, Oscar Griswold diary, Box 1, Oscar W. Griswold Papers, 1917–45, USAHEC.

83 **"It is one":** Entry for January 8, 1945, ibid.

83 **"It has been":** Douglas MacArthur to Jean MacArthur, January 8, 1945, RG 10, General Douglas MacArthur's Private Correspondence, 1848–1964, MMAL.

83 **The propeller:** John T. Warren to Commander in Chief, U.S. Fleet, "Action Report, Bombardment and Close Covering in Support of the Assault and Occupation of Beachheads on the Shores of Lingayen Gulf, Luzon, P.I., 3–18 January 1945," USS *New Mexico*, January 18, 1945.

83 **Such attacks:** A snapshot of the varying wounds caused by kamikaze attacks can be found in "Luzon Operation, Lingayen Gulf, January 9, 1945" by the Medical Department of the USS *Harris*. That report is included with Marion Emerson Murphy to Commander in Chief, U.S. Fleet, "Report of Action—Amphibious Attack on Lingayen Gulf," USS *Harris*, January 19, 1945.

83 **An orange-sized:** Ibid.

83 **"The penis":** Ibid.

84 **"Men were most":** OPNS Narrative, Hist., M-1 OPN, Luzon Campaign, drafts, 37th Infantry Division, October 11–December 22, 1944.

84 **"Everybody's dreaming":** Dos Passos, *Tour of Duty*, p. 124.

84 **"As the sun sank":** "Life Aboard the Transports," undated public affairs narrative.

84 **Sixty-five minesweepers:** Thomas C. Kinkaid to Commander in Chief, U.S. Fleet, "Action Report—Luzon Attack Force, Lingayen Gulf—Musketeer Mike One Operation," May 15, 1945.

84 **"As I swam":** Entry for January 7, 1945, Joseph Moretti diary, in Patric, *To War in a Tin Can*, p. 150.

84 **A lack of charts:** Thomas C. Kinkaid to Commander in Chief, U.S. Fleet, "Action Report—Luzon Attack Force, Lingayen Gulf—Musketeer Mike One Operation," May 15, 1945.

85 **American warships:** After Action Report, XIV Corps, M-1 Operation, July 29, 1945, Box 1475, RG 407, Records of the Adjutant General's Office, Philippine Archives Collection, Liberation/Post-War, NARA.

85 **Navy fighters:** Thomas C. Kinkaid to Commander in Chief, U.S. Fleet, "Action Report—Luzon Attack Force, Lingayen Gulf—Musketeer Mike One Operation," May 15, 1945.

85 **"These sketches":** Ibid.

85 **"a naval bombardment":** Sixth Army, Report of the Luzon Campaign, January 9–June 30, 1945, p. 1:17.

85 **In sickbays:** Drury, *History of Chaplain Corps*, p. 2:197; Ingram C. Sowell to Commander in Chief, U.S. Fleet, "Action Report, Bombardment of and Fire Support for Landings, Lingayen Gulf, Luzon Island, Philippine Islands, 1 January 1945 to 18 January 1945, Inclusive," Battleship Division Four, January 29, 1945.

85 **"At the height":** Patric, *To War in a Tin Can*, pp. 151–52.

85 **"The sun came up":** After Action Report, XIV Corps, M-1 Operation, July 29, 1945.

85 **A twin-engine:** "Revised Form for Reporting A.A. Action by Surface Ships," USS *Hodges*, January 9, 1945.

85 **At seven-forty-five:** "Revised Form for Reporting A.A. Action by Surface Ships," USS *Columbia*, January 9, 1945.

85 The *Boise*: "Revised Form for Reporting A.A. Action by Surface Ships," USS *Boise*, January 9, 1945.

86 "Most of the wounded": Drury, *History of Chaplain Corps*, p. 2:197.

86 "Now hear this": Mathias, *GI Jive*, p. 111.

86 "Well, here we go": Ozzie St. George, "Return to Luzon," *Yank*, February 16, 1945, p. 4.

86 "It sounded": Robert J. Conrad, "Regiment Played Big Role during Invasion of Luzon," *Hartford Courant*, January 8, 1945, p. 1.

86 Included this morning: Thomas C. Kinkaid to Commander in Chief, U.S. Fleet, "Action Report—Luzon Attack Force, Lingayen Gulf—Musketeer Mike One Operation," May 15, 1945.

86 "Our troops": Fahey, *Pacific War Diary*, p. 264.

86 "It is one": Courtney Whitney to Evelyn Whitney, January 8, 1945, Box 10, RG 16, Papers of Maj. Gen. Courtney Whitney, MMAL.

87 "My heart was sad": Entry for January 8, 1945, Griswold diary.

87 "Only the tops": St. George, "Return to Luzon," p. 4.

87 "Shells whirred": Ibid.

87 "He had given": Ibid.

87 "Gun fire on beach": Thomas C. Kinkaid to Commander in Chief, U.S. Fleet, "Action Report—Luzon Attack Force, Lingayen Gulf—Musketeer Mike One Operation," May 15, 1945.

87 "The bombardment": Patric, *To War in a Tin Can*, p. 152.

87 "Boys are on the beach": Walter S. Macaulay to Commander in Chief, U.S. Fleet, "Action Report, Lingayen Gulf Operation, Luzon Island, Philippine Islands, 1 January 1945 to 18 January 1945, Inclusive," USS *Colorado*, February 2, 1945.

88 "The first wave": Ibid.

88 "No apparent": Spencer Davis, "Luzon Invasion Step by Step during First Hour Described," *Joplin* (Missouri) *News Herald*, January 10, 1945, p. 1.

88 "There is no": Ibid.

88 "No enemy movement": Ibid.

88 "When I came": Letter dated January 13, 1945, in Stroup, *Letters from the Pacific*, p. 180.

88 "He left Luzon": Yates McDaniel, "General at Rail of Warship as Bomb Drops Near-by," *Chicago Daily Tribune*, January 10, 1945, p. 1.

88 "Many 2½-ton trucks": I Corps, History of Luzon Campaign, Philippine Islands 1945.

88 Kamikazes returned: Herman J. Redfield to Commander in Chief, U.S. Fleet, "Action Report—Bombardment Operations in Lingayen Gulf, Luzon, Philippine Islands During Period 6–9 January 1945 and Including Collateral Supporting Actions and Operations During Period 3–18 January 1945," USS *Mississippi*, January 30, 1945.

89 Seconds later: John M. Armstrong to Commodore Commanding Australian Squadron, "Action Report—Mike 1 Operation," HMAS *Australia*, January 22, 1945.

89 "The *Australia*": Ingram C. Sowell to Commander in Chief, U.S. Fleet, "War Diary for the Month of January, 1945—Transmittal of," Battleship Division Four, February 7, 1945.

89 A little more: Entry for January 9, 1945, Douglas MacArthur diary, Box 66, RG 5, Records of General Headquarters, SCAP, 1941–51, MMAL; Willard M. Downes to Commander in Chief, U.S. Fleet, "War Diary of USS *Boise* for January 1945," February 21, 1945.

89 "On our way": Egeberg, *General*, p. 105.

89 "We won't be seeing": Ibid.

89 "All of these": MacArthur, *Reminiscences*, p. 241.

90 "I slept well": William C. Dickinson, "On Fifteen-Mile Beachhead," *New York Times*, January 10, 1945, p. 1.

90 "The Jap": Ibid.

90 "Our troops": "Krueger Men Plan Gift of Manila for Birthday," *New York Times*, January 11, 1945, p. 3.

90 "Ignoring the fine": Dunn, *Pacific Microphone*, p. 277.

90 "I've taken part": Dunn broadcast transcript, January 10, 1945.

90 "In a series": MacArthur, *Reminiscences*, p. 241.

90 "We'll bury him": William Dunn, broadcast transcript, January 15, 1945, RG 52, Papers of William J. Dunn, MMAL.

91 MacArthur climbed: Willard M. Downes to Commander in Chief, U.S. Fleet, "War Diary of USS *Boise* for January 1945," February 21, 1945.

91 "His back door": "'We Are Now at the Japs' Rear; Back Door Shut,'" *Chicago Daily Tribune*, January 10, 1945, p. 1.

91 "It is Mac's": Bonner Fellers to Dorothy Fellers, January 9, 1945, Box 2, RG 44a, Papers of Brig. Gen. Bonner F. Fellers, MMAL.

91 "We expected rice": Potter, *Life and Death*, p. 130.

91 "The American army": Ibid., p. 132.

92 "He has the air": Ibid.

92 "Here on these islands": Ibid.

92 "It is easy": Ibid., p. 131.

92 Japanese Rear Adm.: Ricardo Trota Jose, "Postscript: Here Lies 'The Butcher of Manila,'" *Philippines Daily Inquirer*, February 16, 2005, p. A1.

92 During the late night: Hornfischer, *Neptune's Inferno*, pp. 353–66.

94 Until late December: Denshichi Okochi testimony, November 16, 1945, YTT, pp. 2532–56.

94 Despite the army's plan: See the statements of Kenichiro Asano (February 20, 1950), Shigeichi Yamamoto (December 16, 1949), Yorio Ishikawa (December 1, 1949), and Koichi Kayashima (December 10, 1949, and March 8, 1950), all found in General Headquarters, Far East Command, Military Intelligence Section, Historical Division, "Statements of Japanese Officials on World War II," LOC.

95 In addition to Manila: Shizuo Yokoyama testimony, November 4, 1945, Box 1905, RG 331, SCAP, Legal Section, Manila Branch, Statements & Affidavits, Alphabetical File, 1945–49, NARA.

95 To defend it: Smith, *Triumph in Philippines*, p. 244.

95 "The repair work": Manila Naval Defense Opn Order no. 39, February 2, 1945, Box 1276, RG 331, SCAP, Legal Section, Administrative Division, Documents & Maps, 1945–48, NARA.

95 Iwabuchi divided: Military History Section, Headquarters, Army Forces Far East, "Philippine Area Naval Operations," pt. IV, January–August 1945, Japanese Monograph no. 114, pp. 9–10, Roderick Hall Collection, FHL; Smith, *Triumph in Philippines*, pp. 244–46. Various documents contain different spellings for Takesue Furuse. I have used the spelling of his name as it appears in his war crimes trial records.

95 "Hold Manila City": Manila Naval Defense Force Opn Order no. 17, January 21, 1945, Box 1276, RG 331, SCAP, Legal Section, Administrative Division, Documents & Maps, 1945–48, NARA.

95 Iwabuchi's battle plan: Details of the Japanese fortification of Manila come from "Combat in Manila," April 21, 1945, Box 1957, RG 407, Records of the Adjutant General's Office, WWII Operations Reports, 1940–48, NARA. A modified version of this report was later released as "Japanese Defense of Cities as Exemplified by the Battle for Manila," July 1, 1945, Box 1997, RG 407, Records of the Adjutant General's Office, WWII Operations Reports, 1940–48, NARA.

99 "All Manila highways": Serial no. 1378, January 31, 1945, G-2 Journal, Box 8624, RG 407, Records of the Adjutant General's Office, WWII Operations Reports, 1940–48, 37th Infantry Division, NARA.

99 "All main bridges": General Headquarters, SWPA, Military Intelligence Section, General Staff, "Report on the Destruction of Manila and Japanese Atrocities," February 1945, Box 1116, RG 331, SCAP, Legal Section, Administrative Division, War Crimes Files, 1946–50, NARA.

99 "Defensive preparation": Ibid.
100 "People began to disappear": Garcia, *It Took Four Years*, p. 98.
100 "It looks": Entry for January 18, 1945, in Lichauco, *"Dear Mother Putnam,"* p. 200.
100 "The Japanese were": Garcia, *It Took Four Years*, p. 95.
100 "Big fighting": Ibid., p. 100.
100 "I know": Entry for October 29, 1942, in Labrador, *Diary of Japanese Occupation*, p. 234.
100 "We shall fight": Monaghan, *Under Red Sun*, p. 230.
101 "Very few of you": "Fires Are Still Burning in Manila," *New York Times*, February 8, 1945, p. 3.
101 "Defeat is a bitter": Entry for October 21, 1944, in Pestaño-Jacinto, *Living with the Enemy*, p. 238.

CHAPTER 5

102 "Hunger had become": Entry for January 26, 1945, in Cates, *Drainpipe Diary*, p. 242.
102 Abram Hartendorp: Background on Hartendorp's personal life is drawn from vols. 1–3 of his unpublished memoirs, *I Have Lived*, which can be found in Box 1 of his personal papers at the Library of Congress.
103 "Three deaths": Hartendorp, *Japanese Occupation*, p. 2:502, 512–13.
103 Conditions at Santo Tomas: An invaluable resource in learning about the experience of internees at Santo Tomas can be found in Report no. 91, "Mis-Treatment and Imprisonment Under Improper Conditions of Civilian Internees at Santo Tomas University, Manila, P.I., by the Japanese During the Period January 1942 to February 1945," November 22, 1945, Box 1118, RG 331, SCAP, Legal Section, Administrative Division, War Crimes File, 1946–50, NARA. All testimony below, unless otherwise noted, comes from this report or the folders marked as containing "excess materials."
103 Founded in 1611: Hartendorp, *Japanese Occupation*, pp. 1:8–9.
103 "Santo Tomas was never": Eunice J. Young and Frank J. Taylor, "Three Years Outside This World," *Saturday Evening Post*, May 5, 1945, p. 89.
103 Americans comprised: Hartendorp, *Japanese Occupation*, p. 1:11.
103 "You had bankers": Terry Meyers Johnson, oral history by Elizabeth Norman, July 5, 1992, RG 135, Papers of Drs. Michael and Elizabeth Norman, MMLA.
103 "The rich": Young and Taylor, "Three Years Outside This World," p. 89.
104 The Japanese made: Earl Carroll, "How 3 Brave Captives Were Murdered by Japs," *San Francisco Examiner*, August 14, 1945, p. 12.
104 "I'll die": Earl Carroll, "Brutal Japs Execute Three British Martyrs," *San Francisco Examiner*, August 15, 1945, p. 22.
104 "Then the Japs stood": Ibid.
104 "The lesson": Entry for April 19, 1943, in Vaughan, *Ordeal of Elizabeth Vaughan*, p. 208.
104 "Two things": Mydans, *More Than Meets*, p. 73.
104 A nine-person: Stevens, *Santo Tomas Internment Camp*, pp. 12–21; Hartendorp, *Japanese Occupation*, pp. 1:12–42.
104 "We had offices": Earl Carroll, "The Secret War of Santo Tomas," *San Francisco Examiner*, August 13, 1945, p. 8.
104 The Japanese did not: Hartendorp, *Japanese Occupation*, pp. 1:17–20; A.V.H. Hartendorp testimony, August 16–18, 20–22, 1945.
105 William Hoffman spent: William John Hoffman testimony, December 4, 1945.
105 "Leading members": Hartendorp, *Japanese Occupation*, pp. 1:18–19.
105 Internees converted: Marie Adams, "Conditions at Santo Tomas," June 7, 1945, Box 222, RG 112, Surgeon General's Office, Operations Service, Mobilization and Overseas Operations Division, Inspection Branch, Interviews with Officers Visiting S.G.O. Installations, 1943–45, NARA; Emmet F. Pearson, "Morbidity and

Mortality in Santo Tomas Internment Camp," *Annals of Internal Medicine,* 24, no. 6 (1946): 988–1013; Hartendorp, *Japanese Occupation,* pp. 1:28–30; Stevens, *Santo Tomas Internment Camp,* pp. 109–34.

105   **An army of six hundred:** Hartendorp, *Japanese Occupation,* pp. 1:26–34; Pearson, "Morbidity and Mortality in Santo Tomas Internment Camp," pp. 993–94; Stevens, *Santo Tomas Internment Camp,* pp. 102–5, 263.

106   **"The cluttered rooms":** Hartendorp, *Japanese Occupation,* p. 1:43.

106   **Internees planted thirty:** Ibid., pp. 1:33–34; Hartendorp testimony, August 16–18, 20–22, 1945.

106   **"A bucket":** Sams, *Forbidden Family,* p. 97.

106   **"One could have":** Mydans, *More Than Meets,* p. 74.

106   **To relieve crowding:** Hartendorp testimony, August 16–18, 20–22, 1945.

106   **Residents nicknamed:** Young, "Three Years Outside This World," p. 90.

106   **"Though such a shanty":** Hartendorp, *Japanese Occupation,* p. 1:42.

106   **"The shanties were private":** Williams, *To the Angels,* p. 166.

107   **The adults set out:** Don H. Holter to Any Educational Official Concerned, January 17, 1945, included with the above-referenced Report no. 91; Hartendorp, *Japanese Occupation,* pp. 1:34–36.

107   **Students even received:** Caroline Jane Bailey, Academic Record, 1942–43, Box 1, RG 98, Papers of Fay C. Bailey and Family, MMLA.

107   **"While every pupil":** Don H. Holter to Any Educational Official Concerned, January 17, 1945.

107   **"Previous to that":** Hartendorp, *Japanese Occupation,* p. 1:114.

107   **"If you want privacy":** Ibid., p. 44.

107   **"There seemed to be no":** Adams, "Conditions at Santo Tomas," June 7, 1945.

108   **To distract internees:** Hartendorp, *Japanese Occupation,* p. 1:38.

108   **The captives went so far:** Baseball Schedule at Santo Tomas Internment Camp, February 17, 1943, Box 1, RG 98, Papers of Fay C. Bailey and Family, MMLA.

108   **Internee Archie Taylor:** Boxing Program, March 12, 1943, ibid.

108   **"Once in a while":** Helen M. Nestor, oral history by Thomas Beeman, April 9, 1983, RG 135, Papers of Drs. Michael and Elizabeth Norman, MMLA.

108   **"Santa Claus came":** Madeline M. Ullom, "Army Nurse Corps in the Philippines," n.d., Box 41, RG 15, Materials Donated by the General Public, MMLA.

108   **"The Little Theater under the Stars":** Stevens, *Santo Tomas Internment Camp,* p. 192.

108   **"Independent, Curt, Concise":** Hartendorp, *Japanese Occupation,* p. 1:373.

108   **"We lived in the past":** Inez Moore, oral history by Colonel Slewitzke, n.d., RG 135, Papers of Drs. Michael and Elizabeth Norman, MMLA.

110   **"Beer-bellies":** Hartendorp, *Japanese Occupation,* p. 1:112.

110   **Many had no concept:** Frank Hewlett, "66 Children from Santo Tomas Take Long, Hungry Look at U.S.," *Racine* (Wisconsin) *Journal Times,* March 31, 1945, p. 2.

110   **"To many of these":** Entry for September 20, 1944, in Cates, *Drainpipe Diary,* p. 218.

110   **"She worked to earn money":** Entry for April 21, 1943, ibid., p. 161.

110   **"It used to aggravate":** Wygle, *Surviving,* p. 81.

111   **"I am in very bad need":** Hartendorp, *I Have Lived,* p. 3:458.

111   **"I want only":** Ibid., p. 3:459.

111   **"I have been picturing":** Entry for July 27, 1942, Abram Hartendorp diary, ibid., pp. 3:462–463.

112   **"The typed note":** Entry for July 10, 1943, in Vaughan, *Ordeal of Elizabeth Vaughan,* p. 234.

112   **"Oh, Jim, Jim":** Ibid.

112   **Popular Manila radio:** Don Bell, "Wrong Story," *Life,* May 21, 1945, pp. 4, 6.

112   **"When the Americans entered":** Young, "Three Years Outside This World," p. 90.

112   **"Our ration decreased":** Adams, "Conditions at Santo Tomas," June 7, 1945.

112   **"Paunches, of course":** Hartendorp, *Japanese Occupation,* p. 2:48.

113   **One hundred eighty-five:** Peter C. Richards, "The Liberation Bulletin of Philippine

Internment Camp no. 1 at Santo Tomas University, Manila, Philippines," February 3, 1945, copies of which can be found with Report no. 91, the Santo Tomas papers at LOC, and in the Wisconsin Veterans Museum.

113 "Each day as I climbed": Prising, *Manila, Goodbye*, p. 147.

113 "There was a tension": Adams, "Conditions at Santo Tomas," June 7, 1945.

113 "Each day, we examined": Entry for August 2, 1944, in Cates, *Drainpipe Diary*, pp. 212–13.

114 "If MacArthur doesn't": Entry for August 14, 1944, ibid., p. 214.

114 "It seemed every time": Frank Eugene Long testimony, July 3, 1945.

114 "As I waited": Prising, *Manila, Goodbye*, p. 161.

114 "That's a rather dangerous": Hartendorp, *Japanese Occupation*, p. 2:364.

114 "That's a real fight": Ibid.

114 To the amazement: Potter, *Bull Halsey*, p. 278.

114 "Men, women, and children": Entry for September 21, 1944, in Cates, *Drainpipe Diary*, p. 218.

115 "This is a raid": Prising, *Manila, Goodbye*, p. 148.

115 "They're here": Ibid.

115 "Look at that one dive": Entry for September 21, 1944, in Cates, *Drainpipe Diary*, p. 219.

115 "We pounded": Ibid.

115 Elizabeth Vaughan celebrated: Entry for September 21, 1944, in Vaughan, *Ordeal of Elizabeth Vaughan*, p. 296.

115 "For an hour or more": Entry for September 21, 1944, in Cates, *Drainpipe Diary*, p. 218.

115 "Blood plasma": Entry for September 23, 1944, ibid., p. 220.

115 "We have no deaths": Entry for November 14, 1944, Albert Holland diary, Watkinson Library, Trinity College, Hartford, Conn.

115 The Japanese guards: Hartendorp testimony, August 16–18, 20–22, 1945; entry for November 4, 1944, in Cates, *Drainpipe Diary*, p. 225.

115 "We reached a point": Margaret Gillooly, oral history by Richard W. Byrd, March 18, 1995, UNT.

115 "Pennies from Heaven": Hartendorp, *Japanese Occupation*, p. 2:367.

116 "Lover, Come Back to Me": Entry for September 27, 1944, in Cates, *Drainpipe Diary*, p. 220.

116 "The body": Gillooly oral history.

116 "Many people complained": Hartendorp, *Japanese Occupation*, p. 2:452.

116 Caroline Bailey's parents: Undated photo caption of Caroline Bailey Pratt and her stuffed animals on file at the MMAL.

116 Children picked: Fernie Naylor testimony, June 12, 1945.

116 "Such a wonderful": Elsa Colquhoun note, January 18, 1945, in Robert Colquhoun, "Santo Tomas: A War Memoir, 1941–1945," unpublished manuscript, Roderick Hall Collection, FHL, p. 30.

116 Medical officer Maj.: Adams, "Conditions at Santo Tomas," June 7, 1945; Naylor testimony.

116 Even rats: Entry for December 23, 1944, Anne Louise Goldthorpe diary, Archives of the Episcopal Church, Austin, Tex.

116 "One man": Nixon, *Delayed Manila*, p. 66. A copy of this diary is at MMAL.

116 "How was it": Entry for November 15, 1944, in Cates, *Drainpipe Diary*, p. 230.

116 "Dogs or old tomcats": Prising, *Manila, Goodbye*, pp. 150–51.

117 "I was fond": Colquhoun, "Santo Tomas," p. 14.

117 "The poor splendid": Hartendorp, *Japanese Occupation*, p. 2:464.

117 Internees likewise ate: Ibid., pp. 2:435–36; entry for November 20, 1944, in Cates, *Drainpipe Diary*, pp. 230–31; Entry for December 6, 1944, Goldthorpe diary.

117 One of those was: Entry for December 6, 1944, Goldthorpe diary.

117 "It must again": Hartendorp, *Japanese Occupation*, p. 2:436.

117 "Our hunger": Entry for December 15, 1944, in Cates, *Drainpipe Diary*, p. 234.

117 The Japanese, in contrast: Entries for January 20 and February 2, 1945, in Cates, *Drainpipe Diary*, pp. 241, 245.

117 "Just as soon": Entry for February 1, 1945, ibid., p. 244.

117 Another forty-three: Richards, "The Liberation Bulletin of Philippine Internment Camp no. 1 at Santo Tomas University, Manila, Philippines," February 3, 1945.

118 A kilo of sugar: Pearson, "Morbidity and Mortality in Santo Tomas Internment Camp," p. 1001.

118 "The money lenders": "Internees Stole Food from Pigs at Jap Camp, Says S. M. Letter," *San Mateo Times*, March 2, 1945, p. 7.

118 "There is as much": Entry for December 5, 1944, Holland diary.

118 "I weighed 92 lbs today": Entry for December 23, 1944, Goldthorpe diary.

118 "I weigh 110 today": Entry for November 17, 1944, Holland diary.

118 "I'm hungry": Fernie Naylor testimony, June 12, 1945.

118 "The tremendously active": Entry for January 17, 1945, in Cates, *Drainpipe Diary*, p. 241.

118 "Starvation is taking": Prising, *Manila, Goodbye*, p. 168.

118 "Even the vomit": Ibid.

118 "It is hard": Entry for December 11, 1944, Goldthorpe diary.

119 "When I went to bed": Adams, "Conditions at Santo Tomas," June 7, 1945.

119 The average caloric intake: Pearson, "Morbidity and Mortality in Santo Tomas Internment Camp," p. 1000; Hartendorp testimony.

119 "I was worried": Entry for January 5, 1945, Goldthorpe diary, in Neil Henry, "A Journal of Human Endurance," *Washington Post*, March 20, 1983, p. A1.

119 As much as 90 percent: Pearson, "Morbidity and Mortality in Santo Tomas Internment Camp," p. 1003.

119 Army nurse Gwendolyn Henshaw: Gwendolyn Henshaw Deiss, oral history by Esther Jane McNeil, March 7, 1984, RG 135, Papers of Drs. Michael and Elizabeth Norman, MMLA.

119 "When I'd stand up": Sally Blaine Millett, oral history by Elizabeth Norman, September 20, 1990, ibid.

119 "Many of us believed": Entry for December 20, 1944, in Cates, *Drainpipe Diary*, p. 235.

119 A mass mania: These recipes come from a journal on file in Box 1, RG 98, Papers of Fay C. Bailey and Family, MMLA.

119 "People would be": Anna Williams Clark, oral history by Mary Ellen Condon, September 1, 1983, RG 135, Papers of Drs. Michael and Elizabeth Norman, MMLA.

120 "What made the mania": Entry for December 10, 1944, in Cates, *Drainpipe Diary*, p. 233.

120 "Many prisoners": Prising, *Manila, Goodbye*, p. 168, 19, 169.

120 "Every waking hour": Bertha Dworsky Henderson, oral history by Mary Horan, n.d., RG 135, Papers of Drs. Michael and Elizabeth Norman, MMLA.

121 "Food is getting": Entry for January 15, 1945, Goldthorpe diary.

121 "Some stayed": Entry for January 1, 1945, in Cates, *Drainpipe Diary*, p. 239.

121 "This place is a living": Elsa Colquhoun note, January 1, 1945, in Colquhoun, "Santo Tomas," p. 22.

121 Even then desperate internees: Millett oral history.

121 "I saw many cases": Adams, "Conditions at Santo Tomas," June 7, 1945.

121 "What bothered me": Raymond E. Abbitt, oral history by Ronald E. Marcello, February 25, 1975, UNT.

121 The camp's doctors: Hartendorp, *Japanese Occupation*, pp. 2:406–7.

121 "If there were any milk": Ibid., p. 2:407.

122 "The aged and infirm": Lemuel Earl Carroll testimony, August 9, 13, 14–15, 1945.

122 "In the last year": Ray Perez, "4 Decades Later, Civilian POWS Reunite to Remember," *Los Angeles Times*, February 14, 1986, p. 1.

122 "Day in, day out": Entry for December 26, 1944, Holland diary.

122 The Japanese often left: Madeline M. Ullom testimony, June 11, 1945.

122 "As I watched": Entry for October 31, 1944, in Cates, *Drainpipe Diary*, p. 224.

122 "What a pitiful": Entry for December 6, 1944, Goldthorpe diary.

122 The January 21 passing: Hartendorp, *Japanese Occupation*, pp. 2:499–500.

122 "Uncle John Shaw": Prising, *Manila, Goodbye*, p. 171.

123 Chairman of the internee: Earl Carroll, Memorandum to All Camp Doctors, January 31, 1945.

123 "He was": Carroll testimony.

123 "There were twenty-three": Adams, "Conditions at Santo Tomas," June 7, 1945.

123 "For the last week": Entry for January 10, 1945, in Cates, *Drainpipe Diary*, p. 240.

123 "Still here, still waiting": Letter dated February 1, 1945, in Cary, *Letters from Internment Camp*, p. 118.

123 "In the anguish": Prising, *Manila, Goodbye*, p. 172.

123 "We survived": Carroll testimony.

PART II

125 "The stage was now": Sixth Army, Report of the Luzon Campaign, January 9–June 30, 1945, p. 1:36.

CHAPTER 6

127 "No one will ever know": Milton Sandberg, December 5, 1945, YTT, p. 3913.

127 "Go to Manila": Chase, *Front Line General*, p. 80.

128 "I still cannot": Robert Eichelberger to Emma Eichelberger, January 16, 1945, in Luvaas, *Dear Miss Em*, p. 195.

128 "I do not": Entry for January 14, 1945, Griswold diary.

128 "Bunk!": Clyde D. Eddleman, oral history by Lowell G. Smith and Murray G. Swindler, February 11, 1975, Box 2, Clyde D. Eddleman Papers, USAHEC.

128 "Mac has made": Bonner Fellers to Dorothy Fellers, January 16, 1945, Box 2, RG 44a, Papers of Brig. Gen. Bonner F. Fellers, MMAL.

128 "If I were commanding": Dunn, *Pacific Microphone*, p. 279.

129 "The next twenty minutes": Henry A. Mucci, "We Swore We'd Die or Do it," *Saturday Evening Post*, April 7, 1945, p. 110.

129 "What a barbaric": Bonner Fellers to Dorothy Fellers, January 29, 1945, Box 2, RG 44a, Papers of Brig. Gen. Bonner F. Fellers, MMAL.

129 "I know there are": William Dunn, broadcast transcript, January 23, 1945, RG 52, Papers of William J. Dunn, MMAL.

129 "I presume": Douglas MacArthur to AGWAR, January 27, 1945, Box 2, RG 3, Records of Headquarters, SWPA, 1942–45, MMAL.

129 "best clerk": Manchester, *American Caesar*, p. 166.

129 "Eisenhower's curve": Luvaas, *Dear Miss Em*, p. 251.

130 He did so: Rogers, *MacArthur and Sutherland*, pp. 1:262–66.

130 Out of the 142: Manchester, *American Caesar*, p. 230.

130 In a sign: "Stadium Now MacArthur Field," *New York Times*, March 17, 1942, p. 27; "Capital Street Named MacArthur," *New York Times*, March 6, 1942, p. 6; "Bridge Named for MacArthur," *New York Times*, February 19, 1942, p. 4.

130 Couples had danced: "MacArthur Glide Is New Dance," *New York Times*, March 16, 1942, p. 9; "The Wave of Fame," *New York Times*, March 23, 1942, p. 12; "Babies, Highways and Parks Are Being Named for MacArthur," *Pittsburgh Post-Gazette Daily Magazine*, April 2, 1942, p. 1.

130 So confident: R. K. Sutherland, "Plan for Entry of the Commander-in-Chief and Official Party into the City of Manila," February 2, 1945, and "Draft of Proposed Jeep Assignments for Formal Entry into Manila," February (n.d.), 1945, both in Box 14, RG 3, Records of Headquarters, SWPA, 1942–45, MMAL.

130 **"It would be"**: McCallus, *MacArthur Highway*, p. 128.
130 **"He is"**: Entry for February 4, 1945, Griswold diary.
131 **"We're the battling bastards"**: Wainwright, *General Wainwright's Story*, p. 54.
131 **"She insisted"**: Frank Hewlett, "Reporter Finds Wife Among 3700 Rescued in Jap Camp at Manila," *Pittsburgh Press*, February 5, 1945, p. 1.
131 **"Under the stress"**: Mydans, *More Than Meets*, p. 116.
132 **"Santo Tomas was his last"**: Dunn, *Pacific Microphone*, p. 297.
132 **"Everything will be stripped"**: Serial no. 1, January 31, 1945, S-2–3 Journal, Box 13367, RG 407, WWII Operations Reports, 1941–48, First Cavalry Division, NARA.
133 **"Mudge's plan"**: Chase, *Front Line General*, p. 81.
133 **Guerrilla reports reflected**: "Extracts from Daily Philippines Messages Sheets," Box 310, RG 496, Records of General Headquarters, SWPA and U.S. Army Forces, Pacific, MIS Administrative Section, General Correspondence, 1942–46, NARA.
133 **"Nips moving out"**: Message no. 218, December 28, 1944, ibid.
133 **"Nips bored holes"**: Message no. 232, January 12, 1945, ibid.
133 **"Barricades constructed"**: Message no. 234, January 14, 1945, ibid.
133 **"I don't see how"**: Robert Eichelberger to Emma Eichelberger, January 23, 1945, in Luvaas, *Dear Miss Em*, p. 198.
133 **"We still do not know"**: Robert Eichelberger to Emma Eichelberger, January 29, 1945, ibid., p. 204.
134 **American forces had**: Max Myers to Commanding General, XXIV Corps, "Atrocities," January 17, 1945, Box 1060, RG 331, SCAP, Legal Section, Administrative Division, Closed Case Files, 1945–46, NARA.
134 **"The head, arms"**: Burdette L. Andrews, affidavit, February 22, 1945, ibid.
134 **"I don't know when"**: Dunn, *Pacific Microphone*, p. 290.
134 **"It was impossible"**: Ibid.
134 **"Your jeep"**: Mydans, *More Than Meets*, p. 186.
135 **"Again we insisted"**: Dunn, *Pacific Microphone*, p. 292.
135 **"We're traveling light"**: Mydans, *More Than Meets*, p. 186.
135 **"It had been"**: Dunn, *Pacific Microphone*, p. 292.
135 **"Behind stretched"**: Mydans, *More Than Meets*, p. 186.
135 **"Morning came"**: Ibid., pp. 186–87.
135 **"Almost all"**: Ibid., p. 187.
136 **"the greatest ovation"**: William Dunn, broadcast transcript, February 2, 1945, RG 52, Papers of William J. Dunn, MMAL.
136 **"Thousands of people"**: Ibid.
136 **"The whole column"**: Chase, *Front Line General*, p. 84.
136 **"Mabuhay"**: Mydans, *More Than Meets*, p. 187.
136 **"God bless you"**: Ibid.
136 **"I was more moved"**: Carl Mydans, "'My God! It's Carl Mydans,'" *Life*, February 19, 1945, p. 21.
136 **"Any member"**: Dunn, *Pacific Microphone*, p. 294.
136 **"As our column"**: Historical Record, Fifth Cavalry, Luzon Campaign, July 12, 1945, Box 13367, RG 407, WWII Operations Reports, 1941–48, First Cavalry Division, NARA.
136 **"Evidence all along"**: Ibid.
137 **"No football team"**: Mydans, "'My God! It's Carl Mydans,'" p. 21.
137 **"Our pauses"**: Dunn, *Pacific Microphone*, p. 295.
137 **"Suddenly," Dunn recalled**: Dunn, *Pacific Microphone*, p. 297.
137 **"Bill, this has"**: Ibid.
137 **"I had no information"**: Ibid.
137 **"Let's go"**: Mydans, *More Than Meets*, p. 187.
137 **"The Japanese had mined"**: Mydans, "'My God! It's Carl Mydans,'" p. 22.
138 **"Many Japs"**: Serial no. 1483, February 3, 1945, G-2 Journal, Box 8624, RG 407, Records of the Adjutant General's Office, WWII Operations Reports, 1940–48, 37th Infantry Division, NARA.

138 "Be alert": Mydans, "'My God! It's Carl Mydans,'" p. 22.
138 "There was not a rifle": Ibid.
138 "We were entering Manila": Historical Record, Fifth Cavalry, Luzon Campaign, July 12, 1945.
138 "God Bless America": Buenafe, *Wartime Philippines*, p. 254.
138 "Tell me you think": Mydans, *More Than Meets*, p. 188.
138 "I think I will have": "Captain Colayco Was First Casualty at Santo Tomas," *Free Philippines*, February 13, 1945, p. 2.
139 "We're there": Mydans, *More Than Meets*, p. 188.
139 "I felt a flush": Mydans, "'My God! It's Carl Mydans,'" p. 96.
139 "Fires were burning": Ibid.
139 "Maybe they've gone": Mydans, *More Than Meets*, p. 188.
139 "I'm sure the Japs": Mydans, "'My God! It's Carl Mydans,'" p. 96.
139 "We lay there": Ibid.
140 "You all right": Mydans, *More Than Meets*, p. 189.
140 "I want two men": Ibid.
140 "Grenade": Mydans, "'My God! It's Carl Mydans,'" p. 98.
140 "Run that tank": Ibid.
140 "The snorting tank": Dean Schedler and Fred Hampson, "Liberation of Americans at Santo Tomas Described," *Tuscaloosa News*, February 5, 1945, p. 3.
140 "Any Americans": Mydans, "'My God! It's Carl Mydans,'" p. 98.
140 "I'm an American": Mydans, *More Than Meets*, p. 189.
140 "You Americans": Mydans, "'My God! It's Carl Mydans,'" p. 98.
140 "Thanks, Mac": Mydans, *More Than Meets*, p. 189.
140 "That's the Main Building": Ibid.
141 "I'm going in across": Mydans, "'My God! It's Carl Mydans,'" p. 98.
141 "I tripped once": Ibid.
141 "Thank God": Ibid.
141 "Crowds pressed": Ibid.
141 "Who are you": Mydans, *More Than Meets*, p. 189.
141 "Carl Mydans": Mydans, "'My God! It's Carl Mydans,'" p. 98; Bruce Montgomery, "Widow Recalls Terror, Hunger of War Camp," *Sarasota Herald-Tribune*, December 27, 1977, p. 2B.
141 "I was unable": Mydans, "'My God! It's Carl Mydans,'" p. 98.
142 "No, darling, no": Ibid.
142 "God Bless America": Ibid.
142 "I found a little girl": Hewlett, "Reporter Finds Wife among 3700 Rescued," p. 1.
142 "He's gone": Lucas, *Prisoners of Santo Tomas*, p. 121.
142 In recent months: Rita G. Palmer as told to Adna N. Hayes, "Three Years in a Prison Camp," *Hampton Union*, May 10, 1945, p. 1.
142 "Where's my wife": Young, "Three Years Outside This World," p. 92.
142 "I found her there": Hewlett, "Reporter Finds Wife among 3700 Rescued," p. 1.
142 "I found her": Dunn, *Pacific Microphone*, p. 301.
143 "Frank grabbed me": Ibid.
143 "Your skin prickled": Margaret Gillooly, oral history by Richard W. Byrd, March 18, 1995.
143 "The Americans are coming": Ibid.
143 "They came so close": Entry for February 3, 1945, in Cates, *Drainpipe Diary*, p. 245. Various accounts differ slightly on how many planes buzzed Santo Tomas that afternoon as well as precisely what was written in the note that was dropped.
143 "We always thought": Minnie Bresse Stubbs, oral history by Peg Baskfield, April 9, 1983, RG 135, Papers of Drs. Michael and Elizabeth Norman, MMLA.
144 "Each day may": Frank Cary letter, February 3, 1945, in Cary, *Letters from Internment Camp*, p. 120.
144 "Not bombers": Prising, *Manila, Goodbye*, p. 179–82.
144 "From our windows": Alice R. Clarke, "Thirty-Seven Months as Prisoners of War," *American Journal of Nursing* 45, no. 5 (1945): 344.

145 **"Many stayed up"**: Hartendorp, *Santo Tomas Story*, p. 405.
145 **"We watched"**: Entry for February 3, 1945, in Cates, *Drainpipe Diary*, pp. 245–46.
145 **"Turn right"**: Clarke, "Thirty-Seven Months as Prisoners of War," p. 345.
145 **"Honey, they're here"**: Entry for February 3, 1945, in Cates, *Drainpipe Diary*, p. 246.
145 **"Well, this is it"**: Raymond E. Abbitt, oral history by Ronald E. Marcello, February 25, 1975.
145 **"Mama, Mama"**: Entry for February 3, 1945, Goldthorpe diary.
145 **"The Americans"**: Ibid.
146 **"As in a dream"**: Entry for February 3, 1945, in Cates, *Drainpipe Diary*, p. 246.
146 **"Over here"**: Entry for February 3, 1945, Margaret Bayer (Pittam) diary, Box 2, RG 112, Santo Tomas Internment Camp Papers, MMAL.
146 **"This way"**: Ibid.
146 **"It was then"**: Entry for February 3, 1945, in Cates, *Drainpipe Diary*, p. 246.
146 **"There was a sea"**: Gillooly oral history.
146 **"Like the last day"**: Entry for February 3, 1945, in Cates, *Drainpipe Diary*, pp. 246–47.
147 **"This was liberation"**: William Dunn, broadcast transcript, February 4, 1945, RG 52, Papers of William J. Dunn, MMAL.
147 **"Come on, now"**: Williams, *To the Angels*, p. 204.
147 **"It makes me sick"**: Ibid., p. 205.
147 **"I only wanted"**: Ibid.
148 **"They're here"**: Prising, *Manila, Goodbye*, p. 183–84.
148 **"Look what I found"**: David Boguslav, "Internee Describes Liberation Eve," *Hope Star*, February 4, 1947, p. 6. The byline mistakenly spells his surname Goguslav.
148 **"My land"**: Rose Meier, oral history by Margaret Lauer, March 12, 1984, RG 135, Papers of Drs. Michael and Elizabeth Norman, MMLA.
149 **"My God"**: Gwendolyn Henshaw Deiss, oral history by Esther Jane McNeil, March 7, 1984, RG 135, Papers of Drs. Michael and Elizabeth Norman, MMLA.
149 **"It was just"**: Bertha Dworsky Henderson, oral history by Mary Horan, n.d., RG 135, Papers of Drs. Michael and Elizabeth Norman, MMLA.
149 **"Where are the Japs"**: Entry for February 3, 1945, in Cates, *Drainpipe Diary*, p. 246.
149 **"Let us out"**: Hartendorp, *Japanese Occupation*, p. 2:524.
150 **"Kill them"**: Ibid., p. 2:525.
150 **"Why do you wear"**: Ibid.
150 **"When I got over"**: Wygle, *Surviving*, p. 132.
150 **"Here, take that"**: Prising, *Manila, Goodbye*, p. 184–85.
151 **"Enough, ladies"**: Williams, *To the Angels*, p. 208–10.
152 **"I went and looked"**: Sally Blaine Millett, oral history by Elizabeth Norman, September 20, 1990.
152 **"Dead"**: Prising, *Manila, Goodbye*, p. 185.
153 **"To us"**: Entry for February 4, 1945, in Cates, *Drainpipe Diary*, pp. 248–49.

CHAPTER 7

154 **"Food and freedom"**: "Four Internees Express Joy at Liberation," *Salt Lake Tribune*, February 6, 1945, p. 4.
154 **"We forced"**: Robert Yelton Robb, "Nightmare in Santo Tomas," *Collier's*, February 5, 1949, p. 64–65.
155 **"The only reason"**: Percy H. Ripka testimony, June 2, 1945, in Report no. 91.
155 **"The Commandant"**: Frank Cary letter, dated February 11, 1945, in Cary, *Letters from Internment Camp*, p. 123.
155 **"We'll give you"**: Robb, "Nightmare in Santo Tomas," p. 65.
156 **"The machine-gun fire"**: Wilkinson, *Surviving*, p. 154.
157 **"Mommy"**: Robb, "Nightmare in Santo Tomas," p. 65.
157 **"A very little"**: Stevens, *Santo Tomas Internment Camp*, p. 363.

157 "American machine-gun": Rupert Wilkinson, "Standoff at Santo Tomas," *World War II*, March–April 2014, p. 63.

157 "Take it easy": Robb, "Nightmare in Santo Tomas," p. 65.

158 "No sleep tonight": Diary entry for February 3, 1945, in Wygle, *Surviving*, pp. 130–31.

158 "Blackout regulations": Entry for February 3, 1944, in Cates, *Drainpipe Diary*, p. 247.

158 "One of the unforgettable": Frank Robertson, "Pure Joy Fills Camp," *San Antonio Light*, February 5, 1945, p. 1.

159 "Don't you know": "Little Girl Would Save Her Candy to Give Her Sick Daddy," *Corsicana Daily Sun*, February 9, 1945, p. 4.

159 "The old army chow": Van Sickle, *Iron Gates*, p. 320.

159 "Oh, can I": Rose Meier, oral history by Margaret Lauer, March 12, 1984.

159 "Sat up all night": Diary entry for February 4, 1945, in Wygle, *Surviving*, p. 133.

159 "I remember the first":" Rita James, oral history by Patricia Murphy, June 5–6, 1984, RG 135, Papers of Drs. Michael and Elizabeth Norman, MMLA.

159 "The fascination": Robertson, "Pure Joy Fills Camp," p. 1.

160 "It sure is good": Van Sickle, *Iron Gates*, p. 318.

160 "We kept the poor": Entry for February 3, 1945, Bayer diary.

160 "What in the world": Entry for February 3, 1945, in Cates, *Drainpipe Diary*, pp. 247–48.

160 "This is a new": Ibid., p. 248.

160 Despite the celebration: Chase, *Front Line General*, p. 88.

160 "The internees": Francis J. McCarthy, "Internees in Manila in Deplorable Condition," *Pittsburgh Post-Gazette*, February 5, 1945, p. 2.

161 "We had civilians killed": Helen M. Nestor, oral history by Thomas Beeman, April 9, 1983.

161 "What's wrong": Minnie Bresse Stubbs, oral history by Peg Baskfield, April 9, 1983.

161 "We worked that night": Ibid.

161 "You may be needed": Williams, *To the Angels*, p. 210.

161 "The heck with it": Eleanor Garen, oral history by Elizabeth Norman, October 15, 1990, RG 135, Papers of Drs. Michael and Elizabeth Norman, MMLA.

161 "You're not supposed": Ibid.

161 "I walked up": Sally Blaine Millett, oral history by Patricia Rikli, April 9, 1983, RG 135, Papers of Drs. Michael and Elizabeth Norman, MMLA.

161 "You have no idea": Ibid.

161 "I'm free": Williams, *To the Angels*, p. 210.

162 "Call your Mother": Garcia, *It Took Four Years*, p. 104.

162 "From every section": Entry for February 3, 1945, in Lichauco, *"Dear Mother Putnam,"* p. 204.

162 The room: Details on the tower room come from Montinola, *Breaking the Silence*, pp. 28–32.

163 "By evening": Ibid., pp. 67–68.

163 "by the rich odor": Prising, *Manila, Goodbye*, p. 186–87.

163 General Chase: Chase, *Front Line General*, p. 88.

164 "Steadily through the night": Prising, *Manila, Goodbye*, p. 187.

164 "On Sunday": Williams, *To the Angels*, p. 210.

164 "With the dawn": "Liberated Manila Returns to the Air," *Broadcasting*, February 12, 1945, p. 14.

164 "Complete with fielders'": Boguslav, "Internee Describes Liberation Eve," p. 6.

164 "Hey Prising": Prising, *Manila, Goodbye*, p. 187.

164 "You had sort of": Millett oral history.

165 "Say, you nurses": Williams, *To the Angels*, p. 211.

165 "To a certain extent": Headquarters, 37th Division Artillery, Report After Action, November 1, 1944, to March 5, 1945, Box 8764, RG 407, Records of the Adjutant

General's Office, WWII Operations Reports, 1940–48, 37th Infantry Division, NARA.

165 "In a few hours": Robert S. Beightler, "Report on the Activities of the 37th Infantry Division, 1940–1945," n.d. (ca. 1946), USAHEC.
165 "This," he declared: Dick Hanley, "Hike to Manila," *Yank*, March 9, 1945, p. 5.
165 "Manila," one tank: Contey-Aiello, *50th Anniversary Album*, p. 151.
165 The crowds: Charles A. Henne, "Battle History of the 3d Battalion, 148th Infantry, Manila, The Unwanted Battle (4 February through 7 March 1945)," April 18, 1988, unpublished manuscript, USAHEC, p. 42.
165 "A few Filipinos": Beightler, "Report on the Activities of the 37th Infantry Division, 1940–1945," n.d.
165 "Every time an army truck": Entry for February 4, 1944, in Cates, *Drainpipe Diary*, p. 248.
166 "If ever I've prayed": Frank Robertson, "Santo Tomas Internee's Story," *Milwaukee Sentinel*, February 6, 1945, p. 2.
166 "I can't resist": Mydans, *More Than Meets*, p. 193.
166 "Our camp was buzzing": Entry for February 4, 1944, in Cates, *Drainpipe Diary*, p. 248.
166 If Noguchi's Northern Force: Smith, *Triumph in Philippines*, p. 252.
166 "We were short": Chase, *Front Line General*, p. 89.
166 "Enemy strength": Robert F. Goheen, G-2 Periodic Report no. 78, February 4, 1945, Box 13295, RG 407, Records of the Adjutant General's Office, WWII Operations Reports, 1941–48, First Cavalry Division, NARA.
166 Throughout the day: Historical Record, Fifth Cavalry, Luzon Campaign, July 12, 1945.
167 "The Japs were starting": Ibid.
167 "Numerous wrecked cars": Ibid.
167 "All the men": Ibid.
167 "All bridges across": Ibid.
168 "Yesterday's guards": Prising, *Manila, Goodbye*, p. 188.
168 "All the streets": Ibid.
168 "My spirits sagged": Ibid.
168 Laborers buried: Hartendorp, *Japanese Occupation*, p. 2:530.
168 "The man held": Mydans, *More Than Meets*, p. 198.
168 "Tell me honestly": Ibid., pp. 198–99.
169 "He was distinctly": Ibid., p. 199.
169 "Spike": Ibid., pp. 200–1.
170 "Almost everyone": Robertson, "Pure Joy Fills Camp," p. 1.
170 "If our arrival": Dunn broadcast transcript, February 4, 1945.
170 "We're going to let": Mydans, *More Than Meets*, p. 198.

CHAPTER 8

172 "We never believed": Celedonia de Arquillo testimony, July 23, 1945, in Report no. 53, "Investigation of the Massacre of Civilians of Various Nationalities at, and in the Vicinity of, St. Paul's College in Malate, Manila, Philippine Islands on 9 February 1945," August 28, 1945, Box 1112, RG 331, SCAP, Legal Section, Administrative Division, War Crimes File, 1946–50, NARA.
172 "We were transfixed": James V. Thompson, oral history by Eleanor Swent, April 24, 1991, University of California, Berkeley.
172 "It's the boys": Johnson, *I Was a Prisoner*, p. 137.
172 "American tanks!": Miles, *Captive Community*, p. 160.
172 "Hell, Harvey": Ibid., p. 161.
173 "Never had profanity": Ibid.
173 "Manila was in flames": Brown, *Bars from Bilibid*, p. 120.

173 "I was so excited": Entry for February 3, 1945, in Crouter, *Forbidden Diary*, p. 467.

174 "The dead man": Mansell with Mansell, *Under the Shadow*, p. 248.

174 Around ten-thirty a.m.: Warren A. Wilson report, n.d., HIA.

174 "The Japanese army": Major Ebiko message, February 4, 1945, exhibit II, ibid. This is a true copy of the handwritten original, which Warren kept.

175 "I don't get it": Carlton B. Vanderboget, "Report of Medical Department Activities in the Philippines," May 21, 1945, Box 222, RG 112, Surgeon General's Office, Operations Service, Mobilization and Overseas Operations Division, Inspection Branch, Interviews with Officers Visiting SGG Installations, 1943–45, NARA.

175 "A number of baseball": Wilson report, n.d.

175 "Gangway": Entry for February 4, 1945, in Crouter, *Forbidden Diary*, p. 469.

175 "A hush swept over": Miles, *Captive Community*, p. 162.

175 "I just held": Entry for February 4, 1945, Ethel Herold diary, Box 1, Renee Ream Collection, HIA.

175 "They filed through": Entry for February 4, 1945, in Crouter, *Forbidden Diary*, p. 469.

175 "They all went out": Ibid.

176 "Not a shot": Vanderboget, "Report of Medical Department Activities in the Philippines," May 21, 1945.

176 "I could never": Miles, *Captive Community*, p. 162.

176 "I have our official release": Ibid.

176 "Here we are": Entry for February 3–4, 1945, Donald Mansell diary, Box 1, Renee Ream Collection, HIA.

176 "I put my arm": Entry for February 4, 1945, in Crouter, *Forbidden Diary*, pp. 469–70.

176 "We waved": James V. Thompson, oral history by Eleanor Swent, April 24, 1991.

176 "I began to feel horribly": Entry for February 4, 1945, in Crouter, *Forbidden Diary*, p. 470.

177 "We didn't want": Frankel, *Frankel-y Speaking*, p. 104.

177 "All right, boys": Robert Shaplen, "The Freeing of Bilibid," *New Yorker*, March 3, 1945, p. 64.

178 "The windows": Ibid.

178 "I stuck my eye": Ibid.

178 "Hey!": Ibid.

178 "By Jesus": Frankel, *Frankel-y Speaking*, p. 106.

178 "I'm Sergeant Anderson": Shaplen, "Freeing of Bilibid," p. 64.

178 "I just wanted": Ibid., p. 65.

179 "Who are you": Russell Brines, "Old Bilibid Now Citadel of Freedom," *Evening Independent*, February 6, 1945, p. 1.

179 "The camp": Entry for February 4, 1945, Robert Kentner diary, Navy Bureau of Medicine and Surgery, Falls Church, Va.

179 "Mummie, come, come": Entry for February 5, 1945, in Crouter, *Forbidden Diary*, p. 470.

179 "I was too worn": Ibid.

179 "The demolition": Manila Naval Defense Force Order no. 43, February 3, 1945, in "Analysis of A.T.I.S. Translations of Captured Japanese Documents Bearing on Yamashita Case," October 19, 1945, Box 1998, RG 331, SCAP, Legal Section, Manila Branch, Illegal Acts by Japanese in Philippines, 1945–47, NARA.

180 "As large a quantity": Ibid.

180 "The demolition": Manila Naval Defense Force Order no. 44, February 3, 1945, in "Combat in Manila," April 21, 1945.

180 "The enemy may use": Manila Naval Defense Force Opn Order no. 40, February 2, 1945, Box 1276, RG 331, SCAP, Legal Section, Administrative Division, Documents & Maps, 1945–48, NARA.

180 North of the Pasig: Report no. 80, "Investigation of Burning of Downtown Manila by the Japanese Between 3 February and 7 February 1945," August 21, 1946, Box

1116, RG 331, SCAP, Legal Section, Administrative Division, War Crimes File, 1946–50, NARA. All testimony cited below, unless otherwise noted, comes from this report.

180 "A few minutes": Dominador Santos testimony, October 11, 1945.
180 "The whole ground floor": Angel Dionzo testimony, October 3, 1945.
181 "There were explosions": Yu Cheng Pho testimony, October 18, 1945.
181 "By this time": Vicente Arias testimony, October 13, 1945.
182 At the same time: Report no. 64, "Investigation of the Murder of Fifty-One Filipino and Chinese Civilians and Sixty-Four Unidentified Civilians, and the attempted Murder of Four Filipino Civilians, at the Dy-Pac Lumberyard, 1032 Juan Linda Street, Tondo District, Manila, Philippine Islands, Between 13 January and 4 February 1945," June 17, 1947, Box 1114, RG 331, SCAP, Legal Section, Administrative Division, War Crimes File, 1946–50, NARA. Additional details can be found in the testimonies of Flora Reyes Mabagos and Ricardo Mendoza, October 29, 1945, YTT, pp. 189–95, and Jose Lacson, Ricardo San Juan, Ricardo Trinidad, and Beato Vitan, November 14, 1945, YTT, pp. 2165–75, 2204–9. Unless otherwise noted, all testimony cited below comes from victim statements included in Report no. 64.
182 "When we reached": Ricardo San Juan testimony, July 25, 1945.
183 "His head": Ibid.
183 "I fell forward": Ricardo Trinidad testimony, August 9, 1945.
183 "Oh!" Yap cried: San Juan testimony.
183 "When the Japanese": Ibid.
184 "His head": Ibid.
184 "When the executioner": Ibid.
184 "Some of the babies": Ibid.
185 "That baby of mine": Ricardo San Juan testimony, December 14, 1948, p. 306 of the trial transcript of *People of Philippines v. Shizuo Yokoyama*, Box 1698, RG 331, SCAP, Legal Section, Prosecution Division, Philippines versus Japanese War Criminals, Case File, 1947–49, NARA.
185 "Oh, how painful": San Juan testimony, July 25, 1945.

CHAPTER 9

186 "The American flag": William Dunn, broadcast transcript, February 5, 1945, RG 52, Papers of William J. Dunn, MMLA.
186 "The moustached Brady": Mydans, "'My God! It's Carl Mydans,'" p. 100.
186 "Under no condition": Ibid.
186 "But if they fire": Frank Hewlett, "66 Japanese Freed to Save Hostages," *New York Times*, February 6, 1945, p. 4.
186 "It was still dark": Mydans, *More Than Meets*, p. 195.
187 "As they appeared": Mydans, "'My God! It's Carl Mydans,'" p. 100.
187 "Let's go": Mydans, *More Than Meets*, p. 195.
187 "Two limped": Hewlett, "66 Japanese Freed to Save Hostages," p. 4.
187 "All arrangements": Historical Record, Fifth Cavalry, Luzon Campaign, July 12, 1945.
187 "Hey, Shack": Williams, *To the Angels*, p. 213.
187 "Our former captors": Ibid., pp. 213–14.
187 "Be quiet": Ibid., p. 214.
188 "Make them bow": Mydans, "'My God! It's Carl Mydans,'" p. 103.
188 "Who would like": Madeline M. Ullom, "Experiences of a U.S. Army Nurse in the Philippines," Conference of Army Historians, 50th Anniversary of World War II, June 13–16, 1994, Box 41, RG 15, Materials Donated by the General Public, MMLA.
188 "Small bands": Prising, *Manila, Goodbye*, p. 189.

188 "This, the first": Eighth Cavalry, History of the Luzon Campaign, January–June 1945, Box 13378, RG 407, WWII Operations Reports, 1941–48, First Cavalry Division, NARA.

188 "They got off too easy": Van Sickle, *Iron Gates*, p. 318.

188 "How about chow!": Hewlett, "66 Japanese Freed to Save Hostages," p. 4.

188 "The Japanese marched": Mydans, *More Than Meets*, p. 195.

188 "Well, I just elbowed": Delphino M. Peña, oral history by Domingo Marquez and Paul Zepeda, August 16, 2001, Nettie Lee Benson Latin American Collection, University of Texas, Austin.

189 "Tell the colonel": Mydans, *More Than Meets*, p. 196.

189 "This is as far": Mydans, " 'My God! It's Carl Mydans,' " p. 100.

189 "This is where we": Ibid.

189 "V for Victory": Mydans, *More Than Meets*, p. 196.

189 "Brady raised his arms": Ibid.

189 "Brady returned it": Mydans, " 'My God! It's Carl Mydans,' " p. 100.

189 "Stand back": Ibid.

190 "Under orders": Mydans, *More Than Meets*, pp. 196–97.

190 "Behind them": Ibid., p. 197.

190 "Bill Chase was ecstatic": Dunn, *Pacific Microphone*, p. 302.

191 "Many prisoners put on": Prising, *Manila, Goodbye*, p. 190.

191 "It was simple": Dunn broadcast transcript, February 5, 1945.

191 "We nearly all broke": Williams, *To the Angels*, p. 216.

191 "For three years": Ford Wilkins, "Internees in Tears as Old Glory Rises," *New York Times*, February 6, 1945, p. 1.

191 "No fanfare": Dunn broadcast transcript, February 5, 1945.

191 With the cavalry: After Action Report, XIV Corps, M-1 Operation, July 29, 1945.

192 "Intelligence reports": Sixth Army, Report of the Luzon Campaign, January 9–June 30, 1945, p. 1:36.

192 "This operation places": "The Texts of the Day's Communiques on the Fighting in Various War Zones," *New York Times*, February 2, 1945, p. 2.

192 fourteen food trucks: Hartendorp, *Japanese Occupation*, p. 2:538.

192 "Food, Food, Food": Entry for February 5, 1945, Bayer diary.

192 "We had good army": Entry for February 5, 1945, in Cates, *Drainpipe Diary*, p. 249.

193 "As they tore": Hartendorp, *Japanese Occupation*, p. 2:538.

193 "There were several": Hartendorp, *I Have Lived*, p. 3:480.

193 Two had died: Hartendorp, *Japanese Occupations*, p. 2:540.

193 "Paul Whitaker died": Entry for February 5, 1945, Bayer diary.

193 "It was when": Mydans, *More Than Meets*, p. 199.

193 "You know": Ibid.

193 "Nothing had changed": Ibid.

194 "I don't know just": Sid Huff and Joe Alex Morris, "The General Keeps His Word," *Saturday Evening Post*, October 13, 1951, p. 197.

194 "I had to look again": Ibid.

194 "Take care of these": Ibid.

194 "I've got something": Ibid.

195 "Mrs. Seals weighs": Bonner Fellers to Dorothy Fellers, February 5, 1945, Box 2, RG 44a, Papers of Brig. Gen. Bonner F. Fellers, MMAL.

195 "The condition of these": Courtney Whitney to Evelyn Whitney, February 6, 1945, Box 10, RG 16, Papers of Maj. Gen. Courtney Whitney, MMAL.

195 "My visit to Santo Tomas": Courtney Whitney to Evelyn Whitney, February 7, 1945, ibid.

196 "Never have I": Dunn, *Pacific Microphone*, p. 302.

196 An inventory: Bonner F. Fellers to Douglas MacArthur, February 5, 1945, Box 2, RG 3, Records of Headquarters, SWPA, 1942–45, MMAL.

196 "The Japanese tried": Ibid.

196 "Manila is now": Entry for February 5, 1945, Robert Kentner diary.

196 "holocaust": McCracken, *Very Soon Now*, p. 184.
196 "Several times": Ibid.
197 "Japanese troops": "Internees Rescued from Bilibid Fires," *New York Times*, February 7, 1945, p. 4.
197 At 9:11: Report after Action, Operations of the 37th Infantry Division, Luzon, P.I., November 1, 1944, to June 30 1945 (M-1 Operation), September 10, 1945, Box 8601, RG 407, Records of the Adjutant General's Office, WWII Operations Reports, 1940–48, 37th Infantry Division, NARA.
197 "Stretcher cases": "Internees Rescued from Bilibid Fires," p. 4.
197 "It was a thrill": Entry for February 5, 1945, Ethel Herold diary.
197 "You guys": Beightler, "Report on the Activities of the 37th Infantry Division, 1940–1945," n.d.
197 The fires: Monaghan, *Under Red Sun*, p. 272.
197 "Japs going thru Tondo": Serial no. 40, February 5, 1945, G-2 Journal, Box 8624, RG 407, Records of the Adjutant General's Office, WWII Operations Reports, 1940–48, 37th Infantry Division, NARA.
198 "Alert all your": Serial no. 35, February 5, 1945, S-2-3 Journal, Box 13367, RG 407, WWII Operations Reports, 1941–48, First Cavalry Division, NARA.
198 "The guerrilla reports": Robert Eichelberger to Emma Eichelberger, February 3, 1945, in Luvaas, *Dear Miss Em*, p. 209.
198 "The fires in Manila": Robert Eichelberger to Emma Eichelberger, February 5, 1945, ibid., p. 210.
198 "The smoke and the dust": After Action Report, XIV Corps, M-1 Operation, July 29, 1945.
198 "The spectacle": Diary entry for February 4, 1945, in Rhoades, *Flying MacArthur*, pp. 350–51.
198 "We were powerless": Beightler, "Report on the Activities of the 37th Infantry Division, 1940–1945," n.d.
199 "Japs popped out": Charles A. Henne, "Battle History of the 3d Battalion, 148th Infantry, Manila, The Unwanted Battle (4 February through 7 March 1945)," pp. 44–45.
199 "We made quite": Ibid., p. 45.
199 "It was the first time": Ibid.
199 "Every time I ran": Ibid.
199 "It was a once": Ibid., p. 46.
200 "The Nips are systematically": Williams, *To the Angels*, p. 217.
200 "With the coming": Historical Record, Fifth Cavalry, Luzon Campaign, July 12, 1945.
200 "Well, boys": "Desperate Japs Set Fire to Manila," *Mercury*, February 8, 1945, p. 4.
200 "Last night was": Courtney Whitney to Evelyn Whitney, February 6, 1945.
200 "I hear the fire crackle": Diary entry for February 5, 1945, in Nixon, *Delayed Manila*, pp. 86–87.
201 "No please": Rosa Calalang testimony, October 16, 1945, in Report no. 94, "Investigation of the Atrocities Committed by the Japanese at Intramuros, Manila, Philippine Islands, During February 1945," October 30, 1945, Box 1118, RG 331, SCAP, Legal Section, Administrative Division, War Crimes File, 1946–50, NARA.
201 "Mama": Rosa Calalang testimony, November 13, 1945, YTT, p. 2046.
201 "Today should have": Entry for February 4, 1945, in Lichauco, *"Dear Mother Putnam,"* p. 204.
201 "Discouragement, despair": Ibid.
202 "The heat": Entry for February 5, 1945, ibid., p. 205.
202 "A big bang": Garcia, *It Took Four Years*, p. 106.
202 "There were no": Ibid., p. 107.
203 "The nights turned": Montinola, *Breaking the Silence*, p. 12.
203 "Our forces": "The Texts of the Day's Communiques on the Fighting in Various War Zones," *New York Times*, February 6, 1945, p. 2.

203 "The fall of Manila": "Commenting on the Fall of Manila," February 2, 1945, Box 4, RG 16, Papers of Maj. Gen. Courtney Whitney, MMAL; "MacArthur's Slogan Now Is 'On to Tokyo,'" *New York Times*, February 6, 1945, p. 1.
203 "Manila fell": "Prize of Pacific War, Manila Fell to MacArthur Like Ripened Plum," *Newsweek*, February 12, 1945, p. 36.
203 "a spectacular climax": "Return to Manila," *New York Times*, February 5, 1945, p. 14.
203 "a masterpiece": Barnet Norver, "Manila Redeemed," *Washington Post*, February 6, 1945, p. 6.
203 "Given the far-reaching": Ibid.
204 "It completes": Ernest Lindley, "Return to Manila," *Washington Post*, February 7, 1945, p. 9.
204 Personal congratulations: Letters and cables of congratulations can be found in Folder 1, Box 2, RG 3, Records of Headquarters, SWPA, 1942–45, MMAL.
204 "The lustre": "Chiang Hails Free Manila," *New York Times*, February 7, 1945, p. 3.
204 "This is": Franklin Roosevelt to Douglas MacArthur, February 7, 1945, Box 2, RG 3, Records of Headquarters, SWPA, 1942–45, MMAL.
204 "culmination of one": MacArthur, *Reminiscences*, p. 248.
204 "more pleasure": "Joy Over Manila Widespread Here," *New York Times*, February 6, 1945, p. 5.
204 The House of Representatives: Ibid.; Washington to ADV ECH GHQ (MacArthur), February 14, 1945, Box 2, RG 3, Records of Headquarters, SWPA, 1942–45, MMAL.
204 The city of Philadelphia: "Philadelphia to Hail Manila," *New York Times*, February 6, 1945, p. 3.
204 "Well done": Washington to ADV ECH GHQ (MacArthur), February 11, 1945, Box 2, RG 3, Records of Headquarters, SWPA, 1942–45, MMAL.
205 "The view of Manila": Robert Eichelberger to Emma Eichelberger, February 6, 1945, in Luvaas, *Dear Miss Em*, pp. 211–12.
205 "It was something": Ibid., p. 212.
205 "The sky was": Robert S. Beightler, "Report on the Activities of the 37th Infantry Division, 1940–1945," n.d. (ca. 1946), USAHEC.
205 "MacArthur has visions": Entry for February 7, 1945, Griswold diary.
206 "What fighting": Lindesay Parrott, "Japanese Cut Off," *New York Times*, February 6, 1945, p. 1.
206 "Fires were spreading": George E. Jones, "Foe Making Stand in South of Manila," *New York Times*, February 6, 1945, p. 4.
206 "Why does he do this?": Entry for January 26, 1945, Griswold diary.
206 "When soldiers are dying": Entry for March 3, 1945, ibid.
206 "It seemed to me": Eichelberger and MacKaye, *Our Jungle Road*, p. 182.
206 "Mop-up is": Martin, *GI War*, p. 314.
207 "I shall be honored": CG 8TH Army to CINC SWPA Advance, February 11, 1945, Box 14, RG 3, Records of Headquarters, SWPA, 1942–45, MMAL.
207 "All at once": Dunn, *Pacific Microphone*, p. 306.
207 "General MacArthur had": Ibid.
207 "If this announcement": Ibid., pp. 306–8.

CHAPTER 10

208 "They beat me": Ko King Hun testimony, October 5, 1945, in Report no. 109, "Investigation of the Atrocities Committed at Fort Santiago, Intramuros, Manila, P.I. by Members of the Military Police of the Imperial Japanese Forces, from January 1942 to February 1945," November 27, 1945, Box 1120, RG 331, SCAP, Legal Section, Administrative Division, War Crimes File, 1946–50, NARA.
208 Around eight-thirty: Report no. 94.

208 **For almost four centuries:** Details on Fort Santiago are drawn from Report no. 109. All testimony cited below, unless otherwise noted, comes from this report.

209 **"The ceilings and walls":** Raymond P. Cronin, "Ancient Spanish Torture Chamber Revived by Japs," *Manitowoc Herald-Times*, December 14, 1943, p. 5.

209 **"It is alive again":** Entry for March 16, 1942, in Pestaño-Jacinto, *Living with the Enemy*, p. 25.

209 **"slaves in the Spanish":** Elvira Llanes testimony, February 6, 1946.

209 **"In a period":** Frank Bacon testimony, October 1, 1945.

209 **"I was so thin":** Ko King Hun testimony, October 5, 1945.

209 **American prisoner:** Margaret Morgan testimony, July 30, 1945.

209 **"Each time":** Jose Lichauco testimony, October 22, 1945.

209 **"The shock":** Generose Provido testimony, September 21, 1945.

210 **"I felt so bad":** Jose Syyonping testimony, October 27, 1945.

210 **"I was given":** Erik Friman testimony, September 6, 1945.

210 **"When they put":** Ko King Hun testimony, October 5, 1945.

210 **"This was the most":** Provido testimony.

210 **"I saw men":** Ladislao Joya testimony, October 26, 1945.

210 **"After that":** Richard Beck testimony, September 6, 1945.

210 **"Come on":** Joya testimony.

211 **"It took me two":** Ibid.

211 **"It was horrible":** Ibid.

211 **"Some of them":** Santiago Nadonga testimony, October 26, 1945.

211 **"Don't worry":** Ester Aenlle testimony, October 11, 1945, in Report no. 94.

211 **"We watched them":** Rosa Calalang testimony, October 16, 1945, ibid.

212 **"Chase":** Chase, *Front Line General*, p. 96.

212 **"This is my":** Ibid.

212 **"Retrieved own":** Entry for February 7, 1945, Douglas MacArthur diary.

212 **"Welcome to Bilibid":** Egeberg, *General*, p. 135.

213 **"Some eyes":** Ibid.

213 **"If I'd known":** Entry for February 11, 1945, James Halsema diary, Box 1, Renee Ream Collection, HIA.

213 **"They remained silent":** MacArthur, *Reminiscences*, p. 248.

213 **"I never thought":** Egeberg, *General*, p. 136.

213 **"Dear God":** Ibid.

213 **"You're back":** MacArthur, *Reminiscences*, p. 248.

213 **"I'm long overdue":** Whitney, *MacArthur*, p. 189.

213 **"My boys":** Egeberg, *General*, p. 136.

214 **"Awfully glad":** Whitney, *MacArthur*, p. 189.

214 **"To those":** Entry for June 22, 1944, in Vaughan, *Ordeal of Elizabeth Vaughan*, p. 274. See also Thomas W. Houston, "MacArthur's Memoirs," *Life*, August 7, 1964, p. 18.

214 **"I will never know":** MacArthur, *Reminiscences*, p. 248.

214 **"The general walked":** Chase, *Front Line General*, p. 96.

214 **"He grabbed my hand":** Entry for February 7, 1945, in Crouter, *Forbidden Diary*, p. 478.

214 **"He must have":** Ibid.

214 **"Hello, sonny":** Whitney, *MacArthur*, p.188.

214 **"Arrangements are being":** Egeberg, *General*, p. 136.

215 **"I passed":** MacArthur, *Reminiscences*, p. 248.

215 **"Burn Tokyo":** "Fires Are Still Burning in Manila," *New York Times*, February 8, 1945, p. 3.

215 **Barely twenty-four:** Quarterly Report of Medical Activities, 893d Medical Clearing Company, APO #74 (First Quarter, 1945), April 1, 1945, Box 179, RG 112, Records of the Office of the Surgeon General (Army), HUMEDS, Records Used for Preparing WWII-era Medical Unit Histories, NARA.

215 **"Every available":** Frederick H. Martin, After Action Report, M-1 Operations, 893d Medical Clearing Company (Separate), July 29, 1945, ibid.

215   "The litter and rubble": Ibid.

216   "These pathetic": Ibid.

216   "The surgical theater": Quarterly Report of Medical Activities, 893d Medical Clearing Company, APO #74 (First Quarter, 1945), April 1, 1945.

216   "For the first week": Martin, After Action Report, M-1 Operations, 893d Medical Clearing Company (Sep).

217   "There's MacArthur": Fred Hampson, "MacArthur Returns to Manila," *Racine Journal-Times*, February 7, 1945, p. 1.

217   "People ran": Frank Robertson, "Manilans Greet M'Arthur with Wild Acclaim," *Washington Post*, February 8, 1945, p. 1.

217   "He received": Walter Simmons, "M'Arthur Back in Manila," *Chicago Daily Tribune*, February 8, 1945, p. 3.

217   "At nearly every step": Russell Brines, "Gen. MacArthur Greets Friends at Prison Camp," *Wilmington News-Journal*, February 7, 1945, p. 1.

217   "Oh, General": William Wilson, "Shells Strike Santo Tomas As MacArthur Visits Camp," *Pittsburgh Press*, February 27, 1945, p. 1.

217   "Well, Margaret": Robertson, "Manilans Greet M'Arthur," p. 1.

217   Seals was far: "General Seals Wife Succumbs," *Anniston Star*, May 23, 1945, p. 2.

217   "General": Ralph Teatsorth, "Damage to Manila Is Already Estimated at Two Billions; MacArthur Making Inspections," *Dunkirk Evening Observer*, February 7, 1945, p. 1.

217   "I would have": Robertson, "Manilans Greet M'Arthur," p. 1.

218   "In the lobby": Hartendorp, *I Have Lived*, p. 3:480.

218   "In their ragged": MacArthur, *Reminiscences*, p. 247.

218   "I ran out": Entry for February 7, 1945, Edith Shacklette diary, RG 135, Papers of Drs. Michael and Elizabeth Norman, MMLA.

218   "His five stars": Entry for February 7, 1945, Margaret Bayer diary.

218   "My visit": Douglas MacArthur to Harold S. Smith, February 7, 1945, Box 14, RG 3, Records of Headquarters, SWPA, 1942–45, MMAL.

219   "He was much": Entry for February 7, 1945, Griswold diary.

219   "This has been": Egeberg, *General*, p. 139.

219   "Chase": Chase, *Front Line General*, p. 97.

219   "Chase, you will": Ibid.

219   "Turning a corner:" Egeberg, *General*, p. 140.

220   "Here he stopped": Chase, *Front Line General*, p. 98.

220   "Manuel, you will": Douglas MacArthur, " 'They Died Hard—Those Savage Men,' " *Life*, July 10, 1974, p. 73.

220   "When they find": Ibid.

220   "Aurora": Day, *Manila Hotel*, p. 120.

221   "the bitterest": Report After Action, Operations of the 37th Infantry Division, Luzon, P.I., November 1, 1944, to June 30, 1945 (M-1 Operation), September 10, 1945.

221   As Beightler remembered: Smith, *Triumph in Philippines*, p. 260.

221   "He seemed to think": Entry for February 7, 1945, Griswold diary.

221   "I want to visit": Chase, *Front Line General*, p. 98.

221   "Viva": Ibid.

221   "Obviously much pleased": Ibid.

222   "My tongue": Ibid., pp. 98–99.

222   Second Lt. John Hanley: Report no. 64; unless otherwise noted, all affidavits and testimony cited below come from this report.

222   "On the adult": John C. Hanley affidavit, February 14, 1945.

222   "These were": Paul G. Smith affidavit, February 14, 1945.

222   "It appeared": Claude R. Higdon, Jr., affidavit, February 14, 1945.

223   "Her head": Manuel D. Mendoza testimony, August 7, 1945.

223   "Many had wounds": Hobert O. Mason affidavit, February 8, 1945.

223   "I saw eight piles": Antonio Lamotan testimony, August 6, 1945.

223   "It was fastened": Daniel Simon testimony, August 3, 1945.

224 **"Her neck"**: Benjamin Chome testimony, August 7, 1945.
224 **Maj. David Binkley**: David V. Binkley affidavit, March 9, 1945; Francisco del Rosario and Manuel del Rosario joint affidavit, March 11, 1945; Mariano del Rosario testimony, July 25, 1945; Francisco del Rosario testimony, August 2, 1945.
224 **"Whole families"**: Report no. 64.
225 **"In general"**: Robert F. Goheen, G-2 Periodic Report #82, February 8, 1945, Box 13295, RG 407, Records of the Adjutant General's Office, WWII Operations Reports, 1941–48, First Cavalry Division, NARA.
225 **"Neither the sketch"**: Ibid.
227 **Officers had selected**: Historical Record, Report after Action, pt. 1, Operations of the 148th Infantry, Luzon, Philippine Islands, November 1, 1944–March 4, 1945, Box 8770, RG 407, Records of the Adjutant General's Office, WWII Operations Reports, 1940–48, 37th Infantry Division, NARA; Report After Action, Operations of the 37th Infantry Division, Luzon, P.I., November 1, 1944, to June 30, 1945 (M-1 Operation), September 10, 1945.
227 **"Quietly"**: Charles Henne, "Battle History of the 3d Battalion, 148th Infantry, Manila, The Unwanted Battle (4 February through 7 March 1945)," p. 53.
227 **"Any idea"**: Ibid., pp. 53–54.
228 **"No, Major"**: Ibid., p. 54.
228 **"The fire slashed down"**: Ibid.
228 **"When we were hit"**: Ibid., p. 55.
228 **"Hollywood could not"**: Ibid., p. 54.
228 **"With only the rush"**: Ibid., p. 55.
229 **"Lots of guys"**: Frankel, *Frankel-y Speaking*, p. 117.
229 **"I'm hit"**: Ibid., p. 118.
229 **"I can run"**: Ibid.
229 **"This man is dead"**: Ibid.
229 **"He was killed"**: Ibid.
229 **"Look"**: Entry for February 7, 1945 in Nixon, *Delayed Manila*, p. 88.
230 **"While we sat"**: Ibid.
230 **"Did you hear that"**: Ibid.
230 **"I don't have any shrapnel"**: Ibid.
230 **"Stay away"**: Ibid., p. 89.
230 **"We huddled against"**: Ibid.
230 **"We huddled together"**: Ibid.
230 **"Our God"**: Ibid.
231 **"Immediately the first"**: Entry for February 7, 1945, Margaret Bayer diary.
231 **"Stretchers began"**: Ibid.
231 **"The stairs"**: Ibid.
231 **"Hot American chow"**: Ford Wilkins, "MacArthur Enters Manila; Hailed by Freed Prisoners," *New York Times*, February 8, 1945, p. 1.
231 **"She should be"**: Terry Meyers Johnson, oral history by Elizabeth Norman, July 5, 1992, RG 135, Papers of Drs. Michael and Elizabeth Norman, MMLA.
231 **"I was holding"**: Ibid.
231 **"You're hit"**: Ibid.
232 **"I remember"**: Ibid.
232 **"There was a woman"**: Sally Blaine Millett, oral history by Patricia Rikli, April 9, 1983.
232 **"I was going"**: Sally Blaine Millett, oral history by Elizabeth Norman, September 20, 1990.
232 **"Sally, you know"**: Ibid.
233 **"Jane, Jane"**: Ibid.
233 **"Jane was wild"**: Ibid.
233 **"Where is she"**: Stevens, *Santo Tomas Internment Camp*, p. 380.
233 **"He saw a"**: Ibid., pp. 380–81.
233 **"Oh Lord"**: Ibid., p. 381.
233 **"He came back"**: Ibid.

233 The afternoon shelling: Hartendorp, *Japanese Occupation*, p. 2:545.
233 "The Educational Building": Martin, After Action Report, M-1 Operations, 893d Medical Clearing Company (Sep).
234 "Stunned and weeping": Entry for February 7, 1945, in Cates, *Drainpipe Diary*, pp. 250–51.
234 The fifty-five-year-old: "John McFie Killed In Luzon Action," *Albuquerque Journal*, February 27, 1945, p. 2.
234 "I knew a good thing": Entry for May 4, 1943, in Cates, *Drainpipe Diary*, p. 163.
234 "They seemed closer": Ibid.
234 "They had never": Entry for February 28, 1944, ibid., p. 203.
235 "His breathing": Entry for February 7, 1945, ibid., p. 251.
235 "Where's Mrs. Mack": Ibid.
235 "There was one": Monahan and Niedel-Greenlee, *All This Hell*, p. 160.
235 "We all worked all nite": Entry for February 7, 1945, Edith Shacklette diary.
235 "This day had been": Entry for February 7, 1945, in Cates, *Drainpipe Diary*, p. 250.
235 "In bombing raids": Stevens, *Santo Tomas Internment Camp*, p. 380.
235 "To be shelled": Ibid.
236 "Nobody is brave": Ibid.
236 "Night shelling was": Van Sickle, *Iron Gates*, p. 322.
236 "We spent the entire": Entry for February 7, 1945, Margaret Bayer diary.
236 According to figures: Hartendorp, *Japanese Occupation*, pp. 2:545–46.
236 "I picked up": Entry for February 7, 1945, in Nixon, *Delayed Manila*, pp. 87–88.

CHAPTER 11

237 "High and low": Entry for March 8, 1945, in Crouter, *Forbidden Diary*, p. 497.
237 "The only ones": Lourdes Lecaroz testimony, October 3, 1945, in Report no. 94. All testimony cited below, unless otherwise noted, comes from this report.
237 "Listen everybody": Rosa Calalang testimony, October 16, 1945.
237 "We thought it was": Ibid.
238 "Where is the director?": Benita Lahoz testimony, September 12, 1945.
238 "Fire": Rosa Calalang testimony, October 16, 1945.
238 "We ran out": Ibid.
238 "This is not water": Candida Ocampo testimony, November 7, 1945, YTT, p. 1282.
239 "We moved everyone": Sister Nelly de Jesus Virata testimony, October 16, 1945.
239 "We found them": Sister Nelly de Jesus Virata testimony, November 6, 1945, YTT, p. 1154.
239 Thirty-seven-year-old: Miguel Blanco testimony, September 27, 1945.
239 "The breeze": Mariano Agilada testimony, October 6, 1945.
239 "It was like": Rosa Calalang testimony, October 16, 1945.
239 "The fire became": Renee Pena testimony, September 5, 1945.
239 "We were being suffocated": Lourdes Lecaroz testimony, October 3, 1945.
240 "The bell was ringing": Remedio Huerta Beliso testimony, October 6, 1945.
240 "150 guerrillas": "Report on the Destruction of Manila and Japanese Atrocities," February 1945. A copy of this diary entry, albeit with a slightly different translation, can be found in "Analysis of A.T.I.S. Translations of Captured Japanese Documents Bearing on Yamashita Case," October 19, 1945.
241 "I've been hit": Charles Henne, "Battle History of the 3d Battalion, 148th Infantry, Manila, The Unwanted Battle (4 February through 7 March 1945)," p. 60.
241 "The bullet": Ibid.
241 "Very limited progress": Historical Record, Report After Action, pt. 1, Operations of the 148th Infantry, Luzon, Philippine Islands, November 1, 1944–March 4, 1945.
242 "At least during the war": Murphy, *Heroes*, p. 300–1.
243 "The intrepid team": Senate Committee on Veterans Affairs, *Medal of Honor*

Recipients, 1863–1978, 96th Cong., 1st sess. (Washington, D.C.: U.S. Government Printing Office, 1979) p. 664.

244 **Bounded by the Pasig:** Smith, *Triumph in Philippines*, p. 261; Terrain Handbook 41A, Manila City, December 6, 1944, pp. 52, 90.

244 **"Battleship Island":** Charles Henne, "Battle History of the 3d Battalion, 148th Infantry, Manila, The Unwanted Battle (4 February through 7 March 1945)," p. 62.

244 **"I'll fire three bursts":** Royal Arch Gunnison, "The Burning of Manila," *Collier's*, April 7, 1945, p. 44.

245 **"The doughboys":** Ibid.

246 **"Hey, Joe":** Ibid.

246 **"There was no escape":** Ibid.

246 **"Inch by inch":** Ibid.

246 **"The large steam":** Sixth Army, Report of the Luzon Campaign, January 9–June 30, 1945, p. 4:134.

246 **"It was the damnedest":** Gunnison, "Burning of Manila," p. 44.

247 **"We had almost":** Flanagan, *Angels* (1948), p. 79.

247 **Eichelberger's army had:** J. M. Swing, Headquarters 11th Airborne Division, "Report after Action with the Enemy, Operation Mike VI, Luzon Campaign," January 24, 1946, USAHEC.

247 **"From now on":** Flanagan, *Angels* (1948), p. 81.

248 **"Destruction and chaos":** Ibid., p. 84.

248 **"Tell Halsey":** Ibid., p. 85.

248 **"The Japs":** Ibid.

248 **"We were trapped":** Garcia, *It Took Four Years*, p. 107.

249 **"Every night":** Ibid., p. 108.

249 **"Luckily it failed":** Entry for February 9, 1945, in Lichauco, *"Dear Mother Putnam,"* p. 208.

249 **"Tomorrow it will":** Ibid.

249 **"My knees turned":** Montinola, *Breaking the Silence*, p. 69.

250 **"It will be our turn":** Ibid., p. 13.

250 **"Units must be":** Manila Naval Defense Opn Order no. 55, February 7, 1945, Box 1276, RG 331, SCAP, Legal Section, Administrative Division, Documents & Maps, 1945–48, NARA.

250 **On the morning:** Koichi Kayashima statement, December 10, 1949, in "Statements of Japanese Officials on World War II," LOC.

250 **Since American soldiers:** Shizuo Yokoyama interrogation, October 9, 1945, Box 2023, RG 331, SCAP, Legal Section, Manila Branch, Misc. File, 1945–49, NARA.

250 **The night of his arrival:** Kayashima statement.

251 **"I sensed":** Kenichiro Asano statement, February 20, 1950, in "Statements of Japanese Officials on World War II," LOC.

251 **The list of those attacked:** See Atrocity Report nos. 16, 26, and 48, which can be found in Boxes 1109 and 1111, RG 331, SCAP, Legal Section, Administrative Division, War Crimes File, 1946–50, NARA.

251 **"The Americans":** Kobayashi Group Order, February 13, 1945, in "Analysis of A.T.I.S. Translations of Captured Japanese Documents Bearing on Yamashita Case," October 19, 1945.

252 **"When Filipinos":** Manila Naval Defense and Southwestern Area Fleet Opn Orders, December 23, 1944–February 14, 1945, ibid.

PART III

253 **"Everyone who escaped":** James T. Walsh, "Report of Investigation of Alleged Mass Murders of Civilians In the Intramuros (Walled City) Area of Manila, P.I., by Japanese Imperial Forces," April 5, 1945, Box 245, RG 407, Records of the Adjutant General's Office, Philippine Archives Collection, NARA.

CHAPTER 12

255 "The screams": Engracio Losa testimony, September 12, 1945, in Report no. 66, "Investigation of the Murder of at Least Five Hundred Civilians of Filipino, French, Spanish, Indian, American and German Nationalities of Whom Seventy Victims Are Identified, and the Wounding of Five Filipino and Spanish Civilians on 10 February 1945," October 3, 1945, Box 1114, RG 331, SCAP, Legal Section, Administrative Division, War Crimes File, 1946–50, NARA.

255 Japanese marines fanned: See Report no. 53. Additional details can be found in the testimonies of Anna de Jesus, Luisa Barahona, Camilo Diego, Luis Vazquez, Winifred Colma, Angeles Barahona, and Herminio Velarde, Jr., October 31, 1945, YTT, pp. 442–95. Unless otherwise noted, all testimony cited below comes from victim statements included in Report no. 53.

255 "You have to leave": Angeles Barahona testimony, July 24, 1945.

255 "Wake up": Domingo Giocado testimony, July 7, 1945.

256 "Ma'am": Clara Rice testimony, August 6, 1945.

256 "You can't": Daniel Vazquez testimony, July 2, 1945; Luis Vazquez testimony, June 19, 1945.

256 "Kura": Josefina Punzalan testimony, July 9, 1945.

256 "You go to see": Gurmuksing Kanusing testimony, June 11, 1945.

256 "This is the one": Salvador Sepulveda testimony, July 28, 1945.

256 "Don't bring": Josefina Punzalan testimony, July 9, 1945.

257 "We said some": Ibid.

257 "All the people": Serafin Sepulveda testimony, June 20, 1945.

257 "In case": Angeles Barahona testimony, July 24, 1945.

257 "Stay near": Ibid.

257 "Wait and be quiet": Josefina Punzalan testimony, July 9, 1945.

257 "Who knows": Honorio David testimony, June 18, 1945.

257 "Get the candies": Salvador Sepulveda testimony, July 28, 1945.

258 "Do not stand": Josefina Punzalan testimony, July 9, 1945.

258 "Maybe it's poison": Luisa Barahona testimony, August 3, 1945.

258 "Don't stand": Angeles Barahona testimony, July 24, 1945.

258 "Miss": Luisa Barahona testimony, October 31, 1945, YTT, p. 454.

258 "The college": Anna de Jesus testimony, July 20, 1945.

258 "I saw my right": Pacifico Benito testimony, August 1, 1945.

258 "I vomited blood": Eutiquio Antipolo testimony, July 21, 1945.

259 Thirty-two-year-old: Virginia Sepulveda testimony, June 20, 1945.

259 "I could hear": Marcelino Punzalan testimony, July 10, 1945.

259 "We walked": Theodore Blendo testimony, August 7, 1945.

259 "Let's run": Murli Kundanmal testimony, June 1, 1945.

259 "Another Japanese": Angeles Barahona testimony, July 24, 1945.

259 "I could see": Cayetano Barahona testimony, July 24, 1945.

259 "She was pleading": Rosario Fernandez testimony, June 20, 1945.

260 "She was holding": Winfred Colma testimony, July 6, 1945.

260 "My child": Orlando Colma testimony, July 6, 1945.

260 "Her right leg": Winfred Colma testimony, July 6, 1945.

260 "Father": Camilo Diego testimony, August 3, 1945.

260 "Kill me": Rosario Fernandez testimony, June 20, 1945.

260 "He got his knife": Herminio Velarde, Jr., testimony, July 11, 1945.

261 "That child": Camilo Diego testimony, August 3, 1945.

261 At the same time: See Report no. 61. Additional details can be found in the testimonies of Esther Garcia Moras, Priscilla Garcia, Evangeline Garcia, Virginia Velasco, Maria Luisa Sotelo, Josefina Ramos, Uliran Pedro, and Eloisa Chicote, November 1, 1945, YTT, pp. 500–599. Unless otherwise noted, all testimony cited below comes from victim statements included in Report no. 61.

261 "Matte, matte": Lucy A. Tani testimony, June 27, 1945.

261 "It was bare": Ibid.
262 "We tried": Esther Garcia Moras testimony, June 25, 1945.
262 "We pulled our hair": Ibid.
262 "You go": Priscilla Garcia testimony, June 26, 1945.
262 "What else": Priscilla Garcia testimony, November 1, 1945, YTT, p. 518.
262 "He pulled": Evangeline Garcia testimony, June 25, 1945.
262 "Kill": Ibid.
262 "She was crying": Esther Garcia Moras testimony, June 25, 1945.
262 "Nothing happened": Ibid.
262 "Where is Pris?": Esther Garcia Moras testimony, November 1, 1945, YTT, p. 508.
263 "Everybody in the room": Ibid.
263 "I was not strong": Esther Garcia Moras testimony, June 25, 1945.
263 "I leave you": Evangeline Garcia testimony, June 25, 1945.
263 "He took me": Priscilla Garcia testimony, June 26, 1945.
263 "He told me": Ibid.
263 "He placed his pistol": Ibid.
263 "He took his knife": Priscilla Garcia testimony, November 1, 1945, YTT, p. 519.
263 "You will have": Priscilla Garcia testimony, June 26, 1945.
263 "She was perspiring": Esther Garcia Moras testimony, November 1, 1945, YTT, p. 508.
264 "Esther": Ibid.
264 "She seemed": Pacita Tapia testimony, July 27, 1945.
264 "Get up": Priscilla Garcia testimony, November 1, 1945, YTT, p. 520.
264 "No, no": Priscilla Garcia testimony, June 26, 1945.
264 "I was struggling": Esther Garcia Moras testimony, June 25, 1945.
264 "He stood up": Ibid.
264 "When he finished": Ibid.
264 "I crawled": Ibid.
265 "I was raped": Ibid.
265 "On each occasion": Ibid.
265 "I was raped": Ibid.
265 "They were like": Paquita Coastas Garcia testimony, June 25, 1945.
265 "They were not": Pacita Tapia testimony, July 27, 1945.
265 "I wanted to die": Fanny Gadol testimony, June 21, 1945.
265 "My God!": Erlinda Querubin testimony, June 30, 1945.
265 "I want to die": Paquita Coastas Garcia testimony, June 25, 1945.
266 "These Japanese beasts": Yolanda Entrala Guerrero testimony, June 12, 1945.
266 "The girls were": Vicky Gadol testimony, June 21, 1945.
266 "Everything was in confusion": Margarita Salado Ghezzi testimony, June 29, 1945.
266 "We could smell": Erlinda Querubin testimony, June 30, 1945.
266 "He showed the girls": Margarita Salado Ghezzi testimony, June 29, 1945.
266 "I took out": Rebecca Habibi testimony, July 14, 1945.
266 "I stuck my finger": Julia Ghezzi testimony, June 28, 1945.
266 "No good": Pilar Garcia Viuda de Castaner, June 19, 1945.
266 "When he saw": Carmencita Veloso Ballesteros testimony, July 10, 1945.
267 "We grabbed": Erlinda Querubin testimony, June 30, 1945.
267 "Every night": Luisa Guevara testimony, July 28, 1945.
267 "I was so upset": Paquita Coastas Garcia testimony, June 25, 1945.
267 The days of terror: Rebecca Habibi testimony, July 14, 1945.
267 "I could hear": Raymunda Decena Guevara, July 30, 1945.
267 "All of us": Pilar Ubago Miranda testimony, July 4, 1945.
267 "It was so terrible": Erlinda Querubin testimony, June 30, 1945.
268 "He told me": Trinidad Llamas de Garcia testimony, June 12, 1945.
268 "He had a pistol": Isabel Caro testimony, July 24, 1945.
268 "The place was in bedlam": Paquita Coastas Garcia testimony, June 25, 1945.
268 "The hotel was burning": Trinidad Llamas de Garcia testimony, June 12, 1945.

268 "No matter": Entry for February 9, 1945, in Cates, *Drainpipe Diary*, pp. 252–53.
268 "She tried": William Dunn, broadcast transcript, February 8, 1945, RG 52, Papers of William J. Dunn, MMLA.
269 "It was a loaf": Colquhoun, "Santo Tomas," p. 32.
269 "I particularly": Ibid.
269 "One gave me": Ibid
269 A February 11 report: Courtney Whitney to Douglas MacArthur, February 11, 1945, "Report on Conditions at Santo Tomas Internment Camp," Box 4, RG 16, Papers of Maj. Gen. Courtney Whitney, USA, Philippine Section, SWPA, MMAL.
269 "I cannot bring": Douglas MacArthur to the Internees at Santo Tomas, n.d., ibid.
269 "The nights": Entry for February 12–13, 1945, in Wygle, *Surviving*, pp. 143–44.
270 "There's something unreal": Dunn, *Pacific Microphone*, p. 309.
270 "A few days ago": Monahan and Neidel-Greenlee, *All This Hell*, p. 161.
270 "The worst": Joaquin, *Mr. F.E.U.*, p. 102.
270 "It is your turn": Montinola, *Breaking the Silence*, p. 69.
271 "There was a shocked": Ibid., p. 79.
271 "Safe in there": Joaquin, *Mr. F.E.U.*, p. 164.
272 "They're here": Montinola, *Breaking the Silence*, p. 69.
272 "Be brave": Ibid., p. 70.
272 "We're only civilians": Ibid.
272 "The strange sounds": Ibid., p. 79.
272 "Candy": Joaquin, *Mr. F.E.U.*, p. 166.
272 "Side by side": Montinola, *Breaking the Silence*, p. 96.
272 "Pray": Ibid.
273 "Remember, O most": Ibid., p. 80.
273 "No words": Ibid.
273 "Go look": Joaquin, *Mr. F.E.U.*, p. 167.
273 "Look for Ching": Ibid.
273 "In her white": Montinola, *Breaking the Silence*, p. 95.
274 "Help her!": Ibid., p. 97.
274 "His lifeless": Ibid.
274 "It's useless": Ibid.
274 "Night came": Ibid., p. 80.
275 "Is Nanay mad": Ibid., p. 98.
275 "Night had descended": Ibid., p. 99.
275 "Don't leave me": Ibid.
275 "Stay with": Ibid.
275 "Stop it": Ibid., p. 100.
275 "Avenge us": Ibid.
276 "She was not": Ibid.
276 "It is all right": Ibid., p. 101.
276 "Sagrado Corazon": Ibid.
276 "She's alive": Joaquin, *Mr. F.E.U.*, p. 169.
276 To capture southern Manila: After Action Report, XIV Corps, M-1 Operation, July 29, 1945.
277 "It was now evident": Historical Record, Report after Action, pt. 1, Operations of the 148th Infantry, Luzon, Philippine Islands, November 1, 1944–March 4, 1945.
277 "Surely they heard us": Charles Henne, "Battle History of the 3d Battalion, 148th Infantry, Manila, The Unwanted Battle (4 February through 7 March 1945)," p. 68.
277 "Gains were measured": Ibid., p. 67.
278 "The fighting in South Manila": Entry for February 10, 1945, Griswold diary.
278 "The fighting": Beightler, "Report on the Activities of the 37th Infantry Division, 1940 1945," n.d.

CHAPTER 13

279 "The Japanese caught": Esperanza Esteban testimony, September 24, 1945, in Report no. 66.

279 Francisco Lopez hid: Ibid. See also Dumana, *German Club-Manila*, pp. 58–60. Additional details can be found in the testimonies of Francisco Lopez, Helena Rodriguez, Engracio Losa, and Asuncion R. Marbas, November 2, 1945, YTT, pp. 666–712. Unless otherwise noted, all testimony cited below comes from victim statements included in Report no. 66.

279 "We had to stoop": Francisco Lopez testimony, November 2, 1945, YTT p. 669.

280 "You can just imagine": Francisco Lopez testimony, January 24, 1949, p. 603 of the trial transcript of *People of Philippines v. Shizuo Yokoyama*, Box 1698, RG 331, SCAP, Legal Section, Prosecution Division, Philippines Verses Japanese War Criminals, Case File, 1947–49, NARA.

280 "Women and the kids": Francisco Lopez testimony, November 2, 1945, YTT p. 669.

280 "*Tomodachi*": Ibid.

280 "*Tomodachi*": Ibid., p. 670.

280 "The others laughed": Ibid., pp. 670–671.

281 "I saw the Japanese": Francisco Lopez testimony, September 3, 1945.

281 "We might as well": Francisco Lopez testimony, November 2, 1945, YTT, p. 671.

281 "I half-way fainted": Ibid., p. 672.

282 "She fell to the ground": Ibid., p. 683.

282 "This fellow right away": Ibid.

282 "I heard my brother": Ibid., p. 678.

282 "I survived": Helena Rodriguez, December 22, 1994, unpublished narrative, Memorare Manila 1945 Foundation Collection, FHL.

283 "It was almost impossible": Helena Rodriguez testimony, September 5, 1945.

283 "Everybody was crying": Helena Rodriguez testimony, November 2, 1945, YTT, p. 695.

283 "Let the children": Ibid.

283 "Your youngest brother": Ibid.

283 "I just sat there": Ibid., p. 696.

283 "We told him": Ibid.

284 "Everybody began": Ibid.

284 "After a while": Ibid., p. 698.

284 "I heard the slashes": Ibid., p. 699.

285 "It felt like": Helena Rodriguez, December 22, 1994, unpublished narrative.

285 "It was a miracle": Helena Rodriguez, "My Tragic 11-Day Diary," n.d.

285 "Look out for my wound": Francisco Lopez testimony, November 2, 1945, YTT, p. 684.

285 "That muddy": Ibid., p. 685.

286 "This is worse": Ibid., pp. 686–87.

286 "There was blood": Ibid., p. 687.

286 "I don't want": Ibid., pp. 687–88.

287 Since his withdrawal: Muto, "Truth of the Philippines Campaign," June 17, 1947.

287 The general would: Michio Kitayama interrogation, November 10, 1945, Box 2023, RG 331, SCAP, Legal Section, Manila Branch, Misc. File, 1945–49, NARA; Shizuo Yokoyama testimony, November 4, 1945, Box 1905, RG 331, SCAP, Legal Section, Manila Branch, Statements & Affidavits, Alphabetical File, 1945–49, NARA.

287 "With the information": Denshichi Okochi Sworn Deposition, May 27, 1947, Box 1276, RG 331, SCAP, Legal Section, Administrative Division, Documents & Maps, 1945–48, NARA.

288 "There are gardens": Dos Passos, *Tour of Duty*, p. 161.

289 At the same time: Report no. 59, "Investigation of the Murder and Attempted Murder of More Than Four Hundred Male Civilians in Paco District, Manila,

Philippine Islands, on 10 February 1945," September 9, 1945, Box 1113, RG 331, SCAP, Legal Section, Administrative Division, War Crimes File, 1946–50, NARA. Additional details can be found in the testimonies of Jose Cabanero, Federico P. Davantes, Natividad Bonifacio, Aquilino Rivera, Benjamin Urrutia, Ricardo Esquerra, Go Hong, Cayetano Lagdameo, Julieta Milanes, and Francisco del Rosario, November 3, 1945, YTT, pp. 796–865. Unless otherwise noted, all testimony cited below comes from victim statements included in Report no. 59.

289 "Don't": Eva Gregorio testimony, July 7, 1945.
289 "Forced labor": Conrada Balleta testimony, August 4, 1945.
289 "You come along": Lourdes Garon testimony, August 4, 1945.
290 "May I see him": Celestina Mandanas Capili testimony, July 12, 1945.
290 "He can work": Ibid.
290 "I looked": Ibid.
290 "When he was": Ibid.
290 "Why": Ricardo Esquerra testimony, November 3, 1945, YTT, p. 830.
290 "I was so frightened": Conrada Balleta testimony, August 4, 1945.
290 "Pass!": Ricardo Esquerra testimony, November 3, 1945, YTT, pp. 832–833.
291 "The bullet": Godofredo G. Rivera testimony, June 22, 1945.
291 Rivera's seventeen: Aquilino Rivera testimony, June 26, 1945.
292 "When I was facing": Jose Cabanero testimony, August 16, 1945.
292 "Tomodachi!": Federico P. Davantes testimony, August 14, 1945.
292 "Japanese and Philippines": Benjamin Urrutia testimony, July 19, 1945.
292 "When the hand": Ibid.
292 "We are all going": Ibid.
292 "I could hardly": Ibid.
293 "I then felt": Eugene Bayot testimony, August 21, 1945.
293 During that time: Sy Chia testimony, July 13, 1945; Cayetano Lagdameo testimony, July 19, 1945; Julio Ramirez testimony, August 1, 1945.
294 "Perhaps this is": Virginio Suarez testimony, August 17, 1945.
294 "This is my house": Ruben Musngi Magat testimony, August 7, 1945.
294 "I am here": Pablo C. Martinez testimony, August 7, 1945.
294 "Teodoro!": Ricardo Esquerra testimony, November 3, 1945, YTT, p. 834.
294 "I saw one": Feliz Plata testimony, July 10, 1945.
294 "Banzai": Ricardo Esquerra testimony, November 3, 1945, YTT, p 835.
294 "I placed my hand": Virginio Suarez testimony, August 17, 1945.
295 "I saw": Angel Enriquez testimony, February 20, 1945.
295 By then: Fidel Merino testimony, July 11, 1945.
295 "The pile": Eustaquio Batoctoy testimony, July 25, 1945.
295 "Within two or three": Bessie Wakefield Chase testimony, June 28, 1945.
295 "We counted": Francisco del Rosario testimony, August 21, 1945.
295 "The evidence clearly": Report no. 59.
296 "There were so many": Hartendorp, *Japanese Occupation*, p. 2:548.
296 "Their arrival": Frederick H. Martin, After Action Report, M-1 Operations, 893d Medical Clearing Company (Sep).
296 "How strong": Entry for February 8, 1945, in Cates, *Drainpipe Diary*, p. 252.
296 "The civilians": Martin, After Action Report, M-1 Operations, 893d Medical Clearing Company (Sep).
296 "They were in a pitiful": Entry for February 5, 1945, in Cates, *Drainpipe Diary*, p. 249.
296 "They are so far": Entry for February 16, 1945, in Wygle, *Surviving*, p. 146.
297 "In a sweat": Prising, *Manila, Goodbye*, p. 194.
297 "No, you go": Ibid.
297 "The woman's face": Ibid., pp. 194–95.
297 "The armless": Ibid., p. 194.
297 "I know I am": John W. Osborn letter, February 15, 1945, John Osborn Santo Tomas Internment Transcriptions, William L. Clements Library, UM.
297 "Often, during the two": Ibid.

298 "The whole street": Flanagan, *Angels* (1989), p. 266.
298 "Many nursing women": Ibid.
298 "It is now": William Dunn, broadcast transcript, February 7, 1945, RG 52, Papers of William J. Dunn, MMLA.
298 "Manila was secured!": Entry for February 12, 1945, in Cates, *Drainpipe Diary*, p. 253.
298 "Most of the officers": Ibid.
298 "They won't be coming": Van Sickle, *Iron Gates*, p. 319.
299 "I had never": Prising, *Manila, Goodbye*, p. 196.
299 "Well": Ibid.
299 "Thereafter we fired": "Japanese Defense of Cities as Exemplified by the Battle for Manila," July 1, 1945.
299 The attack that Saturday: Hartendorp, *Japanese Occupation*, p. 2:547.
299 "A grim morning": Entry for February 10, 1945, in Wygle, *Surviving*, p. 142.
300 "Still no sleep": Entry for February 10, 1945, in Cates, *Drainpipe Diary*, p. 253.
300 "She was wandering": Wygle, *Surviving*, p. 191.
300 "Part of a skull": Ibid.
300 "Still she did not": Prising, *Manila, Goodbye*, p. 192.
300 "No": Ibid.
300 "You know": Nixon, *Delayed Manila*, p. 91.
300 "Who wants to die": Ibid.
300 "We stood": Ibid.
301 "Are you one of our": Sally Blaine Millett, oral history by Patricia Rikli, April 9, 1983.
301 "The shelling of Santo Tomas": Dos Passos, *Tour of Duty*, p. 172.
301 "Why the hell": Ibid.
301 "Might as well": Ibid.

CHAPTER 14

302 "They liquidated": Agustin Garcia testimony, August 17, 1945, in Report no. 52, "Investigation of the Murder of Alexander Bachrach, Four Filipino Civilians and Three to Five Unidentified Filipino Civilians, and the Attempted Murder of Jesus Quintero at 914 Indiana Street, Malate, Manila, Philippine Islands, on 12 February 1945," March 6, 1947, Box 1112, RG 331, SCAP, Legal Section, Administrative Division, War Crimes File, 1946–50, NARA.
302 Modesto Farolan had hustled: Report no. 11, "Investigation Pertaining to the Massacre in the Philippine Red Cross Building at the Intersection of Isaac Peral and General Luna Streets, Manila, Philippine Islands, on 10 February 1945," June 8, 1945, Box 1109, RG 331, SCAP, Legal Section, Administrative Division, War Crimes File, 1946–50, NARA. Additional details can be found in the testimonies of Patrocinio Abad (Corazon Noble), Gliceria Andaya, Florita Loveriza, John K. Lewy, and Juan P. Juan, October 29, 1945, YTT, pp. 132–87. Unless otherwise noted, all testimony and records cited below come from victim statements and reports included in Report no. 11.
302 "From February 4": Modesto Farolan testimony, May 12, 1945.
303 "Nothing will happen": John K. Lewy testimony, May 11, 1945.
304 "How many refugees": Modesto Farolan testimony, May 12, 1945.
304 "Japanese, *tomodachi*": Isabel Tabaque testimony, May 11, 1945.
304 "No good": Modesto Farolan testimony, February 14, 1945.
304 "Philippine Red Cross": Ibid.
304 "I explained": Modesto Farolan testimony, May 12, 1945.
305 "We heard shots": Patrocinio Abad testimony, October 29, 1945, YTT, p. 136.
305 "Doctor, doctor": Patrocinio Abad testimony, May 8, 1945.
305 "I lay prone": Ibid.
305 "She was": Patrocinio Abad, testimony, October 29, 1945, YTT, p. 138.

306 "When she started": Gliceria Andaya testimony, May 9, 1945.
306 "Wait a moment": Marina de Paz testimony, May 8, 1945.
306 "Wait a moment": Ibid.
307 "He is our": Modesto Farolan testimony, May 12, 1945.
307 "Aruy!": Gliceria Andaya testimony, May 9, 1945.
307 "One bayonet thrust": Modesto Farolan testimony, February 14, 1945.
307 "The wounded": Gliceria Andaya testimony, May 9, 1945.
308 "From where": Modesto Farolan testimony, February 14, 1945.
308 "Americans": Gliceria Andaya testimony, May 9, 1945.
308 "Escusi": Ibid.
308 "Please have mercy": John K. Lewy testimony, May 11, 1945.
308 "I was laying": John K. Lewy, "I Survived Japanese Cold Blooded Slaughter and Brutality in the Manila Red Cross Building," March 4, 1945.
308 "I told her": John K. Lewy testimony, May 11, 1945.
309 "I didn't give": Lewy, "I Survived Japanese Cold Blooded Slaughter and Brutality in the Manila Red Cross Building," March 4, 1945.
309 "We were all": Juan P. Juan testimony, May 10, 1945.
309 "After they left": Corito Fiel, "War Survivors Speak Up, Finally," *Philippine Daily Inquirer*, March 6, 1995, clipping in files of Memorare Manila 1945 Foundation Collection, FHL.
309 "She was pale": Juan P. Juan testimony, October 29, 1945, YTT, p. 177.
309 "What happened": Ibid.
309 "Finally she broke": Juan P. Juan testimony, May 10, 1945.
310 "Boys": Vicente Abad testimony, May 8, 1945.
310 "All the people": Ibid.
310 "When I came": John K. Lewy testimony, May 11, 1945.
310 "Take the baby": Vicente Abad testimony, May 8, 1945.
310 "The baby": Ibid.
310 "I just lay": Patrocinio Abad testimony, May 8, 1945.
311 "He could not stand": Koichi Kayashima statement, December 10, 1949, in "Statements of Japanese Officials on World War II," LOC.

CHAPTER 15

312 "This is a doomed": Robert Shaplen, "Manila's Stunned Survivors Can Only Stare and Weep," *Newsweek*, February 26, 1945, p. 32.
312 "The types of casualties": Ross J. Porritt, "Historical Report, 9 January 1945 to 30 June 1945, Inclusive," July 28, 1945, Box 81, RG 112, Records of the Office of the Surgeon General (Army), HUMEDS, Records Used for Preparing WWII-era Medical Unit Histories, NARA.
312 "It had been used": Robert G. Swearingen, "History of the 71st Evacuation Hospital (SEM), From 11 January 1945 to 30 June 1945," August 11, 1945, Box 83, ibid.
313 The 54th Evacuation Hospital: Thomas M. Kirk, "Quarterly Historical Report," April 10, 1945, ibid.
313 To do so: Report after Action, Operations of the 37th Infantry Division on Bougainville, BSI and Luzon, P.I, From 1 November 44 to 30 June 45, Annex no. 2 Intelligence, Appendix B Order of Battle, Ninth Order of Battle Team, Box 8604, RG 407, Records of the Adjutant General's Office, WWII Operations Reports, 1940–48, 37th Infantry Division, NARA.
314 Captured enemy documents: Headquarters Sixth Army, G-2 Weekly Report no. 75, February 14, 1945, Box 1969, RG 407, Records of the Adjutant General's Office, WWII Operations Report, 1940–48, Sixth Army, NARA.
314 "polyglot": Robert F. Goheen, G-2 Periodic Report #83, February 9, 1945, Box 13295, RG 407, Records of the Adjutant General's Office, WWII Operations Reports, 1941–48, First Cavalry Division, NARA.
314 "puny opponents": Ibid.

314 **"potpourri":** Robert F. Goheen, G-2 Periodic Report #82, February 8, 1945, ibid.

314 **"It is a hastily":** Robert F. Goheen, G-2 Periodic Report #83, February 9, 1945, ibid.

314 **American forces seized:** Serial no. 1906, February 11, 1945, G-2 Journal, Box 8624, RG 407, Records of the Adjutant General's Office, WWII Operations Reports, 1940–48, 37th Infantry Division, NARA.

314 **"All of the essentials":** Charles Henne, "Battle History of the 3d Battalion, 148th Infantry, Manila, The Unwanted Battle (4 February through 7 March 1945)," p. 73.

314 **"I spent the night":** Ibid.

314 **"only official to welcome":** Counter Intelligence, Area Study no. 10, Manila and Environs, n.d., Box 15, RG 319, Army Staff, Office of the Assistant Chief of Staff for Intelligence, G-2, NARA.

314 **Valuable records:** Report after Action, Operations of the 37th Infantry Division on Bougainville, BSI and Luzon, P.I, From 1 November 44 to 30 June 45, Annex no. 2 Intelligence, Appendix B Order of Battle, Ninth Order of Battle Team.

314 **In a seminary:** Ibid.

314 **"This life of mine":** Robert F. Goheen, G-2 Periodic Report #85, February 11, 1945, Box 13295, RG 407, Records of the Adjutant General's Office, WWII Operations Reports, 1941–48, First Cavalry Division, NARA.

315 **On the battlefield:** Report after Action, Operations of the 37th Infantry Division, Luzon, P.I., November 1, 1944, to June 30, 1945 (M-1 Operation), September 10, 1945.

315 **"The platoons":** Battle of Luzon, 754th Tank Battalion, January 9–June 3, 1945.

315 **"Massed artillery":** Headquarters Sixth Army, G-2 Weekly Report no. 75, February 14, 1945, Box 1969, RG 407, Records of the Adjutant General's Office, WWII Operations Report, 1940–48, Sixty Army, NARA.

315 **"Unable to restrain":** Historical Record, Fifth Cavalry, Luzon Campaign, July 12, 1945.

315 **"In the peaceful":** Ibid.

316 **"will not understand":** General Staff, *Reports of General MacArthur*, p. 1:191.

316 **"From then on":** Robert S. Beightler, "Report on the Activities of the 37th Infantry Division, 1940–1945," n.d. (ca. 1946), USAHEC.

316 **Over the course:** Kurt J. Sellers, Technical Memorandum 10–89, "Artillery Ammunition Expenditures in Urban Combat: A Comparative Case Study of the Battles of Clark Field and Manila," September 1989, U.S. Army Human Engineering Laboratory, Aberdeen Proving Ground, Maryland, p. 108.

316 **"Some districts":** Krueger, *From Down Under*, p. 251.

316 **"It was like a bowling alley":** Dos Passos, *Tour of Duty*, p. 188.

316 **"We lived like dogs":** Hans Steiner, "Life and Death During the Occupation," *Philippines Free Press*, February 21, 2004, pp. 22, 29, clipping in Memorare Manila 1945 Foundation Collection, FHL.

316 **"The shelter was filled":** William C. Brady, "War Is Hell," unpublished narrative.

317 **"I came out":** Sundri Kishinchand testimony, June 1, 1945, in Report no. 21, "Investigation of the Violent Deaths of Mira Kishinchand, Pari Kishinchand and Radhi Kishinchand, Indians, in Paco, Manila, Philippine Islands, on 11 February 1945," June 24, 1945, Box 1109, RG 331, SCAP, Legal Section, Administrative Division, War Crimes File, 1946–50, NARA.

317 **"When the shelling":** Benjamin Santander Ramis, undated Malate Martyrs Information Sheet, Memorare Manila 1945 Foundation Collection, FHL.

317 **"When she came back":** Sancho Enriquez testimony, October 24, 1945, in Report no. 109.

317 **"I can see little":** "Use as Forts Dooms Manila Buildings," *Washington Post*, February 13, 1945, p. 9.

317 **"The reduction":** Robert S. Beightler to the Adjutant General, "Citation of the 112th Medical Battalion," September 14, 1945, Ortigas Foundation Library, Pasig City, Philippines.

317 **"The only Japs":** Hugh Hoffman, Headquarters First Cavalry Division, "Historical Report of the 1st Cavalry Division in the Luzon Campaign, 27 January 45–30 June 45," July 12, 1945, Box 13284, RG 407, Records of the Adjutant General's Office, WWII Operations Reports, 1941–48, First Cavalry Division, NARA.

318 "A double-barrel": Headquarters First Battalion, 145th Infantry, "Japanese Tactics and Employment of Weapons," March 25, 1945, Box 8764, RG 407, Records of the Adjutant General's Office, WWII Operations Reports, 1940–48, 37th Infantry Division, NARA.

318 "The heat had glued": Karnow, *In Our Image*, p. 321.

318 On Gilmore Street: Robert F. Goheen, G-2 Periodic Report #82, February 8, 1945.

318 "Tanks attempting": Eighth Cavalry, History of the Luzon Campaign, January 27–June 1945, Box 13378, RG 407, WWII Operations Reports, 1941–48, First Cavalry Division, NARA.

318 "For a split": Dean Marks, "The Day the Tank Blew Up," unpublished narrative, Box 3, Edward M. Flanagan, Jr., Papers, USAHEC.

318 "The turret was off": William H. Swan, "Recollection of Luzon, 1945," unpublished narrative, MMAL.

318 In another case: R. G. Langham, S-2 Periodic Report, no. 11, February 17, 1945, Box 13367, RG 407, WWII Operations Reports, 1941–48, First Cavalry Division, NARA.

318 The enemy likewise: Ozzie St. George, "The Two Faced City," *Yank*, April 27, 1945, p. 7.

319 "Outwardly these pillboxes": Sixth Army, Report of the Luzon Campaign, January 9–June 30, 1945, p. 4:124.

319 Between the National Psychopathic: Robert F. Goheen, G-2 Periodic Report #85, February 11, 1945, Box 13295, RG 407, Records of the Adjutant General's Office, WWII Operations Reports, 1941–48, First Cavalry Division, NARA.

319 "In his physical resemblance": Headquarters Sixth Army, G-2 Weekly Report no. 77, February 28, 1945, Box 1969, RG 407, Records of the Adjutant General's Office, WWII Operations Report, 1940–48, Sixth Army, NARA.

319 "Enemy morale": R. G. Langham, S-2 Periodic Report, no. 11, February 17, 1945.

319 "The old Escolta": William Dunn, broadcast transcript, February 14, 1945, RG 52, Papers of William J. Dunn, MMLA.

319 "A lot of this destruction": Oscar Griswold as quoted in the *Evening Star*, February 10, 1945; a clipping, minus the headline and page number, can be found in Report no. 80.

319 "Mac": Bonner Fellers to Dorothy Fellers, February 10, 1945, Box 2, RG 44a, Papers of Brig. Gen. Bonner F. Fellers, MMAL.

320 "Day after day": Robert S. Beightler to the Adjutant General, "Citation of the 112th Medical Battalion," September 14, 1945.

320 "Not only furniture": George E. Jones, "Manila Is Ravaged by Fire and Shell," *New York Times*, February 9, 1945, p. 3.

320 "They killed": Ann Bachrach testimony, June 3, 1945, in Report no. 52.

320 "The Japanese seemed": Elsie Hamburger testimony, June 1, 1945, in Report no. 28, "Investigation of the Murder of Fifteen Unknown Filipino Civilians in the Singalong District, Manila, Philippine Islands, on 12 February 1945," July 5, 1945, Box 1110, RG 331, SCAP, Legal Section, Administrative Division, War Crimes File, 1946–50, NARA.

320 "We ran up": Entry for February 10, 1945, in Lichauco, *"Dear Mother Putnam,"* pp. 208–9.

321 "They gave Cornelia": Ibid., p. 209.

321 "From their incoherent": Entry for February 19, 1945, ibid., p. 211.

321 "I met thousands": Ibid., pp. 211–12.

321 "Farther up the road": Ibid., p. 212.

321 Absent any relief: Fung, *Beneath the Banyan Tree*, p. 170.

321 "I never realized": Entry for February 19, 1945, in Lichauco, *"Dear Mother Putnam,"* p. 213.

322 "The stench": Ibid., p. 212.

CHAPTER 16

323 "The Western mind": "Report on the Destruction of Manila and Japanese Atrocities," February 1945.
323 Hundreds of refugees: Report no. 94; unless otherwise noted, all testimony cited below comes from this report.
323 "My mother caught": Rosalinda Andoy testimony, October 11, 1945.
324 "Mother": Ibid.
324 "She received seven": Rosario Nieves testimony, October 12, 1945.
324 "I went to my mother": Ibid.
325 "My mother brushed": Rosalinda Andoy testimony, October 11, 1945.
325 "You must leave now": Garcia, It Took Four Years, p. 11.
325 "Very dangerous": Ibid.
326 "Was it Japanese": Ibid.
326 "Quick, go now": Ibid., p. 113.
326 "There were": Ibid., p. 114.
327 "Who is it": Ibid.
327 "There goes": Ibid., p. 115.
327 "Help me": Ibid., p. 118.
328 "Where's the doctor": Ibid.
328 "What next": Ibid., p. 119.
328 Just one block away: Report no. 27, "Investigation of the Massacre of Forty-One Civilians; Attempted Murder of Fifteen Civilians, All of Various Nationalities; Rape and Attempted Rape of Four Filipinos at De La Salle College, 1501 Taft Avenue, Manila, Philippine Islands, Between 7 and 14 February 1945," July 4, 1945, Box 1110, RG 331, SCAP, Legal Section, Administrative Division, War Crimes File, 1946–50, NARA. See also Gonzalez and Reyes, These Hallowed Halls. Additional details can be found in the testimonies of Francis J. Cosgrave, Anton Heitmann, Martin C. Hain, Rosario Carlos, and Servillano Aquino, October 30, 1945, YTT, pp. 263–322. Unless otherwise noted, all testimony and documents cited below come from victim statements included in Report no. 27.
329 "She was tall": Olaguer, Terror in Manila, p. 34.
329 "That boy looked": Servillano Aquino testimony, May 29, 1945.
329 "If I die": Ibid.
330 "They were pretty rough": Anton Heitmann (Antonius von Jesus) testimony, May 26, 1945.
330 "From then on": Francis J. Cosgrave testimony, October 30, 1945, YTT, p. 265.
330 "Everybody got scared": Servillano Aquino testimony, May 29, 1945.
331 "We could hear": Francis J. Cosgrave testimony, October 30, 1945, YTT, p. 265.
331 "You can't do this": Anton Heitmann testimony, May 26, 1945.
331 "They're going to kill": Francis J. Cosgrave testimony, May 26, 1945.
331 "Father": Fernando Vasquez-Prada, transcript of Rotary Speech, March 1, 1994, Memorare Manila 1945 Foundation Collection, FHL.
331 "I raised my hand": Francis J. Cosgrave testimony, October 30, 1945, YTT, p. 271.
332 "They were hit": Fernando Vasquez-Prada, transcript of Rotary Speech, March 1, 1994.
332 "My mother seeing": Ibid.
332 "My mother was slashed": Ibid.
332 "Let her take": Ibid.
332 "Some of the women": Antonio Madrileno testimony, June 6, 1945.
332 "When the Japanese": Francis J. Cosgrave, "La Salle College Massacre," March 6, 1945.
333 "I raised": Juanita Tamayo testimony, May 29, 1945.
333 "We heard four": Filomeno Inolin testimony, June 1, 1945.
334 "She was sitting": Servillano Aquino testimony, October 30, 1945, YTT, p. 312.
334 "When the nurse": Servillano Aquino testimony, May 29, 1945.

334 "Oh": Ibid.

334 "I received four": Filomeno Inolin testimony, June 1, 1945.

334 "He was stabbed": Servillano Aquino testimony, May 29, 1945.

334 "He let me": Ibid.

334 "He decided to push": Servillano Aquino testimony, October 30, 1945, YTT, p. 314.

335 "At that instant": Servillano Aquino testimony, May 29, 1945.

335 "It's all over": Antonius von Jesus, "The Holocaust in Manila," in Gonzalez and Reyes, *These Hallowed Halls*, p. 66.

336 "I am a German": Anton Heitmann testimony, May 26, 1945.

336 "We remained": Francis J. Cosgrave, "La Salle College Massacre," March 6, 1945.

336 "Don't drink": Joan Orendain, "Children of War," in Constantino, *Under Japanese Rule*, p. 122.

337 "My father and I": Ibid.

337 "I was more": Francis J. Cosgrave, "La Salle College Massacre," March 6, 1945.

337 "As far as I could": Francis J. Cosgrave testimony, May 26, 1945.

337 "I could not lift": Servillano Aquino testimony, May 29, 1945.

337 "I am here": Ibid.

338 "I preferred death": Ibid.

338 "I wanted to faint": Ibid.

338 "She was dead": Servillano Aquino testimony, January 27, 1949, p. 700 of the trial transcript of *People of Philippines v. Shizuo Yokoyama*, Box 1699, RG 331, SCAP, Legal Section, Prosecution Division, Philippines versus Japanese War Criminals, Case File, 1947–49, NARA.

338 "I heard them": Rosario Carlos testimony, October 30, 1945, YTT, p. 302.

338 "I felt my dress": Ibid.

338 "He was": Servillano Aquino testimony, May 29, 1945.

338 "Let us pray": Ibid.

339 "As the hours passed": Fernando Vasquez-Prada, transcript of Rotary Speech, March 1, 1994.

339 "My father was killed": Ibid.

339 "Bastards": Servillano Aquino testimony, May 29, 1945.

339 "My mother lasted": Fernando Vasquez-Prada, transcript of Rotary Speech, March 1, 1994.

339 "Father Cosgrave would come": Servillano Aquino testimony, May 29, 1945.

340 "I had difficulty": Ibid.

340 "Every minute": Ibid.

340 "Father": Ibid.

340 "Anybody alive?": Ibid.

340 "Yes": Ibid.

341 "The high buildings": Charles Henne, "Battle History of the 3d Battalion, 148th Infantry, Manila, The Unwanted Battle (4 February through 7 March 1945)," pp. 71–72.

341 "The preferred solution": Ibid., p. 72.

341 "Based on reports": Ibid.

341 "It was astonishing": Ibid., p. 75.

342 "A Filipino": Ibid.

342 "Jap": Ibid.

342 "Picking their way": Ibid., p. 79.

CHAPTER 17

343 "Cannibals in the lowest": Report no. 13, "Investigation of the Alleged Shooting, Bayonetting and Burning of Civilians at the Perez Rubio Residence, 150 Vito Cruz Street, Singalong, Manila, Philippine Islands, on 12 February 1945," June

11, 1945, Box 1114, RG 331, SCAP, Legal Section, Administrative Division, War Crimes File, 1946–50, NARA.

343 **"The Manila Defense Force":** Military History Section, Headquarters, Army Forces Far East, "Philippine Area Naval Operations," pt. 4, January–August 1945, Japanese Monograph no. 114, p. 17.

343 **From his headquarters:** Smith, *Triumph in Philippines*, p. 272.

344 **"Withdraw at once":** Potter, *Life and Death*, p. 136.

344 **"Counterattacks in our area":** Military History Section, Headquarters, Army Forces Far East, "Philippine Area Naval Operations," pt. 4, January–August 1945, Japanese Monograph no. 114, p. 17.

344 **"Today, Shimbu Group":** Ibid., pp. 17–18.

344 **"The headquarters":** Ibid., p. 18.

344 **"In anticipation":** Ibid.

345 **"In view":** Ibid.

345 **"The night of the 18th":** Ibid., p. 19.

345 **"We can hold out":** Ibid.

345 **The Japanese went so far:** Report no. 18, "Investigation of the Murder of Boris Semenovich Gurevich, His Son, Leonid Borisovich Gurevich, and Victor George Vantchurin, Russians, 610 Kansas Street, Manila, Philippine Islands, on 10 February 1945," June 20, 1945, Box 1109, RG 331, SCAP, Legal Section, Administrative Division, War Crimes File, 1946–50, NARA.

346 **Troops murdered:** Report no. 70, "Investigation of the Massacre of Approximately One Hundred Filipino and Spanish Civilians at the Price House, 535 Colorado Street, Ermita, Manila, P.I., on 10 February 1945," August 20, 1946, Box 1114, RG 331, SCAP, Legal Section, Administrative Division, War Crimes File, 1946–50, NARA.

346 **Two days later:** Report no. 13.

346 **A similar atrocity:** Report no. 63, "Investigation of the Murder of Over One Hundred Civilians, Including Twenty-Six Identified Filipino and Four French Civilians, and Attempted Murder of Seventeen Filipino Civilians, Four of Whom Are Identified, at 1462 Taft Avenue, Pasay, Rizal, Philippine Islands, on 13 February 1945," March 17, 1947, Box 1114, RG 331, SCAP, Legal Section, Administrative Division, War Crimes File, 1946–50, NARA.

346 **Thirty-five more:** Report no. 88, "Investigation of the Murder of Thirty-Five and Wounding of Twenty-Eight Spanish, Filipino, and Chinese Civilians at Dr. Moreta's House, 417 Isaac Peral Street, Manila, on 17 February 1945," October 21, 1945, Box 1117, ibid.

346 **Russian immigrant Helen Kremleff:** Report no. 6, "Investigation of the Alleged Atrocities Committed on Eugene Andreewitz Kremleff and Mrs. Helen Kremleff, His Wife, 34 Den Pan St., Pasay, Rizal, Philippine Islands, and Julian Jawai and Alfredo Gana, 47 Ignacio St., Pasay, Rizal, Philippine Islands, 9 February 1945," April 29, 1947, Box 1108, RG 331, SCAP, Legal Section, Administrative Division, War Crimes File, 1946–50, NARA.

346 **Fellow Russian native:** Report no. 18.

346 **"Go":** Eva M. Gurevich testimony, May 26, 1945, ibid.

346 **"When I was":** Ibid.

346 **That's where troops:** Report no. 52.

346 **"Goodbye, Darling":** Anne Bachrach testimony, August 15, 1945, ibid.

346 **"I looked around":** Ibid.

346 **"Japanese patrols":** Augusto S. Besa testimony, August 7, 1945, in Report no. 68, "Investigation of the Murder of Felix Isla, Angel Francisco, and Three Other Civilian Male Filipinos, and the Attempted Murder of Silverios T. Braganza, Filipino, in Malate, Manila, Philippine Islands, on 13 February 1945," March 12, 1947, Box 1114, RG 331, SCAP, Legal Section, Administrative Division, War Crimes File, 1946–50, NARA.

347 **"I heard them shooting":** Max Hahn testimony, June 2, 1945, in Report no. 20, "Investigation of the Murder of Messrs. Lazar Braun, Robert Markus and Alexan-

der Farmakowski in Manila, Philippines Islands, on 12 February 1945," February 26, 1947, Box 1109, RG 331, SCAP, Legal Section, Administrative Division, War Crimes File, 1946–50, NARA.

347 **"Many mothers":** Stella Mary Best testimony, August 16, 1945, in Report no. 59.

347 **News reporters flocked:** Ozzie St. George, "Bankers' Hours," *Yank*, April 27, 1945, p. 7.

348 **"The gunner sat":** Ibid.

348 **"Here I found":** Mydans, *More Than Meets*, pp. 202–3.

348 **"A short distance":** Robert Shaplen, "Manila's Stunned Survivors Can Only Stare and Weep," *Newsweek*, February 26, 1945, p. 32.

348 **"There is":** William Gray, Cable 9, February 19, 1945, Box 252, Dispatches from *Time* Magazine Correspondents, HL.

348 **"They are not trying":** William Dunn, broadcast transcript, February 12, 1945, RG 52, Papers of William J. Dunn, MMLA.

349 **"Before moving the artillery":** Ira Rosenberg testimony, May 21, 1946, in Report no. 80.

349 **"To facilitate":** Ibid.

349 **"Just have a chair":** Walter Simmons, "Tribune Writer in Ringside Seat Sees Japs Get 'It,'" *Chicago Daily Tribune*, February 17, 1945, p. 2.

349 **"Just across the river":** Ibid.

349 **"Twelve, thirteen":** Ibid.

349 **"Just watch":** Ibid.

349 **"One of those":** Ibid.

350 **"The Japs":** Ibid.

350 **"That's all right":** Ibid.

350 **"God":** St. George, "Bankers' Hours," p. 7.

350 **"Each time the Long Toms":** Dos Passos, *Tour of Duty*, p. 175.

350 **"Boy":** St. George, "Bankers' Hours," p. 7.

350 **"It was like smashing":** Gunnison, "Burning of Manila," p. 40.

350 **"The hotel":** St. George, "Bankers' Hours," p. 7.

350 **"This is like a $2.20":** Ibid.

351 **"There goes our drink":** Dos Passos, *Tour of Duty*, p. 195.

352 **In one such case:** Report no. 19, "Investigation of the Murder of Bartolome Pons, Rosario Garcia (Pons), Eva V. Garcia (Pons), Pacita King, Edward King, Delfin Marquez, and Three Filipinos Identified by Their First Names as Candida, Virginia and Isaac at Paco, Manila, Philippine Islands, on 7 February 1945," June 21, 1945, Box 1109, RG 331, SCAP, Legal Section, Administrative Division, War Crimes File, 1946–50, NARA.

352 **"The baby":** Donald D. Forward, "Atrocity Report," February 15, 1945, ibid.

352 **"One of the persons":** Steven W. Loska testimony, May 11, 1945, ibid.

352 **"There is no visible":** Lynn B. Griffith to Staff Judge Advocate, War Crimes Branch, "Report by War Crimes Branch on the Death of Don Bartolome Pons, Rosario Garcia Pons, Eva Garcia, Pacita King, Edward King, Delfin Marquez, and Three Servants by the Names of Candida, Virginia and Isaac, Last Names Unknown," May 23, 1945, ibid.

352 **"Desire full details":** ADV ECH GHQ to CG SIXTH ARMY ATTN G-2, February 17, 1945, Box 1993, RG 331, SCAP, Legal Section, Manila Branch, Illegal Acts by Japanese in Philippines, 1945–47, NARA.

352 **"All four":** Serifine F. Ruggio testimony, February 13, 1945, in Report no. 67, "Investigation of the Murder of Forty-Three Chinese and Filipino Civilians and Attempted Murder of Twelve Chinese and Filipino Civilians in Ermita, Manila, Philippine Islands, on 11 February 1945," August 20, 1946, Box 1114, RG 331, SCAP, Legal Section, Administrative Division, War Crimes File, 1946–50, NARA.

353 **"Japanese":** Ibid.

353 **"The woman had one":** William Kropf testimony, February 18, 1945, ibid.

353 **"I examined the body":** William C. Gardner testimony, February 18, 1945, ibid.

353 **"A short distance":** Ibid.

353   "The woman lay": David V. Binkley testimony, March 9, 1945, ibid.
353   "The building shook": Garcia, *It Took Four Years*, p. 120.
354   "We're getting out": Ibid.
354   "Ceilings were collapsing": Ibid., p. 121.
354   "Stick together": Ibid.
354   "Only a moment before": Ibid., p. 122.
355   "Everyone was running": Ibid., p. 123.
355   "It was an eerie sight": Ibid.
355   "Most distressing": Ibid., p. 124.
356   "Quickly": Ibid., p. 127.
356   "No more than ten minutes": Ibid., p. 128.
356   "There was no let-up": Ibid.
356   "Can't he see": Ibid.
356   "That's enough": Ibid., p. 129.
356   "The sound": Ibid., p. 131.
357   "Fragments of red-hot": Ibid.
357   "The Japanese have come": Ibid., p. 133.
357   "Pray my son": Ibid.
357   "Don't be afraid": Ibid.
357   "Don't move": Ibid., p. 134.
358   "The sound of distant": Ibid., p. 135.
358   "My brother and I": Ibid., p. 136.
358   "You should go": Ibid., p. 137.
358   "There was no": Ibid., p. 140.
359   "For four days": Joaquin, *Mr. F.E.U.*, p. 170.
359   "Be brave": Montinola, *Breaking the Silence*, p. 70.
359   "I forgive them": Ibid., p. 101.
359   "What's the matter": Joaquin, *Mr. F.E.U.*, p. 171.
359   "There were no flags": Ibid.
360   "Relaxing is impossible": Charles Henne, "Battle History of the 3d Battalion, 148th Infantry, Manila, the Unwanted Battle (4 February through 7 March 1945)," p. 80.
360   "As the noose tightened": Hugh Hoffman, Headquarters 1st Cavalry Division, "Historical Report of the 1st Cavalry Division in the Luzon Campaign, 27 January 45–30 June 45," July 12, 1945.
360   "The strain of this battle": Entry for February 18–22, 1945, Griswold diary.
361   "Intramuros": Ibid.
361   "The Japs offered": Charles Henne, "Battle History of the 3d Battalion, 148th Infantry, Manila, The Unwanted Battle (4 February through 7 March 1945)," p. 80.
362   "Jimmy, killed instantly": Ibid., p. 81.

CHAPTER 18

363   "South of the Pasig": St. George, "Two Faced City," p. 6.
363   "We encountered": Garcia, *It Took Four Years*, p. 141.
364   "There was no way": Ibid.
364   "We moved slowly": Ibid., p. 142.
364   "The stone building": Ibid.
364   "We wouldn't": Ibid., p. 143.
364   "Don't look": Ibid.
365   "I could not move": Ibid.
365   "No, not in there": Ibid., p. 144.
365   "Where the hell": Ibid.
365   "Show them in": Ibid., p. 145.
365   "But only for the night": Ibid.

365 "Don't stand": Ibid., p. 146.
366 "The sound of rifle": Ibid.
366 "Block after block": Ibid., p. 155.
366 "No two corpses": Ibid.
366 "A very poignant": Ibid.
367 "Unlike the other": Ibid., p. 157.
367 "It's not the Ritz": Ibid., p. 160.
368 "I was so weary": Ibid., p. 161.
368 The Fifth and Twelfth: Historical Record, Fifth Cavalry, Luzon Campaign, July 12, 1945.
368 "When the smoke died": Bonner Fellers to Dorothy Fellers, February 16, 1945, Box 2, RG 44a, Papers of Brig. Gen. Bonner F. Fellers, MMAL.
369 "During the lull": "Yanks Tag Jap Trying to Steal Home—For Keeps," *Washington Post*, February 19, 1945, p. 1.
369 "Those Japs remaining": Historical Record, Fifth Cavalry, Luzon Campaign, July 12, 1945.
369 Despite red crosses: Report no. 60, "Investigation of the Fortification of the Philippine General Hospital for Military Purposes; the Rape of [redacted], 20-year-old Female Filipino Civilian; and the Murder of Unidentified Civilians in Ermita, Manila, Philippine Islands, During February, 1945," March 10, 1947, Box 1113, RG 331, SCAP, Legal Section, Administrative Division, War Crimes File, 1946–50, NARA.
370 "The halls": Ann C. Keily testimony, November 5, 1945, Box 1997, RG 331, Supreme Commander for the Allied Powers, Legal Section, Manila Branch, Illegal Acts by Japanese in the Philippines, 1945–47, NARA.
370 "Every Japanese soldier": "PGH Staff Carried on Despite Shelling, Menace of Japanese," *Free Philippines*, February 22, 1945, p. 2.
370 Sixteen-year-old: Edgar Krohn, Jr., interview by author, September 14, 2015.
370 "A man in front": Edgar Krohn, Jr., "The Way It Was: A Teenager's Experience During the Battle for Manila," in Guillermo and Parsons, *Manila 1945*, p. 52.
370 "He turned around": Ibid.
371 "In a corner": Ibid.
371 "I have always": Ibid., p. 54.
371 That quest: James Litton, interview by author, September 17, 1945.
371 "She lay moaning": James Litton, "The Battle of Manila: February 3–March 3, 1945," unpublished narrative.
371 "She was bandaged": Ibid.
372 "From a peep hole": Ibid.
372 "This direct fire": Historical Record, Report after Action, pt. 1, Operations of the 148th Infantry, Luzon, Philippine Islands, November 1, 1944–March 4, 1945.
372 "Fighting continued": Ibid.
372 "All resistance was": Ibid.
372 "By midmorning": Miguel P. Avanceña, "PGH 1945: Days of Terror, Nights of Fear," *Philippine Daily Inquirer*, February 18, 2012, p. A1.
373 "How many are you": Krohn, Jr., "The Way It Was," in Guillermo and Parsons, *Manila 1945*, p. 56.
373 "*Amerikano!*": James Litton, "The War Years: Reminiscences of a Young Boy," February 25, 2015, lecture, Ortigas Foundation Library, Pasig City, Philippines.
373 "I am alive": Ibid.
373 "Don't do that": Luis R. Esteban, "My War: A Personal Narrative," unpublished memoir, AWM.
373 "Casualties ran": Robert S. Beightler to the Adjutant General, "Citation of the 112th Medical Battalion," September 14, 1945.
373 "The evacuation continued": Report after Action, Operations of the 37th Infantry Division, Luzon, P.I., November 1, 1944, to June 30, 1945 (M-1 Operation), September 10, 1945.

374 "The area we are": Historical Record, Fifth Cavalry, Luzon Campaign, July 12, 1945.
374 "A fair bag": Ibid.
374 "Both of the deceased": John H. Amesse testimony, February 24, 1945, Box 310, RG 496, Records of General Headquarters, SWPA and U.S. Army Forces, Pacific, MIS Administrative Section, General Correspondence, 1942–46, NARA.
374 "with the rain": Historical Record, Fifth Cavalry, Luzon Campaign, July 12, 1945.
374 "A terrific explosion": Ibid.
375 "Their complete": Ibid.
375 "Numerous holes": Ibid.
375 "Looking through a crack": Ibid.
375 "The holding force": Ibid.
376 "At first they seemed": Ibid.
376 "An appalling sight": Ibid.
376 "In the five adjoining": Ibid.
377 For the surviving: Report no. 94. All testimony cited below, unless otherwise noted, comes from this report.
377 "They were burned": Sister Nelly de Jesus Virata testimony, October 16, 1945.
377 "The dogs": Rosa Calalang testimony, October 16, 1945.
377 Twenty-four-year-old: Pacita Vasquez Siguenza testimony, October 20, 1945.
377 "We could never": Conchita Huerta testimony, October 5, 1945.
377 "Rape won't hurt": Ibid.
377 "My family killed": Andrea P. Lopez testimony, October 13, 1945.
378 "Sometimes, as twilight": Joaquin, *Intramuros*, p. 36.
378 "We found her torso": Ibid.
378 "We tried to help": Ester Aenille testimony, October 11, 1945.
378 "I think Japan": Antonio O. Gisbert testimony, October 23, 1945.
378 "We will all die": Lourdes Locsin Godino testimony, October 17, 1945.
379 "How many": Rosa Calalang testimony, October 16, 1945.
379 "What are they": Ibid.
379 "You've hit me": Ibid.
380 "Doctor, doctor": Consolaction Cordero testimony, October 10, 1945.
380 "All nurses": Benita Lahoz testimony, September 12, 1945.
380 "I could see": Rosa Calalang testimony, October 16, 1945.
380 "The Japanese bayonetted": Ibid.
380 "Somebody please": Ibid.
380 "We don't know": Ibid.
381 "One of the women": Benita Lahoz testimony, September 12, 1945.
381 "What are you doing": Conrado Tauro testimony, March 4, 1945.
381 "Don't sit down": Jose Maria Barrullo testimony, September 11, 1945.
381 "There was no room": Epifanio Guitierrez, Jr., testimony, October 2, 1945.
381 "Those killed": Jose Maria Barrullo testimony, September 11, 1945.
381 "I am hit": Eduardo W. Carceller testimony, October 13, 1945.
382 "The worst part": Jose Maria Barrullo testimony, September 11, 1945.
382 "We made up": Ibid.
382 "I was able": Belarmino de Celis testimony, September 27, 1945.
382 "Many were still breathing": Ibid.
383 "A profound silence": Julio Rocamora testimony, March 1, 1945.
383 "I did not find": Belarmino de Celis testimony, September 27, 1945.
383 "A representation": Hartendorp, *Japanese Occupation*, p. 2:560.
383 "We won't be": Entry for February 18, 1945, in Cates, *Drainpipe Diary*, p. 256.
383 "We cheered madly": Ibid.
384 "I saw": Prising, *Manila, Goodbye*, p. 195.
384 "We consumed vast": Entry for February 18, 1945, in Cates, *Drainpipe Diary*, p. 255.
384 "Give the poor bastards": Ibid.
384 "It was the same": Ibid.

384   "The food still seems": John W. Osborn letter, February 8, 1945, John Osborn Santo Tomas Internment Transcriptions, UM.

384   "The camp children": Entry for February 18, 1945, in Cates, *Drainpipe Diary*, p. 256.

384   "They haven't any idea": Bonner Fellers to Dorothy Fellers, February 16, 1945, Box 2, RG 44a, Papers of Brig. Gen. Bonner F. Fellers, MMAL.

385   "We had to shout": Entry for February 14, 1945, in Cates, *Drainpipe Diary*, pp. 253–54.

385   "The guns still crash": Entry for February 20–23, 1945, in Wygle, *Surviving*, p. 149.

385   "The last time": Entry for February 20, 1945, in Cates, *Drainpipe Diary*, p. 256.

385   "We looked to the north": Ibid.

385   "There was a soldier": St. George, "Two Faced City," p. 6.

386   "Across the river": Ibid.

386   "South of the River": Ibid.

386   "The other side": Ibid.

386   "The stories that come": William Dunn, broadcast transcript, February 16, 1945, RG 52, Papers of William J. Dunn, MMLA.

386   "But I do": William Dunn, broadcast transcript, February 21, 1945, RG 52, Papers of William J. Dunn, MMLA.

386   "I cannot understand": Henry Keys, "The Horror of Manila," *Daily Express*, February 15, 1945, p. 1; George E. Jones, "Filipino Civilians Massacred by Foe," *New York Times*, February 15, 1945, p. 1. Keys and Jones have slightly different spellings for Dr. Josephina Bulatao. The spelling used here is as it appears in the *New York Times*.

386   "It was painful": Robert Shaplen, "Manila's Stunned Survivors Can Only Stare and Weep," *Newsweek*, February 26, 1945, p. 32.

386   "At last the Japanese": Keys, "Horror of Manila," p. 1.

386   "The Jap is a fiend": Bonner Fellers to Dorothy Fellers, February 14, 1945, Box 2, RG 44a, Papers of Brig. Gen. Bonner F. Fellers, MMAL.

387   "Thank you": Ibid.

387   "How she could": Ibid.

387   "Since yesterday": Carl Mydans, "These Are the War Victims," *Saturday Evening Post*, September 1, 1945, p. 6.

387   "All morning": Ibid.

388   "Everything you ever": Ibid.

388   "He was not the same": Felipe Buencamino III, "Refugees Salvage Hope, Little Else, From Ruins," *Free Philippines*, February 20, 1945, p. 2.

388   "At a spot": Water Simmons, "Peace and Quiet, Horror of War, Manila Is Both," *Chicago Daily Tribune*, February 16, 1945, p. 5.

388   "Mothers and children": Shaplen, "Manila's Stunned Survivors Can Only Stare and Weep," p. 32.

389   "It's plenty hot": Simmons, "Peace and Quiet, Horror of War," p. 5.

389   "Americans have formed": William Gray, Cable 4, 5, 6, February 18, 1945, Box 252, Dispatches from *Time* Magazine Correspondents, HL.

389   Gray visited: John Dos Passos also described this church in *Tour of Duty*, pp. 181–82.

389   "A Filipino woman": Gray, Cable 4, 5, 6, February 18, 1945.

389   "Progress is slow": William Dunn, broadcast transcript, February 12, 1945, RG 52, Papers of William J. Dunn, MMLA.

389   "A beaten enemy": George E. Jones, "Filipino Civilians Massacred by Foe," *New York Times*, February 15, 1945, p. 1.

390   "That bank's full": Simmons, "Peace and Quiet, Horror of War, Manila Is Both," p. 5.

390   "The floor is covered": Ibid.

390   "It was heartbreaking": Gunnison, "Burning of Manila," p. 40.

390   "There, propped": Ibid.

391 "Here we saw": George E. Jones, "Vast Area of Ruin Is Left in Manila," *New York Times*, February 21, 1945, p. 4.

391 "Block after ruined": Ibid.

391 "I understand": Robert Eichelberger to Emma Eichelberger, February 21, 1945, in Luvaas, *Dear Miss Em*, p. 225.

391 This de facto: Robert Eichelberger to Emma Eichelberger, February 28, 1945, ibid., p. 228.

391 "MacArthur was shattered": Rogers, *MacArthur and Sutherland*, p. 2:263.

392 "I do not believe": Robert Eichelberger to Emma Eichelberger, February 14, 1945, in Luvaas, *Dear Miss Em*, p. 216.

392 "I must say": Robert Eichelberger to Emma Eichelberger, February 18, 1945, ibid., p. 218.

392 "The long drawn-out": Bonner Fellers to Dorothy Fellers, February 14, 1945, Box 2, RG 44a, Papers of Brig. Gen. Bonner F. Fellers, MMAL.

CHAPTER 19

393 "The old Walled City": George E. Jones, "Intramuros a City of Utter Horror," *New York Times*, February 25, 1945, p. 25.

393 An estimated two thousand: Smith, *Triumph in Philippines*, p. 301.

393 Japanese troops had: Charge no. 52, Bill of Particulars, *United States v. Tomoyuki Yamashita*, Box 1959, RG 331, SCAP, Legal Section, Manila Branch, Records of Trial Exhibits, 1945–49, NARA.

393 "The entire area": "Combat in Manila," April 21, 1945.

393 "Tremendous fire": After Action Report, 716 Tank Battalion, January 9–February 8, 1945, March 18, 1945–February 8, 1945 (sic).

393 Troops finally: Report after Action, Operations of the 37th Infantry Division, Luzon, P.I., November 1, 1944, to June 30, 1945 (M-1 Operation), September 10, 1945.

394 "The tedious process": Ibid.

394 Civilian escapees: After Action Report, XIV Corps, M-1 Operation, July 29, 1945.

394 "Your situation": Ibid.

394 "So it is": Entry for February 11–17, 1945, Griswold diary.

394 "The use of air": Rogers, *MacArthur and Sutherland*, p. 2:263.

394 "Horrid as it seems": Entry for February 11–17, 1945, Griswold diary.

394 "I understand": Ibid.

395 The plan for: After Action Report, XIV Corps, M-1 Operation, July 29, 1945.

395 "The element": Ibid.

395 "The huge guns": Rogers, *MacArthur and Sutherland*, p. 2:264.

396 "I have witnessed": William Dunn, broadcast transcript, February 24, 1945, RG 52, Papers of William J. Dunn, MMLA.

396 "Forty feet thick": Jones, "Intramuros a City of Utter Horror," p. 25.

396 In one hour: Archibald M. Rodgers, "Artillery Ammunition Expenditure for Preparation for Attack on Intramuros, 0730–0930 23 February 1945," February 24, 1945, Box 8706, RG 407, Records of the Adjutant General's Office, WWII Operations Reports, 1940–48, Sixth Army, NARA.

396 That was combined: Sixth Army, Report of the Luzon Campaign, January 9–June 30, 1945, p. 1:40.

396 "The old soft stones": Charles Henne, "Battle History of the 3d Battalion, 148th Infantry, Manila, The Unwanted Battle (4 February through 7 March 1945)," p. 84.

396 Inside the dark: Antonio O. Gisbert testimony, October 23, 1945, in Report no. 94.

396 "We could not": Benita Lahoz testimony, September 12, 1945, ibid.

397 "The firing": Belarmino de Celis testimony, September 27, 1945, ibid.

397 "The ensuing silence": Dunn broadcast transcript, February 24, 1945.

397 "Now there's nothing": Dunn, *Pacific Microphone*, pp. 313–14.

397 "It was a breathless": Ibid., p. 314.

397 "Not a shot": Jones, "Intramuros a City of Utter Horror," p. 25.
397 At the same time: After Action Report, XIV Corps, M-1 Operation, July 29, 1945.
397 "A lone sniper": Dunn broadcast transcript, February 24, 1945.
397 "God bless them!": Ibid.
397 "Retaking the Intramuros": Sixth Army on Luzon, Lingayen to Manila, January 9–March 3, 1945, Box 1957, RG 407, Records of the Adjutant General's Office, WWII Operations Reports, 1940–48, Sixth Army, NARA.
398 "A short rattle": Jones, "Intramuros a City of Utter Horror," p. 25.
398 "Come on": Belarmino de Celis testimony, September 27, 1945.
398 "I knew by the voice": Ibid.
398 "The soldiers": Jones, "Intramuros a City of Utter Horror," p. 25.
398 "I don't know": Ibid.
399 "Damn it": Frankel and Kirker, 37th Infantry Division, p. 291.
399 "That sounds": Ibid., p. 292.
399 "How do you like": Ibid.
399 "We had better leave": Ester Aenlle testimony, October 11, 1945, in Report no. 94.
400 "Don't be afraid": Felicidad Villez Ocampo testimony, September 28, 1945, ibid.
400 "We are Filipinos!": Ester Aenlle testimony, October 11, 1945, ibid.
400 "Go forward": Lourdes Lecaroz testimony, October 3, 1945, ibid.
400 "She too, was shot": Ibid.
400 "American soldiers": Mary Tormey testimony, September 4, 1945, ibid.
400 "Over it streamed": Jones, "Intramuros a City of Utter Horror," p. 25.
401 "Come along": Henry Keys testimony, November 7, 1945, YTT, p. 1334.
401 "I knelt down": Ibid.
401 "She bore": Ibid., p. 1335.
401 "Look at this!": Ibid., p. 1336.
401 "She told us": Ibid.
401 "He was the only": Ibid.
402 "Come here!": Ibid.
402 "The flies": Ibid., p. 1337.
402 "Every building": David S. Conner testimony, August 24, 1945, in Report no. 109.
402 "The hands": Ibid.
402 "He said that": Frank E. Pitchek testimony, February 28, 1945, ibid.
402 "Every thinkable": After Action Reports, M-1 Operation, Drafts, Luzon Campaign, 37th Infantry Division, November 16, 1944–February 24, 1945, Box 8603, RG 407, Records of the Adjutant General's Office, WWII Operations Reports, 1940–48, 37th Infantry Division, NARA.
403 Four hundred enemy dead: Report After Action, Operations of the 37th Infantry Division, Luzon, P.I., November 1, 1944, to June 30 1945 (M-1 Operation), September 10, 1945.
403 "When the Japanese": Report no. 109.
403 "There were ashes": David S. Conner testimony, August 24, 1945, ibid.
403 "These bodies": Frank J. Middelberg testimony, March 1, 1945, ibid.
403 "The bodies": Jacob E. Klein testimony, February 28, 1945, ibid.
403 "Bodies in the rear": J. D. Frederick, "Report of Atrocities at Fort Santiago, Intramuros, City of Manila," March 1, 1945, ibid.
404 "These double doors": Ibid.
404 "Some enlisted men": Frank J. Middelberg testimony, March 1, 1945, ibid.
404 "So thick": Frederick, "Report of Atrocities at Fort Santiago, Intramuros, City of Manila," March 1, 1945, ibid.
404 "a more diabolical": Ibid.
404 "All indications": Frank J. Middelberg testimony, March 1, 1945, ibid.
404 "The starved": Frederick, "Report of Atrocities at Fort Santiago, Intramuros, City of Manila," March 1, 1945, ibid.
405 "The total number": John D. Frederick testimony, March 2, 1945, ibid.
405 "God has been good": Entry for February 23, 1945, Griswold diary.

405 **In a daring:** After Action Report, XIV Corps, M-1 Operation, July 29, 1945; Kenney, *General Kenney Reports*, pp. 523–24.

405 **The family had fled:** H.V.W., memorandum, February 15, 1945, including "Inventory of General Douglas MacArthur's and Manila Hotel's Properties in the Presidential Suite," Box 2, RG 3, Records of Headquarters, SWPA, 1942–45, MMAL.

406 **On February 14 the general:** George D. Sears to Douglas MacArthur, February 14, 1945, with Inventory of Silver, ibid.

406 **U.S. soldiers later found:** William T. Holladay to Robert Beightler, February 15, 1945, with Inventory of Silver, ibid.

406 **"House still unharmed":** Douglas MacArthur to Jean MacArthur, February 16, 1945, Box 14, RG 3, Records of Headquarters, SWPA, 1942–45, MMAL.

406 **"I saw the Manila Hotel":** Bonner Fellers to Dorothy Fellers, February 24, 1945, Box 2, RG 44a, Papers of Brig. Gen. Bonner F. Fellers, MMAL.

406 **"Do not":** Douglas MacArthur to Jean MacArthur, February 18, 1945, Box 14, RG 3, Records of Headquarters, SWPA, 1942–45, MMAL.

406 **At six a.m. on February 23:** Entry for February 23, 1945, Douglas MacArthur diary.

407 **"300 lbs":** Serial no. 3416, February 22, 1945, G-2 Journal, Box 8624, RG 407, Records of the Adjutant General's Office, WWII Operations Reports, 1940–48, 37th Infantry Division, NARA.

407 **MacArthur's sedan:** Historical Record, Fifth Cavalry, Luzon Campaign, July 12, 1945.

407 **"I watched":** MacArthur, *Reminiscences*, p. 247.

408 **"The higher the stairs":** Manchester, *American Caesar*, p. 416.

408 **"Nothing was left":** MacArthur, *Reminiscences*, p. 247.

408 **"The books":** Manchester, *American Caesar*, p. 416.

408 **"Nice going":** MacArthur, *Reminiscences*, p. 247.

408 **"But there was nothing":** Ibid.

CHAPTER 20

409 **"The Japs have murdered":** John W. Osborn letter, February 25, 1945, John Osborn Santo Tomas Internment Transcriptions, UM.

409 **Gen. Douglas MacArthur:** Entry for February 27, 1945, Douglas MacArthur diary.

409 **The windows:** William Gray, Cable 24, February 25, 1945, Box 254, Dispatches from *Time* Magazine Correspondents, HL.

409 **"As I passed":** MacArthur, *Reminiscences*, p. 251.

410 **Much of the damage:** Frankel, *Frankel-y Speaking*, pp. 118–21.

410 **"It had scarcely been":** Kenney, *General Kenney Reports*, p. 525.

410 **An American band:** Details of the ceremony come from the following sources: William Gray, Cable 29, March 2, 1945, Box 256, Dispatches from *Time* Magazine Correspondents, HL; "Filipinos Regain Full Civil Control; MacArthur Says U.S. 'Kept Faith,'" *New York Times*, February 27, 1945, p. 1; "Osmeña Civil Government Installed by MacArthur," *Free Philippines*, February 28, 1945, p. 1; "Home to the Rock," *Newsweek*, March 12, 1945, p. 34.

410 **"For me":** MacArthur, *Reminiscences*, p. 251.

410 **"Mr. President":** "Text of Gen. MacArthur's Speech at Malacañan," *Free Philippines*, February 28, 1945, p. 1. A copy of MacArthur's speech can also be found in Box 1, RG 16a, Papers of Maj. Gen. Courtney Whitney, MMAL.

411 **"His bronze features":** Whitney, *MacArthur*, p. 192.

411 **"I could not":** MacArthur, *Reminiscences*, p. 251. MacArthur's recollection of the moment his voice broke differs from news accounts at that time. Given the passage of time before he wrote his memoirs, I have opted to use the news accounts.

411   "We mourn": "Text of President Osmeña's Address," *Free Philippines*, February 28, 1945, p. 2.

411   "As Osmeña began": William Gray, Cable 29, March 2, 1945.

412   "I am so glad": Ibid.

412   He was joined: Entry for March 2, 1945, Douglas MacArthur diary.

412   "So this is the 373": Barbey, *MacArthur's Amphibious Navy*, p. 308.

412   "We had departed": MacArthur, *Reminiscences*, p. 250.

412   "Once the PTs": Barbey, *MacArthur's Amphibious Navy*, p. 308.

412   "Go ahead": Kenney, *General Kenney Reports*, p. 519.

413   From January 23: Sixth Army on Luzon, Lingayen to Manila, January 9–March 3, 1945, Box 1957, RG 407, Records of the Adjutant General's Office, WWII Operations Reports, 1940–48, Sixth Army, NARA.

413   "The fight": Ibid.

413   U.S. soldiers: Templeman, *Return to Corregidor*, pp. 10–24.

413   "In several instances": Sixth Army, Report of the Luzon Campaign, January 9–June 30, 1945, p. 1:54.

413   "I sat down": Smith, *Triumph in Philippines*, p. 348.

413   "Corregidor": Kenney, *General Kenney Reports*, p. 521.

413   "Malinta Hill": "MacArthur Revisits Corregidor," *Free Philippines*, March 5, 1945, p. 1.

414   "They made it tough": "Home to the Rock," *Newsweek*, March 12, 1945, p. 34.

414   "The odor": George E. Jones, "M'Arthur Raises Corregidor Flag," *New York Times*, March 3, 1945, p. 1.

414   "They were so thick": Karig, Harris, and Manson, *Battle Report*, p. 242.

414   "I am home again": Jones, "M'Arthur Raises Corregidor Flag," p. 1.

414   "On the way": Rogers, *MacArthur and Sutherland*, pp. 2:264–65.

414   "Corregidor's dusty": William Gray, Cable 29, March 2, 1945.

415   "Sir": Templeman, *Return to Corregidor*, p. 20.

415   "The capture": Jones, "M'Arthur Raises Corregidor Flag," p. 1.

415   "Colonel": Ibid.

415   "The buildings": "Combat in Manila," April 21, 1945.

415   Unlike earlier battles: Frankel, *37th Infantry Division*, p. 293.

415   War planners: Smith, *Triumph in Philippines*, p. 302.

416   "The reduction": After Action Report, XIV Corps, M-1 Operation, July 29, 1945.

416   Of the three: Smith, *Triumph in Philippines*, p. 303.

416   "We made a churned-up": Beightler, "Report on the Activities of the 37th Infantry Division, 1940–1945," n.d.

416   "Your life": Headquarters Sixth Army, G-2 Weekly Report, no. 78, March 7, 1945, Box 1969, RG 407, Records of the Adjutant General's Office, WWII Operations Reports, 1940–48, Sixth Army, NARA.

417   "The ranks": Historical Record, Fifth Cavalry, Luzon Campaign, July 12, 1945.

417   "Only the battered": Smith, *Triumph in Philippines*, p. 304.

417   "If we run out": Friend, *Blue-Eyed Enemy*, p. 205.

418   The well his troops: PW Preliminary Interrogation Report no. 37–62, Hanichi Nishioka, February 27, 1945, and PW Preliminary Interrogation Report no. 37–61, Kensaburo Uchida, February 26, 1945, both in Box 8640, RG 407, Records of the Adjutant General's Office, WWII Operations Reports, 1940–48, NARA.

418   "If anyone": Friend, *Blue-Eyed Enemy*, p. 205.

418   "After the number": Historical Record, Fifth Cavalry, Luzon Campaign, July 12, 1945.

419   "A last minute": Ibid.

419   "The man who": Headquarters Sixth Army, G-2 Weekly Report, no. 78, March 7, 1945.

419   "You have ten": Ibid.

419   "At this point": Ibid.

419   "At the end": Smith, *Triumph in Philippines*, p. 306.

CHAPTER 21

420 **"It may never"**: War Department Release, "Statement on Japanese Atrocities in Manila," April 17, 1945, Box 1060, RG 331, SCAP, Legal Section, Administrative Division, Closed Case Files, 1945–46, NARA.

420 **"The list"**: Entry for February 19, 1945, in Lichauco, *"Dear Mother Putnam,"* p. 214.

420 **"My son's body"**: Jose Herman testimony, June 7, 1945, in Report no. 16.

421 **"I just dug"**: Juan Gonzalez testimony, June 1, 1945, in Report no. 48.

421 **Fred Canillas visited**: Fred F. Canillas testimony, July 28, 1945, in Report no. 50, "Investigation of the Murder of Felipe Canillas, and His Wife, Five Daughters and Two Sons and Zoilo Llave, All of Malate, Manila, Philippine Islands, on 8–9 February 1945," March 5, 1947, Box 1112, RG 331, SCAP, Legal Section, Administrative Division, War Crimes File, 1946–50, NARA.

421 **"My wife was wearing"**: Prudencio Chicote Lalana testimony, September 17, 1945, in Report no. 88.

421 **Some survivors**: Elisa Bonifacio testimony, August 8, 1945, in Report no. 59.

421 **The Japanese had gone**: "Russian Civilians Victims of Japanese Brutality in Manila," April 29, 1945, in Report no. 52.

421 **"The skin"**: Henry J. Muller, Jr., testimony, May 11, 1945, in Report no. 6.

421 **"I was able"**: Armando Valdes testimony, June 28, 1945, in Report no. 48.

421 **"There was no"**: Eva M. Gurevich testimony, May 26, 1945, in Report no. 18.

421 **Rita Losinas was**: Rita Losinas testimony, June 11, 1945, in Report no. 27.

421 **"With a heavy"**: John W. Osborn letter, March 4, 1945, John Osborn Santo Tomas Internment Transcriptions, UM.

422 **Every day**: " 'Free Philippines' Jams City Traffic," *Free Philippines*, March 1, 1945, p. 1.

422 **"Ana Mari Gomez"**: "Missing Persons," *Free Philippines*, March 14, 1945, p. 4.

422 **"Isabelo de los Reyes, Jr."**: "Missing Persons," *Free Philippines*, March 19, 1945, p. 4.

422 **"Victor Vantchurin, 19"**: "Missing Persons," *Free Philippines*, March 20, 1945, p. 4.

422 **The fight to retake**: After Action Report, XIV Corps, M-1 Operation, July 29, 1945; Smith, *Triumph in Philippines*, p. 307.

422 **"There were graves"**: Hartendorp, *Japanese Occupation*, p. 2:606.

423 **"When we grabbed"**: George W. Simmie testimony, May 30, 1945, in Report no. 13.

423 **"We used a spading"**: Faustino Gonzalez testimony, June 1, 1945, in Report no. 48.

423 **"As is our village"**: Hashmatrai Hotchand testimony, June 11, 1945, in Report no. 30, "Investigation of the Murder of Hotchand Hassamal, Lachmandas Parmanand, Vassanmal Pokardas, Kimatrai Vensimal, British Indians, and Felix Diaz, Emilio Tubayang, Purita and Vicente (Full Names Unknown), Filipinos, at 1588 Taft Avenue, Malate, Manila, Philippine Islands, on or about 11 February 1945," January 28, 1947, Box 1110, RG 331, SCAP, Legal Section, Administrative Division, War Crimes File, 1946–50, NARA.

423 **"I left the bodies"**: Paciencia Montano testimony, July 11, 1945, in Report no. 59.

423 **Few witnessed**: Mariano del Rosario testimony, October 31, 1945, YTT, pp. 387–89; Jose Quiogue testimony, July 19, 1945, in Report no. 58, "Investigation of the Massacre of Thirty-Six Civilians; Wounding of Nine Other Civilians; Attempted Murder of Thirteen Other Civilians, All of Various Nationalities, in Ermita, Manila, Philippine Islands, on 10 February 1945," March 13, 1947, Box 1112, RG 331, SCAP, Legal Section, Administrative Division, War Crimes File, 1946–50, NARA.

423 **"Those in the dungeon"**: David S. Conner testimony, August 24, 1945, in Report no. 109.

423 **The family of twelve-year-old**: Roderick Hall, interview by author, February 25, 2015; Roderick Hall to author, May 17, 2017.

423 **"In the night"**: Entry for March 7, 1945, in Crouter, *Forbidden Diary*, p. 496.

424 **"There was an overpowering"**: Rogers, *MacArthur and Sutherland*, p. 2:265.

424 **"holy godawful"**: Entry for February 27, 1945, Ethel Herold diary.
424 **"No amount of spitting"**: Charles Henne, "Battle History of the 3d Battalion, 148th Infantry, Manila, The Unwanted Battle (4 February through 7 March 1945)," p. 95.
424 **"I didn't sweep"**: George E. Jones, "Manila Hospitals Also Waging War," *New York Times*, February 23, 1945, p. 8.
424 **Exhausted doctors**: "203,928 Have Received PCAU Aid in Manila," *Free Philippines*, March 5, 1945, p. 2.
424 **"If I told you"**: Jones, "Manila Hospitals Also Waging War," p. 8.
424 **"We never believed"**: George E. Jones, "Filipino Civilians Massacred by Foe," *New York Times*, February 15, 1945, p. 1.
424 **"It is beastly"**: Bonner Fellers to Dorothy Fellers, March 24, 1945, Box 2, RG 44a, Papers of Brig. Gen. Bonner F. Fellers, MMAL.
424 **"Not only beds"**: Maurice C. Pincoffs, "Health Problems in Manila," in Pincoffs, *Letters from Two World Wars*, p. 267.
425 **"There are hideous"**: Entry for February 27, 1945, in Crouter, *Forbidden Diary*, p. 490.
425 **"So many families"**: Entry for February 18, 1945, in Labrador, *Diary of Japanese Occupation*, p. 269.
425 **"The tales told"**: Entry for March 17, 1945, James Halsema diary.
425 **"Eddy!"**: Hartendorp, *I Have Lived*, p. 3:483.
425 **"I took him"**: Ibid.
426 **"That night"**: Montinola, *Breaking the Silence*, p. 25.
426 **The combination**: Survey of War Damage in the Philippines, "Report of the Special Investigating Mission Sent to the Philippines in June 1945 by the War Damage Corporation and Completed in September 1945," 79th Cong., 1st Sess. (Washington, D.C.: U.S. Government Printing Office, 1945), p. 14.
426 **The battle had left**: "Philippine Civil Affairs," August 25, 1945, Box 5, RG 5, Records of General Headquarters, SCAP, 1941–51, MMAL.
426 **"Men, women and children"**: George E. Jones, "Hungry Filipinos Fed by Americans," *New York Times*, February 22, 1945, p. 4.
426 **Some eight hundred thousand people**: Pincoffs, *Letters from Two World Wars*, pp. 266–67.
426 **"Sanitation had broken"**: Sharpe, *Brothers beyond Blood*, p. 185.
426 **Residents resorted**: "It May Be Primitive, But Manila Still Has Transportation," *Free Philippines*, March 9, 1945, p. 2.
426 **"The morale"**: "Philippine Civil Affairs," August 25, 1945.
427 **A postwar American survey**: Survey of War Damage in the Philippines, "Report of the Special Investigating Mission Sent to the Philippines in June 1945 by the War Damage Corporation and Completed in September 1945," pp. 2, 9.
427 **"There is some damage"**: Ibid., p. 14.
427 **"Houses wanted"**: Advertisements, *Free Philippines*, March 1, 1945, p. 2.
427 **"Wanted to buy"**: Advertisements, *Free Philippines*, February 27, 1945, p. 2.
427 **"Loan wanted"**: Advertisements, *Free Philippines*, March 17, 1945, p. 4.
427 **The battle had destroyed the:** "Draft of the Unpublished 1945 Annual Report of President Osmeña to the President of the United States," *Bulletin* 2, no. 2 (1974): 55–56.
427 **The battle had destroyed not:** "Manila Observatory and Its Library Destroyed," *Free Philippines*, February 23, 1945, p. 2.
427 **The Philippine General Hospital**: "Draft of the Unpublished 1945 Annual Report of President Osmeña to the President of the United States," *Bulletin* 2, no. 1 (1974): p. 90.
427 **"Nothing is standing"**: "Manila Botanical Gardens Destroyed," *Free Philippines*, March 16, 1945, p. 4.
428 **In the short term**: "203,928 Have Received PCAU Aid in Manila," p. 2; Walter Simmons, "Business Ruined for Many Years in the Philippines," *Chicago Daily Tribune*, March 6, 1945, p. 5.

428 "War damage to coconut": "Destruction and Rehabilitation in the Philippines," *American Chamber of Commerce Journal* 22, no. 3 (1946): 7.
428 The American Chamber: Advertisements, *Free Philippines*, April 2, 1945, p. 4.
428 "The manager": Hartendorp, *Japanese Occupation*, p. 2:606.
428 "To me the loss": Beightler, "Report on the Activities of the 37th Infantry Division, 1940–1945," n.d.
428 "I spat on": Carmen Guerrero Nakpil, "Benevolence," *Sunday Times Magazine* (Manila), April 23, 1967, p. 14.
428 "Damn you": Ibid.
428 "I had no conception": Entry for March 3, 1945, in Crouter, *Forbidden Diary*, p. 493.
429 "For one who": Entry for March 17, 1945, in Labrador, *Diary of Japanese Occupation*, p. 283.
429 "All this ruin": Entry for February 21, 1945, Ethel Herold diary.
429 "I have seen": Entry for March 3, 1945, in Wygle, *Surviving*, p. 166.
429 "There seemed nothing": Hartendorp, *Japanese Occupation*, p. 2:605.
429 "So much for Manila": Beightler, "Report on the Activities of the 37th Infantry Division, 1940–1945," n.d.
429 "There was no joy": Rogers, *MacArthur and Sutherland*, p. 2:265.
429 "The tables": Ibid.
430 "Warning: Mines & Booby Traps": Entry for March 17, 1945, James Halsema diary.
430 "I wandered": Entry for February 23, 1945, in Cates, *Drainpipe Diary*, p. 258.
430 "I am appalled": Entry for March 8, 1945, in Crouter, *Forbidden Diary*, p. 497.
430 "Manila had become": Prising, *Manila, Goodbye*, p. 201.
430 "Suddenly someone shouted": Ibid., p. 202.
430 "Flies swarmed": Ibid., p. 203.
430 "Sex, which I had": Ibid.
431 "Hey, you": Ibid.
431 Doctors examined: After Action Report, XIV Corps, M-1 Operation, July 29, 1945.
431 "It is anticipated": Ibid.
431 "What?": Egeberg, *General*, pp. 166–67.
432 "Morals and convention": Sharpe, *Brothers Beyond Blood*, p. 185.
432 "Yamashita is finished": Bonner Fellers to Dorothy Fellers, February 24, 1945, Box 2, RG 44a, Papers of Brig. Gen. Bonner F. Fellers, MMAL.
432 "a most effective": Smith, *Triumph in Philippines*, p. 579.
432 "The arrogant conqueror": Charles A. Willoughby, "The Liberation of the Philippines," *Military Review* 26, no. 5 (1946): 17.
432 "To breathe clean": Historical Record, Fifth Cavalry, Luzon Campaign, July 12, 1945.
432 "beating the tin": Charles Henne, "Battle History of the 3d Battalion, 148th Infantry, Manila, The Unwanted Battle (4 February through 7 March 1945)," p. 82.
432 "It was not unusual": Ibid.
433 The Americans killed: Serial no. 3719, March 6, 1945, and Serial no. 3722, March 6, 1945, G-2 Journal, Box 8625, RG 407, Records of the Adjutant General's Office, WWII Operations Reports, 1940–48, 37th Infantry Division, NARA.
433 Two days later: Serial no. 3740, March 7, 1945, ibid.
433 The following day: Serial no. 3761, March 8, 1945, ibid.
433 Others worked: Headquarters Sixth Army, G-2 Weekly Report, no. 76, February 21, 1945, Box 1969, RG 407, Records of the Adjutant General's Office, WWII Operations Reports, 1940–48, Sixth Army, NARA.
433 "This explosion": Report after Action, Operations of the 37th Infantry Division, Luzon, P.I., November 1, 1944, to June 30, 1945 (M-1 Operation), September 10, 1945.
433 Bulldozers helped: "Philippine Civil Affairs," August 25, 1945.
433 The city's sanitation: Ibid.

433 **The army also looked:** Report after Action, Luzon Campaign, November 1, 1944–
June 30, 1945, G-1 Section, pt. 6, Box 8604, RG 407, Records of the Adjutant
General's Office, WWII Operations Reports, 1940–48, 37th Infantry Division,
NARA.

433 **"The theater":** Ibid.

433 **The army likewise:** Report after Action, Operations of the 37th Infantry Division,
Luzon, P.I., November 1, 1944, to June 30, 1945 (M-1 Operation), September 10,
1945; "Organized Baseball Resumes at Rizal Park," *Free Philippines*, March 31,
1945, p. 2.

433 **Famed composer:** "Berlin Presents His Filipino Song to Commonwealth Gov't,"
Free Philippines, March 29, 1945, p. 4.

434 **"Manila is free":** Jean MacArthur to Sara E. King, February 5, 1945, Box 5, RG
13, Papers of Jean MacArthur, MMAL.

434 **"Doc":** Egeberg, *General*, p. 184.

434 **"Now":** Jean MacArthur, oral history transcript 7, Box 15, RG 13, Papers of Jean
MacArthur, MMAL.

434 **He climbed aboard a tender:** Entry for March 6, 1945, Douglas MacArthur diary.

434 **On deck:** "Mrs. MacArthur and Son Rejoin General in Manila," *New York Times*,
March 8, 1945, p. 11; Manchester, *American Caesar*, pp. 422–24.

435 **"Isn't it wonderful":** Kenney, *MacArthur I Know*, p. 128.

435 **"George, I did":** George C. Kenney, oral history by D. Clayton James, July 16,
1971, MMAL.

435 **"Manila was practically":** Bonner F. Fellers to Alice Chitwood, April 6, 1945, Box
14, RG 3, Records of Headquarters, SWPA, 1942–45, MMAL.

435 **"Lord":** Jean MacArthur, oral history transcript 10, Box 15, RG 13, Papers of Jean
MacArthur, MMAL.

436 **"I had a horrible feeling":** Huff and Morris, *My Fifteen Years*, p. 100.

436 **"Your coming to Manila":** Mary Fairchild to Jean MacArthur, March (n.d.), 1945,
Box 5, RG 13, Papers of Jean MacArthur, MMAL.

436 **"It was just heartbreaking":** Jean MacArthur oral history transcript 10.

436 **"Well":** Entry for March 7, 1945, in Crouter, *Forbidden Diary*, p. 496.

436 **"It may be":** Ibid.

436 **The MacArthurs called:** Entry for March 6, 1945, Douglas MacArthur diary.

436 **"I think I'd better":** Jean MacArthur oral history transcript 10.

437 **A few days later:** Entry for March 17, 1945, Douglas MacArthur diary.

437 **The roof was gone:** Huff and Morris, *My Fifteen Years*, p. 100.

437 **"I had learned":** MacArthur, *Reminiscences*, p. 35.

437 **"You wanted to know":** Jean MacArthur to Sara E. King, April 6, 1945, Box 5, RG
13, Papers of Jean MacArthur, MMAL.

PART IV

439 **"In a way":** Servillano Aquino testimony, January 27, 1949, p. 699 of the trial
transcript of *People of Philippines v. Shizuo Yokoyama,* Box 1699, RG 331, SCAP,
Legal Section, Prosecution Division, Philippines versus Japanese War Criminals,
Case File, 1947–49, NARA.

CHAPTER 22

441 **"What the Japanese":** Entry for March 17, 1945, in Labrador, *Diary of Japanese
Occupation*, p. 286.

441 **Shortly before:** Carlisle, *Red Arrow Men*, pp. 213–14.

441 **"One cannot imagine":** Muto, "Truth of the Philippines Campaign," p. 37.

442 **"Tears flowed":** Ibid., p. 62.

442 "It knifed": "When He Heard of Japan's Surrender," in Potter, *Life and Death*, p. 183.

442 "Don't worry": Ibid., p. 149.

442 "If I kill myself": Ibid.

442 On August 24: Blakeley, *32nd Infantry Division*, pp. 266–73; Eichelberger, *Our Jungle Road*, pp. 256–58.

442 "My men have": "Before Giving Himself Up," in Potter, *Life and Death*, p. 184.

443 "I have been charged": "Yamashita Yields in Philippines; Wainwright Takes the Surrender," *New York Times*, September 3, 1945, p. 1.

443 "General Yamashita": Ibid.

443 "The war is over": Muto, "Truth of the Philippines Campaign," p. 73.

444 "We had nothing": Ibid.

444 "This is typical": Bob MacMillan, "Yamashita Gives Up," *Yank*, October 12, 1945, pp. 3.

444 "This is like a cinema": Ibid.

444 "As he walked": Blakeley, *32nd Infantry Division*, p. 273.

444 "We were served": Muto, "Truth of the Philippines Campaign," p. 73.

445 "The insults": Ibid.

445 The general presented: Kenworthy, *Tiger of Malaya*, pp. 29–38.

445 MacArthur would later: "Yamashita Sword Coming to U.S.," *New York Times*, September 7, 1945, p. 5.

445 "It's a heck": "The Bandwagon," *New Republic*, September 10, 1945, p. 317.

445 "Not only was": Muto, "Truth of the Philippines Campaign," p. 73.

446 "He ordered it": Joseph Hearst, "Gen. Yamashita Gives Army Up to Wainwright," *Chicago Daily Tribune*, September 3, 1945, p. 5.

446 "No": Ibid.

446 Though the High Commissioner's: Wainwright, *General Wainwright's Story*, p. 284.

446 Guerrilla leaders: Dean Schedler, "P.I. Campaign Ends as Yamashita Signs Surrender," *Manila Times*, September 5, 1945, p. 2.

447 "Manila was shockingly": Wainwright, *General Wainwright's Story*, p. 276.

447 "I saw one eyebrow": Percival, *War in Malaya*, p. 326.

447 "Percival and Yamashita": Rodolfo L. Nazareno, "Signature Formally Ends P.I. Campaign," *Star Reporter*, September 4, 1945, p. 1.

447 "Please be seated": Ibid.

447 "You have heard": " 'Butcher' of Bataan Yields to U.S. Hero," *Los Angeles Times*, September 3, 1945, p. 1.

447 "I am": Ibid.

447 "He was rigid": "Yamashita Yields in Philippines," p. 1.

448 "General Yamashita": Muto, "Truth of the Philippines Campaign," p. 74.

448 "He walked up": Wainwright, *General Wainwright's Story*, pp. 285–86.

448 "General": Ibid., p. 285.

448 "From our speeding": Muto, "Truth of the Philippines Campaign," p. 74.

449 The dogged work: Breakdown of Atrocity Reports, n.d., Box 1993, RG 331, SCAP, Legal Section, Manila Branch, Illegal Acts by Japanese in Philippines, 1945–47, NARA.

449 "Kill Americans troops": Loose Handwritten Sheet Containing Instructions Given by the Commanding Officer of a Group (Heidan), Names of Officer and Group Not Stated, Dated 8 March, Year Not Stated, But Presumably 1945, Doc. 47, in "Analysis of A.T.I.S. Translations of Captured Japanese Documents Bearing on Yamashita Case," October 19, 1945.

449 "Four prisoners": Entry for December 28, 1944, handwritten diary, November 23, 1944, to February 1945, belonging to a member of MBI Unit, Doc. no. 40, ibid.

449 "All natives": Entry for March 17, 1945, notebook kept by MG Co of West of the Lake Sector Unit, February 13–March 12, 1945, Doc. no. 39, ibid.

449 "Taking advantage": Entry for March 27, 1945, bound handwritten notebook,

December 19, 1944–March 27, 1945, belonging to Pvt 1st Cl Matsuoka, Itoji of Asahi 1111 Force, Doc. no. 41, ibid.

449 **"I have already killed":** Captured Japanese diary (neither owner nor unit listed), February (n.d.) 1945, Doc. no. 33, ibid.

450 **"He's not fit":** Sidney Mashbir, oral history by D. Clayton James, July 27, 1971, MMAL.

450 **"That was that":** Ibid.

450 **"The witness":** Rukmani Kishinchand testimony, June 11, 1945, in Report no. 21.

450 **"They speak flawless":** Report no. 66.

450 **"She does not speak":** Ibid.

450 **"Yes, I know":** Belarmino de Celis testimony, September 27, 1945, in Report no. 94.

450 **"I didn't tell":** Remedio Huerta Beliso testimony, October 6, 1945, ibid.

451 **"Do you know":** Ismael Sedro testimony, September 20, 1945, in Report no. 67.

451 **"Many people were killed":** Ichiro Sato statement, November 23, 1945, included in *People of Philippines v. Shizuo Yokoyama,* Box 1698, RG 331, SCAP, Legal Section, Prosecution Division, Philippines versus Japanese War Criminals, Case File, 1947–49, NARA.

451 **"I killed my 15":** Sohei Michishita statement, November 20, 1945, ibid.

452 **"It is hard":** Joaquin Maranon testimony, September 15, 1945, in Report no. 70.

452 **"They all look":** Elsie Hamburger testimony, June 1, 1945, in Report no. 28.

452 **"He had slit eyes":** Cayetano Lagdameo testimony, July 19, 1945, in Report no. 59.

452 **"My future":** Walter K. Frankel testimony, February (n.d.) 1945, in Report no. 47, "Investigation of the Murder of Justice Antonio Villa-Real and Fifteen Other Civilians and the Attempted Murder of Three Civilians at Pax Court, Pasay, Rizal, Philippine Islands, on 12 February 1945," August 12, 1945, Box 1111, RG 331, SCAP, Legal Section, Administrative Division, War Crimes File, 1946–50, NARA.

452 **"What the Japanese":** Jose C. Yulo testimony, September 4, 1945, in Report no. 63.

452 **"I honestly believe":** Joaquin Maranon testimony, September 15, 1945, in Report no. 70.

452 **"diabolical":** Report no. 53.

452 **"inhuman":** Emil Krause and R. Graham Bosworth, "Report of Investigation of Alleged Atrocities by Members of the Japanese Imperial Forces in Manila and Other Parts of Luzon, Philippine Islands," April 9, 1945, Box 1993, RG 331, SCAP, Legal Section, Manila Branch, Illegal Acts by Japanese in Philippines, 1945–47, NARA.

452 **"savage":** Ibid.

452 **"This orgy":** Report no. 63.

452 **"Such a cruel":** Report no. 51, "Investigation of the Massacre at 612–614 Kansas Street, Paco, Manila, Philippine Islands, of Twelve Civilians; Attempted Murder of Three Civilians, All of Various Nationalities, Committed on 10 February 1945," March 1, 1945, Box 1112, RG 331, SCAP, Legal Section, Administrative Division, War Crimes File, 1946–50, NARA.

452 **"They were simply":** Report no. 47.

452 **The sack of Manila:** Krause and Bosworth, "Report of Investigation of Alleged Atrocities by Members of the Japanese Imperial Forces in Manila and Other Parts of Luzon, Philippine Islands," April 9, 1945.

453 **"It is recommended":** Ibid.

CHAPTER 23

454 **"There can be":** Edmund P. Stone, "Report of Investigation of Authenticated Cases of Atrocity Committed by Imperial Japanese Forces in Manila," February

26, 1945, Box 1993, RG 331, SCAP, Legal Section, Manila Branch, Illegal Acts by Japanese in Philippines, 1945–47, NARA.

454 "one of the most hated": " 'Malaya Tiger' in Bilibid, on Fish and Rice," *Washington Post*, September 4, 1945, p. 10.

454 "I feel sure": "Atlanta Wife against Mate in This Case," *Atlanta Constitution*, October 9, 1945, p. 12.

454 "How do you feel": William Kibler, "The Fight of His Life," *Altoona Mirror*, December 9, 2012, p. 1.

455 "Our feelings": J. Gordon Feldhaus, "The Trial of Yamashita," *Current Legal Thought* 13 (August 1947): 255.

455 "We had all seen": George F. Guy, "The Defense of Yamashita," *Wyoming Law Journal* 4 (Fall 1949): 154.

455 "So you're the guys": Reel, *Case of Yamashita*, p. 13.

455 "as intelligent": Report of Interrogations of Tomoyuki Yamashita and Akira Muto, September 4–6, 1945, Box 7, RG 44a, Papers of Brig. Gen. Bonner F. Fellers, MMAL. See also Samuel S. Stratton, "Tiger of Malaya," *Proceedings*, February 1954, pp. 136–43.

455 "the real brains": Ibid.

455 "an almost childish": Ibid.

455 "He was a terrific": "Local Navy Lt. Interrogates Yamashita," *Schenectady Gazette*, December 11, 1945, p. 15.

456 Through those broadcasts: "Spain Severs Relations With Japan over Killing of Officials in Manila," *New York Times*, April 12, 1945, p. 1.

456 "Neither Gen. Yamashita": "Summary of Interrogations of General Yamashita and Other Responsible Commanders and Staff Officers," n.d., Box 8640, RG 407, Records of the Adjutant General's Office, WWII Operations Reports, 1940–48, NARA.

456 "I don't know": "Summary of Interrogations of General Yamashita and Other Responsible Commanders and Staff Officers," n.d.

456 "Another explanation": Ibid.

457 "It must have been": Feldhaus, "Trial of Yamashita," p. 255.

457 "His head seemed": Guy, "Defense of Yamashita," p. 155.

457 "Harvard": Reel, *Case of General Yamashita*, p. 14.

457 "To me the idea": Akira Muto testimony, November 22, 1945, YTT, p. 3052.

457 "We cut him short": Reel, *Case of General Yamashita*, p. 16.

458 "Where did the city": Ibid., p. 22.

458 "I decided to put": Ibid.

458 "The Japanese army": Ibid.

458 "It was entirely": Ibid., p. 24.

458 "His forthright manner": Guy, "Defense of Yamashita," p. 156.

458 "When surrender": Reel, *Case of General Yamashita*, p. 26.

459 heavy rains prompted: Joyce Velde, interview by author, February 19, 2015.

459 American engineers: Hartendorp, *Japanese Occupation*, pp. 2:647–48.

459 "Manila was": Ibid., 648.

459 A rash of bootleg: "Liquor Poisoning Deaths Drop to Zero," *Free Philippines*, May 4, 1945, p. 3.

459 "The fearsome Japs": "Peace and Order in Manila," *Sunday* (Manila) *Post*, September 30, 1945, p. 4.

459 Leftover land mines: "Jap Land Mines Still Taking Toll in Manila," *Courier*, September 21, 1945, p. 2.

459 "This country": A.V.H. Hartendorp, "Fascist Machinations in Manila," *Sunday (Manila) Post Magazine*, September 30, 1945, p. 1.

460 Outside the High Commissioner's: Robert Cromie, "Yamashita Wins 2 Jap Officers as His Counsel," *Chicago Daily Tribune*, October 9, 1945, p. 2.

460 "Allied legal laboratory": "Court to Try Yamashita Neither Civil Nor Military But Laboratory," *Courier*, October 28, 1945, p. 2.

460 "would have probative": B.M. Fitch to Commanding General, AFWESPAC, "Reg-

ulations Governing Trial of War Criminals," September 24, 1945, Box 1925, RG 331, SCAP, Legal Section, Manila Branch, 201 File, 1945–48, NARA.

460 **"The rule of evidence"**: Robert Trumbull, "Yamashita Trial Sets Precedents," *New York Times*, November 11, 1945, p. 65.

461 **"It was"**: Reel, *Case of General Yamashita*, p. 41.

461 **"mere soldier"**: Ibid., p. 34.

461 **"I'm amazed"**: Robert Cromie, "First Jap War Trial Today," *Chicago Daily Tribune*, October 8, 1945, p. 1.

461 **The courtroom**: Reel, *Case of General Yamashita*, pp. 27–28; Joseph Laitin, "Yamashita Pleads Not Guilty, Scores Point in Legal Battle," *Manila Post*, October 9, 1945, p. 1; Robert Trumbull, "Much Evidence Arrayed," *New York Times*, October 8, 1945, p. 7; Kenworthy, *Tiger of Malaya*, p. 41.

461 **Many dignitaries**: "Yamashita Enters 'Not Guilty' Plea," *Manila Chronicle*, October 9, 1945, p. 1; "Plea of 'Not Guilty' Entered by Yamashita; Trial Set for October 29," *Manila Times*, October 1, 1945, p. 1; Leon O. Ty, " 'Not Guilty!'— Yamashita," *Courier*, October 9, 1945, p. 1.

462 **"The arraignment"**: Feldhaus, "Trial of Yamashita," p. 255.

462 **"Attention"**: "Yamashita Enters 'Not Guilty' Plea," p. 1.

462 **"He hesitated"**: George Mountz letter, October 9, 1945, George Mountz Collection, ACPL.

462 **"Sweat gleamed"**: " 'Butcher of Bataan' Is Fat Again, Still Cruel Looking," *Courier*, October 9, 1945, p. 1.

462 **"Toothless Tiger"**: "Toothless Tiger," *Newsweek*, October 15, 1945, p. 54.

462 **"Gopher of the Philippines"**: "Gen. Yamashita Arraigned for Crimes in Manila," *Los Angeles Times*, October 9, 1945, p. A4.

462 **"beady"**: "Yamashita enters 'Not Guilty' Plea," *Manila Chronicle*, October 9, 1945, p. 1.

462 **"rat-like eyes"**: Ty, " 'Not Guilty!'—Yamashita," p. 1.

462 **"He looked like"**: "The Gentleman or the Tiger?" *Time*, December 10, 1945, p. 23.

462 **"They've fattened him"**: " 'Butcher of Bataan' Is Fat Again," p. 1.

462 **The same day**: "Aussies Want Hand on Gen. Yamashita," *Courier*, October 9, 1945, p. 1.

463 **"It probably is"**: Robert Kerr to L. H. Redford, November 29, 1974, in L. H. Redford, "The Trial of General Tomoyuki Yamashita: A Case Study in Command Responsibility," Thesis, Old Dominion University, September 1975, p. 98.

463 **"Guards keep"**: Entry for November 29, 1945, in James J. Halsema, "The End of the War (III)," *Bulletin* 20, no. 4 (1992): 39.

463 **"The proceedings"**: Russel Reynolds, October 8, 1945, YTT, p. 3.

463 **"Whom does"**: Ibid., p. 26.

463 **"I am happy"**: Tomoyuki Yamashita, ibid.

463 **"There are a number"**: Ibid., p. 27.

463 **"The Accused"**: Russel Reynolds, ibid., p. 28.

464 **"Thank you"**: Tomoyuki Yamashita, ibid.

464 **"We maintain"**: Robert Kerr, ibid., p. 29.

464 **"We have certain"**: Ibid., p. 36.

464 **The massacres outlined**: Bill of Particulars, *United States v. Tomoyuki Yamashita*, Box 1959, RG 331, SCAP, Legal Section, Manila Branch, Records of Trial exhibits, 1945–49, NARA.

464 **"The charges"**: "Toothless Tiger," p. 54.

464 **"The Accused"**: Henry Clarke, October 8, 1945, YTT, p. 58.

464 **"General Tomoyuki Yamashita"**: Russel Reynolds, ibid.

465 **"My plea"**: Tomoyuki Yamashita, ibid.

465 **"There were"**: Guy, "Defense of Yamashita," p. 158.

465 **The job**: Reel, *Case of General Yamashita*, pp. 76–77.

465 **"We worked"**: Ibid., p. 77.

465 **"By virtue"**: Guy, "Defense of Yamashita," pp. 158–59.

466 **At four p.m. on October**: Frank Reel, YTT, October 29, 1945, p. 72.

466 **"We were dumbfounded"**: Reel, *Case of General Yamashita*, p. 77.

466 "The power behind": Ibid., p. 78.
466 "That's very good": Pat Robinson, "Yamashita Sure He'll Be Freed by Army Court," *Washington Post*, October 29, 1945, p. 1.
466 "I don't see how": Ibid.

CHAPTER 24

467 "Nothing has seared": Carlos P. Romulo, "Our Morning," *Free Philippines*, February 22, 1945, p. 2.
467 "It was first": "Gen. Yamashita Put on Trial," *Los Angeles Times*, October 29, 1945, p. 1.
467 Adding to the excitement: "Discover Jap Land Mine Near High Commissioners House," *Courier*, October 30, 1945, p. 1.
467 The trial that kicked: Robert Cromie, "Yamashita's Trial to Air 123 Offenses," *Chicago Daily Tribune*, October 28, 1945, p. 1; Robert Trumbull, "Yamashita Trial Begins Tomorrow," *New York Times*, October 28, 1945, p. 7.
467 The 123 specific charges: Jim Gianladis, "Tiger's Trial," *Yank*, November 30, 1945, p. 4.
468 "repeatedly raping": Bill of Particulars, *United States v. Tomoyuki Yamashita*.
468 "entire settlements": Ibid.
468 "killing approximately": Ibid.
468 "The list goes on": "Court to Distinguish between Yamashita Moral, Legal Guilt," *Manila Chronicle*, October 27, 1945, p. 5; Kenneth L. Dixon, "Yamashita's Legal Guilt Is Problem," *Hartford Courant*, October 14, 1945, p. 14.
468 "From the very beginning": Gianladis, "Tiger's Trial," p. 4.
468 "We believe": Frank Reel, October 29, 1945, YTT, p. 72.
468 "Defense Counsel": Robert Kerr, ibid., p. 84.
468 "The case": Russel Reynolds, Ibid., p. 85.
468 "permanently mutilated": Robert Kerr, ibid., p. 98.
468 "We Americans": Ibid., pp. 97–98.
469 "That is the charge": Ibid., p. 99.
469 Kerr jumped: Vicente L. del Fierro, "Japs Killed My Baby!—Noble," *Star Reporter*, October 29, 1945, p. 1. Other news accounts of that day's proceedings include Robert Trumbull, "Horror Recital on in Yamashita Trial," *New York Times*, October 29, 1945, p. 1; Robert Cromie, "Yamashita Goes on Trial," *Chicago Daily Tribune*, October 29, 1945, p. 1; Zacarias Nuguid, Jr., "Atrocities Told at Yamashita Trial," *Daily Standard*, October 30, 1945, p. 1.
469 "My name": Patrocinio Abad (Corazon Noble) testimony, October 29, 1945, YTT, p. 132.
469 "hell on the loose": "Yamashita Unmoved as Witnesses Describe Scenes of Horror, Murder," *Manila Times*, October 30, 1945, p. 1.
469 "I saw them aiming": Patrocinio Abad testimony, October 29, 1945, YTT, pp. 137–38.
470 "bloodbath": "Yamashita Unmoved," p. 1.
470 "a story of horror": Trumbull, "Horror Recital on in Yamashita Trial," p. 1.
470 "nightmare of doom": Fierro, "Japs Killed My Baby!—Noble," p. 1.
470 "Yamashita appeared": "Corazon Noble Describes Massacre at Infirmary," *Courier*, October 30, 1945, p. 1.
470 "Can you tell": Patrocinio Abad testimony, October 29, 1945, YTT, p. 138.
470 The prosecution hurried: Redford, "Trial of General Tomoyuki Yamashita," pp. 28–29; George Mountz letter, November 5, 1945, George Mountz Collection, ACPL.
471 "foul a tale": "Japanese Savagery," *New York Times*, November 6, 1945, p. 18.
471 "Not even the wholesale": Robert Cromie, "Mass Murder in Manila Club Told on Stand," *Chicago Daily Tribune*, November 2, 1945, p. 1.
471 "The Japanese soldier": Leoncio Tolentino testimony, November 12, 1945, YTT, p. 1825.

471 "One of my sisters": Justine Manlisik testimony, November 14, 1945, ibid., p. 2186.
471 "They burned": Beatriz Sapinoso testimony, November 16, 1945, ibid., p. 2454.
471 "Oh my God!": Priscilla Garcia testimony, November 1, 1945, ibid., p. 519.
471 "I couldn't even think": Esther Garcia testimony, November 1, 1945, ibid., pp. 513–14.
472 "The girl's feet": Robert Trumbull, "Girl, 11, Stirs Yamashita Hearing by Story of Stabs, Parents' Slayings," *New York Times*, November 6, 1945, p. 1.
472 Tears ran down: "The General and Rosalinda," *Time*, November 19, 1945, p. 22.
472 "Before your mother": Rosalinda Andoy testimony, November 6, 1945, YTT, p. 1168.
472 "Her simple honest": Armando J. Malay, "Survivors Relate Jap Brutalities in Fort Santiago," *Manila Chronicle*, November 7, 1945, p. 1.
472 "American generals": Trumbull, "Girl, 11, Stirs Yamashita Hearing by Story of Stabs, Parents' Slayings," p. 1.
472 "Do not weep": "Rosalinda Andoy—Age 11," poem included with George Mountz letter, November 16, 1945, George Mountz Collection, ACPL.
472 "Gripping the sides": Mac. R. Johnson, "Yamashita Asks Manila Court to Halt His Trial," *New York Herald Tribune*, November 13, 1945, p. 6.
473 "After I was stabbed": An Kim Ling testimony, November 12, 1945, YTT, p. 1183.
473 "The audience": Johnson, "Yamashita Asks Manila Court to Halt His Trial," p. 6.
473 "Let me get": "Angry Mother Tries to Claw at Yamashita," *Manila Times*, November 3, 1945. p. 1.
473 "As they led": Ibid.
473 "You still have face": Robert Trumbull, "Filipino Escaped Beheading by Foe," *New York Times*, November 13, 1945, p. 5.
473 "On the chairman's order": Ibid.
474 Esquerra stood up: Robert Cromie, "Filipinos Tossed in Hole, Buried Alive by Japs," *Chicago Daily Tribune*, November 3, 1945, p. 3.
474 "You, first": Ricardo Esquerra testimony, November 3, 1945, YTT, p. 834.
474 "I just picked": Armando J. Malay, "Woman Witness Found Carrying Pieces of Rock," *Manila Chronicle*, November 15, 1945, p. 1.
474 "I found it hard": Henry Keys, "Reporter Accuses Yamashita," *Daily Express*, November 8, 1945, p. 4.
474 "Was the ration": A.V. H. Hartendorp testimony, November 7, 1945, YTT, p. 1386.
474 "It really brought": George Mountz letter, November 7, 1945, George Mountz Collection, ACPL.
474 Each day the atrocities: "Quiet Room in Manila," *Time*, November 12, 1945, p. 23.
474 "The prosecution's map": Trumbull, "Filipino Escaped Beheading by Foe," p. 5.
474 "Revolting testimony": Cromie, "Filipinos Tossed in Hole, Buried Alive by Japs," p. 3.
474 Manila radio announcers: Army Airways Communications System, 7th Wing Historical Report, October 1–December 31, 1945, Air Force Historical Research Agency, Montgomery, Ala.
475 " 'Rape Pools' ": " 'Rape Pools' Described by City's Prettiest Women," *Manila Post*, November 2, 1945, p. 1.
475 "Courtroom Tearful": Vicente L. del Fierro, "Courtroom Tearful as Girl Speaks," *Star Reporter*, November 6, 1945, p. 1.
475 "Defense Silent": "Defense Silent as Orgy of Murder, Rape Is Told," *Manila Post*, October 31, 1945, p. 1.
475 "Perhaps enough testimony": "Editorial Points," *Boston Globe*, November 13, 1945, p. 10.
475 "The Japanese soldiers": "Japanese Ethics," *Hartford Courant*, November 7, 1945, p. 10.
475 "Day after day": Reel, *Case of General Yamashita*, pp. 91–92.

475   **"Yamashita sits"**: George Mountz letter, November 1, 1945, George Mountz Collection, ACPL.
475   **"His reddish eyes"**: "Days of Terror," *Newsweek*, November 12, 1945, p. 45.
476   **"Hearsay evidence"**: Frank A. Reel, "Even His Enemy," *Ohio Bar Association Report* 19, no. 10 (1946): 170.
476   **"Imagine"**: George Mountz letter, November 4, 1945, George Mountz Collection, ACPL.
476   **"Who is this Mr. Jackson"**: Reel, *Case of General Yamashita*, p. 119.
476   **"The trial stinks"**: Entry for November 12, 1945, Norman Sparnon diary, Norman James Sparnon Collection, AWM.
477   **"There was not one word"**: Guy, "Defense of Yamashita," pp. 162–63.
477   **"It's like a man"**: "Yamashita: Too Busy," *Newsweek*, December 10, 1945, p. 44.
477   **"I was convinced"**: Robert L. Schwartz, "Justice for Yamashita?" *Time*, November 28, 1949, p. 4.
477   **"In the opinion"**: "Yamashita: Too Busy," p. 44.
477   **"There are wide"**: "Filipinos Fear Yamashita May Go Scot Free," *Los Angeles Times*, November 19, 1945, p. 7.
478   **"Yamashita complains"**: "Editorial Points," *Boston Globe*, November 15, 1945, p. 140.
478   **"Commander in Chief"**: CINCAFPAC ADV (Marshall) to CINCAFPAC FOR WHITLOCK, November 12, 1945, Box 1944, RG 331, SCAP, Legal Section, Manila Branch, Radiograms, 1945–49, NARA.
478   **"Among the people"**: Keichoku Yoshida testimony, November 27, 1945, YTT, p. 3454.
478   **"General Yamashita believed"**: Shigetaro Amakasu testimony, November 27, 1945, ibid., pp. 3468–69.
478   **"Among the Army men"**: Shigemasa Sunada testimony, November 28, 1945, ibid., p. 3483.
478   **"Did General Yamashita"**: Akira Muto testimony, November 21, 1945, ibid., p. 3038.
479   **"Have you ever seen"**: Norman James Sparnon testimony, November 27, 1945, ibid., pp. 3393–95.
479   **"There were no deaths"**: John Shizuo Ohashi testimony, November 26, 1945, ibid., p. 3358.
479   **"General Yamashita"**: Harry Clarke, November 28, 1945, ibid., p. 3518.
479   **"The sleepy court"**: "Yamashita Takes Stand as P.I. High Court Turns Down His Habeas Corpus Petition," *Courier*, November 29, 1945, p. 1.
479   **"electrified"**: Felix G. Gonzalez, " 'Tiger' Gives Blanket Denial," *Manila Post*, November 29, 1945, p. 1.
479   **"courtroom into a mild"**: Armando J. Malay, " 'Tiger' Claims He Did Not Control Troops," *Manila Chronicle*, November 29, 1945, p. 1.
480   **"Yamashita wants"**: "Yamashita: Too Busy," p. 44.
480   **All eyes focused**: Other news accounts that detail Yamashita's testimony include: "Yamashita Takes Stand in Defense," *New York Times*, November 28, 1945, p. 5; Robert Trumbull, "Yamashita Denies Any Atrocity Link," *New York Times*, November 29, 1945, p. 3; Robert Trumbull, "Yamashita Firm in Denying Guilt," *New York Times*, November 30, 1945, p. 3; Robert Cromic, "Tiger Denies All in Court Fight for Life," *Chicago Daily Tribune*, November 29, 1945, p. 3; "Tiger Testifies, Denies Charges," *Manila Times*, November 29, 1945, p. 1.
480   **"The burly general"**: Robert Cromie, "Yamashita on Stand; Shifts Atrocity Blame," *Chicago Daily Tribune*, November 28, 1945, p. 1.
480   **"He spoke"**: "Yamashita: Too Busy," p. 44.
480   **"Did you ever"**: Tomoyuki Yamashita testimony, November 29, 1945, YTT, pp. 3556, 3558.
481   **"Each red pin"**: Tomoyuki Yamashita testimony, November 30, 1945, ibid., pp. 3654, 3656–57, 3659–60.

482 "When the defense rested": "The Gentleman or the Tiger?" *Time*, December 10, 1945, p. 23.

482 At eight-thirty on: In addition to the trial transcript, the following news accounts detail the proceedings: Robert Trumbull, "Defense Sums up Yamashita's Case," *New York Times*, December 5, 1945, p. 3; Robert Trumbull, "Hanging Demanded as Yamashita Fate," *New York Times*, December 6, 1945, p. 3; Robert Cromie, "Free Yamashita, He Didn't Know, Counsel Pleads," *Chicago Daily Tribune*, December 5, 1945, p. 10; "Death by Hanging Asked for General Yamashita," *Manila Times*, December 6, 1945, p. 1; Felix G. Gonzalez, " 'Hang Yamashita,' Court Urged," *Manila Post*, December 6, 1945, p. 1; "Hanging of Gen. Yamashita Asked by Chief Prosecutor," *Courier*, December 6, 1945, p. 1; Robert L. Stewart, "Death for 'Tiger' Asked," *Daily Standard*, December 6, 1945, p. 1.

482 "It is directed": "Proposed Announcement in Open Session," n.d., Box 1, Morris C. Handwerk Papers, USAHEC.

483 "The prosecution contends": Milton Sandberg closing arguments, December 5, 1945, YTT, pp. 3918–19.

483 "The battle of the south": Ibid., pp. 3921–22.

484 "To us the guerrillas": Frank Reel closing arguments, December 5, 1945, YTT, p. 3962.

484 "We don't say": Ibid., p. 3970.

484 "They were led": Robert Kerr closing arguments, December 5, 1945, YTT, pp. 3997–98.

484 "The whole length": Ibid., p. 4042.

484 "All natives": Ibid., p. 4031.

484 "Burned 1,000": Ibid., p. 4027.

484 "Kill even women": Ibid., p. 4026.

484 "Is this warfare?": Ibid., p. 4032.

485 "If we accept": Ibid., p. 4013.

485 "It was his duty": Ibid., p. 4004, 4053.

485 "Anything less": Ibid., pp. 4053–54.

486 "I am ready": Kenworthy, *Tiger of Malaya*, p. 84.

486 "There can be only": Ibid.

486 Spectators turned out: In addition to the news accounts cited below, the following accounts proved helpful: "Tiger Hears Verdict Today," *Manila Chronicle*, December 7, 1945, p. 1; Robert Trumbull, "Yamashita Is Found Guilty," *New York Times*, December 7, 1945, p. 1; "Death Decreed," *Washington Post*, December 8, 1945, p. 3; "General Yamashita, Found Guilty, Sentenced to Hang Until Dead," *Manila Times*, December 8, 1945, p. 1; Armando J. Malay, "Tiger Is Unmoved as He Receives Death Sentence," *Manila Chronicle*, December 8, 1945, p. 1.

486 "Every inch": "Will Hang General Yamashita for Manila Atrocities; Pearl Harbor Sneak Attack Atoned," *Courier*, December 8, 1945, p. 1.

486 "The verdict": "Newspaper Men Against Execution of Yamashita," *Barrier Minder*, December 7, 1945, p. 1; Robert Cromie, "Doom Yamashita to Hang," *Chicago Daily Tribune*, December 7, 1945, p. 1.

486 "Hanging would be": "Newspaper Men Against Execution of Yamashita," p. 1.

486 "It is inconceivable": Ibid.

486 "The prosecution": Entry for November 28, 1945, in Halsema, "End of the War (III)," p. 39.

486 "The Defense were": Entry for December 5, 1945, Sparnon diary, Norman James Sparnon Collection, AWM.

487 "They have discharged": Armando J. Malay, "Yamashita to Hear Sentence on Friday," *Manila Chronicle*, December 5., 1945, p. 1.

487 "Rumor has it": George Mountz letter, December 6, 1945, George Mountz Collection, ACPL.

487 To beat the competition: Entry for December 7, 1945, in Halsema, "End of the War (III)," p. 41.

487 "He carefully laid": Reel, *Case of General Yamashita*, p. 168.

487   "There will be no": Ibid.
488   "Attention!": "Attention!" *Time*, December 12, 1945, p. 20.
488   "We agreed": Russel B. Reynolds to John H. Tucker, Jr., December 6, 1970, Box 1, Morris C. Handwerk Papers, USAHEC.
488   "The Commission is in session": Russel Reynolds, December 7, 1945, YTT, p. 4057.
488   "The crimes": Ibid., p. 4058.
488   "Many of the witnesses": Ibid.
489   "Taken at full": Ibid., p. 4060.
489   "An unearthly silence": George Mountz letter, December 7, 1945, George Mountz Collection, ACPL.
489   "It is absurd": Russel Reynolds, December 7, 1945, YTT, p. 4061.
489   "The Accused": Ibid.
489   "I have been": Tomoyuki Yamashita statement, ibid., p. 4062.
490   "The room was": Kenworthy, *Tiger of Malaya*, p. 85.
490   "It was as though": "Will Hang General Yamashita for Manila Atrocities; Pearl Harbor Sneak Attack Atoned," p. 1.
490   "Accordingly upon secret": Russel Reynolds, December 7, 1945, YTT, p. 4063.
490   "I feel that he": Guy, "Defense of Yamashita," p. 172.
490   "Not a muscle": "General Yamashita, Found Guilty, Sentenced to Hang Until Dead," *Manila Times*, December 8, 1945, p. 1.
490   "As the convicted": "Will Hang General Yamashita for Manila Atrocities," p. 1.
490   "He maintained": "'Yamashita Will Die,'" *Newsweek*, December 17, 1945, p. 51.
491   "If I ever": Entry for October 30, 1945, in Halsema, "End of the War (III)," p. 29.
491   "I still don't think": Entry for December 7, 1945, ibid., p. 41.
491   "C'mon": Reel, *Case of General Yamashita*, p. 175.
491   "Yamashita will die": "'Yamashita Will Die,'" p. 51.
491   "Yamashita gets justice": "Yamashita Gets Justice," *Manila Chronicle*, December 9, 1945, p. 4. For more details on reaction of American papers, see "U.S. Papers Hail Yamashita's Death Sentence," *Courier*, December 9, 1945, p. 1.
491   "The death sentence": "The Yamashita Trial," *Star Reporter*, December 8, 1945, p. 2.
491   "The Filipino people": "Yamashita Verdict Draws Praise from President Osmeña," *Star Reporter*, December 8, 1945, p. 1.
491   "Manila has suffered": "Wants Tiger Hanged Here," *Daily Standard*, December 9, 1945, p. 1.
491   "The American method": "Attention!" *Time*, December 12, 1945, p. 20.
491   "Why must they": "Yamashita Awaits M'Arthur's Final Word on Death Sentence," *Courier*, December 8, 1945, p. 1.
491   As a token: "Yamashita, Due to Die, Presents Gifts to Yanks," *Los Angeles Times*, December 8, 1945, p. 4; Reel, *Case of General Yamashita*, p. 175; Guy, "Defense of Yamashita," pp. 155, 173.
492   "You're the only": Reel, *Case of General Yamashita*, p. 175.
492   "That is my last": Ibid.
492   "General was lying": Milton P. Thomson, Memorandum to Judge Advocate, December 10, 1945, Box 1937, RG 331, SCAP, Legal Section, Manila Branch, War Crimes Trials Status Reports, 1945–47, NARA.

CHAPTER 25

493   "An uncurbed": Frank Murphy, dissenting opinion, *In re Yamashita*, 327 U.S. 1 (1946), February 4, 1946, Box 898, RG 331, SCAP, Legal Section, Administrative Division, Investigation Reports for War Crimes, 1945–48, NARA.
493   The lawyers had argued: Robert Cromie, "Seek to Halt Yamashita War Crime Hearing," *Chicago Daily Tribune*, November 12, 1945, p. 10.
493   "Under no circumstances": TELECON 11180900/Z, "War Crimes Trials," Box

1944, RG 331, SCAP, Legal Section, Manila Branch, Radiograms, 1945–49, NARA.

493 **The Philippine Supreme Court:** Guy, "Defense of Yamashita," pp. 168–71.

493 **"We contend":** "MacArthur Rapped by Tiger's Counsel for Trial Handling," *Manila Chronicle*, November 24, 1945, p. 1.

494 **"Europe is one":** "Army Court Hit before P.I. Tribunal," *Manila Post*, November 24, p. 1.

494 **"As far as":** "MacArthur Rapped by Tiger's Counsel," p. 1.

494 **"Why don't you":** "MacArthur Rapped by Tiger's Counsel," p. 1.

494 **"I don't think":** "Army Court Hit before P.I. Tribunal," p. 1; "Score MacArthur for Making Rules Re 'Tiger' Trial," *Courier*, November 24, 1945, p. 1.

494 **Hendrix's passion:** Felix G. Gonzalez, "Supreme Court Denies Yamashita Plea, Has No Jurisdiction," *Manila Post*, November 29, 1945, p. 1.

495 **"General Tomoyuki":** Reel, *Case of General Yamashita*, p. 203.

495 **"It is believed":** CINCAFPAC ADVANCE to WARTAG, December 8, 1945, Box 763, RG 331, SCAP, Adjutant General's Section, Operations Division, Mail & Records Branch, Classified Decimal File, 1945–47, NARA.

495 **"Secretary of War":** WASHINGTON to CINCAFPAC, CINCAFPAC ADVANCE (Personal to MacArthur and Styer), December 9, 1945, ibid.

495 **"The Supreme Court":** Reel, *Case of General Yamashita*, p. 204.

495 **"Court requested":** WASHINGTON to CINCAFPAC ADV (MacArthur), December 17, 1945, Box 763, RG 331, SCAP, Adjutant General's Section, Operations Division, Mail & Records Branch, Classified Decimal File, 1945–47, NARA.

496 **"high-grade lynching":** Harlan Stone to Sterling Carr, December 4, 1945, Box 9, Harlan Stone Papers, LOC.

496 **"I don't mind":** Ibid. Stone elaborated on his views in a November 13, 1945, letter to Louis Lusky, in Box 19, ibid.

496 **On the side:** Draft Release, December 19, 1945, Box 283, Hugo Black Papers, LOC.

496 **"It was a battle":** Wiley Rutledge to John Frank, February 13, 1946, Box 137, Papers of Wiley B. Rutledge, LOC.

496 **"It was only":** Wiley Rutledge to John Frank, February 22, 1946, ibid.

496 **"emphasize the dissension":** Fine, *Frank Murphy*, p. 453.

496 **"I fail to see":** J. K. Roach to Hugo Black, n.d., Box 283, Hugo Lafayette Black Papers, LOC.

496 **"A dead snake":** J. W. Smith to Hugo Black, n.d., ibid.

497 **"I realize":** Reel, *Case of General Yamashita*, p. 208.

497 **"That is not to say":** Ibid.

497 **"The Honorable":** Ibid., pp. 213–14.

497 **"I glanced around":** Ibid., p. 213.

497 **Throughout six hours:** No transcript of the hearings exist, though the following news accounts detail the proceedings: Jay Walz, "High Court Hears Yamashita's Pleas," *New York Times*, January 8, 1946, p. 2; "Yamashita's Case Now under Study," *New York Times*, January 9, 1946, p. 8; "Highest Court Weighs Fate of Yamashita," *Washington Post*, January 9, 1946, p. 9; Willard Edwards, "Highest Court Hears Plea for Yamashita Life," *Chicago Daily Tribune*, January 8, 1946, p. 1; Willard Edwards, "Supreme Court Weighs Ruling on Yamashita," *Chicago Daily Tribune*, January 9, 1946, p. 8.

497 **"The case at bar":** Reel, *Case of General Yamashita*, p. 211.

498 **"No decision":** WASHINGTON to CINCAFPAC, January 29, 1946, Box 763, RG 331, SCAP, Adjutant General's Section, Operations Division, Mail & Records Branch, Classified Decimal File, 1945–47, NARA.

498 **"Corrections of their":** *In re Yamashita*, 327 U.S. 1 (1946), February 4, 1946, Box 898, RG 331, SCAP, Legal Section, Administrative Division, Investigation Reports for War Crimes, 1945–48, NARA.

498 **"For reasons already":** Ibid.

498 **"Those provisions":** Ibid.

498   "More is at stake": Wiley Rutledge, dissenting opinion, February 4, 1945, ibid.
499   "That there were": Frank Murphy, dissenting opinion, February 4, 1945, ibid.
499   "They belong to": Ibid.
500   "The high feelings": Ibid.
500   "I wholly respect": Fine, *Frank Murphy*, p. 458.
500   In a letter to a friend: Wiley Rutledge to John Frank, February 22, 1946, Box 137, Papers of Wiley B. Rutledge, LOC.
500   "These trials cannot": Rutledge to Frank, February 13, 1946, ibid.
500   "The Yamashita case": "Yamashita's Appeal," *New York Times*, February 5, 1946, p. 20.
500   "The decision of": "Legality of Military Commissions Upheld," *Los Angeles Times*, February 6, 1946, p. A4.
501   "We shall not": "Yamashita Case," *Washington Post*, February 6, 1946, p. 6.
501   "This case rises": "Making Our Own Liberty Secure?" *St. Louis Star-Times*, March 22, 1946, p. 22.
501   "Thank God": Mrs. D.C. Cowles to Wiley Rutledge, February 5, 1946, Box 137, Papers of Wiley B. Rutledge, LOC.
501   "tornado": Rutledge to Dave Rosner, March 5, 1946, ibid.
501   "I never thought": Willard S. Fraser to Rutledge, n.d., ibid.
501   "The effect": Fred A. Dewey to Rutledge, February 13, 1946, ibid.
501   "May it be": Robert B. Burch to Rutledge, March 6, 1946, ibid.
501   "It is not easy": Orders no. 2, February 11, 1946, Box 763, RG 331, SCAP, Adjutant General's Section, Operations Division, Mail & Records Branch, Classified Decimal File, 1945–47, NARA. A handwritten copy of MacArthur's review can be found in RG 10, General Douglas MacArthur's Private Correspondence, 1848–1964, MMAL.
502   "stripped of uniform": Ibid.
502   "chill, scathing": "M'Arthur Dooms Yamashita," *Los Angeles Times*, February 7, 1946, p. 1.
502   Allied occupation forces: Lindesay Parrott, "Yamashita Order Shocks Japanese," *New York Times*, February 8, 1946, p. 13; James, *Years of MacArthur*, p. 3:95.
502   "I thought and prayed": "Yamashita Wins Stay; Truman's Mercy Asked," *Los Angeles Times*, February 8, 1946, p. 1.
502   "We are heirs": Ibid.
502   "I have been prepared": "Yamashita Death Up to Truman," *Chicago Daily Tribune*, February 8, 1946, p. 1.
502   "did not even": "Gen. Yamashita Plea to Truman Proves Futile," *Los Angeles Times*, February 9, 1946, p. 1.
502   "The War Department": "Truman Seals Yamashita's Fate," *New York Times*, February 9, 1946, p. 6.
503   "The doom of": "Gen. Yamashita Plea to Truman Proves Futile," p. 1.
503   "It was indeed": Reel, *Case of General Yamashita*, p. 239.
503   "The Secretary of War": CINCAFPAC to COMGEN AFWESPAC, February 10, 1946, Box 1944, RG 331, SCAP, Legal Section, Manila Branch, Radiograms, 1945–49, NARA.
503   "You are authorized": CINCAFPAC to AFWESPAC, February 20, 1946, ibid.
503   "Intramuros, hallowed": "Resolution Requesting the United States Army Authorities to Hang General Yamashita, the Tiger, In Public, In Intramuros," December 11, 1945, Box 1937, RG 331, SCAP, Legal Section, Manila Branch, War Crimes Trials Status Reports, 1945–47, NARA.
503   American authorities: CG AFWESPAC, SGD STYER to CINCAFPAC (Personal Attention General MacArthur), February 7, 1946, Box 1944, RG 331, SCAP, Legal Section, Manila Branch, Radiograms, 1945–49, NARA.
503   "the most closely": V. G. Miller and W. C. Wilson, "Yamashita Pays with His Life for the Rape of Manila," *Manila Post*, February 24, 1946, p. 1.
503   "After the execution": CG AFWESPAC, SGD STYER to CINCAFPAC (Personal Attention General MacArthur), February 7, 1946.

504 **"at an hour":** W. D. Styer to Commanding Officer, Philippine Detention and Rehabilitation Center, February 21, 1946, Box 1937, RG 331, SCAP, Legal Section,
Manila Branch, War Crimes Trials Status Reports, 1945–47, NARA.
504 **In preparation for:** Styer to Commanding General, Base X, February 21, 1946,
ibid.
504 **"I don't blame":** "Yamashita Hanged Near Los Baños Where Americans Were
Tortured," *New York Times*, February 23, 1946, p. 1.
504 **"The world I knew":** Potter, *Life and Death* , p. 184.
504 **For his final:** Ibid., p. 173.
504 **"We were sorry":** Ibid.
504 **Guards escorted:** Background on the hanging of Yamashita is drawn in part from
the following sources: "Gen. Yamashita Hanged as Disgraced Soldier," *Los Angeles Times*, February 23, 1946, p. 1; "Gen. Yamashita Executed," *Chicago Daily
Tribune*, February 23, 1946, p. 1; "I Thank You!" *Time*, March 4, 1946, p. 25;
"Yamashita: By the Neck," *Newsweek*," March 4, 1946, p. 45; "Tiger's Death
Described," *Manila Chronicle*, February 26, 1946, p. 1; "Yamashita, Ohta Die on
First Anniversary of Freedom of US PWs," *Manila Times*, February 24, 1946, p.
1; Kenworthy, *Tiger of Malaya*, pp. 87–88.
505 **Lt. Charles Rexroad:** "Yamashita Hangman," *Chicago Daily Tribune*, February
24, 1946, p. 5; Pat Robinson, "'Tiger of Malaya' Predicts He'll Hang as War Criminal," *San Antonio Light*, September 13, 1945, p. 1; "Job of Hanging 130 Japs Just
'Assignment,'" *Evening Times*, March 23, 1949, p. 7.
505 **"Putting a rope":** Harold H. Martin, "Hanging Is His Trade," *Saturday Evening
Post*, June 5, 1948, p. 22.
505 **"One man catches":** Charles Rexroad, handwritten account of Yamashita's hanging, February 23, 1946, copy courtesy of Nathaniel Helms.
505 **"There is no lost":** Ibid.
505 **"Have you any":** Charles Rexroad, handwritten account of Yamashita's hanging,
February 23, 1946.
505 **"I will pray":** "Yamashita Hanged Near Los Baños," p. 1.
506 **The trapdoor:** Joseph T. Gohmann to Commanding Officer, Phil Detn & Rehab
Ctr, APO 75, "Time of Death of War Criminals," February 23, 1946, copy courtesy of Nathaniel Helms.
506 **"I pronounce this man":** Charles Rexroad, handwritten account of Yamashita's
hanging, February 23, 1946.
506 **"among soldiers":** "Yamashita Is Buried in Prisoners' Cemetery," *Hartford Courant*, February 24, 1946, p. 2.

Epilogue

507 **"The Manila of 1941":** Dunn, *Pacific Microphone*, p. 20.
507 **"The past is dead":** Entry for March 3, 1945, in Crouter, *Forbidden Diary*, p. 493.
508 **"By the end":** Orendain, "Children of War," in Constantino, *Under Japanese Rule*,
p. 68.
508 **Yamashita's wife:** S. Iguchi to General Headquarters of the Supreme Commander
for the Allied Powers, "The Ashes of the Late General Yamashita," March 5, 1946,
Box 763, RG 331, SCAP, Adjutant General's Section, Operations Division, Mail &
Records Branch, Classified Decimal File, 1945–47, NARA.
509 **"He was executed":** Potter, *Life and Death* , p. 175.
509 **"I am responsible":** Takesue Furuse pleadings, March 21, 1949, p. 14 in *People of
Philippines v. Takesue Furuse,* Box 1699, RG 331, SCAP, Legal Section, Prosecution Division, Philippines versus Japanese War Criminals, Case File, 1947–49,
NARA.
509 **"May God have mercy":** Jose V. Andrada statement, March 23, 1945, p. 25, ibid.
509 **"I am doing this":** "Freed Japs to Shun Heritage of Hate, Quirino Explains," *Albuquerque Journal*, July 6, 1953, p. 13.

510   "I think we made": John Cornelison, "Hanging of Japanese General Called U.S. Judicial Blunder," *Cedar Rapids Gazette*, April 12, 1967, p. 4C.

510   Maj. Gen. Russel Reynolds: Reynolds to John H. Tucker, Jr., December 6, 1970, Box 1, Morris C. Handwerk Papers, USAHEC.

510   "damning": Ibid.

510   "After weighing": Reynolds to Otto E. Reik, March 8, 1950, ibid.

511   "Douglas MacArthur bears": Aluit, *By Sword and Fire*, p. 395.

511   "One side killed": Brady, "War Is Hell," unpublished narrative.

511   "sentimental journey": MacArthur, *Reminiscences*, p. 418.

511   "My life has": Manchester, *American Caesar*, p. 696.

511   Yamashita's hanging did: Charles T. Brown to Edmund J. Lilly, August 15, 1947, Edmund J. Lilly Papers, J.Y. Joyner Library, East Carolina University, Greenville, N.C.

511   "During cold days": Cayetano Lagdameo testimony, November 23, 1948, p. 97 of *People of Philippines v. Shizuo Yokoyama,* Box 1698, RG 331, SCAP, Legal Section, Prosecution Division, Philippines versus Japanese War Criminals, Case File, 1947–49, NARA.

511   American nun: Sister Mary Trinita Logue testimony, May 19, 1945, in Report no. 10, "Investigation of the Mistreatment and Torture of Sister Mary Trinita Logue (Sister Trinita), Santo Tomas University, Manila, Philippine Islands, Between 15 April and 15 May 1944," June 5, 1945, Box 1108, RG 331, SCAP, Legal Section, Administrative Division, War Crimes File, 1946–50, NARA.

511   "I could not talk": Orendain, "Children of War," in Constantino, *Under Japanese Rule*, p. 127.

511   "It was just total": William Branigin, "50 Years Later, Survivors of Battle of Manila Speak Out," *Washington Post*, October 27, 1994, p. A34.

512   "Landmine explosion": Augusto Jimenez Raymundo questionnaire, n.d., Memorare Manila 1945 Foundation Collection, FHL.

512   "Burned alive": Amelia Briar Casteley questionnaire, n.d., ibid.

512   "Raped and bayonetted": Amparo da Silva de Martinez questionnaire, November 17, 1995, ibid.

512   "I saw them": Loreto Franco Racho questionnaire, November 4, 1994, ibid.

512   "On the morning": Angie Abad Santos letter, February 8, 1995, ibid.

SELECT BIBLIOGRAPHY

Agoncillo, Teodoro A. *The Fateful Years: Japan's Adventure in the Philippines, 1941–1945.* 2 vols. Quezon City, Philippines: R.P. Garcia Publishing, 1965.

Agustin, Conrado Gar. *Men and Memories in Confinement: Excerpts from a Diary Written in Prison during the Japanese Occupation, June 21, 1942–February 5, 1945.* Manila: MCS Enterprises, 1973.

Aluit, Alfonso J. *By Sword and Fire: The Destruction of Manila in World War II, 3 February–3 March 1945.* Manila: National Commission for Culture and the Arts, 1994.

Ashton, Paul. *Bataan Diary.* Santa Barbara, Calif.: Ashton Publications, 1984.

Ashton, Paul, ed. *"And Somebody Gives a Damn!"* Santa Barbara, Calif.: Ashton, 1990.

Associated Press. *Reporting to Remember: Unforgettable Stories and Pictures of World War II by Correspondents of The Associated Press.* New York: Associated Press, 1945.

Astor, Gerald. *Crisis in the Pacific: The Battles for the Philippine Islands by the Men Who Fought Them—An Oral History.* New York: Donald I. Fine Books, 1996.

Baldwin, Hanson W. *Great Mistakes of the War.* New York: Harper & Brothers, 1950.

Barbey, Daniel E. *MacArthur's Amphibious Navy: Seventh Amphibious Force Operations, 1943–1945.* Annapolis, Md.: U.S. Naval Institute, 1969.

Barker, A. J. *Yamashita.* New York: Ballantine, 1973.

Bayly, Christopher, and Tim Harper. *Forgotten Armies: The Fall of British Asia, 1941–1945.* Cambridge, Mass.: Belknap Press of Harvard University Press, 2005.

Beck, John Jacob. *MacArthur and Wainwright: Sacrifice of the Philippines.* Albuquerque: University of New Mexico Press, 1974.

Bergamini, David. *Japan's Imperial Conspiracy.* New York: William Morrow, 1971.

Blair, Clay, Jr. *MacArthur.* Garden City, N.Y.: Doubleday, 1977.

Blakeley, H. W. *The 32nd Infantry Division in World War II.* Madison, Wis.: Thirty-Second Infantry Division History Commission, 1957.

Bland, Larry I., ed. *"Aggressive and Determined Leadership": June 1, 1943–December 31, 1944.* Vol. 4 of *The Papers of George Catlett Marshall.* Baltimore: Johns Hopkins University Press, 1996.

Blount, James H. *American Occupation of the Philippines, 1989–1912.* New York: G.P. Putnam's Sons, 1912.

Borneman, Walter R. *MacArthur at War: World War II in the Pacific.* New York: Little, Brown, 2016.

Braddon, Russell. *The Naked Island.* Garden City, N.Y.: Doubleday, 1953.

Brereton, Lewis H. *The Brereton Diaries: The War in the Pacific, Middle East and Europe, 3 October 1941–8 May 1945.* New York: William Morrow, 1946.

Breuer, William B. *The Great Raid on Cabanatuan: Rescuing the Doomed Ghosts of Bataan and Corregidor.* New York: John Wiley & Sons, 1994.

———. *Retaking the Philippines: America's Return to Corregidor and Bataan, October 1944–March 1945.* New York: St. Martin's Press, 1986.

Brougher, W. *South to Bataan, North to Mukden: The Prison Diary of Brigadier General W. E. Brougher.* Edited by D. Clayton James. Athens: University of Georgia Press, 2010.

Brown, Charles. *Bars from Bilibid Prison*. San Antonio, Tex.: Naylor, 1947.

Buell, Thomas B. *Master of Sea Power: A Biography of Fleet Admiral Ernest J. King*. Boston: Little, Brown, 1980.

Buenafe, Manuel E. *Wartime Philippines*. Manila: Philippine Education Foundation, 1950.

Buencamino, Felipe. *Memoirs and Diaries of Felipe Buencamino III: 1941–1944*. Edited by Victor A. Buencamino, Jr. Makati City, Philippines: Copycat, 2003.

Buencamino, Victor. *Memoirs of Victor Buencamino*. Mandaluyong, Philippines: Jorge B. Vargas Filipiniana Foundation, 1977.

Calero, Ana Mari S. *Three Continents*. Manila: De La Salle University Press, 2001.

Cannon, M. Hamlin. *Leyte: The Return to the Philippines*. Vol. 9 in *The U.S. Army in World War II: The War in the Pacific*. Washington, D.C.: U.S. Army Center of Military History, 1993.

Carlisle, John M. *Red Arrow Men: Stories about the 32nd Division on the Villa Verde*. Detroit: Arnold-Powers, 1945.

Cary, Frank. *Letters from Interment Camp, Davao and Manila, 1942–1945*. Ashland, Ore.: Independent Printing Co., 1993.

Cates, Tressa Roka. *The Drainpipe Diary*. New York: Vantage Press, 1957.

Chang, Iris. *The Rape of Nanking: The Forgotten Holocaust of World War II*. New York: Penguin, 1998.

Chapman, F. Spencer. *The Jungle Is Neutral*. Guilford, Conn.: Lyons Press, 2003.

Chase, William C. *Front Line General: The Commands of Maj. Gen. Wm. C. Chase*. Houston, Tex.: Pacesetter Press, 1975.

Churchill, Winston S. *The Hinge of Fate*. Vol. 4 of *The Second World War*. Boston: Houghton Mifflin, 1950.

Cogan, Frances B. *Captured: The Japanese Internment of American Civilians in the Philippines, 1941–1945*. Athens: University of Georgia Press, 2000.

Condon-Rall, Mary Ellen, and Albert E. Cowdrey. *The U.S. Army in World War II: The Technical Services*. Vol. 3, *The Medical Department: Medical Service in the War against Japan*. Washington, D.C.: U.S. Army Center of Military History, 1998.

Connaughton, Richard. *MacArthur and Defeat in the Philippines*. Woodstock, N.Y.: Overlook Press, 2001.

Connaughton, Richard, John Pimlott, and Duncan Anderson. *The Battle for Manila*. Novato, Calif.: Presidio Press, 1995.

Constantino, Renato, ed. *Under Japanese Rule: Memories and Reflections*. Quezon City, Philippines: Foundation for Nationalist Studies, 2001.

Contey-Aiello, Rose, ed. *The 50th Anniversary Commemorative Album of the Flying Column, 1945–1995*. Tarpon Springs, Fla.: Marrakech Express, 1994.

Cortesi, Lawrence. *The Battle for Manila*. New York: Zebra Books, 1984.

Cowdrey, Albert E. *Fighting for Life: American Military Medicine in World War II*. New York: Free Press, 1994.

Crouter, Natalie. *Forbidden Diary: A Record of Wartime Internment, 1941–1945*. Edited by Lynn Z. Bloom. New York: Burt Franklin, 1980.

D'Este, Carlo. *Eisenhower: A Soldier's Life*. New York: Henry Holt, 2002.

Day, Beth. *The Manila Hotel: The Heart and Memory of a City*. No publisher, no date.

Donovan, Robert J. *Tumultuous Years: The Presidency of Harry S. Truman, 1949–1953*. New York: W. W. Norton, 1982.

Dos Passos, John. *Tour of Duty*. Boston: Houghton Mifflin, 1946.

Dower, John W. *Cultures of War: Pearl Harbor, Hiroshima, 9–11, Iraq*. New York: W. W. Norton, 2010.

———. *War Without Mercy: Race and Power in the Pacific War*. New York: Pantheon, 1986.

Drury, Clifford M. *The History of the Chaplain Corps, U.S. Navy*. 2 vols. Washington, D.C.: U.S. Government Printing Office, 1950.

Dumana, Tessie, ed. *The German Club-Manila, 1906–1986*. Manila: German Club, 1986.

Dunn, William J. *Pacific Microphone*. College Station: Texas A&M University Press, 1988.

Egeberg, Roger Olaf. *The General: MacArthur and the Man He Called "Doc."* New York: Hippocrene Books, 1983.

Eichelberger, Robert L., and Milton MacKaye. *Our Jungle Road to Tokyo*. New York: Viking Press, 1950.

Eisenhower, Dwight D. *At Ease: Stories I Tell to Friends*. Garden City, N.Y.: Doubleday, 1967.

Eisenhower, John S. D. *General Ike: A Personal Reminiscence*. New York: Free Press, 2003.

Eisenhower, Susan. *Mrs. Ike: Memories and Reflections of the Life of Mamie Eisenhower*. New York: Farrar, Straus and Giroux, 1996.

Empie, Evelyn Berg, and Stephen H. Mette. *A Child in the Midst of Battle: One Family's Struggle for Survival in War-torn Manila*. Rolling Hills Estates, Calif.: Satori Press, 2001.

Escoda, Jose Ma. Bonifacio M. *Warsaw of Asia: The Rape of Manila*: Quezon City, Philippines: Giraffe Books, 2000.

Fahey, James J. *Pacific War Diary, 1942–1945: The Secret Diary of an American Sailor*. Boston: Houghton Mifflin, 2003.

Falk, Stanley L. *Seventy Days to Singapore*. New York: G.P. Putnam's Sons, 1975.

Farrell, Brian, and Sandy Hunter, eds. *Sixty Years On: The Fall of Singapore Revisited*. Singapore: Eastern Universities Press, 2002.

Ferrell, Robert H., ed. *The Eisenhower Daries*. New York: W. W. Norton, 1981.

———. *Off the Record: The Private Papers of Harry S. Truman*. New York: Harper & Row, 1980.

Feuer, A.B., ed. *Bilibid Diary: The Secret Notebooks of Commander Thomas Hayes, POW, the Philippines, 1942–45*. Hamden, Conn.: Archon Books, 1987.

Fine, Sidney. *Frank Murphy: The Washington Years*. Ann Arbor; University of Michigan Press, 1984.

Finn, Richard B. *Winners in Peace: MacArthur, Yoshida, and Postwar Japan*. Berkeley: University of California Press, 1992.

Flanagan, Edward M., Jr. *The Angels: A History of the 11th Airborne Division, 1943–1946*. Washington, D.C.: Infantry Journal Press, 1948.

———. *The Angels: A History of the 11th Airborne Division*. Novato, Novato, Calif.: Presidio Press, 1989.

Frankel, Stanley A. *Frankel-y Speaking about World War II in the South Pacific*. Scarsdale, N.Y.: Stanley A. Frankel, 1992.

Frankel, Stanley A., and Frederick Kirker, eds. *The 37th Infantry Division in World War II*. Washington, D.C.: Infantry Journal Press, 1948.

Friend, Theodore. *The Blue-Eyed Enemy: Japan against the West in Java and Luzon, 1942–1945*. Princeton, N.J.: Princeton University Press, 1988.

Fung, Cornelia Lichauco. *Beneath the Banyan Tree: My Family Chronicles*. Hong Kong: CBL Fung, 2009.

Garcia, Joaquin L. *It Took Four Years for the Rising Sun to Set, 1941–1945: Recollections of an Unforgettable Ordeal*. Manila: De La Salle University Press, 2001.

General Staff. *Reports of General MacArthur: The Campaigns of MacArthur in the Pacific*. Washington, D.C.: U.S. Government Printing Office, 1994.

Glusman, John A. *Conduct under Fire: Four American Doctors and Their Fight for Life as Prisoners of the Japanese, 1941–1945*. New York: Viking, 2005.

Goldhagen, Juergen R., ed. *Manila Memories: Four Boys Remember Their Lives Before, During and After the Japanese Occupation*. Exeter, U.K.: Old Guard Press, 2008.

Gonzalez, Andrew, and Alejandro T. Reyes. *These Hallowed Halls: The Events of February 1945 at De La Salle College*. Manila: De La Salle University Press, 1982.

Greenfield, Kent Roberts, ed. *Command Decisions*. Washington, D.C.: U.S. Army Center of Military History, 1987.

Güell, Carmen. *La Última de Filipinas*. Barcelona, Spain: Belacqva, 2005.

Guillermo, Lucky, and Peter C. Parsons, eds. *Manila 1945: The Rest of the Story.* Manila: AV Manila Creative Production Co., 2015.

Gunnison, Royal Arch. *So Sorry, No Peace.* New York: Viking Press, 1944.

Hamilton, Nigel. *Mantle of Command: FDR at War, 1941–1942.* Boston: Houghton Mifflin Harcourt, 2014.

Harper, Fowler V. *Justice Rutledge and the Bright Constellation.* Indianapolis: Bobbs-Merrill, 1965.

Harriman, W. Averell, and Elie Abel. *Special Envoy to Churchill and Stalin, 1941–1946.* New York: Random House, 1975.

Hartendorp, A.V.H. *The Japanese Occupation of the Philippines.* 2 vols. Manila: Bookmark, 1967.

———. *The Santo Tomas Story.* New York: McGraw-Hill, 1964.

Hassett, William D. *Off the Record with F.D.R., 1942–1945.* New Brunswick, N.J.: Rutgers University Press, 1958.

Hastings, Max. *Retribution: The Battle for Japan, 1944–45.* New York: Alfred A. Knopf, 2008.

Hayashi, Saburo, and Alvin D. Coox. *Kogun: The Japanese Army in the Pacific War.* Quantico, Va.: Marine Corps Association, 1989.

Henderson, Bruce. *Rescue at Los Baños: The Most Daring Prison Raid of World War II.* New York: William Morrow, 2015.

Herman, Arthur. *Freedom's Forge: How American Business Produced Victory in World War II.* New York: Random House, 2012.

Hibbs, Ralph Emerson. *Tell MacArthur to Wait.* New York: Carlton Press, 1988.

Holland, Robert B. *100 Miles to Freedom: The Epic Story of the Rescue of Santo Tomas and the Liberation of Manila, 1943–1945.* New York: Turner Publishing, 2011.

Holt, Daniel D., ed. *Eisenhower: The Prewar Diaries and Selected Papers, 1905–1941.* Baltimore: Johns Hopkins University Press, 1998.

Holzimmer, Kevin C. *General Walter Krueger: Unsung Hero of the Pacific War.* Lawrence: University Press of Kansas, 2007.

Hornfischer, James D. *The Last Stand of the Tin Can Sailors: The Extraordinary World War II Story of the U.S. Navy's Finest Hour.* New York: Bantam Books, 2004.

———. *Neptune's Inferno: The U.S. Navy at Guadalcanal.* New York: Bantam Books, 2011.

Howard, J. Woodford, Jr. *Mr. Justice Murphy: A Political Biography.* Princeton, N.J.: Princeton University Press, 1968.

Hoyt, Edwin P. *Three Military Leaders: Heihachiro Togo, Isoroku Yamamoto, Tomoyuki Yamashita.* Tokyo: Kodansha International, 1993.

Huff, Sid, and Joe Alex Morris. *My Fifteen Years with General MacArthur.* New York: Paperback Library, 1964.

Hunt, Frazier. *The Untold Story of Douglas MacArthur.* New York: Devin-Adair, 1954.

Hyland, Judy. *In the Shadow of the Rising Sun.* Minneapolis.: Augsburg, 1984.

Ishida, Jintaro. *The Remains of War: Apology and Forgiveness.* Guilford, Conn.: Lyons Press, 2001.

James, D. Clayton. *The Years of MacArthur.* 3 vols. Boston: Houghton Mifflin, 1970–85.

Joaquin, Nick. *Manila, My Manila.* Makati City, Philippines: Bookmark, 1999.

———. *Mr. F.E.U.: The Culture Hero That Was Nicanor Reyes.* Manila: Far Eastern University, 1995.

Joaquin, Nick, ed. *The Philippine Daily Inquirer Presents Intramuros.* Manila: Philippine Daily Inquirer, 1988.

Johnson, Leland E. *I Was a Prisoner of the Japs.* Saratoga, Calif.: Leland E. Johnson, 1947.

Jordan, David M. *FDR, Dewey, and the Election of 1944.* Bloomington: Indiana University Press, 2011.

Jordan, Jonathan W. *American Warlords: How Roosevelt's High Command Led America to Victory in World War II.* New York: NAL Caliber, 2015.

Karig, Walter, Russell L. Harris, and Frank A. Manson. *Battle Report: Victory in the Pacific*. New York: Rinehart & Co., 1949.

Karnow, Stanley. *In Our Image: America's Empire in the Philippines*. New York: Random House, 1989.

Kenney, George C. *General Kenney Reports: A Personal History of the Pacific War*. Washington, D.C.: U.S. Air Force History and Museums Program, 1997.

———. *The MacArthur I Know*. New York: Duell, Sloan and Pearce, 1951.

Kenworthy, Aubrey Saint. *The Tiger of Malaya: The Story of General Tomoyuki Yamashita and "Death March" General Masaharu Homma*. New York: Exposition Press, 1953.

King, Ernest J., and Walter Muir Whitehill. *Fleet Admiral King: A Naval Record*. New York: W. W. Norton, 1952.

Korda, Michael. *Ike: An American Hero*. New York: Harper, 2007.

Krueger, Walter. *From Down Under to Nippon: The Story of Sixth Army in World War II*. Washington, D.C.: Zenger, 1979.

Labrador, Juan. *A Diary of the Japanese Occupation: December 7, 1941–May 7, 1945*. Manila: Santo Tomas University Press, 1989.

Lael, Richard L. *The Yamashita Precedent: War Crimes and Command Responsibility*. Wilmington, Del.: Scholarly Resources, 1982.

La Follette, Philip. *Adventure in Politics: The Memoirs of Philip La Follette*. Edited by Donald Young. New York: Holt, Rinehart and Winston, 1970.

Langone, Louis C. *The Star in the Window: Select Stories of World War II Veterans*. Bloomington, Ind.: iUniverse, 2011.

Larrabee, Eric. *Commander in Chief: Franklin Delano Roosevelt, His Lieutenants, and Their War*. New York: Harper & Row, 1987.

Leahy, William D. *I Was There: The Personal Story of the Chief of Staff to Presidents Roosevelt and Truman Based on His Notes and Diaries Made at the Time*. New York: Whittlesey House/McGraw-Hill, 1950.

Leary, William M. *MacArthur and the American Century: A Reader*. Lincoln: University of Nebraska Press, 2001.

Leasor, James. *Singpore: The Battle That Changed the World*. Garden City, N.Y.: Doubleday, 1968.

Lee, Clark. *They Call It Pacific: An Eye-Witness Story of Our War against Japan, from Bataan to the Solomons*. New York: Viking Press, 1943.

Lee, Clark, and Richard Henschel. *Douglas MacArthur*. New York: Henry Holt, 1952.

Lichauco, Marcial P. *"Dear Mother Putnam": A Diary of the War in the Philippines*. No place or publisher, 1949.

Lucas, Celia. *Prisoners of Santo Tomas: Based on the Diaries of Mrs. Isla Corfield*. London: Leo Cooper, 1975.

Luvaas, Jay, ed. *Dear Miss Em: General Eichelberger's War in the Pacific, 1942–1945*. Westport, Conn.: Greenwood Press, 1972.

MacArthur, Douglas. *Reminiscences*. New York: McGraw-Hill, 1964.

Maga, Tim. *The Judgment at Tokyo: The Japanese War Crimes Trials*. Lexington: University Press of Kentucky, 2001.

Mañalac, Fernando J. *Manila: Memories of World War II*. Quezon City: Giraffe Books, 1995.

Manchester, William. *American Caesar: Douglas MacArthur, 1880–1964*. Boston: Little, Brown, 1978.

Manning, Paul. *Hirohito: The War Years*. New York: Dodd, Mead, 1986.

Mansell, Donald E., and Vesta W. Mansell. *Under the Shadow of the Rising Sun: The True Story of a Missionary Family's Survival and Faith in a Japanese Prisoner-of-War Camp during World War II*. Nampa, Id.: Pacific Press, 2003.

Martin, Ralph G. *The GI War: 1941–1945*. Boston: Little, Brown, 1967.

Mashbir, Sidney Forrester. *I Was an American Spy*. New York: Vantage Press, 1953.

Mason, Alpheus Thomas. *Harlan Fiske Stone: Pillar of the Law*. New York: Viking, 1956.

Mathias, Frank F. *GI Jive: An Army Bandsman in World War II*. Lexington: University of Kentucky Press, 1982.

McCallus, Joseph P. *The MacArthur Highway and Other Relics of American Empire in the Philippines*. Washington, D.C.: Potomac Books, 2010.

McCracken, Alan. *Very Soon Now, Joe*. New York: Hobson Book Press, 1947.

Mellnik, Steve. *Philippine Diary: 1939–1945*. New York: Van Nostrand Reinhold, 1969.

Miles, Fern Harrington. *Captive Community: Life in a Japanese Internment Camp, 1941–1945*. Jefferson City, Tenn.: Mossy Creek Press, 1987.

Miller, Merle. *Plain Speaking: An Oral Biography of Harry S. Truman*. New York: Berkley Publishing, 1974.

Miller, Stuart Creighton. *Benevolent Assimilation: The American Conquest of the Philippines, 1899–1903*. New Haven, Conn.: Yale University Press, 1982.

Molina, Antonio M. *Dusk and Dawn in the Philippines: Memoirs of a Living Witness of World War II*. Quezon City: New Day, 1996.

Monaghan, Forbes J. *Under the Red Sun: A Letter from Manila*. New York: Declan X. McMullen Co., 1946.

Monahan, Evelyn M., and Rosemary Neidel-Greenlee. *All This Hell: U.S. Nurses Imprisoned by the Japanese*. Lexington: University Press of Kentucky, 2010.

Montinola, Lourdes R. *Breaking the Silence*. Quezon City: University of the Philippines Press, 1996.

Moore, Charles. *Daniel H. Burnham: Architect, Planner of Cities*. 2 vols. Boston: Houghton Mifflin, 1921.

Moore, Stephen. *As Good as Dead: The Daring Escape of American POWs from a Japanese Death Camp*. New York: Caliber, 2016.

Morison, Samuel Eliot. *The Liberation of the Philippines: Luzon, Mindanao, the Visayas, 1944–1945*. Vol. 13 of *History of the United States Naval Operations in World War II*. Boston: Little, Brown, 1959.

Morton, Louis. *The Fall of the Philippines*. Vol. 2 of *The United States Army in World War II: The War in the Pacific*.Washington, D.C.: U.S. Army Center of Military History, 1993.

Moule, William R. *God's Arms around Us*. Nevada City, Calif.: Blue Dolphin, 1960.

Murphy, Edward F. *Heroes of World War II*. New York: Ballantine Books, 1990.

Mydans, Carl. *More Than Meets the Eye*. New York. Harper & Brothers, 1959.

Nakpil, Carmen Guerrero. *A Question of Identity: Selected Essays*. Manila: Vessel Books, 1973.

National Historical Institute. *Remembering World War II in the Philippines: Proceedings of the Oral History Conference Marking the 60th Anniversary of the Battle for Manila*. 2 vols. Manila: National Historical Institute, 2007.

Nixon, Eva Anna. *Delayed Manila: 1941–1945*. Newberg, Ore.: no publisher, 1981.

Norman, Elizabeth. *We Band of Angels: The Untold Story of American Nurses Trapped on Bataan by the Japanese*. New York: Random House, 1999.

Norman, Michael, and Elizabeth M. Norman. *Tears in the Darkness: The Story of the Bataan Death March and its Aftermath*. New York: Farrar, Straus and Giroux, 2009.

O'Brien, Niall, ed. *Columban Martyrs of Malate*. Manila: Kadenda Press, 1995.

Onorato, Michael P. *Forgotten Heroes: Japan's Imprisonment of American Civilians in the Philippines, 1942–1945*. Westport, Conn.: Meckler, 1990.

Ooka, Shohei. *Fires on the Plain*. Translated by Ivan Morris. Baltimore: Penguin, 1972.

Parillo, Mark P. *The Japanese Merchant Marine in World War II*. Annapolis: Naval Institute Press, 1993.

Patric, James H. *To War in a Tin Can: A Memoir of World War II aboard a Destroyer*. Jefferson, N.C.: McFarland, 2004.

Percival, A. E. *The War in Malaya*. London: Eyre and Spottiswoode, 1949.

Pérez de Olaguer, Antonio. *Terror in Manila: February 1945*. Edited by Bernardita Reyes Churchill. Translated by Trinidad Ongtangco Regala. Manila: Memorare Manila 1945 Foundation, 2005.

Perret, Geoffrey. *Old Soldiers Never Die: The Life of Douglas MacArthur*. New York: Random House, 1996.

Perry, Mark. *The Most Dangerous Man in America: The Making of Douglas MacArthur*. New York: Basic Books, 2014.

Pestaño-Jacinto, Pacita. *Living with the Enemy: A Diary of the Japanese Occupation*. Pasig City, Philippines: Anvil, 1999.

Petillo, Carol Morris. *Douglas MacArthur: The Philippine Years*. Bloomington: Indiana University Press, 1981.

Piccigallo, Philip R. *The Japanese on Trial: Allied War Crimes Operations in the East, 1945–1951*. Austin: University of Texas Press, 1979.

Picornell, Pedro M. *The Remedios Hospital, 1942–1945: A Saga of Malate*. Manila: De La Salle University Press, 1995.

Pincoffs, Maurice C. *Letters from Two World Wars and a Sketch of His Life by his Wife*. Baltimore: Garamond/Pridemark, 1967.

Pogue, Forrest C. *George C. Marshall: Organizer of Victory*. New York: Viking, 1973.

Poston, Madeleine. *My Upside-Down World*. Portland, Ore.: Benneta, 2002.

Potter, E. B. *Bull Halsey*. Annapolis, Md.: Naval Institute Press, 1985.

———. *Nimitz*. Annapolis, Md.: Naval Institute Press, 1976.

Potter, John Deane. *The Life and Death of a Japanese General*. New York: Signet Books, 1962.

Pownall, Sir Henry. *Chief of Staff: The Diaries of Lieutenant-General Sir Henry Pownall*. Edited by Brian Bond. 2 vols. London: Archon Books, 1974.

Prising, Robin. *Manila, Goodbye*. Boston: Houghton Mifflin, 1975.

Pu Yi, Henry. *The Last Manchu: The Autobiography of Henry Pu Yu, Last Emperor of China*. Edited by Paul Kramer. New York: Skyhorse, 2010.

Quezon, Manuel Luis. *The Good Fight*. New York: D. Appleton-Century, 1946.

Redmond, Juanita. *I Served on Bataan*. Philadelphia: J.B. Lippincott, 1943.

Reel, A. Frank. *The Case of General Yamashita*. New York: Octagon Books, 1971.

Regimental Staff. *The 129th Infantry in World War II*. Washington, D.C.: Infantry Journal Press, 1947.

Reyes, Jose G. *Terrorism and Redemption: Japanese Atrocities in the Philippines*. Translated by Jose Garcia Insua. Manila: n.p., 1947.

Rhoades, Weldon E. *Flying MacArthur to Victory*. College Station: Texas A&M University Press, 1987.

Rielly, Robin L. *Kamikaze Attacks of World War II: A Complete History of Japanese Suicide Strikes on American Ships, by Aircraft and Other Means*. Jefferson, N.C.: McFarland & Co., , 2010.

Robertson, William G., ed. *Block by Block: The Challenges of Urban Operations*. Fort Leavenworth, Kans.: U.S. Army Command and General Staff College Press, 2003.

Rogers, Paul P. *MacArthur and Sutherland*. 2 vols. New York: Praeger, 1990–91.

Romulo, Carlos P. *I Saw the Fall of the Philippines*. Garden City, N.Y.: Doubleday, Doran, 1943.

Roosevelt, Elliott, ed. *F.D.R., His Personal Letters*. New York: Duell, Sloan and Pearce, 1950.

Rosenman, Samuel I. *Working with Roosevelt*. New York: Harper & Brothers, 1952.

Ryan, Allan A. *Yamashita's Ghost: War Crimes, MacArthur's Justice, and Command Accountability*. Lawrence: University Press of Kansas, 2012.

Sams, Margaret. *Forbidden Family: A Wartime Memoir of the Philippines, 1941–1945*. Madison: University of Wisconsin Press, 1989.

Savary, Gladys. *Outside the Walls*. New York: Vantage Press, 1954.

Sayre, Francis Bowes. *Glad Adventure*. New York: Macmillan, 1957.

Schultz, Duane. *Hero of Bataan: The Story of General Jonathan M. Wainwright*. New York: St. Martin's Press, 1981.

Sharpe, George. *Brothers beyond Blood: A Battalion Surgeon in the South Pacific*. Austin, Tex.: Diamond Books, 1989.

Shortal, John F. *Forged by Fire: General Robert L. Eichelberger and the Pacific War*. Columbia: University of South Carolina Press, 1987.

Sides, Hampton. *Ghost Soldiers: The Forgotten Epic Story of World War II's Most Dramatic Mission*. New York: Doubleday, 2001.

Sloan, Bill. *Undefeated: America's Heroic Fight for Bataan and Corregidor.* New York: Simon and Schuster, 2012.

Smith, Colin. *Singapore Burning: Heroism and Surrender in World War II.* New York: Penguin, 2006.

Smith, Jean Edward. *Eisenhower: In War and Peace.* New York: Random House, 2012.

Smith, Robert Ross. *The Approach to the Philippines.* Vol. 8 of *The U.S. Army in World War II: The War in the Pacific.* Washington, D.C.: U.S. Army Center of Military History, 1996.

———. *Triumph in the Philippines.* Vol. 10 of *The U.S. Army in World War II: The War in the Pacific.* Washington, D.C.: U.S. Army Center of Military History, 1993.

Snodgrass, John E., comp. *History and Description of the Philippine General Hospital: Manila, Philippine Islands, 1900–1911.* Manila: Bureau of Printing, 1912.

Steinberg, David Joel. *Philippine Collaboration in World War II.* Ann Arbor: University of Michigan Press, 1967.

Stevens, Frederic H. *Santo Tomas Internment Camp, 1942–1945.* New York: Stratford House, 1946.

Stirling, Yates. *Sea Duty: The Memoirs of a Fighting Admiral.* New York: G.P. Putnam's Sons, 1939.

Storey, Moorfield, and Julian Codman. *Secretary Root's Record: "Marked Severities" in Philippine Warfare—An Analysis of the Law and Facts Bearing on the Action and Utterances of Presidents Roosevelt and Secretary Root.* Boston: Geo. W. Ellis Co., 1902.

Storey, Moorfield, and Marcial P. Lichauco. *The Conquest of the Philippines by the United States, 1898–1925.* New York: G.P. Putnam's Sons, 1926.

Stroup, Russell Cartwright. *Letters from the Pacific: A Combat Chaplain in World War II.* Edited by Richard Cartwright Austin. Columbia: University of Missouri Press, 2000.

Swinson, Arthur. *Defeat in Malaya: The Fall of Singapore.* New York: Ballantine Books, 1969.

———. *Four Samurai: A Quartet of Japanese Army Commanders in the Second World War.* London: Hutchinson, 1968.

Taft, Helen Herron. *Recollections of Full Years.* New York: Dodd, Mead, 1914.

Taylor, Lawrence. *A Trial of Generals: Homma, Yamashita, MacArthur.* South Bend, Ia.: Icarus Press, 1981.

Templeman, Harold. *The Return to Corregidor.* New York: Strand Press, 1945.

Toland, John. *But Not in Shame: The Six Months after Pearl Harbor.* New York: Random House, 1961.

———. *The Rising Sun: The Decline and Fall of the Japanese Empire, 1936–1945.* New York: Random House, 1970.

Tomblin, Barbara. *G.I. Nightingales: The Army Nurse Corps in World War II.* Lexington: University Press of Kentucky, 2003.

Torres, Cristina Evangelista. *The Americanization of Manila, 1898–1921.* Quezon City: University of the Philippines Press, 2010.

Tsuji, Masanobu. *Singapore: The Japanese Version.* Edited by H.V. Howe. Translated by Margaret E. Lake. New York: St. Martin's Press, 1960.

Tugwell, Rexford G. *The Brains Trust.* New York: Viking, 1968.

Van Sickle, Emily. *The Iron Gates of Santo Tomas: The Firsthand Account of an American Couple Interned by the Japanese in Manila, 1942–1945.* Chicago: Academy Chicago, 1992.

Vaughan, Elizabeth Head. *The Ordeal of Elizabeth Vaughan: A Wartime Diary of the Philippines.* Edited by Carol Morris Petillo. Athens: University of Georgia Press, 1985.

Villamor, Jesus. A., and Gerald S. Snyder. *They Never Surrendered: A True Story of Resistance in World War II.* Quezon City: Vera-Reyes, 1982.

Volckmann, R. W. *We Remained: Three Years behind the Enemy Lines in the Philippines.* New York: W. W. Norton. 1954.

Wainwright, Jonathan M. *General Wainwright's Story: The Account of Four Years of*

Humiliating Defeat, Surrender, and Captivity. Edited by Robert Considine. Garden City, N.Y.: Doubleday, 1946.

Weintraub, Stanley. *15 Stars: Eisenhower, MacArthur, Marshall: Three Generals Who Saved the American Century.* New York: Free Press, 2007.

Whan, Vorin E., Jr., ed. *A Soldier Speaks: Public Papers and Speeches of the General of the Army Douglas MacArthur.* New York: Praeger, 1965.

Whitney, Courtney. *MacArthur: His Rendezvous with History.* New York: Knopf, 1956.

Wilkinson, Rupert. *Surviving a Japanese Internment Camp: Life and Liberation at Santo Tomas, Manila, in World War II.* Jefferson, N.C.: McFarland, 2014.

Williams, Denny. *To the Angels.* San Francisco: Denson Press, 1985.

Willoughby, Amea. *I Was on Corregidor: Experiences of an American Official's Wife in the War-torn Philippines.* New York: Harper & Brothers, 1943.

Willoughby, Charles A., comp. *The Guerrilla Resistance Movement in the Philippines: 1941–1945.* New York: Vantage Press, 1972.

Willoughby, Charles A., and John Chamberlain. *MacArthur: 1941–1951.* New York: McGraw-Hill, 1954.

Wolfe, Robert, ed. *Americans as Proconsuls: United States Military Government in Germany and Japan, 1944–1952.* Carbondale: Southern Illinois University Press, 1984.

Worcester, Dean C. *The Philippines: Past and Present.* New York: Macmillan, 1921.

Wright, Bertram C., comp. *The 1st Cavalry Division in World War II.* Tokyo: Toppan, 1947.

Wygle, Peter R. *Surviving a Japanese POW Camp: Father and Son Endure Internment in Manila During World War II.* Ventura, Calif.: Pathfinder Publishing of California, 1991.

INDEX

Page numbers in *italics* refer to illustrations.

Abad, Maria Lourdes Vera, 303, 305,
310, 469
Abad, Patrocinio, *see* Noble, Corazon
Abad, Ramon, 309, 310
Abad, Vicente, 303, 310
Abbitt, Raymond, 121, 145
Abellera, Corazon, 304, 306
Abiko, Nanakazu, 150–52, 168, 188
Acuna, Regina, 335
Adams, Marie
on constant chaos at Santo Tomas, 107
on deaths at Santo Tomas, 123
on declining rations, 112
on starvation, 113, 119, 121
Aenille, Ester, 378
Agilada, Mariano, 239
Agoncillo, Teodoro
on black markets, 70
on collective collapse of morality, 74
on starvation, 73
on substitute cigarettes, 68
Ah Cheu (Arthur's nanny), 68, 436
Alba, Leticia, 309
Alda, Robert, 383
Allied Translator and Interpreter Section, 449
Aluit, Alfonso, 511
Amakasu, Shigetaro, 478
American battleships
Boise, 9, 85–86, 91
Colorado, 87
Columbia, 85, 86
Mississippi, 89
Missouri, 443
Montpellier, 86
Pennsylvania, 7
Washington, 93
American Chamber of Commerce, 58, 428
American forces
First Cavalry Division, *see* First Cavalry Division
Second Battalion, 241
Third Battalion, 241
Third Fleet, 114
Fifth Cavalry Regiment, *see* Fifth Cavalry Regiment
Sixth Army, 77, 85, 127, 246, 413
report on battle for Provisor Island, 246
report on enemy intending to destroy or possibly pollute water for Manila area, 192
report on the Luzon campaign, 85, 125, 246, 413
Eighth Army, 77, 192, 225, 247, 250
Eighth Cavalry Regiment, 188, 318–19
Eleventh Airborne Division
advance on Manila, *78,* 192
convergence to trap Japanese forces in Manila, 343, 360
division boundary for Manila, 225, *226, 276, 315*
XI Corps, *78*
Twelfth Cavalry Regiment, 360–61, 368
XIV Corps, 77, *78,* 85, 395, 416, 453
(*see also* First Cavalry Division; Thirty-Seventh Infantry Division)
Thirty-Second Infantry Division, 442, 443, 445
Thirty-Seventh Infantry Division, *see* Thirty-Seventh Infantry Division
Thirty-Eighth Infantry Division, 212
112th Medical Battalion, 317, 320, 373
128th Infantry Regiment, 443, 444
129th Infantry Regiment
in battle for Provisor Island, 227, 244–47
crossing of the Pasig River, 227, 240–41
discovery of massacres, 352–53, 404–5
report on number of bodies in Fort Santiago's sealed dungeon, 404–5
in seizure of Intramuros, 395

American forces (*continued*)
140th Field Artillery, 313
145th Infantry Regiment, 318, 395
148th Infantry Regiment
crossing of the Pasig River, 227
expansion of American bridgehead
through Pandacan and Paco to
Harrison Boulevard, 240
fatigue and frazzled nerves as closing
in on Manila Bay, 360
push towards Manila Bay, 342, 360
reports of
on assault on Philippine General
Hospital, 372
on battle for Paco Railroad Station,
241
on Japan reaching point of making
stand, 277, 372
role in constricting the Japanese
between America's advancing front
line and the waterfront, 340–42,
343
taking of Legislature and Finance
buildings, 416, 417, 419
716th Tank Battalion, 393
754th Tank Battalion, 315
893rd Medical Clearing Company,
215–16, 233, 296
see also intelligence forces, American
American hospitals
71st Evacuation Hospital, 312–13
29th Evacuation Hospital, 312
54th Evacuation Hospital, 313
American Red Cross, *see* Red Cross
American Revolution, 42
American submarines
Narwhal, 95
Swordfish, 220
American tanks
Battlin' Basic, 140
Georgia Peach, 146, 359
Amesse, John, 374
Andaya, Gliceria, 306, 307, 310
Anderson, Arthur, 86
Anderson, Neil, 199
Anderson, Rayford, 177–79
Anderson, Robert, 10
Andoy, Adelaida, 323, 324–25, 472
Andoy, Isabel, 324
Andoy, Rosalinda, 323–25, 399, 471–72,
473
Ang Tibay Shoe Factory, 197
Aniban, Francisco, 289, 290
Antipolo, Eutiquio, 258
Antonio, Dominador, 183–84

Antonio, Pablo, 270
Aquino, Servillano, 329–31, 333–35,
337–40, 439
Aquino, Trinidad, 331, 334–35, 337
Archer, Gladys, 236
Arias, Vicente, 181
Arima, Kaoru, 446
Arnold, Henry ("Hap"), 204
Arquillo, Celedonia de, 172
Asagumo, 93
Asano, Kenichiro, 251
Atlanta Constitution, 454
atrocities, *see* massacres and atrocities
Australia, 2, 203, 462–63
Australia, 89
Avanceña, Miguel, 372
Avila Camacho, Manuel, 204

Bachrach, Alexander, 346
Bachrach, Emil, 435
Bachrach, Mary, 435
Bacon, Frank, 209
Bailey, Caroline, 107, 116
Balfour, Nick, 156
Balintawak Monument, 138, 211–12
Ballesteros, Carmencita, 266
Balleta, Aniban, 289
Balleta, Conrada, 290
Balleta, Eugenio, 289
Barahona, Angeles, 259
Barahona, Cayetano, 255, 257, 258, 259
Barahona, Luisa, 258
Barahona, Maria, 255
Barbey, Daniel, 412
Barcelona, Santiago, 182
Barlow, Ernest, 443
Barullo, Jose, 381, 382
Bataan Death March, 5, 111, 173, 511
Batangas Province, massacre in, 464,
471, 474
Batoctoy, Eustaquio, 295
Battlin' Basic, 140
Bauman, Russell, 443
Bayer, Helen, 231
Bayer, Margaret
on food trucks from Lingayen, 192
on internees' interest in soldiers, 160
on MacArthur's visit to Santo Tomas,
218
on Paul Whitaker's death, 193
on shelling of Santo Tomas, 231, 236
Bayot, Eugene, 293, 294
Bay View Hotel, rapes at, 261–68, 449,
450, 471
Be, Ang, 473
Beck, Richard, 210

Beightler, Robert, 212, 433
    on destruction in Manila from artil-
        lery, 316, 416, 428, 429
    on Filipinos' reaction to soldiers'
        arrival in Manila, 165
    on fires in Manila, 197, 198–99, 205
    frustration with slow progress in
        Manila, 278
    refusal to shake Yamashita's hand, 444
Beliel, Clarence, 112
Beliso, Remedio Huerta, 240, 450
Bell, Don, 112
Belsen prison camp, 471
Benitez, Jesus, 289
Benito, Pacifico, 258
Bennett, Edward, 72
beriberi, 113–14, 121, 168
Berlin, Irving, 433
Besa, Augusto, 346
Best, Stella Mary, 347
B.F. Goodrich, 58
Bilibid Prison
    Douglas MacArthur's visit to,
        212–15
    internees and POWs at
        anxieties about violence during liber-
            ation, 173–74
        during fires, 197, 212
        hope for liberation, 172–73
        Japanese Army's release of, 174–75
        MacArthur's worry over fate of,
            128–29
        number of, 77, 172
    Japanese soldiers' departure from,
        175–76
    Jean MacArthur's visit to, 436
    liberation of, 177–79
    parading of POWs through streets on
        way to, 64–65
Bill of Particulars, 464, 465, 466, 467–68,
    483
Binkley, David, 224, 353, 404–5
Binondo district, 180, 427
Bishop, George, 447–48
Black, Hugo, 496
black market, 459
    for Red Cross medical supplies, 269
    for stolen food at Santo Tomas, 118
    for stolen goods in Manila, 70
Blaine, Sally, 301
    on American soldiers at Santo Tomas,
        161, 164
    on death of Abiko, 152
    on internees' weak bladder muscles,
        119
    on shelling of Santo Tomas, 232–33

Blanco, Miguel, 239
Blendo, Theodore, 259
Blitz, 467
Bloom, Samuel, 116
Bogue, Douglas, 79–80
Boguslav, David, 148, 164
Boguslav, Peggy, 148
Boise, 9, 85–86, 91
bootleg liquor, 432, 459
Boss, Irene, 303
Boss, Margaret, 303, 308
Boss, Martin, 303, 308
Boston Globe, 475, 478
Brady, Carmen Berlanga, 68, 74
Brady, Charles ("Todd"), 171, 186–87,
    188, 189–90
Brady, William, 74, 316, 511
Breese, Minnie, 143, 161
Brines, Russell, 217
Brooks, Louise Cromwell, 18
brothels, 431
Brougher, William, 11
Brown, Bob, 165, 241
Brown, Charles, 173
Brugger, Sylvia, 311
Buckland, Larry, 86
Buenafe, Manuel, 62
Buencamino, Felipe, 62, 69, 320, 388
Bulatao, Josephina, 386
Bulfer, Harry, 399
Bulkeley, John, 6
Burch, Robert, 501
Burgess, Henry, 298
Burnham, Daniel, 56–57, 58, 77, 97, 342,
    507
By Sword and Fire (Aluit), 511

Cabanatuan internment camp, 77, 79,
    111, 128–29, 134, 215
Cabanero, Jose, 292
Calalang, Aurora, 379
Calalang, Jesus, 211, 237, 379
Calalang, Rosa
    on fires, 238, 239
    on last time seeing husband, 211,
        237–38
    on massacre at Santo Domingo
        Church, 379–80
    on men burned while alive, 377
    rescue of, 399
Calinog, Manuel, 223–24
Calub, Bernardino, 280–81
Campbell, Mike, 277
Camp O'Donnell, 65
Campos, Pedro, 346
Canillas, Fred, 421

Capili, Ambrosio, 290
Capili, Celestina, 290
Carceller, Eduardo, 381
Carceller, Emilio, 381
Carlisle, John, 424
Carlos, Asela, 331, 337, 338
Carlos, Cecilia, 333
Carlos, Jose, 329, 330
Carlos, Juanita, 333
Carlos, Rosario, 331, 333, 334, 337, 338
Carlos, Tony, 331, 335
Caro, Isabel, 268
Carroll, Earl, 104, 122, 123, 149
Cary, Frank
    as an interpreter in Hayashi's surren-
        der, 149, 155
    on fires, 123
    on liberation, 143–44
Case of General Yamashita, The (Reel),
    510
Cassiani, Helen, 108, 161
Castaner, Pilar Garcia Viuda de, 266
Castle, Myrtle, 194–95
Catale, Daniel, 165
Cates, Lowell, 160, 384
Celis, Belarmino de, 382–83, 396–97,
    398, 450
Central Force, 95, 227, 250, 415
    in battle for Paco Railroad Station,
        244–46
    defense of government offices, 377
    escalation of attacks against civilians
        suspected of guerrilla ties, 251
    use of pillboxes, 277
    use of vertical landscape to target
        infantrymen, 341
Chambers, Beatrice, 235
Chapman, Spencer, 38
Chase, Bessie, 295
Chase, William ("Bill"), 163–64, 190, 295
    as commander of the Thirty-Eighth
        Infantry Division, 212
    on food and ammunition shortage at
        Santo Tomas, 166
    as leader of forces seizing Manila,
        132–33
    on MacArthur's tour of Malacañan
        Palace, 219–21
    on MacArthur's visit to Bilibid, 214
    order to secure the Quezon Bridge,
        167
    on physical condition of internees, 160
    plan to end standoff with the Japanese
        at Santo Tomas, 170–71
    visit to brewery with MacArthur, 222
Chia, Sy, 293

Chiang Kai-shek, 204
Chicago Tribune, 471
Chickering, Bill, 10, 389
Chome, Benjamin, 224
Churchill, Winston, 10, 39, 40, 43
Clark, Harlow, 352
Clark, Henry, 374
Clarke, Harry, 454
    on clothing for Yamashita's arraign-
        ment, 462
    first meeting with Yamashita, 457
    oral arguments presented to the U.S.
        Supreme Court, 496, 497
    reaction to verdict, 491
    at Yamashita's arraignment, 464
    Yamashita's gifts to, 491
    during Yamashita's trial, 474, 479–80
coconut trees, cost of war damage to,
    428
Cojuangco, Antonio, 329, 331, 334,
    337–38
Cojuangco, Antonio, Jr., 329
Cojuangco, Ricardo, 330
Colayco, Manuel, 138, 140
Colma, Camilo, 260
Colma, Concepcion, 260
Colma, Illuminada, 260
Colma, Violeta, 260
Colma, Winfred, 260
Colorado, 87
Colquhoun, Elsa, 116, 121
Colquhoun, Robert, 117, 269
Columbia, 85, 86
Columbia Express, 434
Conner, David, 402, 403, 423
Conner, Haskett ("Hack"), Jr., 134–35,
    136–37, 138, 140, 164
Cooper, Rosario ("Dimples"), 26–27
Coralles, Leandro, 380
Cornwallis, Charles, 42
Corregidor Island
    American forces' seizure of, 412–15
    Japan's seizure of, 11, 64, 107
    MacArthurs' escape from, 1–3, 4–6, 9,
        30, 214, 511
    MacArthur's return visit to, 412–15
    statue of MacArthur on, 511
Cosgrave, Francis, 329, 330–33, 336, 337,
    339–40
Courier (Manila), 470, 479, 486, 490
Cowles, Mrs. D. C., 501
Crichton, Jean, 118
Cromie, Robert, 474, 480
Cronin, Raymond, 209
Crouter, Jerry, 173, 176
Crouter, June, 176

Crouter, Natalie, 237, 507
  on destruction from the battle, 428, 430
  on Douglas MacArthur's visit to Bilibid, 214
  on Japanese soldiers' departure from Bilibid, 175
  on Jean MacArthur's visit to Bilibid, 435–36
  on liberation of Bilibid, 179
  on smell of death in the air, 423–24
  on watching the battle, 173, 176–77
Crowder, Enoch H., 15
Cruz, Pedro, 294
Cruz, Vito, 100
Crystal Arcade, 181
Cuba, 21, 22
Curtin, John, 43, 204

Dagupan, 91
Davantes, Federico, 292
Davis, Marjorie Ann, 231
Davis, Paul, 231
De La Salle College, 328
  American soldiers' liberation of, 340
  Japanese occupation of, 328–29
  refugees at, 328, 329–31
De La Salle massacre, 331–39, 366, 464, 511
Dempsey, Jack, 57
Dewey, Fred, 501
Dewey, George, 22, 24
Diaz, Anacleto, 311
Diego, Alicia, 260
Diego, Camilo, 260, 261
Diego, Cocha, 260
Diego, Lydia, 260, 261
Diego, Romeo, 260
Diego, Rosalinda, 260
Diller, LeGrande, 207, 391
Dionzon, Angel, 180
Dominador, Antonio, 183–84, 224
Dominador, Arturo, 224
Dominador, Cecilia, 224
Doolittle, Jimmy, 510
Dos Passos, John
  on army censorship, 301
  on artillery during the battle, 316
  exploration of abandoned homes, 390
  on MacArthur's headquarters, 288
  on shelling of Manila Hotel, 350, 351
Douglas, William, 496
Dred Scott case, 500
Dugong Hinugasan, 303
Dunn, William ("Bill"), 129
  on conditions at Santo Tomas, 170
    decision to no longer report on atrocities, 386
  on enemy troops entrenched in Manila, 298
  on fires, 319
  on Hewlett's search for his wife, 132, 137, 142–43
  on hunger at Santo Tomas, 159, 268–69
  on internees raising American flag, 191
  on Intramuros from artillery observation post, 348
  on liberation of Santo Tomas, 147, 170, 186
  on Lingayen Gulf invasion, 76, 90
  on MacArthur's censorship, 391
  on the Manila of 1941, 60, 507
  on needing a break from Santo Tomas, 196
  reaction to a victory parade for MacArthur, 207
  riding with First Cavalry into Manila, 131, 134–36, 137
  on seizure of Intramuros, 396, 397
  on slow progress of battle, 389
Duran, Tita, 303–4, 310
Durango, Teresita, 303–4, 310
Dworsky, Bertha, 120–21, 270
Dy Pac Lumberyard, massacre at, 182–85, 222–24
dysentery, 3, 5, 105, 121, 377, 441

Ebiko, Major, 174, 176
Eddleman, Clyde, 128
Egeberg, Roger, 89, 410, 434
  on dead Japanese soldiers in truck, 219
  trip to Manila Hotel with MacArthur, 406, 408
  on venereal disease among troops, 431
  on visit to Bilibid, 212, 213, 215
Eichelberger, Robert, 291
  on fires in Manila, 198, 205
  on house-to-house defense, 392
  on MacArthur's plans for a victory parade, 207, 391
  on MacArthur's premature declaration of victory, 206
  questioning Japan's motivations in lack of opposition, 127–28, 133
  role in MacArthur's invasion plan, 77
Eighth Army, 77, 192, 225, 247, 250
Eighth Cavalry Regiment, 188, 318–19
Eisenhower, Dwight, 12, 20, 21, 28, 60, 129–30

electricity, Japanese interrogators' use of, 209–10

Eleventh Airborne Division
  advance on Manila, 78, 192
  convergence to trap Japanese forces in Manila, 343, 360
  division boundary for Manila, 225, 226, 276, 315

Enriquez, Angel, 289, 295

Enriquez, Eva, 289

Enriquez, Sancho, 317

Ermita district
  destruction in, 427, 430
  fires in, 279–84
  German Club massacre in, 279–82, 283, 471
  Southern Force's defense of, 95, 97
  Thirty-Seventh Infantry's seizure of, 276

Erwin, Leroy, 350

Eschbach, Carl, 174, 175, 176

Espiritu, Fausta, 474

Esquerra, Ricardo, 290–91, 294, 295, 473–74

Esteban, Esperanza, 279

Esteban, Luis, 373

Fahey, James, 86

Fairbanks, Douglas, 57

Fairchild, Mary, 436

Faircloth, Jean, see MacArthur, Jean Faircloth

Fajardo, Celia, 184, 223

Fajardo, Faustino, 223, 224

Fajardo, Florencia, 223

Fajardo, Lourdes, 223

Fajardo, Melita, 223

Falls, Jimmy, 227, 341, 361–62

Far Eastern University, 67, 215

Farolan, Modesto
  on Japanese troops' tour of Red Cross headquarters, 304
  opening of refugee center, 201, 302
  on Red Cross massacre, 305, 306–8, 310

Feldhaus, Gordon, 454, 455, 457, 491–92

Fellers, Bonner, 89, 432
  on Cabanatuan liberation, 129
  on condition of Santo Tomas internees, 384–85
  confidence in MacArthur, 128
  on destruction of Manila, 319
  escorting of Jean and Author to Manila, 434
  on fight at Manila Hotel, 406
  on housing shortage, 435
  inventory of Santo Tomas, 196
  on Japanese forces' behavior, 386–87, 424
  on Lingayen Gulf invasion, 91
  on long drawn-out battle, 392
  on MacArthur's intellect, 20
  prediction about Luzon campaign, 77
  on Rizal Memorial Stadium battle, 368
  visit to Santo Tomas, 194, 195, 217

Fernandez, Rosario, 259

Fifth Amendment, 499

Fifth Cavalry Regiment, 360–61
  in assault on Harrison Park and Rizal Memorial Stadium, 368, 369
  reports of, 136
    on departure of Japanese from Santo Tomas, 187
    on fires in Manila, 200
    on University of the Philippines, 374–76
    on waiting for Japanese to surrender, 417
  seizure of Agriculture Building, 416, 417, 418–19

Filipinas Heritage Library, 512

fires, 319
  in covering up massacres, 252, 352
  in districts north of the Pasig River, 196–201
  in Ermita district, 279–84
  families attempts to escape from, 202–3
  fears about, 248–59, 271
  in Intramuros, 238–40, 402
  in Paco district, 295, 439
  as weapons of attack, 180–81

First Cavalry Division, 192, 315, 340
  advance on Manila, 78, 134–39
  attempt to secure the Quezon Bridge, 166–67
  convergence to trap Japanese forces in Manila, 343, 360, 368
  crossing of the Pasig River, 225, 226, 227, 228, 237, 276
  landing in Lingayen, 127
  in Leyte, 127
  liberation of Santo Tomas camp, 139–40, 143, 145–49
    escorting of Japanese from camp after, 186–90
    fortification of camp after, 160, 164, 166
    standoff with Japanese during, 149–50, 154–57, 164, 170–71
  reports of, 225, 360
  in seizure of Intramuros, 395

Fisher, Harrison, 120
Flanagan, Edward, 247, 248
Flatiron Building in New York, 56
Foley, Frances Helen, 232–33
Foley, Mary, 232
Foley, Walter B., 232, 236
food
    at Santo Tomas internment camp, 102,
        104–5, 110
    after liberation, 158–60, 165–66, 192,
        268–69, 384–85
    declining average caloric intake, 119
    ethical dilemmas for doctors about,
        121–22
    food theft, 118, 121
    sources of, out of desperation,
        116–17, 121
    testimony at Yamashita's trial on,
        479
    withholding of, as a weapon, 112–14,
        119
    see also starvation
Formosa, 10, 12, 288
Fort McKinley
    in Iwabuchi's defense plan, 225
    Iwabuchi's move to, 250, 311
    orders for Iwabuchi to move to, 94,
        344–45
    Southern Force's defense of, 95, 247
    Yamashita's arrival at, 47
    Yamashita's departure from, 53, 54
Fort Santiago, 423, 511
    Americans' methods for fighting in,
        402–3
    atrocities at, listed in Yamashita's
        trial, 464
    final orgy of mass murder and burning
        prisoners alive at, 403–5
    Japanese guards' use of torture at,
        209–10, 402, 404, 511
    killings of males from Intramuros
        taken to, 208, 211, 237, 240, 377,
        402
    memorial plaques outside dungeons
        of, 508
    removal of the dead from dungeon
        of, 423
    during the Spanish Inquisition, 208–9
Forward, Donald, 352
Fox, Billy, 177–78
Frankel, Stanley, 228–29
Frankel, Walter, 452
Frankfurter, Felix, 500
Fraser, Willard, 501
Frederick, John, 405
Free Philippines, 422, 427

Friedinger, Henry ("Friday"), 212
Friman, Erik, 210
Fujiwara, Kanenaga, 445
Furuda-san, 325–26, 331
Furuse, Takesue, 95, 225, 247, 250, 509

Gadol, Fanny, 265
Gadol, Vicky, 266
Gallaher, Joseph, 349
Garcia, Agustin, 302
Garcia, Esther, *see* Moras, Esther Garcia
Garcia, Evangeline, 262–63
Garcia, Ida
    departure from St. Scholastica,
        354–56, 357
    escape to St. Scholastica, 326–27
    Furuda-san's warning to, 325, 331
    preparations for fighting, 100
    reaction to MacArthur's return, 162
    return to Paco, 367
    shelter in Santa Ana, 365–66
    stocking of bomb shelter, 202
Garcia, Joaquin ("Jack")
    on American air raids, 72
    on arduous hike to Santa Ana, 363–64
    departure from St. Scholastica, 354–56
    on difficulty finding shelter in Santa
        Ana, 365–66
    on escape to St. Scholastica, 326–28
    on fires in Manila, 202, 249, 326
    friendship with Arthur MacArthur,
        67–68, 366
    on Furuda-san's warning, 325–26
    on Japanese troops' sniping of civil-
        ians, 248
    on murder of priest and nuns, 364–65
    on new currency, 63
    on news of MacArthur's return, 162
    on people disappearing, 100
    reaction to American troops, 357–58
    return to Paco, 366–68
    on shelling of St. Scholastica, 327–28,
        353–55
Garcia, Paquita Coastas, 265, 267, 268
Garcia, Priscilla, 262–64, 471
Garcia, Ramon (father), 363
    bomb shelter of, 202
    departure from St. Scholastica,
        354–56
    efforts to find shelter in Santa Ana,
        364–65
    escape to St. Scholastica, 327
    hope for MacArthur's return, 75
    preparing items to take during fires,
        249
    return to Paco, 366–67

Garcia, Ramon (son)
    departure from St. Scholastica, 354–56
    reaction to American troops, 358
    return to Paco, 367
    school attended by, 325
Garcia, Trinidad Llamas de, 267–68
Gardner, William, 353
Garen, Eleanor, 161
Garrett, Glidden, 145
Garrett, Margaret, 145
Gebhard, Adolf, 335
General Electric, 58
Geneva Convention, 99, 369, 448
Genko Line, 247, 250
George F. Badger, 85
Georgia Peach, 146, 359
Gerhart, James, 137, 150, 155
German Club massacre, 279–82, 311,
    345, 508
Gershwin, George, 383
Ghezzi, Julia, 266
Ghezzi, Margarita Salado, 266
Gill, William, 442
Gillooly, Margaret, 115, 116, 143, 146
Giocado, Domingo, 255–56
Gisbert, Antonio, 378
Godino, Lourdes, 378–79
Goebbels, Joseph, 11
Goldthorpe, Anne Louise
    on drastic weight loss at Santo Tomas,
        118, 119
    on liberation of Santo Tomas, 145
    on scarcity of food, 121
    sickness from eating canna lily bulbs,
        117
    on Ulmstad's funeral, 122
Gonzalez, Faustino, 423
Gonzalez, Juan, 421
Graetz, Martha, 303, 308
Graetz, Waldemar, 303, 308
Gray, Bill, 348, 389, 411, 414
Great Britain
    defeat in Singapore, 30, 31, 36, 37–42,
        43
    naval base in Singapore, 36–38
    number of civilian deaths during
        World War II in, 467
Grew, Joseph, 204
Griswold, Oscar, 77, 212, 361, 396
    on destruction of Manila, 205, 319
    division of responsibility for Manila's
        north, 191–92
    frustration with slow progress, 278,
        360
    on kamikaze attacks, 83
    on MacArthur's impatience, 221

on MacArthur's plans for a victory
    parade, 130
on MacArthur's premature declara-
    tion of victory, 128, 206
on MacArthur's refusal to use bomb-
    ers, 394–95
on MacArthur's visits to Bilibid and
    Santo Tomas, 219
sadness on eve of Lingayen invasion,
    87
on seizure of Intramuros, 397, 405
Guadalcanal, 32, 92
Guam, 12, 22, 31
Guevara, Luisa, 267
Guevara, Raymunda, 267
Guido, Jose, 251, 421, 423
Gunita, 303
Gunnison, Royal Arch, 246–47, 350, 390
Gurevich, Boris, 346
Gurevich, Eva, 346, 421
Gurevich, Leonid, 346
Gutierrez, Epifanio, Jr., 381
Guy, George, 454, 477
    on appointment to Yamashita's
        defense team, 455
    on fairness of Yamashita's trial, 510
    first meeting with Yamashita, 457, 458
    gift from Yamashita to, 492
    on press buildup to trial, 465–66
    on Yamashita's reaction to verdict, 490
Guzman, Peter de, 512

H. E. Heacock Company, 58, 62, 143
Habibi, Rebecca, 266, 267
Hague Convention, 99
Hahn, Max, 347
Hall, Roderick "Rod," 423
Halsema, James, 225, 487
    on American forces guarding Japanese
        POWs, 463
    conversation with POW at Bilibid, 213
    on redundancy of survivors' stories,
        425
    on Yamashita's trial, 486
Halsey, William ("Bull"), 114, 248
Hamamoto, Masakatsu, 457, 475, 489,
    497
Hamburger, Elsie, 320, 452
Hamilton, Fred, 191
Hanley, John, 222
Hara, Mamoru, 502
Hardy, Mary Pinkney, *see* MacArthur,
    Mary Pinkney Hardy ("Pinky")
Harper, Mildred, 236
Harrington, Fern, 172–73, 175, 176
Harrison Park, 368

Hartendorp, Abram, 383, 429
  on anticipation before liberation, 145
  as camp historian at Santo Tomas,
    102–3, 104
  on camp's mascot, 117
  on companies rebuilding after the
    battle, 428
  on death certificates and funerals,
    422
  on deaths from shelling on Santo
    Tomas, 236
  on decline of internees from poor diet,
    110, 112–13, 116
  on food options at Santo Tomas, 105
  on housing crisis, 459
  on letters received by internees, 193
  on MacArthur's visit to Santo Tomas,
    218
  nervous breakdown after liberation,
    425
  on population as shell-shocked, 459
  on refugees clamoring for admittance
    to Santo Tomas, 296
  separation from family while at Santo
    Tomas, 110–11, 425
  on shanties at Santo Tomas, 106
  testimony at Yamashita's trial, 474
Hartendorp, Eddy, 111, 425
Hartendorp, Henry, 425
Hartford Courant, 475
Hauser, Gus, 228
Hayashi, Toshio
  departure from Santo Tomas, 186,
    189, 190
  negotiation of surrender, 149–50, 155,
    170–71
  reaction to Americans firing on build-
    ing, 156
"Heaven Watch the Philippines" (Berlin),
    433
Hemingway, Ernest, 57
Henderson, Bertha, 149
Henderson, John, 270
Hendrix, Mary, 454
Hendrix, Walter, 454, 492, 493–94
Henne, Chuck, 240–41, 340, 361
  on crossing the Pasig River, 227–28
  on finding Japanese hiding after the
    battle, 432–33
  on frazzled nerves of troops, 360
  on Jimmy Falls' death, 362
  on Laurel's house, 314
  on measuring gains, 277
  on oblivious civilians, 341–42
  on searching for cover during fires,
    199–200

  on seizure of Intramuros, 396
  on smell and taste of death, 424
Henshaw, Gwendolyn, 119, 149
Herman, Jose, 251, 420–21
Herold, Ethel, 175, 197, 424, 429
Hewlett, Frank
  escape from Corregidor, 131
  on Japanese troops' departure from
    Santo Tomas, 187
  on malaria and malnutrition among
    troops, 3
  reunion with wife, 142–43
  riding with First Cavalry into Manila,
    131, 135, 138–40
  search for wife, 131–32, 137, 138–41
Hewlett, Virginia, 131–32, 137, 142
Heyward, Spike, 169–70
Hick, Howard, 166
Hick, Maybell, 166
Higdon, Claude, Jr., 222
High Commissioner's Summer Resi-
    dence, 445, 446
Hirohito, Emperor, 32, 46, 441, 442
Hirose, Toshio, 149
Hiroshima, atomic attack on, 441
Hitler, Adolf, 35
Hodges, 85
Hoffman, William, 105
Holland, Albert, 115, 118, 122
Homma, Masaharu, 4, 63
hospitals
  71st Evacuation Hospital, 312–13
  29th Evacuation Hospital, 312
  54th Evacuation Hospital, 313
Hotchand, Hashmatrai, 423
Howard, Sam, 194
Hubert, Hartmann, 335
Huerta, Conchita, 377
Huff, Sidney, 194–95
Hughes, Robert, 23
Hun, Ko King, 208, 209
hunger
  among civilians in Japan, 32
  among internees at Santo Tomas, 102,
    112–14, 118, 120–21
  among MacArthur's troops on Bataan
    Peninsula, 3–4
  during Battle of Leyte, 49–50
  in Manila under Japanese occupation,
    55–56, 70–71
  see also starvation

Ickes, Harold, 20–21
I Corps, 77, 88
Indian Wars, 15, 22
Inolin, Filomeno, 329, 331, 333, 334

intelligence forces, American
on Dy Pac Lumberyard massacre,
222
estimate of reinforcements to Southern Force, 247
focus of, 313–15
on Iwabuchi's defense plan, 133, 225
MacArthur and, 128
reports of
on intentional destruction or pollu-
tion of Manila's water, 192
on Japanese troops setting fires,
197–98
on low enemy morale, 319
on minefields in Lingayen Gulf, 84
on Yamashita, 31
internment camps, 53
Bilibid Prison, *see* Bilibid Prison
Cabanatuan internment camp, 77, 79,
111, 128–29, 134, 215
Japanese Americans in, 496
at Los Baños, 77, 79, 160, 197, 346,
405
MacArthur's worry about invasion
jeopardizing lives at, 77, 79, 81,
128–29
at University of Santo Tomas, *see*
Santo Tomas internment camp
interracial relationships, 60
Intramuros
Americans' observation of Japanese
in, 347–49
Americans' seizure of, 415
fighting during, 395–99, 402–3
plan for, 276, 394–95
preparations for, 393–94
rescue of refugees during, 398, 399,
400
terror for refugees during, 396–97
artillery attacks on, 378–79
destruction in, 427
elaborate tunnels dug by Japanese in,
394
history of, 56, 393
in Iwabuchi's battle plan, 95, 97
Japanese' killing of men in, 208, 211,
237, 240, 377, 381–83, 393
Japanese' sealing gates of, 201, 208,
225
massacre at Santo Domingo Church
in, 323–24, 379–81, 471–72
rapes in, 201, 378
resolution requesting Yamashita's
hanging in, 503
torture of refugees in, 209–10, 401–2,
403, 404–5
tourists' exploration of, 508

Iwabuchi, Sanji, 458, 511
American forces' isolation of, 343,
409–10, 415–17
battle plan for Manila, 92–95, *96*, 97,
98, 99, 133, 225, 241
daily reports sent to Yokoyama,
250–51, 287
final stand in the Agriculture Building,
416, 417–18
move to Fort McKinley, 250, 311
naval career of, 92–94
orders for the final destruction of
Manila, 179–80
orders for troops to fight to the death,
314, 417
orders to blow the Ayala and Quezon
bridges, 167
physical description of, 92
refusal to retreat to Fort McKinley,
344–45
return to Manila, 311
as scapegoat, 456, 458
suicide of, 418, 419

Jackson, Robert, 495–96
James, Rita, 159
Japan
atomic attacks on, 441
defeat of British in Singapore, 30, 31,
36, 37–42, 43
firebombing of, 441
hunger among civilians in, 32
Sook Ching Massacre by, 42–43
surrender of, 443
see also Japanese forces; Manila,
Battle of
Japanese Americans, interning of, 496
Japanese forces
Central Force, 95, 227, 250, 415
in battle for Paco Railroad Station,
244–46
defense of government offices, 377
escalation of attacks against civilians
suspected of guerrilla ties, 251
use of pillboxes, 277
use of vertical landscape to target
infantrymen, 341
Northern Force, 95, 250, 418
detonation of buildings, 198, 225
hunkering down behind walls of
Intramuros, 377
Iwabuchi's orders to blow Ayala and
Quezon bridges, 167
retreat across the river to form second line of defense, 179
pillboxes used by, 97, 98, 99, 241, 242,
247, 248, 277

Southern Force, 95, 225, 247, 509
86th Air Corps, 451
Japan Times and Advertiser, 11, 43
Jenkins, Paul B., 16
Jesus, Anna de, 258
Jesus, Antonius von, 330, 335, 336, 337
Joaquin, Nick, 65
Johnson, Mac, 472, 473
Jolson, Al, 383
Jones, George, Col., 414–15
Jones, George E. (*New York Times*
    reporter), 393
  on daily lines at army aid stations, 426
  on death and destruction as punitive,
    389–90
  on fires in Manila, 206
  on former Manila dead, 391
  on MacArthur's return visit to Cor-
    regidor, 414
  on refugees from Intramuros, 400
  on seizure of Intramuros, 396, 397, 398
  tour of hospitals after the battle, 424
  on worthless Japanese occupation
    bills, 390
journalists
  censorship of, 301, 391–92
  with the Lingayen Gulf invasion, 84,
    87, 90
  with MacArthur on return visit to
    Corregidor, 413–14
  observation of Intramuros, 347–49
  riding with First Cavalry into Manila,
    127, 130–31, 132, 134–35
  on Yamashita's war crimes trial, 462,
    468, 470, 472–75, 477–80, 482, 486,
    490
  see also specific journalists
Joya, Ladislao, 210–11
Juan, Juan P., 302–3, 307, 309–10
Juan, Lucia Santos de, 303, 307

kamikaze attacks
  after Lingayen Gulf invasion, 88–89,
    90
  as a new type of weapon, 10, 32
  on ships during voyage for Lingayen
    Gulf, 76, 83–84, 85–86
Kanusing, Gurmuksing, 256
Kapica, Edward, 446
Karatsu, 95
Karnow, Stanley, 24
Katz, Bernard, 472
Kayashima, Koichi, 250–51, 311
Keily, Ann, 370
Kelly, Patrick, 251
Kembu Group, 52
Kenney, George, 410, 412, 413, 435

Kentner, Robert, 179, 196
Kenworthy, Aubrey Saint, 445, 448,
    485–86, 487–88, 490
Kerr, Robert
  background of, 461
  on raw emotions surrounding
    Yamashita's trial, 463
  at Yamashita's arraignment, 463–64
  at Yamashita's trial, 468–74, 478, 479,
    480–82, 484–85
  closing statements of, 484–85
  cross-examination of Yamashita,
    480–82
  opening arguments of, 468–69
  witnesses for, 469–70, 471–73, 476
Keys, Henry, 386, 400–402, 474
Kinkaid, Thomas, 87
King, Charles, 16
King, Robert, 375
Kirishima, 92–93
Kishinchand, Mira, 317
Kishinchand, Pari, 317
Kishinchand, Radhi, 317
Kishinchand, Sundri, 317
Klein, Jacob, 403
Knipp, Labin, 199
Knowlting, Eda, 217
Kohnke, Bertha, 303, 308
Kohnke, George, 303, 308
Kohnke, Irene, 303, 308, 310
Konrad, Victor, 335
Kou, Shiyoku, 479
Kozuki, Yoshio, 502
Kremleff, Eugene, 346, 421
Kremleff, Helen, 346
Krohn, Edgar, Jr., 370–71, 373
Kropf, William, 353
Krueger, Walter, 192
  at crossing of the Pasig River, 227
  on destruction of districts of Manila,
    316
  landing at Lingayen Gulf, 77, 87, 88,
    90
  MacArthur's frustration with slow
    progress of, 127
  MacArthur's refusal of request to use
    bombers, 394
  on MacArthur's return visit to Cor-
    regidor, 412

Labrador, Juan, 429, 441
  on hunger in Manila, 71
  on Japanese officer's warning, 100
  on murders and mutilations, 425
  on poverty, 71
  on unemployment, 65–66
  on wide use of bicycles, 69

Ladies Home Journal, 120
La Follette, Philip, 20
Lagdameo, Cayetano, 452, 511
Lahoz, Benita, 381, 396
Lalana, Prudencio Chicote, 421
La Loma Cemetery, 97, 104, 318–19, 433
Lamotan, Antonio, 223
land mines
    in battle for Nichols Field, 247
    civilian deaths from, 364, 459, 512
    clearing of, 433
    Iwabuchi's battle plan using, 97, *98*
    at La Loma Cemetery, 318–19
    leftover, 433, 459, 467
    warning sign to refugees about, 430
La Salle, John Baptist de, Saint, 328
Laurel, Jose, 70–71, 133, 314, 410
Leavey, Edmond, 447–48
Lecaroz, Lourdes, 237, 239, 400
Lehrbas, Lloyd, 212, 406, 410, 434
Leo, Flavius, 331–32
Levy, Rene, 284
Lewy, John, 303, 305, 308–9, 310
Leyte, Battle of, 9, 49–51, 52, 127, 134, 298
Lichauco, Cornelia, 321
Lichauco, Jessie, 320–21
Lichauco, Jose, 209
Lichauco, Marcial
    on arrival of U.S. army, 7, 320–21
    on avoiding Japanese sentries, 63
    on emaciated and starving people, 73
    on fears of American artillery, 249
    on fires, 202
    on guerrilla assassinations, 66–67
    on high food prices, 71
    on hunger, 55
    items sold by, 69
    on Japanese propaganda, 64
    on Japanese scorched- earth policy, 100
    on Japanese troops' retreat, 201
    on list of known dead from the battle, 420
    on POWs paraded through streets, 65
    on torture and beatings, 66
    on wounded and dying refugees, 321–22
Life magazine, 24, 37, 42, 168, 188
Limpus, Lowell, 486
Lindley, Ernest, 204
Ling, Ang Kim, 472–73
Ling, Elisa Ang, 472, 473
Lingayen Gulf
    American invasion of
        eve of, 84

    first wave of, 86–89, 90
    kamikaze attacks on ships during
        voyage for, 76, 83–84, 85–86
    MacArthur's invasion plan for,
        76–77, 82, 84–85
    Pennsylvania entering the, *7*
    U.S. ships crowding the, 76
    First Cavalry Division's landing in, 127
    Japanese invasion of, 29
liquor, bootleg, 432, 459
Litonjua, Anatolio, 486
Litton, George, 371
Litton, Jim, 371–72, 373
Lloyd, Sam, 149
Loewinsohn, Carl, 162
Logue, Mary Trinita, 511
Long, Frank, 114
Lopez, Andrea, 377
Lopez, Carmen, 281
Lopez, Francisco, 279–82, 285–87, 450, 471
Lopez, Jose, 281
Lopez, Julia, 282
Lopez, Maria, 282
Losa, Engracio, 255
Los Angeles Times, 462, 467, 477, 500, 502
Los Baños internment camp, 77, 79, 160, 197, 346, 405
Losinas, Rita, 421
Loska, Stevens, 352
Loveriza, Florita, 306
Lucian, Alemond, 335
Lumsden, Herbert, 10
Luzon
    invasion of, 7
        eve of, 84
        first wave of, 86–89, 90
        kamikaze attacks during voyage for,
            76, 83–84, 85–86
        preparations for, 84–85
        voyage for, 76, 82–86
    Japanese supply shortages on, 52–53
    railroads on, 53
    Yamashita's defense strategy for, 46, 51–52
    see also Manila
Luzon Prisoner of War Camp No. 1, 492, 506

MacArthur, Arthur (DM's brother), 17
MacArthur, Arthur (DM's father)
    career aspirations of, 19
    career in the Philippines, 15, 21, 25, 27, 219, 410, 507–8
    during the Civil War, 11–12
    death of, 15–16, 25

egotism of, 15, 20–21
home in the Philippines, 219
progressive racial views of, 26
testimony at congressional hearing, 24
vases Hirohito's grandfather gave, 29
MacArthur, Arthur (DM's son), 9
birth certificate of, 3
birth of, 28
evacuation from Corregidor, 1, 5, 30
evacuation from Manila, 29, 406
Garcia's friendship with, 67–68, 366
godfather of, 28, 220
return to Manila, 434, 435, 436–37
MacArthur, Douglas
on artillery vs. bombing, 316
censorship of press, 391–92
at ceremony handing over power to
Osmeña, 409, 410–11
death of, 511
depression over the destruction of
Manila, 319
donation of Yamashita's sword to
West Point, 445
education of, 17–18, 26
efficiency reports on, 1, 19
egotism of, 20–21
evacuation from Corregidor, 1–3, 4–6,
9, 11, 30, 214, 406, 511
evacuation from Manila, 29–30, 61,
405, 406
family background of, 14–17, 19, 21
Filipina mistress of, 26–27
headquarters in San Miguel, 287–88
impatience with progress in retaking
Manila, 127–28, 130, 133
intellect of, 20
Irving Berlin's dedication to, 433
Japan and Germany's mocking of, 4,
11, 12
at Japan's surrender ceremony, 443
jealousy of Eisenhower, 129–30
lax attitude about venereal diseases
among troops, 431
on Leyte victory, 51
Luzon campaign
comments to journalists after Lingayen invasion, 89–90
forty-day voyage for, 83
invasion plan for, 76–77, 79, 81, 82,
88
marriages of
first marriage, 18, 26
second marriage to Jean, 20, 27, 28,
434
military assignments in the Philippines, 25–26, 27

military honors and promotions, 18,
19
move into mansion in Santa Mesa
district, 435
order for all massacres to be investigated, 352
order for evacuation of Manila, 3, 29
order for Mudge to retake Manila, 127
penthouse in Manila Hotel, 3, 28, 57,
405, 406–8, 437
physical toll of war on, 1
premature declaration of victory in
the Philippines, 203–6, 208, 298, 391
progressive racial views of, 26–27
promise to return to the Philippines, 6,
11, 12–13
public image of, construction of, 130
reaction to father's death, 16
reception by Filipinos, 429, 510–11
return to Manila, 211
return to the Philippines, 9, 511
return visit to Corregidor, 412–15
statue on Corregidor of, 511
tour of Malacañan Palace, 219–20
victory parade planned in honor of,
130, 203, 207, 391, 412
visit to Balintawak Monument, 211–12
visit to Bilibid, 212–15
visit to Santo Tomas, 216–19
on war, 9
Yamashita's case and
order for Yamashita's execution,
501–2, 503, 504
U.S. Supreme Court and, 495, 497–98
war crimes trial and, 450, 460, 477,
478, 483, 493–94, 510
MacArthur, Jean Faircloth, 13
evacuation from Corregidor, 1, 3, 5,
6, 30
evacuation from Manila, 29, 405–6
first home in Manila, 261
meeting Douglas, 20, 27
penthouse in Manila Hotel, 28, 405–6,
407–8, 437
return to Manila, 434–37
visits to Bilibid and Santo Tomas,
435–36
wedding of, 28
MacArthur, Malcolm, 17
MacArthur, Mary Pinkney Hardy
("Pinky"), 16–18, 19–20, 27–28, 410
Madrileno, Antonio, 332
Magtal, Ubaldo, 294
Mahan, Maynard, 398–99
Makapili, 66
Makati, 508

Malacañan Palace, 166, 219–20, 410
malaria, 3, 5, 441
Malate district
    destruction in, 427, 430
    First Cavalry Division's seizure of, 276
    Southern Force's defense of, 95
    St. Paul's College massacre in, 255–61,
        471
    wounded and dying refugees from,
        321–22
Malay, Armando, 487
Malaya
    Australia's interest in charging
        Yamashita for atrocities committed
        in, 462–63, 510
    rubber production in, 36
    Yamashita's defeat of the British in,
        30, 31, 99, 510
Malay Peninsula, 36, 38
    see also Malaya; Singapore
malnutrition, 3, 68, 72, 123, 170, 196, 214
Mañalac, Alfredo, 65
Mañalac, Fernando, 65, 69, 70, 72–73
Mango, Carl, 80
Manila
    in 1945, 59
    American hospitals opened to treat
        wounded people in, 312–13
    Binondo district, 180, 427
    Burnham's plan for, 56–57
    destruction from the battle in, 253,
        316–17, 426, 427–29, 511 (see also
        fires)
        cultural losses, 427–28
        economic losses, 428, 507
        municipal losses, 426–27
    Ermita district, see Ermita district
    founding of, 56
    housing crisis in, 435, 459
    Japanese Army's seizure of, 61–62, 131
    Japanese occupation of
        American air raids during, 72,
            99–100, 114–15, 211
        collapse of collective sense of moral-
            ity during, 74–75
        dwindling of basic goods during, 68
        fuel shortages during, 68–69
        guerrilla assassinations during,
            66–67
        guerrilla attacks on collaborators
            during, 66
        hunger during, 55–56, 70–71
        malnutrition during, 68, 72
        orphans during, 71–72
        puppet government installed during,
            63
        rape during, 66, 74
        rebranding process during, 62–64
        ruined economy during, 65–66, 67,
            73–75, 508
        starvation during, 5, 55, 73, 508
        suppression of populace during,
            64–65
        thefts during, 69–70, 73–74
        torture and beatings during, 66
        unemployment during, 65–66
    MacArthur's order for evacuation of,
        3, 29
    Malate district, see Malate district
    Paco district, see Paco district
    population of, on eve of World War
        I, 57
    prior to World War II, life in, 57–58,
        60, 507, 508
    racial prejudices in, 58, 60
    Santa Ana district, see Santa Ana
        district
    Santa Cruz district, 180, 312, 427, 484
    transportation in, 57–58
Manila, Battle of
    American forces' convergence to trap
        Japanese forces in, 343, 360, 368,
        376–77
    American troops' crossing of the Pasig
        River during, 225, 226, 227–29, 237,
        240–41, 250, 276, 313
    attacks against civilians suspected of
        guerrilla ties during, 251, 252
    battles in Agriculture, Finance, and
        Legislature buildings during,
        415–19
    block-by-block combat of, 277, 287,
        360, 375
    deaths during, 422
        corpses populating urban wasteland
            from, 342, 363–64, 366
        stench from, 423–24
        survivors' burial of relatives and
            neighbors, 422–23
    devastation from artillery on refugees
        during, 316–17, 420, 426, 511–12
    as ending American imperialism in the
        Philippines, 507
    end of, 419
        clearing land mines after, 433
        Japanese hiding after, 432–33
    Intramuros during, Americans' seizure
        of, 276, 393–400, 402–3, 415
    Japanese troops' destruction of Manila
        during, 179–81 (see also fires)
    Japanese troops' sniping of civilians in
        public during, 248, 345, 346–47

Japanese' troops' use of urban land-
    scape in, 221, 276–77, 298, 317–18
liberation of Bilibid during, 177–79
liberation of Santo Tomas during,
    139–40, 143, 145–49
standoff with Japanese troops,
    149–50, 154–57, 164, 170–71
transformation into a military base,
    160, 164, 166, 216
massacres during
    American troops' discovery of tor-
        ture and, 351–53
    De La Salle massacre, 331–39, 366,
        464, 511
    at Dy Pac Lumberyard, 182–85,
        222–24
    in Fort Santiago's sealed dungeon,
        404–5
    German Club massacre, 279–82, 311,
        345, 508
    of men in front of Philippine Gen-
        eral Hospital, 311
    of men in Intramuros, 208, 211, 237,
        240, 377, 381–83, 393
    of men in Paco district, 289–95, 311,
        473
    Red Cross massacre, 305–10, 311,
        345, 464, 469–70
    Santo Domingo Church, massacre at
        ruins of, 323–24, 379–81, 471–72
    Shell Service Station, massacre
        behind, 311, 352–53, 473
    at Singalong death house, 293–95,
        473–74, 511
    small-scale atrocities against fami-
        lies, 345–47
    St. Paul's College massacre, 255–61,
        345
    Suloc massacre, 451
    Tabacalera Cigar and Cigarette
        Factory, massacre in yard of, 311,
        352–53
    use of fire in attempts to cover up,
        252, 352
mass graves used during, 224, 292–93,
    353, 388, 421, 423
medical care during
    Americans' opening of hospitals to
        provide, 312–13, 320
    struggle to provide, for wounded
        patients, 424–25
    wounded refugees seeking, at Santo
        Tomas, 295–97
Nichols Field battle during, 247, 248
Paco Railroad Station battle during,
    241–43, 244, 276–77

Philippine General Hospital battle
    during, 345, 369–73
pillboxes used by Japanese forces in,
    97, 98, 99, 241, 242, 247, 248, 277
Provisor Island battle during, 227,
    244–47, 250, 276–77
rapes during, see rape
Rizal Hall battle during, 374–76
sections of city controlled by each side
    during, 191–92, 201, 276, 315
shelling of Santo Tomas during,
    229–36, 299–301
survivors' physical and emotional
    wounds after, 511–12
survivors seeking loved ones after,
    420–22
see also American forces; intelligence
    forces, American; Japanese forces
Manila Cathedral
    explosives rigged in, 239
    Intramuros residents ordered to report
        to, 201
    massacre at, 381–83
    men taken from, to be massacred, 208,
        211, 237
Manila Chronicle, 472, 479, 491
Manila Electric Railway and Light Com-
    pany, 57–58
Manila Hotel, 29, 57, 508
    Americans' shelling of, 350–51,
        406–7
    battle to retake, 407–8
    description of, 57
    MacArthur's penthouse in, 3, 28, 57,
        405, 406–8, 437, 508
    opening of, 57
Manila Post, 459, 479, 503
Manila Times, 473, 490
Manlisik, Justina, 471
Mansell, Donald, 173–74, 176
Manzano, Jaime H., 55
Maranon, Joaquin, 452
Marcelo, Ana Maria, 308
Marcelo, Armando, 307
Marcelo, Carlos, 307
Marcelo, Ernesto, 307
Maria, Arcadius, 337
Maria, Maximin, 335–36
Marianas, 32, 44, 298
Marks, Deane, 318
Marshall, George, 11, 12–13
Marshall, Richard, 20
Martin, Frederick, 215
Martin, Robert, 206
Martinez, Pablo, 294
Mashbir, Sidney, 450

massacres and atrocities, 42
    American troops' discovery of, 351–53
    Batangas Province massacre, 464, 471, 474
    behind Shell Service Station, 311, 352–53, 473
    against civilians suspected of guerrilla ties, 251, 252
    during defeat of British in Singapore, 42–43
    De La Salle massacre, 331–39, 366, 464, 511
    of families at Dy Pac Lumberyard, 182–85, 222–24
    in Fort Santiago's sealed dungeon, mass starvation, 404–5
    German Club massacre, 279–82, 311, 345, 508
    near Tabacalera Cigar and Cigarette Factory, 311, 352–53
    Philippine General Hospital, killing of men in front of, 311
    of POWs on Palawan, 79–81, 464
    Red Cross massacre, 305–10, 311, 345, 464, 469–70
    Santo Domingo Church, massacre at ruins of, 323–24, 379–81, 471–72
    at Singalong death house, 293–95, 473–74, 511
    slaughter of men in Intramuros, 208, 211, 237, 240, 377, 381–83, 393
    slaughter of men in Paco district, 289–95, 311, 473
    small-scale atrocities by marauding troops attacking families, 345–46
    Sook Ching Massacre, 42–43
    St. Paul's College massacre, 255–61, 345
    Suloc massacre, 451
    survivors' physical and emotional wounds after, 511, 512
    by U.S. troops against Filipinos, 22–24
    use of fire to cover up, 252, 352
    in Yamashita's war crimes trial
        Bill of Particulars for atrocities in, 464, 466, 467
        prosecution on, 461
        testimony of survivors on, 469–70, 471–73
    see also torture
Mayfield, Frank, 167
McCracken, Alan, 196–97
McDaniel, Yates, 88
McDole, Glenn, 79, 80–81
McFie, Dorothy, 234–35
McFie, John, Jr., 234–35, 236
McKinley, William, 21–22, 24, 25

McMurray, Roy ("Bus""), 199
Mellnik, Steve, 3–4, 60
Memorare Manila 1945 Foundation, 512
Mendoza, Agapita, 224
Mendoza, Greta, 223
Mendoza, Manuel, 223–24
Mendoza, Ricardo, 223
Menoher, Charles T., 1
Merino, Fidel, 295
Meyers, Terry, 231–32
Michishita, Sohei, 451
Middelberg, Frank, 403, 404
Milagros (orphaned girl), 71–72, 272, 275
Milanes, Julieta, 473
Mindoro, 9, 50, 90, 112
mines
    Iwabuchi's battle plan using, 97, 98, 99, 133
    scouring Lingayen Gulf for, 84
    tank trap made of, 167
    see also land mines
Mintz, Lew, 228
Miranda, Pilar, 267
Mississippi, 89
Missouri, 443
Mitsui Mining Company, 67
Miyazawa, Hoichiro, 417
Monaghan, Forbes, 66, 100
Montaner, Enrique, 354
Montaner, Mrs., 354–55
Montano, Artemio, 423
Montano, Manuel, 423
Montano, Paciencia, 423
Montenegro, Elvira, 491
Montpellier, 86
Moore, George, 5
Moore, Inez, 108, 110
Moras, Esther Garcia, 262–65, 471
Moreno, Isabelita, 400
Moreta, Rafael, 346
Moretti, Joseph, 84
Morgan, Margaret, 209
Morse, William, 29
Mountz, George
    on Judge's lack legal knowledge, 476
    on moment of levity during Yamashita trial, 474
    on verdict in Yamashita's trial, 478
    on Yamashita at his arraignment, 462
    on Yamashita's reactions during trial, 475
Mucci, Henry, 129
Mudge, Verne, 135, 160, 212
    MacArthur's order to retake Manila, 127

plan for seizure of Manila, 132–33
selection of journalists to accompany
    cavalry to Manila, 127, 130–31,
    132, 134
Murphy, Frank, 493, 498, 499–500
Mussolini, Benito, 11
mutilation
    among survivors at Santo Tomas, 296
    of dead American troops, 134, 374
    at De La Salle massacre, 332, 334, 339
    difficulty identifying bodies in, 223
    at Dy Pac Lumberyard massacre, 183
    at Fort Santiago, 210, 401
    in German Club massacre, 280, 282
    in Indian Wars, 22
    physical and emotional wounds after,
        511, 512
    in Singalong death house, 293–95, 473
    testimony of survivors on, 468, 471,
        473, 474
Muto, Akira, 478
    on Americans' landing at Lingayen, 91
    appointment to Philippines, 47–48
    defense of Yamashita in later writings,
        509
    execution of, 509
    imprisonment of, 445, 448, 455
    on lack of knowledge of conditions in
        the Philippines, 48
    on living in the jungle, 441–42
    as part of Yamashita's defense coun-
        sel, 463–64, 476
    reaction to method of execution, 491
    reaction to indictment of Yamashita,
        457
    on supply shortages from the Leyte
        campaign, 52–53
    surrender to Americans, 443–44, 445,
        446–48
    testimony at Yamashita's trial, 478
    on U.S. planes hindering battle prepa-
        rations, 52
    at Yamashita's first meeting with his
        defense team, 457
    Yamashita's last command to, 492
    on Yamashita's snoring, 54
Mydans, Carl, 81
    as an internee at Santo Tomas, 104,
        106, 108, 131
    on arrival of Japanese troops into
        Manila, 61
    on artillery observation post, 348
    on Brady's negotiation with Hayashi,
        171
    on Hewlett's search for his wife,
        131–32, 138–41
    on Japanese troops' departure from
        Santo Tomas, 186–87, 188, 189–90
    on liberation of Santo Tomas, 139–40,
        169–70
    on MacArthur's oratorical skills, 20
    on physical condition of internees,
        168–69
    on refugees not complaining, 387–88
    riding with First Cavalry into Manila,
        131, 135–40, 169–70
    on struggle to adjust at Santo Tomas,
        193
Mydans, Shelley, 131–32, 141
Myers, Terry, 103

Nadonga, Santiago, 211
Nagako, Empress, 46
Nagano, Osami, 44
Nagasaki, atomic attack on, 441
nail treatment as torture, 210
Nakpil, Carmen Guerrero, 74–75, 428
Nanking Massacre, 61, 99, 481, 509,
    510
Narwhal, 95
National City Bank of New York build-
    ing, 347
National Mall, 56
National Museum of Fine Arts, 508
Navarro, Adela, 285, 286
Navarro, Angela, 286
Navarro, Concepcion, 286
Navarro, Joaquin, 285, 286–87
Navarro, Joaquin, Jr., 281, 285, 286
Navarro, Natividad, 286
Navarro, Pilar, 286
Nazareno, Rodolfo, 447
New Guinea, 12, 13, 30, 32, 246, 298
Newland, Vernon, 154
New Mexico, 10, 83
Newsweek, 203, 462, 464, 475
New York Times, 206
    on MacArthur in Manila, 203
    on Supreme Court's ruling on
        Yamashita case, 500
    on witness testimony in Yamashita's
        trial, 471, 472, 473
Nichols Field, 95, 114, 247, 248, 250
Nielsen, Eugene, 79, 80, 81
Nieves, Balbina, 324
Nieves, Rosario, 324
Nixon, Eva Anna, 116, 200, 229–30, 236,
    300–301
Noble, Corazon, 303, 305, 309, 310,
    469–70
Noguchi, Katsuzo, 95, 182, 199, 208, 225,
    237, 250, 418

Northern Force, 95, 250, 418
　　detonation of buildings, 198, 225
　　hunkering down behind walls of Intra-
　　　muros, 377
　　Iwabuchi's orders to blow Ayala and
　　　Quezon bridges, 167
　　retreat across the river to form second
　　　line of defense, 179
Norver, Barnet, 204
Nuremburg trial, 495–96

Ohashi, Shizuo, 149, 150, 479
Ohaus, Martin, 280
Okochi, Denshichi, 94, 287, 344, 446, 448
O'Laughlin, Cal, 28
Olmsted, Frederick Law, Jr., 56
Ommaney Bay, 10, 86
Opinion, Glicerio, 461
Orendain, Joan, 68, 72, 508
Osaka Mainichi, 43
Osborn, John, 297, 384, 409, 422
Osmeña, Emilio, 462
Osmeña, Esperanza, 412, 436, 461–62,
　　470
Osmeña, Mary, 462
Osmeña, Rosie, 462
Osmeña, Sergio, 130, 288
　　background of, 409
　　ceremony for handing over power to,
　　　409, 410–11
　　leaflets dropped from planes with
　　　message from, 90
　　MacArthur's friendship with, 25, 436
　　on verdict in Yamashita's trial, 491
Owens, Russell, 57
Ozaeta, Ramon, 494

Paco district
　　destruction in, 427
　　fires in, 295, *439*
　　massacre of men in, 289–95, 311, 473
　　photo of wounded refugee in, *439*
　　Southern Force's defense of, 95, 97
　　Thirty-Seventh Infantry's seizure of,
　　　276
Paco Railroad Station, battle for, 241–43,
　　244, 276–77
Palawan, massacre of POWs on, 79–81,
　　464
Palmer, Rita, 142
Pangan, Narda, 371
Parrott, Lindesay, 206
Pasig River
　　American troops' crossing of, 250, 313
　　First Cavalry Division, 225, *226*, 227,
　　　228, 237, 276

129th Infantry Regiment, 227,
　　240–41
148th Infantry Regiment, 227
Thirty-Seventh Infantry, 225, *226*,
　　227, 237
　　bisecting of Manila, 57
　　explosion of bridges over, 95, 99, 167
Patric, James, 85, 87
Patriotic Association of Filipinos, 66
Patterson, Robert, 495
Patton, George, 204
Paul, Paternus, 335
Paulino, Carlos, 138
Pearl Harbor, attack on, 64, 441, 486
Pedret, Jose Sansó, 367
Peña, Delphino, 188–89
Pena, Renee, 239
Pennsylvania, 7
Percival, Arthur, 40–42, 446, 447, 448
Perez-Rubio, Carlos, 346, 422
Pershing, John, 18, 20, 204
Pestaño-Jacinto, Pacita, 31, 63, 209
　　on fears under Japanese occupation,
　　　61
　　on food shortage, 71
　　on Japanese' distrust of Filipinos, 64
　　on Japanese' reaction to defeat, 101
　　on Japanese' use of civilians property,
　　　62
　　on starvation, 73
　　on thefts, 69, 70
Petillo, Carol, 25, 26–27
Philippine Detention and Rehabilitation
　　Center, 504
Philippine General Hospital, 238
　　Americans' liberation of, 372–73
　　artillery attacks on, 369, 370, 371, 372
　　battle at, 372
　　description of, 57
　　hostages at, 369
　　Iwabuchi's plan for men to hunker
　　　down at, 345
　　men massacred in front of, 311
　　patient records lost at, 427
　　rapes at, 370, 371
Philippine National Library and
　　Museum, 427
Philippines
　　America's early involvement in massa-
　　　cres and atrocities in, 22–24
　　independence of, 507, 511
　　Japanese occupation of, *see* Manila:
　　　Japanese occupation of
　　Spanish-American War and, 21–22
Philippine Supreme Court, 493–94
Pho, Yu Cheng, 181

pillboxes used by Japanese forces, 277
   construction of, 97, *98*, 99, 277
   in Nichols Field battle, 247, 248
   in Paco Railroad Station battle, 241,
      242
Pimentel, Leonora Fajardo, 223
Pimentel, Venancio, 183
Pincoffs, Maurice, 424–25
Pitchek, Frank, 402
Plata, Felix, 294
Plazuela de Santa Isabel, 512–13
Poe, Fernando, 433
Pons, Bartolome, 352
Pons, Rosario, 352
Pope, Jean, 71
Pownall, Henry, 42
POWs, *see* prisoners of war (POWs)
Price, Ed, 154–55
Price, Walter, 346
Prince of Wales, 39
Prising, Frederick, 120, 144, 300
Prising, Marie, 120, 148, 152, 300
Prising, Robin
   on anxiety waiting for rescue, 123
   on attacks on Abiko, 150–51
   on conditions outside Santo Tomas
      after liberation, 168
   on death of American soldier friend,
      299
   on flyover before liberation, 144
   on food at Santo Tomas, 116–17, 163
   on hunger at Santo Tomas, 113, 114,
      120
   on internees raising of American flag,
      191
   on John Shaw, 122–23
   on liberation of Santo Tomas, 148
   on MacArthur's visit to Santo Tomas,
      218
   reaction to survivors, 430
   on refugee's laughter while watching
      movie, 383–84
   on sex between female internees and
      American soldiers, 430
   on shelling of Santo Tomas, 300
   on toll of starvation, 118
   on transformation of Santo Tomas to
      military base, 164
   on wounded refugees at Santo Tomas,
      297
prisoners of war (POWs)
   American fighter pilot captured by
      Yamashita's forces, 442
   MacArthur's worry over fate of, with
      slow progress, 77, 79, 81, 128–29
   on Palawan, massacre of, 79–81, 464

paraded through streets on way to
      Bilibid, 64–65, 77
   Yamashita's decision to turn over, 53
prostitutes, 103, 108, 267, 431, 432, 459
Provido, Generoso, 210
Provisor Island, battle for, 227, 244–47,
      250, 276–77
Puerto Rico, 22
Punzalan, Josefina, 256–57, 258
Punzalan, Marcelino, 259
Pu Yi, Henry, 45

Querubin, Erlinda, 76, 266, 267
Quezon, Aurora, 220
Quezon, Manuel, 25, 28, 29, 220, 409
Quirino, Alicia, 388, 509
Quirino, Armando, 388, 509
Quirino, Elpidio, 388, 509
Quirino, Fe, 388, 509
Quirino, Norma, 388, 509

Racho, Loreto Franco, 512
racial prejudices in Manila, 58, 60
racism of U.S. troops against Filipinos,
      22–24
Ramirez, Julio, 293
Ramis, Benjamin, 317
Ramis, Francisco, 317
rape
   at the Bay View Hotel, 261–68, 449,
      450, 471
   in De La Salle massacre, 338
   fear of, 66
   in German Club massacre, 280, 282
   in Intramuros, 201, 377
   in Leyte, 134
   during occupation of Manila, 66, 74
   at Philippine General Hospital, 370,
      371
   at San Agustin Church, 377
   venereal diseases after, 425
   victims feelings of dishonor after, 450
   in war crimes trial of Yamashita
      Bill of Particulars on, 467, 468
      difficulty of interviews about, 450
      testimony of survivors on, 471
Rape of Nanking, *see* Nanking Mas-
      sacre
Red Cross
   black market for medical supplies
      from, 269
   food and medicine supplied to Santo
      Tomas, 105
   headquarters as refugee center and
      emergency hospital, 302, 304–5
   letters delivered to Santo Tomas, 192

Red Cross massacre, 305–10, 311, 345, 464, 469–70
Reed, Thomas, 22
Reel, Frank, 454
on allowance of third and fourth degree hearsay testimony, 476
The Case of General Yamashita, 510
final arguments of, 484
first meeting with Yamashita, 457–58
on judges in Yamashita trial, 461
on need for personal vengeance, 475
oral arguments presented to the U.S. Supreme Court, 496, 497
on order for MacArthur to postpone Yamashita's execution, 495
on preparing for trial, 465
reaction to verdict, 491
request for a continuance, 468
on supplemental Bill of Particulars, 466
on Truman's refusal to intervene, 503
on Yamashita's behavior before the verdict, 487
Yamashita's gift to, 492
Reese, John, 242–43
Repulse, 39
Rexroad, Charles, 505, 506
Reyes, Amparing, 271, 272, 273–74, 275–76, 359
Reyes, Josefina, 66
Reyes, Lourdes
on American liberation, 359
on crowds' plundering of home, 73–74
on father's plan to hide family, 271
on fires, 203
hiding under makeshift lean-to, 274–76, 326, 358
on Japanese's merciless flogging of family horse, 271
on Japanese rounding up men from homes, 249–50
life before Japanese occupation of Manila, 67
massacre of family of, 272–74
on Milagros, 71–72
on return to family home, 425–26
watching the battle, 162–63
Reyes, Luis, 271, 272
Reyes, Nicanor ("Nick")
crowds' plundering of home of, 73–74
mansion of, 67, 270
moving of family during fires, 202–3
murder of, 272, 273–74, 359, 449
orphaned girl taken in by, 71–72
plan to hide family, 271

reaction to Japanese rounding up men from homes, 249–50
struggle to support family, 67, 69
Reyes, Teresita ("Ching"), 67, 271, 272, 273, 426
Reynolds, Russel, 460, 476, 510
at arraignment, 463–64
delivery of verdict, 490
directions about final arguments, 482–83
on judges' pact to never speak publicly about the trial, 488, 510
lack of legal training, 463–64, 476
remarks before verdict, 488–89
ruling on defense's request for a continuance, 468
Rhapsody in Blue, 383
Rhoades, Weldon ("Dusty"), 198
Rice, Clara, 256
Rieper, Rose, 159
right to due process, 499
Ripka, Percy, 155
Rivera, Aquilino, 291–92
Rivera, Arturo, 291
Rivera, Godofredo, 291
Rizal Hall, 374–76
Rizal Memorial Stadium, 326, 345, 361, 368, 433
Roach, J. K., 496
Robb, Robert, 154, 156–57
Roberts, Joseph, 412
Roberts, Kenneth, 158
Robertson, Frank, 158–60, 170, 217
Robinet, Alex, 443
Robinson, Hugh, 132
Robinson, Pat, 466, 486
Robohm, John, 349–50
Rocamora, Julio, 383, 398
Rocha, Juan Jose P., 511–12
Rocque, Louis, 424
Rodriguez, Alfonso, 283
Rodriguez, Alvaro, 283
Rodriguez, Augusto, 283
Rodriguez, Helena, 282–85, 450
Rodriguez, Remedios, 283, 284
Rodriguez, Vicente, 283, 284
Rodriquez, Cleto ("Chico"), 242–43
Rogers, Paul, 424
on Bataan and MacArthur, 11
on disposal of bodies on Corregidor, 414
on Filipinos reactions to MacArthur, 429
on MacArthur's censorship of the press, 391–92
on Manila burning during evacuation, 30
on seizure of Intramuros, 396

Roka, Tressa
    on Abiko's death, 153
    on American air raids, 114–15
    on arrival of doctors and nurses from
        Leyte, 296
    on constant artillery fire, 385
    on deaths at Santo Tomas, 122
    on exploring Malate and Ermita after
        the battle, 430
    on flyover before liberation, 143
    on food at Santo Tomas, 116, 192,
        268, 384
    on fortifications of Santo Tomas, 160
    on hunger, 102, 113, 117
    illness at Santo Tomas, 165
    on inequality among internees at, 110
    on liberation of Santo Tomas, 145,
        146–47
    on loss of hope U.S. forces would
        return, 121
    on popularity of soldiers, 158, 166
    on shelling of Santo Tomas, 234–35
    on soldiers' exhaustion, 298
    on sounds of battle nearing Manila,
        123
    on starvation, 118, 119–20
    on watching newsreels, 383
Romanus, Lambert, 330, 335
Romero, Jose, 60
Romulo, Carlos, 412, 467
Roosevelt, Franklin, 288
    decision to intern Japanese Ameri-
        cans, 496
    MacArthur's berating of, on returning
        to Manila, 13, 288
    on MacArthur's egotism, 21
    Marshall's recommendation of
        MacArthur for Medal of Honor
        to, 12
    order for MacArthur to evacuate
        Corregidor, 2, 220
    reaction to news of Manila's fall, 204
Root, Elihu, 25
Rosario, Francisco del, 224, 295
Rosario, Mariano del, 224, 423
Rosenberg, Ira, 348–49
Ruggio, Serifine, 352
Rutledge, Wiley, 496, 498–500, 501

Salang, Anselmo, 371
Salonga, Fortunata, 333, 338
Sams, Margaret, 106
San Agustin Church
    artillery attacks on, 377–78
    burning of adjoining convent to,
        239–40

Intramuros residents ordered to report
    to, 201
refugees escape from, 399–400
refugees taken from, to be massacred,
    237, 377, 381
Sandberg, Milton, 127, 454, 483–84, 492,
    496
San Fabian, 88–89, 91
sanitation
    in Manila, after battle, 426
    at Santo Tomas, 105–6
San Juan, Corazon, 185
San Juan, Cresencio, 184
San Juan, Jose, 184–85
San Juan, Ricardo, 182–83, 184–85, 222
San Juan, Virginia, 182, 184, 185, 222
San Juan de Dios Hospital, 238, 323,
    380, 402
Santa Ana district
    Americans' capture of, 276
    artillery damage in, 249
    displaced refugees in, 321–22, 358,
        363, 364, 389
    priest and nuns hung in, 364–65
Santa Cruz district, 180, 312, 427, 484
Santa Rosa College
    evacuation of refugees to, 238–39, 323
    massacre of refugees from, 379–80,
        381
Santo Domingo Church, massacre at
    ruins of, 323–24, 379–81, 471–72
Santos, Amelia, 307
Santos, Angie Abad, 512
Santos, Dominador, 180
Santos, Edward, 307
Santo Tomas internment camp, 77, 112
    American air raids as raising spirits
        at, 114–16
    deaths at, 103, 113, 117–18, 122–23,
        216, 231–36, 299
    Douglas MacArthur's visit to, 216–19
    emotional trauma of, on non-intern-
        ees, 194–96
    escape from, 104
    food at, 102, 104–5, 110, 112, 114
        after liberation, 158–60, 165–66, 192,
            268–69, 384–85
        declining average caloric intake, 119
        ethical dilemmas for doctors about,
            121–22
        food theft, 118, 121
        sources of, out of desperation,
            116–17, 121
    funerals at, 122
    grounds of, 109
    internal broadcast system at, 112, 116

Santo Tomas internment camp
(*continued*)
Japanese' departure from, 186–90
Japanese guards' abuse at, 150
Jean MacArthur's visit to, 435–36
liberation of, 139–40, 142–43, 145–49,
169–70, 173, 190–91
Americans' standoff with Japanese
after, 149–50, 154–57
anticipation before, 143–45
female internees' relationships with
American soldiers after, 166, 430
fortification of camp after, 160, 166,
216
Hayashi's negotiation of surrender
after, 149–50, 155
Internees' selling of Red Cross medical supplies after, 269
inventory of, after, 196
letters received by internees after,
192–93
transformation into a military base
after, 160, 164, 166, 216
transformation to military base after,
164
MacArthur's aides visit to, 194–96
MacArthur's worry over fate of,
128–29
medical care at, 105, 121
after liberation, 161, 164–65, 215–16,
233–34
wounded refugees seeking, 295–97
mental toll of internment on internees
at, 106–8, 110–12
anxiety/hope waiting for rescue, 123
inequality among internees at, 110
internees resorting to fantasy due to,
119–20
internees separated from family
members at, 110–12
irritability from hunger, 113
loss of hope for rescue, 121
mental breakdowns, 120, 131–32
nothing to look forward to, 108, 110
overcrowding and, 106–7
from shelling of Santo Tomas,
300–301
suicide attempts, 120
mix of internees at, 103–4, 110
physical condition of internees at, 105
beriberi, 113–14, 121, 168
dysentery and diarrhea, 121
hunger, 102, 112–14, 118, 120–21
starvation among internees at, 102,
103, 113, 116, 118–21, 123, 161,
215–16

recreation organized at, 108, 118–19,
383–84
required daily work at, 106
sanitation at, 105–6
school at, 107, 118
shanties at, 106–7
shelling of, 229–36, 299–301
small city within, 104–7, *109*
testimony at Yamashita's trial on, 479
U.S. civilians rounded up and taken
to, 62, 77
Sapinoso, Beatriz, 471
Sato, Ichiro, 451
Sato, Masahiko, 79
Sayre, Francis, 467
Sayson, Antonio, 509
Schedler, Dean
escape from Corregidor, 131
on MacArthur's return visit to Corregidor, 413–14
riding with First Cavalry into Manila,
131, 136, 137, 140
at Yamashita's trial, 487
Schwartz, Robert, 477
Seals, Carl, 195
Seals, Margaret, 195, 217
Second Battalion, 241
Sedro, Ismael, 450–51
Sepulveda, Salvador, 256
Sepulveda, Serafin, 257
Sepulveda, Virginia, 259
sexual assault, *see* rape
sexual torture, 210
Shacklette, Edith, 218, 235
Shannon, Francis, Jr., 348
Shaplen, Robert, 312
on artillery observation post, 348
on difficulty of interviewing refugees,
386
on military commission of Yamashi-
ta's trial, 477
on verdict in Yamashita's trial, 490
on wounded refugees, 388–89
on Yamashita's testimony, 480
Sharpe, George, 426, 432
Shaw, John, 122–23
Shell Service Station, massacre behind,
311, 352–53, 473
Sherman, William, 14
Shimbu Group, 52, 250–51, 456
Iwabuchi's dispatch to, 311
on progress of counterattacks, 344
as tasked with completing evacuation
of supplies from Manila, 54
territory defended by, 52
Yokoyama as leader of, 52, 94, 509

Shobu Group, 52
Shulter, Sayre, 229
Siguenza, Pacita, 377
Siguenza, Sebastian, 399, 400
Silen, Bert, 164
Simmie, George, 422–23
Simmons, Walter, 389, 390
    on artillery observation post, 349
    on MacArthur's visit to Santo Tomas,
        217
    on mass graves, 388
Simon, Daniel, 223
Singalong death house, 293–95, 473–74,
    511
Singapore
    atrocities by Japanese forces in, 42–43,
        99
    British naval base at, 36–38
    Japans defeat of British in, 30, 31, 36,
        37–42, 43
        atrocities during and after, 42–43,
            99, 481
        British surrender to Japan, 40–42,
            446
        casualties in, 40
Sison, Antonio, 370
Sixth Army, 77, 85, 127, 246, 413
    report on battle for Provisor Island,
        246
    report on enemy intending to destroy
        or possibly pollute water for Manila
        area, 192
    report on the Luzon campaign, 85,
        125, 246, 413
Smith, Charles, 79
Smith, J. W., 496
Smith, Jacob ("Hell-Roaring Jake"),
    23–24
Smith, Paul, 222
Smith, Robert Ross, 417, 419, 432
Solomon, Elaine, 219
Sook Ching Massacre, 42–43
Soriano, Andres, 212, 220, 222, 406, 410,
    434
South Dakota, 93
Southern Force, 95, 225, 247, 509
South Seas Caper, 433
Spain, 21–22, 138, 456
Spanish-American War, 21–22
Spanish Inquisition, 209
Sparnon, Norman James, 476–77, 479,
    486–87
"squaw men," 60
St. George, Ozzie, 87, 348, 350, 363,
    385–86
St. Louis Star-Times, 501

St. Paul's College massacre, 255–61, 345
Stanley, Ernest, 149, 187, 189
Star Reporter, 491
starvation
    among internees at Santo Tomas, 102,
        103, 113, 116, 118–21, 123, 161,
        215–16
    soldiers' reactions to, at liberation
        of, 147, 163
    testimony at Yamashita's trial on,
        479
    Japanese forces use of, as a weapon,
        112–14, 119, 404
    in Manila under Japanese occupation,
        55, 73, 508
Stauffer, Tank, 241
Steiner, Hans, 316
Stevens, Frederick, 233, 235
Stevenson, Ted, 123, 151–52, 161
Stewart, Robert, 486
Stimson, Henry, 204
Stirling, Yates, 23
Stone, Edmund, 454
Stone, Harlan Fiske, 495–96, 497, 498
Stratton, Samuel, 455
Streegan, Emil, 284
Streegan, Inez, 284
Stroup, Russell, 88
Styer, William, 503–4
    Reynolds' mention of, in directions
        about final arguments, 483
    at Yamashita's arraignment, 461
    at Yamashita's formal ceremony for
        surrender, 447, 448
Suarez, Virginio, 293–94
suicide
    attempts by Santo Tomas internees,
        120
    see also kamikaze attacks
Suloc massacre, 451
Sunada, Shigemasa, 478
Supreme Court, U.S., *see* U.S. Supreme
    Court
Supreme Court Library, 427
Sutherland, Dick, 89, 128, 412
Sutton, James, 137–38
Suzuki, Sosaku, 50
Swan, William, 318
Swift, Innis, 77
Swordfish, 220
Syyonping, Jose, 210

Tabacalera Cigar and Cigarette Factory,
    massacre in yard of, 311, 352–53
Tabaque, Isabel, 308
Taft, William, 15, 25, 56, 120

Tama Reien Cemetery, 508
Tamayo, Juanita, 333, 337–38
Tani, Lucy, 262
Tanquilot, Jose, 294
Tapia, Pacita, 264, 265
Taylor, Archie, 108
Templeton, Sgt., 315
Terauchi, Hisaichi, 49, 50, 53
thefts in Manila during Japanese occupation, 69–70, 73–74
Third Battalion, 241
    see also American forces: 148th Infantry Regiment
Third Fleet, 114
Thirty-Eighth Infantry Division, 212
Thirty-Second Infantry Division, 442, 443, 445
Thirty-Seventh Infantry Division, 340, 368
    advance on Manila, 78, 165
    arrival in Manila, 165
    convergence to trap Japanese forces in Manila, 343, 360
    crossing of the Pasig River, 225, 226, 227, 237
    on eve of Luzan invasion, 84
    liberation of Bilibid, 177–79, 197
    reports of
        on evacuation of Philippine General Hospital, 373
        on explosion from artillery duds and mines collected after Battle of Manila, 433
        on Fort Santiago, 402–3
        on tedious process of securing the General Post Office by Intramuros, 394
        on venereal disease rates from troops visiting brothels, 431
    sector of Manila responsible for, 192, 276, 315
Thomas, Shenton, 38
Thompson, James, 172, 176
Time magazine, 462, 472, 482
Tojo, Hideki
    execution of, 509
    on Japan refusing to surrender to any nation, 33
    ouster of, 44
    rivalry with Yamashita, 34–35, 36, 43–44, 46
Tokyo, firebombing of, 441
Tokyo Rose, 4
Tolentino, Leoncio, 471
Tormey, Mary, 400
Torres, Antonio, 314

torture
    burning to death people while still alive, 79, 80–81, 377, 403, 512
    burns with cigarettes, 471
    of captured cavalryman Henry Clark, 374
    on collaborators during Japanese occupation of Manila, 66
    in De La Salle massacre, 331–36, 338–39
    in Dy Pac Lumberyard massacre, 182–85
    at Fort Santiago, 209–10, 402, 404–5
    in German Club massacre, 279–82
    in massacre of POWs on Palawan, 79–81
    nail treatment, 210
    during occupation of Manila, 66
    in Santo Domingo Church massacre, 323–24
    of Santo Tomas internees, 150
    sexual torture, 210
    survivors discovery of, on bodies of, 421
    survivors' physical and emotional wounds after, 511, 512
    of U.S. troops left in Philippines, 5
    waterboarding, 24, 209–10, 511
    see also rape
Trinidad, Ricardo, 183
Trinidad, Tony, 378
Truman, Harry, 502–3
Trumbull, Robert, 460, 474
Tsuji, Masanobu, 38, 39, 41
Tsukada, Rikichi, 52
Tupas, Rodolfo, 71
Twelfth Cavalry Regiment, 360–61, 368

Ullom, Madeline, 108
Umezu, Yoshijiro, 46
Umstad, Henry, 122
unemployment during Japanese occupation of Manila, 65–66
Union Station in Washington, 56
University of Manila, killings at, 381
University of Santo Tomas
    founding of, 103
    internment camp at, see Santo Tomas internment camp
University of the Philippines, 361, 369, 373–76
Urrutia, Benjamin, 292–93
U.S. Army Corps of Engineers, 428
U.S. forces, see American forces
U.S. Supreme Court
    decision against Yamashita, 498–500

defense team's appeal to, 494–95, 496, 497
defense team's oral arguments before, 496, 497
justices' debate whether to hear Yamashita's case, 495–96
order staying execution of, 495
press reviews of decision on Yamashita's case, 500–501
Utsunomiya, Naokata, 445, 457, 463
Uychuico, Clemente, 329, 330

Valdes, Alejo, 251, 421
Valdes, Armando, 421
Valdes, Basilio, 410
Valdes, Ramon, 421
Valdez, Teodoro, 294
Valencia, Al, 487
Vanderboget, Carlton, 175, 176
Van Sickle, Emily, 159, 160, 236, 298
Vasquez-Prada, Alfonso, 332
Vasquez-Prada, Enrique, 329, 332, 339
Vasquez-Prada, Fernando, 330, 332, 336–37, 338–39, 366, 511
Vasquez-Prada, Helen, 325, 329, 330, 332, 336–39, 340, 366
Vasquez-Prada, Herman, 332
Vaughan, Elizabeth, 104, 111–12, 115, 214
Vazquez, Daniel, 256
Vazquez, Luis, 256
Velarde, Herminio, 260–61
Velde, Joyce Brady, 72, 74
Venecia, German de, 304–5, 306–7
venereal diseases
    after rape by Japanese soldiers, 425
    increase in, among troops visiting brothels, 431
Virata, Nelly de Jesus, 239, 377
Viri, Fructuoso, 182–83

Wack Wack Golf and Country Club, 60, 315, 432
Wainwright, Jonathan, 2, 447, 448
Waller, Littleton, 23–24
Walsh, James T., 253
war crimes, German, Nuremburg trial prosecuting, 495–96
war crimes trial of Yamashita
    American investigators' preparation for, 448–53, 465
    deciphered Japanese orders, letters, and diaries, 449
    identification of list of major atrocities, 449
    interviews with Japanese survivors/soldiers, 451, 452–53

interviews with victims, 448–49, 450–51, 452
report created for each atrocity, 449, 452
arraignment of Yamashita, 459, 460–65
Bill of Particulars in, 464, 466, 467–68
charge in, 457
defense team for Yamashita in, 454
    challenges for, 475–76
    final arguments of, 483–84
    first meeting with Yamashita, 454, 455, 456–59
    preparation for trial, 465–66
    reaction to verdict, 490–91
    request for a continuance, 466, 468
    Reynolds' remarks before verdict about, 488–89
    witnesses for, 478–80
evidentiary elasticity in, 460, 476–77, 509–10
judges in
    as anxious to wrap up the trial as soon as possible, 470
    background of, 460–61, 494
    pact to never speak publicly about the trial, 488, 510
    reading of verdict, 490
    remarks before reading of verdict, 488–89
    as subordinate to MacArthur, 460, 477, 510
press on, 462, 468, 470, 472–75, 477–80, 482, 486, 490
prosecution in
    background of, 461
    closing statements of, 484–85
    cross-examination of defense witness, 479
    cross-examination of Yamashita, 480–82
    opening arguments of, 468–69
    witnesses for, 469–73, 471–73, 476
spectators for, 467, 470, 482, 486, 490
translators required for, 467
verdict in, 486–87
    reactions to, 490–91
    Reynolds delivery of, 490
    Yamashita's prepared statement before, 489
War Damage Corporation, 427
War of 1812, 61
Wasatch, 87
Washington, 93
Washington Post, 203, 204, 454, 500–501
waterboarding, 24, 209–10, 511

Weidmann, William, 157
Welborn, Betty, 141
West, George, 245
West, Leon, 349
Whitaker, Paul, 193
White, Lawrence, 317
Whitney, Courtney, 86–87, 194, 195–96, 200, 411
Wilkins, Ford, 191
Wilkinson, Rupert, 156–57
William, Mutwald, 335
Williams, Anna, 119
Williams, Denny
    on attacks on Abiko, 151, 152
    on fires in Manila, 200
    on internees raising of American flag, 191
    on Japanese troops' departure, 187
    on liberation of Santo Tomas, 147–48, 161, 164, 165
    on shanties at Santo Tomas, 106
Willoughby, Charles, 13, 128, 432
Wilson, Sam, 190
Wilson, Warren, 174–75, 176, 178–79, 212, 215
Winship, Theodore, 179
Witthoff, Evelyn, 230
Wood, Walter, Jr., 447
Wygle, Peter, 150, 296–97, 300
Wygle, Robert
    on aggravation of smelling rich internees' food, 110
    on constant artillery fire, 385
    on destruction of Manila, 429
    on fire in Manila, 269–70
    on night of Santo Tomas' liberation, 158, 159
    on shelling of Santo Tomas, 299

Xavier, Egbert, 100, 325, 329, 330
XI Corps, *78*
XIV Corps, 77, *78*, 85, 395, 416, 453
    see also First Cavalry Division; Thirty-Seventh Infantry Division

Yamashita, Hisako, 33, 46, 508
    on husband's departure for Philippines, 45
    husband's farewell to, before departing for Singapore, 37
    husband's inability to leave Tokyo to visit, 44
    husband's letter to, after Americans' landing at Lingayen Gulf, 91
    on MacArthur's order of execution of husband, 502

petition to American government for husband's remains, 508
statement after verdict in husband's trial, 491
Yamashita, Tomoyoshi, 33
Yamashita, Tomoyuki
    affair with German woman, 33–34, 35
    American troops' hunt for, 432, 441, 448
    at Bilibid, 448, 467
    burial in Tama Reien Cemetery in Tokyo, 508
    claim of ignorance of any atrocities, 455–56, 480, 481, 490
    claim that poor communications left him ignorant of the battle, 287, 456, 481, 485
    as commander in the Philippines, 92, 287
        appointment, 44–45, 94
        Battle of Leyte, 49–51
        censuring of Yokoyama for failing to rein in Iwabuchi, 343
        concerns about defense strategy at Tokyo meeting, 45–46
        decision to turn over POWs and internees, 53
        defense strategy for Luzon, 51–52
        at Fort McKinley, 47–49, 53–54, 133
        at Ipo, 53, 54, 287
        as leader of the Shobu Group, 52
        order for all Japanese women and children to return Japan, 53
        order for Iwabuchi to withdraw from Manila, 343–44
        threats in the press against Filipinos fighting against Japan, 47
        view of assignment as destined for defeat, 45–46, 47–48
    defeat of British in Singapore, 30, 31, 36, 37–38, 39–42, 99, 446
    defense team and, 454, 455, 458, 491–92
    execution of, 495, 501–6, 511
    family background of, 32–33, 42
    interview with press before trial, 466
    Manchuria assignment of, 43–44
    military career of, 33–36, 43–44
    nicknames of, 31, 43
    opposition to Japan entering the war, 35–36
    physical description of, 31, 457
    poetry written by, 32, 37, 442, 504
    reaction to verdict, 490
    reaction to indictment as a war criminal, 457
    reputation as an eccentric officer, 34
    role in Sook Ching Massacre, 42–43

snoring of, 54
study of MacArthur as an opponent, 49
surrender to Americans, 442–48
Tojo and, 34–35, 36, 43–44, 509
transfer to Luzon Prisoner of War
    Camp, 492
war crimes trial of, *see* war crimes
    trial of Yamashita
Yank magazine, 467, 468
Yap, Twan, 182, 183
Yette, Joe, 108
Yokoyama, Shizuo, 52, 94, 456
    forwarding of Iwabuchi's daily reports
        to Yamashita, 287
    Iwabuchi's daily reports sent to,
        250–51

orders for Iwabuchi retreat from
    Manila, 344–45
plan for group to retreat into moun-
    tains east of Manila, 94
war crimes trial of, 509
Yamashita's censuring of, 343–44
Yamashita's order to fight a protracted
    battle, 54
Yonai, Mitsumasa, 46, 51
Yoshida, Keichoku, 478
Yotsuide, General, 45
Young, Eunice, 103–4, 112, 142, 270
Yulo, Jose, 452

Zabala, Paulina, 303, 305, 307
Zabala, Rene, 303, 305, 307, 310